Summary of Contents

Professional
Visual Basic 5.0
Business Objects

Rockford Lhotka

Wrox Press Ltd. ®

Professional Visual Basic 5.0 Business Objects

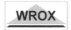

Published by Wrox Press Ltd. 30 Lincoln Road, Olton, Birmingham, B27 6PA
Printed in CANADA
ISBN 1-861000-43-X

Trademark Acknowledgements

Credits

Authors
Rockford Lhotka

Editors
Tim Briggs
Dominic Shakeshaft

Technical Reviewers
Allan Emery
Mike Erickson
Brian Francis
Richard Grimes
Christian Gross
John Harris
Mark Harrison
Steve Jakab

Technical Reviewers
Jesse Liberty
Greg Peele
John Smiley
Mike Sussman
Dorai Thodla

Design/Layout
Graham Butler

Cover
Andrew Guillaume

Index
Simon Gilks

Cover photo supplied by The Image Bank

About the Author

Rockford Lhotka has over 10 years experience in software development. He worked in Pascal, FORTRAN and Basic on VAX/VMS computers for a number of years until Windows NT and Visual Basic 1.0 first became available. Rockford has worked on many projects in various roles, including software development and design, network administration, help desk management and project management.

With the release of Visual Basic 4.0, Rockford began designing and developing n-tier client/server systems using component-based technology and has been doing so ever since. Rockford has been involved in the design and development of a number of successful, enterprise-level applications based on the techniques discussed in this book.

In addition to designing and writing software, Rockford is an avid proponent of component-oriented design using Visual Basic and COM. He regularly speaks on these topics, as well as evangelizing the concepts to friends, coworkers and clients.

Rockford currently works for BORN Information Services, an IT consulting group based out of Wayzata, Minnesota. He is a Technical Manager in the Minneapolis Microsoft Client/Server Business Unit, and is responsible for managing the technical direction of the business unit.

Dedication

To my wife, Teresa, and our sons, Timothy and Marcus.

Acknowledgments

Writing this book has been a lot of fun, and a lot of work. Without the continued support of my family it would not have been possible, and to them I owe my greatest thanks.

Many of the ideas and concepts in this book have evolved out of discussions with a number of other people and I would like to thank them:

Thanks go to Greg Nyberg and J.C. Hamlin for the hours we spent discussing how distributed object applications are implement in Forte'. Kevin Ford has always made himself available to bounce ideas off from, and always has ideas of his own in return. Thank you to Andy Anderson for helping to solidify my arguments in favor of the n-tier architecture used in the book. Dan Boerner helped set the direction for the ASP code in the chapter with his support. Thanks also, to the BORN Information Services Visual Basic Framework Team.

My deepest thanks to the excellent team of reviewers and editors from Wrox Press. Their feedback and support have been outstanding and I appreciate them greatly!

Finally, thank YOU for purchasing this book. I sincerely hope that you find it as enjoyable and useful to read as it has been to write!

Windows programming, and more specifically Visual Basic programming has an incredibly bright future in both conventional client/server and Internet environments. I am firmly convinced that, by using object-oriented design along with COM, MTS and other Win32 services, that we'll see Visual Basic become the pre-eminent development tool for enterprise-level solutions.

Thanks, code well and have fun!

Table of Contents

Introduction

It seems that every time I discuss developing programs in Visual Basic using object-oriented design techniques, I'm met with skepticism or even outright disbelief. The fact is that many people have misconceptions about Visual Basic and its ability to create object-oriented applications.

However, most object-oriented design folks would agree that the language, or development tool, is secondary, and that the key to successful object-oriented design is to have the right mindset, create the design correctly, and then implement the application with the tool of your choice. Following this philosophy, it's theoretically possible to create object-oriented software using FORTRAN or COBOL. Of course, the correct choice of tool can save you many problems in the actual implementation of your design.

Fortunately, Visual Basic 5.0 provides us with almost every tool we need to implement an object-oriented design. In fact, I've developed quasi-object designs in Visual Basic 3.0, and full-blown object-oriented designs in Visual Basic 4.0. With the advent of Visual Basic 5.0, we have even more powerful object tools at our disposal, making the use of object-oriented techniques even more attractive.

This book is about designing business software using Visual Basic 5.0 and following an object-oriented design philosophy. We'll be studying a number of examples to demonstrate how we can create a solid object model and implement it using Visual Basic. Along the way, we'll cover a number of specific techniques that make this whole concept work well in the Visual Basic environment. In addition, we'll demonstrate some general architectural techniques that can apply equally well to almost any tool.

First, I'll define business objects and discuss why they are so useful and important. Then we'll consider how to package these business objects into components to be reused. Once we've covered these basics, we'll look at how to build a number of user interfaces on top of the business objects, and how to provide a set of services so that the objects can be stored in a relational database.

Introduction

We'll discuss different types of application design, from single-tier to multi-tier to Internet Web development. All the sample applications in this book will fit into a three-tier logical model, but the techniques can be used on one computer, on several or across the Internet.

If you're one of the skeptics I mentioned earlier, I intend to convince you that Visual Basic is entirely up to the task of creating object-oriented software, with all the benefits that entails. If, on the other hand, you're already convinced, then this book should provide you with plenty of valuable techniques and concepts about how to create distributed and object-oriented software with Visual Basic 5.0.

What's Covered in This Book

Professional Visual Basic 5.0 Business Objects will take you from a broad discussion of what business objects are, and why they're such a powerful theme in modern OO programming, through to the implementation of a full project using business objects within Visual Basic. This project will also involve some of the newest and most exciting server-side technologies, including DCOM, MTS and ASP.

In Chapter 1, I present the rationale for the book, which is that object-oriented design, business objects, and Visual Basic 5 allow us to develop highly scalable and reusable code. We define what business objects are, we consider the benefits of using business objects and we begin to think about how object-oriented principles can be implemented in Visual Basic.

In Chapter 2, we review traditional Visual Basic development techniques, and see how business objects and components can improve the way we develop software. We consider various architectures that support component-based applications, and I introduce the ideas behind the component-based scalable logical architecture (CSLA) we'll be implementing. For those of you who aren't familiar with programming objects in Visual Basic 5.0, I provide an introduction in Appendix A.

In Chapter 3, we take the 'real-world' scenario of a video rental store, and analyze it in order to identify a series of representative software objects. The principles necessary to implement these objects and their interactions in Visual Basic are then introduced. Appendix B covers the details of the UML used in the design diagrams within this chapter.

In Chapter 4, we take Chapter 3's object model and apply it to possible physical architectures. We also code some examples to implement some basic business object functionality, and to highlight issues involved in coding UI and database access for these architectures.

By Chapters 5 and 6 it's time to code the video store's business objects. First we decide on some common interface elements, and then code a template class we can reuse for each business object. Chapter 5 concentrates on the simpler, standalone business objects and utility objects, while Chapter 6 implements parent-child relationships, hybrid (sometimes a child, sometimes standalone) and sibling objects.

At the end of Chapter 6, the code is functional but not very useful. It lacks both a user interface and persistence code. In Chapter 7, we code a Visual Basic client for the business objects, while in Chapter 8, we implement code to save each object's state to a local Access database.

In Chapter 9, I'll show how to implement an Excel front end to the video store project using VBA. The ease with which we accomplish this should prove how reusable business objects can be.

In Chapter 10, I'll split off the persistence code into a separate project. This is necessary to implement a fully scalable solution, where code resides near its 'client', the database. We want to be able to put the persistence code and the database on a separate machine from the client, and ideally on separate machines themselves. The need for efficient use of the underlying transport, DCOM, drives the implementation of the communication between the business objects and their persistence counterparts. In Chapter 11, we package up the client and server code using the Setup Wizard that comes with Visual Basic.

In Chapter 12, I'll upsize the database to SQL Server 6.5, and run the persistence code within Microsoft Transaction Server. This emerging technology simplifies issues of object management, database connection pooling and transaction management.

Finally, in Chapter 13, we implement a simple web interface using IIS and Active Server Pages. This is quite easy, as we have the business objects' DLL available to the scripting code within the page.

What You Need to Use This Book

Obviously, this book requires Visual Basic 5.0, preferably the Enterprise Edition (for the Class Wizard and the Setup Wizard), and definitely with the Visual Studio Service Pack 2 installed (to take advantage of the Apartment Threading option on ActiveX servers).

At various times, this book requires the following Microsoft technologies:

- ❑ Visual Modeler
- ❑ Access, Excel from Office 97
- ❑ A Windows NT 4.0 Server to host DCOM Servers on a local network
- ❑ MTS 1.1
- ❑ SQL Server 6.5
- ❑ IIS 3.0 with ASP 1.0

The Source Code

The source code for the book is available from the Wrox web site, **http://www.wrox.com**. It focuses mainly on the **VideoStore** application discussed above.

Conventions

We use a number of different styles of text and layout in the book to help differentiate between the various types of information. Here are examples of the styles we use along with explanations of what they mean:

Bulleted information is shown like this:

- ❑ **Important Words** are in a bold font.
- ❑ Words that appear on the screen, such as menu options, are a similar font to the one used on screen, e.g. the File menu.
- ❑ Keys that you press on the keyboard, like *Ctrl* and *Enter*, are in italics.
- ❑ All file, function names and other code snippets are in this style: `Video.mdb`.
- ❑ We've also italicized the first mention of classes like *Video*, when the discussion involves no code.

Code shown for the first time, or other relevant code, is in the following format,

```
Dim intVariable1 As Integer

intVariable1 = intVariable1 + 1
Debug.Print intVariable1
```

while less important code, or code that has been seen before, looks like this:

```
intvariable1 = intvariable1 + 1
```

Code you need to type into an Immediate window, or for a browser's URL appears like this:

```
http://www.wrox.co.uk
```

And code which will need to be filled in with appropriate values for your system is represented like this:

```
http://www.myserver.com/myapplication/
```

Finally, background information will look like this,

> **And vital, not-to-be-missed information looks like this.**

Professional Visual Basic 5.0 Business Objects

Tell Us What You Think

We have tried to make this book accurate and enjoyable, and reading it worthwhile. But what really matters is whether or not *you* find it useful, and we would really appreciate your views and comments. You can return the reply card in the back of the book, or contact us at:

feedback@wrox.com
http://www.wrox.com
or
http://www.wrox.co.uk

Introducing Business Objects

Overview

In the introduction, I presented the rationale for this book, which is that object-oriented design, business objects, and Visual Basic 5 allow us to develop highly scalable and reusable code. In this first chapter, we'll look at these concepts and the arguments for them in more detail. Specifically, we'll review:

- ❑ Defining objects
- ❑ Defining business objects
- ❑ Using Visual Basic 5.0 to create objects
- ❑ Re-using code with components
- ❑ Business objects in action - application types
- ❑ Object-oriented principles in Visual Basic 5.0

What are Business Objects?

This book is about developing applications using business objects. So the first thing we need to do is define how we'll be using the term **business objects**. Since this term means different things to different people, we need to make sure that we're all talking about the same thing before proceeding any further.

Just looking at the words, you might decide that these are *objects* that reflect or represent your *business*. And you'd pretty much be right - at a high level, it really is that simple. The programs we write can be viewed as models of the real world. We create programs to simulate parts of the world around us - to record what's happening or to make predications about what might happen.

What is an Object?

To understand business objects, we need to understand the concept of an **object**. An object is a code-based abstraction of a real-world entity or relationship. In the computer, an object consists of some data (state information) and behavior (a set of routines).Our programs use an **interface** to get access to an object's data and behavior. We can represent the object as something like the following diagram:

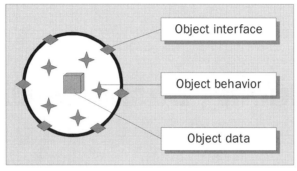

Objects and Classes

All objects are defined by a **class**. A class is essentially a template from which the object is created, which means that we can create many objects based on a single class. Each object is referred to as an **instance** of the class.

The word class is pretty descriptive, since we're basically classifying our objects. For instance, if we have a couple of objects, *Squirrel* and *Rabbit*, they could be instances of a *Mammal* class.

To use a more business-like example, we may have a *Customer* class. From this class we could create instances to represent each our customers, such as *Fred Smith* and *Mary Jones*. Each actual customer would have its own object, but all the objects would be created from the same template, the Customer class:

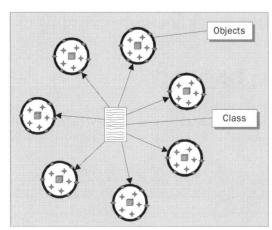

In Visual Basic, we define classes using **class modules**. We can then create objects based on the class module, with each object being an instance of the class.

Class modules are like form or standard modules, in that they have a declaration section followed by a series of **Sub**, **Function** and **Property** subroutines. The difference is that the variables and code in a class module can only be used by creating an instance of the class.

Let's take a look at how Visual Basic's class modules are used to provide a template for our objects.

Objects Contain Data

All objects contain data about themselves. For instance, an object representing a simple cardboard box might have data about the box's height, width, and depth. The object might also know whether the box is open or closed. Furthermore, we might have many box objects, each with its own height, width and depth. Each of these objects could be an instance of a *Box* class.

Data values in objects are stored in **instance variables**. Each instance of an object has its own set of variables, separate from the variables of any other object, even those of the same class. In this way, two objects of the same class can each have their own individual data, so each of our earlier box objects can have its own height, width, and depth.

In Visual Basic, a class's instance variables are stored as module-level variables inside a class module. For example:

```
Option Explicit

Private dblHeight As Double
Private dblWidth As Double
Private dblDepth As Double
Private blnOpen As Boolean
```

As with any other module, module-level variables in a class module can be declared as either **Public** or **Private**.

Private variables are only accessible to code within the class module, and they are the preferable way to manage data within objects. For any client code to manipulate a **Private** variable, it must call our object's code to do the manipulation; it can't do anything directly. This gives us a lot of control, since we can implement business or validation rules against any values that the client code attempts to change.

Instance variables declared as **Public** are accessible to code within our object, but they are also directly accessible to any client code written to use our object. Use of **Public** instance variables is very bad practice. Any client code can directly manipulate a **Public** instance variable, without going through any of our object's code. This means our object gives up all control over the value, trusting the author of the client code not to break any rules or do anything that is invalid.

One of the primary principles of object design is **encapsulation**, a concept we'll explore throughout the rest of the book. Encapsulation means that objects should hide their internal design and data from the code that uses them.

Private variables help by forcing any client code to use our code to change our object's data, thus allowing us to change how the object is implemented at any time with little or no impact on other programs that use this object. **Public** variables directly break the principal of encapsulation, providing a client with direct and uncontrolled access to an object's data.

Objects Have Behaviors

Of course, the whole idea behind having an object is so our programs can interact with it. If we're encapsulating an object's data then we need to provide the ability for the client programmer to access the information that the object holds.

Objects need to provide an interface to allow their client programs to gain access to these services. Just as in the real world, where objects interact - it is our aim in programming with objects to facilitate and control their interaction - via properties, methods and events. These form the interface the object presents to the world.

In Visual Basic, an object's interface is composed of **Property**, **Sub** and **Function** routines, as well as any events declared using the **Event** keyword. Any of these routines declared as **Public** within the class module become part of the object's interface.

In reality, an object can have many interfaces, allowing client code to use the object in different ways as appropriate. We'll cover this in more detail in the next section.

Properties

A property is an attribute that describes the object. Objects often have many properties to provide client code with access to all of their attributes.

It's important to make that an object's properties are not the same as its data. Objects often contain data that would not be considered to be an attribute of the object. For instance, a *Person* object may have an *Age* property, but the underlying data might be a birth date. The birth date itself may or may not be available as a property of the object.

Properties allow us, as the object's designer, to pick and choose what information we want to make available about our object. We can also choose which property values can be changed by our object's users. Some of that information may come directly from our object's data, while other information may come from calculated values or other sources.

So in our earlier box example we may not care to let other programs see the box's dimensions, but we may want them to be able to get at the box's volume:

```
Public Property Get Volume() As Double
   Volume = dblHeight * dblWidth * dblDepth
End Property
```

Visual Basic provides us with three different types of **Property** routines. **Property Get** routines are used to retrieve a property from an object. Then there are two routines to put values into a property, depending on whether the value is a reference to an object or not. **Property Let** routines allow client code to put any value into a property other than a reference to an object, while **Property Set** routines are used only for object references.

10

Properties can be read-only (**Property Get**), write-only (**Property Let/Set**) or read-write (both properties). Even if we include a **Property Let** or **Property Set** routine for a property, we can include code in that routine to validate the new value or check any other business rules before allowing the client code to change the value.

Methods

Objects, like their real-world counterparts, need to provide services (or functions) when they interact. Using their own data, or data passed as parameters to the method, they manipulate information to yield a result.

Methods are simply routines that we code within the class to implement the services we want to provide. Some methods return values or provide information back to the calling code. These are called **interrogative methods**. Others, called **imperative methods**, just perform a service and return nothing to the calling code.

In Visual Basic, methods are implemented using **Sub** or **Function** routines within the class module that defines our object. **Sub** routines may accept parameters, but they do not return any result value when they are complete. **Function** routines can also accept parameters, and they always generate a result value that can be used by the calling code.

> *The difference between a **Function** routine and a **Property Get** routine is quite subtle. Both return a value to the calling code and, either way, our object is running a subroutine defined by our class module to return the value.*
>
> *The difference is less programmatic than it is a design choice. We could create all our objects without any **Property** routines at all, just using methods for all interactions with the object. However, **Property** routines are obviously attributes of the object, while a **Function** might be an attribute or a method. By carefully implementing all attributes as **Property Get** routines, and any interrogative methods as **Function** routines, we will create more readable and understandable code.*

Using our now familiar box example, programs may need to open or close the box - so we need to provide a way to do this:

```
Public Sub OpenBox()
   blnOpen = True
End Sub

Public Sub CloseBox()
   blnOpen = False
End Sub
```

With this approach, our client code might look like this:

```
Dim objBox As New Box

objBox.Open
objBox.Close
```

Where this gets more useful is when we add code to check our rules. We shouldn't be able to open an already open box, or close an already closed box. With absolutely no impact to our client code, we can add the following rules to the **Box** class:

```
Public Sub OpenBox()
   If Not blnOpen Then Err.Raise vbObjectError, _
      "Box already open"
   blnOpen = True
End Sub

Public Sub CloseBox()
   If Not blnOpen Then Err.Raise vbObjectError, _
      "Box already closed"
   blnOpen = False
End Sub
```

In this case, we're simply raising an error if the client code tries to call either the **OpenBox** method when the box is already open or the **CloseBox** method when it's already closed. The real key, here, is that the implementation of these methods is totally encapsulated within our class module. We were able to make these changes without having to make any changes to our client code.

Events

In object-oriented design, the concept of an event is pervasive. In OO parlance, objects act in response to events, such as a user providing a value, or another object calling one of our object's methods. In the Visual Basic 5.0 environment, we have access to a somewhat different type of event.

Any Visual Basic developer is used to writing code to respond to events. Controls on forms generate events continually, and we write code behind those events to take appropriate action. For instance, a **CommandButton** control provides a **Click** event, firing it any time the user clicks on the button. We then write code to respond appropriately:

```
Private Sub Command1_Click()
   MsgBox "The user clicked the button"
End Sub
```

Before Visual Basic 5.0, there was no way for a Visual Basic developer to *cause* events, only to respond to them. Now we can use the **Event** statement to declare an event and the **RaiseEvent** command to fire it off.

Going back to our **Box** class, let's allow the user to stretch our box by implementing a **Stretch** method:

```
Public Sub Stretch(Percentage As Double)
   dblHeight = dblHeight * Percentage
   dblWidth = dblWidth * Percentage
   dblDepth = dblDepth * Percentage
End Sub
```

As a convenience, perhaps we want to raise an event to let any client programs know that our box has a new size. Visual Basic makes this very easy. We just need to add an **Event** declaration in the (General) (Declarations) section of our **Box** class module:

```
Event Stretched()
```

Events are always **Public** in scope, since they're always raised back to whatever client code has a reference to our object.

With our event declared, we can now fire it off using the **RaiseEvent** command:

```
Public Sub Stretch(Percentage As Double)
   dblHeight = dblHeight * Percentage
   dblWidth = dblWidth * Percentage
   dblDepth = dblDepth * Percentage
   RaiseEvent Stretched
End Sub
```

We'll go into much more detail about events in Chapter 3.

Multiple Interfaces

So far, we've looked at an object as having a single interface composed of its **Public Sub**, **Function**, and **Property** routines, along with any events it has declared. With Visual Basic 5.0, things are a bit more complex. Our objects can actually have many different interfaces simultaneously, although a client can only use one at a time.

If we create an object from a class we built in Visual Basic, that object will have at least the one interface we defined in our class module. In this simple case, it appears as though our program has direct access to the object, although in reality we're getting at the object through an interface defined by the class:

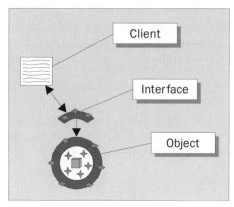

> With Visual Basic 5.0, a client program never has direct access to an object, only to one of the object's interfaces.

Sometimes, one interface isn't enough. Our object may represent more than one real world entity, and we need to be able to model this in Visual Basic. For instance, a *Customer* object is great, but a real customer is also a person. To model this in our application, we might need our Customer object to also act like a *Person* object from time to time.

To accomplish this, we can just add the Person interface to our object. Then a client program can use our object through the Customer interface with its set of properties and methods. It might also use the object through the Person interface, with its own separate set of properties and methods. This way, the client can use the object in whichever way is appropriate at any given time:

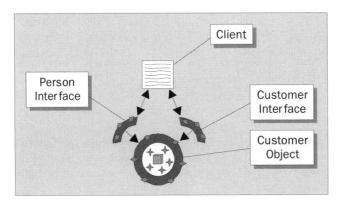

As we've seen, when we create a class in Visual Basic, its **Public** members comprise the interface for our object. However, we can also use the **Implements** statement to add another interface to our object. The **Implements** keyword requires that we supply a class name with which it will work.

With our **Box** example, for instance, we might also include an interface for a more generic **Container** class. To do this, we'd need to add an **Implements** statement in the general declarations section of our **Box** class module:

```
Implements Container
```

As soon as we add this line, Visual Basic will require that we add code to our class module to implement all the **Public** properties and methods from the **Container** class. Suppose the **Container** class module contains a single method, called **PutIn**, and a property, called **IsOpen**:

```
Public Sub PutIn(Item As Object)

End Sub

Public Property Get IsOpen() As Boolean

End Property
```

The property and method may or may not have code in them. As I've shown them in this example, there's no code. It doesn't really matter to our **Box** class, since we need to add our own code in the **Box** class module regardless. For instance, the **Box** class's implementation of **PutIn** may add any new items into a **Private** collection variable, and **IsOpen** may just return our **blnOpen** flag:

```
Option Explicit
```

```
Implements Container

Private colItems As New Collection
```

```
Private dblHeight As Double
Private dblWidth As Double
Private dblDepth As Double
Private blnOpen As Boolean

Public Sub OpenBox()
  If Not blnOpen Then Err.Raise vbObjectError, _
    "Box already open"
  blnOpen = True
End Sub

Public Sub CloseBox()
  If Not blnOpen Then Err.Raise vbObjectError, _
    "Box already closed"
  blnOpen = False
End Sub
```

```
Private Sub Container_PutIn(Item As Object)
  colItems.Add Item
End Sub

Private Property Get Container_IsOpen() As Boolean
  Container_IsOpen = blnOpen
End Property
```

There are a couple interesting things about these new routines we've added. First off, they are declared as **Private** routines, so at first glance they don't appear to be available to any client code. This is deceptive, however, since they are available to clients through the **Container** interface.

If these routines were declared as **Public**, they'd be part of the **Box** interface. That's not what we are after though. Instead of declaring them as **Public**, we declare them as **Private**, and then indicate that they belong to the **Container** interface by putting **Container_** in front of the name of the routine.

We'll discuss multiple interfaces in more detail later in the book.

Business Objects

The world around us is made up of both physical objects and concepts. To effectively model or simulate the real world and human processes in our code, it would be good if our software could be made up of representations of these real-world objects. As we have seen in the previous section, object-oriented programs attempt to do just that.

Business objects are designed to represent real 'objects' and concepts in our business. Here are some examples of these real 'objects':

- ❏ An employee
- ❏ A purchased part
- ❏ A manufactured part
- ❏ A work order
- ❏ A customer

All of these are objects in the physical world, and the whole idea behind using software business objects is to create representations of these same objects inside our applications. Then our application can make these objects interact with each other just as they would in the physical world. For instance, an *employee* might create a *work order* to build a *manufactured part* from one or more *purchased parts* that are then sold to the *customer*.

Following this logic, we can create a *work order* business object that contains all the code it needs to manage itself - so we never need to replicate code to create work orders, we just use the object.

Similarly, a *customer* object contains and manages its own data. A well-designed customer object can contain all the data and routines needed to represent a customer throughout an entire business and this can be used across all the applications for that business. We may use our customer object when taking an order. We might later use it when sending out a bulk mailing and analyzing sales patterns - without affecting any of the code that uses the object to take an order. Of course, over time, the customer object may evolve: it may gain new properties or new methods to support more functionality; the point is that the previous properties and methods can and should remain the same, so that existing applications need not be changed.

Why Use Business Objects?

Having defined the essence of a business object, let's look at the reasons we might want to use them.

Modeling Our Business

Of course, the reason we're developing applications in the first place is to solve some problem or automate some process. Having a set of abstract objects in software that represent physical objects can simplify this whole process.

As we'll see in Chapter 3, we can identify and design our objects in such a way that they provide a model of our business domain. With our initial identification of these business objects, we can then begin to model the business process we want to automate - or the problem we need to solve.

We can draw a picture showing how these objects relate or interact with each other in the real world. Using that picture, we can make our software objects work with each other in the same way. Essentially, we're defining **relationships** between our various business objects, showing how each object calls methods of other objects in order to simulate the real-world process.

This is a very intuitive approach to software development, since our applications become software models of the real world.

We've already started to do this with our description of an employee creating a work order and so forth. If we break that statement down into pieces, we can see a number of similar interactions between these objects:

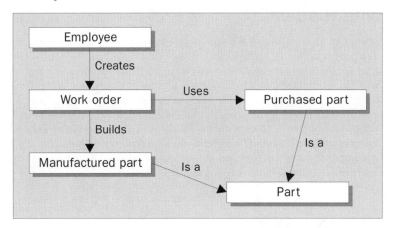

I'll demonstrate the whole process of creating and modeling objects in Chapter 3, when we get into some more specific examples.

Code Reuse

Most applications developed today are essentially built from scratch. Over and over, we recreate many of the same processes and procedures from earlier programs. Granted, many programmers copy code from existing programs into their new programs, and then modify the copied code to fit any new requirements. But this means that the same code is copied over and over again. If we need to change something in the original code, we'll also have to find and change that same code everywhere it's been used. Which is far from ideal.

> *You've probably done this type of code reuse many times over. And you've probably spent countless hours going through dozens of programs making the same code change. Then you've spent hours debugging all the changed programs. Talk about expensive!*

In other situations, code reuse is managed through libraries of code, or maybe even precompiled routines. But even in these cases, code reuse is difficult. In one of the best environments I've ever worked, we had a large and complete library of precompiled routines. By using these routines, we were able to dramatically improve the productivity of our development team.

Still, it wasn't uncommon to run into a program that required a change to our library. Unfortunately, a change to the library required modifying and rebuilding all the applications that relied on the library. Worse yet, sometimes the new functionality required actually going back and changing all the programs that used the library to bring them up to date. This was expensive, and required us to modify what was otherwise stable program code, thereby increasing the risk of bugs.

So copying code helps, but it's far from ideal. Creating libraries of code, or pre-compiled routines, can help a lot; but both techniques still leave a lot to be desired. What we really need is a solution that allows code reuse yet retains the flexibility of selective changes based on the need of the particular application. It would be great if we could derive what we needed and modify or extend the behavior. Fortunately, objects provide just this capability.

Creating Building Blocks

Traditional programs are centered around the processes and procedures that the program is trying to model. Object-oriented programs, on the other hand, are centered around the real-world objects that the program is trying to model. Once these objects have been identified and modeled, we can write programs that use these objects to simulate the processes and procedures in a much simpler and cleaner way than other programming approaches would accomplish.

If we base our applications on business objects then we'll create a collection of reusable building blocks that we can use time and time again in applications throughout our business. And, perhaps more importantly, we can continue to change and evolve our objects, over time, with little or no impact on the older applications that are already using those objects.

What are Components?

If you've followed the software industry for long then you'll have realized that object-oriented technology is not exactly new any more. In fact, it's been around for many years; but only now is it really becoming a popular concept in business. Why is that?

There are probably a lot of different reasons, but there is one in particular that we need to explore. As we discussed earlier in the chapter, a lot of the impetus for new development techniques is to facilitate code reuse. Unfortunately, just creating objects in code is not enough to maximize reuse.

Until recently, if we had the code for a *Customer* object in one program, and we wanted to use that object in another application, we'd have to copy the *code* into our application. We got to reuse the code, but, if anything changed, we had to find and change each copy of the customer object in all the different applications where it could be in use.

The problem is that as soon as there are two or more different copies of the same code, there's no easy way to keep them all synchronized. In many ways, we're back where we started - with simple copy-paste code reuse. At best, we've simply come up with a new way to create source code libraries:

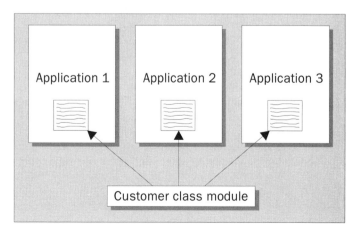

This is where **component-oriented design** comes in. Components build on object technologies to provide a better way of achieving reuse of our objects.

The term **component** is one of those overloaded words that has a different meaning to just about anyone you'd care to ask. Even within the OO community, there's a great deal of disagreement about the meaning of the term. Many people would argue that a component is nothing more than a large or complex business object.

In fact, the terms 'object' and 'component' are often used interchangeably, but there's a distinct and important difference between them:

1   Objects are created from classes. Classes are made up of source code that defines the object's data and the routines that are needed to manipulate that data.
2   Components are precompiled *binary* code. Since components are precompiled, they are independent of the language in which they were created.

Since we're using a Microsoft development tool to create software for Microsoft operating systems, we'll stick with Microsoft's definition of a component. In their view, components are ActiveX servers or ActiveX controls. They are precompiled units of code that expose one or more interfaces for use by client programs:

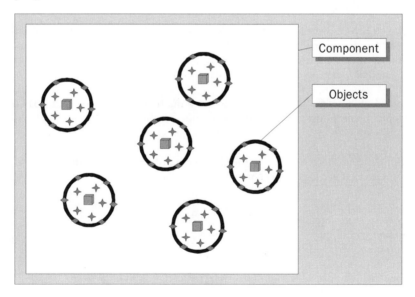

Even within the Microsoft world you'll find some confusion. To many people, ActiveX controls and components are synonymous. In reality, however, ActiveX controls are merely one type of component, along with various other types of ActiveX servers. We'll look at all these different types of components in the next section.

With binary components, we can achieve a whole new level of reuse in our applications. Going back to our *Customer* object, we can put the code into our component rather than into each individual application. The applications can then use the object directly from the component:

We get the same functionality as when we copied the source code into each application, but now we only need to maintain that code in a single place - the component.

Component Interfaces

Basically, what we're saying is that a component is a pre-compiled group of objects. Some of these objects can be used by client programs, while others may be hidden from the outside world, available for use only within the component itself. In many ways, a component is like a small application, but one that makes its functionality available for use by other applications.

Earlier, we discussed object interfaces and how they are made up of the object's **Public** properties, methods, and events. Since a component is really a group of objects, the component's interface is made up of its public objects.

Of course, this implies that there is a way to indicate which of our objects are to be public and which are private. There's no real analog to this concept within traditional object-oriented design.

Object-oriented design always assumes that any object can interact with any other object within our application. Component-oriented design gives us greater control, since we can choose which of our component's objects are available for use by other applications:

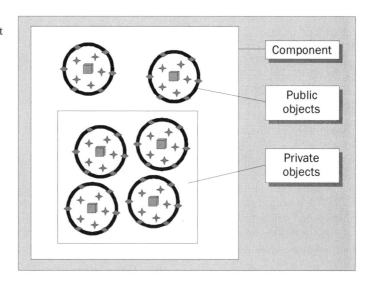

Types of Components

Components can be designed for use in different areas within our programs. In general, there are three different types of components in an application:

- ❑ Standard/general components
- ❑ Application-specific components
- ❑ Industry-specific components

Standard/General Components

I like to think of general components as the sort of thing you can buy out of just about any programmer's catalog. In fact, there are many components that are generally available from Windows itself or that come with Visual Basic. These are components that provide services so broadly useful that you can use them just about anywhere. Some good examples include DAO, RDO, graphing controls, grid controls and mathematical library components.

For the most part, we're better off purchasing general components rather than rolling our own. Most companies that sell components make their living off the sales, so the components are likely to be of pretty decent quality. Furthermore, just about any popular type of component will be developed by multiple vendors, so competition will tend to get us better quality and more features as well.

Of course, with Visual Basic 5.0, we can easily create components that are quite general in nature. If we can't find a component that fits our needs then we can just create our own. Better still, if we find a component that's *close* to what we need, we can use it inside a new Visual Basic component and just build on what it provides.

Application-Specific Components

Each application is unique, and provides some specific functionality. We can put all of those components that belong entirely to an application into the application-specific component category.

Perhaps our program needs to do some specific graphical display, or some complex calculations. These might be built as components - even though they aren't useful to any other applications.

Clearly, since we're not likely to find this type of component on the commercial market, we'll be writing our own. I'll touch on this concept here and there throughout the rest of the book, but the majority of these components will be controls to customize our interface - so they really aren't going to contain business objects.

Industry-Specific Components

These are components that are targeted at a specific industry, or perhaps a specific area of a business. As we'll discuss later in the chapter, there are a number of efforts underway to develop vertical market components, and those efforts are almost always industry-specific.

Vertical components are rather rarer in the commercial area. Still, if we look around we can find more and more components that fit into this area. Many standalone products are beginning to expose public object interfaces, so we can write our programs to use parts of the product as a component. Products such as accounting systems, or shop floor control systems, can be used as components if they're designed to provide a public interface.

On the other hand, we may find that there simply aren't components for our particular industry to suit our needs. In that case, we'll have to develop our own components for use in our applications.

Business objects really come into play here. By using business objects to build a model of the actual 'objects' used in our industry, we can create very powerful components. It is primarily this type of component that we'll be focusing on throughout the remainder of the book.

Creating Business Components in Visual Basic

Hopefully, by now, you're beginning to get a solid feel for the benefits that business objects can offer. Business objects provide both code reuse and an understandable, manageable way to model our business processes in our software. With the ability to organize and group our business objects into precompiled binary components, we can fully realize the benefits of the technology.

Visual Basic allows us to create components in a variety of ways, and we can organize our business objects into these components. Using Visual Basic, we can create ActiveX servers, both in-process (DLL's) and out-of-process (EXE's). Additionally, we can create ActiveX controls (OCX's), which are another form of component. Any of these types of components can house our business objects, each with different strengths and weaknesses.

Out-of-Process Servers

An out-of-process server is a component that is effectively a separate program containing objects. This type of server will always run in its own process space, and will thus be largely independent from any client programs.

There are two main options with out-of-process servers. We can create the server so that each object runs in its own process, or we can create the server so that all the objects in the server run within a single process.

There are cases where our business objects will be running in a number of separate processes. The most notable scenario is where we have a full-blown application that can also be used as a component. We might also create out-of-process servers when we want to start some task and let it run in the background while the user continues to work with our application.

There is a cost to this approach however. Most applications require many different business objects to be active all at the same time and, if each object runs in its own process, we'll have a lot of processes running concurrently. Having a great many processes active on a workstation can be devastating to performance.

The Windows operating system does some work every **quantum** (20 milliseconds or so) to determine which process should get to run next. Even if a process is idle, it is still in the list of processes to check, and so the operating system has to do some extra work to check our idle process. If we have a lot of processes, this can add up and become a problem:

On the other hand, we can create a server where all of our objects exist inside a single process. If we put business objects inside this type of server, all of the objects can work together, sharing resources and memory. Many clients can use the objects in our server, and all the objects from all those clients can easily communicate and work with each other inside the same process.

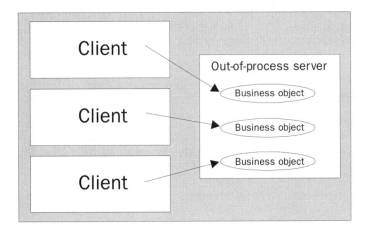

Either type of out-of-process server suffers from one very significant drawback: performance.

All Windows components use the Component Object Model (COM) to allow communication with objects in other processes. We'll discuss COM in more detail later in the chapter. For now, all we need to know is that COM handles all communication between objects in different processes.

Unfortunately, COM imposes a very high overhead on each call from one process to another (cross-process calls). Therefore, on each reference to a property and each call to a method, we take the hit of this overhead - and performance can suffer substantially.

There are techniques that can be used to help minimize the impact of this overhead, and I'll demonstrate those later in the book.

In-process Servers

An in-process server is a component where our objects run inside the *client's* process. Each client essentially gets its own private copy of our component - and therefore a copy of all our objects.

In-process servers avoid the overhead of running in their own process, thus conserving resources and memory for the system. Additionally, the communication between the client and our objects does not have to go from one process to another - and so we avoid almost all of the overhead imposed by COM on out-of-process server communication.

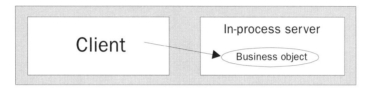

Since in-process components run inside the client's process, we use less memory and we don't create extra processes. We'll also improve performance, but we do give up some capabilities. Since each server is running in each client's process space, our business objects are effectively split up - so they can't share resources or memory with each other, but only with each client.

By judicious use of out-of-process servers combined with in-process servers, we can create applications that draw on the strengths of each. I will demonstrate this at various points throughout the book.

ActiveX Controls

Finally, let's look at ActiveX controls. These are yet another type of component, but one that's typically used to create visual objects as part of an interface design. Some ActiveX controls are invisible; but if we get right down to it, there's very little difference between an invisible ActiveX control and a regular in-process server.

Business objects can be placed in an ActiveX control just as easily as they can be placed in an in-process server. Many developers may find it easier to work with objects packaged in this type of component, since they can literally drop the component on a form and work with it from there - just as if it were a regular control.

Also, ActiveX controls can be very powerful in a Web application. Microsoft's Internet Explorer will automatically download and install controls, but not in-process servers. This makes it far easier to include a control into a Web page than to include an in-process server.

One significant drawback to ActiveX controls is that they require our client programs to have at least one form that can be a container to hold the control. More than simply having to include the form in the project, we actually have to have the form loaded in memory in order to gain access to the objects inside the control. This is somewhat less efficient than getting the objects directly from an in-process server.

Fitting Business Objects into Applications

Now that we've established what business objects are, and we've explored the different types of components that can contain them, we need to look at just where the objects fit into our typical application. We'll discuss this in much more detail in Chapter 2, but it will be useful to take a quick, high-level look at some different application models, and where business objects fit into them.

> *For the client/server experts reading this, I should point out that we're really blurring the lines between the physical and logical models in this overview. In each case, I'm really proposing a 3-tier logical model; but it is useful to see where everything falls physically regardless. In Chapter 2, we'll be more precise, as we get into more detail on the architecture we'll use throughout the book.*

Single-tier Applications

A single-tier application is the simplest of the models that we'll look at. This type of application is simply a program that runs on the user's machine. It might talk to a database, but that database resides on the same machine (or perhaps on a mapped network drive). The key thing, here, is that all the work takes place on the same machine: the user interface, business- and data-processing are all on the user's computer.

A diagram of this type of application would look like this:

Now let's look at where the business objects fit into the picture:

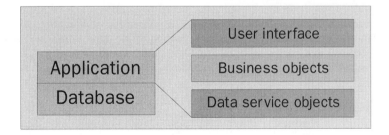

In this type of application, everything is pretty simple. Since our entire application is running on a single machine, the business objects just fit right into the application.

Don't worry about the data service objects just yet. We'll discuss what they are and what they do in Chapter 2. For now, let's just look at them as being the code that communicates between business objects and the database.

Two-tier Client/Server

The simplest type of distributed computing is two-tier client/server. In this type of application, the data processing is moved off the user's machine on to a dedicated database server machine. Two-tier client/server is the most common type of client/server application built today. It offers significant benefits over a simple application, since the processing of data is centralized and becomes a shared resource between all the users:

Still, with two-tier client/server, the only work that has really been moved off the user's machine is the data management - storing and retrieving data. The user-interface and any processing done by the application remain pretty much where they were:

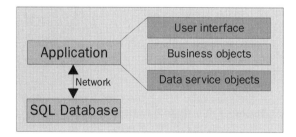

The primary difference lies in the role of the data service objects. In this model, they have to do much less work, since a lot of the data processing is moved to the database server - usually in the form of stored procedures and triggers written in SQL. Again, we'll talk in more detail about these data service objects in Chapter 2.

Three-tier Client/Server

Over time it has become apparent that two-tier client/server is simply not powerful enough or flexible enough to handle many larger applications. Since each client workstation maintains a dialog with the central database server, the network traffic can be quite high. Furthermore, the central database server can become a performance bottleneck - as many users try to access the same resources at the same time.

Three-tier client/server helps address these issues by putting another physical server between the users and the database. This central **application server** can more efficiently manage network traffic and the load on the database server.

Better still, it is typically much easier to add more application servers than it is to add more database servers. Adding a database server would require us to split our data between the database servers, whereas adding an application server should just require some relatively minor changes to parts of our application:

Just like two-tier client/server, the data processing is handled primarily on the database server. However, we now have an application server that can do a lot of work. This means that we can move a substantial part of our application off the user's workstation and onto the application server.

There are a number of benefits to distributed processing, including:

- ❑ Centralization of shared resources
- ❑ Rich, flexible client interfaces to the data
- ❑ Spreading our workload across various machines
- ❑ Putting processing in the most efficient location possible

How much processing is moved to the application server may vary. It depends on many factors, but mostly we need to decide how much work we want our client workstations to do. Designs range from having the client workstation do virtually nothing to the client workstation doing almost everything. We'll discuss the pros and cons of each approach in Chapter 2.

As I've shown it in this diagram, much of our business logic remains on the user workstation. In Chapter 2, we'll explore why it can be very beneficial to have the business objects on the client workstation as shown here.

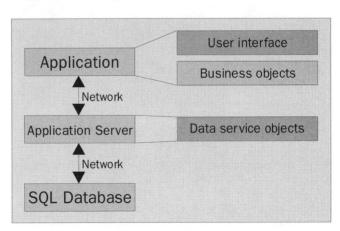

Web-based Applications

The models that I've presented so far leave a fair amount of the application on the client workstation. Applications designed for the World Wide Web take an entirely different approach. Web applications put as little of the application as is physically possible on the client, and keep all the processing centralized on one or more servers:

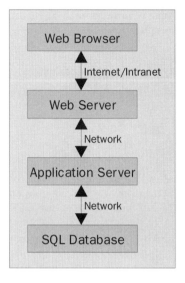

Since the browser will only provide a user-interface, the rest of our application needs to move down to the server:

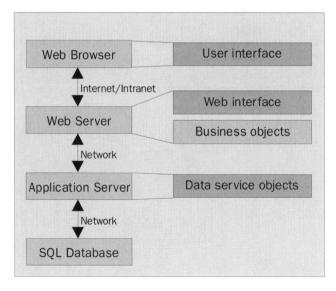

In this figure, we still have an interface, our business objects, and our services. What we've done is moved virtually everything down to the server, leaving a very light user interface on the user's workstation.

The big difference is that instead of a *user*-interface on top of our business objects, we now have a *web*-interface. This is a layer of code that interacts with the web server to communicate with the client. The web-interface is basically a layer of 'glue' between the business objects and the HTML that gets sent to the user's browser.

The web interface provides HTML to the browser via the web server and accepts the user's input through the browser and web-server. There are many technologies available to build this web interface - including CGI, ISAPI, Active Server Pages and others.

There are some other fairly significant issues with this type of architecture. In Chapter 11, we'll implement a browser-based user-interface using Active Server Pages as the glue between the business objects and the web server.

Object-based vs. Object-oriented Approaches

Visual Basic has always been object-based, meaning that we could always use objects in our programs; but the language provided no way to create objects until Visual Basic 4.0.

Perhaps it would be more accurate to say that it has always been component-based, since, until Visual Basic 4.0, we've been unable to use objects per se but rather we've used pre-built binary components.

Originally, these components came in the form of VBX's (Visual Basic Custom Controls), which really set the stage for where we are today. VBX components provided us with pre-built functionality that we could just plug into our programs and start using. They were so useful, in fact, that an entire cottage industry grew up around them - and various development tools have now been enhanced to support their use.

Unfortunately, VBX technology was pretty limiting in a number of ways. VBX controls were difficult to create, and the way they communicated with Visual Basic was strict and somewhat limited. Because of these problems, Microsoft developed a new standard for component development. These new components were called OLE Controls, and are now called ActiveX controls. Either way, they are commonly known as OCX's (OLE Custom Controls).

Visual Basic 4.0 added a number of actual object-oriented abilities to the language, by adding the *class module,* and allowing us to create objects based on our own classes. Now, with version 5.0, we have even more capabilities with the addition of the **Friend** and **Implements** keywords, along with the ability to raise our own events - all of which we'll discuss in detail later in the book.

Visual Basic 4.0 also introduced the ability to create our own components. This has given us the ability to easily package our objects together into reusable binary modules, as we discussed earlier in the chapter.

Most people look at four criteria when deciding if a language is object-oriented. These criteria are abstraction, encapsulation, inheritance and polymorphism. Let's look briefly at each of these from Visual Basic's viewpoint. I don't want to get into too much detail, here, since there are entire books written about this subject alone; but I do want to quickly illustrate where Visual Basic stands.

Abstraction

Abstraction is the process by which we can think about specific properties or behaviors without thinking about a particular object that has those properties or behaviors. We know that most cars have four wheels, a steering and an engine, without thinking of any particular car, or how the internals of the engine operates.

Abstraction allows us to recognize how things are similar and ignore differences - to think in general terms, and not the specifics. A **TextBox** control is an abstraction, because we can place it on a form, and then tailor it to our needs by setting properties. Visual Basic allows us to define abstractions using class modules.

Any language that allows a developer to create a class from which objects can be instantiated meets this criteria, and Visual Basic is no exception. We can easily create a class to represent a car, essentially providing an abstraction. We can then create instances of that class, where each object can have its own attributes such that it represents a specific automobile.

Encapsulation

Encapsulation is the concept that an object should be a 'black box'. Another way to put this is that an object should totally separate its interface from its implementation.

This means that an object should completely contain any data it requires, and that it should also contain all the code required to manipulate that data. Programs should interact with our object through an interface, using properties and methods. Client code should never work directly with the data owned by the object.

> *In object-speak, programs interact with objects by sending messages to the object. These messages are generated by other objects, or by external sources such as the user. The way the object reacts to these messages is through methods. What Visual Basic calls properties would otherwise be called attributes.*

Both Visual Basic 4.0 and 5.0 provide full support for encapsulation through class modules. Using these modules, we can create classes which entirely hide their internal data and code, providing a well-established interface of properties and methods to the outside world.

For example, if we create a class module and add the following code:

```
Option Explicit

Public Property Set Form(Target As Form)

End Property

Public Property Let CurrentX(X As Single)

End Property

Public Property Let CurrentY(Y As Single)

End Property
```

Then we've created an interface for the class. From here, we could do virtually anything in terms of *implementing* the class. For instance, we could just store the values:

```
Option Explicit

Private frmForm As Form
Private sngX As Single
Private sngY As Single

Public Property Set Form(Target As Form)
    Set frmForm = Target
End Property

Public Property Let CurrentX(X As Single)
    sngX = X
End Property

Public Property Let CurrentY(Y As Single)
    sngY = Y
End Property
```

Or maybe we just want to move to the coordinates:

```
Option Explicit

Private frmForm As Form

Public Property Set Form(Target As Form)
    Set sngForm = Target
End Property

Public Property Let CurrentX(X As Single)
    frmForm.CurrentX = X
End Property

Public Property Let CurrentY(Y As Single)
    frmForm.CurrentY = Y
End Property
```

Either way, we haven't changed the *interface* of the class, and so any program working with this class would have no idea if we have switched from one implementation to the other. This is the essence of encapsulation.

> *Obviously, the user might have a problem if we made such a change to our object. If applications were developed expecting the first set of behaviors, and then we changed to the second, there could be some interesting side effects. However, the point here is that the client programs would continue to function, even if the results were quite different than when we started.*

We'll be making heavy use of encapsulation throughout this book, so you'll become very familiar with it if you haven't seen it before.

Polymorphism

Polymorphism is often considered to be directly tied to inheritance (which we'll discuss next). In reality, however, it's independent to a large degree. Polymorphism means that we can have two classes with different implementations or code, but with the same interface. We can then write a program that operates upon that interface and doesn't care about which type of object it operates at runtime.

Polymorphism through Late Binding

For example, if we have a class called **Square** and another one called **Cowboy** then they may both have a method called **Draw**. We can write a program that tells an object to draw by calling the **Draw** method. This program won't care if it is working with a **Square** or a **Cowboy** - even though each object must obviously implement the **Draw** method differently.

If the **Square** class contains the following code:

```
Option Explicit

Public Sub Draw(Target As Form)
   Target.Line Step(0, 0)-Step(0, 100)
   Target.Line Step(0, 0)-Step(100, 0)
   Target.Line Step(0, 0)-Step(0, -100)
   Target.Line Step(0, 0)-Step(-100, 0)
End Sub
```

And the **Cowboy** class contains this code:

```
Option Explicit

Public Sub Draw(Target As Form)
   Target.Print "Draw from holster"
   Target.Print "Aim"
   Target.Print "Fire"
End Sub
```

Then we can put this routine in a form:

```
Public Sub DoDraw(SomeObject As Object)
   SomeObject.Draw Me
End Sub
```

This routine doesn't care if it is passed a **Square** or a **Cowboy**, even though the two classes are implemented in an entirely different fashion. Notice that the routine accepts a parameter of type **Object**. By doing this, we have allowed the routine to accept literally any object we care to send it. This simple example of polymorphism works in Visual Basic 4.0 as well as Visual Basic 5.0.

Visual Basic 4.0 implements polymorphism in the same manner as Smalltalk, by using something called **late binding**. We've just seen an example of late binding with the **Draw** method of the **Square** and **Cowboy** objects.

Late binding means that the Visual Basic compiler makes no effort to determine if calls to our objects are valid. All the checking takes place while the program is running. Each call to an object is checked as it's called, and an error is raised if the call turns out to be invalid.

Polymorphism with Early Binding

Visual Basic 5.0 retains this ability, but also implements a stricter form of polymorphism (similar to that found in C++) through its support of **interface inheritance** using the **Implements** keyword.

For example, if we create a **Shape** class with the following code:

```
Option Explicit

Public Sub Draw(Target As Form)

End Sub
```

Then we can use **Shape** as a base to create a **Square** class:

```
Option Explicit

Implements Shape

Public Sub Shape_Draw(Target As Form)
   Target.Line Step(0, 0)-Step(0, 100)
   Target.Line Step(0, 0)-Step(100, 0)
   Target.Line Step(0, 0)-Step(0, -100)
   Target.Line Step(0, 0)-Step(-100, 0)
End Sub
```

And we can also create a **Circle** class, again using the **Shape** class as a base class:

```
Option Explicit

Implements Shape

Public Sub Shape_Draw(Target As Form)
   Target.Circle Step(0, 0), 200
End Sub
```

With these classes defined, we can try them out. The following code accepts a parameter and then calls its **Draw** method:

33

```
Public Sub DrawShape(objSomeShape As Shape)
   SomeShape.Draw Me
End Sub
```

Notice the difference between this example and the previous one with the **Square** and **Cowboy** classes. Instead of accepting an **Object** type as a parameter, we're now able to accept a parameter of type **Shape**. We've ensured that the only objects passed to our routine will be shapes. Since we'd probably never use the **Shape** class as a base to build a **Cowboy** class, we don't have to worry about getting a **Cowboy** when we wanted a **Square** or **Circle**.

This uses **early binding**. Early binding occurs as the program is being compiled, which means that the compiler can help us out by doing type checking and by verifying that the properties and methods we call on the object are valid.

Inheritance

Inheritance is the concept that a new class can be based on an existing class, inheriting its interface and functionality from the original class. With inheritance, a class gains all the properties and methods that make up the interface of the base class, and it can then extend the interface by adding properties and methods of its own. The new class can also extend or change the implementation of each of the properties and methods from the original base class.

For instance, if we had a class called *Fruit* that had all the properties and methods which apply to all types of fruit, then inheritance would make it very easy to create classes for *Apple*, *Orange* and so forth. We wouldn't have to recreate all the code for an apple to be a fruit: it would get that automatically from the original Fruit class.

Interface Inheritance

Visual Basic 5.0 doesn't directly support the concept of inheritance. It does provide something called **interface inheritance** using the **Implements** keyword. We've already used this keyword when we discussed polymorphism, but it can be applied here to help simulate a form of inheritance.

Interface inheritance lets us inherit the interface of one class into a new class. The downside is that all we get is the interface, not the original object's data or behavior. Worse still, we can't extend an interface created with the **Implements** keyword. One of the key benefits of inheritance is the ability to extend the base interface, so this is a substantial drawback.

If we look at a **Fruit** class, we'll find an interface that includes elements appropriate for any type of fruit. In this example, we've got a growing climate and color for the fruit:

```
Option Explicit

Public Property Get GrowingClimate() As String

End Property

Public Property Get Color() As String

End Property
```

```
Public Property Get Bites() As Integer

End Property
```

Notice that there's no code in the routines shown here. That's because all we'll be inheriting is the interface; any code in these routines wouldn't be used anyway.

Now we can create a new class, **Apple**, and inherit the interface from the **Fruit** class by using the **Implements** keyword:

```
Option Explicit

Implements Fruit

Private Property Get Fruit_GrowingClimate() As String
   Fruit_GrowingClimate = "Moderate"
End Property

Private Property Get Fruit_Color() As String
   Fruit_Color = "Red"
End Property

Private Property Get Fruit_Bites() As Integer
   Fruit_Bites = 20
End Property
```

Earlier in the chapter, we discussed multiple interfaces and how the **Implements** keyword works. Instead of declaring **GrowingClimate**, **Color** and **Bites** directly, we need to make them **Private** in scope and put **Fruit_** in front of each name so Visual Basic knows that these routines belong to the **Fruit** interface.

We might also create an **Orange** class, again based on the **Fruit** interface:

```
Option Explicit

Implements Fruit

Private Property Get Fruit_GrowingClimate() As String
   Fruit_GrowingClimate = "Warm"
End Property

Private Property Get Fruit_Color() As String
   Fruit_Color = "Orange"
End Property

Private Property Get Fruit_Bites() As Integer
   Fruit_Bites = 20
End Property
```

Now, contrary to what we'd expect, we can write code to compare apples and oranges:

```
Public Function CompareColor(AnApple As Fruit, AnOrange As Fruit)
   CompareColor = (AnApple.Color = AnOrange.Color)
End Function
```

More importantly, we've created two different classes, both having inherited the same interface from **Fruit**. This is a very powerful technique when we have otherwise dissimilar classes that have a number of the same interface elements. We can write client code to treat all the objects the same - even though they are different.

Unfortunately, this technique doesn't allow us to extend the interface, and so it is less a way to implement inheritance than it is to implement polymorphism, as in the last section. The **Orange** class can't add properties or methods to its version of the **Fruit** interface. This limits our flexibility, and really prevents us from using this to simulate full-blown inheritance.

Containment and Delegation

Fortunately, it is possible, with a little extra work, to roll our own inheritance using Visual Basic - and thus gain many of the advantages we'd get in other languages that fully support inheritance. This is achieved by combining a concept called **containment** with another called **delegation**.

Containment is the idea that an object can have a private instance of another object inside itself. Were we to have a *Human* object, it might *contain* a *Heart* object. The Heart object would be private to the *Human* object, since no client code would normally interact with the Heart.

Delegation means that one object delegates work to another object rather than doing the work itself. If our *Human* object has a *PulseRate* property, it might ask the *Heart* object for the rate rather than figuring it out by itself. It has effectively delegated the responsibility for the *PulseRate* to the *Heart* object.

If we combine these two concepts, we can simulate inheritance. Let's look at how that can work with our fruit example.

Again, we'll create a class called **Fruit**; but this time we'll put some code in the **GrowingClimate** routine. With inheritance, we'd expect to be able to use this behavior in any new classes we create based on **Fruit**:

```
Option Explicit

Public Property Get GrowingClimate() As String
  GrowingClimate = "Moderate"
End Property

Public Property Get Color() As String

End Property

Public Property Get Bites() As Integer

End Property
```

Now we'll create an **Apple** class, but this time we won't use the **Implements** keyword. Instead, we'll manually recreate the interface from the **Fruit** class - with absolutely no changes to the declarations of either property:

```
Option Explicit

Private objFruit As New Fruit

Public Property Get GrowingClimate() As String
  GrowingClimate = objFruit.GrowingClimate
End Property

Public Property Get Color() As String
  Color = "Red"
End Property

Public Property Get Bites() As Integer
  Bites = 20
End Property
```

The first thing you might notice is that we're creating a **Private Fruit** object within our new class. Our new **Apple** class is using the concept of containment to have an instance of the **Fruit** class inside itself:

```
Private MyFruit As New Fruit
```

In the **GrowingClimate** routine, our new **Apple** class just delegates the work down to the private **Fruit** object:

```
GrowingClimate = objFruit.GrowingClimate
```

Now let's create an **Orange** class by following the same technique:

```
Option Explicit

Private objFruit As New Fruit

Public Property Get GrowingClimate() As String
  GrowingClimate = "Warm"
End Property

Public Property Get Color() As String
  Color = "Orange"
End Property

Public Property Get Bites() As Integer
  Bites = objFruit.Bites
End Property

Public Property Get Slices() As Integer
  Slices = Bites / 2
End Property
```

Since the **GrowingClimate** for an **Orange** is different, it doesn't delegate that call down to the **Fruit** object. Instead, it replaces, or overrides, the functionality by implementing the routine itself.

We have also extended the interface for our **Orange** object by adding a **Slices** property. While we've simulated the inheritance of the **GrowingClimate**, **Color** and **Bites** properties, we're also able to extend the interface as needed for each specific class.

Back to our client code, which compares apples and oranges, we need to change how we accept our parameters:

```
Public Function CompareColor(AnApple As Object, _
    AnOrange As Object)
  CompareColor = (AnApple.Color = AnOrange.Color)
End Function
```

The code within this routine is the same as we had before, but now our parameters are of type **Object** instead of type **Fruit**. Since our new classes don't use the **Implements** keyword, we can't have Visual Basic treat these objects like a **Fruit** object.

However, we do know that they have the same set of properties and methods, and so we can write our code to treat them identically. We just need to tell Visual Basic that they are generic objects rather than objects of a specific class.

COM - The Plumbing behind the Scenes

The Common Object Model (COM) is Microsoft's standard for object interaction. COM provides a standard mechanism by which objects and components can communicate, independent of the language in which the components were created.

Other major Windows technologies rely on COM to function. The two most notable of these technologies are OLE (Object Linking and Embedding) and ActiveX. These both use COM to facilitate all the interaction between objects. OLE uses COM to communicate between applications, allowing users to link or embed parts of one application's data and display into another application. ActiveX is broader, using COM to support communication between controls, in-process, and out-of-process servers.

Microsoft has designed Visual Basic to fit seamlessly into COM. Components created with Visual Basic are ActiveX components, which means that they use COM to communicate with each other and with their client programs. In many other languages, it can be very complex to create components that fit into this model, but Visual Basic takes care of all that complexity behind the scenes.

Distributed COM (DCOM) extends the communication capabilities across the network. With DCOM, any COM object can transparently communicate with objects on other machines over the network. This works with components created in Visual Basic as well, which means that Visual Basic developers can create objects and distribute them across the network with very little effort.

Visual Basic 5.0's object capabilities are very well matched to those of COM. COM objects typically have multiple interfaces and, as we've seen, Visual Basic objects can have multiple interfaces using the **Implements** keyword. COM, like Visual Basic, has no direct support for inheritance, but instead relies upon aggregation so we can group objects together to provide more complex functionality.

Because Visual Basic 5.0's capabilities are so closely matched with COM's capabilities, it is an ideal development tool when we're working in a COM environment.

Other Industry Efforts

COM isn't the only distributed object platform on the market, so we'll take a quick look at a couple of other options, mainly to try and see how important communicating components and business objects are in modern computing.

CORBA

The Object Management Group (OMG) is a consortium of companies that have banded together to develop an object communication standard. The Common Object Request Broker Architecture (CORBA) is a standard that competes with Microsoft's Component Object Model (COM) in many ways.

The various companies involved, and the industry press, tend to dwell on the differences between the two competing standards. While it's true that there are differences, what I want to emphasize here is the similarities between these standards.

Both CORBA and COM provide standardized mechanisms for objects to communicate with each other. They specify how components and applications can be built in a distributed and organized fashion. CORBA, like DCOM, provides for communication between objects distributed across a network, providing for complex multi-tiered applications based on the standard.

Perhaps most importantly, CORBA and COM both encourage the use of business objects in their architectures. And they both advocate a separation of business rules from the presentation layer, in such a way that the main application logic is contained in an object model that's largely independent of the user-interface.

Vertical Market Groups

Another major effort underway by various companies and organizations is the creation of business object frameworks that support specific vertical markets, such as IBM's San Francisco initiative. These are collections or groups of objects that are built to service specific business needs.

For instance, a vendor might build an object framework that encompasses the typical requirements of managing a shop floor in a factory. The vendor can then market their framework to companies who are building shop floor control software. These companies can then base their software development on the pre-existing business objects, extending or modifying them as needed to meet their specific business needs.

It remains to be seen whether this type of object framework will be viable in the marketplace. While many business processes are generally similar from company to company, it is also true that every company is unique. The level of modification required to take a framework and make it useful in a given situation could be quite large, and it could offset the benefits to be gained.

Summary

In this chapter, we've introduced the concepts that will be covered through the remainder of the book. At this point, you should have a good understanding of what business objects are - and why they're so important to the future of software development. You should also have a general understanding of component technology and how business objects can be managed and distributed through components.

From here, we'll explore these concepts in more practical detail. We'll look at:

- ❏ The design and creation of business objects
- ❏ How these objects fit into our applications
- ❏ How business objects interact with the user-interface
- ❏ How business objects interact with the database
- ❏ How business objects can interact with each other

2

Application Architecture with Business Objects

Overview

In Chapter 1, we ran through a quick overview of what business objects are and why they're so important to software development. We also took a brief look at the concept of component-oriented design, which allows us to group business objects together into reusable binary components.

In this chapter, we'll review traditional Visual Basic development techniques, and see how business objects and components can improve the way we develop software.

Traditional Visual Basic development is very fast and very powerful, but it doesn't necessarily lend itself very well to large and complex applications. Using the capabilities of objects and components, we can more easily create and maintain very complex applications. The best part of this is that we can continue to leverage our existing Visual Basic skills, because working with business objects is really an evolutionary change rather than an entirely revolutionary approach.

The most significant change in our development, when we use objects, is that we follow a somewhat different architecture than we've used in traditional development. As we go through this chapter, we'll be looking at traditional Visual Basic architectures and the impact of business objects and binary components upon those traditional architectures.

Most large applications are implemented in a client/server environment, with the application's processing spread across a number of machines, including the user's workstation, a database server, and possibly an application server that sits in the middle. We'll look at this type of architecture, and see how we can use our business objects to take full advantage of all these machines.

Building Applications with Components

To begin with, let's take a quick look at some of the key techniques and concepts we've used to develop applications, and how these traditional techniques can be used when we're working with business objects. Most of these techniques will carry over, though sometimes there will be some subtle differences.

Event-Driven Programming

Visual Basic programming (and Windows programming, more generally) is almost entirely geared towards event-driven programming. This means that our programs are typically composed of subroutines that are run only in response to external events - such as a mouse click. It is a rare Windows program that runs a series of procedures from top to bottom and is done.

Most mini-computer, mainframe and DOS-based applications were sequential in nature. They gathered the user's input in a specific order, processed it, and generated specific output. This was all very predictable, since the application itself was very much in control.

In an event-driven environment, such as Windows, our applications effectively give control over to the user. The user gets to choose in which order they want to enter any input, when it should be processed and often how and where the results should be displayed. Rather than being in control, our application code sits in the background waiting for the user to indicate what should be done.

For instance, let's look at how we might get input from the user. In a sequential application, we'd prompt the user for input when we needed it. In some form of DOS BASIC, that process might look like this:

```
Print "Name? ";
Input strName
Print "Age? ";
Input intAge
Call DoProcessing(strName, intAge)
```

Here, the program is in control: it asks the user for each bit of information in turn, and the user has no choice but to follow the program's flow from top to bottom.

Within Visual Basic, the approach is entirely different. We display a form to the user, allowing them to choose into which field, if any, they want to enter information:

Our code, rather than being a single sequential list of commands, now becomes a series of subroutines that are only run when specific events occur. For instance, as the user enters values into each text box on the screen, we may react to the input events and store the values in variables:

```
Private Sub txtName_Change()
  strName = txtName
End Sub

Private Sub txtAge_Change()
  intAge = Val(txtAge)
End Sub
```

Then, in response to the **Click** event caused when the user clicks the OK button, we might perform some processing:

```
Private Sub cmdOK_Click()
  DoProcessing(strName, intAge)
End Sub
```

Either approach gets the job done, but the event-driven approach turns a lot of control back over to the user. This is, generally, a positive thing: users usually like to have a choice about how they use their applications.

Events and Objects

Event-driven programming works well when we're dealing with objects. This is because an event is basically a type of message. When the user clicks on a button, our program gets a message saying, "*Hey, the user clicked the button*". Of course, the message comes to us in the form of an event - in this case, the **Click** event for our button. Still, what we basically received was a message that something happened.

When we're dealing with objects, we always interact with an object though its interface; that is, its properties and methods. When we call an object's method, we do so by *sending it a message*. This may not be very obvious, since, within our code, it looks as if we just called a method on the object. Take this line of code, for example:

```
objCustomer.CreateInvoice
```

This code *looks* like a call to the **CreateInvoice** subroutine within the **Customer** class module. However, it's important to remember, when dealing with objects, that this kind of code actually sends a **CreateInvoice** *message* to the **objCustomer** object.

Our objects react to such events in the same way that Visual Basic programs have always reacted to events: using a subroutine.

```
Public Sub CreateInvoice()
  ' create the invoice here
End Sub
```

Any time we interact with an object, we're doing so by sending it a message. From the object's perspective, a message is basically an event caused by some outside force (typically, our program's code or some other object), and so our objects are always driven by events - just like our traditional Visual Basic applications.

Code Behind Forms

In traditional Visual Basic applications, most programs have tended to respond to the events caused by the user - through the forms and controls that we've provided on our forms. So it's been very common to find the code to handle these events directly behind the controls that raise them.

Many developers have therefore written the bulk of their code in the subroutines that run when particular events fire:

```
Private Sub cmdButton_Click()
    ' do all the work here
End Sub
```

Meanwhile, other developers have tended to call centralised subroutines in the module's **General** section, or subroutines that have been placed in a separate code module:

```
Private Sub cmdButton_Click()
    DoWork()
End Sub

Private Sub DoWork()
    ' do all the work here
End Sub
```

Either way, the results have been the same: Visual Basic code has been directly invoked by the events raised in the user-interface (UI).

Putting code behind events from the UI hasn't provided us with much in the way of code reuse. The most that we've been able to hope for is to use code modules - so that we can call our code from multiple forms.

To use code in other projects, we've had to copy original code into our new projects, causing duplicate code and maintenance problems down the line. Another approach has been to include the same code module in multiple projects; but then we run the risk that modifying the code in the module will break any other programs that rely on the module. Even if we don't break the programs, they need to be recompiled and redistributed to take advantage of our changes.

By designing our applications with business objects and components, we now have the opportunity to make it significantly easier to reuse our code. Instead of trying to reuse source code, we can package that code into binary components and use those components anywhere we need them.

If we create a component that provides some key functionality - everything to do with our customers, for instance - then we can use that component in any program that needs to deal with customers. As long as we are careful not to change or remove any properties or methods from our objects, we can change or add anything we want to our customer component with little risk of breaking existing programs.

Access to Data

Most business applications deal with data. Traditional Visual Basic applications have implemented code to work directly with the database. The database could be local, or on a mapped network drive, such as a Microsoft Access database. Others would be maintained by an actual database server such as Microsoft SQL Server or Oracle.

Visual Basic hasn't always had easy access to databases. In fact, it wasn't until Visual Basic 3.0 that we had easy access to databases - through a data access model and the infamous data control. Using the JET database engine, we could finally open up databases and work with the data using native elements of the Visual Basic language. Through JET we even had access to SQL database servers through Open DatabaseOpen Database Connectivity (ODBC).

The JET engine worked well enough to create two-tier client/server applications, but it tended to be slow and inflexible. There was no easy way to tap into the power of the SQL database server from our applications. Without resorting to direct calls to the ODBC API, or using proprietary database libraries, there was no way to avoid the use of the JET engine for database access.

Visual Basic 4.0 added a couple of important capabilities: Remote Data Objects (RDO), and an enhanced data access model in the form of Data Access Objects (DAO). RDO is a thin object layer built on top of the ODBC API that provides a substantial performance boost over JET - as well as giving us more capabilities to use the power of a database server. The enhanced DAO with Visual Basic 4.0 offered powerful new capabilities for working with Access databases, but provided little help for dealing with ODBC data sources.

Now, with Visual Basic 5.0, we have even more capabilities. RDO 2.0 offers even more powerful and faster access to ODBC data sources. We can use the familiar DAO model to efficiently access ODBC data sources using ODBCDirect. ODBCDirect provides us with the same DAO object model we use for Access databases, but it uses RDO behind the scenes to provide us with significant performance benefits.

Even more importantly, Visual Basic 5.0 allows us to create components. These components can be run on the user's workstation, on the database server, or on an application server sitting in the middle. Using the current data access technologies, such as RDO and ODBCDirect, we can create components that interact with the database. We can then use those components to develop our applications - and the application won't have to know about or deal with any database issues at all. We'll get into a lot more detail through the remainder of this chapter and at various points throughout the book.

Use of Controls

As we observed in Chapter 1, controls are one of the distinguishing features of Visual Basic, and probably Visual Basic's greatest contribution to the software industry.

VBX Controls

Unfortunately, VBX technology has some severe limitations. In particular, there's very little flexibility in the way that Visual Basic interacts with the controls. VBX controls have to provide a predefined list of methods, regardless of what the control actually does. Furthermore, a control developer can't add new methods to a control, making it very difficult to provide advanced functionality to the end developer. Instead, many controls provide an **Action** property, where the developer can set the property to a whole range of values to get different effects. This certainly doesn't lead to readable code; who knows what this might do:

```
myControl.Action = 21
```

To cap it off, Microsoft chose not to support the VBX standard in the Win32 environment. This means that VBX controls are now only available to developers working in 16-bit Windows. For 32-bit development, we need to use ActiveX controls.

ActiveX Controls

ActiveX controls have largely removed the limitations of VBX controls by extending the VBX concept with more flexibility and more powerful capabilities. Like VBX controls, ActiveX controls typically provide a visual 'widget' for use in developing user-interfaces. However, they are also binary components; that is, they can contain multiple objects. This means that ActiveX controls can implement a complex interface, including any properties or methods that are needed to make the control useful.

Rather than implementing a generic and hard-to-read **Action** property, an ActiveX control can implement a descriptive method, for example:

```
myControl.SpinLeft
```

As the Visual Basic tool has matured, so have its capabilities with regard to controls. Today, ActiveX controls are a specialised form of component for use in building user-interfaces. As a component, ActiveX controls can contain objects, and they can make those objects available to help implement any required functionality in a program.

With Visual Basic 5.0, we have the ability to create our own ActiveX controls. We can create them as purely visual widgets for use in developing user-interfaces, or we can make them more complex by treating the control as a component and including objects.

Certainly, most controls are just visual widgets, and that is their primary function. At the same time, there are more techniques available for the distribution of controls to client workstations, or across the Internet, than there are for other ActiveX servers such as DLLs or EXEs. There are times when it's preferable to package objects within a control simply because that control can be automatically downloaded to a Web browser or other client where the objects are needed.

Use of Components

Components, as I've defined them, are binary entities that contain one or more objects that can be used by applications. The components we can create with Visual Basic are always ActiveX servers:

either in-process servers (DLLs) or out-of-process servers (EXEs). With Visual Basic 5.0, we can also create ActiveX controls, which are a more specialised form of component.

Let's review the benefits of using components, which we discussed in Chapter 1.

Reuse

One of the key benefits of binary components is a high level of reuse. We can use a single component in many applications, continually enhancing and improving the component without having to recompile or redistribute the client programs. For instance, we can create an application that uses version 1.0 of a component, as shown in the figure:

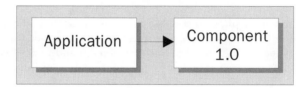

If we then find that this component would be useful in another application, with minor enhancements, we can use it as shown in the next figure:

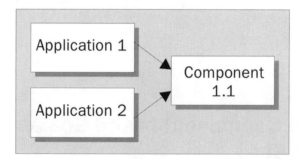

As long as we make sure the properties and methods in version 1.0 of the component are not changed as we enhance it to version 1.1, our original application can continue to use the component without change. This means that we don't need to recompile or redistribute the first application - a very important consideration if our application is installed on hundreds or thousands of client workstations.

Flexibility

The components that we create using Visual Basic are always ActiveX servers. This is important, because ActiveX servers can be used by many development languages and tools - even ones that we may not foresee, as we create our applications.

For instance, we may create an application where our business objects are in an ActiveX DLL. We could then create a user-interface for those objects using Visual Basic forms and controls, pretty much just like any other program. After we deploy our application (both the UI program and our DLL), someone else may create *their own* user interface for our DLL, perhaps using Microsoft Excel, Active Server Pages or just about any other Windows development environment.

This is a powerful advantage to us as developers. We can provide an unprecedented level of flexibility to our customers, since they can use part or all of our application as building blocks for the development of their own custom solutions. While we may provide a base application with a standard user-interface, our customers may choose to create their own user-interface - or extend our application's functionality to suit their specific needs.

Client/Server

The ability to create components that contain one or more objects is key to the development of applications that are highly scalable. Since version 3.0, it's been practical to develop two-tier client/server applications using Visual Basic. Using components, we're now able to create more complex applications across any number of tiers.

This is true regardless of how many physical computers are involved. Even on a single machine, we can separate our application's business functionality from the user-interface through the use of components. If our business logic is contained in business objects, and those objects are in an ActiveX DLL, then we've effectively separated our objects from any user-interface that might be created to use that DLL.

Alternatively, we might put our business objects in an ActiveX EXE, or use Microsoft Transaction Server, so that they're running on another physical machine across the network. This technique allows our applications to utilise the processing power of many machines and to minimise the amount of information that's sent back and forth over the network.

In the next section, we'll look at a specific application architecture, which we'll call the **Component-based Scalable Logical Architecture** (CSLA for short), that can be used on a single workstation and yet easily be converted to run across many machines on a network.

Introducing the Component-based Scalable Logical Architecture (CSLA)

To effectively use business objects and components to develop our applications, it's very helpful to start with a good **logical architecture**. This means that we want to start with a firm idea about what types of services our application will provide, and whether we want to implement them in our user-interface, in components or in a SQL database server.

In this section, we'll look in detail at the logical architecture that we'll be using throughout the remainder of the book. The CSLA is designed to work well whether it's placed entirely on a single workstation or whether it's spread across a number of machines in a network. With this type of design, we can scale an application from a single to many users with relative ease.

A logical architecture includes all the parts of an application. For instance, a typical three-tier application is composed of the following parts:

- ❏ Presentation
- ❏ Business processing
- ❏ Data processing

The following diagram shows how these parts, or tiers, work together to make up an application:

The presentation tier, or user-interface, acts as a client to our business objects. The business processing is handled by the middle tier. This tier is composed of our business objects, all working together to implement the functionality required for our application. The business objects themselves rely on the third tier to manage data processing, storing, retrieving and manipulating data within our databases.

The best way to see how an application can be divided into tiers is to look at a traditional application and break it apart - so that's what we'll do now.

Splitting Up a Traditional Application

Let's take a simple Visual Basic application, like any we may have created in Visual Basic 3.0. An application typically has at least one form for the user-interface, along with some code to do any work that needs to be done, and the application probably talks to a database to store and retrieve data.

The Application

To keep this very simple, let's build a quick Visual Basic application that has a single form and uses a simple text file as a logical database. This example demonstrates the distinct layers of an application.

We'll just have a simple form, as shown below. The text box is called **txtName** and the command buttons are **cmdGet** and **cmdPut**:

Let's suppose that we have two business rules. The first is that the name must be in uppercase, and the second is that the name is required.

To ensure that the name is uppercase, we'll add the following code:

```
Option Explicit

Private Sub txtName_LostFocus()
  txtName.Text = UCase$(txtName.Text)
End Sub
```

And to make sure we don't save a blank name, we'll add this code:

```
Private Sub cmdPut_Click()
  If Len(Trim$(txtName.Text)) = 0 Then
    MsgBox "You must enter a name", vbInformation
    Exit Sub
  End If
End Sub
```

Now let's just add some code to save the name to a file. This would normally be saving to a database, but we want to keep the program very simple to illustrate the different processes that are happening:

```
Private Sub cmdPut_Click()

  Dim lngFile As Long

  If Len(Trim$(txtName.Text)) = 0 Then
    MsgBox "You must enter a name", vbInformation
    Exit Sub
  End If

  lngFile = FreeFile
  Open "C:\TEMP.TMP" For Output As file
  Print #lngFile, txtName.Text
  Close lngFile

End Sub
```

Finally, we'll add some code in behind **cmdGet** to pull the name back in from our 'database':

```
Private Sub cmdGet_Click()
  Dim lngFile As Long
  Dim strInput As String

  file = FreeFile
  Open "C:\TEMP.TMP" For Input As lngFile
  Line Input #file, strInput
  txtName.Text = strInput
  Close file
End Sub
```

Now run the program. As you can see, we're able to store and retrieve a name. Furthermore, we won't save a blank name, and any name that we do save is stored in uppercase.

Now let's examine the program from the viewpoint of a three-tier logical model. We'll try to determine which parts of the program perform the presentation, which parts the business logic and which parts the data processing.

The Presentation Tier

This is really the user-interface, or how the program presents information to the user and collects information from the user. In our simple example, the presentation layer certainly includes the form itself:

The presentation layer also includes some of the code that we put behind the form, but certainly not all the code is directly related to the presentation. In the following listing, the presentation code is highlighted:

```
Option Explicit

Private Sub cmdGet_Click()
    Dim lngFile As Long
    Dim strInput As String

    lngFile = FreeFile
    Open "C:\TEMP.TMP" For Input As lngFile
    Line Input #file, strInput
    txtName.Text = strInput
    Close file
End Sub

Private Sub cmdPut_Click()
    Dim lngFile As Long

    If Len(Trim$(txtName.Text)) = 0 Then
        MsgBox "You must enter a name", vbInformation
        Exit Sub
    End If

    lngFile = FreeFile
    Open "C:\TEMP.TMP" For Output As lngFile
    Print #lngFile, txtName.Text
    Close file
End Sub

Private Sub txtName_LostFocus()
    txtName.Text = UCase$(txtName.Text)
End Sub
```

Out of all that code, almost none of it is involved in actually presenting data to the user. Take a look at the lines that we've highlighted. For instance, we need to display the name after we've retrieved it from storage:

```
txtName.Text = strInput
```

Notice, however, that this line is stuck right in the middle of several other lines of code that have nothing to do with presenting the data.

Detecting that **txtName** is blank is a business rule, so that is not part of the presentation. Notifying the user that it is blank, however, is indeed part of the user interface:

```
MsgBox "You must enter a name", vbInformation
```

Again, our presentation code is in the middle of other code that is not interface-related. The upshot of this is that if we want to change the business rule, or we want to change the presentation, then we're going to be changing the same code block for either task.

That wasn't too bad, but the line in the **LostFocus** event is not so cut and dried. This line does two things: it converts the name to uppercase (a business rule), and it displays the name back into the form so that the user can see the final result (a presentation choice):

```
txtName.Text = UCase$(txtName.Text)
```

Looking at these lines of code, you can see just what a mess we've gotten ourselves into. We have no way of changing the interface without tampering with business-related code, and we can't change our business rules without affecting the interface code.

The Business Tier

Let's now look at the parts of the program that handle the business logic or business rules. Again, it's only a part of the overall program, so we'll highlight the areas that we need to examine:

```
Option Explicit

Private Sub cmdGet_Click()
  Dim lngFile As Long
  Dim strInput As String

  lngFile = FreeFile
  Open "C:\TEMP.TMP" For Input As lngFile
  Line Input #lngFile, strInput
  txtName.Text = strInput
  Close file
End Sub

Private Sub cmdPut_Click()
  Dim lngFile As Long

    If Len(Trim$(txtName.Text)) = 0 Then

      MsgBox "You must enter a name", vbInformation
```

```
      Exit Sub
   End If

   lngFile = FreeFile
   Open "C:\TEMP.TMP" For Output As lngFile
   Print #lngFile, txtName.Text
   Close lngFile
End Sub

Private Sub txtName_LostFocus()
   txtName.Text = UCase$(txtName.Text)
End Sub
```

In the **cmdPut_Click** event, we need to make sure that the name is not blank - and avoid saving the value if it is:

```
If Len(Trim$(txtName.Text)) = 0 Then
   MsgBox "You must enter a name", vbInformation
   Exit Sub
End If
```

Once again, notice how there is code managing the presentation layer right in the middle of our business processing.

The situation is worse (but now rather familiar) within the **LostFocus** event: we see the *same line* that we saw in the presentation layer, now working for our business processing to make sure that the name is in upper case:

```
txtName.Text = UCase$(txtName.Text)
```

Furthermore, suppose we need to provide access to this name to some other program, or from some other part of the same program: since the business logic is so tied into the display of this form, we'd have to duplicate the business code elsewhere.

Clearly, this is not an ideal way to organise an application.

The Data Services Tier

In our simple example, the data service code (highlighted in the following code) is fairly straightforward:

```
Option Explicit

Private Sub cmdGet_Click()
   Dim lngFile As Long
   Dim strInput As String

   lngFile = FreeFile
   Open "C:\TEMP.TMP" For Input As lngFile
   Line Input #lngFile, strInput

   txtName.Text = strInput
```

```
      Close file
   End Sub

   Private Sub cmdPut_Click()
     Dim lngFile As Long

      If Len(Trim$(txtName.Text)) = 0 Then
        MsgBox "You must enter a name", vbInformation
        Exit Sub
      End If

      lngFile = FreeFile
      Open "C:\TEMP.TMP" For Output As lngFile
      Print #1lngFile, txtName.Text
      Close file
   End Sub

   Private Sub txtName_LostFocus()
      txtName.Text = UCase$(txtName.Text)
   End Sub
```

Still, in both the **cmdGet_Click** and **cmdPut_Click** event code, the data processing is mixed right in with the presentation and business logic, making it difficult to change the data processing without risking the other parts of the program.

The n-tier Solution

Certainly, there are conventional solutions to help deal with these problems - including putting code in BAS modules, or creating class modules to hold this code. Unfortunately, these solutions don't fully meet the needs of code reuse and separating (or partitioning) the various parts of the application.

The ideal solution is to pull the user-interface code into one area, the business logic into another and the data processing into a third. By breaking our application into these tiers, we can make it much easier to change any section of our program with less risk of causing bugs in the other tiers. By avoiding the case where a single routine includes code for both presentation and business logic for instance, we can change our presentation code without impacting the business code itself.

We can also facilitate code reuse. For instance, the code in the business tier may be useful to more than one form in the user-interface tier. If our business code is intermingled with the presentation code, it can be very difficult to use that business logic across various different presentations. By separating the code, we can make it very easy for our application to show the same business information through various presentations.

Splitting up Business Processing

Developing a logical multi-tier architecture for our applications helps to partition code by separating the presentation, business and data processing. Once we've partitioned the application into manageable parts, we can build components to hold the objects at each level within the program.

Deciding exactly where to split the functionality is not easy. Even in the simple example that we just looked at, the code to convert the name to uppercase essentially belongs to both the presentation and business layers:

```
txtName.Text = UCase$(txtName.Text)
```

If we choose to put this line in the presentation tier then we're able to give the user timely feedback - indicating that the name has been converted to uppercase. But this means that we've put a business rule in the presentation tier, which is far from preferable.

We could put the code in the business tier - a good place for it, since it's a general rule that should be enforced regardless of the interface. Doing this, however, can make it much more difficult for the user-interface to provide timely feedback to the user. It's entirely possible that the business tier will be running on another machine somewhere in the network, so we could be adding a lot of network traffic if the presentation tier is asking the business layer for field-by-field information all the time.

Another possibility is to put the code in both locations. This provides timely feedback to the user, and lets the business tier centrally enforce the rule. Of course, we've duplicated the code by doing this, and so the program becomes much harder to maintain in the long run.

None of these are optimal solutions. This is one of the hardest issues we face as developers of distributed systems. It would be nice if there was a definite answer, so we could say *this is the way to do it*. Unfortunately, the choice depends on many factors, and these factors are different for each project.

So, the question remains: what are we to do about this partitioning problem? In general, there are two possible approaches: the rich (interactive) interface, and the batch interface. We'll take a look at each of these now.

Rich Interface

Advocates of the rich interface look at the evolution of software from dull, non-interactive screens, to highly-interactive, graphical displays, and want to provide that experience for the user.

Word processing is an excellent example. Years ago, people entered their text, along with various arcane codes, into what was essentially a glorified text editor. From there, they could print their text and see what it looked like after it was formatted. User demand pressured vendors into developing what-you-see-is-what-you-get word processing, so the user eventually received a highly interactive interface with immediate feedback on appearance. Even more recently, tools such as Microsoft Word have begun to subtly provide feedback on spelling by underlining misspelled words as the user types. In short, users *like* highly interactive, well-designed interfaces.

However, there is a cost to providing this rich interface: it requires that many of the business rules be easily and quickly accessible from the presentation layer. If the rules are located on a server out on the network, then the presentation layer will have to make calls across that network - which will probably result in dismal interface performance.

The solution is to put some or all of the business rule processing on the clients, thus allowing the presentation layer to easily and quickly access those rules - which should provide a highly interactive experience for the user.

The major drawback to this solution is that it requires that we run part of our application on the client workstation. This can be a serious problem if we need to distribute the application to hundreds or thousands of client workstations. Fortunately, there are many new technologies becoming available, in the Windows environment, to automatically manage this distribution. For example, Microsoft Internet Explorer and Microsoft's Zero Administration Initiative both automate the installation of client-side components.

Batch Interface

On-Line Transaction Processing (OLTP) developers have long subscribed to a *batch input* concept. Web browser interfaces also follow along this line, since it minimises network traffic and leaves virtually no processing on the client.

Interfaces constructed with this technique allow the user to enter virtually anything on the screen, and perform little or no screening of input while the data is being entered. When the user accepts the screen, the business rules check all the entries and report a list of problems with the data.

The benefit to this approach is significant. All the business rules are centralised and so easily maintained. The presentation layer does virtually no work beyond that required by the controls with which the user interacts. This approach virtually eliminates the logistic problems of maintaining hundreds or thousands of clients.

The downside to batch interfaces is that the user-interface is very much non-interactive, since it gives the user no immediate feedback. In many cases, this type of interface will be unacceptable to the end users, who often want their application moved to Windows specifically to escape a batch-style interface.

The Best of Both Worlds

The conflict between rich and batch interfaces is significant. As developers, we want to provide the user with the best, most interactive interface that we can manage. At the same time, we need to provide good performance, and design the application to be easily manageable - since it's going to be deployed to hundreds or thousands of client machines.

Visual Basic provides us with the tools to overcome these problems. To do this, we need to adopt an architecture where we split the business processing into two parts:

1   User-interface (UI)-centric business processing
2   Data-centric business processing

The idea behind splitting the business processing apart is to keep processing as physically close to where it is needed as possible. This means that the processing needed by the presentation layer should be physically close, typically on the client. Processing that mostly works with data should be closer to the data source, often on a central application server.

If we look at a typical business object, we'll find that it provides some services that are only useful for developing an interface. We'll also find that it provides some services that are mostly useful for supporting data processing.

For instance, let's consider a simple *Product* object. Such an object might implement the following services:

Service	Purpose
ID	ID value of the product
Name	Product's name
Price	Product's price
QOH	Quantity of the product on hand
Receive(Quantity)	Receive some amount of the product into the inventory
Allocate(Quantity)	Allocate some amount of the product from the inventory
Load(ID)	Load the object from the database
Save()	Save the object into the database
Delete()	Delete the object from the database

Typically, we'd implement a Product object such that it implements all of these services. The problem is that we're left with a single object that needs to run on one machine - either the client or the server.

This puts us back at the rich versus batch interface crossroads. If we put the object on the client, we can provide a rich interface, but we've also put the data access methods on the client. If we put the object on the server, the client will need to go across the network to use any of the services provided by the object, so the user-interface would typically communicate with the object in a batch format; in other words, we're back to providing a batch interface for the user.

However, suppose we split our Product object into two separate objects: a UI-centric Product object, and a data-centric Product object. Let's consider this now.

UI-centric Business Processing

Our UI-centric Product object would provide the following services:

Property/Method	Purpose
ID	ID value of the product
Name	Product's name
Price	Product's price

Table continued on following page

Property/Method	Purpose
QOH	Quantity of the product on hand
Receive(Quantity)	Receive some amount of the product into the inventory
Allocate(Quantity)	Allocate some amount of the product from the inventory

All these services would very likely be used only by the user-interface. By making these available in their own object, we have the option of putting that object in a component that will be installed on each client. Now the UI code will be able to interact with this object locally, without any network traffic. Any business rules that are implemented by these services will be enforced interactively. Thus we can implement a rich, highly interactive interface for the user.

In general, the UI-centric business processing resides on the client machine, so it's readily accessible to the presentation layer. This is processing that does not require interaction with the database or with other centralised resources. We're including a lot of business rules and business processing in this category.

For instance, if a data field can only accept a future date, this is the place for that rule. If a series of values need to be totalled together and run through a mathematical formula, this too is where the processing belongs.

On the other hand, if a field needs to be checked against a column in a large table, or verified against some external data source (like a credit check), then this is the wrong place to do the work.

By keeping the UI-centric processing close to the client, we can build some very nice, highly interactive user-interfaces. While we can't tell the user about *every* business rule violation that they might cause, we can probably catch the majority of them and present it to the user in a timely fashion.

Data-centric Business Processing

The data-centric Product object would provide the following services:

Property/Method	Purpose
Load(ID)	Load the object from the database
Save()	Save the object into the database
Delete()	Delete the object from the database

These services interact exclusively with the database to retrieve, add, update or remove our object's data. These are not the type of service that the user-interface requires on a field-by-field basis, so we won't take any serious performance hit by running them on a separate machine from the client workstation.

A lot of business rules require quick access to the data source or some other centralised resource, such as a credit checking service via TCP/IP or messaging such as a central fax service. Again, in keeping with the philosophy that processing should be performed physically close to the source, this type of business rule belongs on some central machine. Usually, this would be an application server, although that may vary. We'll discuss physical architectures more thoroughly in Chapter 4.

> It's important to understand that data-centric business processing is not the same as data services. Data services are mostly concerned with storage, retrieval and integrity of data; business processing, on the other hand, is all about enforcing business rules and performing any business logic.

A good example of a data-centric business rule is that of verifying a user's entry against a column in a very large table. It is not practical, or desirable, to download all that data to the client machine, so the rule can't be enforced there.

Such a rule might belong in the data services (implemented in SQL) if it's just a simple lookup. But suppose the business rule is more complex - such that more processing is required beyond just the lookup. This is often much easier to do in a high-level language, such as Visual Basic, than it is to do in a SQL stored procedure.

As another example, suppose we have an order entry application, and our users want automatically generated sequential order numbers that need to be displayed as soon as the order screen is presented to the user. Generating sequential order numbers is a form of business processing, but to make them sequential across all clients requires centralised processing. We *could* do this at the database level, but it would probably make more sense to handle it through our business logic. Implementing a simple business service to provide the next sequential order number is easy, and keeping it at this level can help reduce the load on the database server.

Tying Together the Business Logic

Even though we've split the business processing into two parts, they are still integral. In fact, they *must* work together efficiently, since neither the UI-centric nor data-centric processing can, by themselves, provide all the business logic required for an application.

> What we need is for the two parts of the business processing to handle all their communications internally, so that neither the presentation layer, nor the data processing layer, is aware that the business logic has been split apart. Essentially, we want it to appear as single layer of software.

Each UI-centric (client-side) business object must be able to efficiently communicate with any corresponding data-centric (server-side) object. The communication between these objects will typically be across a network, and so the goal is to minimise the dialog between the objects.

In Chapter 4, we'll go into the details and see how we can make this communication fast and practical.

An n-tier Architecture

So far, we've looked at a three-tier architecture and how we can split our business processing into two distinct parts: UI-centric and data-centric. What we've really done is move from a three-tier architecture to an **n-tier** architecture. The new architecture consists of the following four layers:

- ❑ Presentation
- ❑ UI-centric business objects
- ❑ Data-centric business objects
- ❑ Data services

If you look back at the three-tier diagram in Chapter 1 and compare it to the following figure, you'll note that all we've done is split the business tier into two parts:

This may seem like a small change, but in reality it is very significant. By splitting the UI-centric processing from the data-centric processing, we've given ourselves much more flexibility. We can now keep the UI-centric processing on the client, so we can provide a rich interface for the user. At the same time, we have the option of moving the data-centric processing away from the client to a machine with faster access to the database, so we can gain significant performance benefits.

Let's go through each part of this architecture and see how it works. We'll be using this architecture throughout the remainder of the book, so we need to make sure it's clear in our minds as we go forward.

Presentation Tier

To start off, we have the most visible part of the whole application: the user-interface. Traditionally, these are the forms, menus, and controls that the user uses to interact with our program. It's quite reasonable, however, that we might need to expand this definition to fit into today's environment. The presentation layer for our application might not just be made up of Visual Basic forms anymore. Rather, it might be an HTML page, a spreadsheet, a word processor, or another entire application.

The key thing to keep in mind about the user-interface is that *it is not the application*. As we'll see shortly, the business objects are the application; the user-interface is just how the user chooses to interact with our objects.

> The goal is to create programs that are independent of the presentation to the user. This means that our application can have many different user-interfaces implemented in different tools and technologies.

As we discussed earlier, in a typical Visual Basic application almost all the code, and therefore almost all the processing, lives in the user-interface. Programmers put most of their code behind controls on their forms. Other programmers put the code in code modules to be called from the forms, but really the processing is still entirely centered around the interface:

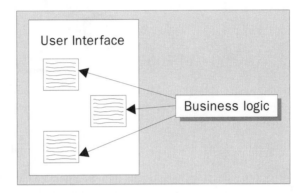

This is an ideal technique when we're writing event-driven programs, and so it has worked well for us so far. The events come from the user-interface, and so it makes perfect sense for all the code to be directly linked to that interface.

Unfortunately, this approach doesn't work nearly so well when we're trying to develop an object-oriented model for our program, since the focus of the program is on the interaction between objects rather than on an interaction with events in the interface.

Our users often want more than just a traditional user-interface; they may also want a web browser interface, for instance. A more advanced user might even want access to our application from Visual Basic for Applications (VBA), so they can work with the application from within their spreadsheet or word processor.

Also, the part of an application that typically changes the most is the user-interface. Users like to tweak their interface almost continually, and so it seems as if there is a constant stream of requests to move the controls around or replace radio buttons with a combo box and so forth. If our code is primarily placed behind the controls on forms then even an apparently simple interface change can be complex. Not only do we have to change the interface, but we probably have to rearrange the actual business logic to compensate for the changes.

This is not an easy request to fulfil if we have a substantial amount of code tied to our Visual Basic form interface. Even putting much of the code in BAS modules doesn't help, since neither Excel nor browser-based interfaces will have easy access to the code.

On the other hand, if our program is built based on components that contain business objects then we can easily write a flexible interface, or even a number of interfaces, to talk to our application:

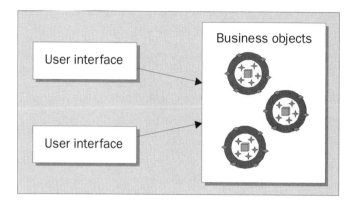

Changes to a Visual Basic form interface now become much simpler, and safer, since our business code is independent of the code inside the form.

Also, our application automatically supports any program that can act as a client to an ActiveX server. This includes most Windows development tools and productivity software (such as Microsoft Excel). Even the Web browser problem becomes much simpler, since we can use Active Server Pages to directly access the application's business objects to create HTML pages for the browser:

At this point, it may not be entirely clear how this architecture can be implemented with Visual Basic. As we get further into business objects, we'll delve into the details and see just how well this whole idea works out. This architecture has been used in the development of a number of large projects with great success - that's happy users, good performance and long term maintainability!

UI-centric Business Objects

Instead of putting the bulk of the code for our application behind Visual Basic forms, we'll move that code into business objects. By doing this, we can apply object-oriented design techniques to build an object model, and put the business rules and processing into the objects of that model.

In Chapter 1, we defined what a business object is - on a fairly high level. In summary:

> **Business objects are the core of your business solution. With Visual Basic, they are instances of class modules that are designed to represent the real-world 'objects' with which our application is dealing.**

In Chapter 3, we'll go through some techniques that we can use to identify real-world objects and translate them into software objects.

The user-interface is really a client, or user, of the business objects. While the user-interface displays and retrieves data from the user, the business objects need to provide all the business functionality and capabilities required by the user interface. At the same time, the business objects need to enforce all the business rules and relationships to meet the design requirements of our application.

The business objects should provide appropriate access to all the functionality of the application. The presentation tier, even including macros in other applications such as Microsoft Word, should be able to use the components containing our business objects to do their work.

The business objects contain the business rules for the real-world entities that they represent. For instance, if a business rule says that a customer must have a last name, there should be code in the customer business object to make sure that the last name isn't blank. You might find something like the following code in the **LastName** property of a customer object:

```
Public Property Let LastName(Name As String)
   If Len(Name) = 0 Then
      Err.Raise vbObjectError + 10, "Customer class", _
         "Last name can not be blank"
   Else
      strLastName = Name
   End If
End Property
```

Business objects interact with each other by following the rules laid out by our object model. Business rules dictate how the objects work with, or relate to, each other.

As an example, perhaps a customer can have many phone numbers. Translating this into business objects, our customer object will have many phone objects. There is a relationship between the customer object and each phone object, in that each phone object is owned by a customer. This relationship needs to be coded somehow into either the customer or the phone objects. For instance, the phone objects may be stored as a collection inside the customer object:

```
Option Explicit

Private PhoneNumbers As New Collection
```

Our UI-centric business objects should be designed to accurately reflect the real-world business entities that our application needs to model. This means that each object should represent some entity, along with any attributes, methods and business rules that affect that entity. Our overall object model should also enforce any business rules regarding how objects interact.

Any user-interface will interact exclusively with our UI-centric business objects, and so these objects must not only implement and enforce all our business rules, but they need to provide all the capabilities that the UI developer will require to create a rich, interactive interface for the user.

Data-centric Business Objects

By splitting the data-centric processing out of our business objects, we've provided ourselves with a great deal of flexibility in terms of how we deploy our application. We can choose to implement the data-centric business objects in a DLL, so that it runs on the client workstation, or we can put them in an EXE running on another machine on the network. We can easily compile them into a DLL and run them within Microsoft Transaction Server (as we'll see later in the book).

Our data-centric business objects typically provide certain services that are used by our UI-centric business objects. When a UI-centric business object needs some work done that it can't do by itself, it just has a data-centric object do the work.

Our UI-centric business objects should provide the UI developer with an intuitive and reliable model of the real-world objects in our business. Our data-centric objects need to provide the UI-centric objects with a robust and powerful mechanism by which data can be saved and retrieved as needed. This means that all interaction with data sources should be managed by our data-centric objects; the client-side business objects should have no idea how data is stored or retrieved.

ODBC Data Sources

Most applications deal with data, and most data is stored in some type of database that we can reach using ODBC (Open Database Connectivity). Because of this, most of our data-centric business objects will make heavy use of data access technologies such as DAO, RDO and ADO.

Since our server-side business objects will handle all the database interaction, this is where we'll find all the SQL statements, recordsets, resultsets, database objects and so forth. It's the job of the data-centric business objects to translate all these relational database concepts into data that is useful to our client-side business objects.

As an added bonus, our data-centric business objects can be used to shield much of our application from the differences across various SQL databases. Since all the database interaction is managed by our server-side objects, we have only one place to change code when we need to support a new database.

While it's true that we can use ODBC to help minimise the differences between various databases, there is a cost. A prime example is an application that needs to run on a single workstation with an Access database *and* in a WAN environment with an Oracle database. Using ODBC, we can write a single set of data-centric objects that work with both databases. Unfortunately, our code will be optimised for neither Access nor Oracle, very possibly leading to unacceptable performance.

With little or no impact to our user-interface or the UI-centric business objects, we can make our data-centric business objects smart enough to deal with both types of database. These objects can be written to detect the type of database and to run the appropriate queries and use the appropriate data access techniques for either Access or Oracle as needed.

Along the same line, if we need to migrate from one kind of database to another then we only need to change the server-side business objects, not all the business objects on the clients. Perhaps our database was a legacy system, and we used screen-scraping technology to get at the data. If we later convert to Microsoft SQL Server, we can just change the data-centric business objects to get the data from the new source - with no impact to our user-interface or the client-side business objects.

Non-ODBC Data Sources

It's important to remember that data isn't always stored in a relational database. Many applications need access to specialised hardware or software. For instance, we may have objects that represent information that is stored in a proprietary laboratory information management system (LIMS) or some equivalent type of system. Perhaps our objects represent physical devices that load trucks with an appropriate mix of cement, sand and gravel to make ready-mix concrete.

As we discuss 'data-centric' business objects, we need to keep in mind that we aren't always working with ODBC, SQL, and other relatively simple data sources. Fortunately, the CSL architecture we're talking about allows us to shield our client-side business objects from all these details through the use of server-side objects. Our data-centric objects can interact with whatever data source we need to deal with, whether complex or not. At the same time, our UI-centric business objects can provide an easy, consistent interface for use by the UI developers.

Minimise Licensing Costs

If we're implementing our architecture across multiple physical machines, we have the option of moving the data-centric objects off the client workstations and on to a central application server machine. We might do this by putting the objects in an ActiveX EXE server and using DCOM, or we might put them into an ActiveX DLL server running within Microsoft Transaction Server. We'll look at examples of each approach later in the book.

By centralizing the data-centric objects on a separate application server machine, we've also centralised all the database interaction. This means that the clients don't need to have any direct access to the database, only to the application server.

This has a couple of benefits. Logistically, we may have simplified the client desktop - since we don't need to install and maintain ODBC drivers and data connections out there. Also, suppose we have 100 client workstations: traditionally, we'd have to buy 100 client licenses for our database. By using a centralised set of data services, we can let the clients share the connections to the database, thus reducing the number of client licenses that we need to purchase. Since most database vendors charge licensing on a *per connection* basis, we can save on licensing costs.

Data Services Tier

The final area we need to discuss is the data services tier. At a minimum, this tier is responsible for creating, updating, retrieving and deleting data from a data source. In many cases, it also includes more complex features, such as enforcement of relational integrity and other data-related rules.

In most cases, this data handling will actually take place on a database server. This allows us to put quite a bit of processing on the database server, using SQL-stored procedures and triggers. This can often provide important performance benefits, since most SQL database servers can optimise stored procedures so they run very efficiently.

It's important to note, however, that much of the work that a database server might have done in a application may actually be more appropriately placed in our data-centric business objects rather than in SQL code. SQL is notoriously difficult to work with. It doesn't compare to tools such as Visual Basic for features such as debugging and flexibility. While it's still very valid to do some SQL coding in an application, it is often much more cost effective to move the processing to a different layer of the application - where we can bring more powerful development tools to bear on the problem.

Summary

In this chapter, we've looked at event-driven programming, code behind forms, and other traditional design concepts. We saw how Visual Basic 5.0's object- and component-oriented features build upon older concepts to provide us with new and more powerful capabilities for software design.

We also walked through the concept of a logical three-tier application model, separating presentation, business logic and data processing. We developed a specific application model including a presentation tier, UI-centric business objects, data-centric business objects and a data services tier. We discussed how this CSL architecture can be implemented in environments ranging from a single workstation to a network where the processing is spread across multiple machines.

At this point, you should have a good understanding of how this architecture works and how business objects and binary components are used to implement it. As we progress through the remainder of the book, we'll build on these concepts and implement an application by making use of them.

From here, we'll explore these concepts in more practical detail. We'll look at:

- ❑ The design and creation of business objects
- ❑ How business objects are implemented in Visual Basic
- ❑ How business objects are used to create components
- ❑ The different types of components we can create using Visual Basic

Specifically, in the next chapter, we'll cover:

- ❑ Analysis of our business domain
- ❑ Identification of business objects
- ❑ Design of individual business objects
- ❑ How business objects interact
- ❑ Using business objects to model our business

3

Business Object Analysis

Overview

We've done some important work in the first two chapters. We've defined what we mean by business objects, we've considered the benefits of using business objects, and we've looked at some of the logical architectures that can use business objects to their best advantage. Now it's time to think about the relationship between our business objects and the real world they represent. Specifically, we're going to take a look at some of the techniques that can help us identify, in the very first instance, the actual business objects that we need to create when we're modeling business situations in the real world.

In this chapter, and through the rest of this book, we'll be creating three interrelated systems that are designed to help run a video rental store. We'll perform a detailed business object analysis of these systems within this chapter, which will provide us with a sound introduction to object analysis.

We'll be making extensive use of the **use case** technique in this chapter. This is a form of analysis that can be very useful for identifying and designing business objects. We'll also look at some of the common types of object relationship that can be found in real-world business systems, and we'll consider how we can design our business objects to support these relationships.

So here are the main business analysis themes in this chapter:

- ❑ Identifying and defining business objects
- ❑ Object attributes and behaviors
- ❑ Object relationships
- ❑ Analysis: our Video Store example project

In this chapter, we'll be focusing on the UI-centric business objects that were located within the Component-based Scalable Architecture (CSLA) that I presented in the last chapter:

The UI-centric business objects are the objects that most closely represent the real-world entities that we're trying to model with our software. As such, UI-centric objects also happen to be the heart of any application that's built upon this particular model.

> **Any presentation layer will be built directly on top of these UI-centric business objects, so a key requirement is that they provide a robust, easy-to-use model of our business processes.**

In this chapter, we'll look at real-world business entities and determine how to represent them as software objects. The technique we'll use to represent these business entities will be to model them, and the particular part of the business that we want to model will be our business **domain**. As we'll see, within this chapter, there are two major steps that we must accomplish if we are to successfully model our domain:

1 We need to figure out which real-world entities need to be part of our object model. From there, we can decide which attributes (properties) and behaviors (methods) these objects will need if they are to successfully represent our business entities.

2 We need to evaluate the relationships between our different objects. Objects can interact with or relate to each other in many different ways. We need to add properties, methods, and events to our objects so that they can work together to model our business processes.

*Another major aspect to the design comes when we decide which objects should go into different binary components, such as EXE's or DLL's. This is part of the **implementation design** of our objects, and we'll cover these issues in Chapter 4, where we discuss the creation of business object components.*

Once we've identified our business objects and their relationships, we'll have created a **logical object model**, which will help us decide how we can implement those relationships using Visual Basic.

The relationships we'll be discussing are commonly used in object-oriented design, but exactly how we implement them in Visual Basic may vary from implementation methods commonly seen in other languages.

Identifying and Defining Business Objects

Here's a question that I'm often asked when I'm talking about business objects: how do you figure out what objects to create? It's a good question. Sometimes, objects are pretty obvious; a *customer* object in a sales system, for instance. Unfortunately, not all business objects are so obvious, and it can take some work to identify them.

> **It's always important to do a good job of analysis when we're developing any software; but it's even more critical when we're designing software using object-oriented techniques. Since one of the main aims in using objects and components is to promote reuse, it's important to identify and design our objects effectively.**

There are plenty of books and articles that tell us all about rapid development and how we should quickly put together some objects and then let the object model evolve to meet future needs. This seems like an excellent idea; but unfortunately, this approach goes a long way toward defeating the reusability of the objects in the model.

If our evolutionary process requires that we change certain properties or methods that we've already added to an object, or that we must replace a single object with multiple objects, then we'll have to change all our client programs as well.

While it's true that we don't have to design every detail of our objects up front, it is very important that we identify our objects carefully. It's also very important that we get to the central behaviors of each object *right from the start*. The better the job that we can do during the analysis and design of our objects, the less risk we run of having to make substantial and costly changes later.

There are a number of approaches we can use to analyze and identify our business objects. These techniques include:

- ❑ Decomposition of business concepts and processes
- ❑ Deriving our objects from a data model
- ❑ CRC (Class, Responsibility and Collaborator) cards
- ❑ Use cases or scenarios

In an ideal world, we'd be able to design our applications without ever having to worry about an existing data model. And if we're lucky enough to be in this situation, we can start with our business object design and then build our data model to support our objects.

Since this is rarely an ideal world, however, it's much more likely that we'll be using an existing data source with a preset structure. But even in this case, we should still start by creating a business object model - with the understanding that we may have to compromise our model later on to fit it in with the existing database.

> **Using the CSLA, we can minimize the impact of the database design, since the data-centric business processing is handled separately from the objects that represent our business entities.**

Use Case Analysis

At its most basic level, a **use case** is simply a written description of a business process. We can employ this technique as a high-level analysis tool to determine overall system requirements, and to identify broad business objects that are involved in high-level processes. At the other end of the spectrum, we can get very specific in the use case description, defining detailed functionality and objects.

The process of starting with high-level use cases, and then zooming in to a number of increasingly detailed functional use cases, until we reach a set of specific objects and behaviors, is a technique known as **functional decomposition**.

This is very much a top-down approach to software analysis, and one that end users can usually relate to very well. It's easy to get a user to describe their high-level requirements, and then just continue to ask more and more questions to get a more detailed view of what they need. Usually, we can take the written use cases back to the user to make sure that what we heard and wrote down was actually what they meant.

Requirements Use Case or Scenario

At the broadest level, we can create use cases that help to define overall system requirements. This type of use case is known as a **requirements use case**, or a **scenario**. A requirements use case can help to identify some of the more major business objects in our business domain - despite the fact that the process is actually geared more towards gathering requirements than describing any specific functionality.

Use Case 1: Renting a Video

Here's an example of a requirements use case for a common activity: renting a video. Obviously, there are a number of other high-level use cases involved in the store's overall operation, but this case covers one broad process that's central to the store's business:

Requirements Use Case for Video Rental

The video store maintains an inventory of rentable videos for perusal by customers. A customer enters the store and browses the inventory to select any number of videos to rent.

The customer then brings the videos to the front counter where an attendant identifies the customer, makes note of each video, and calculates the total rental price. The attendant gives the customer an invoice, which lists the videos and shows the total amount due.

The customer pays for the rental and leaves with the videos. To avoid setting off the security alarm, the attendant hands the rented videos to the customer as they leave.

Use Case 2: Problem Recording

Here's another example of some related requirements that might be implemented, in a separate system, to track problems with videos:

Requirements Use Case for Video Problem Recording

The video store maintains an inventory of rentable videos. As the videos age they begin to have problems. By tracking the number of problems over time, the store can stop renting the videos before they get too bad.

The customer reports the problem to an attendant, either when the video is returned or sometimes over the phone. The attendant records the video's ID into the computer and indicates the nature or category of the problem, along with the date and (optionally) a text description.

Use Case 3: Rental Analysis Reporting

Finally, here are some requirements for a system that reports an analysis of video rentals.

Reporting requirements are often quite different from the rest of an application. Actual reporting is typically done through a reporting package that works directly against the data source. Data analysis is often best done by within business objects, since we can take full advantage of the logic we've coded into our objects.

Requirements Use Case for Rental Analysis

In order to decide what kinds of videos to provide for renting in the future, the store owner wants to analyze the inventory to identify which types of video make the most profit.

To do this, the computer needs to look at the number of times each video was rented and what the rental price was for each rental – essentially looking at the revenue generated by the video. This needs to be compared to the purchase cost of each video to determine whether the video recouped its cost effectively.

All this data needs to be consolidated to show the profitability of the videos - both by producing studio and by video category.

Identifying High-Level Requirements

The requirements use case descriptions are not very specific. There are a number of areas where we've identified requirements but not specific functionality. For example, some of the requirements we can derive from the *video rental* use case could include:

- ❑ The store maintains an inventory
- ❑ The inventory must be available for browsing
- ❑ The store employs an attendant
- ❑ There is a mechanism by which the attendant can identify a specific customer
- ❑ The attendant can identify specific videos
- ❑ There is a security system triggered by videos leaving the store

Identifying High-Level Objects

We can also pick out some potential high-level objects. This is an important step, since these objects are likely to be the ones that are shared across multiple use cases, and very likely across multiple applications within our organization. Basically, we just want to look through the use case and pick out all the nouns. Each noun has the potential to become a business object. Whether it ends up as a business object is something we'll determine through the rest of the process.

Here's a list of potential high-level business objects from the *video rental* use case:

Store	Attendant
Inventory	Invoice
Video	Rental price
Customer	Payment
Front counter	Security alarm

We'll use this list later on, as we go through the functional use cases and analysis. During that process, we'll identify some of the objects listed here as actual objects in our application; others, of course, won't be required. In this first phase, our objective is to identify any objects within the business domain - not just those that we'll code into our application.

Functional Use Case

A functional use case is much more specific than the requirements use case we just saw. Most requirements use cases will actually encompass a number of more detailed functional use cases. These are used less for determining system requirements than for defining required functionality. They are also very useful for identifying business objects.

Let's use a single sentence from the Video Rental requirements use case, above, as an example of a functional use case:

> The customer then brings the videos to the front counter where an attendant identifies the customer, makes note of each video, and calculates the total rental price.

There are a lot of things going on here, but the description is not nearly detailed enough to fully describe the functionality. All it does describe, of course, are the requirements. So let's develop a use case that defines the functionality to support these requirements:

Functional Use Case for Video Checkout

The customer places the videos on the counter and provides an ID card to the attendant. The attendant chooses the video rental menu option on the screen, then enters the customer's ID number by scanning the ID card with a barcode reader. This automatically retrieves the customer's name and address from the database, and displays the information on the screen. The entry point is left in position to enter the first video's ID number.

The attendant takes each video, in turn, and uses the barcode reader to enter the video's ID number by scanning the video jacket. This automatically retrieves the video's description and rental price, and displays them on the screen next to the video ID number.

As each video ID number is entered, a subtotal price is calculated and displayed at the bottom of the screen. Based on the subtotal price, the system automatically calculates and displays the tax and the end total.

Of course, this is only a small part of the whole picture. If this was more than just an example, we would continue through the requirements use case, building more functional use cases to fill in the rest of the details. But let's keep up our momentum: it's time to identify some real functionality from this use case.

Identifying Functionality

Our functional use case for Video Checkout, above, is still focused on the business process; but its level of detail is sufficient for us to be able to define specific functionality - and get right to the business objects that we'll need to create. First, let's go through and list the functionality that's described:

- ❑ The customer has an ID number
- ❑ The video rental transaction is handled via a specific screen
- ❑ The customer's ID number is sufficient to retrieve the customer's information
- ❑ The customer's name and address are in the database
- ❑ Videos each have an ID number
- ❑ Once the customer data is shown, the cursor moves to the video entry field
- ❑ The video's ID number is sufficient to retrieve the video's information
- ❑ The video's title and rental price are in the database
- ❑ The system must keep a running subtotal for all videos entered
- ❑ The system must calculate the tax
- ❑ The system must calculate a total rental fee

Notice that not all the functionality that's been described fits into business objects. For instance, the requirement that 'once the customer data is shown, the cursor moves to the video entry field' is not a business rule, but a presentation rule. This functionality is no less important to the end user of the system, but we do need to make sure that presentation rules are handled by the user-interface, not the business objects.

Identifying Business Objects

Now let's find the business objects that are required to support this functionality. As before, a good technique for this process is to pick out the nouns from the use case. Of course, this could get carried to an extreme, so your judgement is required. What we need to do is to pick out possible real-world objects that might need to be modeled in the software:

Customer	ID number
Video	Barcode reader
ID card	Database
Attendant	Subtotal price
Screen	Tax
ID number	Total Price

Clearly, some of the possible objects we've listed won't end up being created as objects in the software; nevertheless, this is a good starting point. The next step is to determine how these objects relate to each other. During this process, we'll find out which of the objects are important to the software and which are not.

Defining Object Relationships

Although it may sound old-fashioned, it can be very valuable to write the name of each object that we listed on to a small card or piece of paper, one note per object. Then we can use a white-board, or any other large surface we can draw on, and stick the objects to the surface. This lets us move the objects around as needed, and lets us draw lines between the objects to show how they're connected.

> There are commercial case tools on the market that make this very easy to perform on a computer. Rational Rose for Visual Basic and Microsoft Visual Modeler are good examples. These programs can be very useful, as they offer the same abilities as putting cards on a white-board, but allow us to save the diagrams to disk, add comments to our objects and relationships, and sometimes even generate code based on the object design.

Once our objects are written down and placed on a surface, we're ready to move on and figure out how they relate to each other. This is fairly straightforward, since all we need to do is go back through the use case and look for verbs and other connecting phrases between the nouns. Again, this could get carried to an extreme, so some judgement is required!

Types of Relationships

There are some key types of relationships that we need to find. Other relationships exist, and are important, but these are ones we need to make sure we get:

Relationship	Description/Example
Ownership (owns, has)	Parent-child relationships
User (uses)	One object uses or employs the services of another object
Aggregate (contains, made of)	One object is made up of other (subordinate) objects
Generalization (is a)	One object is a specific type of another object

Something else to keep in mind is that we might need to add some new objects as we go along. Picking out the nouns from the use case is great, but the use case might have *implied* some other objects that we don't have yet. For instance, we may find that we need objects to represent some of the verbs in our use cases. That's fine, just don't be surprised if it happens.

Following the same logic, there will be objects that we don't need, and we'll be getting rid of those.

Example Relationships

So let's look through the use case and pick out some relationships:

- ❑ A customer **owns** an ID card
- ❑ An ID card **contains** a customer number
- ❑ A customer **has** an ID number
- ❑ A video **has** an ID number
- ❑ Attendant **uses** the screen
- ❑ Attendant **chooses** a menu option
- ❑ Barcode reader **scans** the ID card
- ❑ The screen **displays** (**or uses**) the customer information
- ❑ The screen **displays** (**or uses**) the video information
- ❑ The screen **displays** (**or uses**) the subtotal, tax, and total
- ❑ The subtotal price **uses** the video prices
- ❑ The tax **uses** the subtotal price
- ❑ The total is **made up of** the subtotal and tax

There are other relationships that we could identify; these are just some examples that illustrate the common relationships we'll encounter. This information is more clearly presented in diagrammatic form:

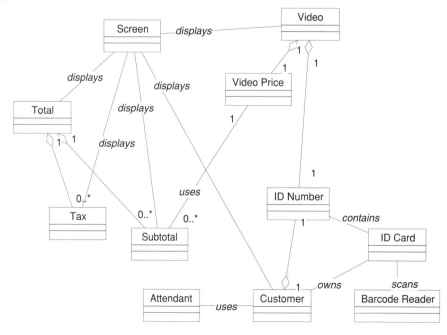

The figure shown here was drawn using Microsoft Visual Modeler, part of the Visual Studio package. The notation used is the Universal Modeling Language (UML). Appendix B contains a brief explanation of UML as used here.

Eliminating Unneeded Objects

Now the challenge is to eliminate the objects that we don't need to put into our software model. There are two main things to look at:

1   Objects that just aren't needed in this particular use case
2   Objects that fit into other layers of the application, such as the presentation layer

The first thing we should do is look at those objects that don't have a lot of relationships in the diagram. Neither the attendant nor the barcode reader are well connected, so they need to be looked at carefully.

It's unlikely that we'll need to have an attendant object to handle the functionality in this use case, since the attendant just interacts with the screen. We won't completely write it off as an object, however, because it was also listed in the requirements use case - so it may be used to provide some other functionality. Still, we don't need it here, so we can remove it from our diagram.

The barcode reader is probably not required either. This is more of a common sense issue, but barcode readers usually just provide input to the software that's indistinguishable from keyboard input, so it's hard to imagine what such a business object would do for our program.

Now look at the objects that the attendant and barcode reader touched. The screen object is still very connected, but the ID card is a borderline case. Since the ID card is just a way of expressing the customer's ID number, we can probably eliminate it from the picture as well.

The next step is to look at each object and eliminate those that belong in either the presentation or data processing layers of the application. In our case, the screen object certainly fits the bill for belonging in the presentation layer.

However, it's very useful to leave something representing the presentation layer in the model, for the sake of clarity. At the same time, we don't want to mistake it to be an actual business object, so we need to keep that in mind when we look at the figure.

After all the changes, our diagram looks like this:

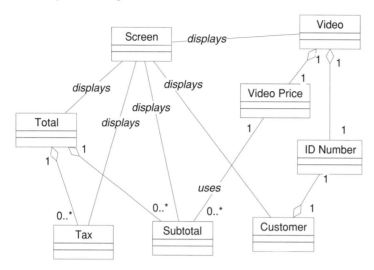

Consolidating Objects

At this point, we've got a pretty clear picture of the objects that we need, and how they're all related to each other. Now is a good time to look at the diagram with a critical eye to determine if there are objects that can be consolidated to form a more general object.

> *There may also be objects in our diagram that are really attributes of other objects, but we won't worry about those yet. We'll discuss attributes and properties in the next section.*

Looking at the diagram, there are three objects that are all very much interrelated. The *tax* and *total* objects are both generated upon the basis on the *subtotal* object. It would make a lot of sense to add a new object to the diagram that would give us a more general view of these objects.

If we look back at our requirements use case, we'll see that there is a potential business object called an *invoice*.

> **It is important to keep looking back at the requirements use case, and to look at all the other related functional use cases, to find objects that overlap or have relationships with the objects at hand. Our functional analysis is not happening in isolation, so it's important to regularly stop and take a look at the bigger picture.**

The *invoice* object needs to display the total amount along with some other information, so it's a good candidate to use as an object to contain the *total*, *tax* and *subtotal* objects. Here's a list the relationships for our new *invoice* object:

- ❏ The invoice **has a** total
- ❏ The invoice **has a** subtotal
- ❏ The invoice **has a** tax
- ❏ The invoice **refers to** customer
- ❏ The invoice **has a** list of videos

Looking back at the previous example, we can see how complex the model is for the presentation designer. The *screen* entity is communicating with a lot of different objects in our model, so it may be very difficult for the programmer of the presentation layer to use our model effectively. In this new model, however, the UI developer only needs to worry about interacting with three objects: *invoice*, *video* and *customer*. All the other objects are available through one of those three.

If we add in the *invoice* object, we end up with the following diagram for our objects:

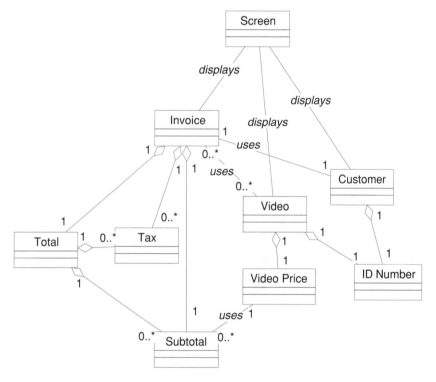

At this point, we have a pretty good understanding of the business objects that we need to handle for the functional use case. We may not be done yet, however: it's possible that we'll still need to add or remove some objects as we finish up the analysis.

Now we need to move on to figure out some specifics about the objects; in particular, we need to list the properties, methods, and events that each object needs in order to support the use case's functionality. First, let's look at the properties.

Identifying Object Attributes (or Properties)

Our programs interact with objects using the interface (properties, methods, and events) that the object provides. Properties are the attributes, or elements, that describe an object.

Although the analytical processes to determine the properties and methods are similar and interrelated, it is often easier to start with the properties, keeping the behaviors in mind, and then move on to finalize the methods.

We'll get our properties using two primary techniques:

1   We'll go back to our functional use case to find any properties that we need to meet the requirements listed there.
2   We'll look at the object model diagram from the previous section, since some of the objects in our model might be better expressed as attributes of other objects - something we'll cover in much more detail shortly.

Additionally, some of our objects have relationships to other objects, such as the *invoice* having a reference to a *customer* object. In this case, we'll want to add a property to the *invoice* object so that the *customer* object is accessible.

As well as the properties needed to fulfil the business requirements, the objects will also have properties to support the way we implement our components. We'll ignore these particular properties for now, and cover them in Chapter 5.

Identifying Attributes - Looking through the Use Case

So, our first technique to identify object attributes involves us going through each object in our model, looking at the relevant use case to decide what attributes are appropriate.

A simple example is the *customer* object. Looking at the use case, we can see some fairly obvious attributes that will be required; in particular, the name and address. The customer's ID number may also be an attribute, although we've put it into our model as an object. We'll talk about the ID number shortly.

Of course, the address is likely to contain a number of attributes, such as street, city, state, and zip code.

Alternatively, we may determine that we have other addresses from other functional use cases, so perhaps the address is really a separate object. Translating from use cases into an object design is a holistic process: we need to continually look back at other use cases and related object models to see where and how they overlap. This is how code re-use is tied in to the object model we are building.

In this case, we'll just assume that a customer has a single address with a street, city, state, and zip code. Here is a list of the objects from our model, along with the properties that we're likely to derive from the use case:

Object	Object's Attributes
Tax	Tax amount
Subtotal	Subtotal amount
Total	Total amount for invoice
Invoice	Since the invoice isn't actually in our use case, and we added it later, we won't get any properties from the use case
Customer	Name
	Street
	City
	State
	Zip
Video price	Rental price
Video	Description
ID number	ID Number

Identifying Attributes - Looking at the Object Model Diagram

Our second technique to identify object attributes involves an examination of each object in our object model to make sure that it really is an object - and not just an attribute of a related object. This distinction is somewhat subtle, and requires us to step back and look at the requirements use case and any other related functional use cases that might impact the model.

A good clue to start with is to examine the attributes we've assigned to each object at this point. Any object with just a single property is a good candidate to become a simple property of its parent object. Look at the *ID number* object. It only has a single property, so does it really warrant the status of being an object, or is it just an attribute of the *customer* and *video* objects?

This depends very much on how the ID number object is used in other use cases. In this particular use case, it is simply an attribute - but if it's used the same way elsewhere then it should probably just become a property.

We need to keep in mind that properties are not the only thing that might define an object. As we'll discuss shortly, methods and behaviors can also define an object. Before assuming that the ID number object is just an attribute, we need to ensure that it doesn't provide any behaviors that make it more appropriate to being an object.

In going through the object model, look for objects that have a single property and those that have a parent. A parent is typically an object that *has* or *owns* or is *made up of* the object that we're looking at. Another way to look at it is that the child object *belongs to* the parent. The following objects look like good candidates to become properties of other objects:

Object	Parent
Video price	belongs to the video object
ID number	belongs to the customer and video objects
Tax	belongs to the invoice object
Subtotal	belongs to the invoice object
Total	belongs to the invoice object

At the end of this process, we have the following objects and properties:

Object	Attributes
Invoice	Tax
	Subtotal
	Total
Customer	ID number
	Name
	Address
	City
	State
	Zip
Video	ID number
	Description
	Price

At this point, we have properties for each of the objects individually; but, according to our diagram, the *invoice* object contains both the *customer* and *video* objects. We need to decide how the presentation layer will get at the *customer* and *video* objects through the *invoice* object. This is a very complex issue with a lot of different solutions.

> *To give this issue the space it deserves, we'll discuss it fully in the next section of this chapter. Therefore, we'll leave the object properties as they are for now.*

Remember that everything we've done so far is tentative; we may still need some of the objects that we've eliminated if we find that they have methods in the following step. Still, it's a pretty good bet that we're close - so it is worth putting together an object model diagram that we can use to figure out the methods:

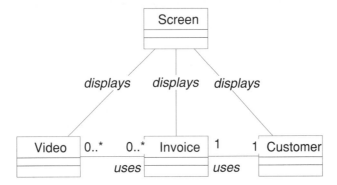

The object model has been simplified dramatically through this process. The analysis is geared toward building a simple model with just the objects that we need to represent the business process within our application. Since we chose not to remove the *screen* entity in the diagram during this process, we've also been able to simplify the model so that it will be easy to use when it's time to develop the presentation layer.

Identifying Object Behaviors (or Methods)

Objects do not only have attributes; they also have behaviors. Our programs ask an object to act out its behaviors by using **methods**. A method is very much like a subprogram, or function, that our program can call; but whereas a subprogram is simply a routine in our program, a method is a routine defined for our object.

Objects have behaviors that help model their role in business process. Very often, they also have behaviors, or methods, that let them interact with the other objects in the model - in ways that aren't necessarily obvious from the use cases.

> *We're going to discuss business process behaviors in this section. We'll cover object relationship behaviors in the next section.*

The technique we need to follow to determine an object's behavior is very similar to that which we've just seen for an object's properties. First, we need to go through the functional use case to find any methods that are required. Then, we need to look at our object model and add any methods that are required for objects to interact with each other.

Identifying Behaviors - Looking through the Use Case

Let's look through each object in our object model and read through the use case to decide what behaviors or actions each object might be able to take. Many business objects primarily provide data, so don't be surprised if many of our objects don't have methods.

Looking at the *customer* object, we can see that the actual person does a lot of things, like putting the videos on the counter, and providing an ID card. However, our software doesn't need to be aware of these actions - so we don't need to provide methods for them. But our software does need to retrieve and display the customer's name and address once the ID number is entered. Now, since these are attributes of the customer object, it's a good bet that our *customer* object will have some behavior to load this information.

Next, let's look at the *video* object. Again, the *video* object doesn't play an active part in the use case as far as our application is concerned - other than that it needs to load the description and rental price once its ID number is entered.

Our last object is the *invoice* object. This object isn't directly in the use case at all, but it does have the subtotal, tax and total values as attributes. The use case indicates that these values are calculated, so the *invoice* object will probably need a method to support this behavior.

At this point, our objects have the following behaviors:

Object	Behavior
Customer	Load customer data
Video	Load video data
Invoice	Calculate subtotal
	Calculate tax
	Calculate total

If we look back at the requirements use case, we can see that there are other behaviors that we are not taking into account. For instance, the invoice needs to be printed, and it is implied that the rented videos will be recorded in the inventory system. We don't need to worry about these issues at this point, since they would normally be covered by other functional use cases. This illustrates how closely all the different use cases are related to each other, and how they are all used together to come up with a comprehensive object model.

Identifying Behaviors - Looking through the Object Model

The *customer* and *video* objects both have behaviors that comprise loading data from a database. This type of behavior is integral in making objects persistent, as we discussed in Chapter 2. In Chapter 4, we'll get into the code for implementing this behavior. For now, however, we're just interested in defining our objects' interfaces, so we'll add a **Load** method to support this behavior, and worry about the details later.

We've listed three different calculation behaviors for the *invoice* object, all of which are closely related. This is an interesting situation that requires some thought. There are three ways to approach these behaviors:

❑ Implement three calculation methods
❑ Implement a single calculation method
❑ Automatically recalculate when properties are changed

When we're making decisions about our objects' interfaces, we need to keep our customer in mind. We have two main design issues: modeling the business entities, and making our objects easy to use at the presentation layer. Here, our customer is the programmer who is writing the user interface.

Implementing three different calculation methods means that the UI programmer needs to understand and call all three methods where appropriate. Since all the calculations are directly tied to each other, it would surely be much better to combine them into a single method for the programmer to call.

Better still, suppose the programmer didn't need to call *any* method to do the calculation. The calculation would only need to happen when a video was added or removed from the list of rentals. The invoice object owns the list of videos, so it should be able to detect when a video is added or removed - and automatically recalculate the values.

All three solutions are valid, and we could choose any of them and have a working program. We should always strive to provide the simplest object interface for the UI programmer, since it helps them to be more productive and it makes the code less prone to bugs. In this case, the upshot is that we'll opt to automatically recalculate the subtotal, tax and total, so that those values are always correct. This means we don't need any calculation methods on our *invoice* object.

Ideally, we'd be able to notify the UI when the values have been recalculated, thus making it easy for the programmer to update the display. Fortunately, Visual Basic 5.0 provides the `RaiseEvent` command to let us do just that.

Notification (or Events)

There are many times when objects can perform some action in response to a property being set or a method being called. This has traditionally been difficult to implement, since an object has usually needed to notify the calling program that the action has taken place.

In the previous section, we discussed the *invoice* object and how it can detect when a video is added or removed from the list of rentals. Either of these conditions should cause the subtotal, tax and total amounts to be recalculated. The challenge is that the UI needs to be notified that these values have changed so that the display can be updated.

Traditional Solutions

Traditionally, this would have been handled either by having the UI refresh the values when it added or removed a video, or by calling a special *Calculate* method to force the calculation.

If the UI updates the values when adding or removing a video, we've effectively coded some business logic into the UI. After all, the UI would have to know all the conditions under which the values might change, so that it could know when to refresh the display.

Using an explicit *Calculate* method is also far from ideal. If we have such a method, then we're relying on the UI code to call it, rather than recalculating our values automatically. If the UI doesn't call the method when appropriate, we could end up in a situation where the subtotal, tax, and total properties on the object would be incorrect. This solution can not only lead to bugs, but it also requires that the UI programmer must have more knowledge about how our object works than we might otherwise prefer (such as a more appropriate time to call the *Calculate* method).

Callbacks

A more complex solution to the problem would be to have the *invoice* object call a method of another object and have that object update the UI. This solution solves most of our problems, but it's definitely harder to implement for the UI developer.

To implement this, the UI itself would have to create an object to receive the message sent by the invoice object. Of course, the invoice object would need to know about the UI's object so that it could call it; we'd therefore need to add a method to the invoice object so that the UI could pass a reference to its object!

Once the invoice object had a reference to the UI's object (let's call it *Displayer*), it could call some predefined method on the *Displayer* object whenever a message needed to be sent to the UI. This is shown in this diagram:

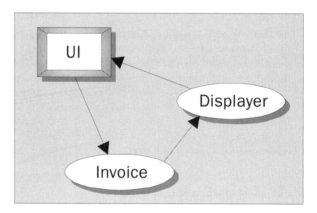

Let's look through some code that could handle this.

Displayer Object

First off, our UI developer will need to provide an object to update the display. Create an ActiveX DLL project, create a new class module called **Displayer**, and add this sample code:

```
Option Explicit

Public Sub UpdateValues()
  ' in this routine we'd update our display
  ' with the properties from the Invoice
  ' object
End Sub
```

This example assumes that we've implemented our business objects in an ActiveX DLL, and that the UI is in a different EXE or DLL. We'll keep our **Displayer** class in a separate ActiveX DLL for now, which will allow us to create a simple UI test harness in a Standard EXE. (Alternatively, if we had created our UI in a ActiveX DLL, then the **Displayer** class could have been included within the main UI project.)

The **Displayer** class must also have its **Instancing** property set to 5 - MultiUse so that we can make it available to the **Invoice** object.

The upshot of all this is that if we did want our **Displayer** class to be within the main UI program, then our UI project would need to be an ActiveX server - whereas it may have only needed to be a regular program prior to the introduction of the callback mechanism.

Invoice Objects

Within the main DLL project for our business objects, the **Invoice** class also needs some special code to support the callback. It needs a method that will allow the UI to give it a reference to the **Displayer** object.

For our current example, add a sample DLL for our business objects, using the File-Add Project menu option, then add a class module, using the Project-Add Class Module menu option, and call that class module **Invoice**. Now add the following sample code to **Invoice**:

```
Option Explicit

Private objCallback As Object

Public Sub SetCallback(Display As Object)
  Set objCallback = Display
End Sub
```

Performing the Callback

Then, in the routine where the **Invoice** object does the calculations, we need to call the **UpdateValues** method of the **Displayer** object:

```
Public Sub Calculate()
  ' here we'd do the calculations

  objCallback.UpdateValues
End Sub
```

Releasing Object References

Finally, we need to make sure that the **Invoice** object releases its reference to the **Displayer** object before the **Invoice** goes away. If we don't do this, we run the risk of having objects hanging around in memory after we've tried to close down the program:

```
Private Sub Class_Terminate()
  Set objCallback = Nothing
End Sub
```

The UI Code

Now that all that has been set up, we can write some UI code that creates the **Invoice** object. Since we're going to use a Standard EXE to hold our sample UI and test our callback mechanism, add a Standard EXE project using the File-Add Project menu option, add a standard module to that project, using the Project-Add Module menu option, and enter this example code:

```
Private objInvoice As Invoice
Private objDisplayer As Displayer
```

```
Set objDisplayer = New Displayer
Set objInvoice = New Invoice

objInvoice.SetCallback objDisplayer
objInvoice.Calculate
```

Notice that, as well as creating an **Invoice** object, we create a **Displayer** object, and give the **Invoice** object a reference to it.

> *You'll need to make a reference to the **Invoice** object from the UI project. Select the UI project in the Project window, and use the Project-References menu option to select the project containing our **Invoice** object.*

> *Since we've created a separate EXE for the UI test harness, we also need to add references to the projects containing the **Displayer** object and the **Invoice** object. Select the UI EXE project in the Project window, and use the Project-References menu option to select the appropriate references to the other projects.*

If you run the sample program as it stands, you won't see much happen: but if you step through the program execution, you'll see the callback mechanism alive and well. The UI code successfully establishes the **Displayer** callback method to itself before it calls the **Invoice** object's **Calculate** method. Within the **Calculate** method, the callback is then made to the **Displayer** class's **UpdateValues** routine.

This solves our problem, in that it allows an object to notify our program when something has happened. In our example, the **Invoice** object notifies the UI object that **Calculate** method has been called. In some ways, this is very attractive, since the interaction between the two objects is very well defined, and the UI can give the **Invoice** object a reference to any object that implements an **UpdateValues** method. Since this technique uses regular method calls between the two objects, we can write our code to pass any parameters that our program might need.

On the other hand, this solution is somewhat complex: it forces the UI developer to add a new class to the project, or make the UI program an ActiveX server. It also tightly couples the business object to the UI implementation, since it requires that the UI provide an object with a specific method.

Raising Events

Visual Basic 5.0 introduced the ability to raise **events** from our objects. This means that we can write code in our class module that will raise an event in the calling code, just as a button control can raise a **Click** event in a form.

This is done by introducing three new keywords to the Visual Basic 5.0 language. In our class module, we need to use the **Event** and **RaiseEvent** keywords, respectively, to declare and raise events. In the calling code (Form or Class module), we need to declare the object using the new **WithEvents** keyword.

Sticking with the **Invoice** object example, we could have the **Invoice** object raise an event when the subtotal, tax and total amounts have changed. Then the UI programmer would just need to write code behind the event to update the display. This is a very nice model, since all Visual Basic programmers are familiar with writing code to respond to events - so the learning curve for the UI programmer is very small.

Invoice Objects

Inside our **Invoice** object, we need to have a line to declare our event:

```
Public Event UpdateValues()
```

Then in the routine where we calculate the amounts, we can add a line to raise the event:

```
Private Sub Calculate()
   ' here we'd do the calculations

   RaiseEvent UpdateValues

End Sub
```

All references to our **objCallback** object are now unnecessary, and we no longer need our **SetCallback** routine, since we've managed to create the same mechanism using events.

The UI Code

The UI programmer just needs to make a change to the declaration of the **Invoice** object to include the **WithEvents** keyword:

```
Private WithEvents objInvoice As Invoice
```

At this point, the **objInvoice** object will appear in the Object dropdown in the upper-left of the code window, along with any other controls or objects available to the module. If we choose **objInvoice**, then the Procedure dropdown in the upper right will list all the events that are declared in the **Invoice** class - just **UpdateValues** in this case. This means we can write a regular event procedure:

```
Private Sub objInvoice_UpdateValues()
   ' here we'd put the code to update the
```

```
      ' values on the display
    End Sub
```

All references to our **objDisplayer** object are now unnecessary; and, since we no longer need our **Displayer** class module, the UI no longer needs to be an ActiveX server.

This solution is not very different from implementing a callback, but it does have some significant advantages. The UI programmer doesn't need to implement a special class. In fact, the UI programmer can draw on existing knowledge and techniques to write code behind the object's events - just as if they were events from a control on a form. Furthermore, the **Invoice** object author doesn't need to worry about being passed some external object, or any specifics about the calling program at all. They may appreciate that.
The bottom line is that the **RaiseEvents** command works independently of whether anyone actually receives the event that's raised. This means that we've effectively separated the UI programmer's tasks from the object developer's tasks.

Other Use Case Formats

The concept of a use case is pretty broad. There are many different things called use cases that are written up in many different ways. That's fine - it's the concept of having a detailed description of a business process that is important.

The format that we used earlier in this chapter is a simple prose or text description of the process. A couple of other popular formats that we might encounter include: a step-by-step outline in a table format, a flowchart or a flow diagram.

Functional use cases are typically grouped together with the higher-level requirements use case from which they flowed. All of these use cases, when combined, provide a solid and traceable base of documentation for the subsequent design, development, testing and documentation of the system.

Functional use cases frequently include user-interface mock-ups, often created in Visual Basic to look somewhat like the screen that the users will see at the end. This can be very useful, because it can help the users visualize the flow of the system as they proof our use case descriptions.

Developing prototype screens using Visual Basic can be very powerful. Not only can we create screens to assist our users in visualizing the system, but, if we're careful, we can get a significant head start on the development of the UI itself. Visual Basic is not only good for prototyping - it's also good for easily converting prototypes into full-blown applications without having to start over from scratch.

Object Relationships

At this point, we've gone through our use case scenarios, and we've defined all the objects that we need to model our business process. We've even gone so far as to determine how all the objects are related to each other at a high level.

Thus far, however, our objects don't have any properties or methods that actually let them interact with each other. Essentially, we've identified relationships between objects; but we haven't added any way to implement those relationships.

Earlier in the chapter, we discussed the common types of object relationships:

Relationship	Description/Example
Ownership (owns, has)	Parent-child relationships
User (uses)	One object uses or employs the services of another object
Aggregate (contains, made of)	One object is made up of other (subordinate) objects
Generalization (is a)	One object is a specific type of another object

Let's go through each relationship and discuss how to implement that relationship with Visual Basic.

The Ownership Relationship - Implementing Collections

Ownership really defines a parent-child type relationship between objects. There may be one child, or this may be a one-to-many relationship. In this section, we're going to focus on the situation where one parent has many children.

> If there can only be one child, it's often more appropriate to view the relationship as a form of aggregation, which we'll talk about later in this chapter.

This ownership relationship is the basis for most object hierarchies we'll find in Windows applications. It is usually viewed as a **collection** of child objects that are owned or controlled in some way by the parent. The best way to manage this type of relationship is to build a collection class to contain the child objects, and then implement a read-only property on the parent object to provide access to the collection object.

The Invoice Object

If we consider our video store example, our **Invoice** object is likely to have a list of line items: one line item for each video that the customer rents. This is a parent-child type relationship, where it would be good to have a collection of **LineItem** objects available through the **Invoice** object.

In our **Invoice** object, we'll add a property so that the calling program can access the collection of videos. We'll call the new property **LineItems**, since it will be a list of **LineItem** objects. The code to handle this in the **Invoice** class would look something like this:

```
Option Explicit

Private WithEvents objLineItems As InvoiceItems

Private Sub Class_Initialize()
  Set objLineItems = New InvoiceItems
End Sub

Public Property Get LineItems() As InvoiceItems
  Set LineItems = objLineItems
End Property

Private Sub objLineItems_AddItem(strID As String)
  CalculateAmounts
End Sub

Private Sub objLineItems_RemoveItem(strID As String)
  CalculateAmounts
End Sub

Private Sub CalculateAmounts()
  ' here we'd recalculate the subtotal, tax
  ' and total amounts for the invoice
End Sub
```

The **LineItems** property is the key, since it allows the calling program to get at the **InvoiceItems** collection. We've also included events so that the **Invoice** object will be notified when a **LineItem** object is added or removed from the collection. This ties in with our earlier discussion about raising events to recalculate the subtotal, tax and total amounts on the invoice.

The InvoiceItems Collection Object

The **InvoiceItems** collection class is based on Visual Basic's native **Collection** class. Our collection uses a Visual Basic **Collection** object, internally, to store all the **LineItem** objects - but we've enhanced the **Add** method so that it only supports **LineItem** objects.

> *The normal Visual Basic* **Collection** *will accept just about anything to store, which doesn't bode well if we only want to get* **LineItem** *objects.*

Here's what the code to support our **InvoiceItems** collection object might look like:

```
Option Explicit

Event AddItem(strID As String)
Event RemoveItem(strID As String)

Private colItems As Collection

Private Sub Class_Initialize()
  Set colItems = New Collection
End Sub

Public Function Add(strID As String) As LineItem
  Dim objItem As LineItem

  Set objItem = New LineItem
```

```
    objItem.Load strID
    colItems.Add objItem, strID
    Set Add = objItem
    RaiseEvent AddItem(strID)
End Function

Public Sub Remove(ByVal varIndex As Variant)
   Dim strID As String

   strID = colItems.Item(varIndex).ID
   colItems.Remove varIndex
   RaiseEvent RemoveItem(strID)
End Sub

Public Function Count() As Long
   Count = colItems.Count
End Function

Public Function Item(ByVal varIndex As Variant) As LineItem
   Set Item = colItems.Item(varIndex)
End Function

Public Function NewEnum() As IUnknown
   Set NewEnum = colItems.[_NewEnum]
End Function
```

In this code, we've simply encapsulated a **Collection** object, **colItems**, by creating a **Private** variable and exposing our own **Add**, **Remove**, **Item**, and **Count** elements.

The key here is that the new **Add** method only supports **LineItem** objects, so that no unexpected object types can get into our collection. The **Add** method is also responsible for creating the **LineItem** object, and arranges to load any data based on the ID value supplied - by calling the **Load** method.

```
Set objItem = New LineItem
objItem.Load strID
```

Although we can't see it in the code, the **Item** method has been made the default by using a new capability of Visual Basic 5.0. This means that where we'd previously have written code like this:

```
Set objLineItem = objItems.Item(1)
```

We can now write the same line like this:

```
Set objLineItem = objItems(1)
```

To set a method as the default, choose the Tools-Procedure Attributes menu, and click on the Advanced button when the dialog comes up:

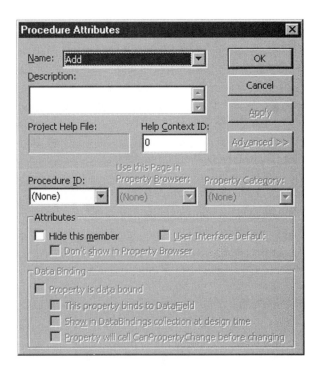

In the Name field, choose the method name to be changed. Then, in the Procedure ID field, choose the (Default) setting and click OK.

Our new class also contains a **NewEnum** method. This is a special method that allows the calling code to use the **For Each...Next** style of accessing the contents of our collection. This means that we can write client code like this:

```
For Each objLineItem In objItems
   Debug.Print objLineItem.Price
Next
```

Until Visual Basic 5.0, the **For Each** structure was only available for native Visual Basic **Collection** objects. Now, by implementing the **NewEnum** method, we can make our user-defined **Collection** objects support the **For...Each** structure as well.

Our **NewEnum** method simply returns a hidden object within the native Visual Basic **Collection** class, called **_NewEnum**. Like the **Item** method, we need to use the Tools-Procedure Attributes menu option to set some special values for the **NewEnum** method. The following diagram shows the settings that are required:

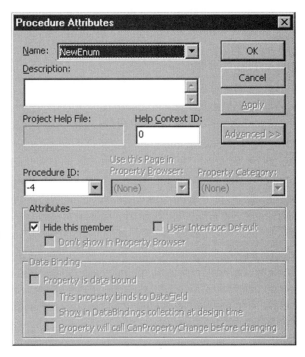

The Procedure ID field is set to −4, which is the value required to work with **For...Each** structures. Also, the Hide this member box is checked, to make our method hidden in the COM type library.

Notice that the **InvoiceItems** class declares and raises two events: **AddItem** and **RemoveItem**. These events allow the **Invoice** object to know when the calling program has added or removed a video from the collection, so that the invoice amounts can be recalculated.

The LineItem Object

We'll keep the **LineItem** object simple. We'll just give it an **ID** and a **Price** property, along with the **Load** method. Here's the code:

```
Option Explicit

Private strID As String
Private dblPrice As Double

Public Sub Load(ID As String)
  strID = ID
  ' eventually there will be code here to go
  ' load the video information from the
  ' database, but for now we'll just make up
  ' a price
  dblPrice = 1.99
End Sub

Public Property Let ID(strValue As String)
  strID = strValue
End Property

Public Property Get ID() As String
  ID = strID
End Property

Public Property Let Price(dblValue As Double)
  dblPrice = dblValue
End Property

Public Property Get Price() As Double
  Price = dblPrice
End Property
```

The **LineItem** object has no extra code to support collections or any other relationships. The object is entirely designed around modeling the real-world video entity.

The Calling Program

In order to bring this whole thing together, let's look at some code that will add some line items to the invoice and then interrogate the price of the first item:

```
Dim objInvoice As Invoice
Dim strPrice as String

Set objInvoice = New Invoice
objInvoice.LineItems.Add "1"
```

```
objInvoice.LineItems.Add "2"

strPrice= objInvoice.LineItems(1).Price
```

Notice how we've just used the **InvoiceItems** method as though it were a collection, calling its **Add** method for each video.

This approach to implementing parent-child relationships is very powerful, and yet it provides a very easy interface for the end programmer who'll be using our objects to develop the application.

The User Relationship - Calling Objects

When an object holds a reference to another object, and calls its properties or methods, we have a *uses* type relationship. Another way to look at this is as a client-server relationship between the two objects. The client calls properties or methods on the server, and gets an appropriate response.

This is the simplest of the relationships, and is one that virtually all Visual Basic programmers are familiar with - so we won't spend much time discussing it.

The user or client simply declares a variable and creates an object:

```
Dim objItem as LineItem

Set objItem = New LineItem
```

And then the user calls the object's properties or methods:

```
objItem.Load "ABC"
MsgBox objItem.Price
```

When the user is done with the object, they just releases it by setting its reference to **Nothing**:

```
Set objItem = Nothing
```

Probably all of us have used objects, or at least controls, in the Visual Basic programs we've written. Having an object use another object is no more difficult than using an object from a form or code module.

The Aggregate Relationship - Combining Objects

There are many times when an object is composed of other objects, in whole or in part. For instance, our **Invoice** object is partially composed of the **Customer** object. Without the **Customer** object, our **Invoice** doesn't have enough information to be useful. The **Customer** is subordinate to the **Invoice**, but the **Invoice** can't exist without the **Customer**.

There are two different approaches that we can use to handle this situation. The first of these is simple aggregation; the second involves combining interfaces.

Our discussion will therefore run as follows:

1   We'll look at a simple aggregation example
2   We'll alter that example to use a combined interface technique
3   We'll investigate how one object might expose another object's data
     as a read-only property

Technique 1 - Simple Aggregation

The first approach we'll look at is simple aggregation. With this approach, we can simply expose the subordinate objects as properties of the top-level object. For instance, look at the following code:

```
Option Explicit

Private objCustomer As Customer

Private Sub Class_Initialize()
  Set objCustomer = New Customer
End Sub

Public Function Customer() As Customer
  Set Customer = objCustomer
End Function
```

All we've done, here, is create a private **Customer** object, and allowed the calling program to gain access to it through our **Customer** method. This is very simple to implement, and it gives the calling program full access to any of the objects we've aggregated into our top-level object.

There are, however, a couple of drawbacks to simple aggregation. The most obvious problem is that the calling program can do virtually anything to the aggregated object. In the example above, the calling program has full access to the **Customer** object, so it can change any properties or call any methods. In some cases, this might be fine, but we may want greater control over what the calling program can do, such as validation and error handling.

> When we're designing an object model, it's important to assume that everything will get misused or called incorrectly. Objects need to protect themselves, and if an object is composed of other objects then it needs to protect the subordinate objects as well.

Technique 2 - Combining Object Interfaces

Now that we've seen how easy it is to implement simple aggregation, let's look at an approach that gives us more control over how the client code can use the aggregated object.

Although this doesn't follow true object-oriented design, it's often a better idea to simply merge the properties and methods of all the objects into a single object interface. With this approach, we can still have the aggregated objects instantiated inside our top-level object, but we don't make them directly available to the calling program.

Consider the following code from the **Invoice** class:

```
Option Explicit

Private objCustomer As Customer
Private curTax As Currency

Private Sub Class_Initialize()
  Set objCustomer = New Customer
End Sub

Public Property Let Name(strValue As String)
  objCustomer.Name = strValue
End Property

Public Property Get Name() As String
  Name = objCustomer.Name
End Property

Public Property Get Tax() As Currency
  Tax = curTax
End Property
```

Note that this class is made up of both its own data and the **Customer** object; but rather than exposing the **Customer** object itself, this implementation has its own **Name** property that just calls the **Customer** object's **Name** property. This technique passes a lot of control to the **Invoice** object - at the expense of object-oriented philosophy.

Of course, this approach also has some drawbacks. If an aggregated object's interface changes, perhaps by adding a new property, then the new interface elements aren't immediately available to client programs. In that situation, we would need to add the new elements to the top-level object's interface first. With simple aggregation, on the other hand, where we would expose the aggregated object as a property, this problem would never arise.

Technique 3 - Combining Data

As we've seen, simple aggregation and aggregation through combined interfaces are very good ways to solve the problem where one object relies on another for data or functionality. Unfortunately, neither solution is truly ideal in a client/server setting.

Let's diverge a bit from object theory, and look at a common scenario in business programming. Most of us work with data that is stored in relational tables. Even if we choose to represent that data as objects, such as **Customer** or **Invoice**, we'll often run into cases where the data needs to be consolidated (or aggregated) together across object boundaries.

With our current example, the **Invoice** object needs data from the **Customer** object to function - in our case, the **Customer** object's **Name** property. Essentially, we're trying to consolidate some of the **Customer** object's data into the **Invoice**. So far, we've done that using a couple different techniques to implement aggregation.

Unfortunately, this can be very inefficient. In order to get the **Name** property from the **Customer** object, our **Invoice** object has to load the *entire* **Customer** object from the database. This means that we're loading two whole objects - one of them just to get a single property value. Most relational database engines can pull information together much faster than we can when we load individual objects and put them together ourselves.

Let's take an example. Here's a functional use case from the *Rental Analysis* requirements:

Consolidated Reporting

This use case covers the specific steps used to consolidate the rental counts and prices for each video.

The system must scan all invoice detail lines for each video. Each invoice for a video will count as a single rental, and so the system must count the invoices. For this analysis, the system must also calculate an average rental price, based on each invoice for the video. Prices may change over the life of the video, and so the analysis needs to use the average price.

Once the system has calculated a video's rental count and average price, it needs to provide these numbers - along with the name of the producing studio and the video's category for analysis. The studio and category are stored with the other video information.

We'll discuss two different ways of solving this business situation. First, let's look at how we might solve it using pure aggregation of objects; then, we'll look at an alternative solution that provides much better performance.

Object Method

Looking at this problem with a pure object focus, we can quickly pick out the **LineItem** and **Video** objects as containing the data we need. We'll add in a **VideoData** object, which will contain the business logic to accumulate all the data together. So far, we have the objects and properties as shown in the table on the following page.

Using objects, our **VideoData** object would contain the logic to load all the **LineItem** objects for each invoice, and accumulate a rental count and average price for each **Video**. It would also aggregate the **Video** object to get the **Studio** and **Category** data.

> In Chapter 4, we'll discuss a couple of efficient techniques for loading and saving object data in a database. As good as these are, they don't compare to the performance we can get by processing a lot of data in the data tier.

Object	Properties
LineItem	VideoID
	Price
Video	VideoID
	Studio
	Category
VideoData	VideoID
	RentalCount
	AveragePrice
	Studio
	Category

It's relatively inefficient for the **VideoData** object to load all the **LineItem** objects from the database. The rental count and average price can be calculated with a simple SQL statement in the database itself, and this would be much faster. With an extra **JOIN**, the SQL statement can pull in the **Studio** and **Category** data without even having to load a separate **Video** object.

Database Method

Following a database train of thought, we would have one type of object: **VideoData**. This object would be loaded directly from the database using a SQL statement to pull together all the data at once, very efficiently. The following is an example SQL statement that we could use in Microsoft Access to achieve this:

```
SELECT InvoiceDetail.VideoID, Count(InvoiceDetail.VideoID) AS CountOfVideoID,
Avg(InvoiceDetail.Price) AS AvgOfPrice, Videos.Studio, Videos.Category
FROM InvoiceDetail INNER JOIN Videos ON InvoiceDetail.VideoID = Videos.VideoID
GROUP BY InvoiceDetail.VideoID, Videos.Studio, Videos.Category;
```

The following figure (overleaf) shows this query in Access.

Of course, there are some drawbacks to building objects this way rather than through regular aggregation. Suppose the **LineItem** object had business logic behind the **Price** property. By pulling the price directly from the database, we will have bypassed that logic. This might force us to replicate the code inside the **VideoData** object. In that case, we'd want to think hard about which solution is the most appropriate.

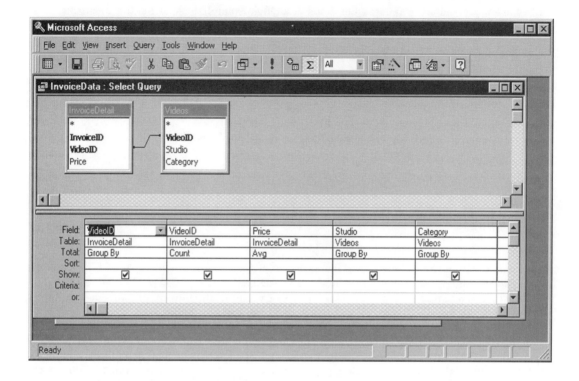

The Generalization Relationship - Containing Objects

Generalization is an analysis technique used to find common ground between a number of objects. Once we've established that a group of objects have a set of common behaviors and properties, we can create a more generalized class to represent all those common elements. We can then use that generalized class as a base from which we can create all the other, more specialized, classes.

We can view this new, general class as a sort of *parent* to all the more specialized classes. The process of creating the specialized classes from the general class is called **inheritance** - something we discussed in a different context in Chapter 1. When we view our generalized class as a parent of the specialized classes, we're creating what's called a **class hierarchy**.

A class hierarchy is like a family tree for our objects. As we trace back from one object to the next, we become more and more general. Let's look at a quick example to see what this means:

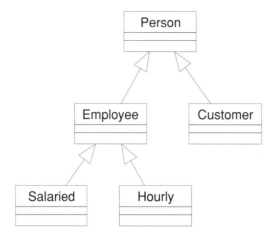

This diagram demonstrates how a class hierarchy might appear for various types of *Person*. If we look at an *Hourly* employee, we can see that they're a specialized type of *Employee*. In other words, the *Employee* class is a parent to *Hourly* and *Salaried*. We can follow the flow all the way back to the most general class, *Person*. All of these classes are derived from the *Person* class.

Generalization is a very powerful analysis technique. By identifying the commonalities between various objects, we provide ourselves with an opportunity to achieve a high level of reuse. Since we can implement all the common functionality in one class, we can then use that functionality in all the more specialized classes. The more specialized classes *inherit* the functionality from the generalized class.

Inheritance is the technique used to implement objects that are identified using the generalization technique. Visual Basic 5.0 doesn't provide a direct mechanism to support inheritance, but it's such an important concept that we need to provide it. As we discussed in Chapter 1, we can use containment and delegation together to simulate inheritance in Visual Basic.

To see how we can implement inheritance, let's use an example from our video rental store. Suppose the store decides to not only rent videos, but also to sell popcorn, candy bars and other snacks.

Looking for Common Ground

We've already considered that our *Invoice* object has *LineItem* objects to reflect the videos that are rented. Now we're saying that we've got two different types of line item - a video rental line item and a line item for snacks the customer wants to purchase.

Let's look at the possible properties and methods for the video rental line item, which we'll call **RentalItem**:

Properties	Methods
Title	CheckOut
Price	MarkAsPaid

Now let's look at the possible properties and methods we might find in the line item to purchase a snack (**PurchaseItem**):

Properties	Methods
Price	ReduceInventory
TaxableFlag	MarkAsPaid

We have a couple of indications that we may be able to come up with a more general class from these two. First off, we know they are both used in a similar way - they're both line items of an **Invoice** object. Secondly, in looking at their respective properties and methods, we can see that they share some interface elements.

Taking the common properties and methods from each, we derive the following list:

Properties	Methods
Price	MarkAsPaid

We can look at this as being a new, more general line item object, called **LineItem**. If we then use **LineItem** as a base from which to implement both the **RentalItem** and **PurchaseItem** objects, we'll have a class hierarchy.

This diagram illustrates how each of our specialized line item classes, **RentalItem** and **PurchaseItem**, will inherit behaviors from the more general **LineItem** class.

Now let's implement this relationship using Visual Basic. To start with, we'll create our general class, **LineItem**. Once that's done, we'll use it as a base class to implement the **RentalItem** class. Once we've seen how to implement **RentalItem**, the implementation of the **PurchaseItem** class would be trivial, so we won't rehash the same material again.

LineItem Class

Our general **LineItem** class will implement the properties and methods that are common to all line items. In this case, we're talking about a **Price** property and a **MarkAsPaid** method. Let's take a look at the code for the **LineItem** class:

```
Option Explicit

Private dblPrice As Double
Private flgPaid As Boolean

Public Property Get Price() As Double
  Price = dblPrice
End Property

Public Property Let Price(dblValue As Double)
  dblPrice = dblValue
End Property

Public Sub MarkAsPaid()
  flgPaid = True
End Sub

Private Sub Class_Initialize()
  flgPaid = False
End Sub
```

This code is very straightforward. Our **Price** property merely stores and retrieves its value from the **dblPrice** variable, while the **MarkAsPaid** method simply sets the **flgPaid** variable to **True**. Obviously, any real business object would be more complex, but this should be enough code to demonstrate how inheritance works.

RentalItem Class

Now we're getting into the interesting part. Since Visual Basic doesn't directly support inheritance, we'll use a combination of containment and delegation to simulate it. We covered this briefly in Chapter 1, but we'll get a good taste for the process as we implement the **RentalItem** class.

Setting up the RentalItem Class

Before we inherit the behaviors of the **LineItem** class, let's set up the basics of our **RentalItem** class. We don't need to worry about the **Price** property or the **MarkAsPaid** method, since we'll inherit them from the **LineItem** class. We do need to implement the **Title** property and **CheckOut** method however:

```
Option Explicit

Private strTitle As String
Private flgCheckedOut As Boolean

Public Property Get Title() As String
  Title = strTitle
End Property

Public Property Let Title(strValue As String)
  strTitle = strValue
```

```
End Property

Public Sub CheckOut()
   flgCheckedOut = True
End Sub

Private Sub Class_Initialize()
   flgCheckedOut = False
End Sub
```

We've kept this code very simple as well. The **Title** property just stores and retrieves its value from the **strTitle** variable, with the **CheckOut** method setting the **flgCheckedOut** variable to **True**.

Containing a LineItem Object

With the basics of the class down, we can move on to inherit the **LineItem** class's functionality. The first thing we need to do is use the technique of containment to make our **RentalItem** object *contain* a **LineItem** object. This means declaring a **Private** variable to hold the reference to our **LineItem** object. Add the following line to the **RentalItem** class:

```
Option Explicit

Private strTitle As String
Private flgCheckedOut As Boolean
```

```
Private objLineItem As LineItem
```

We also need to create an instance of the **LineItem** class. The best place to do this is in the **Class_Initialize** routine, so the object is created right up front and is available any time we need it. Add this line to the **RentalItem** class:

```
Private Sub Class_Initialize()
   flgCheckedOut = False
```
```
   Set objLineItem = New LineItem
```
```
End Sub
```

Inheriting Behavior Using Delegation

Our **RentalItem** object now has access to its own private **LineItem** object. Rather than implementing its own **Price** property, it can rely on its **LineItem** object's **Price** property to do the work. The same goes for the **MarkAsPaid** method, where the **RentalItem** object can *delegate* the work to its private **LineItem** object.

Of course, the **LineItem** object is **Private**, so any client code working with our **RentalItem** object won't be able to get at it. In order to make a **Price** property and **MarkAsPaid** method available to the client code, our **RentalItem** object will need to implement them. The implementation is simple however, since we'll just delegate the work down to our private **LineItem** object.

Add this code to the **RentalItem** class:

```
Public Property Get Price() As Double
  Price = objLineItem.Price
End Property

Public Property Let Price(dblValue As Double)
  objLineItem.Price = dblValue
End Property

Public Sub MarkAsPaid()
  objLineItem.MarkAsPaid
End Sub
```

When the client code calls the **MarkAsPaid** method, for instance, our **RentalItem** code merely echoes the call to the **LineItem** object's **MarkAsPaid** method, rather than trying to do any work itself.

Trying It Out

Let's take a quick look at some client code that we might use to work with the **RentalItem** object at this point. Rather than creating a UI for such a simple example, let's look at how we might test this object in Visual Basic's Immediate debug window. With our two classes in place, we can enter the following into the Immediate window:

```
set x=New RentalItem
x.Price=1.99
print x.Price
 1.99

x.MarkAsPaid
x.CheckOut

x.Title="Video X"
print x.Title
 Video X
```

This example shows how we're able to work with the properties and methods from the **RentalItem** object itself, as well as those from the **LineItem** object. To the client code, there is no difference at all. This is exactly the behavior that we'd get using actual inheritance, were it available.

This would, of course, be a lot easier if Visual Basic directly supported inheritance; but, at the same time, this shows that we can do inheritance in Visual Basic - after a fashion. Since generalization is such an important part of object design, it's very important for us to be able to implement it in some manner.

Summary

In this chapter, we've discussed the analysis and design process for developing a logical business object model. Our discussion included:

- ❏ Requirements use cases (or scenarios)
- ❏ Functional use cases
- ❏ How to identify objects from our use cases
- ❏ How to determine the properties, methods and events for our objects
- ❏ Object relationships and how to implement them using Visual Basic

Object-oriented analysis and design techniques provide us with very powerful and useful tools. These techniques can be useful whether we're going to implement our application using object technology or not, since they offer a general way to model our business entities and processes.

From here, we'll move on to look at implementing robust, real-world business objects and components using Visual Basic. Then, in Chapter 5, we'll start to tie everything together as we implement a full-blown example application based on the video rental store example that we studied in this chapter.

4

Designing Business Objects

Overview

In Chapter 2, we looked at the logical parts, or tiers, of a client/server application. In this chapter, we'll walk through the common *physical* architectures that we're likely to encounter as we develop our applications. We'll look at how the different logical tiers of the application fit into each physical model, and we'll discuss some different options in each case.

The physical architectures that we'll discuss include:

- ❑ 2-tier (client workstations and a database server)
- ❑ 3-tier (client workstations, application servers, and database servers)
- ❑ Internet (browser-based client, Web server, and database servers)

We'll also look at some specific design concerns for our business objects. Our UI-centric business objects need to communicate with a user-interface, and there are some issues that we need to be aware of when we're designing our objects to make this work well.

Furthermore, our objects need to be **persistent**. This means that they must have a way to be saved and restored from a database. The CSLA (Component-based Scalable Logical Architecture) provides for this, and in this chapter we'll get right into the details on how it's all done. As ever, what sounds easy enough in principle can be challenging in practice, so we'll take a good look at some of the techniques available in Visual Basic to make it fast and easy to persist objects.

Physically Distributed Architectures

When we discussed the CSLA, in Chapter 2, we didn't dictate which machines were to run any particular part of our application. In this section, we're going to go through the most common physical architectures. We'll explore how we can place the logical tiers of our application on physical machines to provide a rich, interactive user-interface, good application performance, and scalability.

2-tier Physical Architecture

So far, I've portrayed 2-tier applications as the 'old way' of doing things. In reality, however, this is still the most common physical client/server architecture, so it's important that we look at how we can use the CSLA within this physical 2-tier environment.

Traditional 2-tier

In a traditional 2-tier design, each client connects to the data server directly, and the processing is distributed between the data server and each client workstation.

Take a look at the following diagram. On the left, we can see the physical machines that are involved; on the right, we can see the logical layers - next to the machines on which they'll be running:

In this case, we've put virtually all the processing on the client, except for the data processing itself. This is a very typical 2-tier configuration, commonly known as an **intelligent client design**, since quite a lot of processing occurs on the client workstation.

This approach makes the most use of the horsepower on the user's desktop, relying on the central database only for data services.

Just how much processing is performed on the server can have a great impact on the overall performance of the system. In many cases, the data processing can add up to a lot of work, and if the data server is being used by a great many clients then it can actually become a performance bottleneck. By moving most of the processing to the clients, we can help reduce the load on the data server.

Of course, the more processing that's moved to the client, the more data is typically brought from the server to the client to be processed. For example, suppose we want to get a list of customers in a given zip code and whose last name starts with the letter 'L'. We could have the server figure out which customers match the criteria and send over the result, or we could send over details of all the customers and have the client figure it out.

Here's the point: the more processing we move to the client, the more load we tend to put on the network. Of course, if we have *no* processing on the client, we might also have to send a lot of material over the network - since the server becomes responsible for creating each screen that's seen by the user, and those screens need to be sent across to the client.

> **Ideally, we can find a balance between the processing on the server, the processing on the client, and the load on the network, which uses each to their best advantage.**

2-tier with Centralized Processing

Traditional 2-tier architectures lack one very important feature. Typically, no *business* logic runs on the server: it is all located in the clients. Certainly, there may be a fair amount of work done on the server to provide data services, but the bulk of the business processing is almost always limited to the clients.

Even in a 2-tier setting, it would be very nice if we could put some services on our database server to provide shared or centralized processing. If our data server can support the extra processing, and it's running Windows, then we can most certainly design our application to match the following diagram:

With this approach, we have objects that are running on a central server machine. This means that they can easily interact with each other, allowing us to create shared services, such as a message service, that allow a business object to send messages to other business objects on other client workstations.

This model might also reduce the network traffic. Our data-centric business objects can do a lot of preprocessing on the data from the database *before* sending it over the network - so we can reduce the load on the network.

Another benefit to this approach is that it means the database doesn't have to be a SQL database. Since the application service objects sit between the database and the actual business objects on the clients, they can allow us to use a much less sophisticated database in a very efficient manner. This could also allow us to tap into multiple data sources, and it would be entirely transparent to the code running on the client workstations.

For instance, our application may need to get at simple text files on a central server - maybe hundreds or thousands of such files. We could create an application service object that sent the data from those files to the business objects on the client workstations and updated the data when it was sent back. From the business object's viewpoint, there would be no way of knowing whether the data came from text files or from memo fields in a complex SQL database.

Of course, this model puts a lot of extra processing on the database server. Before jumping on this as a perfect solution, we would need to evaluate whether that machine could handle both the data processing and the application service processing without becoming a bottleneck.

3-tier Physical Architecture

In a 3-tier design, the client workstations communicate with an application server, and the application server communicates with the data server that holds the database.

This is a very powerful and flexible way to set things up. If we need to add another database, we can do so without changing the clients. If we need more performance, we just add another application server - again with little or no change to the clients.

In the following diagram, the physical machines are on the left, and the various tiers of the application on the right. You can see which parts of the application would be running on the different machines:

Client: Presentation and UI-centric Business Objects

With this approach, both the presentation layer and some objects are placed on the client workstations. This may appear a bit unusual, since it's commonly thought that the business objects go on the central application server machine.

In an ideal world, keeping all the business processing on the application server would make sense. This would put all the business rules in a central place where they would be easy to maintain. As we discussed in Chapter 2, however, this typically leads to a batch-oriented user-interface rather than the rich interface most users desire.

By moving all our processing off the client workstations, we're also failing to make good use of the powerful computers on the user's desktops. Most companies have invested immense amounts of money to provide their users with powerful desktop computers. It seems counterproductive to ignore the processing potential of these machines by moving all the applications processing to a central machine.

Another view might be that the objects should be on both the client *and* the server, moving back and forth as required. This might seem better still, since the processing could move to the machine where it was best suited at any given time. This is the basic premise of the CSLA, where we've split each business object between its UI-centric and data-centric behaviors - effectively putting half the object on the client and half on the application server.

Unfortunately, Visual Basic has no innate ability to move objects from machine to machine. From Visual Basic's perspective, once an object has been created on a machine, that's where it stays. This means we need to come up with an effective way of moving our objects back and forth between the client and the application server. We'll look at some powerful techniques for handling this later in the chapter.

Performance issues play a large role in deciding where we should place each part of our application. Let's look at our 3-tier physical model and see how the tiers of our application will most likely communicate:

When we're using ActiveX servers like the ones we create with Visual Basic, the client workstations typically communicate with the application server through Microsoft's Distributed Component Object Model (DCOM). Our data-centric objects will most likely use ODBC to communicate with the database server, although this is certainly not always the case.

> *In Visual Basic 4.0, we would have used Remote OLE Automation. This was often quite slow and somewhat limiting. DCOM is a substantial improvement over Remote Automation, providing the same benefits but with much better performance.*

When we're working with DCOM, we have to consider some important performance issues. As we go through this chapter, we'll look at various design and coding techniques that we can use to achieve an excellent performance. In general, however, due to the way DCOM works, we don't want to have a lot of communication going on across the network. The problem is not that DCOM is slow, or less powerful than other network communication alternatives, such as Distributed Comnputing Environment (DCE) or Common Object Request Broker Architecture (CORBA). The bottom line is that this problem happens to be common to all of these related technologies.

> It is always important to minimize network traffic and calls to objects or
> procedures on other machines.

Regardless of performance arguments, we should always keep our objects phyically close to whatever
it is that the objects interact with the most. The user-interface should be close to the user, and the
data processing should be close to the data. This means that the user-interface should be on the
client, and the data services should be on the data server. By keeping the objects in the right place
we can avoid network communication and gain a lot of performance.

Our UI-centric business objects primarily interact with the user-interface, so they belong as close to
that interface as possible. After all, the user-interface is constantly communicating with the business
objects to set and retrieve properties and to call methods. Every now and then, a business object
talks to its data-centric counterpart, but the vast bulk of the interaction is with the user-interface.

Application Server: Data-centric Business Objects

As we discussed in the last section, the data-centric business objects run on the application server.
Typically, these objects will communicate with the database server using ODBC:

Depending on the situation, we'll probably use one of the technologies available within Visual Basic
5.0 to interact with ODBC. The most common technologies include:

- Remote Data Objects (RDO)
- ODBCDirect
- Active Data Objects (ADO/OLEdb)

> *ADO is not actually included with Visual Basic. To use it, you need to get it from the*
> *Microsoft Web site,* **http://www.Microsoft.com/** *or with another Microsoft product*
> *where it is included. One such product is Microsoft Internet Information Server.*

If we're working with a typical database server, such as Oracle or SQL Server, then RDO is probably
the best bet. It provides very good performance, and allows us to tap into many of the features of the
database server very easily. RDO is just a thin object layer on top of the ODBC API, so there's very
little overhead to degrade performance.

Alternatively, we could decide to use ODBCDirect, which is a new addition to Data Access Objects
(DAO) 3.5. ODBCDirect is a thin layer on top of RDO, so it's nearly as fast as using RDO itself. The
benefit of ODBCDirect is that we get to use the same familiar DAO object model that we use when
we're talking to an Access database - so we don't have to learn a new object model.

The newest entry to the data access arena is Active Data Objects (ADO). ADO is a relatively new technology for accessing data, and it's built on top of OLEdb. It provides the application programmer with a very simple and easy model for data access. Since ADO uses OLEdb for data access, it's relatively easy for database vendors to provide powerful and efficient access to their databases. Microsoft has indicated that ADO is the future strategic choice for data access in the Windows environment.

Something to keep in mind is that the application server can talk to the data server in whatever way really works best. For instance, our application server may use TCP/IP sockets, some form of proprietary DLL, or screen-scraping technology, to interact with the data source:

This illustrates a major benefit to this whole design, and one that a lot of companies can use. If our data is sitting on some computer that's hard to reach, or expensive in terms of licensing or networking, then we can effectively hide the data source behind the application server and still let our UI-centric business objects work with the data, regardless of how we accessed it.

Internet Architecture

Now that we've looked at a fairly traditional 3-tier physical architecture, let's examine a couple of different architectures for Internet/intranet development. These architectures are not the typical Web browser-based designs that most people are familiar with. Instead, we're going to blur the browser approach together with the CSLA to demonstrate a multi-tier architecture with a browser interface.

Architecture #1

The first architecture we'll look at is the closest to today's typical Web development. On the left is the physical layout, which is very typical of a Web environment. On the right, though, we're using our now familiar CSLA, with one exception:

Web browser	Presentation tier
	ASP interface
Web server	UI-centric objects
	Data-centric objects
Database server	Data services tier

One of the primary goals for Internet development is to keep the client as thin as possible to provide compatibility across all the different Web browsers out there. This means that we should avoid putting any processing on the client if at all possible.

Ideally, all we'd ever send to a client would be pure HTML, since that would let any browser act as a client to our program. Of course, HTML provides no ability to do any processing of program logic on the client side, and so this provides the ultimate in thin clients.

Since the Web browser client provides no real processing capabilities, we need a layer of code on the Internet Information Server (IIS) to act as a surrogate or proxy user-interface for the business objects.

We could actually implement this layer using a variety of technologies, but I've shown it here using Active Server Pages (ASP). ASP provides direct and easy communication with ActiveX server objects such as our UI-centric business objects. With ASP, we simply write scripting code that will be executed on the web server itself.

This assumes that the business objects are contained inside ActiveX DLLs. This is a requirement for objects that are accessed from ASP code.

Our newly added ASP interface layer accepts input from the browser and uses it to act like a traditional business object client. What this really means is that the VBScript code in this layer takes the place of the Visual Basic forms that we'd normally be using as an interface to the business objects.

Without getting too deep into ASP (since we'll cover this in detail later in the book), here's some sample code that we could place in an ASP page to make a call to a simple Visual Basic ActiveX DLL. The **ASPmessenger** Visual Basic object just returns a simple text string that's then displayed in the user's browser:

```
<HTML>
<BODY>
<% Set MyObject = Server.CreateObject("ASPtest.ASPmessenger") %>
<% = MyObject.GetMessage %> <P>
</BODY>
</HTML>
```

The VBScript code is the two lines within the **<%** and **%>** brackets. The code is pretty much identical to what we'd use in Visual Basic itself to create an object and call a method.

The **ASPtest** server is a simple ActiveX DLL developed in Visual Basic 5.0. It has a single class module, called **ASPmessenger**, with a single string function named **GetMessage**. Here is the **GetMessage** code:

```
Option Explicit

Public Function GetMessage() As String
  GetMessage = "Here is a message from ASPtest"
End Function
```

This code illustrates how practical and easy it is to use Visual Basic components within an Active Server Page script. With this technology, and a good set of components containing business objects, we can build an application based on business objects and then use ASP to create the user-interface. We'll cover this in more detail in Chapter 13, where we'll build an ASP interface. This interface will use the same underlying business objects as the Visual Basic form-based interface that we'll create in Chapter 7 and the Microsoft Excel interface that we'll create in Chapter 9.

Architecture #2

The second design that we'll look at here is very similar to the first, but it's more scaleable. In this design, we retain the application server from the 3-tier model that we discussed earlier to offload some of the processing from the web server:

Web browser	Presentation tier
Web server	ASP interface
	UI-centric objects
Application server	Data-centric objects
Database server	Data services tier

In this diagram, we've moved the data-centric business objects off the Web server and back on to the application server. This can be particularly useful if we have a mixed environment where we're providing a browser interface for some users and a Visual Basic forms interface to others.

The code running in the Active Server Pages takes the place of the Visual Basic forms in a more tradition user-interface. This means that any code that would have been behind our Visual Basic forms, to format data for display, or to modify any user input, will be coded using VBScript or JavaScript in our ASP pages. Either way, this code should be pretty minimal, since any actual business logic should always be placed in the business objects or application services.

If we want to get real fancy, we can create an ActiveX DLL that contains objects that know how to format our data for display. These objects could then be used when we're developing our Visual Basic interface as well as our ASP interface.

The ASP code also needs to generate the HTML responses for the user, essentially creating a dynamic display of our data. Fortunately, this is very easy to do using VBScript, as we can draw on our experience as Visual Basic developers. There's a very small learning curve to move from Visual Basic development to developing Web pages using ASP.

COM/DCOM Performance

Most of the physical architectures that we've been looking at use DCOM (Distributed Component Object Model) for communication between machines on the network. But even with the speed improvements over Remote Automation, DCOM can still be pretty slow. In particular, there is substantial overhead on a *per call basis*.

Each time our program calls an object's property, or method, there's a speed hit. We get pretty much the same speed hit regardless of whether our call sends a single byte to the object or a thousand bytes. Sure, it takes a little longer to send a thousand bytes than a single byte, but the COM *overhead* is the same either way - and that overhead is far from trivial.

Calling Single Properties

From a high-level view, each time we access a property or call a method, COM needs to find the object that we want to talk to; and then it needs to find the property or method. Once it's done all that work, it moves any parameter data over to the other process, and calls the property or method. Once the call is done, it has to move the results back over to our process and return the values.

Take the following code, for example:

```
Set objObject = CreateObject("MyServer.MyClass")
With objObject
   .Name = "Mary"
   .Hair = "Brown"
   .Salary = 31000
End With
```

This code has four cross-process or cross-network calls (depending on whether **MyServer** is on the same machine or across the network). The **CreateObject** call is remote and has overhead. Each of the three property calls is also remote, and each has similar overhead. For three properties, this might not be too bad; but suppose our object had 50 properties, or suppose that our program was calling these properties over and over in a loop. We'd soon find this performance totally unacceptable.

Passing Arguments to a Method

Passing multiple arguments to a method, rather than setting individual properties, is significantly faster. For example:

```
Set objObject = CreateObject("MyServer.MyClass")
objObject.SetProps "Mary", "Brown", 31000
```

But too much overhead still remains, because of the way COM and DCOM process the arguments on this type of call. Furthermore, this technique doesn't allow us to design our business objects in the way we discussed in Chapter 4. With this technique, we'd end up designing our object interfaces around technical limitations.

Manual Marshalling of Data

Many programmers have tried the techniques we've just seen, and they've eventually given up, saying that COM is too slow to be useful. This is entirely untrue. Like any other object communication technology, COM provides perfectly acceptable performance, just as long as we design our applications using an architecture designed to work with it.

Due to COM's overhead, when we're designing applications that communicate across processes or across the network we need make every effort to minimize the number of calls between objects. Preferably, we'll bring the number of calls down to one or two, with very few parameters on each call.

> Instead of setting a series of parameters, or making a method call with a list of parameters, we should to design our communication to call a method with a single parameter that contains all the data we need to send.

There are two main approaches we can take to move large amounts of data in a single method call:

- **Variant** arrays
- User defined types with the **LSet** command

In both cases, what we're doing is **marshalling** our data. This means that we're collecting the data into a single unit that can be efficiently passed to another object and then pulled out for use by that object.

Variant Arrays

The **Variant** data-type is the ultimate in flexibility. A **Variant** variable can contain virtually any value of any data-type - including numeric, string, or even an object reference. As you can imagine, an *array* of **Variants** extends that flexibility so that a single array can contain a collection of values, each of a different data-type.

For instance, consider this code:

```
Dim vntArray(3) As Variant

vntArray(0) = 22
vntArray(1) = "Fred Jones"
vntArray(2) = 563.22
vntArray(3) = "10/5/98"
```

Inside the single array variable **vntArray** we've stored four different values, each of a different type. We can then pass this entire array as a parameter to a procedure:

```
PrintValues vntArray
```

In a single call, we've passed the entire set of disparate values to a procedure. Since methods of objects are simply procedures, we could also pass the array to a method:

```
objMyObject.PrintValues vntArray
```

The **PrintValues** procedure or method might look something like this:

```
Public Sub PrintValues(Values() As Variant)
  Dim intIndex As Integer

  For intIndex = LBound(Values) To UBound(Values)
    Debug.Print Values(intIndex)
  Next intIndex
End Sub
```

This simple code just prints the values from the array to the immediate window in the Visual Basic development environment. It does, however, illustrate how easy it is to get at the array data within an object's method.

Of course, the **Variant** data-type is highly inefficient compared to the basic data-types, such as **String** or **Long**. Using a **Variant** variable can be many times slower than a comparable variable with a basic type. For this reason, we need to be careful about how and when we use **Variant** arrays to pass data.

The **Variant** data-type is generic, meaning that a **Variant** variable can hold virtually any piece of data we provide. The downside to this is that, each time we go to use the variable, Visual Basic needs to check and find out what kind of data it contains. If it isn't the right type of data then Visual Basic will try to convert to a type we can use. All this adds up to a lot of overhead, and thus our performance can suffer.

If our object's data is stored in a **Variant** array, we'll incur this overhead every time we use any of our object's data from that array. The code in most objects work with data quite a lot, so we really do run the risk of creating objects with poor performance if we use **Variant** arrays.

Using GetRows

Many of our objects will need data from a database. If we're going to use a **Variant** array to send this data across the network, we'll need some way to get the data from the database into the array. Usually, we'll get the data from the database in the form of a DAO **Recordset** or RDO **Resultset**.

Both **Recordset** and **Resultset** objects provide us with an easy way to copy the database data into a **Variant** array. This is done using the **GetRows** method that's provided by both of these objects. The **GetRows** method simply copies the data from the object into a two-dimensional **Variant** array.

The following code, for instance, copies the entire result of a query into a **Variant** array named **vntArray**:

```
Dim vntArray As Variant

rsMyRecordset.MoveFirst
vntArray = rsMyRecordset.GetRows(rsMyRecordset.RecordCount)
```

vntArray now contains the contents of the recordset as a two-dimensional array. The first dimension indicates the column or field from the recordset; the second dimension indicates the row or record:

```
vntMyValue = vntArray(intColumn, intRecord)
```

Of course, the subscripts for the column are numeric, so they aren't as descriptive as the field name would be if we had access to the actual recordset. Instead of the following:

```
MyValue = rsMyRecordset("MyValue")
```

We're reduced to using something like this:

```
MyValue = vntArray(2)
```

The order of columns is entirely dependent upon the field order returned in the recordset. This means that if we add a field to our SQL SELECT statement, in the middle of other fields that we're retrieving, then we'll have to change all of our programs that rely on **Variant** arrays to pass data.

Passing User-Defined Types with LSet

Many people store their object's data in a variable based on a UDT, because it's a very concise and convenient way to handle the values. If we could pass a UDT variable to another ActiveX component then we'd be able to send an entire object's data in a single parameter to a method.

Unfortunately, things aren't quite that simple, because Visual Basic doesn't allow us to pass a UDT variable as a parameter. Luckily, there is a very nice solution that enables us to efficiently pass a UDT's data to another ActiveX component. We'll take a good look at this solution, but first let's put it in perspective.

Background

Many languages have some equivalent to Visual Basic's UDT. For instance, C has the **struct**, and both FORTRAN and Pascal have similar constructs. Some languages natively support multiply-defined structures, where the programmer can define two different variable definitions for the same chunk of memory. FORTRAN implements **COMMON** memory blocks, while C uses a **union** keyword within a **struct**:

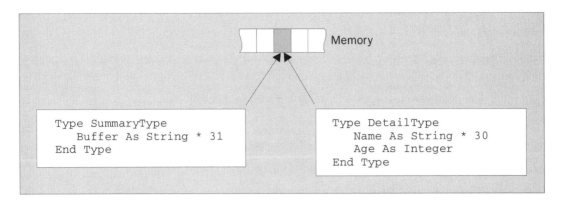

```
Type SummaryType
    Buffer As String * 31
End Type
```

```
Type DetailType
    Name As String * 30
    Age As Integer
End Type
```

Memory

Multiply-defined structures are very powerful. They allow us to set up a user-defined type like this:

```
Private Type DetailType
   Name As String * 30
   Age As Integer
End Type
```

Then we can set up another user-defined type that is exactly as long as **DetailType**:

```
Private Type SummaryType
   Buffer As String * 31
End Type
```

Remember that in Win32 environments such as Windows 95 and Windows NT, strings are all Unicode; therefore, each character in a string will actually consume 2 bytes of memory. This is so Windows can support more complex character sets, such as those required by Arabic or languages in the Far East.

So **DetailType** is a total of 62 bytes in length: 60 for the **Name** field and 2 for the **Age** field. This means that **SummaryType** also needs to be 62 bytes in length. With Unicode, a 62 byte **String** is actually half that many characters. Therefore, dividing 62 by 2, we find that **SummaryType** needs to be 31 characters long.

It's worth noting that if **DetailType** were 61 bytes in length (say **Age** was a **Byte**) then **SummaryType** would still need to be 31 characters long, since we must round up. If we didn't round up, then **SummaryType** would be just 30 characters long and could only hold 60 of the 61 characters: we'd lose one byte at the end.

FORTAN, C, and some other languages would allow a single variable to be referenced as **DetailType** or **SummaryType**. In other words, they would let us get at the same set of bytes in memory in more than one way. This means that we could set the **Name** and **Age** values with **DetailType**, and also treat the memory as a simple String without having to copy any values in memory.

Since Visual Basic doesn't allow us to pass a UDT variable as a parameter to an object, we need some way to convert our UDT variables to a data-type that can be passed. The ideal situation would be one in which we could simply define the same chunk of memory as both a UDT and a simple String variable, as shown above.

Although Visual Basic doesn't allow us to do this, it does provide us with a very efficient technique that we can use to provide an excellent workaround.

Visual Basic Implementation

Visual Basic's approach does require a memory copy, but it's performed with the **LSet** command, which is very fast and efficient. Let's take a look at how **LSet** works.

Open a Standard EXE project and type in the **DetailType** and **SummaryType** UDT's that we just looked at. They need to be entered in the General Declarations section of our form. Then add the following code to the **Form_Click** event:

```
Private Sub Form_Click()
   Dim udtDetail As DetailType
   Dim udtSummary As SummaryType

   With udtDetail
      .Name = "Fred Jones"
      .Age = 23
   End With
End Sub
```

This code simply defines a variable, using each UDT, and then loads some data into the **udtDetail** variable, which is based on the **DetailType** type. So far, this is pretty simple - so here comes the trick. We'll add a line using the **LSet** command:

```
Private Sub Form_Click()
   Dim udtDetail As DetailType
   Dim udtSummary As SummaryType

   With udtDetail
      .Name = "Fred Jones"
      .Age = 23
   End With

   LSet udtSummary = udtDetail

End Sub
```

This new line uses the **LSet** command to do a direct memory copy of the contents of **udtDetail** into **udtSummary**. Visual Basic does not perform any type checking here; in fact, it doesn't even look at the content of the variables; it just does a memory copy. This is very fast and very efficient: substantially faster than trying to copy individual elements of data, for instance.

The result of this code is that the **Name** and **Age** values are stored in the **udtSummary** variable, and can be accessed as a string using **udtSummary.Buffer**. Of course, the values stored aren't all printable text, so if we try to print this value we'll get garbage. That's OK though: the objective was to get the data into a single variable. Now we can pass that string to another procedure using the following code:

```
Private Sub Form_Click()
   Dim udtDetail As tDetail
   Dim udtSummary As tSummary

   With udtDetail
      .Name = "Fred Jones"
      .Age = 23
   End With

   LSet udtSummary = udtDetail

   PrintValues udtSummary.Buffer

End Sub
```

The **PrintValues** subroutine just accepts a simple **String** as a parameter. Of course, we're really passing a more complex set of data, but it's packaged into a simple String at this point so it's easy to deal with. Let's look at the **PrintValues** routine:

```
Public Sub PrintValues(Buffer As String)
   Dim udtDetail As DetailType
   Dim udtSummary As SummaryType

   udtSummary.Buffer = Buffer
   LSet udtDetail = udtSummary

   With udtDetail
      Debug.Print .Name
      Debug.Print .Age
   End With
End Sub
```

Again, we declare variables using **DetailType** and **SummaryType** for use within the routine, and we copy the parameter value into **udtSummary.Buffer**. Both values are simple Strings, so this isn't a problem. We do need to get at the details of **Name** and **Age,** though, so we use the **LSet** command to perform a memory copy and get the data into the **udtDetail** variable:

```
LSet udtDetail = udtSummary
```

Once that's done, we can simply use **udtDetail** as normal: in this case, for just printing the values to the Immediate window in the Visual Basic IDE.

If you run this program, and click on the form, the appropriate output will appear in the Immediate window accordingly.

Memory Alignment

In most languages, including Visual Basic, the compiler will align certain user-defined data-types in memory so that they fall on longword boundaries. This means that the compiler inserts filler space if an element won't start on an even 4-byte boundary.

This slightly complicates how we determine the length of our string buffer UDT. While this memory alignment problem adds some complexity to our use of **LSet** to copy a UDT, it is not hard to overcome. Let's look at the details of the problem, and then we'll see how easy it is to solve.

Consider the following user-defined type:

```
Private Type DetailType
   B1 As Byte
   L1 As Long
End Type
```

If we assume that the compiler starts the type on a memory boundary, then **B1** will be at the start of a 4-byte boundary. But **B1** is only a single byte long, and it's required that **L1** start on a longword boundary; so that leaves 3 bytes of space, between **B1** and **L1**, which need to be taken up. This is where the compiler inserts the filler space.

One way to quickly check the actual length (in bytes) of a UDT is to declare a variable based on the UDT in question and use the **LenB** function. This function will return the length, in bytes, of any variable - including one based on a UDT. For instance, we could write the following code:

```
Private Sub TypeLength()
   Dim udtDetail As DetailType

   MsgBox LenB(udtDetail)
End Sub
```

If we run this subroutine, we get a message box showing the total number of bytes in the **DetailType** UDT, which in this case is 62.

Not all data-types are longword-aligned. To accurately determine where the compiler will be adding filler space, we need to know which data-types will be aligned. The following data-types do not need to be aligned to a longword boundary, so they will always start right at the end of any previous variable:

```
Byte
Integer
Boolean
String
```

The following data-types are longword aligned by the compiler:

```
Long          Single
Double        Date
Currency      Decimal
Object        Variant
```

The compiler will add space as needed in front of any of these data-types, so they always start on a longword boundary.

When the compiler adds these filler spaces, it makes our UDT that much longer. Of course, we're creating another UDT to copy our data into, so we need to know exactly how long to make that UDT so that it can fit all the data. Here's our problem: the length of the string needs to be inflated to include the filler spaces - otherwise it will be too short, and the last few bytes of data will be lost during the copy.

The following UDT will hold 6 bytes of data:

```
Private Type SummaryType
   Buffer As String * 3
End Type
```

At first glance, we might expect **SummaryType** to be able to contain the **DetailType** elements shown above, since a **Byte** and **Long** combined are only 5 bytes in length. But because **L1** (the **Long**) needs to be longword-aligned, the compiler inserts 3 filler bytes before **L1**; therefore, the total length of **DetailType** is actually 8 bytes. This means that we need the following UDT to hold all the data from **DetailType**:

```
Private Type SummaryType
   Buffer As String * 4
End Type
```

While the issue of longword alignment makes it more complicated to determine the length of the buffer UDT, it is a predictable behavior, and it isn't really very hard to ensure we get the length correct.

Designing Our UI-centric Business Objects

So far, we've looked at how the logical tiers of our application can be deployed across various physical machines. We've also looked at the performance ramifications of using COM and Distributed COM to communicate between our objects.

In this section, we'll go through a number of key concepts that are critical to our business objects and the creation of Visual Basic user-interfaces to our objects. Here are the major themes we'll be considering:

- ❑ The UI as a business object client
- ❑ Field-level validation
- ❑ Object-level validation
- ❑ Canceled edits
- ❑ Protecting properties and methods

In the sections that follow, we'll be developing a small project to help us discuss these main themes. And in Chapters 5 and 6, where we'll expand upon this discussion, we'll implement a full set of major business objects and a corresponding user-interface that will become the core of our video rental store project.

The UI as a Business Object Client

One of the primary tenants of the CSLA is that the user-interface will rely on our business objects to provide all the business rules and business processing. This implies that there will be a fair amount of communication between our UI-centric business objects and the user-interface itself:

In the CSLA, the UI-centric business objects typically reside on the same machine as the user-interface. In the first section of this chapter, we looked at 2-tier, 3-tier, and Internet physical architectures - so we've seen where the Presentation tier and UI-centric objects may reside.

In a conventional client/server setting (2-tier or 3-tier), we can put these Presentation tier objects and UI-centric objects directly on the client workstations. If we were developing a browser-based user-interface, we'd put these objects on a Web server using Active Server Pages (ASP) running VBScript.

The following figure shows how all the logical tiers of our application can be deployed across the physical machines in both a 3-tier and Internet scenario:

By keeping the UI-centric business objects as close to the user-interface as possible, we can make it as easy as possible for the UI developer. If they are right there on the client machine then they're easy and safe to work with. This means quick development and a higher quality application.

Most larger projects will be developed in a team setting. Typically, the team will be divided into developers who manage the data, developers who construct the business objects, and developers who use the business objects. The people in each of these groups need different skills and a different focus.

The UI developers are those who use the business objects. Ideally, they don't need to understand OO analysis or design; nor do they need to have full knowledge of the complexities of DCOM, network traffic, or implementing inheritance with Visual Basic. Instead, these people should have skills geared toward creating an intuitive user-interface. Their focus is on providing the user with the best possible experience when using the application.

Designing Our Objects to Support the UI

It's our job, as business object designers and builders, to make the UI developer's job as easy as possible. We need to design our business objects so that they are powerful and provide all the features and functionality that the UI developer will need. At the same time, our objects have to be robust and self-protecting.

> If an object can be misused, it will be misused. If an object can be created outside of its proper place in an object hierarchy, it will be. In short, if our business objects don't protect themselves then the resulting application will be buggy.

What this really boils down to is that the UI is just a client of the business objects. The business objects are the core of the application, and the UI is secondary. This makes it very easy to change the UI without risking the business logic stored in the business objects. It also means that we can change our business logic in one place and, by simply upgrading the ActiveX components that contain our business objects, we can change the application's behavior. Often this can be done with little or no impact on the user-interface itself.

We need to make sure that our objects provide sufficient functionality so that we don't limit the capabilities of the UI. At the same time, we need to make sure that our functionality is not tied to any single UI or interface concept. If we compromise our objects for a specific UI then we set a precedence that might mean we'll change our objects any time the UI is changed - and that is exactly what we want to avoid.

Ideally, we should design our UI-centric business objects so they provide a robust and consistent set of services for use by the user-interface. It isn't enough that the objects simply represent real-world entities; they also need to make it easy for the UI developer to create rich and interactive user-interfaces.

Business Behaviors vs UI Behaviors

The business-related behaviors of each object will vary - depending on the real-world entity that each object represents. At the same time, we should be able to provide a consistent set of behaviors, across all our business objects, to support the user-interface. We don't want the UI developer to have to learn a whole new set of rules to work with each and every business object. Instead, we want all our business objects to basically behave in the same manner.

As we've already seen, our objects provide an interface that is composed of properties, methods, and events that represent real-world objects. This is sufficient to create a simple UI that just lets the user enter information in the hope that it's correct. However, there are a couple other types of interaction that a UI will need if we want to provide more feedback to the user. These include raising errors and having some way to indicate when an object is in a valid state.

We also need to take steps to ensure that the UI developer can't easily break our objects by calling inappropriate methods or setting inappropriate properties. And we need to prevent the UI from creating or accessing objects that need to be protected.

A Basic Object and User-Interface

We've just covered a number of concepts that are very important if we're going to provide a consistent set of behaviors to the users of our objects. To illustrate these concepts, we'll use a simple example. This will let us try out each concept in turn.

The Person Class

For our example, let's create a single class that represents a person. It's going to be easy to work with this class, because we can all understand the properties and behaviors that might make up a Person object. This class also makes a good example for us because there isn't very much difference between a person, a customer, and an employee - and the latter two are both typical business objects that we might need to create.

Defining the Person Object's Interface

We won't get too carried away with the attributes of a person. Certainly we could list hundreds, if not thousands, of attributes, but we'll limit the list to four:

- ❑ **SSN** (social security number)
- ❑ **Name**
- ❑ **Birthdate**
- ❑ **Age**

In Chapters 1 and 3, we discussed events and how they could be used to allow our objects to indicate when certain things happened. In our **Person** object, we'll implement an event to indicate when the person's age has been changed:

- ❑ **NewAge**

As we'll see, this event will need to be fired any time the **BirthDate** property is set, since that is when the person will get a new **Age** property value.

Setting up the Project

If we're going to do some coding, we'll need to set up a project in Visual Basic where we can work. Following the CSLA, we'll actually want to create two different projects: one for our business object (**Person**), and one for the user-interface.

Putting the UI in a separate project from the business object will help enforce the separation between the presentation and business tiers. The UI itself will be in a program that the user can run, just like any other program we'd normally create. For our business objects, we'll use an ActiveX DLL, since we don't want the overhead of running a whole other EXE for our **Person** object.

Right now, we're going to concentrate on the **Person** object. We'll create a project for the UI once we're done with the Person object. So create a new ActiveX DLL project, and change the name of the project to **PersonObjects** using its Properties window.

Coding the Person Object

Once we've opened our new **PersonObjects** project, we should see the code window for **Class1**. Use the Properties window for the class to change the name of the class to **Person**.

Here is the code for the **Person** class:

```
Option Explicit

Event NewAge()

Private Type PersonProps
   SSN As String * 11
   Name As String * 50
   Birthdate As Date
   Age As Integer
End Type

Private udtPerson As PersonProps

Public Property Let SSN(Value As String)
   udtPerson.SSN = Value
End Property

Public Property Get SSN() As String
   SSN = Trim$(udtPerson.SSN)
End Property

Public Property Let Name(Value As String)
   udtPerson.Name = Value
End Property

Public Property Get Name() As String
   Name = Trim$(udtPerson.Name)
End Property
```

```
   Public Property Let Birthdate(Value As Date)
      Static intOldAge As Integer

      udtPerson.Birthdate = Value
      If DatePart("y", udtPerson.Birthdate) > DatePart("y", Now) Then
        udtPerson.Age = _
           DateDiff("yyyy", udtPerson.Birthdate, Now) - 1
      Else
        udtPerson.Age = DateDiff("yyyy", udtPerson.Birthdate, Now)
      End If
      If udtPerson.Age <> intOldAge Then
        intOldAge = udtPerson.Age
        RaiseEvent NewAge
      End If
   End Property

   Public Property Get Birthdate() As Date
      Birthdate = udtPerson.Birthdate
   End Property

   Public Property Get Age() As Integer
      Age = udtPerson.Age
   End Property
```

This class contains a very straightforward set of code. We just accept the values for properties and return them when requested. The exception being that we recalculate the **intAge** value each time the **Birthdate** property is set, so that it can be returned in the read-only **Age** property.

Also notice that we have code to raise the **NewAge** event in the **Property Let** routine for the **BirthDate** property. When we get a new birthdate for the person, we always need to check to see if we've changed the person's age. If we have changed their age, we can raise this event to indicate to our client program that the age is now different.

That's all there is to this class, for the moment. We'll expand on its functionality shortly, but, right now, we need make sure that we can create a user-interface to work with this simple version.

The PersonDemo User-Interface

Adding the project

Let's put together a very simple form to act as an interface for a **Person** object. We'll build this in a new Standard EXE project called **PersonDemo**. We can add this project to the same Visual Basic session that we used to build the **PersonObjects** project: simply choose the File-Add Project option, rather than File-New Project, and choose Standard EXE. Don't forget to change the name of this second project to **PersonDemo** using its Properties window.

> *The ability to have multiple projects inside the same session of Visual Basic is new with version 5.0. When we run our project in this type of setting, Visual Basic will break us into the debugger in any of the projects that are loaded, making this a very attractive feature for debugging. In Visual Basic 4.0, we would have had to run a copy of Visual Basic for each project we wanted to debug interactively.*

Creating the Form

Here's what we want the **EditPerson** form to look like:

The form has three text boxes so that the user can supply values for the social security number (**txtSSN**), name (**txtName**), and birth date (**txtBirthDate**). It also has a label set up to display the person's age (**lblAge**), as well as standard OK, Cancel and Apply buttons (**cmdOK**, **cmdCancel** and **cmdApply**). Set the **Enabled** properties of **cmdOK** and **cmdApply** to **False**, and set the **BorderStyle** property of **lblAge** to 1 - Fixed Single.

Referencing the PersonObjects project

Before we start putting code behind the form, we need to make sure our new project has access to our **Person** class. Even though both projects are running within the same Visual Basic window, we still need to add a reference from our UI project back to the ActiveX DLL we created.

To do this, we need to choose the Project-References menu option to bring up the References dialog window. Then find the entry for **PersonObjects** and check the box to the left:

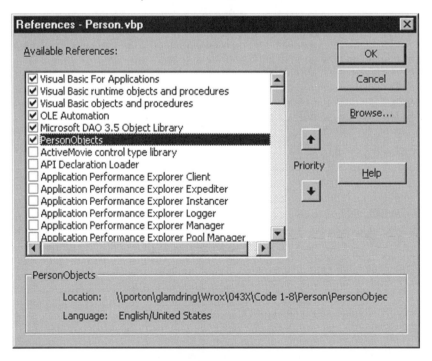

When we click OK, we'll establish a reference from our UI project back to our in-process server, **PersonObjects**. This will give our program access to all the public classes in that project. In this case, we'll get access to the **Person** class.

Adding the code

Now let's put some code behind the Edit Person form:

```
Option Explicit

Private WithEvents objPerson As Person

Private Sub cmdApply_Click()
  ' save the object
End Sub

Private Sub cmdCancel_Click()
  ' do not save the object
  Unload Me
End Sub

Private Sub cmdOK_Click()
  ' save the object
  Unload Me
End Sub

Private Sub Form_Load()
  Set objPerson = New Person
End Sub

Private Sub objPerson_NewAge()
  lblAge = objPerson.Age
End Sub

Private Sub txtBirthdate_Change()
  If IsDate(txtBirthdate) Then objPerson.Birthdate = txtBirthdate
End Sub

Private Sub txtName_Change()
  objPerson.Name = txtName
End Sub

Private Sub txtSSN_Change()
  objPerson.SSN = txtSSN
End Sub
```

There's nothing terribly complex going on here.

At the top, we declare a variable to hold our **Person** object and then, in the **Form_Load** event, we create a **Person** object and store a reference to it in the **objPerson** variable. The only point worth making, here, is that we're using the **WithEvents** keyword as we declare the **objPerson** variable. This is what allows our program to receive the **NewAge** event that the **Person** object might raise. We don't have to use the **WithEvents** keyword, but without it we won't be able to receive the event.

If we do receive a **NewAge** event, it will be handled in the **objPerson_NewAge** routine. In this case, we want to update the age value that's displayed in **lblAge** with the **objPerson.Age** property.

Each text box has a **Change** event subroutine that simply takes the value from the control and puts it into the corresponding property of our **Person** object. We are trusting the business object, **Person**, to handle any validation or business rules, so there's no reason to worry about that here in the UI.

The OK, Cancel and Apply button code is intentionally vague. How we support these buttons from within our business object is tricky. The solution we're going to see is both elegant and powerful, but we'll need to beef up our **Person** object a bit before we're ready to cover it.

Running the Program

Since it is from the **PersonDemo** project that our UI calls the business objects, we need to make sure that it's from the **PersonDemo** project that the program starts to run. To set this up, select the **PersonDemo** project in the Project Group window, right-click the mouse to get the context menu, and select Set as Start Up. Now, when we run the program, Visual Basic will begin execution within the PersonDemo project.

At this point, we should be able to choose the Run-Start menu option or press F5 to run the program and interact with our **Person** object.

This seems like a pretty nice, straightforward solution. However, we'll soon find that we have a couple problems with our implementation, so let's take a look at them.

Enforcing Field-level Validation

Looking at the **Person** class, we see that it should only store 11 characters for the **SSN** and 50 characters for the **Name** - at least according to our user-defined type, **PersonProps**:

```
Private Type PersonProps
  SSN As String * 11
  Name As String * 50
  Birthdate As Date
  Age As Integer
End Type
```

Here's the situation: if we run the program and enter text into the **SSN** or **Name** fields on the form, we'll find that we can enter as many characters as we like. This is obviously a problem.

While we could simply set the **MaxLength** property on the form's fields, we haven't solved the underlying problem. After all, suppose the next interface is an Excel spreadsheet, where we don't have a **MaxLength** property. This is a clear case where the object needs to protect itself.

Raising an Error from the Person Object

The easiest way for the object to indicate that it has a problem with a value is just to raise an error. So let's alter the **SSN Property Let** in our **Person** class as follows:

```
Public Property Let SSN(Value As String)
   If Len(Value) > 11 Then _
      Err.Raise vbObjectError + 1001, "Person", "SSN too long"

   udtPerson.SSN = Value
End Property
```

Now the form will be notified if the user's entry is invalid. We might still want to set the **MaxLength** property on the form's field but, if we don't, then at least there will be some indication that there was a problem - and the object will have protected itself.

Trapping the Error in the UI

Of course, the form will need some extra code to handle the error that's raised. How that error is handled is up to the individual UI designer. It could be handled as simply as sounding a beep and resetting the displayed value. Add this code to the **txtSSN_Change** routine in the Edit Person form:

```
Private Sub txtSSN_Change()

   On Error GoTo HandleError

   objPerson.SSN = txtSSN

   Exit Sub

HandleError:
   Beep
   txtSSN = objPerson.SSN
   txtSSN.SelStart = Len(txtSSN)

End Sub
```

Since we're handling our own error situation here, it's necessary to set the Visual Basic environment to break only on those errors that we aren't handling ourselves. To set this up, we need to make sure that the Visual Basic environment will only Break on Unhandled Errors. *In Visual Basic 5.0, choose the* Tools-Options *dialog, select the* General *tab, and make sure that* Break on Unhandled Errors *is selected.*

*Also note that we didn't use **On Error Resume Next**, but instead used a labeled error handler. With Visual Basic 5.0, this is an important performance consideration, since the native code compiler adds a lot of extra code to support **On Error Resume Next**, so a labeled error handler is much more efficient.*

Running the Program

At this point, we should be able to run our program and see how this works. Go to the SSN field and try to enter a value longer than 11 characters. The code we just added should prevent us from entering any value longer than 11 characters.

The beauty of this solution is that the code in the form only deals with the presentation; it doesn't enforce any business rules. We could add extra checks in the **Person** class to prevent entry of alpha characters in the field, or change the maximum length, and there would be no impact on the code in the form.

Enforcing Object-level Validation

By raising errors when a field is given an invalid value, we've provided **field-level validation** through our business object. It's also important to provide **object-level validation** to the largest degree possible.

Object-level validation checks the entire object - all the properties and internal variables - to make sure that everything is acceptable and all business rules have been met. This is important to the UI developer, since they may want to disable the OK and Apply buttons when the object is not valid and cannot be saved.

Object-level validation is more difficult to implement than field-level validation, since it depends upon more factors. An object might be valid only when all fields have values filled in; or perhaps a field is required only when another field contains a specific value. Virtually anything is possible, since the rules are dictated by the business requirements for the object.

Worse still, some object-level validation may not be possible in the business object on the client. Some business rules might really be relational rules in the database, so it's possible that we won't know they aren't being met until we try to save the object's data.

Granted, we can't guarantee that an object is valid according to rules enforced by the application services; but that shouldn't stop us from indicating whether the object meets all the conditions that *can* be checked right there on the client workstation. If we do that, then at least the UI can disable the OK and Apply buttons most of the time it's actually appropriate to do so, and we'll be moving towards a better interface.

An IsValid Property

To provide this functionality for the UI, let's just add a single **Boolean** property to the **Person** object, called **IsValid**. This property will return a **True** value if all the business rules are met (or at least, as far as our object can tell that they've all been met).

If our object has an **IsValid** property, then the form can check to see if the object is valid at any point. If the **IsValid** property returns **False** then the form knows that the object has at least one broken business rule, and the OK and Apply buttons can be disabled.

This implies that the **IsValid** property's value is based on *all* the business rules in the object. That can make things pretty complex, since an object might have a lot of business rules to check. For instance, we may have rules specifying which properties are required. We may also have rules that specify that a field must be blank if another has a value - or just about anything else we can think up.

There are a number of ways to implement an **IsValid** property. For instance, we could code all the business rules into the **IsValid** routine itself. Then, every time the property was checked, we'd just run through a series of checks to make sure all the conditions were met. This approach can be a serious performance problem, however, if we have a lot of rules - or if some of our rules are complex and hard to check.

Another possibility is to keep a **Private** variable to keep track of the number of rules that are broken at any given time. As property values change, we can check all the appropriate rules and change this counter as needed. This solution can provide better performance, but can be very difficult to implement.

In particular, when we check a rule we have no way of knowing if it was already broken or if it is newly broken due to some new data. If it was already broken then we don't want to increment our rule-broken count; but if it's a newly broken rule, then the rule-broken count needs to be upped by one.

One very good way to implement the **IsValid** property is to keep a collection of the rules that are broken within the object. If there are no broken rules in our collection, then we know the object is valid. As we check each rule, we can also use the collection to track whether the rule was already broken, is broken now, or is unbroken. This is a very useful concept, and one that we'll use in Chapter 5 - where we implement quite a number of business objects.

To make all this easier, let's create a **BrokenRules** class to help manage this collection for us. We'll then be able to use this class whenever we need to implement an object-level **IsValid** property in our business objects. We'll certainly be seeing it in action when we implement the objects for our video rental store application, in Chapter 5.

The BrokenRules Class

The **BrokenRules** class has one purpose, and that is to make it easy for our business objects to keep track of their business rules and how many are broken at any given time. If there are no broken business rules then our business object can return a **True** value from its **IsValid** property.

Creating the BrokenRules Class

Since this class will be used exclusively by our business objects as they keep track of their broken business rules, we'll need to add the **BrokenRules** class module to any business object projects we may be developing.

For instance, in the **Person** project that we've been developing in this chapter, we will need to add the **BrokenRules** class to our **PersonObjects** project - since that's where our business object resides in this example.

So add a new class module to the **PersonObjects** project, using the Project-Add Class Module menu option, and change the name of the new class module to **BrokenRules** using its Properties window.

Go ahead and enter the following code for the **BrokenRules** class, and then we'll walk through how it works.

```
Option Explicit

Event BrokenRule()
Event NoBrokenRules()

Private colBroken As Collection
```

```
Private Sub Class_Initialize()
  Set colBroken = New Collection
End Sub

Public Sub RuleBroken(Rule As String, IsBroken As Boolean)
  On Error GoTo HandleError
  If IsBroken Then
    colBroken.Add True, Rule
    RaiseEvent BrokenRule
  Else
    colBroken.Remove Rule
    If colBroken.Count = 0 Then RaiseEvent NoBrokenRules
  End If

HandleError:
End Sub

Public Property Get Count() As Integer
  Count = colBroken.Count
End Property
```

Once you've entered this code, make sure you save it, because we'll be using it throughout the development of our video rental project.

Our **BrokenRules** class first declares a collection variable and two events:

```
Event BrokenRule()
Event NoBrokenRules()

Private colBroken As Collection
```

The **colBroken** collection will be used to store exactly which rules have been broken; meanwhile, the events that we've declared will be raised when a rule is broken or when the broken-rule count goes to zero.

The real work in the class is done in the **RuleBroken** routine:

```
Public Sub RuleBroken(Rule As String, IsBroken As Boolean)
  On Error GoTo HandleError
  If IsBroken Then
    colBroken.Add True, Rule
    RaiseEvent BrokenRule
  Else
    colBroken.Remove Rule
    If colBroken.Count = 0 Then RaiseEvent NoBrokenRules
  End If

HandleError:
End Sub
```

The calling code, in our **Person** object, just passes this routine a label for the rule and a **Boolean** flag to indicate whether the rule was broken or not. Then, we just check that **Boolean** flag: if it's **True** then the rule was broken, so we make sure it's in the collection:

```
        If IsBroken Then
           colBroken.Add True, Rule
           RaiseEvent BrokenRule
```

If it is already in the collection, we'll get an error and exit the routine; but if it isn't already there, then we'll not only add it to the collection but also raise the **BrokenRule** event so the calling program knows that at least one rule has been broken.

Likewise, if **IsBroken** is **False** then we'll remove the entry from the collection:

```
        Else
           colBroken.Remove Rule
           If colBroken.Count = 0 Then RaiseEvent NoBrokenRules
        End If
```

If the entry is not in the collection, an error will occur and we'll exit the routine via the **HandleError** label. If the entry was in the collection, then we'll see if the overall count of broken rules is down to zero. When the count reaches zero, the **NoBrokenRules** event will be fired so the calling code can tell that everything is valid.

*Of course, events aren't universally supported: we can't get them just anywhere within Visual Basic itself, and we can't necessarily use them in all other environments. Other environments can still use this class, but if they don't support events then they'll need to check the **Count** property for these event conditions: when **Count** is zero, there are no broken rules and everything should be valid.*

Using the BrokenRules Object within our Person Object

Now let's see how we can use this **BrokenRules** class in our **Person** object. To keep this fairly simple, let's just enforce a rule that states that the **SSN** field is required and must be exactly 11 characters in length. We've already implemented code to prevent the user from entering more than 11 characters in this field; but now we're making the rules even more restrictive.

In order to use the **BrokenRules** object within our **Person** object, we need to declare and create a **Private** variable to hold the new object. Add the following line of code to the General Declarations section of our **Person** class module:

```
    Private WithEvents objValid As BrokenRules
```

We also need to add code in the **Person** object's **Class_Initialize** routine to create an object for this variable:

```
    Private Sub Class_Initialize()
       Set objValid = New BrokenRules
       objValid.RuleBroken "SSN", True
    End Sub
```

Notice, here, that we're forcing the **"SSN"** rule to be considered broken straight away. This is important, because, as the programmer, we know that the value is blank to begin with, so we need to make sure the business rule is enforced right from the start by indicating that it's broken.

> An important note about events. An object can't raise events until it has
> been fully instantiated, and an object isn't instantiated until *after* the
> `Class_Initialize` routine is complete. This means that any
> `RaiseEvent` statements called during the `Class_Initialize` routine
> won't actually raise any events.
>
> In this example, we're indicating that a rule is broken, so the `BrokenRule`
> event should fire; but it won't, because we're still in the
> `Class_Initialize` routine.

Handling the BrokenRule and NoBrokenRules Events

Our **Person** object needs to handle the events that will be created by the **BrokenRules** object we just created. To make it easier for the UI developer, we'll also have our **Person** object raise an event to let the UI know when the **Person** object becomes valid or invalid.

This first line that we'll add to handle these events goes in the General Declarations section of the **Person** class module, and it declares the **Valid** event. We'll use this event to indicate when our **Person** object switches between being valid and invalid:

```
Event Valid(IsValid As Boolean)
```

As we've seen, our **BrokenRules** object raises two events of its own: **BrokenRule** and **NoBrokenRules**. The **BrokenRule** event will be fired whenever a new rule is broken, while the **NoBrokenRules** will be fired any time the number of broken rules reaches zero.

By adding the following code to our **Person** object, we'll be able to react to these events by raising our own **Valid** event to tell the UI whether the **Person** object is currently valid:

```
Private Sub objValid_BrokenRule()
  RaiseEvent Valid(False)
End Sub

Private Sub objValid_NoBrokenRules()
  RaiseEvent Valid(True)
End Sub
```

If the **BrokenRule** event is fired then we know that at least one of our **Person** object's rules is broken. We can then raise our **Valid** event with a **False** parameter to indicate to the UI that the **Person** object is currently invalid. Likewise, when we receive a **NoBrokenRules** event, we can raise our **Valid** event with a **True** parameter to indicate to the UI that there are no broken rules and that our **Person** object is currently valid.

Implementing the IsValid Property

When we started this discussion, it was with the intent of creating an **IsValid** property on our **Person** object so that the UI could check to see if the object was valid at any given point. By implementing the **Valid** event in the previous section, we've actually provided a better solution; but we can't assume that the UI can actually receive events, since not all development tools provide support for them. The **IsValid** property is therefore remains very important.

Fortunately, our **BrokenRules** object makes implementation of the **IsValid** property very trivial. The **BrokenRules** object provides us with a count of the number of broken rules, and if that count is zero then we know that there are no rules broken. No broken business rules translates very nicely into a valid **Person** object.

To implement our **IsValid** property, let's enter the following code into the **Person** class module:

```
Public Property Get IsValid() As Boolean
  IsValid = (objValid.Count = 0)
End Property
```

This property simply returns a **Boolean** value that's based on whether the broken rule count equals zero or not.

Enforcing the SSN business Rules

In our **Person** object's **Class_Initialize** routine, we added a line to indicate that our **SSN** field was invalid. Since we're making it a required field, and all fields in a brand new object are blank, we know that the rule is broken during the initialization of the class.

We can therefore finish the job by adding some code to check our business rules within the **Person** object's **Property Let** routine for our **SSN** property:

```
Public Property Let SSN(Value As String)
  If Len(Value) > 11 Then
    Err.Raise vbObjectError + 1001, "Person", "SSN too long"
  End If
  udtPerson.SSN = Value
  objValid.RuleBroken "SSN", (Len(Trim$(udtPerson.SSN)) <> 11)
End Property
```

What we've done, here, is simply call the **RuleBroken** method of our **BrokenRules** object, passing it the name of our rule "**SSN**" and a **Boolean** to indicate whether the rule is currently broken. In this case, the rule just checks to make sure the value is exactly 11 characters long.

Anywhere that we need to enforce a rule in our object, we just need to add a single line of code with the rule's name and a **Boolean** to indicate if it's broken or unbroken. All the other details are handled through the **BrokenRules** object and the events that it fires.

Using the Valid Event and IsValid Property in the UI

At this point, we've implemented the **BrokenRules** object to keep track of how many business rules are broken within a business object. We've also enhanced our business object, **Person**, to take advantage of the new **BrokenRules** object. All that remains is to enhance our user interface to take advantage of the **Valid** event and **IsValid** property that we just added to our **Person** object.

A rich user-interface should be able to enable or disable the OK and Apply buttons as appropriate, so that they're only available to the user if the object is actually valid at the time. Most users dislike clicking on a button only to be told that the requested operation can't be performed. Ideally, when an operation can't be performed, the associated buttons should be disabled.

In our case, the OK and Apply buttons are only valid if the business object itself is valid. If the business object isn't valid then we can't save it, so both the OK and the Apply button should be disabled.

Adding the EnableOK Subroutine

The easiest way to manage the enabling and disabling of these buttons is to put the code in a central routine in the form. In our case, we'll need to add the following routine to our Edit Person form in the **PersonDemo** project:

```
Private Sub EnableOK(IsOK As Boolean)
   cmdOK.Enabled = IsOK
   cmdApply.Enabled = IsOK
End Sub
```

Using the IsValid Property

When the Edit Person form loads, the first thing it needs to do is make sure that the buttons are enabled properly. We need to check the **Person** object's **IsValid** property in our **Form_Load** routine to find out if the business object is valid at this point. Add this line of code to the Edit Person form's **Form_Load** routine:

```
Private Sub Form_Load()
   Set objPerson = New Person

   EnableOK objPerson.IsValid

End Sub
```

All we need to do is call our **EnableOK** subroutine, passing the **Person** object's **IsValid** property value as a parameter. If the object is valid, we'll be passing a **True** value, which will indicate that the OK and Apply buttons are to be enabled.

> *It might look as if we could rely on the **Person** object's **Valid** event to fire as the object was created. We could then act on that event to enable or disable the two buttons on our form. Unfortunately, objects can't raise events as they are being created, so there is no way for our **Person** object to raise its **Valid** event while it's starting up. This means we can't rely on the **Valid** event to tell us whether the object is valid as our form is first loading.*

Responding to the Valid Event

Once the Edit Person form is loaded and the user is interacting with it, we can rely on the **Person** object to raise its **Valid** event to tell the form whether it is currently valid. In our Edit Person form, we can add code to respond to this event, enabling and disabling the OK and Apply buttons as appropriate:

```
Private Sub objPerson_Valid(IsValid As Boolean)
   EnableOK IsValid
End Sub
```

Since the object will raise this event any time it changes from valid to invalid or back, the UI developer can rely on this event to enable or disable the buttons for the life of the form. All we need to do is call our **EnableOK** subroutine, passing the **IsValid** parameter value to **EnableOK** to indicate whether to enable or disable the two buttons.

Running the Program

We can now run our program and see how well this works. When the Edit Person form first appears, the OK and Apply buttons are disabled. As a result of the code we've just entered, these buttons will only be enabled when there are exactly 11 characters in the SSN field.

Handling Canceled Edits

Most forms have OK and Cancel buttons, and many have an Apply button as well. We've included these on our sample form to illustrate how to support them within the object, since there have been some extra steps involved.

So far, we've left the code in the buttons' click events somewhat vague. Now let's think through the behaviors we require of the business object to support OK, Cancel and Apply.

We've implemented our form so that our **Person** object's properties are being set every time a field changes on the form. This is important, because it means that any business rules are validated as the user presses each key. A further ramification is that the business object's internal variables are always changing as the user changes values on the screen.

If the OK button is clicked, we just need to save the **Person** object's variables - and the form goes away. We'll cover different ways of saving the object later in the chapter, but the point here is that the OK button is pretty easy. After all, the object already has its internal variables set and ready to be saved. Since the form goes away when OK is clicked, we don't have to worry about any subsequent editing of the data.

The Cancel button is a different story. When the user clicks this button, the form goes away, but the **Person** object might have different data stored in its variables, since the user may well have been typing into some fields before they clicked the Cancel button.

On the surface, this might not seem like a problem: the form holds a reference to the **Person** object and, when it releases that reference, the object, along with its changed data, will just go away – or will it? Unfortunately, the object won't go away if some other form or object also holds a reference to it. Perhaps we have a **Family** object that holds references to a number of **Person** objects. If we were editing one of those **Person** objects and we clicked Cancel, we'd expect the **Person** object itself to stick around as part of the **Family** object; but we'd also expect any changes to its data to be reset to the original values.

The Apply button ties in here as well. When the user clicks Apply, the **Person** object's variables will be saved (as we'll see later). However, the user can keep editing the object - because the form doesn't get unloaded by the Apply button.

To make matters just a bit more complicated, there are also combinations: the user might do some editing, then Apply the edits, do some more work, and then click Cancel. Given that sequence of events, we'd need to keep all the changes up to when the Apply was clicked.

Enhancing the Person object

Let's look at how we can make it easy for a UI developer to support these three buttons. What we're talking about, here, is the ability to start editing the object, and then either **commit** (Apply) or **roll back** (Cancel) the edits that were made.

Let's add three methods to our **Person** object: **BeginEdit**, **ApplyEdit** and **CancelEdit**:

```
Public Sub BeginEdit()
  LSet udtSaved = udtPerson
  flgEditing = True
End Sub

Public Sub ApplyEdit()
  flgEditing = False
  ' data would be saved here
End Sub

Public Sub CancelEdit()
  LSet udtPerson = udtSaved
  flgEditing = False
End Sub
```

We'll walk through the details of these routines over the next few pages.

> The **ApplyEdit** routine contains a comment to indicate where we need to add some code to save the object to a database. In the section on Making Objects Persistent, later in this chapter, we'll discuss saving objects to a database and we'll get into more details about this process.

Right now, let's see how these three new routines provide support for the OK, Cancel and Apply buttons. The code in these routines makes use of two new module-level variables that we need to add to the General Declarations section of the **Person** class module:

```
Private udtSaved As PersonProps
Private flgEditing As Boolean
```

Are We Editing the Object?

The **flgEditing** variable is easy to follow: we just set it to **True** when we start editing the object and **False** when we're done.

We do need to initialize this variable up front, however; so add the following line to the **Class_Initialize** method of the **Person** class module:

```
Private Sub Class_Initialize()
  flgEditing = False
```

```
   Set objValid = New BrokenRules
   objValid.RuleBroken "SSN", True
End Sub
```

By keeping track of whether our object is currently being edited or not, we can make sure that our object's data is only changed when appropriate. We can use this flag to disable all the **Property Let** routines in our object, so the only time a value can be changed is when the object is in **edit mode**. By edit mode, I mean when the **flgEditing** flag is set to **True** by the **BeginEdit** method.

Essentially, we are making the object somewhat self-aware. The object will know whether it should allow any client code to change its data. The technique of viewing an object as a self-aware entity is called anthropomorphization. The term is derived from anthropus for human, and morph for change; we are changing our view of the object from a chunk of code to an intelligent entity. This is one of the core tenants of object-oriented design.

Saving a Snapshot of the Object's Data

The **udtSaved** variable deserves a bit of explanation. Here's how we declare it:

```
Private udtSaved As PersonProps
```

Within our **BeginEdit** routine, above, the **Person** object's data is stored in this **udtSaved** variable, which is based on the user-defined type **PersonProps**:

```
LSet udtSaved = udtPerson
```

There are a couple of important reasons for doing this, one of which is to make it easy to handle canceled edits, since we've stored a version of the Person's object data prior to the edit. The other reason is to make it easy to save the object to a database - but again, we'll discuss this later on in the *Making Objects Persistent* section of this chapter.

The **Person** object uses the **udtPerson** variable to store all its data values. The **udtSaved** variable is a snapshot of the object's state at the time the **BeginEdit** method was called. The copy is very fast and simple, since we use the **LSet** command to copy one user-defined variable directly into another very efficiently. Visual Basic does virtually no extra work during this call: it is, essentially, a memory copy function, and so it's incredibly fast.

*It is certainly possible to store an object's data in **Private** variables, then declare a second set of the variables, and copy them all one by one to create a snapshot. But the technique we're using with the **LSet** command is far faster, and it's easier to code.*

Using the BeginEdit Method

The **BeginEdit** method starts the editing process for the object:

```
Public Sub BeginEdit()
   LSet udtSaved = udtPerson
   flgEditing = True
End Sub
```

The routine simply copies the object's current data into the **udtSaved** variable, in case we need to get back to where we started. It also sets the **flgEditing** variable to **True,** to establish that the object is being edited.

This method needs to be called by the UI before any editing takes place, so we'll now add a line to call it from the Edit Person form's load routine:

```
Private Sub Form_Load()
    Set objPerson = New Person
    EnableOK objPerson.IsValid
    objPerson.BeginEdit
End Sub
```

Using the ApplyEdit Method

Once the Person Edit form has called the **BeginEdit** method on the **Person** object, the object knows that it's being edited. The user can change data on the form to their heart's content, but they'll eventually have to either save any changes or try to cancel them.

If the user clicks either OK or Apply, we need to save the changes in the object. Therefore, we'll also add these lines to the Edit Person form:

```
Private Sub cmdApply_Click()
    ' save the object
    objPerson.ApplyEdit
    objPerson.BeginEdit
End Sub

Private Sub cmdOK_Click()
    ' save the object
    objPerson.ApplyEdit
    Unload Me
End Sub
```

Both routines call the **ApplyEdit** method, and the Apply button's code also calls the **BeginEdit** method to resume the editing process for the object. We need to do this because the Apply button doesn't make the form unload, so the user must be able to continue editing the data at this point.

As you can see from the code above, the **ApplyEdit** routine sets the **flgEditing** variable to **False**, indicating to the **Person** object that editing is complete. The **ApplyEdit** method is also responsible for saving the object's data to the database: once again, a topic we'll cover in more detail in the section on *Making Objects Persistent.*

Using the CancelEdit Method

The user might also click the Cancel button, so we'll add the following line to the Person Edit form:

```
Private Sub cmdCancel_Click()
    ' do not save the object
    objPerson.CancelEdit
```

```
      Unload Me
   End Sub
```

All this line does is call the **CancelEdit** method within our Person business object. Here's that CancelEdit method again:

```
Public Sub CancelEdit()
   LSet udtPerson = udtSaved
   flgEditing = False
End Sub
```

This routine does a couple things, including setting the **flgEditing** variable to **False**, because the editing process is over, and restoring the **Person** object's data to the values stored in **udtSaved**:

```
   LSet udtPerson = udtSaved
```

Again, this is essentially a memory copy of the data that was saved in the **BeginEdit** routine back into the object's central repository of data, **udtPerson**.

> It's important to remember that for this to work, all the object's data must be in the user-defined type. If data values were kept in module-level variables, we'd need some extra code to save and restore those values.

Disabling Edits when flgEditing is False

The final set of changes we need to make to the **Person** object are to make sure that the object doesn't allow itself to be edited until the **BeginEdit** method has been called. We just need to add a line to each **Property Let** and **Property Set** to raise an error unless we're in the middle of editing. We may also choose to disable certain methods; in particular, those methods that impact our object's internal variables.

For example, we'd add this line to the **Property Let Name** routine:

```
Public Property Let Name(Value As String)
   If Not flgEditing Then Err.Raise 383
   udtPerson.Name = Value
End Property
```

Error 383 is an error that indicates a property is read-only, so if we don't want our property to be editable we can just raise that error. Of course, we only need to raise it if **flgEditing** is **False**, so once the **BeginEdit** method has been called the error won't be raised.

This line just needs to be added to the top of each **Property Let** in the **Person** class module. And we'll do essentially the same thing with the **ApplyEdit** and **CancelEdit** methods in the Person class module, but we'll use error 445 for these instead. This error is 'Object doesn't support this action' and it's more appropriate for disabling methods:

```
Public Sub CancelEdit()
```

```
    If Not flgEditing Then Err.Raise 445
        LSet udtPerson = udtSaved
        flgEditing = False
End Sub
```

Testing the Code

These changes are easy enough to test by slightly breaking the code in our Edit Person form. Just comment out the call to **BeginEdit** that we put in the **Form_Load** routine and then run the program.

Now, any attempt to change values in the form's fields will result in error 383 being raised. Clicking the Cancel button should result in error 445.

> *When you've finished this test, don't forget to uncomment the call to BeginEdit!*

While a well-behaved form will never actually encounter these errors, they are vitally important during development of the UI. Again, our objects must be written with the assumption that the UI developer is not going to write the perfect set of code on the first pass, so what we're doing here is helping the UI developer do their job while protecting our objects from errant code.

Protecting Properties and Methods

In the previous section, we effectively switched some properties from read-write to read-only, based on whether the object is flagged as editable. We also disabled some methods using a similar technique.

In this section, we'll quickly run through the reasons why we might want to disable properties or methods. We'll also consider exactly how to implement this disabling.

Read-only Properties

There are various reasons why we might need a read-only property. The most common is where we have a property that's calculated from other data within the object. A good example of this is the **Age** property in our **Person** object, which is read-only and is based on the **Birthdate**.

Other properties might switch between read-write and read-only, depending upon business rules or other criteria. We saw an example of this behavior in the previous section, where we made properties read-only when the object was not in an editable state.

There are two techniques available to us for creating read-only properties. The simplest technique is to provide no **Property Let** or **Property Set** routines for the property. Of course, this technique allows no flexibility, in that we can't then make the property read-write at runtime. The second technique available to us is to still create the **Property Let** or **Property Set** routines, but to raise error 383 'Set not supported (read-only property)' at the top of the routine when we want to make the property read-only:

```
Public Property Let X(Value As Integer)
```

```
      If condition_met Then Err.Raise 383

   Regular code goes here
End Property
```

Disabling Methods

As we've seen, there are situations where we need to temporarily disable methods, **Sub**, or **Function** code within our object. Depending on the state of the object, or various business rules, we may need to effectively turn off a method.

Disabling a method is as simple as generating error 445 'Object doesn't support this action' at the top of a method's code when we want that method disabled:

```
Public Sub X()
   If condition_met Then Err.Raise 445

   Regular code goes here
End Sub
```

We did this earlier, in the **ApplyEdit** and **CancelEdit** methods of our **Person** class. They weren't appropriate unless the object was currently being edited and the **flgEditing** flag was set to **True**.

Write-once Properties

There are also cases where we may wish to create a property that is only written once. This is an excellent technique to use for unique key values that identify an object, and for those situations where business rules dictate that data can not be changed once entered. Real-world examples of this would include an electronic signature or an identity stamp where an object is stamped with a security code that must not be changed.

Write-once properties are implemented using the same error raising technique as a read-only property, but with a bit more logic to support the concept. As an example, let's enhance our **Person** object's **SSN** property to be write-once. After all, once a person gets assigned a social security number, they've got it for life.

Indicating when the Object is 'New'

We can't consider the SSN to be entered until the object is first saved by the user when they click the OK or Apply buttons. At that point, we need to lock down the **Property Let SSN** and any other write-once properties.

To lock down the value, we'll add a module-level variable to our **Person** class module to indicate whether the **Person** object is 'new'. This same variable will come in useful, later, when we talk about saving and restoring objects from a database, since a restored object also needs its write-once properties locked out. Add this variable declaration to the General Declarations section of our **Person** class module:

```
Private flgNew As Boolean
```

Since the UI might also care to know if an object is new or not (so it can alter its appearance appropriately), we'll also create a read-only property for this purpose by adding the following code to the **Person** object:

```
Public Property Get IsNew() As Boolean
   IsNew = flgNew
End Property
```

Now let's implement the **flgNew** variable's operation. We need to start out assuming the object is indeed new:

```
Private Sub Class_Initialize()
   flgEditing = False

   flgNew = True

   Set objValid = New BrokenRules
   objValid.RuleBroken "SSN", True
End Sub
```

Then we just need to flip the switch, when the **Person** object is saved, via the **ApplyEdit** method:

```
Public Sub ApplyEdit()
   If Not flgEditing Then Err.Raise 445
   flgEditing = False

   flgNew = False

   ' data would be saved here
End Sub
```

Disabling the Property

All that remains is to change the **Property Let SSN** routine to become disabled when the object is no longer considered new:

```
Public Property Let SSN(Value As String)
   If Not flgEditing Then Err.Raise 383

   If Not flgNew Then Err.Raise 383

   If Len(Value) > 11 Then _
      Err.Raise vbObjectError + 1001, "Person", "SSN too long"
   udtPerson.SSN = Value
   objValid.RuleBroken "SSN", (Len(Trim$(udtPerson.SSN)) <> 11)
End Property
```

With these changes, the SSN can be entered and changed by the user up to the point where they click OK or Apply. At that point, the **Person** object will be saved to the data, the **flgNew** flag would be set to **False,** and the user will no longer be able to edit the SSN field.

Testing the Code

We can test this in our program, even though the data isn't actually saved to the database, since the **ApplyEdit** method still sets the **flgNew** flag to **False** when the Apply button is clicked.

Run the program, enter 11 characters into the SSN field, and click the Apply button. Now try to change the SSN field again. As a result of the code we've just entered, you'll find that the SSN is fixed, because we've just written to SSN, and it's now a write-once property.

Write-only Properties

Write-only properties are less common than read-only properties, but they do have their uses. A good example of a write-only property is a password property on a security object. There's no reason to read the password back, but we would, sometimes, want to set it.

As with read-only properties, there are two ways to create write-only properties. If we don't need to dynamically change the status at run-time, we can implement a write-only property by simply not writing a **Property Get** routine for the property.

However, if we do need to dynamically change a property from read-write to write-only for some reason, we just need to raise error 394 'Get not supported (write-only property)' at the top of the **Property Get** when the property needs to be write-only:

```
Public Property Get X() As Long

    If condition_met Then Err.Raise 394


    Regular code goes here
End Property
```

Making Objects Persistent

Throughout our discussion, so far, we've danced around the idea of making an object persistent. Objects are great, but if we can't save an object into a database and then retrieve it later, they're somewhat limited in their use.

As we've seen, business objects are intended to represent real-world entities. An entity in the real world, such as a customer, has no concept of saving, adding, updating, or deleting itself - those things just don't make sense. However, when we create an object in software to model a customer or product, we need to compromise the model slightly in order to handle these activities.

> **A primary goal in persisting business objects is to minimize the impact to the logical business model. We want a customer object to be a model of a customer, not a model of a database record.**

In this section, we'll discuss a couple of techniques that we can use to efficiently save business objects to a database without compromising the integrity of the CSLA. Then, we'll talk about what part of our program should actually do the work of saving and retrieving the data. And finally, we'll look at the details of the persistence service that we'll be using through the rest of the book.

The first thing we need to look at is exactly how are we're going to save an object to the database. Virtually all the databases used today are relational databases, although there are exceptions - such as hierarchical databases and object databases. Because of the prevalence of relational databases, however, we're going to focus on saving and restoring objects from that type of database, leaving the others to be covered elsewhere.

It is important to decide where to locate the code that takes care of saving or updating an object in the database. The specifics of how to save an object's data will depend upon where we put this code. There are three basic approaches:

1 Saving/restoring is handled by user-interface code
2 Business objects save/restore themselves
3 A specialized object manages the saving/restoring of business objects

The first solution may be valid in certain cases, but we won't cover it in any detail, because it's directly opposed to an object-oriented solution. The second solution is very valid, but not terribly scalable. In the end, we'll settle on the last solution: it works well with our object-oriented design, and yet provides good scalability for our applications.

But let's take a good look at each of these options, and consider their pros and cons in more detail.

Saving Objects within a Form or BAS Module

In keeping with a more traditional Visual Basic development approach, it's possible to put the persistence code in the form itself, or in a BAS module called by the form. Of course, this means putting quite a bit of logic into the user-interface - something that I don't recommended, since it makes our code much less general.

With this approach, every form that wants to use a given object will need the code to save and restore that object from the database. This almost guarantees duplication of code, and largely defeats the goals that we're trying to achieve by using object-oriented design in our applications.

We're not going to go into the details of any code to support this solution, since it's so directly in conflict with the principles we're trying to follow in this book.

Objects that Save Themselves

I've made it very clear, so far, that the business objects are the application, and the user-interface is pretty expendable. Thus it seems quite logical to assume that each object should know how to save itself to the database. By just adding some form of **Load** and **Save** methods to each object, it would appear that we've pretty much solved all our persistence issues. Let's consider this approach.

Implementing a Load Method

We'll consider, as an example, the **Person** object that we developed in the previous section.

Don't actually make any of these changes to the Person project, however, because this is not yet the optimal solution to our problem. I'll clearly signal when we have found the best solution.

Were we to implement a solution where objects saved themselves, we could add a **Load** method like this (against a Microsoft Access database):

```
Public Sub Load(SSN As String)
   Dim dbPerson As Database
   Dim rsPerson As Recordset
   Dim strSQL As String

   strSQL = "SELECT * FROM Person WHERE SSN='" & SSN & "'"
   Set dbPerson = OpenDatabase("h:\wrox\043x\person\person.mdb")
   Set rsPerson = dbPerson.OpenRecordset(strSQL)
   With rsPerson
     If Not .EOF And Not .BOF Then
       udtPerson.SSN = .Fields("SSN")
       udtPerson.Name = .Fields("Name")
       udtPerson.Birthdate = .Fields("Birthdate")
     Else
       rsPerson.Close
       dbPerson.Close
       Err.Raise vbObjectError + 1002, "Person", "SSN not on file"
     End If
   End With
   rsPerson.Close
   dbPerson.Close
End Sub
```

This code would simply open the database, perform a lookup of the person (based on the supplied social security number), and put the data from the recordset into the object's variables. Also, note that the path we've used for **OpenDatabase** is an absolute one; you'll need to change it to point to your own database.

*Since this code makes reference to a **Database** and **Recordset** object, you may need to add a reference in your project to the DAO. Use the Project-References menu option and select the most up-to-date DAO reference, such as Microsoft DAO 3.5 Object Library.*

Using the Load method from the UI

From the UI developer's perspective, this would be pretty nice, since all they'd need to do would be to get the user to enter the social security number. Let's assume the UI programmer stored this SSN number in a variable called **strSSN**. Some simple code to achieve this (which ignores any input validation concerns right now), which could be placed in a button event or the Form_Load routine, might run as follows:

```
Dim strSSN As String

strSSN = InputBox$("Enter the SSN")
```

Remember that we're not actually making these changes to our Person project and PersonDemo UI, because this is not the optimal solution to our problem.

The working UI code would then follow:

```
With objPerson
  .Load strSSN
  txtSSN = .SSN
  txtName = .Name
  txtBirthdate = .Birthdate
  lblAge = .Age
End With
```

Of course, this code would not only put the values from the object into each field on the form, but it would also trigger each field's **Change** event. These events are set up to put the values right back into the object, which is a rather poor solution. We could, perhaps, overcome this with a typical UI trick: a module-level flag to indicate that we were loading the data:

```
Private flgLoading As Boolean
```

Then, at the top of each **Change** event, we'd just add the following line of code:

```
If flgLoading Then Exit Sub
```

And finally, we'd slightly alter the code that copied the values to the form's fields:

```
flgLoading = True
With objPerson
  .Load strSSN
  txtSSN = .SSN
  txtName = .Name
  txtBirthdate = .Birthdate
  lblAge = .Age
End With
flgLoading = False
```

Saving the Object's Data through the ApplyEdit Method

Back in the **Person** object, we already have a method, **ApplyEdit**, to handle updating the object; so we'll just add some code to that routine:

```
Public Sub ApplyEdit()
  Dim dbPerson As Database
  Dim rsPerson As Recordset
  Dim strSQL As String

  If Not flgEditing Then Err.Raise 445
  flgEditing = False
  flgNew = True
```

```
    strSQL = "SELECT * FROM Person WHERE SSN='" & SSN & "'"
    Set dbPerson = OpenDatabase("h:\wrox\043x\person\person.mdb")
    Set rsPerson = dbPerson.OpenRecordset(strSQL)
    With rsPerson
      If Not .EOF And Not .BOF Then
        .Edit
      Else
        .AddNew
      End If
      .Fields("SSN") = udtPerson.SSN
      .Fields("Name") = udtPerson.Name
      .Fields("Birthdate") = udtPerson.Birthdate
      .Update
    End With
    rsPerson.Close
    dbPerson.Close
End Sub
```

Since this would just update an already existing routine, we wouldn't need to make any changes to our form's code to support the new functionality.

This solution is pretty nice. Probably the biggest benefit of objects that save themselves is that they are very easy for the UI developer to understand. They simply need to have some code to support the **Load** method, and they're all set.

> *It's worth nothing that the way we would have coded the **Load** and **ApplyEdit** methods essentially employed **optimistic locking**. Since no database connection was maintained once the data was loaded or saved, there was no lock on the data in the database while the object was in memory. We could very easily modify the code to maintain an open recordset as long as the object existed, thus converting this to use **pessimistic locking**. This could become very resource intensive if there were a lot of objects, however, since each object would have to maintain its own reference to a recordset.*

> *Along the same lines, if we were to implement an application using this technique then we'd want to open the database itself outside the object. Then we could provide the **dbPerson** variable as a global reference, of some sort, for use by all our objects. Opening databases is usually quite time consuming, so we really would need to make this change to get decent performance in a real application.*

There are a couple of drawbacks to this approach of objects saving themselves. One of our primary goals in creating objects is to make them accurate models of the business entities they represent. By putting all the data-handling code into the objects themselves, we've effectively diluted the business logic with the mechanics of data access. While we can't make our objects pure models of the business entities, it is important to keep as close to that ideal as possible.

Another drawback is that we've tied the data handling and the business handling together in a single object. If our intent is to distribute processing following the CSLA then this approach doesn't help us meet that goal. What we really want is to separate the data access code from the code that supports the business rules - so they can be distributed across multiple machines if need be.

On the upside, this technique of objects saving themselves is very good for applications where we know that the solution doesn't need to scale beyond a physical 2-tier setting. If the application will always be communicating with an ISAM database, such as Microsoft Access, or directly with a SQL database, such as Oracle, then this may be an attractive approach. Be warned, however: applications rarely stay as small as they were originally designed, and it may be wise to consider a more scalable solution.

Objects That Save Other Objects

Now that we've discussed how the UI could directly save an object, and how an object might directly save itself, we'll look at how we can design our business objects to rely on another object to manage their data access. This approach has a couple of very important benefits and is the one we'll use to write our video rental store application through the book.

An important benefit of having an object save itself, as in the previous section, is that the UI developer has a very simple and clear interface for loading and saving an object. At the same time, we really don't want the data access code to be located in the object itself, since that doesn't provide a very scalable solution.

One way to design an application's persistence is to create an object that the UI can call when it needs to save a business object to the database. This new object is designed to manage the persistence of the business object, and so it is called an **object manager**. The object manager contains all the code to retrieve, store, and delete a business object from the database on behalf of the UI.

Another alternative utilizes **data-centric business objects**. This is basically the concept that we can take objects as we saw in the previous section, *Objects that Save Themselves*, and pull only the data-centric processing out into a new object. Then the UI-centric business object can make use of the data-centric business object as needed to retrieve, store, and delete its data from the database.

The object manager solution is a valid approach to designing an application with distributed objects, and so we'll walk through how it could be implemented. Once we've coded this solution, we'll see how easy it is to move from an object manager solution to one using data-centric business objects.

An Object Manager

One approach to persisting business objects is to create an object manager object for use by the UI developer. The UI code would simply ask the object manager to load and save objects on its behalf, typically passing the business objects themselves as parameters to the **Load** and **Save** methods of the object manager.

This design is illustrated in the following figure:

As shown, the presentation tier, or UI, will interact with both our UI-centric business objects, such as our **Person** object, and the object manager that knows how to retrieve, save, and delete our business objects.

Sticking with the **Person** object we've used so far, let's take a look at a **PersonManager** class. The **PersonManager** will handle all the details of retrieving, saving, and deleting **Person** objects from the database. The UI code will ask the **PersonManager** to retrieve a **Person** object when it wants one loaded from the database. The UI will also use it to save a **Person** object back to the database or to delete a **Person** object.

An Object Manager as an Out-of-Process Server

One of our goals is to be able to put the **PersonManager** object on a separate machine from the client workstation. This will allow us more flexibility in how we deploy our application, as we can put this object manager on an application server machine and increase the scalability of our application:

Client workstation	Presentation tier
	UI-centric objects
Application server	Object Manager
Database server	Data services tier

This figure shows where an object manager, such as **PersonManager**, would fit into the CSLA. It also shows how the **PersonManager** can be run on an application server machine separate from the client workstation.

For us to be able to run the **PersonManager** object on a separate machine, we'll need to implement this class in a separate Visual Basic project from the **Person** class. This new project needs to be an ActiveX EXE project; or at least we need to design it to that end.

As we discussed earlier in this chapter, there are serious performance concerns when communicating between processes or across a network. Since we're designing the **PersonManager** to be at least out-of-process, and very likely on another machine across the network, we need to take steps to make sure that our communication is very efficient.

Adding GetState and SetState methods to Person

To this end, we'll use the user-defined type and **LSet** technique discussed earlier in this chapter. In order to implement this in the **Person** object itself, we need to add a couple of new methods: **GetState** and **SetState**.

To use the **LSet** technique, we need to make sure our object's data is stored using a user-defined type. Then we need to create a second user-defined type of the same length to act as a buffer for all the detailed **state data** from our object.

> We'll use the word *state* to describe the core data that makes up an object. An object can be viewed as an interface, an implementation of that interface (code), and state (data). An object could have a lot more data than is really required to define its state. The state data includes only that which must be saved and restored to return an object to its original state.

Our **Person** object already stores its state data in a user-defined type, **PersonProps**. However, this type will be needed by both the **Person** object and the **PersonManager** object, so we'll want to make it available to both. The easiest way to do this is to add a new code module to the **PersonObjects** project and move the **PersonProps** type from the **Person** class module into this code module. We'll call this new code module **PersonUDTs**:

```
Public Type PersonProps
    SSN As String * 11
    Name As String * 50
    Birthdate As Date
    Age As Integer
End Type
```

Notice that we've also changed the scope of the user-defined type from **Private** to **Public** so that it will be available outside this code module.

Now we can add the following user-defined type to the **PersonUDTs** code module:

```
Public Type PersonData
    Buffer As String * 67
End Type
```

This type will act as a buffer for the **PersonProps** data, allowing us to use the **LSet** command to easily copy the detailed information from **PersonProps** into the simple string buffer declared here.

With the user-defined types set up, we're all ready to add the **GetState** and **SetState** methods to our **Person** class module:

```
Public Function GetState() As String
    Dim udtBuffer As PersonData

    LSet udtBuffer = udtPerson
    GetState = udtBuffer.Buffer
End Function
```

To get the object's state, we just copy the detailed **udtPerson** variable into **udtBuffer**. The **udtBuffer** variable is just a **String,** so we can return it as the result of the function:

```
Public Sub SetState(ByVal Buffer As String)
    Dim udtBuffer As PersonData

    udtBuffer.Buffer = Buffer
    LSet udtPerson = udtBuffer
End Sub
```

To set the object's state, we simply reverse the process: accepting a string buffer and copying it into **udtBuffer**. Then we just **LSet udtBuffer**'s data into **udtPerson**, and the object is restored.

Given these methods, our **PersonManager** object needs to make only one call to retrieve all of the data from our object, and make only one other call to send all the object's data back. As we discussed earlier, this is very fast and efficient, even over a network connection.

Cloning Business Objects with GetState and SetState

Since **GetState** and **SetState** simply copy and restore the object's state data, we can use them for other purposes than persistence. They make a built-in cloning capability for each object, since we can write code like this:

```
Dim objPerson1 As Person
Dim objPerson2 As Person

Set objPerson1 = New Person
Set objPerson2 = New Person
```
objPerson1.SetState objPerson2.GetState

The **GetState** method of **objPerson2** simply converts that object's data into a string buffer. That buffer is then passed to the **SetState** method of **objPerson1**, which converts it back into detailed state data. We've moved all the detailed state data from **objPerson2** to **objPerson1** in one line of code.

The Person object's ApplyEdit Method

In our original **Person** object's **ApplyEdit** method, we inserted a comment to indicate that this routine would be responsible for saving the object's data:

```
Public Sub ApplyEdit()
  If Not flgEditing Then Err.Raise 445
  flgEditing = False
  flgNew = False
```
  ' data would be saved here
```
End Sub
```

This is not actually true if we intend to use an object manager like **PersonManager**. Instead, the **PersonManager** object itself will be responsible for saving the **Person** object's data. We don't need to make any changes to the **ApplyEdit** method, but it is important to recognize that the work involved in saving the **Person** object won't be done here and that it will be handled by the **PersonManager**.

It could be argued that it's possible to merge the code from **ApplyEdit** into the **GetState** method, since the **GetState** method will be called by **PersonManager** when it's saving the object - so the edit process must be complete. Unfortunately, this would introduce a side-effect into the **GetState** method that is not intuitive. From the outside, just looking at the name **GetState**, you'd never guess that it also ends the editing process. To avoid confusion, methods should always be as descriptive as possible without unexpected side-effects, and merging these two routines could easily cause such confusion.

Creating the PersonManager Object

Now that we've got the **Person** object ready to go, let's build the **PersonManager** object. To start off, make sure you've saved the Person project and, with the File-New Project menu option, start a new ActiveX EXE project. Set the project's Project Name to **PersonServer** under the Project-Properties menu option.

Change the name of **Class1** to **PersonManager** and make sure its **Instancing** property is set to 5-Multiuse.

Since we'll be sending data back and forth between our **Person** object and the **PersonManager** object through the use of the **LSet** technique, it's important that both objects have access to the **PersonProps** and **PersonData** user-defined types. Fortunately, we've put those types into the code module named **PersonUDTs,** so we can choose Project-Add File and add that code module to our new **PersonServer** project. Now both the **PersonObjects** and **PersonServer** projects have access to the exact same code module containing our user-defined types.

Now we're ready to add some code to the **PersonManager** class.

Adding a Load Method to PersonManager

The UI code will use the **PersonManager** object to load object data from the database into a new **Person** object. To do this, we'll implement a **Load** method on the **PersonManager** object for use by the UI developer. This is where things get interesting.

At the very least, we need to pass the **Load** method an identifier so that it can retrieve the right person. In this example, we'll pass the social security number, with the assumption that it provides a unique identifier for an individual.

Now we need to figure out how to get the data back to the client and into an object. Ideally, we'd like to make the **Load** method a function that returns a fully loaded **Person** object. This would mean our UI client code could look something like this:

```
Dim objPersonManager As PersonManager
Dim objPerson As Person

Set objPersonManager = New PersonManager
Set objPerson = objPersonManager.Load(strSSN)
```

Unfortunately, this is difficult at best. In order to return an object reference, the **Load** method needs to create an object. When an object is created, using either **New** or **CreateObject**, it is instantiated in the same process, and on the same machine, as the code that creates it. This means that a **Person** object created by the **PersonManager**'s **Load** method would be created, in the **PersonManager** object, on whatever machine that code is running.

We need the **Person** object to be created on the client machine, inside our client process. This means that the code to instantiate the object needs to be in that process as well. As a compromise, let's make our client code look something like this:

```
Dim objPersonManager As PersonManager
Dim objPerson As Person

Set objPersonManager = New PersonManager

Set objPerson = New Person
objPersonManager.Load strSSN, objPerson
```

This way, the object is created in the client, but we'll pass it as a reference to the **PersonManager** object to be loaded with data.

Given this approach, let's enter the following code, for the **Load** method itself, into the
PersonManager class module:

```
Public Sub Load(ByVal SSN As String, Person As Object)
    Dim dbPerson As Database
    Dim rsPerson As Recordset
    Dim strSQL As String
    Dim udtPerson As PersonProps
    Dim udtBuffer As PersonData

    strSQL = "SELECT * FROM Person WHERE SSN='" & SSN & "'"
    Set dbPerson = OpenDatabase("h:\wrox\043x\person\person.mdb")
    Set rsPerson = dbPerson.OpenRecordset(strSQL)
    With rsPerson
      If Not .EOF And Not .BOF Then
        udtPerson.SSN = .Fields("SSN")
        udtPerson.Name = .Fields("Name")
        udtPerson.Birthdate = .Fields("Birthdate")

        LSet udtBuffer = udtPerson
        Person.SetState udtBuffer.Buffer
      Else
        rsPerson.Close
        dbPerson.Close
        Err.Raise vbObjectError + 1002, "Person", "SSN not on file"
      End If
    End With
    rsPerson.Close
    dbPerson.Close
End Sub
```

*Once again, this code makes reference to a **Database** and **Recordset** object, so you may
need to add a reference in your project to the DAO. Use the Project-References menu option
and select the most up-to-date DAO reference, such as Microsoft DAO 3.5 Object Library.*

For the most part, this is pretty straightforward database programming, but let's walk through the
routine to make sure everything is clear.

The code opens the database and builds a recordset based on a SQL statement using the social
security number:

```
strSQL = "SELECT * FROM Person WHERE SSN='" & SSN & "'"
Set dbPerson = OpenDatabase("h:\wrox\043x\person\person.mdb")
Set rsPerson = dbPerson.OpenRecordset(strSQL)
```

If we successfully retrieve the data, we just load that data into our user-defined type and use **LSet** to
copy the detailed data into a user-defined type that represents a single string buffer:

```
udtPerson.SSN = .Fields("SSN")
udtPerson.Name = .Fields("Name")
udtPerson.Birthdate = .Fields("Birthdate")

LSet udtBuffer = udtPerson
```

Now that we've got all the data in a single string, we can just make a single call to the **Person** object's **SetState** method, as discussed above:

```
Person.SetState udtBuffer.Buffer
```

*This technique does require that both the detail and buffer user-defined types be available to both the business object project and the **PersonManager** object. The best way to handle this is to put the UDT definitions in a BAS module and include that module in both projects. Better yet, if you're using source code control such as Visual SourceSafe then you can link the file across both projects and allow the source control software to keep them in sync.*

Once we've called the **Person** object's **SetState** method to pass it the data from the database, the UI will have a reference to a fully loaded **Person** object. Then the UI code can use that **Person** object through its properties and methods.

Adding a Save Method to PersonManager

At some point, the UI will need to save a **Person** object's data to the database. To do this, it will use the **PersonManager**, so we'll add a **Save** method to the **PersonManager** object to handle the add and update functions.

The **Save** method can have a fairly simple interface, since all we really need to do is send down a reference to the object itself. The code can then directly call the **GetState** method of the **Person** object to retrieve its data. Here is the code:

```
Public Sub Save(Person As Object)
  Dim dbPerson As Database
  Dim rsPerson As Recordset
  Dim strSQL As String
  Dim udtPerson As PersonProps
  Dim udtBuffer As PersonData

  udtBuffer.Buffer = Person.GetState
  LSet udtPerson = udtBuffer

  strSQL = "SELECT * FROM Person WHERE SSN='" & udtPerson.SSN & "'"
  Set dbPerson = OpenDatabase("h:\wrox\043x\person\person.mdb")
  Set rsPerson = dbPerson.OpenRecordset(strSQL)
  With rsPerson
    If Not .EOF And Not .BOF Then
      .Edit
    Else
      .AddNew
    End If
    .Fields("SSN") = udtPerson.SSN
    .Fields("Name") = udtPerson.Name
    .Fields("Birthdate") = udtPerson.Birthdate
    .Update
  End With
  rsPerson.Close
  dbPerson.Close
End Sub
```

A good question, at this point, might be: why pass the object reference when we could just pass the state string returned by **GetState***? In this case, it would accomplish the same thing, but with one less out-of-process or network call.*

Suppose, however, that the **Person** *object also included a comment field, a dynamic string in the object, and a memo or long text field in the database. Since this variable would be dynamic in length, we couldn't put it into a user-defined type, and so we couldn't easily pass it within our state string.*

In a case like this, the **Save** *method may not only need to use the* **GetState** *method, but it may also have to use a* **GetComment** *method - which we'd implement in the* **Person** *object to return the comment string.*

Basically, by passing the object reference, rather than just the state string, we've provided ourselves with virtually unlimited flexibility in terms of communication between the **PersonManager** *and* **Person** *objects.*

To save a **Person** object, the code in our form's **cmdOK_Click** and **cmdApply_Click** event routines will look like this:

```
Dim objPersonManager As PersonManager

Set objPersonManager = New PersonManager
objPersonManager.Save objPerson
```

Of course the **cmdOK_Click** will have an extra line to unload the form:

```
Unload Me
```

Since we're passing the **Save** method a reference to the **objPerson** object, it can retrieve the data from the **Person** object and write the data out to the database.

Adding a Delete Method to PersonManager

At this point, our UI code can use the **PersonManager** object's **Load** method to retrieve a **Person** object and the **Save** method to add or update a **Person** object into the database. The only remaining operation we need to support is removal of a **Person** object from the database.

To provide this support, we'll add a **Delete** method to the **PersonManager** object. We can use the same identity value for **Delete** that we used for the **Load**; in this case, the social security number. And since we don't need the object's data, we don't need to worry about passing the object reference at all:

```
Public Sub Delete(SSN As String)
  Dim dbPerson As Database
  Dim strSQL As String

  strSQL = "DELETE * FROM Person WHERE SSN='" & SSN & "'"
  Set dbPerson = OpenDatabase("h:\wrox\043x\person\person.mdb")
  dbPerson.Execute strSQL
  dbPerson.Close
End Sub
```

To delete a **Person** object, the UI code would look like this:

```
Dim objPersonManager As PersonManager

Set objPersonManager =  New PersonManager
objPersonManager.Delete objPerson.SSN
```

This might be implemented behind a Delete button or a menu option - whatever is appropriate for the specific user-interface.

Testing the Save Method

We should be able to immediately try out the **PersonManager** object's **Save** method. To do this, we'll need to compile our **PersonServer** project into an EXE. This is done using the File-Make PersonServer.exe menu option from within Visual Basic.

Once the **PersonServer** project has been compiled, we're almost ready to run our **PersonDemo** program. Load up the **PersonDemo** project again, and just add a reference to the **PersonServer** using the Project-References menu option.

Now run the **PersonDemo** program. The form will come up as always, allowing us to enter information into our **Person** object. However, with the changes we just made to the code behind the OK and Apply buttons, clicking either one should cause our **Person** object's data to be saved to the database by our **PersonManager** object.

Testing the Load Method

The **Load** method is a bit trickier, since we need to come up with some way to get the SSN value from the user before we can call the method. The UI code we looked at for calling the **Load** method assumed we already had the SSN value.

Enter the following lines into our Person Edit form's **Form_Load** routine; this way, we can load a **Person** object as the form loads:

```
Private Sub Form_Load()
   Set objPerson = New Person

   Dim objPersonManager As PersonManager
   Set objPersonManager = New PersonManager
   objPersonManager.Load strSSN, objPerson

   EnableOK objPerson.IsValid
   objPerson.BeginEdit
End Sub
```

We can easily enhance this by using the **InputBox$** function to ask the user for the SSN:

```
Private Sub Form_Load()
   Set objPerson = New Person

   Dim strSSN As String
   strSSN = InputBox$("Enter the SSN")
```

```
    Dim objPersonManager As PersonManager
    Set objPersonManager = New PersonManager
    objPersonManager.Load strSSN, objPerson

    EnableOK objPerson.IsValid
    objPerson.BeginEdit
End Sub
```

This gets us almost there. If the user supplies a valid SSN value then our **Person** object will be loaded with the data from the database. All that remains is to update the display on the form, so let's add these lines to the **Form_Load** routine:

```
Private Sub Form_Load()
    Set objPerson = New Person
    Dim strSSN As String

    strSSN = InputBox$("Enter the SSN")

    Dim objPersonManager As PersonManager
    Set objPersonManager = New PersonManager
    objPersonManager.Load strSSN, objPerson

    flgLoading = True
    With objPerson
      txtSSN = .SSN
      txtName = .Name
      txtBirthDate = .BirthDate
      lblAge = .Age
    End With
    flgLoading = False

    EnableOK objPerson.IsValid
    objPerson.BeginEdit
End Sub
```

Notice, here, that we're using the module-level variable trick we saw in an earlier discussion where we looked at objects that save themselves: we set **flgLoading** to **True** while we're loading information into our form, so that we can switch off the form's **Change** events of the text fields.

Therefore, we also need to declare this module-level variable in the General Declarations area of our Person Edit form:

```
    Private flgLoading As Boolean
```

and we need to add this line to all the **Change** events in the Person Edit form:

```
Private Sub txtName_Change()

    If flgLoading Then Exit Sub

    objPerson.Name = txtName
End Sub
```

If we run our **PersonDemo** program now, we'll be prompted for an SSN value. Entering a valid SSN should cause that **Person** object to be displayed. Of course, we don't have any error trapping for invalid SSN entries, but this demonstrates the basic concepts of saving and restoring an object from the database. We'll build a more robust application based on these general techniques starting in Chapter 5.

Data-centric Business Objects

The use of an object manager makes the process of retrieving, saving, and deleting an object pretty straightforward. However, compared to having an object save itself, this is a bit more complex from the UI developer's viewpoint. The UI developer not only needs to understand how to create and use the business objects themselves, but they need to understand how to create and use the objects that manage the persistence. This seems like extra work for little gain.

On the other hand, it's a small step from having the UI developer call the persistence manager object, as we've just seen, to having the business object itself call the persistence manager object:

This figure indicates that the presentation tier, or UI, only needs to interact with our UI-centric business objects. The UI developer just uses simple **Load** and **ApplyEdit** methods on the UI-centric business object, and lets the UI-centric business object take care of asking the data-centric object to actually retrieve, save, or delete the data. The UI developer doesn't have to worry about any of the code to persist the object. At the same time, we get the benefit of having the persistence code in a separate object that can be distributed across the network.

Let's look at how we can modify the previous example to use this new and improved technique. Fortunately, the changes aren't too difficult, so this will go quickly.

Simplifying the Code in the Form

First, let's look at the UI code. The whole idea is to simplify it, and we can easily do that. In fact, we can return it to the form it was in earlier in the chapter, before we implemented the **PersonManager**. The **Apply** and **OK** button code needs to be changed:

```
Private Sub cmdApply_Click()
   objPerson.ApplyEdit
   objPerson.BeginEdit
End Sub

Private Sub cmdOK_Click()
   objPerson.ApplyEdit
   Unload Me
End Sub
```

We also have code in the **Form_Load** routine to get an SSN value from the user and to load our **Person** object using the PersonManager object. We'll need to simplify that code as well:

```
Private Sub Form_Load()
  Set objPerson = New Person
  Dim strSSN As String

  strSSN = InputBox$("Enter the SSN")
```

```
  objPerson.Load(strSSN)
```

```
  flgLoading = True
```

In all three routines, the big difference is that our form's code doesn't need to create or deal with a **PersonManager** object. All the UI developer needs to be concerned with are the basic methods provided by the UI-centric business object, which is our **Person object**.

Adding a Load Method to Person

The changes to the **Person** object itself are a bit more extensive. Earlier in the chapter, we discussed having business objects save themselves to the database. To do this, we created a **Load** method for the object and enhanced the **ApplyEdit** method. Basically, we want to do the same thing here, except that the actual database code will be in a separate object, **PersonManager**.

First, let's add a **Load** method to the **Person** object. Enter the following code into the **Person** class module in the **PersonObjects** project:

```
Public Sub Load(SSN As String)
  Dim objManager As PersonManager

  Set objManager = New PersonManager
  objManager.Load SSN, Me
  Set objManager = Nothing
End Sub
```

This should look familiar, as it's pretty much the same code we just dealt with when having the client talk to the **PersonManager**. The code simply creates a **PersonManager** object, and then asks it to retrieve the object's data by passing the social security number and **Me**, a reference to the current object.

> You'll now need to add a reference to the **PersonServer** project from within your **PersonObjects** project. Use the **Project-References** menu option, and select **PersonServer**.
>
> It's worth noting, at this point, that the **PersonManager** object itself is entirely unchanged from our previous example. By simply adding a few extra lines of code into our business objects, we've dramatically simplified the UI developer's job, and we don't even have to change the objects that contain the data access code.

Updating the Person Object's ApplyEdit Method

Back to the **Person** object, we also need to change the **ApplyEdit** method to talk to the **PersonManager**:

```
Public Sub ApplyEdit()
    Dim objManager As PersonManager

    If Not flgEditing Then Err.Raise 445

    Set objManager = New PersonManager
    objManager.Save Me
    Set objManager = Nothing

    flgEditing = False
    flgNew = False
End Sub
```

Again, all we've done is created a **PersonManager** object, just like we did in the UI of the previous example. Then we just call its **Save** method passing **Me**, a reference to the current object, as a parameter. Of course, the UI developer simply calls **ApplyEdit** to save the object to the database; they don't need to worry about any of these details.

Adding a Delete Method to Person

Finally, let's add a **Delete** method to the **Person** business object. After all, we've already got that capability built into **PersonManager**; we just need to make it available to the UI developer via the business object:

```
Public Sub Delete()
    Dim objManager As PersonManager

    Set objManager = New PersonManager
    objManager.Delete udtPerson.SSN
    Set objManager = Nothing
End Sub
```

> *The only real drawback to this implementation of a **Delete** method is that the UI code may cheat and continue to retain a reference to the **Person** object after the **Delete** method has been called. This can make it much harder to debug the UI, since the developer may not immediately spot the fact that they are still using an object that has theoretically been deleted. One solution to this problem is to maintain a **Boolean** variable inside the object to indicate that the object has been deleted. Using this variable, we can add a line at the top of every property and method to raise the appropriate error to disable them, as discussed earlier in the chapter.*

This final approach to object persistence is a combination of the other techniques. It takes the best from each and puts them together to create an object to manage our data access that is transparent to the UI developer, easy to use for the business object developer, and that can be distributed to a central application server machine.

Testing the Code

The project should now run just as it did when we ran it under the full auspices of the **PersonManager** - we're able to perform deletions and apply edits as normal.

This is as far as we shall pursue our **PersonDemo** project. It' still in a pretty rough form, and there are lots of things we could do to improve it, of course; but the main functionality is in place, and it's served our purposes as we've explored a number of key concepts in this chapter. We're now ready to move on to bigger and better things - such as our video rental store project, where we'll develop the techniques we've learnt with our **PersonDemo** project to produce a sophisticated set of business objects and UI.

Summary

In this chapter, we returned to the CSLA. We looked at how that logical architecture can be implemented on a single machine and across multiple machines. As the number of physical tiers is increased, we can gain better distribution of the processing - increasing our flexibility and scalability with each layer. Of course, each extra layer of hardware can add communications overhead to our application.

We explored some of the business object design issues that impact user-interface developers. One of the primary goals of a business object developer is to make it easy for UI developers to work with the objects. At the same time, the business objects must protect themselves. Essentially, the business object developer must assume that the user-interface code will do something to break the objects - and the developer must take steps to prevent that from happening.

We wrapped up the chapter by looking at different techniques that we can use to save and restore object data in a database, or make objects persistent. Making objects persistent is the key to creating client/server applications using business objects. Most of an application's performance issues surround the techniques used to persist objects in a database, so it's important to choose the appropriate technique for each application.

We'll continue to explore the concepts from this chapter throughout the remainder of the book. Using the video store example from Chapter 3, we'll walk through the development of a series of applications by applying the CSLA to each typical physical model. Here's what we'll be looking at through the next few chapters:

Chapter 7   Create a UI using Visual Basic forms
Chapter 8   Add code to our objects to save themselves to the database
Chapter 9   Create a UI using Microsoft Excel
Chapter 10   Using data-centric business objects over Distributed COM
Chapter 11   Distributing objects over DCOM
Chapter 12   Using data-centric business objects with Microsoft Transaction Server
Chapter 13   Active Server Pages and HTML as a front end

5

Implementing Business Objects Using Visual Basic 5.0

Overview

So far, we've looked at business objects, distributed computing and various physical and logical architectures. We've also taken a fairly in-depth look at some techniques for identifying and designing business objects. At the end of the Chapter 4, we also examined a number of approaches to making objects persistent by saving and restoring their core data, or state, within a relational database.

In Chapters 5 through to 13, we're going to build and modify an application to operate a fictitious video rental store. Of course, the whole idea behind using business objects is to conserve code by encapsulating our core business processes within the business objects themselves. This should make it easy to create subsequent applications with minimal changes to the business object code.

It therefore makes sense to implement our business objects first - and then add the user-interface and object persistence based on the physical requirements of the application. When we talk about physical requirements we're referring to whether the application will be running on a single workstation or in either a two- or n-tier client/server setting.

In this chapter, we'll go through the process of implementing all the business objects that will be required to develop the applications in the remaining chapters.

Common Business Object Interface

In Chapter 4, we talked about common interface elements that objects should provide the UI developer. Let's quickly refresh that now, because all the business objects we'll implement need to provide those interface elements. Along the same lines, all our business objects need to implement certain behaviors so that they're consistent and easy to understand and use from the UI developer's viewpoint.

We won't go into this in great detail, as we covered all of this in Chapter 4. On the other hand, we were talking theory, earlier, and here we're getting down to brass tacks - so we need to be clear on what needs to be done.

OK, Cancel and Apply - A Preliminary Discussion

To support a robust user-interface, including OK, Cancel and Apply buttons, we need to provide support for beginning edits, canceling edits and applying edits. We also need to indicate if the object can be saved or not at any given point in time, so the OK and Apply buttons can be enabled and disabled as needed.

> Don't worry about typing this code in yet. After we review the concepts, we'll enter this code into a code template. Code templates make it easy to create new code modules that start out with a lot of basic code already entered into the module.

Transactional Methods

All our public objects need to support methods to be called from the OK, Cancel and Apply buttons:

- ❏ **BeginEdit**
- ❏ **CancelEdit**
- ❏ **ApplyEdit**

Part of the implementation of these methods requires that the object keep track, internally, of whether it can be edited at any given point. This can be handled through a private **flgEditing** variable.

The basic code to support these methods is pretty simple. Of course, each object will have its own private variables to store its state data, but the following code contains the essence of what each object must do:

```
Option Explicit

Private flgEditing As Boolean


Public Sub BeginEdit()
  If flgEditing Then Err.Raise 445
' save object state
```

```
    flgEditing = True
End Sub
```

Remember, don't worry about entering this code yet. Later in the chapter, we'll enter this code into a code template, which will make it easier for us to create new code modules to add to our video rental store project. For now, we're just looking at the ideas behind the code being presented.

BeginEdit is only valid if the object is not already being edited, so it raises an error if it is called while editing is taking place.

If the object is not already being edited, we need to save the object's core data - whatever that may be. This is indicated by the comment in this code, since the specific code will be different for each object.

Finally, we just need to set the **flgEditing** variable to **True**, since everything is now set for editing the object's data.

Here is the code for **CancelEdit**:

```
Public Sub CancelEdit()
    If Not flgEditing Then Err.Raise 445

    flgEditing = False
    ' restore object state
End Sub
```

The **CancelEdit** method is not valid unless **flgEditing** is true, since we can't cancel an edit if the object is not being edited. If this rule is broken, the method just raises an error to the calling code.

If the object was being edited, we just need to set the **flgEditing** flag to **False** to indicate that the editing is done. Then we must restore the object's state to the copy we made in the **BeginEdit** method. Again, the code for this will be different for each object, depending upon the nature of the data involved; so we've just put a comment here to show where that code would be located.

Here's the code for **ApplyEdit**:

```
Public Sub ApplyEdit()
    If Not flgEditing Then Err.Raise 445

    ' save object state
    flgEditing = False
End Sub
```

As with **CancelEdit**, this method is not valid unless the object is being edited, and, rather like applying a database transaction, applying the edits to an object ends the editing session by setting **flgEditing** to a value of **False**.

Virtually all the code in this method will be customized for each object. To apply the edits we need to save the object's current data just as we did in the **BeginEdit** method. A good approach is to create a common private subroutine to hold this code, and then just call that routine from both **BeginEdit** and **ApplyEdit**.

As we'll discuss shortly, **ApplyEdit** is also responsible for saving the object's data to the database. As we saw in Chapter 4, the database code might be right here, or this routine might call a method on an object on another machine to talk to the database instead.

Indicating Validity

Our business objects also need to provide mechanisms for the user-interface to know when the object is valid. That is, the UI needs to know when to enable and disable the OK and Apply buttons on the screen. This can be done through:

❑ A **Valid** event
❑ An **IsValid** property

As we saw in Chapter 4, a very good way to implement the **Valid** event and **IsValid** property is to use a **BrokenRules** object. Using the **BrokenRules** object, we'll have code in all our business objects to manage those rules.

First, we need to declare a variable for the **BrokenRules** object:

```
Private WithEvents objValid As BrokenRules
```

Then we need to add code to the **Class_Initialize** event to create the object. We also need to initialize the list of broken rules with any rules that we know are broken when an object is blank. Examples of this might include a required field that starts out blank, and thus breaks the rule immediately upon creating the object.

Here's the **Class_Initialize** code:

```
Private Sub Class_Initialize()
  Set objValid = New BrokenRules
  ' if we know any rules are broken on startup
  ' then add code here to initialize the list
  ' of broken rules
  '
  ' objValid.RuleBroken "RuleName", True
End Sub
```

Of course, we want to expose a property to allow the UI to find out if the object can be saved, or is valid. We'll call that property **IsValid**:

```
Public Property Get IsValid() As Boolean
  IsValid = (objValid.Count = 0)
End Property
```

Along the same lines, the **BrokenRules** object raises a couple of events indicating when a rule is broken and when there are no broken rules. We need to intercept those events and raise our **Valid** event up to the UI - so that the UI developer can easily enable or disable the OK and Apply buttons if desired. Here's the code to raise those two events:

```
Private Sub objValid_BrokenRule()
   RaiseEvent Valid(False)
End Sub
```

```
Private Sub objValid_NoBrokenRules()
   RaiseEvent Valid(True)
End Sub
```

We can also use the object's **IsValid** property, within the object itself, to disable any properties or methods that shouldn't be called when the object is not in a savable state. One obvious example of this is the **ApplyEdit** method. If the object shouldn't be saved, we want to make sure the **ApplyEdit** method returns an error when called:

```
Public Sub ApplyEdit()
   If Not flgEditing Then Err.Raise 445

   If Not IsValid Then Err.Raise 445


   ' save object state
   flgEditing = False
End Sub
```

Any other properties or methods that we need to disable can be handled by adding the same line of code at the top of those routines.

We can also declare our own **Valid** event, in Visual Basic 5.0, which can be raised when we need to indicate a change in the state of the object's validity:

```
Event Valid(IsValid As Boolean)
```

Persistence: Saving/Restoring Objects

Most of our business objects will have data that's stored and retrieved from a database. While the actual implementation of this persistence can vary, as we saw in Chapter 4, the business objects can provide a consistent interface to the UI developer regardless of the underlying code.

We need to provide support for retrieving, saving and deleting an object's data. It's also very useful for the UI developer to know whether the object can be considered new and whether it's been changed since it was loaded.

> **Don't worry about typing this code in anywhere. After we review the concepts we'll enter this code into a code template. Code templates make it easy to create new code modules that start out with a lot of basic code already entered into the module.**

Load

In order to get data from the database into our object, we'll implement a **Load** method in all our objects. As we discussed in Chapter 4, there are a number of different ways to implement such a method, so the code here will be fairly light. We'll expand on this code in Chapter 8, then again in Chapters 10 and 12.

```
Public Sub Load(KeyValue As Variant)
  If flgEditing Then Err.Raise 445

  ' code to load the object goes here
End Sub
```

Typically, the **Load** method will accept one or more parameters. After all, we need to provide enough information to uniquely identify the object's data within the database.

Also, this method needs to be disabled if the object is already being edited. We don't want a developer to accidentally reload an object after the user has already started entering values into it. To prevent this, the routine just checks **flgEditing** and raises an error if the value is **True**.

ApplyEdit

We've already discussed the **ApplyEdit** method in the context of supporting the OK, Cancel and Apply buttons. This method is also the key to saving our object's data. When we apply the edits, we not only want to update the object's internal state, but we also want to update its data in the database:

```
Public Sub ApplyEdit()
  If Not flgEditing Then Err.Raise 445
  If Not IsValid Then Err.Raise 445

  ' save object state
  ' save object to database if appropriate

  flgEditing = False
End Sub
```

As with the **Load** method, the specific implementation of saving the data to the database can vary greatly. More important is that we know that the **ApplyEdit** method is a consistent place to locate whatever implementation we choose.

Deleting an Object

To facilitate deletion of an object's data from the database, we'll add a **Delete** method to all the persistent objects. Ideally, deleting an object will also be covered by our **CancelEdit** and **ApplyEdit** methods - so that the UI developer can have maximum control over the behavior.

It isn't difficult to work the **Delete** method into the existing methods. First, we need to add a module-level variable to indicate whether the object has been deleted:

```
Private flgDeleted As Boolean
```

The **Delete** method itself should only be called after a call to **BeginEdit**, but beyond that it will just set **flgDeleted** to a value of **True**:

```
Public Sub Delete()
   If Not flgEditing Then Err.Raise 445

   flgDeleted = True
End Sub
```

Finally, we need to change **CancelEdit** and **ApplyEdit**. **CancelEdit** merely needs to restore **flgDeleted** to a **False** value. This effectively cancels the delete operation, since the flag is reset and the data hasn't been removed from the database.

```
Public Sub CancelEdit()
   If Not flgEditing Then Err.Raise 445
   If Not IsValid Then Err.Raise 445

   flgEditing = False

   flgDeleted = False

   ' restore object state
End Sub
```

The changes to **ApplyEdit** are a bit more extensive, since this method needs to actually commit any data changes. In this case, it needs to commit the delete operation:

```
Public Sub ApplyEdit()
   If Not flgEditing Then Err.Raise 445

   If flgDeleted Then
      ' code to delete the object's data goes here
      flgDeleted = False
   Else
      If Not IsValid Then Err.Raise 445
      ' save object state
      ' save object to database if appropriate
   End If

   flgEditing = False
End Sub
```

If **flgDeleted** is **True** then the code to delete the object's data will be run. At the risk of being repetitive, the implementation of this code can vary depending on the persistence strategy we choose. The routine also resets the **flgDeleted** flag back to **False**, since the delete is now complete and the object is almost like a new object that has yet to be saved to the database.

If **flgDeleted** was **False**, on the other hand, we just need to add or update the object's data as we were doing before these changes were made. The trick is that we move the line that checks **IsValid** into this area along with the code that saves the object's state data. Neither of these activities is appropriate when deleting an object - only when we are updating the data in the database.

As a last step, we'll add an **IsDeleted** property to each object. This is mostly a convenience to developers using our objects, as they may have a need to determine if the object will be deleted if they call **ApplyEdit**. This way, the UI code doesn't need to track whether the **Delete** method has been called; we do it instead:

```
Public Property Get IsDeleted() As Boolean
  IsDeleted = flgDeleted
End Property
```

IsNew

It can be very useful to the UI developer to know when an object is new. Frequently, the programmer will choose to adapt the interface to indicate that an object is new. For instance, it may be possible to enter some data fields only on a new object.

To implement this property, we'll simply keep a **Boolean** flag within the object:

```
Private flgNew As Boolean
```

Then, in the **Class_Initialize** method, we'll set this flag to **True**, indicating that the object has not been loaded with any data from the database:

```
Private Sub Class_Initialize()

flgNew = True

  Set objValid = New BrokenRules
  ' if we know any rules are broken on startup
  ' then add code here to initialize the list
  ' of broken rules
  '
  ' objValid.RuleBroken "RuleName", True
End Sub
```

Of course, as soon as we load data into the object from the database, we know that the object is no longer new. Handling this is as simple as adding a line to our **Load** method:

```
Public Sub Load()
  If flgEditing Then Err.Raise 445

  If Not flgNew Then Err.Raise 445

  flgNew = False

  ' code to load the object goes here
End Sub
```

We've also added a line to prevent the **Load** method from being run unless the object is new. This is just a bit of protection for developers using our objects. After an object has been loaded with data, we don't want them accidentally reloading the object with other data from the database.

Even if our object starts out new, as soon as we save it to the database with the **ApplyEdit** method, the object is really no more new than if we'd loaded it from the database with the **Load** method.

Of course, **ApplyEdit** might also delete the object if the **flgDeleted** flag is **True**. In this case, the object basically becomes new once again. The definition of a new object is one where the object's data doesn't exist in the database, and by removing the object's data from the database we sure meet that condition.

All we need to do is add a couple lines to the **ApplyEdit** method:

```
Public Sub ApplyEdit()
  If Not flgEditing Then Err.Raise 445

  If flgDeleted Then
    ' code to delete the object's data goes here
    flgNew = True
    flgDeleted = False
  Else
    If Not IsValid Then Err.Raise 445
    ' save object state
    ' save object to database if appropriate
    flgNew = False
  End If
  flgEditing = False
End Sub
```

With these changes, we now have a **flgNew** variable that always indicates whether our object is new or whether it came from data that is stored in the database or that was entered by the user and saved to the database. All that remains is to implement a simple **IsNew** property so that the UI developer has access to this information as well:

```
Public Property Get IsNew() As Boolean
  IsNew = flgNew
End Property
```

IsDirty

Along the same lines as knowing when an object is new, it can be very useful to know when the object's data has been changed. This, too, can be implemented by simply adding a **Boolean** variable to the object and setting it to true any time the object's data is changed:

```
Private flgDirty As Boolean
```

By default, the variable will start out with the value of **False**, which is just fine, since a new, empty object is obviously not dirty. To indicate that an object has been changed, we need to add the code inside any **Property Let** routines to set **flgDirty** to **True**:

```
flgDirty = True
```

If we subsequently save the data out to the database then we have synchronized the object with the database, and so we can consider the object to be no longer dirty. This is another line in the **ApplyEdit** method, where we save the object's data. Better still, we only need to save the object's data to the database if **flgDirty** is **True**, so we'll add a check for that as well:

183

```
Public Sub ApplyEdit()
  If Not flgEditing Then Err.Raise 445

  If flgDeleted Then
    ' code to delete the object's data goes here
    flgNew = True
    flgDeleted = False
  ElseIf flgDirty Or flgNew Then
    If Not IsValid Then Err.Raise 445
    ' save object state
    ' save object to database if appropriate
    flgNew = False
  End If

  flgDirty = False

  flgEditing = False
End Sub
```

At this point, we have a **flgDirty** variable that continually indicates whether our object's data has been changed since it was last loaded from or saved to the database. By adding an **IsDirty** property, we can give the UI developer access to this information as well:

```
Public Property Get IsDirty() As Boolean
  IsDirty = flgDirty
End Property
```

Creating a Class Template

As you can see, just creating a simple business object can involve quite a lot of code. No one likes typing the same stuff over and over again. Fortunately, Visual Basic 5.0 provides a way to get a jump-start on coding by letting us add our own templates to the development environment.

In this section we'll create a code template for our UI-centric business objects based on the concepts we just reviewed. We'll use this template through the remainder of this chapter, as we build the business objects for our video store application.

Setting up the Class Module

First, open a new ActiveX DLL project in Visual Basic. This should put us right into a new class module named **Class1**.

In the properties window we need to set the Name and Instancing properties of **Class1**. Set the Name to Business and the Instancing to 5-Multiuse.

Adding the Template Code

Now we need to add the template code. The code we need is all the code we just discussed for OK, Cancel and Apply along with the object persistence and all the related properties. Enter this code into the module:

```
Option Explicit

Event Valid(IsValid As Boolean)

Private flgNew As Boolean
Private flgDeleted As Boolean
Private flgDirty As Boolean
Private flgEditing As Boolean
Private WithEvents objValid As BrokenRules

Public Sub BeginEdit()
  If flgEditing Then Err.Raise 445

  ' save object state
  flgEditing = True
End Sub

Public Sub CancelEdit()
  If Not flgEditing Then Err.Raise 445

  flgEditing = False
  flgDeleted = False
  ' restore object state
End Sub

Public Sub ApplyEdit()
  If Not flgEditing Then Err.Raise 445

  If flgDeleted Then
    ' code to delete the object's data goes here
    flgNew = True
    flgDeleted = False
  ElseIf flgDirty Or flgNew Then
    If Not IsValid Then Err.Raise 445
    ' save object to database if appropriate
    ' save object state
    flgNew = False
  End If
  flgDirty = False
  flgEditing = False
End Sub

Private Sub Class_Initialize()
  Set objValid = New BrokenRules
  flgNew = True
  ' if we know any rules are broken on startup
  ' then add code here to initialize the list
  ' of broken rules
  '
  ' objValid.RuleBroken "RuleName", True
End Sub

Public Property Get IsValid() As Boolean
  IsValid = (objValid.Count = 0)
End Property

Private Sub objValid_BrokenRule()
  RaiseEvent Valid(False)
End Sub

Private Sub objValid_NoBrokenRules()
```

```
      RaiseEvent Valid(True)
   End Sub

   Public Sub Load()
      If flgEditing Then Err.Raise 445
      If Not flgNew Then Err.Raise 445

      flgNew = False

      ' code to load the object goes here
   End Sub

   Public Sub Delete()
      If Not flgEditing Then Err.Raise 445

      flgDeleted = True
   End Sub

   Public Property Get IsDeleted() As Boolean
      IsDeleted = flgDeleted
   End Property

   Public Property Get IsNew() As Boolean
      IsNew = flgNew
   End Property

   Public Property Get IsDirty() As Boolean
      IsDirty = flgDirty
   End Property
```

Saving the Template

Now we need to save the class module into the **Template\Classes** directory under the directory where Visual Basic itself is installed. Typically this will be something like:

C:\Program Files\DevStudio\Visual Basic

Right-click on the **Business** class in the Project window and choose the Save Business As option from the menu; then use the Save File As... dialog to save the class module into the **Template\Classes** directory.

That's it, we now have a template ready to use. We'll want to close the current project before trying to use the template to avoid accidentally saving over the file we just created.

Using the Code Template

To see how it works, just choose the Project-Add Class Module menu option. The Add Class Module dialog will appear, with our new **Business** template listed as an option:

Choose the Business option and click Open. Visual Basic will add a new class module to our project, called **Business**, that contains all the code we entered earlier. From now on, any time we need to add a new business object class to our projects we can just use this template.

The BrokenRules Class

The template we just created relies on the **BrokenRules** class being available to the project. We created the **BrokenRules** class in Chapter 4 to simplify the process of tracking which business rules are broken at any given point in time.

We can either add the **BrokenRules** class to every project, or we can compile it into a DLL and just reference it in each project that needs it. The optimum solution is to put it into a **Utility.dll** or **Common.dll** along with any other classes our developers create that are useful to many different applications.

However, in our video store application, our business objects will all be in one Visual Basic project, so we'll just include the **BrokenRules.cls** file into that project.

Video Rental System Overview

If we were developing an application for real, either for our employer, a client or for retail sale, we'd want to do a full analysis of the business requirements and functional requirements. We looked at some techniques for doing this back in Chapter 3.

Of course, these documents tend to be very long and very dry. While they are invaluable in developing an application, they'd make pretty boring material for a technical book. Because of this, we're just going to run through a very quick overview of the application's requirements - so we can see how the various objects fit into the picture - and leave it at that.

As this is a video rental store application, we'll obviously have customers coming in to rent the videos. And we'll have videos for them to rent, probably with a number of tapes for each video title - especially the popular ones. The rental itself is a transaction, and so we'll express it as an invoice, with line items for each tape that gets rented.

In general, then, we have the following objects:

- ❑ Customer
- ❑ Video
- ❑ Tape
- ❑ Invoice
- ❑ InvoiceItem

When we go through each of these business functions, there will be a number of supporting objects that need to be created. Mostly, these will be collection objects, or objects that represent a series of related business objects. For instance, we will have a *Tapes* object that represents all the *Tape* objects for a specific video title.

The following diagram provides an overview of the main objects we'll be implementing for this system.

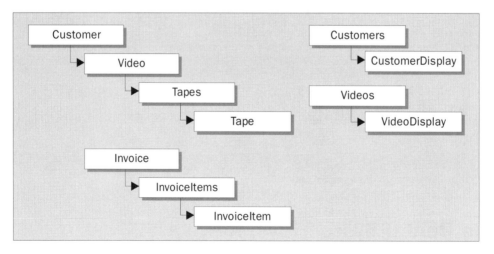

We'll be implementing a few other objects along the way, but this should provide a good picture of all the major objects that are needed to support a video rental store.

Video Rental: Customer Objects

In any retail system, there's always a customer of some sort. Our video store is no exception; someone needs to pay the bills after all. Our customer object needs to contain some pretty basic information about a person - including their name, address and phone number.

We also need to provide a way to find a customer. A typical application would provide some search facility so that the user can enter criteria and get back a list of customers to choose from. The easiest way to support this concept, with objects, is to provide a collection object to contain the list of customers. For this purpose, we'll create a **Customers** object.

In the implementation we'll do here, there is no real relationship between a **Customer** object and a **Customers** object. The **Customer** object will represent a real-world customer. Our **Customers** object will represent a customer list, such as a paper ledger listing some or all of our customer's names.

Customer: A Simple Object

Since this is the first real business object we're creating, we'll go through the process in detail. After this object, we'll gloss over the more repetitive steps so we can focus in on the differences between the objects.

Setting up the Project

To start with, open up a new ActiveX DLL project in Visual Basic. Change the project name to **VideoObjects** by choosing Project-ProjectX Properties... and changing the Project Name field on the Project Properties dialog:

Now right-click on the **Class1** item in the Project window and choose the Remove Class1 option. Answer No when prompted to save any changes.

We'll be adding our classes using the **Business** class template we created earlier in this chapter.

Adding the BrokenRules Class

We'll also need the **BrokenRules** class from earlier in the book. Choose the Project-Add File... menu option and just include the class module directly into this project.

Adding the Customer Class Module

Now we're ready to add our **Customer** class module. Choose the Project-Add Class Module menu option. From the dialog, choose the Business class template that we created earlier and click Open:

We should be looking at a ready-to-go class module with all the template code we built earlier in the chapter. Change the Name property of the class to Customer in the Properties window, and make sure that the Instancing property is 5-Multiuse.

*It's important to restrict the creation of objects, when appropriate, by setting the Instancing property to 1-Private or 2-PublicNotCreatable. In the case of the **Customer** object, however, we want the UI developer to be able to create new **Customer** objects as needed. Later in the chapter, we'll see some objects that can't be directly created from the UI.*

Setting up the Customer Class

Now it's down to adding the code for the class. The first thing we need to do is set up variables to store the object's data. As we discussed earlier in the book, it is a good idea to use user-defined types (UDTs) to store the data, because it makes it easier to save and restore the object's core data - as well as to implement distributed database load and save operations.

Declarations

In the (Declarations) section of the code module, let's add a UDT, **CustomerProps**, to store the object's data. We'll also add declarations for a couple variables based on this type. The first, **udtProps**, will store the object's properties. The other, **udtSave**, will be the copy we'll use when we need to save or restore the object's data within the **BeginEdit**, **CancelEdit** and **ApplyEdit** methods:

```
Option Explicit

Event Valid(IsValid As Boolean)
```

```
Private Type CustomerProps
  CustomerID As Long
  Name As String * 50
  Phone As String * 25
  Address1 As String * 30
  Address2 As String * 30
  City As String * 20
  State As String * 2
  ZipCode As String * 10
End Type

Private udtProps As CustomerProps
Private udtSave As CustomerProps
```

```
Private flgNew As Boolean
Private flgDeleted As Boolean
Private flgDirty As Boolean
Private flgEditing As Boolean
Private WithEvents objValid As BrokenRules
```

Now we need to go through the template code and update it in a few places. In particular, we need to add code to save and restore the object's data as needed.

Load Method

Our template supplied a basic **Load** method, but we need to customize it to suit our needs. In particular, it needs to accept a parameter to uniquely identify the customer data to be loaded. The **CustomerID** field is the unique identifier for our customer objects, so that's the parameter we'll need to accept:

```
Public Sub Load(CustomerID as Long)
  If flgEditing Then Err.Raise 445
  If Not flgNew Then Err.Raise 445

  flgNew = False
```

```
     ' code to load the object goes here
   End Sub
```

There's not much else we can customize in the **Load** method at this point, since the actual data loading code will depend on the data access implementation we choose. Through the remaining chapters of this book, we'll be implementing this method in a couple of different ways.

BeginEdit Method

In the **BeginEdit** method, we need to add a line to save the data in **udtProps** to the **udtSave** variable. As we discussed in Chapter 4, the **LSet** command makes this a very simple process:

```
Public Sub BeginEdit()
  If flgEditing Then Err.Raise 445

  ' save object state

  LSet udtSave = udtProps

  flgEditing = True
End Sub
```

CancelEdit Method

In the **CancelEdit** method, we need to do the reverse, copying the data in **udtSave** back into **udtProps** to restore the object to the last data that was saved:

```
Public Sub CancelEdit()
  If Not flgEditing Then Err.Raise 445

  flgEditing = False
  flgDeleted = False
  ' restore object state

  LSet udtProps = udtSave

End Sub
```

ApplyEdit Method

Similar to the **BeginEdit** method, the **ApplyEdit** method also copies the **udtProps** data into the **udtSave** variable using the **LSet** command:

```
Public Sub ApplyEdit()
  If Not flgEditing Then Err.Raise 445

  If flgDeleted Then
    ' code to delete the object's data goes here
    flgNew = True
    flgDeleted = False
  ElseIf flgDirty Or flgNew Then
    If Not IsValid Then Err.Raise 445
    ' save object to database if appropriate
    ' save object state

    LSet udtSave = udtProps

    flgNew = False
  End If
```

```
        flgDirty = False
        flgEditing = False
      End Sub
```

Note that we're not touching the parts of the code that will eventually save and restore the data from the database. For now, we're just leaving the comments there to remind us that we need to add that code later.

Class_Initialize Routine

Let's say that, at the very least, any customer needs to have a name and a phone number. With a new object, we know that these fields will be blank, and so we need to initialize the **BrokenRules** object to know that these rules are broken. We'll do this by adding a couple of lines to the **Class_Initialize** routine:

```
    Private Sub Class_Initialize()
      flgNew = True
      Set objValid = New BrokenRules
      ' if we know any rules are broken on startup
      ' then add code here to initialize the list
      ' of broken rules
      '
      ' objValid.RuleBroken "RuleName", True

      objValid.RuleBroken "Name", True
      objValid.RuleBroken "Phone", True

    End Sub
```

That's it for the basics. Virtually every business object we create will need the same changes we just made - tailored for that object's specific properties, of course.

Now we can move on to implement any specific properties and methods that the **Customer** object will need. These properties and methods are fairly obvious, since they correspond to the data elements in the UDT that we declared.

Customer Object Properties

Let's go through each property in turn. Most of them will be very similar, but we do have some required fields and one read-only property.

CustomerID Property: Read-only Value

The **CustomerID** property is primarily a key value for the database. Customer numbers are often displayed on forms, or shown on reports, however; so we need to make this available to the UI developer - at least on a read-only basis.

Implementing key values like the **CustomerID** can be a tricky business. We need to decide if the user can enter the initial value, and whether we want to let them change it after it has been entered. The easiest solution, of course, is for the key value to be generated automatically by the computer.

Even if the computer automatically generates the key value, we still need to decide if it should be generated right away when the object is created, or perhaps if it should be generated when the object is first saved to the database. Most databases provide some facility to generate sequential numbers for key values, such as the **AutoNumber** type in Microsoft Access. If we need to provide a key value before saving the object to the database, things get more complex - as we need to generate the number on our own.

For our **Customer** object, we'll assign the key value when the object is saved to the database the first time. If the object is new, we'll just return an ID value of zero. Since we'll be generating the value in code, there is no reason for the UI to ever set the value in our object, and so we'll make it a read-only property - by just implementing a **Property Get** without any **Property Let** procedure:

```
Public Property Get CustomerID() As Long
   CustomerID = udtProps.CustomerID
End Property
```

Name Property: Read-write Value

The **Name** property is read-write, since the user will need to enter a name for the customer, and the UI developer will need to read the **Name** property, later, to display it on any forms.

So here's the **Property Let** procedure for the **Name** property. It accepts a parameter that will contain the name - as entered by the user:

```
Public Property Let Name(Value As String)
   If Not flgEditing Then Err.Raise 383

   If Len(Value) > Len(udtProps.Name) Then _
      Err.Raise vbObjectError + 1001, "String value too long"
   objValid.RuleBroken "Name", (Len(Trim$(Value)) = 0)

   udtProps.Name = Value
   flgDirty = True
End Property
```

The first thing we do in this procedure is check the **flgEditing** flag:

```
If Not flgEditing Then Err.Raise 383
```

If we aren't editing the object, because the UI developer hasn't yet called the **BeginEdit** method, then we need to raise an error. This is less for the end user's benefit than to help the UI developer during the debugging process.

If it's OK to edit the object's data, we need to check any business rules for this field:

```
If Len(Value) > Len(udtProps.Name) Then _
   Err.Raise vbObjectError + 1001, "String value too long"
objValid.RuleBroken "Name", (Len(Trim$(Value)) = 0)
```

> *We'll use the* **BrokenRules** *object that we set up earlier to record and track the rules that are broken. The* **RuleBroken** *method of the* **BrokenRules** *object accepts the rule name as the first parameter and a* **Boolean** *for the second. If we pass it a* **True** *value, it records the rule as being broken, while a* **False** *value indicates that the object's data is valid for this rule.*

One rule that we obviously have is that the field length can't exceed the length of our fixed length **Name** field in the user-defined type. The other rule we have for this field is that it is a required field, so the length can't be zero.

Here's where we can get into a bit of discussion about business rules and their interaction with the UI code. Looking at the code, we can see that we raise an error if the data length is too long, but not when the length is zero. In a sense, we can look at these rules as having two levels of severity. To decide whether to raise an error when a business rule is broken, we need to look at two criteria:

1   First, we need to see if it is possible for our code to even handle the value that we were passed. If the parameter we are passed is too long then we can't even store it, since the UDT's **Name** field can't hold more than fifty characters - and so we have little choice but to raise an error. On the other hand, if the value we are passed is a zero-length string, we can store it without a problem - so we aren't forced to raise an error; instead, we can use the **BrokenRules** object to record the broken business rule.

2   The other criterion we need to consider is what works best for the UI developer. We need to put ourselves in the UI developer's shoes and think about what makes their life easier. If a field is required, the UI needs to disable the OK and Apply buttons, but probably doesn't need to do anything else especially. If the data in the field is too long, however, the UI probably needs to beep or take some other action to let the user know they have typed too much.

If we get past the business rule checks without raising an error, we need to assign the parameter value to the **Name** field of the **udtProps** variable:

```
udtProps.Name = Value
```

This updates the 'live' copy of our data. Since we've required that **BeginEdit** be called before we can edit this field, we know that the original value is stored in the **udtSave** variable - and we can get back to it if the **CancelEdit** method is called later.

We also need to provide a **Property Get** routine for the **Name** property:

```
Public Property Get Name() As String
    Name = Trim$(udtProps.Name)
End Property
```

The routine returns a string value. In this code we're using the **Trim$()** command to trim off any spaces from the **udtProps.Name** value. This is important, as **udtProps.Name** is a fixed length string and would normally return a value out to its full length, padding the end with spaces. This is typically not the expected behavior for a string property on an object; normally, we'd expect to just get the data without trailing spaces. Adding in the **Trim$()** call removes those spaces and gives us the desired result.

Basic Address Properties

The **Address1** property contains the first address line for the customer. It, too, is a read-write property, since the user needs to enter the address and the UI will need to display it. This one is somewhat simpler, since it has no associated business rules and so is about as basic as we can get:

```
Public Property Let Address1(Value As String)
  If Not flgEditing Then Err.Raise 383

  If Len(Value) > Len(udtProps.Address1) Then _
    Err.Raise vbObjectError + 1001, "String value too long"

  udtProps.Address1 = Value
  flgDirty = True
End Property
```

Again, we make sure that it's OK to edit the object's data before doing any real work. If editing is allowed, we check the length of the value to make sure it isn't too long - and raise an error if there is a problem. Finally, we store the parameter value into the UDT variable and we're on our way.

The **Property Get** is also as simple as we'll get. It just returns the value from the UDT, after calling the **Trim$()** command to remove those pesky spaces from the fixed length string:

```
Public Property Get Address1() As String
  Address1 = Trim$(udtProps.Address1)
End Property
```

The **Address2** and **City** properties work the same way:

```
Public Property Let Address2(Value As String)
  If Not flgEditing Then Err.Raise 383

  If Len(Value) > Len(udtProps.Address2) Then _
    Err.Raise vbObjectError + 1001, "String value too long"

  udtProps.Address2 = Value
  flgDirty = True
End Property
```

```
Public Property Get Address2() As String
  Address2 = Trim$(udtProps.Address2)
End Property
```

```
Public Property Let City(Value As String)
  If Not flgEditing Then Err.Raise 383

  If Len(Value) > Len(udtProps.City) Then _
    Err.Raise vbObjectError + 1001, "String value too long"

  udtProps.City = Value
  flgDirty = True
End Property
```

```
Public Property Get City() As String
   City = Trim$(udtProps.City)
End Property
```

State Property: Making a Value Uppercase

With the **State** property, we have an extra bit of work. The codes for states are always shown in upper case, so we essentially have a business rule that says that this field is always uppercase. It would be an easy thing to have the UI just make them uppercase it for us, but it is very important for business objects to protect themselves, and assume that the UI won't necessarily take care of such details:

```
Public Property Let State(Value As String)
   If Not flgEditing Then Err.Raise 383

   If Len(Value) > Len(udtProps.State) Then _
     Err.Raise vbObjectError + 1001, "String value too long"

   udtProps.State = UCase$(Value)
   flgDirty = True
End Property
```

The difference between this and the previous **Property Let** routines is subtle but nevertheless important. We use the **UCase$()** command to make the value uppercase before storing it in the UDT variable:

```
udtProps.State = UCase$(Value)
```

Our other options are to raise an error if the value isn't already uppercase, or to use the **BrokenRules** *object to record this as a broken rule. Recalling our discussion about the basic behavior of a UI form, however, we always use the* **LostFocus** *event on a field to refresh the display with whatever is stored in the business object. This means that the user can enter whatever they like, and the display will be updated with the uppercase version as they leave the field.*

This is a pretty nice compromise for this type of business rule, since it doesn't force the UI developer to do any extra work or worry about errors, but the business rule is still enforced and the display does get updated for the user.

The **State** property also has a **Property Get**, which is no more complex than any of the others:

```
Public Property Get State() As String
   State = Trim$(udtProps.State)
End Property
```

ZipCode Property: Formatting a Value

Like the **State** property, the **ZipCode** property has some extra processing to ensure that it appears correctly:

```
Public Property Let ZipCode(Value As String)
   Dim intDash As Integer
```

```
      If Not flgEditing Then Err.Raise 383

   If Len(Value) > Len(udtProps.ZipCode) Then _
     Err.Raise vbObjectError + 1001, "String value too long"

   intDash = InStr(1, Value, "-")
   If intDash > 0 Then
     udtProps.ZipCode = _
       Format$(Val(Mid$(Value, 1, intDash - 1)), "00000") & _
       "-" & Format$(Val(Mid$(Value, intDash + 1)), "0000")
   Else
     udtProps.ZipCode = _
       Format$(Val(Mid$(Value, 1, 5)), "00000") & _
       "-" & Format$(Val(Mid$(Value, 6)), "0000")
   End If
   If Right$(udtProps.ZipCode, 5) = "-0000" Then _
     udtProps.ZipCode = Left$(udtProps.ZipCode, 5)
   flgDirty = True
End Property
```

```
Public Property Get ZipCode() As String
   ZipCode = Trim$(udtProps.ZipCode)
End Property
```

Zip codes are 5 digits, a dash and then 4 digits. If the last 4 digits are all zeros then the dash and zeros are suppressed.

While the display format data is often controlled within the UI code, it is the business object's job to make sure that the data inside each object is consistent and useful. If we choose to enforce the official zip code format in the UI and the database, then the business object must consider that to be a business rule.

With a method like this, where there is a bit of code to handle the proper formatting of the zip code, it is advantageous to put the logic into the business object. If this field were displayed in a variety of locations in the UI, we would have to duplicate the code in this method in all those places. This way, the code is centralized and easily maintained.

Phone Property

The final property is the **Phone** property. Like the **Name** property, this is a required field, and so we check the length of the parameter value and use the **BrokenRules** object to track whether the field has data:

```
Public Property Let Phone(Value As String)
   If Not flgEditing Then Err.Raise 383

   objValid.RuleBroken "Phone", (Len(Trim$(Value)) = 0)

   udtProps.Phone = Value
   flgDirty = True
End Property
```

```
Public Property Get Phone() As String
   Phone = Trim$(udtProps.Phone)
End Property
```

Customer Object Methods

In the real world, just about everything centers around a customer. Customers rent the videos in the store, return the videos when they are done and pay for any fees that are incurred. Our object's methods need to mimic these activities.

CreateInvoice Method: Creating Another Object

The first method we'll add is **CreateInvoice**. This method will enable the business process where a customer wants to rent one or more videos, since that process is primarily handled through an **Invoice**. We'll create the **Invoice** object later in the chapter, but that doesn't mean we can't add some code to the **Customer** object now:

```
'Public Function CreateInvoice() As Invoice
'   Dim objInvoice As Invoice
'
'   Set objInvoice = New Invoice
'   objInvoice.Initialize Me
'   Set CreateInvoice = objInvoice
'   Set objInvoice = Nothing
'End Function
```

Since we haven't added the **Invoice** class module to our project yet, we'll comment out the routine for now. Once we've added the **Invoice** class to the project we can come back and uncomment those lines.

This routine is a function that returns the **Invoice** object as a result. This means that the calling code will use something like this to create an invoice:

```
Set objInvoice = objCustomer.CreateInvoice
```

We've put in some extra code beyond simply creating the object. At the very least, we can assume that the new **Invoice** object will need to know information about the customer that created it, so we're also assuming that the **Invoice** object will have an **Initialize** method that accepts a **Customer** object as a parameter:

```
objInvoice.Initialize Me
```

We'll need to remember to add this method when we build the **Invoice** object later.

Beyond this code, all the routine does is create a new, blank **Invoice** object, and assign the function's result to be that object:

```
Set CreateInvoice = objInvoice
```

Testing the Customer Object

At this point, the customer object should be done and ready to use. Basic testing of business objects can be done very simply using Visual Basic's interactive debugging capabilities. We can just run an ActiveX DLL project in the IDE and use the Immediate window to test the object's methods and properties.

Press *F5* to run the project. After a short wait the display should change to indicate the program is running.

Now press *Ctrl-Break* to stop the program. If the Immediate window is not visible, use the View-Immediate Window menu option to display it.

We can now create an instance of the **Customer** class with the following line:

Set x = New Customer

x is now a late-bound variable pointing to our new **Customer** object. We can use it to call the object's methods and set and retrieve its properties. For instance, to start an edit of the object type:

x.BeginEdit

Then we can set and check a property value:

x.ZipCode = "123456789"
? x.ZipCode
12345-6789

If we now cancel the edit process, we should be able to prove that the **ZipCode** property gets reset to a blank:

x.CancelEdit
? x.ZipCode
            (blank space)

It's very easy to work with our objects within the Immediate window for simple debugging. Better still, this ease of use carries up to the UI developer, since they just need to use similar code within the interface to accomplish the same work.

Customers: A Read-Only List Object

The **Customer** object was a good example of a very simple business object that represents a single real-world entity. Many business processes, and thus many applications, also need to deal with lists of things - such as a list of customers. Typically, these lists are generated based on some criteria, either because all the items are directly related to each other (such as all the invoices for a customer) or because they share some common data field (such as a zip code).

With a video store application, the user will need a way to search the database for the right customer. They probably won't want to page through individual customers hoping to find the right one; instead, they'll expect to see some sort of search window displaying a list of customers that match a set of search criteria they've supplied.

There are two ways to approach a list object like this. This object can be a collection of **Customer** objects, or it can just be a list of the information that needs to be displayed in the search results window. Each has its benefits and drawbacks:

1   If we choose to make our list object a collection of **Customer** objects, we have a very elegant and simple solution. All the data for each customer will be available for our use, including all the business rules and everything that comes with the **Customer** class. The drawback is a serious one, however: performance. Instead of just retrieving the minimum data required to be displayed, and storing it in an efficient format, we need to retrieve all the data about each customer and create an object for each one. This can turn out to be pretty slow if we are dealing with many customers.

2   We could choose our list object to contain simpler data. In this case it would be a list of only the information that needs to be displayed for the search results. This would, typically, be much faster, since we wouldn't need to retrieve as much data, and we wouldn't need to store it in full-blown **Customer** objects. On the other hand, we'd lose a lot of flexibility, since we'd be tailoring our list object for this one search window. If the UI designer later decides to have a different customer list display, we could end up either extending this object or creating a different customer list object.

This is one of those cases where there is no right answer for all situations. Typically, the second option will be best, since performance is almost always very important for an application.

> **Objects representing lists of other objects or data can be the biggest performance problems in any client/server application. It is very important to weigh performance concerns heavily when deciding how to design your list objects.**

For this example, then, we'll use the second option, just in case our video application ends up having a large number of customers. This option will give us the better performance, though it will require a bit more work to implement. We'll name our new list object **Customers** (note the plural), since it will contain a list of information about multiple customers.

We need to identify the criteria that the user will be supplying to our new list object. Our object will expose properties to the UI developer so they can supply the criteria we'll use when searching for matching **Customer** objects. Since we're going with the option of providing only the required result data (rather than the entire customer object), we also need to identify which fields will be available to the UI developer for display.

For this example, the search criteria will include the customer's name and phone number - our two required fields from the **Customer** class.

Since the **Customers** class represents a list of customer data, it is very much like a **Collection** object. However, unlike a standard Visual Basic **Collection** object, it is a read-only list. Our object won't allow the UI developer to add or remove customers, instead it will just retrieve a list of customers that meet the supplied criteria.

For each item in our read-only collection, we'll be making a number of data elements available: **CustomerID**, **Name** and **Phone**. The easiest way to do this is to add a worker class containing read-only properties for those elements. We'll call this class **CustomerDisplay**.

The CustomerDisplay Class

Using the current project, choose Project-Add Class Module to add a class.

As a simple read-only list of properties, the **CustomerDisplay** class is a far cry from a persistent business class. So, from the Add Class Module dialog, choose the Class Module option and click Open.

Change the Name property for the class to CustomerDisplay. Change the Instancing property to 2-PublicNotCreatable. We want this class to be visible and useful to the UI developer, but we don't want the UI to be able to create instances of this object. Instead, we'll rely on the **Customers** object to actually create any of these objects that we need and supply those instances to the UI developer upon request.

Declarations

Like most objects, **CustomerDisplay** will need a place to store its data. Let's set up a user-defined type to hold the three data elements we'll be using. We'll also declare a variable of this new type, **udtProps**, for use throughout the class module:

```
Option Explicit

Private Type DisplayProps
  CustomerID As Long
  Name As String * 50
  Phone As String * 25
End Type

Private udtProps As DisplayProps
```

Public Properties

Similar to the **Customer** object itself, we need to provide **Public** properties so that the calling code can retrieve the values from our object. These properties just return the values from the UDT variable upon request:

```
Public Property Get CustomerID() As Long
  CustomerID = udtProps.CustomerID
End Property
```

```
Public Property Get Name() As String
  Name = Trim$(udtProps.Name)
End Property
```

```
Public Property Get Phone() As String
  Phone = Trim$(udtProps.Phone)
End Property
```

Friend Properties

At this point, we've defined the object's data storage and public interface. We still need to provide some way to get the data into the object without exposing any new properties or methods to the client code. Fortunately, Visual Basic 5.0 provides the **Friend** keyword, allowing us to create **Property Let** routines that are visible only to other code inside our Visual Basic project:

```
Friend Property Let CustomerID(Value As Long)
   udtProps.CustomerID = Value
End Property
```

```
Friend Property Let Name(Value As String)
   udtProps.Name = Value
End Property
```

```
Friend Property Let Phone(Value As String)
   udtProps.Phone = Value
End Property
```

These property routines look and work just like a regular property routine, except that their scope is limited to the current Visual Basic project. The UI developer will never know that these properties even exist.

Since these properties will only ever be called from the **Customers** class, we don't need to put in any code to catch data errors or broken business rules. The data that will be placed in these properties will come right from the database, through another business object, into the **CustomerDisplay** object. Any data in the database should have gotten there through the **Customer** object, where any business rules would have been enforced before the data could be saved.

The Customers Class

To add the **Customers** class to our project, choose Project-Add Class Module from the menu. Since the **Customers** class won't be a typical persistent business object, but will instead be a form of collection object, choose the Class Module option from the dialog and click Open.

Change the Name property of the class to Customers and make sure the Instancing property is set to 5-Multiuse. The UI developer should be able to create a **Customers** object whenever they want to get a list of customers from the database.

Earlier in the book, we went through the steps to create a full-blown collection class. The **Customers** class will be similar, but it will be read-only, and will have data loaded from the database.

Creating a Base Collection Object

Let's now go through the code that is basic to virtually any collection class. The heart of any collection class is a local variable that contains the actual underlying **Collection** object.

```
Option Explicit

Private colDisplay As Collection
```

It's important to remember that we must create an instance of the collection in the `Class_Initialize` routine so we have it ready for use throughout the rest of the module:

```
Private Sub Class_Initialize()
   Set colDisplay = New Collection
End Sub
```

Count Property

Collections also provide a **Count** property by simply echoing the **Count** value of the underlying **Collection** object:

```
Public Function Count() As Long
   Count = colDisplay.Count
End Function
```

Supporting For...Each

We also want to enable the use of the **For...Each** statement against our collection object. We can do this by implementing a **NewEnum** method on our object:

```
Public Function NewEnum() As IUnknown
   Set NewEnum = colDisplay.[_NewEnum]
End Function
```

> *Our **NewEnum** method returns a reference to an **IUnknown** type object. More accurately, it returns a reference to the **IUnknown** interface of an object. In this case we're returning the interface to whatever is behind the **NewEnum** method of a Visual Basic **Collection** object. We don't need to worry about the composition of this return value, it comes from a Visual Basic object and will be used by Visual Basic to support our **For...Each** functionality – we're just acting as a go-between.*

Choose the Tools-Procedure Attributes... menu option. Under the Advanced button, click on the Hide this member option and set the Procedure ID to −4. If we forget this step, the **NewEnum** method will be visible to client programs and won't be recognized for use with the **For...Each** statement by Visual Basic.

Item Method

In a regular collection class, we'd implement **Add** and **Remove** methods. Since the **Customers** object is read-only, we won't be allowing the client code to add or remove items from our list - and so we don't want to implement those methods. However, we do need to provide the **Item** method - to allow the client code to retrieve the data from our collection.

This is where things get more interesting. The implementation of the **Item** method can vary quite a lot, depending on how the data was retrieved from the database and loaded into the **Customers** object. It is this process of loading data into the object and making it available, via the **Item** method, that dictates the performance of this type of object. We'll look at a couple of different implementations later: one for use with a local database in Chapter 8, and one for use in a multi-tiered application design in Chapter 10.

Since the implementation can vary so greatly, we'll just put comments in the routine for now. Regardless of the implementation, however, the method's name, parameter and return value will remain constant:

```
Public Function Item(ByVal Index As Variant) As CustomerDisplay
    ' find or build a CustomerDisplay object
    ' then return it as a result
End Function
```

The **Item** method, in a normal collection, is the default method. We'll want to emulate that behavior to keep our object as close as possible to a regular collection. To make this property the default, choose the Tools-Procedure Attributes... menu option and click the Advanced button.

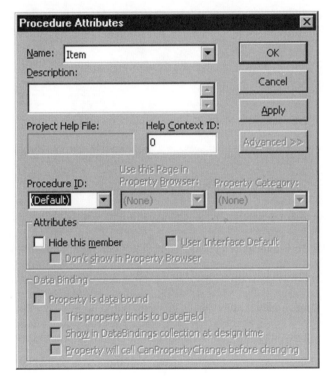

Make sure the **Item** method is selected in the Name option at the top of the dialog. Then just set the Procedure ID field to (Default) as shown in the figure and click OK.

> *The **Index** parameter is passed to the **Item** method using the **ByVal** keyword. This is done because the **Index** parameter on a regular Visual Basic **Collection** object is declared using the **ByVal** keyword and we need to make sure to fully emulate the interface provided by the regular **Collection** object.*

Load Method

One big similarity that the **Customers** object does have with other business objects is that it needs to provide some way to load the data from the database. To be consistent with other business objects, we'll do this through the use of a **Load** method that accepts the criteria as parameters:

```
Public Sub Load(Optional Name As String, _
                Optional Phone As String)
  ' load data from database
End Sub
```

Like the **Item** method, the **Load** method's implementation will vary greatly depending on the data access technique we choose. A lot of performance can be gained or lost depending on this implementation, so it's important to make the appropriate choice. In Chapters 8 and 10, we'll implement this method in a couple of different ways - so we can see how they differ.

Using the Customers Object

Finally, let's consider how the UI developer will use the object. Of course, we can't actually get anything from the object yet, since we don't have any data access code to get data from the database. However, the UI code might look like this:

```
Dim objCustomers As Customers
Dim objDisplay As CustomerDisplay

Set objCustomers = New Customers
objCustomers.Load Phone:="555-1234"
For Each objDisplay In objCustomers
  With objDisplay
    Debug.Print .CustomerID
    Debug.Print .Name
    Debug.Print .Phone
  End With
Next
Set objCustomers = Nothing
```

With similar code, the UI developer could load a list control, such as a **ListView**, to display this information.

Video Rental: Video and Tape Objects

Now that we've got objects to represent our customers, we can move on to the videos that they'll be renting. Video stores typically have a number of tapes for each video title that they rent out. The video itself has a title, rating, production studio and other relevant information. Each individual tape has little more than a unique barcode number, but since it is the tapes that we actually rent out, it's important to keep track of each one individually.

Since we've already gone through the creation of basic business objects with the **Customer** and **Customers** objects, we'll try not to be too repetitive regarding the basic creation process. Instead, we'll focus on those elements and concepts that are new; in particular, the relationship between the object representing a video title and the objects representing the individual tapes.

We'll also introduce a generic class to retrieve lists of text - for use both in validating user input and populating controls like the **ComboBox**. We'll use this class to build the video object.

TextList: a Powerful Utility Object

We'll get to the actual video title object shortly, but first let's go through the more generic class that can be used to represent a list of text items. One of the most common types of entry field is one where the user selects an option from a list. In the case of our video object, we'll have a list of movie ratings and a list of video categories.

Strictly speaking, a list of text fields is probably not analogous to any real-world business entity. At the same time, it is one of the most common concepts that we, as programmers, have to deal with - both from a UI and an object perspective. Most forms have **ComboBox** controls for users to select values, and any underlying business object needs to provide the content for those controls and also screen the supplied values to make sure they're valid. After all, we can't assume that the client code in the UI is going to send us a valid option, since that would break our tenet that the code calling our object will eventually do something that will cause problems in our object.

Like the **Customers** object, the **TextList** object will be read-only. Any calling code will just get the object loaded from the database and then use the object's properties to get at the data. As a collection-style object, our **TextList** will have both text data and a key value for each entry in the list.

Setting up the TextList Class

In our **VideoObject** project, choose the Project-Add Class Module option. As this isn't our basic business object, we'll just use the Class Module option and click Open.

Set the Name property to TextList and the Instancing to 2-PublicNotCreatable. Objects of this class will be created within the context of actual business objects, and so we won't allow the UI developer to create them directly.

Again, our collection object will be based on a normal Visual Basic **Collection** object:

```
Option Explicit

Private colList As Collection
```

In a normal collection, we can do a look-up based on the key value to quickly retrieve an item's value. That is all very useful, but this class will also be used to translate item values back to the original key. The reason for this is because relational databases typically store key values rather than any item's text value. Since the user will be choosing a text value on the screen, at some point we'll need to translate that back to a key value.

To make this easy, we're going to include a second **Collection** object in the class to store the key and item values in reverse - making it possible to use the item's value to quickly do a look-up and retrieve the key value.

```
Option Explicit
Private colList As Collection
Private colKeys As Collection
```

In the **Class_Initialize** we need to create instances of these collections:

```
Private Sub Class_Initialize()
   Set colList = New Collection
   Set colKeys = New Collection
End Sub
```

As with any read-only collection object, we won't have **Add** or **Remove** methods, but we will provide an **Item** method to retrieve the item values based on the keys. In this case, all we need to do is echo the value out of the **colList** collection upon request. The return type is **String** since this object is set up to manage lists of text data:

```
Public Function Item(ByVal Index As Variant) As String
   Item = colList.Item(Index)
End Function
```

Use the Tools-Procedure Attributes... menu option to make the **Item** method the default for this object.

To support the **For...Each** concept, we also need to provide the **NewEnum** method with its Procedure ID set to −4 and the Hide this member option checked:

```
Public Function NewEnum() As IUnknown
   Set NewEnum = colList.[_NewEnum]
End Function
```

Using an Item Value to get a Key

Note that both the **Item** and **NewEnum** methods are based on the **colList** collection. This works great when we use the **TextList** object as a regular collection, but it doesn't give us the ability to do the reverse; that is to easily use a text value to find a key.

So, in addition to the **Item** method, we'll add a corresponding **Key** method. This method works the same as **Item**, but uses the **colKeys** collection instead of **colList**. All we need to do is make sure to load **colKeys** with the item and key values reversed. We'll cover this in more detail shortly:

```
Public Function Key(ByVal Text As String) As String
   Key = colKeys.Item(Text)
End Function
```

Now the user can not only get at an item with this code,

```
strItem = objTextList.Item(strKey)
```

but they can also get at a key value with this code:

```
strKey = objTextList.Key(strItem)
```

The ability to retrieve a key value when provided with a text value is a nice feature. There are many cases where a UI developer has to implement extra code to track not only the items they've listed in a **ListBox** or **ComboBox**, but also the key values corresponding to those items. If we can easily provide support to translate a text value back to its key value, then the UI developer may not have to take these extra steps.

The Load Method

All that remains is to provide a way to get the data from the database into the object. Like our other objects, we'll add a **Load** method to take care of these details. To keep it simple, this **Load** method will just accept a **String** parameter. We can use this parameter to indicate which data should be loaded from the database:

```
Friend Sub Load(ListName As String)
    ' load data from database
    '
    'colList.Add strItem, strKey
    'colKeys.Add strKey, strItem
End Sub
```

Like the other **Load** methods we've looked at, we've commented out the code because it is very much dependent on the persistence model we choose. At the same time, there are a few things that we can take note of here.

First off, this method is declared as **Friend** rather than **Public**. Since we set the Instancing property to PublicNotCreatable, the UI code can't create a **TextList** object directly. By the time they get one of these objects, it should already be populated with data. Our business objects will create **TextList** objects and call their **Load** methods all within the same DLL - so **Friend** is the way to go.

We've also put in comments showing how the two collections will be loaded with data:

```
'colList.Add strItem, strKey
'colKeys.Add strKey, strItem
```

Remember, here, that **colList** is loaded with the item and key values in the proper order, while **colKeys** is loaded with the values in reverse order. This code enables our **Key** method to function properly. Although this technique consumes more memory than a normal collection, because it is storing everything twice, we do get the benefit of being able to quickly retrieve a key value when supplied with an item, as well as just being able to retrieve an item when supplied with a key.

Videos: A Read-only List Object

We need to take one more quick detour before getting into the meat of the **Video** and **Tape** objects. As with customers, the system will need to provide a lookup function for video tapes. To take care of this, we'll implement a **Videos** object along the same lines as the **Customers** object we put together earlier.

Creating the Videos Object

We won't spend much time discussing this object, since it's virtually identical to the **Customers** object. The bulk of the code for objects of this type comes when we implement the database access - so we'll look more closely at it in subsequent chapters.

Add a class module to the **VideoObjects** project, call it **Videos**, and make sure its Instancing property is set to 5-Multiuse so the UI code can create and use the object. Then enter the following code:

```
Option Explicit

Private colDisplay As Collection

Private Sub Class_Initialize()
  Set colDisplay = New Collection
End Sub
```

```
Public Sub Load(Optional Title As String, Optional Studio As String)
  ' load data from database
End Sub
```

```
Public Function Item(ByVal Index As Variant) As VideoDisplay
  ' find or build a VideoDisplay object
  ' then return it as a result
End Function
```

```
Public Function Count() As Long
  Count = colDisplay.Count
End Function
```

```
' NewEnum must return the IUnknown interface of a
' collection's enumerator.
Public Function NewEnum() As IUnknown
  Set NewEnum = colDisplay.[_NewEnum]
End Function
```

As with the **Customers** object, our new **Videos** object is based on a Visual Basic **Collection** object. However, since it is a read-only list we haven't included **Add** or **Remove** methods in our object. The client code can use the **Item** method to retrieve individual elements from our list. In this case, each element will be a new type of object named **VideoDisplay**.

Don't forget to choose the Tools-Procedure Attributes... menu option to make the **Item**
method the default; also, for the **NewEnum** *method, change the Hide this member option
and set the Procedure ID to −4.*

Creating the VideoDisplay Object

In the same way the **Customers** object used a **CustomerDisplay** object to return individual
items, the **Videos** object will use a **VideoDisplay** object. As with **CustomerDisplay**, this object
is a simple read-only object that contains only the fields we'll be retrieving for the UI to display.
Here is the code for the **VideoDisplay** object:

```
Option Explicit

Private Type DisplayProps
  VideoID As Long
  Title As String * 30
  ReleaseDate As Variant
End Type

Private udtProps As DisplayProps
```

```
Public Property Get VideoID() As Long
  VideoID = udtProps.VideoID
End Property
```

```
Public Property Get Title() As String
  Title = Trim$(udtProps.Title)
End Property
```

```
Public Property Get ReleaseDate() As Variant
  ReleaseDate = Trim$(udtProps.ReleaseDate)
End Property
```

```
Friend Property Let VideoID(Value As Long)
  udtProps.VideoID = Value
End Property
```

```
Friend Property Let Title(Value As String)
  udtProps.Title = Value
End Property
```

```
Friend Property Let ReleaseDate(Value As Variant)
  udtProps.ReleaseDate = Value
End Property
```

Video: A Parent Object

We need to have an object to represent each video title. This object will be a bit different from those we've looked at so far. This is the parent object to one or more objects representing the actual tapes of that title. It will also contain a couple of the **TextList** objects that we just defined.

Of course, it will also have regular properties for things like the title of the video and the studio where it was produced.

Setting up the Video Class

In the **VideoObjects** project, add a new class module using the **Business** template we built earlier in this chapter. Change the Name property to Video and make sure the Instancing is set to 5-Multiuse.

Declarations

As usual, we'll set up a UDT to store the object's data, and we'll declare **udtProps** and **udtSave** as variables of that type. In this case, we'll also declare **objCategories** and **objRatings** as type **TextList** to store the lists of valid category and rating codes.

Each **Video** object will also need to have a list of the physical tapes for the title, so we'll declare a variable of type **Tapes** as well. We'll cover the **Tapes** object a bit later, but it's basically a collection object containing all the related **Tape** objects.

Here's what the code for our **Video** object now looks like (remember there's already a lot of code from our **Business** object template):

```
Option Explicit

Event Valid(IsValid As Boolean)
```

```
Private Type VideoProps
  VideoID As Long
  Title As String * 30
  ReleaseDate As Variant
  Studio As String * 30
  Category As String * 20
  Rating As String * 5
End Type

Private udtProps As VideoProps
Private udtSave As VideoProps

Private objCategories As TextList
Private objRatings As TextList
Private objTapes As Tapes
```

```
Private flgNew As Boolean
Private flgDeleted As Boolean
Private flgDirty As Boolean
Private flgEditing As Boolean
Private WithEvents objValid As BrokenRules
```

BeginEdit, CancelEdit and ApplyEdit Methods

As usual, we need to update the **BeginEdit**, **CancelEdit** and **ApplyEdit** methods to manage the object's state:

```
Public Sub BeginEdit()
  If flgEditing Then Err.Raise 445

  ' save object state
  LSet udtSave = udtProps
  objTapes.BeginEdit

  flgEditing = True
End Sub

Public Sub CancelEdit()
  If Not flgEditing Then Err.Raise 445

  flgEditing = False
  flgDeleted = False
  ' restore object state
  LSet udtProps = udtSave
  objTapes.CancelEdit

End Sub

Public Sub ApplyEdit()
  If Not flgEditing Then Err.Raise 445

  If flgDeleted Then
    ' code to delete the object's data goes here
    flgNew = True
    flgDeleted = False
  ElseIf flgDirty Or flgNew Then
    If Not IsValid Then Err.Raise 445
    ' save object state
    ' save object to database if appropriate
    LSet udtSave = udtProps

    flgNew = False
  End If
  objTapes.ApplyEdit udtProps.VideoID

  flgDirty = False
  flgEditing = False
End Sub
```

We don't need to worry about keeping copies of the **objCategories** or **objRatings** objects, as they are essentially static lists of text representing the valid options for those fields.

*The list of tapes contained in a **Tapes** collection object could be a concern. If we have added a tape to that collection, and then we cancel editing on the parent object, **Video**, we need to remove that new tape from the list. Rather than trying to track all that detail here in the **Video** class, we'll let the **Tapes** class manage it. All we need to do in the **Video** code is call the **Tapes** object's **BeginEdit**, **CancelEdit** and **ApplyEdit** methods. Later in the chapter, we'll need to make sure that we implement those methods properly in the **Tapes** class.*

Load Method

Our **Load** method will be implemented based on whatever persistence approach we choose later. However, we do need to add a bit of code now to support the loading of the **Tapes** object:

```
Public Sub Load(VideoID As Long)

    If flgEditing Then Err.Raise 445
    If Not flgNew Then Err.Raise 445

    flgNew = False
    ' code to load the object goes here

    objTapes.Load udtProps.VideoID

End Sub
```

At some point, the list of tapes for this video needs to be loaded from the database. We can let the **Tapes** object's **Load** method do the actual work of loading the data, but that method needs to be called somewhere.

We have two basic options for loading the list of tapes. Firstly, we can load them when the **Video** object itself is loaded, as shown here. This slows down the overall data load process, but gets all the data loaded for use right up front. If we know that the client code is likely to use the collection, it probably makes sense to load it right up front.

Alternatively, we can wait until the first time the UI code tries to access the list of tapes and load the list at that point. This speeds up the loading of the **Video** object itself, but incurs a delay the first time the client code tries to get at a **Tape** object. If the collection data may or may not be used by the client code then we may want to wait to load it. That way, the data won't ever get loaded if the client code doesn't use it - and so we'll get an overall performance gain.

Delete Method

Continuing through the template code, the next method to look at is the **Delete** method. Like the **Load** method, we need to make sure all the related **Tape** objects get deleted if the **Video** object is deleted:

```
Public Sub Delete()
    If Not flgEditing Then Err.Raise 445

    flgDeleted = True

    objTapes.Delete

End Sub
```

Like the previous methods we've looked at, the **Delete** method just calls the **Delete** method on the **Tapes** collection object, and we'll implement it in the **Tapes** class to manage deleting all the associated **Tape** objects.

Class_Initialize Routine

We also need to modify our **Class_Initialize** routine:

```
Private Sub Class_Initialize()
  Set objValid = New BrokenRules
  flgNew = True

  Set objCategories = New TextList
  objCategories.Load "Category"

  Set objRatings = New TextList
  objRatings.Load "Rating"

  Set objTapes = New Tapes

  ' if we know any rules are broken on startup
  ' then add code here to initialize the list
  ' of broken rules
  '
  objValid.RuleBroken "Title", True
End Sub
```

The first change in this routine is to create **TextList** objects for the **objCategories** and **objRatings** variables. Once each of these are created, we call the **TextList** object's **Load** method to load the category and rating lists respectively.

We'll also put some commented lines into this code, which will remind us, when we write our persistence code, to add code to put the first items from the database tables into our respective **udtProps** variables, as default values:

```
Set objCategories = New TextList
objCategories.Load "Category"
' code to assign udtProps.Category with database information

Set objRatings = New TextList
objRatings.Load "Rating"
' code to assign udtProps.Rating with database information
```

Now we need to create an instance of the **Tapes** object for the **objTapes** variable. We don't need to load this object right now, as we'll load it in the **Video** object's **Load** method, as we've already seen:

```
Set objTapes = New Tapes
```

The last change is one we've seen before. In the **Video** object, the **Title** property is a required field - and so we assume that we start out with a broken rule for the **Title** since we know that the field is blank in a new object like this:

```
objValid.RuleBroken "Title", True
```

Video Properties

Most of the properties implemented in the **Video** object use the concepts we looked at with the **Customer** object. The **VideoID** will be a read-only field with a system-generated value, just like **CustomerID**. The **Title** and **Studio** properties are basic text properties, with the **Title** being a required field:

```
Public Property Get VideoID() As Long
  VideoID = udtProps.VideoID
End Property
```

```
Public Property Let Title(Value As String)
  If Not flgEditing Then Err.Raise 383

  If Len(Value) > Len(udtProps.Title) Then _
    Err.Raise vbObjectError + 1001, "String value too long"
  objValid.RuleBroken "Title", (Len(Trim$(Value)) = 0)

  udtProps.Title = Value
  flgDirty = True
End Property
```

```
Public Property Get Title() As String
  Title = Trim$(udtProps.Title)
End Property
```

```
Public Property Let Studio(Value As String)
  If Not flgEditing Then Err.Raise 383

  If Len(Value) > Len(udtProps.Studio) Then _
    Err.Raise vbObjectError + 1001, "String value too long"

  udtProps.Studio = Value
  flgDirty = True
End Property
```

```
Public Property Get Studio() As String
  Studio = udtProps.Studio
End Property
```

ReleaseDate Property: Date Value

The **ReleaseDate** field bears some examination, since it's the first date field we've encountered so far in this chapter. Since Visual Basic provides a **Date** data type, it would seem that implementing a data property would be trivial.

After all, if the **Property Let** just accepts a **Date** parameter and the **Get** returns a **Date** data type, we don't even have to screen the values - since Visual Basic does it for us (*Please don't enter this code*):

```
Public Property Let ReleaseDate(Value As Date)
  If Not flgEditing Then Err.Raise 383

  udtProps.ReleaseDate = Value
  flgDirty = True
End Property

Public Property Get ReleaseDate() As Date
  ReleaseDate = udtProps.ReleaseDate
End Property
```

If there were any business rules, such as requiring the date to be in the past or future, then we'd need to add an extra line or two of code, but, otherwise, one might be tempted to say that there's nothing to it.

Unfortunately, this implementation won't always work. The problem is that **Date** type variables *always* contain some value. As soon as a **Date** variable is created it contains **12/30/1899 12:00:00 AM**.

In many cases, it is important to know whether the date property is blank or whether it's been given a value by the user. The **Date** datatype doesn't provide us with any way to detect this, and so we need an alternative solution.

Instead of using the **Date** data type, we'll use a **Variant**. Then we'll have to add extra code to the **Property Let** to ensure that we really did get passed a valid date. The **ReleaseDate** routine we'll use looks like this:

```
Public Property Let ReleaseDate(Value As Variant)
  If Not flgEditing Then Err.Raise 383

  If Len(Trim(Value)) = 0 Then
    udtProps.ReleaseDate = ""
    objValid.RuleBroken "ReleaseDate", False
  ElseIf IsDate(Value) Then
    udtProps.ReleaseDate = CVDate(Value)
    objValid.RuleBroken "ReleaseDate", False
  Else
    objValid.RuleBroken "ReleaseDate", True
  End If
  flgDirty = True
End Property
```

In this version of the routine, we accept a **Variant** parameter instead of a **Date** data type. This means the calling code can send us virtually any value - so we need to take some extra steps.

Let's look at this code. Since we want to allow entry of a blank, or empty string value, we check for that. We use the **Trim()** command to remove any leading or trailing spaces, and then we check the resulting length. If the length turns up zero then we can just assign an empty string to the **ReleaseDate** variable, and we're all done. We also make sure that the **BrokenRule** object knows that we have a valid value:

```
If Len(Trim(Value)) = 0 Then
  udtProps.ReleaseDate = ""
  objValid.RuleBroken "ReleaseDate", False
```

On the other hand, if the parameter value has a length of greater than zero then we need to find out if it can be translated to a date value. This is easily accomplished by using the **IsDate()** function. **IsDate()** has the benefit of recognizing any date format that Visual Basic can possibly understand, so it provides a great amount of flexibility - with virtually no code:

```
ElseIf IsDate(Value) Then
  udtProps.ReleaseDate = CVDate(Value)
  objValid.RuleBroken "ReleaseDate", False
```

If the parameter value is a valid date then we just need to assign the value to the **ReleaseDate** variable. To make sure that it's stored as a date, we run it through the **CVDate()** function to translate the parameter value to a valid date. **CVDate** returns an error if it can't do the translation, but we don't need to worry about that since we've already used **IsDate()** to make sure it is valid. Once again, we also need to make sure that the **BrokenRule** object knows that we have a valid value.

If both of the previous checks fail then the parameter is neither an empty string nor a valid date. In this case, we'll use the **BrokenRule** object to indicate that a business rule is broken. The business rule that applies here is that we need a valid date and we don't have one:

```
objValid.RuleBroken "ReleaseDate", True
```

Moving on, the **Property Get** for **ReleaseDate** changes very little from our first attempt (which used the **Date** type, as above). We just need to return a **Variant** instead of a **Date** type value, but beyond that there is no change.

Since the **udtProps.ReleaseDate** variable will always contain either an empty string or a valid date value, we can just return whatever it contains without having to perform any conversions to the value:

```
Public Property Get ReleaseDate() As Variant
  ReleaseDate = udtProps.ReleaseDate
End Property
```

TextList-based Properties

Now let's look at some more interesting code. We've already built a general utility class named **TextList** and, within our **Video** object, we have two variables, **objCategories** and **objRatings**, based on that class. We now need to implement some properties to make these variables useful.

There are two main reasons for implementing text list properties with **TextList** objects contained inside a business object:

1   The business object needs to validate any data supplied through a Property Let. To validate data against a list of values, the business object needs to have the list available.

2   The UI will probably want to display the list to the user in a ListBox or ComboBox control. Since the business object already needs to load the list for validation purposes, we don't want to take the performance hit of having the UI load it a second time.

Another possibility is to load the list in the UI and have the UI supply the data to the business object for validation. This keeps performance acceptable, since we don't need to load the list twice; and it does make the list available to the object. This is not a good solution for a couple reasons:

1   The business object becomes dependent on the UI developer. If the UI developer introduces a bug such that the list doesn't load properly, it may be the business object that appears to have a bug rather than the UI.

2   The UI developer is forced to do some extra work and for no benefit. Every part of the UI that uses our business object would need to load the text list data, so there'd be a lot of redundant code and effort.

Category Property

So let's look at the **Category** property and see how this works. We've already loaded the **objCategories TextList** object, back in the **Class_Initialize** routine, so we're all ready to go at this point:

```
Public Property Let Category(Value As String)
  If Not flgEditing Then Err.Raise 383

  udtProps.Category = objCategories.Key(Value)
  flgDirty = True
End Property
```

When the user chooses an option from the **ComboBox** control we'll get the text chosen by the user passed as a parameter to our **Property Let** routine. What we need to store in our UDT variable, **udtProps.Category**, is the key value, not the text value.

To convert from a text value back to a key value we can use the **TextList** object's **Key** method. We implemented this method specifically to accept a text value and to return the corresponding key. If the supplied value isn't found, it will result in an error in the **TextList** object - and we'll just let that error raise right up to the calling code.

The reason we want to store the key value in our internal variable is because that's typically the value we'd find in a database. Most tables containing a list of text values also contain an associated list of key values to be used as foreign keys in other tables.

219

This design makes it easy to change the text values in the table without worrying about losing connections with data in other tables. By structuring our business objects to store these same key values in our object, we make it very easy to load and save the objects from a database. The value we are storing in our object's internal variable is the same as that stored in the database table.

In some more complex scenarios, it's even possible that the content of the list could be different depending on the object's current state. For instance, consider a list of possible surnames on a **Person** *object. If the* **Person** *object's* **Gender** *property is* **Male** *then the list might contain* **Mr**, **Dr**, **Sir** *and so forth; meanwhile, a* **Female Gender** *property might reconfigure the list to contain* **Mrs**, **Ms**, **Dr** *and so on. In this case, the content of the list is dictated by business rules - and that code needs to reside inside the business object.*

The **Property Get** method employs a similar technique:

```
Public Property Get Category() As String
   Category = objCategories.Item(Trim$(udtProps.Category))
End Property
```

Since we stored the key value in our internal variable, we just need to call the **TextList** object's **Item** method to translate the key back into a text value to return to the UI.

Note that we need to use **Trim$()** to remove the trailing spaces from the key value before sending it to the **Item** method. Since the value was stored in a fixed length string, it has trailing spaces - and those would prevent it from matching the key values in the collection.

Interestingly enough, the UI developer in a traditional application would need to know all about the relationship between key values and item values, since they'd be directly reading the tables. The business objects hide the key values entirely, making the UI developer's job much easier - since they just need to load their list control with item values and return the item value chosen by the user, without worrying about translating it to a key value.

The **Property Let** and **Property Get** routines allow the UI developer to give us a value and retrieve the current value. We still need to provide some way for the UI developer to get at the list of valid options. After all, a typical UI will provide the user with this list to make it easy to choose an option that won't generate an error. To do this, we'll implement a **Categories** property that exposes the **objCategories** variable:

```
Public Property Get Categories() As TextList
   Set Categories = objCategories
End Property
```

As we discussed during the implementation of the **TextList** class, the object that the UI developer will get is totally read-only. The UI developer won't even have access to the object's **Load** method, since it's declared as a **Friend** method and is only available within the same Visual Basic project.

The UI developer will be able to retrieve the object's item values, however, by using the property just like a regular Visual Basic **Collection** object. The code might look something like this:

```
For Each vntItem in objVideo.Categories
    cmbComboBox.AddItem vntItem
Next
```

Rating Property

Moving on, we can see that the **Rating Property Let** and **Property Get** are virtually identical to the **Category** property routines:

```
Public Property Let Rating(Value As String)
  If Not flgEditing Then Err.Raise 383

  udtProps.Rating = objRatings.Key(Value)
  flgDirty = True
End Property
```

```
Public Property Get Rating() As String
  Rating = objRatings.Item(Trim$(udtProps.Rating))
End Property
```

Likewise, the **Ratings** property is a carbon copy of the **Categories** routine:

```
Public Property Get Ratings() As TextList
  Set Ratings = objRatings
End Property
```

Tapes Property

The final property that we need to worry about is the **Tapes** property. This one is separated from the others not because it is complex, but because it is very different in concept. This property implements a Parent-Child relationship, making the **Video** object a parent to any number of **Tape** objects:

```
Public Property Get Tapes() As Tapes
  If flgEditing = False Then objTapes.Load Video.ID
  Set Tapes = objTapes
End Property
```

This is a very simple bit of code for such a complex concept. The complexity will come in the **Tapes** object itself, which we'll look at shortly. It is important that this is simple, to help keep the focus of the **Video** object on representing a video. If we'd included a lot of extra code to manage **Tape** objects - adding and removing them from a collection - we would have introduced a lot of code that really had nothing to do with modeling a video - but had everything to do with modeling the relationship.

By pulling the complexity of adding and removing objects from a list out of **Video** and putting it into a specialized **Tapes** object, we have abstracted the relationship management into its own little container.

Summary

In this chapter we've started to code our video rental store example, putting some of the concepts and ideas we've discussed in previous chapters into action. Specifically we've created:

- ❏ A common interface for our code
- ❏ A **Business** template class
- ❏ The start of the video rental system

The **VideoStore** example now has the following defined class:

- ❏ **Customer**
- ❏ **Customers**
- ❏ **CustomerDisplay**
- ❏ **TextList**
- ❏ **Videos**
- ❏ **VideoDisplay**
- ❏ **Video**

This is a good place to take a break. In the next chapter, we'll continue our development of the **VideoStore** set of business objects, but there we need to consider how to handle child objects properly.

6

Implementing Business Objects
Part 2 - Parent and Child Objects

Overview

In the Chapter 5, we started to build up the business objects we needed for our **VideoStore** example. We're about halfway through the initial implementation now - there will be persistence code to add in Chapters 8 and 10. This chapter will be concerned mainly with the more complicated object relationships:

- ❑ Parent-child
- ❑ Hybrid - both child and standalone
- ❑ Polymorphism

We'll implement the following classes:

- ❑ **Tape**
- ❑ **Tapes**
- ❑ **Invoice**
- ❑ **InvoiceItem**
- ❑ **InvoiceFee**
- ❑ **InvoiceTape**
- ❑ **InvoiceItems**

Tape: A Child Object

Before we get into the **Tapes** object, we should really put together the **Tape** object. After all, it's a lot easier to build a collection object when we have something to put into it!

The **Tape** object has some extra complexity when compared to the **Video** or **Customer** objects. Neither **Video** nor **Customer** are child objects, but **Tape** is a child object of **Video**, and so we need to do a fair amount of extra work for **Tape** to work smoothly. We'll get into the details after we get the basic object laid out.

The **Tape** object doesn't have a lot of properties: just a **TapeID**; a flag indicating if it is currently rented out; and the date the tape was acquired. When we rent out a tape to a customer we do it through an invoice. To make it easy to find the invoice on which a tape is rented, we'll also throw in a property to return a reference to the **Invoice** object.

> *Something to keep in mind is that the **Tape** object could also be a parent of other objects. For instance, in Chapter 3 we discussed objects to record problems with tapes. All the **Problem** objects for a tape would be child objects of that particular **Tape** object. To support this, we'd have a **Problems** property and a private **Problems** object to manage the list of child objects.*

The **Tape** object will also have a couple of methods, **CheckOut** and **CheckIn**, to facilitate the rental process. When a tape gets added to an invoice, we'll use the **CheckOut** method to mark it as rented; and then the **CheckIn** method will be used when the tape is returned - so we know it's available for renting again.

Setting up the Tape Class

In the **VideoObjects** project, choose the Project-Add Class Module menu option and use the **Business** class template to add a new class. Change its Name property to Tape.

We'll be creating **Tape** objects from the **Tapes** collection and from the **Invoice** object. Additionally, we'll allow the UI to instantiate a **Tape** object directly - to facilitate the process of returning the tape after it has been rented.

> *When the customer returns the tape, the user simply enters the **TapeID** (typically via a barcode reader) and the tape is recorded as being checked back in.*

To support this, make sure the Instancing property is set to 5-Multiuse.

Updating the Template Code

We'll go through the usual steps of altering the template code to customize it for this object. Rather than walking through the code in detail, I'll just list it here with the alterations highlighted. Then we'll go through the changes we need to make to support the parent-child relationship with the **Video** object.

```
Option Explicit

Event Valid(IsValid As Boolean)

Private Type TapeProps
  TapeID As Long
  VideoID As Long
  Title As String * 30
  CheckedOut As Boolean
  DateAcquired As Variant
  InvoiceID As Long
End Type

Private udtProps As TapeProps
Private udtSave As TapeProps

Private flgDirty As Boolean
Private flgNew As Boolean
Private flgDeleted As Boolean
Private flgEditing As Boolean
Private WithEvents objValid As BrokenRules

Public Sub BeginEdit()
  If flgEditing Then Err.Raise 445

  ' save object state

  LSet udtSave = udtProps

  flgEditing = True
End Sub

Public Sub CancelEdit()
  If Not flgEditing Then Err.Raise 445

  flgEditing = False
  ' restore object state

  LSet udtProps = udtSave

End Sub

Public Sub ApplyEdit()
  If Not flgEditing Then Err.Raise 445

  If flgDeleted Then
    ' code to delete the object's data goes here
    flgNew = True
    flgDeleted = False
  ElseIf flgDirty Or flgNew Then
    If Not IsValid Then Err.Raise 445
    ' save object to database if appropriate
    ' save object state

    LSet udtSave = udtProps

    flgNew = False
  End If
  flgDirty = False
  flgEditing = False
End Sub
Private Sub Class_Initialize()
```

```
      flgNew = True
      Set objValid = New BrokenRules

      ' if we know any rules are broken on startup
      ' then add code here to initialize the list
      ' of broken rules
      '
      ' objValid.RuleBroken "RuleName", True
```
```
   objValid.RuleBroken "DateAcquired", True
```
```
End Sub

Public Property Get IsValid() As Boolean
   IsValid = (objValid.Count = 0)
End Property

Private Sub objValid_BrokenRule()
   RaiseEvent Valid(False)
End Sub

Private Sub objValid_NoBrokenRules()
   RaiseEvent Valid(True)
End Sub
```
```
Public Sub Load(TapeID As Long)
```
```
   If flgEditing Then Err.Raise 445
   If Not flgNew Then Err.Raise 445

   flgNew = False
   ' code to load the object goes here
End Sub

Public Sub Delete()
   If Not flgEditing Then Err.Raise 445

   flgDeleted = True
End Sub

Public Property Get IsDeleted() As Boolean
   IsDeleted = flgDeleted
End Property


Public Property Get IsNew() As Boolean
   IsNew = flgNew
End Property

Public Property Get IsDirty() As Boolean
   IsDirty = flgDirty
End Property
```

We just set up our UDT and the normal **udtProps** and **udtSave** variables. We'll make the **DateAcquired** property a required field - and so the **Class_Initialize** has code to record the field as being invalid using the **BrokenRules** object.

Two of the data elements in the UDT are of particular note. The **VideoID** value is our object's link to its parent. Since **Tape** objects are children of **Video** objects, each child needs to have some mechanism to refer back to its parent.

Even more interesting is the **Title** field. The **Video** object represents a specific video title, with all the related **Tape** objects obviously having the same title as the parent **Video** object. There's a good reason why we've added a **Title** field to our UDT: performance.

There are many cases where an object will need to provide fields that are normally part of another object; in this case, we'll be wanting to display a **Tape** object, including the tape's title. One way to approach this is to instantiate the **Video** object and get the **Title** from that object; and it's a very elegant object-oriented solution. Unfortunately, it also means that to get one simple bit of information we would have to instantiate an entire object, thus incurring the related database and network traffic.

Instead, it is often easier to include data like this as read-only properties of several objects. This way, the data can be loaded and sent over the network all at once, along with the other data belonging to the object. It's much more efficient to do a table join and retrieve the video's title along with the **Tape** object's data than it would be to get the **Tape** object and then turn around and get the entire **Video** object in a separate step.

Child Object Support

The **Tape** object is a bit different from **Video** or **Customer**, since it is a child of the **Video** object. This makes things more complex, since there are some extra behaviors we need to support. Let's look at where this complexity comes from.

A Parent-Child User Interface

Imagine a screen that displays a **Video** object's properties in the top half of the form, and which has a list of the associated **Tape** objects at the bottom. This screen would have OK, Apply and Cancel buttons as we'd expect:

These buttons call the **CancelEdit** and **ApplyEdit** methods of the **Video** object, since that's the object this screen is editing. Calling **ApplyEdit** should cause the **Video** object's data to be saved to the database like normal.

The screen would also have Add, Edit and Delete buttons for the **Tape** objects in the list. If the user clicks Add or Edit then a second screen pops up showing the **Tape** object's data:

This screen would also have OK, Apply and Cancel buttons, each of which would call **CancelEdit** and **ApplyEdit** as we've done so far. But this is where the difference comes in, because the **ApplyEdit** call on the **Tape** object should *not* save the data to the database.

When the user clicks OK or Apply on the tape editing screen, we still don't know that the user won't click Cancel on the Video screen and cancel the entire set of changes. This means that the **Tape** object's **ApplyEdit** method can't work like a normal **ApplyEdit**. Instead, we need to figure out some way for the **Video** object to tell all its children to save their data to the database when its own **ApplyEdit** is called.

The same principal applies to the **CancelEdit** method. When the user clicks Cancel on the Video screen, all the child **Tape** objects need to reset their internal state to the values they held back when the **Video** object's **BeginEdit** was called - even if the user brought up a Tape screen, edited a **Tape** object and clicked the OK button on that screen.

To make things even more complex, the **Tape** object can be brought up directly by the user - since its Instancing is 5-Multiuse. So if the user directly creates the object, it is not part of a **Tapes** collection - and thus is not a child object. We need to implement the **Tape** object such that it knows whether or not it is a child object - so that it can behave properly in either setting.

Indicating if the Tape Object is a Child

Let's update the code for our **Tape** object accordingly. The first thing we'll do is add a module-level variable to indicate whether the object is a child. We can use this flag throughout the class to change the behavior of the methods, depending on the mode of the object:

```
Private flgEditing As Boolean
Private flgChild As Boolean
Private WithEvents objValid As BrokenRules
```

By default, this flag will have the value of **False**, which works well since we don't want the UI developer to have to worry about calling extra properties or methods when using a **Tape** object. Instead, we'll have the parent object call an extra method on the **Tape** object to set the flag's value to **True**. This **SetAsChild** method has a **Friend** scope, so it isn't visible to the UI developer and thus won't be called by accident:

```
Friend Sub SetAsChild()
   flgChild = True
End Sub
```

This will require that we add an extra line of code inside our **Tapes** collection object's **Add** method when it creates a new **Tape** object. We'll actually code this in the next section when we create the **Tapes** object. The code might look something like this:

```
Set objTape = New Tape
objTape.SetAsChild
objTape.Load lngTapeID
```

So, now we have a way for the object to know whether it's actually a child at any time. We're now ready to go through the code and make it act properly - depending on the value of **flgChild**. This is where things get really interesting!

Enhancing BeginEdit, CancelEdit and ApplyEdit

It's important to preserve the same public interface as a normal business object - so that the UI developer doesn't have to worry about an object being a child or not. It shouldn't matter to them what is going on behind the scenes in our object. This means that we need to keep the **BeginEdit**, **CancelEdit** and **ApplyEdit** methods, and make them work basically the same way from the UI developer's viewpoint.

At the same time, we need to build a way for the parent object to tell the child when to save its state (**BeginEdit**), restore its state (**CancelEdit**), or keep any updates (**ApplyEdit**). Basically, we're looking at creating a new set of transaction methods that are only for use by the parent object. This is on top of altering the original three methods so they work properly with the new methods.

> *This stuff can really twist a person's brain. Especially when you consider that we could have* **Problem** *objects as children of a* **Tape** *object. When the user clicks* Cancel *on the* Video *screen, not only do all the* **Tape** *objects need to be reset, but all their respective* **Problem** *objects would need to be reset as well. We'd have to provide for cascading transactional support throughout all the children. Fortunately, the solution I'm presenting here will cover that, hopefully while keeping everyone's sanity.*

Our **Tape** object already has a great deal of code for managing whether it is valid, dirty, new and so forth. Rather than reinventing all of this, we want to tap into it and, with slight alterations, make it work in this new setting. The only new thing we need to keep track of is whether the parent has told us we are editing:

```
Private flgChild As Boolean
Private flgChildEditing As Boolean
```

Along these same lines, we'll be creating a second set of transaction methods to save and restore our object's core data. In the **Tape** object, this means a new variable based on the **TapeProps** UDT:

```
Private udtProps As TapeProps
Private udtSave As TapeProps
Private udtChild As TapeProps
```

BeginEdit and CancelEdit Methods

Before we get into the new methods, let's look at the changes to the existing ones. **BeginEdit** and **CancelEdit** are virtually unchanged from our earlier code; there are just a couple of exceptions:

```
Public Sub BeginEdit()
    If flgChild Then If Not flgChildEditing Then Err.Raise 445

    If flgEditing Then Err.Raise 445

    ' save object state
    LSet udtSave = udtProps
    flgEditing = True
End Sub

Public Sub CancelEdit()
    If flgChild Then If Not flgChildEditing Then Err.Raise 445

    If Not flgEditing Then Err.Raise 445

    flgEditing = False
    flgDeleted = False
    ' restore object state
    LSet udtProps = udtSave
End Sub
```

Both routines have a new line at the top that disables them if the object is a child, and the new **ChildBeginEdit** hasn't been called. What we're doing here is preventing the object from being edited - unless the parent has initiated an editing session as well. We don't want children being edited without the parent's knowledge, since it is the parent that calls the routines to save the data to the database. If the parent is unaware of edits then the save methods won't get called and the data won't be saved.

The nice thing about this approach is that no one can call **BeginEdit** unless the parent has given permission. Since almost everything else in the object's code requires **BeginEdit** to be called, so **flgEditing** is **True**, we essentially make the object read-only until the **ChildBeginEdit** method gets called.

The second change we're going to make will only apply if this object had child objects of its own. As we discussed earlier, we'd need to echo all the **BeginEdit**, **CancelEdit** and **ApplyEdit** calls down to our child collection object. If the **Tape** object itself is a child then those calls should only get echoed when the parent object calls them, not when a screen calls them.

*This is the part that enables cascading transaction support throughout all our children. Suppose we did implement child **Problem** objects with a **Problems** collection to hold them. Then the collection objects, **Tapes** and **Problems**, would both call the **ChildBeginEdit**, **ChildCancelEdit** and **ChildApplyEdit** methods on all their child objects. These methods should only be called by a parent object - never in response to some UI code behind a button.*

*Right now we're implementing the changes so the **Video** object can tell the **Tapes** object to echo the calls to all its child objects. We also need to make sure that each child **Tape** object would also echo the call down to any of its child objects.*

ApplyEdit Method

The **ApplyEdit** method's changes are very similar in concept:

```
Public Sub ApplyEdit()
    If flgChild Then If Not flgChildEditing Then Err.Raise 445
    If Not flgChild And flgNew Then Err.Raise 445

    If Not flgEditing Then Err.Raise 445

    If Not flgChild Then
        If flgDeleted Then
            ' code to delete the object's data goes here
            flgNew = True
            flgDeleted = False
        ElseIf flgDirty Or flgNew Then
            If Not IsValid Then Err.Raise 445
            ' save object to database if appropriate
            ' save object state
            LSet udtSave = udtProps
            flgNew = False
        End If
        flgDirty = False
    End If

    flgEditing = False
End Sub
```

Again, we have the line at the top of the routine to prevent it from being called unless the **ChildBeginEdit** method has been called and set the **flgChildEditing** flag to **True**.

The second new line addresses a more complex concern. We don't want to let the UI code add **Tape** objects without going through a **Video** object. Without going through the **Video** object, the UI could add **Tape** objects with no valid parent, thus creating orphan objects. This means that we need to add a check to disable the routine in the case where the UI has created a new **Tape** object that isn't a child - and then tries to save that object.

Almost all the code in a normal **ApplyEdit** method is geared around deleting an object from the database, or updating the object's data in the database. Since we want all of this activity to happen in the **ChildApplyEdit** method, we need to prevent it from happening here. Basically, this means we've put an **If...Then** check around everything except the code to store the object's state data into **udtSave,** and the code to reset the **flgEditing** flag.

Delete Method

Along with the other transactional methods, the **Delete** method needs some slight alteration:

```
Public Sub Delete()
   If flgChild Then If Not flgChildEditing Then Err.Raise 445

   If Not flgEditing Then Err.Raise 445

   flgDeleted = True
End Sub
```

Since the **Delete** method just sets a flag and lets **ApplyEdit**, or in this case **ChildApplyEdit**, actually do the delete operation, we don't need to change much. Like the other methods, we need to make sure that the method can't be called until **ChildBeginEdit** has 'unlocked' the object.

Load Method

Before moving on to the new methods, we'll visit the **Load** method for a moment. If an object is a child of another object, we can't let the UI code load just anything into that child object. In fact, the data loaded into the child object should be under the control of the parent object. What we really want, is to disable the **Load** method if the object is a child. We'll go through a new **ChildLoad** method for use by the parent in a bit. Right now, let's disable the **Load** method:

```
Public Sub Load(TapeID As Long)
   If flgChild Then Err.Raise 445

   If flgEditing Then Err.Raise 445
   If Not flgNew Then Err.Raise 445

   flgNew = False
   ' code to load the object goes here
End Sub
```

Now let's look at the new methods. All of these methods will have **Friend** scope, so they won't be available to any client code; but they will be usable by the object's parent.

ChildBeginEdit Method

The first is **ChildBeginEdit**, which is called by the parent when an editing session is started:

```
Friend Sub ChildBeginEdit()
   If flgChildEditing Then Err.Raise 445

   ' save object state
   LSet udtChild = udtProps
   flgChildEditing = True
End Sub
```

*What will really happen is that the **Video** object's **BeginEdit** will call **BeginEdit** on the **Tapes** object that we'll implement shortly. The **Tapes** object's **BeginEdit** will then go through all the **Tape** objects in its collection and call **ChildBeginEdit**.*

Notice how similar this new method is to the original **BeginEdit**. The only differences are that it uses the new **flgChildEditing** variable instead of **flgEditing** to avoid confusion with the original **BeginEdit** method, and it stores the object's data in **udtChild** instead of **udtSave**.

ChildCancelEdit Method

Likewise, **ChildCancelEdit** is very similar to the original **CancelEdit** method:

```
Friend Sub ChildCancelEdit()
  If Not flgChildEditing Then Err.Raise 445

  flgChildEditing = False
  flgDeleted = False
  ' restore object state
  LSet udtProps = udtChild
End Sub
```

Again, the only significant differences are that the **flgChildEditing** variable is used instead of **flgEditing**, and the object's data is restored from **udtChild** instead of **udtSave**.

Our object's **BeginEdit**, **ApplyEdit** and **CancelEdit** store a copy of the object's data in **udtSave** as they've always done. By storing a copy of the object's data in **udtChild**, in addition to **udtSave**, we have allowed the user to bring up the **Tape** object and edit it multiple times, getting the normal Cancel and Apply effects they'd expect through the **udtSave** copy.

If the user clicks Cancel on the **Video** object's screen, we're able to ignore all the intervening edits and get back to the **udtChild** copy we made in **ChildBeginEdit**.

> Basically, we've implemented **udtChild** for the express purpose of being able to roll back our child object's state to what it was when the user started editing the *parent* object. This way the user can cancel the edits on the parent object and we can make sure all the edits on any child objects are rolled back as well.

ChildApplyEdit Method

The **ChildApplyEdit** method is also closely based on the original **ApplyEdit** method, so it should look pretty familiar:

```
Friend Sub ChildApplyEdit(VideoID As Long)
  If Not flgChildEditing Then Err.Raise 445
  If Not IsValid Then Err.Raise 445

  If flgDeleted Then
    ' code to delete the object's data goes here
    flgNew = True
    flgDeleted = False
  ElseIf flgDirty Or flgNew Then
    udtProps.VideoID = VideoID
    ' save object to database if appropriate
    ' save object state
```

```
        LSet udtChild = udtProps
        flgNew = False
    End If
    flgDirty = False
    flgChildEditing = False
End Sub
```

Like the other new methods, this method uses **flgChildEditing** instead of **flgEditing** and stores the object's state data in **udtChild** instead of **udtSave**.

One significant difference is the **VideoID** parameter that this routine expects. Since each **Tape** object is a child of a **Video** object, the **Tape** object needs to have some mechanism to know the identity of the parent **Video** object.

The **Video** object's ID number will be assigned as the object is being saved to the database, so the ID number won't be available until after the object has been saved. At this point the **Video** object itself has its ID number, but we still need to provide it to the child **Tape** objects.

The easiest solution is to have the **Video** object pass the ID number as a parameter to the **ApplyEdit** method of the **Tapes** object. That method can then pass the ID number as a parameter to the **ChildApplyEdit** methods of each child **Tape** object.

We've also inserted a comment in this routine to remind us that we need to retrieve the **Video** object's **Title** field during the save process - so that the **Tape** object's **Title** field has a value.

The rest of the code is identical to a normal **ApplyEdit** method, in that the value of the **flgDeleted** flag is queried and, if it's **True**, the data is deleted. Otherwise, the **flgDirty** flag is queried and, if it turns out to be **True**, then the data is saved in the database.

ChildLoad Method

When the **Tape** object is a child rather than a standalone object, the only place that any data is loaded from or saved to the database is in the **ChildLoad** and **ChildApplyEdit** methods. The **Load** is entirely disabled, and the **ApplyEdit** method is relegated to setting some flags and storing an intermediate state value.

Let's take a look at the **ChildLoad** method:

```
Friend Sub ChildLoad(TapeID As Long)
    If flgChildEditing Then Err.Raise 445
    If Not flgNew Then Err.Raise 445

    flgNew = False
    ' code to load the object goes here
End Sub
```

As with the other child methods, this one relies on **flgChildEditing** as a master flag to indicate whether it is a valid method. Beyond that, this routine is identical to a regular **Load** method, which is important, since the **Load** method itself will be disabled if this **Tape** object is a child of a **Video** object (and yet the code to load data from the database is identical either way).

In the final analysis, by adding a couple **Boolean** variables, slightly modifying some existing routines, and adding four new methods, we've altered the **Tape** object so that it can behave as a standalone object or a child object equally well.

> *If our application were to have several child objects, it would be wise to create a*
> ***BusinessChild*** *class template, along the lines of the* ***Business*** *class template we created*
> *earlier in this chapter, to save all the typing involved in doing these changes.*

Tape Properties

Now that the basic operation of the object has been coded, we can move on to the object's properties.

Basic Properties

Like the other ID properties so far, the **TapeID** value will be generated by the database, so it's a simple read-only property in our object:

```
Public Property Get TapeID() As Long
   TapeID = udtProps.TapeID
End Property
```

In our UDT, we have a slot for the title of the tape. As we've discussed, this field is actually part of the **Video** object, but it's more efficient to have a read-only copy here. This way, the UI can display the tape's title without having to go to the expense of instantiating an entire **Video** object.

Now let's look at our **Title** code:

```
Public Property Get Title() As String
   If flgNew Then Err.Raise 483

   Title = Trim$(udtProps.Title)
End Property
```

It's important to note that we load the **Title** data into our object when the object's data is retrieved from the database. Because of this, the **Tape** object's **Title** field needs to be disabled while the object is new.

> *Alternatively, we could have implemented code to update all the* ***Tape*** *objects whenever the*
> ***Video*** *object's* ***Title*** *field changed; but this could have serious performance ramifications of*
> *its own - as you can probably imagine!*

We'll also implement a **Boolean** property called **CheckedOut** to indicate if the tape is currently checked out on an invoice:

```
Public Property Get CheckedOut() As Boolean
   CheckedOut = udtProps.CheckedOut
End Property
```

Later on, we'll go through a couple of methods that maintain the `udtProps.CheckedOut` variable's value. Since this value will be controlled through these methods, we don't want the calling code to be able to directly alter it - and so this needs to be a read-only property.

> *Object purists may argue that* all *properties should be read-only and that only methods should alter property values. While there is something to be said for this approach, from a strict OO viewpoint, it doesn't fit with the historical philosophy of Visual Basic. Visual Basic programmers are used to being able to set properties on forms, controls and other built-in Visual Basic objects. One of our goals with business objects is to make it easy for a Visual Basic UI developer to get up to speed using our objects, and so it makes a lot of sense for Visual Basic business objects to follow in Visual Basic's footsteps and provide read-write properties when appropriate.*

DateAcquired Property: Write Once, Read Many

The `DateAcquired` property is a bit more interesting. Since it's a date property, it will have extra code along the lines of the `ReleaseDate` property in the `Video` object. Also, as we've seen, this will be a required field in the object - so there'll be code to support that as well.

To add another twist to this property, we're going to make it a **WORM** (write once, read many) property. This means that the property can only be set when the object is new, and it becomes a read-only property once the object is saved to the database. While this can be a fairly restrictive business rule, it's nevertheless quite common. In this case, we're assuming that the tape's acquired date will be set when the tape's purchase is recorded into the system - and it shouldn't be changed after that point. Another example of a WORM property might be a digital signature, or personal ID code that's set on an object when it is created. Here's our code for `DateAcquired`:

```
Public Property Let DateAcquired(Value As Variant)
   If Not flgEditing Then Err.Raise 383
   If Not flgNew Then Err.Raise 383

   If Len(Trim(Value)) = 0 Then
     udtProps.DateAcquired = ""
     objValid.RuleBroken "DateAcquired", True
   ElseIf IsDate(Value) Then
     udtProps.DateAcquired = CVDate(Value)
     objValid.RuleBroken "DateAcquired", False
   Else
     objValid.RuleBroken "DateAcquired", True
   End If
   flgDirty = True
End Property
```

In order to implement the WORM concept, we must only allow the `Property Let` code to run if the object is new. Fortunately, our template code already maintains the `flgNew` variable, which indicates whether the object is new or not. All we need to do is add a line at the top of the routine to disable it if `flgNew` is `False`:

```
If Not flgNew Then Err.Raise 383
```

Like the **ReleaseDate** property in the **Video** class, this routine accepts a **Variant** parameter, and checks to make sure that it's either an empty string or a valid date. In this case, however, an empty string breaks the business rule that this field is required, so we need to record that:

```
objValid.RuleBroken "DateAcquired", True
```

Likewise, if the parameter is a valid date then we'll record that the requirement was met, so the object's **IsValid** property returns **True**:

```
objValid.RuleBroken "DateAcquired", False
```

The **Property Get** is quite simple, just like the routine from **ReleaseDate** in the **Video** class:

```
Public Property Get DateAcquired() As Variant
  DateAcquired = udtProps.DateAcquired
End Property
```

Invoice Property: Load on Demand

We'll also implement a read-only **Invoice** property to return a reference to the **Invoice** object - in case this **Tape** object is marked as **CheckedOut**. In the **TapeProps** UDT, at the top of the class, we included an **InvoiceID** variable to store the ID number of the **Invoice** object that represents the transaction that rented out this tape.

This property is a good place to apply a new concept called **load on demand**. Loading an entire object, such as an **Invoice** object, can be very expensive in terms of performance. It would be a shame to take all the time to load the **Invoice** object - unless the calling code actually used the **Invoice** property. Instead, we'll only create an instance of the object when the client code calls the **Property Get Invoice** routine:

```
Public Property Get Invoice() As Invoice
  Dim objInvoice As Invoice

  If Not udtProps.CheckedOut Then Err.Raise 383

  Set objInvoice = New Invoice
  objInvoice.Load udtProps.InvoiceID
  Set Invoice = objInvoice
End Property
```

The first thing that this routine does is declare a placeholder variable for the **Invoice** object we'll be creating:

```
Dim objInvoice As Invoice
```

Then we need to check to see if the current tape is actually rented out. If the **CheckedOut** value is **False** then the tape isn't rented out and so it can't be associated with an invoice. Conversely, if **CheckedOut** is **True** then there must be an invoice associated with the tape, since it can only be checked out through an invoice. We'll implement the **Invoice** object later in the chapter.

```
If Not udtProps.CheckedOut Then Err.Raise 383
```

If the tape is not checked out then we just disable the property by raising an error to the calling code.

All that remains is to create an instance of the **Invoice** class and call its **Load** method with our **InvoiceID** value. As we'll see later, with the implementation of the **Invoice** class, its **Load** method will accept an ID value as a parameter.

```
Set objInvoice = New Invoice
objInvoice.Load udtProps.InvoiceID
```

The final line of the routine assigns the newly loaded **Invoice** object to be the return value of the property:

```
Set Invoice = objInvoice
```

An alternative approach to this routine would be to make **objInvoice** a module-level variable and change the routine to load the object once - and then retain a reference to it from that point forward (*don't enter this code*):

```
Public Property Get Invoice() As Invoice
  Static flgLoaded As Boolean

  If Not udtProps.CheckedOut Then Err.Raise 383

  If Not flgLoaded Then
    Set objInvoice = New Invoice
    objInvoice.Load udtProps.InvoiceID
    flgLoaded = True
  End If
  Set Invoice = objInvoice
End Property
```

This has the advantage of loading the **Invoice** object less often if it's heavily used by the client code. The drawback to it is that the **Invoice** object will remain in memory until the **Tape** object is terminated; if the **Invoice** object is only used a couple times by the calling code, this could be a waste of memory. Either approach works fine - just choose the one that fits the way the property will be used by the client code.

Tape Methods

The **Tape** object will need a couple of methods to interact with the **Invoice** object. As a tape is added to an **Invoice**, the **CheckOut** method will be called to mark the **Tape** object as being checked out. Likewise, when the tape is returned, the **CheckIn** method needs to be called to record that the tape has been checked back in.

CheckOut Method

The only way to check out a tape is to add it to an invoice. Because of this, the UI developer shouldn't be able to call the **CheckOut** method directly, but should instead have to go through the **Invoice** object. This means the routine will be declared with the **Friend** keyword - so that it can only be called by our other business objects.

The routine will accept the ID value of the invoice to which it's being added as a parameter. We'll store this value in our **udtProps** for use in implementing the **Property Get Invoice** we looked at earlier:

```
Friend Sub CheckOut(InvoiceID As Long)
   If Not flgEditing Then Err.Raise 445

   With udtProps
      .CheckedOut = True
      .InvoiceID = InvoiceID
   End With
   flgDirty = True
End Sub
```

The first thing that this routine does is to make sure that the object is being edited. Basically, this means that the method can't be called unless the **BeginEdit** method has been called first. The **CancelEdit** and **ApplyEdit** methods will roll back or commit this method's activities - just as they would with a change to a property value.

> *This is not necessarily a requirement for all methods, but this method will be changing property values in our object, so the ability to support canceling or applying the method is useful to have. Consider the case where the user adds a list of tapes to an invoice, resulting in each tape's* **CheckOut** *method being called as it's added. Then suppose the user clicks the* Cancel *button on the screen, canceling the invoice. All of the* **Tape** *objects need to reset their values now, too, since they are no longer on an invoice. If this can be done by simply calling* **CancelEdit** *on each* **Tape** *object, the process is very easy to implement.*

The rest of the code is not complex. Since we're checking out this tape, we'll just set the **udtProps.CheckedOut** variable to **True**:

```
.CheckedOut = True
```

The parameter to this routine was the **InvoiceID** of the invoice to which the tape is being added. We'll record this value in the UDT as well, so we can use it in the **Invoice** property routine we looked at earlier:

```
.InvoiceID = InvoiceID
```

CheckIn Method

The **CheckIn** method is the reverse of **CheckOut**. When a tape is returned to the store, the system shouldn't require the user to bring up the invoice in order to check in the tape. That would be awkward, so the system needs to allow the UI to directly call the **CheckIn** method on a tape. The UI code would then look something like this:

```
' get the TapeID from a barcode reader
Set objTape = New Tape
With objTape
   .Load lngTapeID
   .BeginEdit
   .CheckIn
```

```
      .ApplyEdit
   End with
   Set objTape = Nothing
```

For this to work, the **CheckIn** method needs to be **Public** in scope rather than the **Friend** scope of **CheckOut**. Beyond that, it just needs to reset the **CheckedOut** and **Invoice** properties to indicate that the tape is checked in:

```
Public Sub CheckIn()
   If Not flgEditing Then Err.Raise 445

   With udtProps
      .CheckedOut = False
      .InvoiceID = 0
   End With
   flgDirty = True
End Sub
```

To be consistent with the behavior of **CheckOut**, this method does require that **BeginEdit** be called first. For all we know, the UI developer might want to build an entire list of tapes to check in, calling the **CheckIn** method on each one. If the UI includes a Cancel button, it might be important to be able to use **CancelEdit** to safely undo all those calls to **CheckIn**.

Tapes: A Parent-Child Relationship Object

In the **Video** object, we implemented a **Tapes** property to contain all the specific **Tape** objects that are children of a specific **Video** object. The **Tapes** property simply exposed a **Tapes** object to the calling code. Now we need to implement the **Tapes** class to support the requirements of the **Video** object's property.

In many cases, collection objects don't represent any real-world entity as much as they represent a real-world relationship between entities. For instance, it is difficult to envision a real-world entity for a **Tapes** object to model. The **Tapes** object will model the parent-child relationship between a video title and all the physical tapes of that title in the store.

When we implemented the **Tape** object itself, we added a bit of extra code so it can act as a standalone object as well as a child object. When we're using **Tape** objects within this new **Tapes** collection object, they'll be child objects - so we'll need to make use of the **SetAsChild**, **ChildLoad**, **ChildBeginEdit**, **ChildCancelEdit** and **ChildApplyEdit** methods.

We already largely defined the **Tapes** object when we implemented the **Video** object earlier. The object's public properties and methods need to make it appear as a collection of **Tape** objects, but we also know there are some methods that will be implemented with **Friend** scope for use by the **Video** object itself.

Setting up the Tapes Class

Add a standard class module to the **VideoObjects** project. Set its Name property to Tapes and its Instancing property to 2-PublicNotCreatable. This object will only be created as a part of the **Video** object, so it shouldn't be creatable by outside code; however, it will be exposed via the **Video** object's **Tapes** property, so it needs to be publicly available.

As with any other collection object, we'll need an actual **Collection** object to build our code around:

```
Option Explicit

Private colTapes As Collection
```

And, of course, the **Class_Initialize** needs to create an instance of a **Collection** object for this variable:

```
Private Sub Class_Initialize()
    Set colTapes = New Collection
End Sub
```

Since this is a collection type object, we'll have the standard **Item**, **Count** and **NewEnum** methods. Don't forget to use Tools-Procedure Attributes... to make the **Item** method the default and the **NewEnum** method have a Procedure ID of −4 and Hide this member attribute.

```
Public Function Item(ByVal Index As Variant) As Tape
    Set Item = colTapes(Index)
End Function
```

```
Public Function Count() As Long
    Count = colTapes.Count
End Function
```

```
Public Function NewEnum() As IUnknown
    Set NewEnum = colTapes.[_NewEnum]
End Function
```

As a collection of **Tape** objects, it's no surprise that the **Item** method returns a **Tape** object when called:

```
Public Function Item(ByVal Index As Variant) As Tape
```

The rest of the code in this object will be a bit different from what we've seen in past collection objects, such as **Customers**. As the owner of a group of child **Tape** objects, the **Tapes** object needs to contain code to manage starting, canceling and applying edits, as well as adding and deleting **Tape** objects.

Edit Methods

When we implemented the **Video** object, we added code in its **BeginEdit**, **CancelEdit** and **ApplyEdit** to call routines of the same names in the **Tapes** object. Now we need to implement those methods so they act as expected.

Since our object will have its own set of these methods, we'll need a module-level variable to make them interact properly, just like all the other objects with these methods:

```
Option Explicit

Private colTapes As Collection

Private flgEditing As Boolean
```

BeginEdit Method

When the **Video** object calls the **BeginEdit** method on the **Tapes** object, it isn't really indicating that the collection should become editable; what it's actually indicating is that all the child **Tape** objects should become editable. When we implemented the **Tape** class, we added a **ChildBeginEdit** method for this very purpose. So here's the **BeginEdit** routine for our **Tapes** object:

```
Public Sub BeginEdit()
  Dim objTape As Tape

  If flgEditing Then Err.Raise 445

  For Each objTape In colTapes
    objTape.ChildBeginEdit
  Next
  flgEditing = True
End Sub
```

This routine is a bit different from any other **BeginEdit** methods we've seen so far. The first couple of lines are pretty simple, just declaring a local variable of type **Tape** and disabling the routine if the editing flag is already set to **True**:

```
Dim objTape As Tape

If flgEditing Then Err.Raise 445
```

The next thing we do is use a **For...Each** to loop through all the items in the **colTapes** collection:

```
For Each objTape In colTapes
    objTape.ChildBeginEdit
Next
```

For each of the **Tape** objects in the collection, we just call **ChildBeginEdit**. This means that when the **Tapes** object's **BeginEdit** method is called by the parent **Video** object, this routine just turns around and calls **ChildBeginEdit** for every child **Tape** object in the collection. Essentially, we've just echoed the **Video** object's **BeginEdit** call down to every child **Tapes** object.

The final line just sets the **flgEditing** flag to **True** so that the **Tapes** object knows it is being edited:

```
flgEditing = True
```

CancelEdit Method

The **CancelEdit** method is quite similar in concept, but it does have an extra twist:

```
Public Sub CancelEdit()
  Dim objTape As Tape
  Dim lngIndex As Long

  If Not flgEditing Then Err.Raise 445

  flgEditing = False
  For lngIndex = colTapes.Count To 1 Step -1
    Set objTape = colTapes.Item(lngIndex)
    With objTape
      If .IsNew Then _
        colTapes.Remove lngIndex
      .ChildCancelEdit
    End With
  Next lngIndex
End Sub
```

Here, again, we just declare a couple of local variables and disable the routine unless the **BeginEdit** method has been called and set **flgEditing** to **True**. Of course, we then set **flgEditing** to **False**, since we're canceling the edit process:

```
Dim objTape As Tape
Dim lngIndex As Long

If Not flgEditing Then Err.Raise 445

flgEditing = False
```

Then the real fun begins. Like the **BeginEdit** method, this routine loops through all the items in the **colTapes** collection, calling each object's **ChildCancelEdit** method. However, this loop looks quite a bit different:

```
For lngIndex = colTapes.Count To 1 Step -1
  Set objTape = colTapes.Item(lngIndex)
  With objTape
    If .IsNew Then _
      colTapes.Remove lngIndex
    .ChildCancelEdit
  End With
Next lngIndex
```

If the user has added any new **Tape** objects to the collection during this editing session, we need to make sure that they're removed if the edit is canceled. After all, canceling the edit should effectively reset all the child **Tape** objects, and the collection itself, back to where they were when the **BeginEdit** method was called. If new **Tape** objects have been added since the call to **BeginEdit**, they need to be removed to get us back to where we were.

This removal is not complex, since each **Tape** object knows if it is new or not, and we can find out by using the object's **IsNew** property. If a **Tape** object is new, we can simply remove it from the collection:

```
If .IsNew Then _
  colTapes.Remove lngIndex
```

Unfortunately, the **Remove** method on a collection requires the index value of the item to be removed. Using **For...Each** to go through a collection, there is no way to find out the index for the current item, and so we'd have no way to call **Remove**. Instead, we have to loop through the collection using a numeric index variable, **lngIndex**.

It's also important to note that all the index values of items in a collection move up by one when an item is removed with the **Remove** method. If we start at index **1** and end up removing it, all the subsequent item index values will be off by one, and we'll have a bug. Instead, we need to start with the bottom item and move back to the top:

```
For lngIndex = colTapes.Count To 1 Step -1
```

The other bit of complexity is that all objects in a collection are effectively late-bound. To get the performance and debugging benefits of early-binding, we need to **Set** each item into our **objTape** variable so that we can use it as an early-bound **Tape** object:

```
Set objTape = colTapes.Item(lngIndex)
```

In the end, our **CancelEdit** routine loops through all the child **Tape** objects and calls **ChildCancelEdit** on each one - so they each reset to the values they held when the **ChildBeginEdit** methods were called. It also removes any new **Tape** objects from the collection, thereby returning the collection itself back to the state it was in when the **BeginEdit** method was called.

ApplyEdit Method

ApplyEdit works the same as **CancelEdit**, though instead of removing new **Tape** objects from the collection, it removes any **Tape** objects that are marked as deleted:

```
Public Sub ApplyEdit(VideoID As Long)
  Dim objTape As Tape
  Dim lngIndex As Long
If Not flgEditing Then Err.Raise 445

  For lngIndex = colTapes.Count To 1 Step -1
    Set objTape = colTapes.Item(lngIndex)
    With objTape
      If .IsDeleted Then _
        colTapes.Remove lngIndex
      .ChildApplyEdit VideoID
    End With
  Next lngIndex
  flgEditing = False
End Sub
```

The routine loops through the items in the collection from bottom to top:

```
For lngIndex = colTapes.Count To 1 Step -1
  Set objTape = colTapes.Item(lngIndex)
  With objTape
```

Since we're committing to the changes at this point, we no longer need any deleted objects. In fact, we want to remove them from our collection since, at the end of **ApplyEdit**, our collection should reflect the contents of the database, and any deleted objects have been removed from the database by the **ChildApplyEdit** code:

```
If .IsDeleted Then _
  colTapes.Remove lngIndex
```

For each child object we also call the **ChildApplyEdit** method. This will cause each **Tape** object to delete or save itself in the database, as appropriate.

```
.ChildApplyEdit VideoID
```

When we implemented the **Tape** object's **ChildApplyEdit** method earlier, we built it to expect the **VideoID** value to be passed. This **ApplyEdit** method accepts that value from the **Video** object and relays it to each **ChildApplyEdit** call.

The end result of the **ApplyEdit** method is that all the child **Tape** object's **ChildApplyEdit** methods have been called, so each one of them has been updated in the database as appropriate. Additionally, any **Tape** objects that were deleted from the database have also been removed from our **Tapes** collection.

Delete Method

The **Video** object's **Delete** method calls a **Delete** method on the **Tapes** object. Of course, the **Video** object's **Delete** method marks the **Video** object itself for deletion, and so we'd expect that all the parent object's children would also get marked for deletion. If the parent is deleted and the children are not, we'd have orphan child objects - and that could be a big problem.

```
Public Sub Delete()
  Dim objTape As Tape

  If Not flgEditing Then Err.Raise 445
  ' code to delete the object's data goes here
  For Each objTape In colTapes
    With objTape
      .BeginEdit
      .Delete
      .ApplyEdit
    End With
  Next
End Sub
```

Like the **BeginEdit** method, our **Delete** method uses a **For...Each** to loop through all the child **Tape** objects and call each of their individual **Delete** methods. Of course, the **Delete** method can't be called without calling **BeginEdit** first, and the deletion won't stick unless the **ApplyEdit** method is called as well.

As with the **Tape** object, the **Delete** method just sets **flgDeleted** to **True**, so the **Tapes** object isn't really deleted at this point, just flagged for deletion. Nothing, including the **Video** object itself, is actually deleted until the **Video** object's **ApplyEdit** method is called. Then, the **Tape** object's **ChildApplyEdit** method will be called and the **Tape** actually deleted.

Adding Tape Objects to the Collection

We need to provide a mechanism for the UI code to add new, blank **Tape** objects to our collection. This capability will be required when the video store purchases a new tape for a video title and needs to add it to the list of tapes to be rented.

Typical collection objects have an **Add** method, and our **Tapes** object will be no exception:

```
Public Function Add() As Tape
  Dim objTape As Tape

  Set objTape = New Tape
  objTape.SetAsChild
  If flgEditing Then objTape.ChildBeginEdit
  colTapes.Add Item:=objTape
  Set Add = objTape
End Function
```

The method will return a new **Tape** object to the calling code, as well as adding the object to the collection:

```
Public Function Add() As Tape
```

Inside the routine, we declare a **Tape** variable and instantiate a new **Tape** object into that variable:

```
Dim objTape As Tape

Set objTape = New Tape
```

Any **Tape** objects added into our collection are obviously child objects of the parent **Video** object, and so we'll call the **SetAsChild** method on the new object:

```
objTape.SetAsChild
```

If our **flgEditing** flag is **True**, it means that we've called the **ChildBeginEdit** methods of all the **Tape** objects in our collection. Since we're adding this new object to the collection, we need to make sure that its **ChildBeginEdit** method is called as well:

```
If flgEditing Then objTape.ChildBeginEdit
```

And, of course, we need to actually add the new object to the collection:

```
colTapes.Add Item:=objTape
```

Finally, we need to set the **Add** method's return value to the new object, so that the calling code can get a direct reference, if so desired:

```
Set Add = objTape
```

Removing Tape Objects

The **Remove** method on our **Tapes** object is conspicuously absent. This is because our object's collection needs to match the list of **Tape** data in the database. The only way to remove a **Tape** object from the collection is to remove it from the database.

To remove a **Tape** object from the database, we need to call its **Delete** method and then call **ChildApplyEdit** to commit the deletion. All of this is handled by allowing the UI code to directly call each **Tape** object's **Delete** method to flag the object for deletion. If the UI code then calls the **ApplyEdit** method on the **Video** object, all the **Tape** objects flagged for deletion will be removed from both the database and the collection.

Loading the Tape Objects

The only remaining issue is how to get all of the child **Tape** objects loaded with data and put into our collection. The **Video** object's **Load** method calls the **Tapes** object's **Load** method, passing it the **VideoID** of the parent object.

Using that ID value, we should be able to write database code to retrieve data for all the **Tape** objects that belong to that **VideoID**. Then, all that remains is to loop through all the retrieved database records, creating a **Tape** object for each one that we can add to our collection.

Like all the other data-related code in this chapter, the actual implementation will vary greatly depending on the physical architecture we choose. We'll go through various approaches to loading this data in chapters 8 and 10. For now, we'll just add some comments to remind us how to loop through the data:

```
Friend Sub Load(VideoID As Long)
   If flgEditing Then Err.Raise 445
```

```
   ' here we'll put looping code to load
   ' each of the Tape objects for the VideoID

   ' For Each TapeID
   '   Set objTape = New Tape
   '   With objTape
   '     .SetAsChild
   '     .ChildLoad TapeID
   '   End With
   '   colTapes.Add Item:=objTape
   ' Loop
End Sub
```

Notice that all we need to retrieve from the database up front is a list of **TapeID** values that correspond to the tapes we need. Then we just loop through the list, creating a new **Tape** object and calling its **ChildLoad** method with each **TapeID** value. Of course, we also call each object's **SetAsChild** method to make sure it knows it is a child object, as we discussed when we implemented the **Tape** class.

> *It's important to note that this approach will work quite well in a single-tier and many two-tier physical architectures, but it will have dismal performance in some two-tier and all three-tier implementations. When we get to a three-tier implementation, we'll see how we can rewrite this **Load** method so that it's very efficient in that setting.*

Video Rental: Invoice Objects

Now we've established our building blocks. We have objects to represent the store's customers, and we have objects to represent the tapes that the store rents out.

So far, our objects have been largely independent of each other. The only relationship that we've looked at in any depth has been the parent-child relationship between the **Video** and **Tape** objects. But the objects that support invoicing will tie the customer objects together with the video tape objects, and so we'll get an opportunity to explore some more complex relationships.

By thinking about how an invoice is put together, a couple of objects readily come to mind. Of course, there's an object representing the invoice itself, but an invoice is really composed of a series of line items - in this case, one for each tape being rented. To represent these line items, we'll have an **InvoiceItem** object that is a child of the **Invoice** object itself:

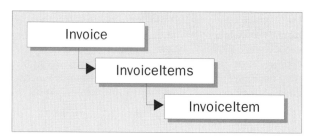

This is a good opportunity to explore **polymorphic** objects and the use of **multiple interfaces** with the **Implements** keyword. To this end, we'll have two types of invoice line items: one for rental of a tape, and one for late fees. Both will be **InvoiceItem** objects, so they'll implement that interface, but they are each unique and different objects - and so we'll create a separate class for each one.

Late Fees: Object Interaction

Before we get too far into the invoicing itself, we should take a short detour to discuss some issues regarding interaction between objects. Late fees provide a good forum for this discussion, since they are the result of some objects interacting with each other.

When someone rents a video tape, there's a specific date by which they need to return the tape, otherwise they're charged a late fee. Typically, rental stores put this late fee on an invoice the next time the customer goes in to rent a tape.

This scenario suggests that each customer has an associated list of late fees that may be outstanding. These fees are added to the list during the process of checking in a tape that is overdue. We have a **CheckIn** method on our **Tape** object, so this seems to be a natural place to add the code to record the late fee.

Adding DateDue to the Tape Object

First, we need to add a **DateDue** property to our **Tape** object. Since it will be automatically calculated, it needs to be a read-only property. We'll add the value to our UDT:

```
Private Type TapeProps
  TapeID As Long
  VideoID As Long
  Title As String * 30
  CheckedOut As Boolean
  DateAcquired As Variant
  DateDue As Variant
  InvoiceID As Long
End Type
```

And we'll add a read-only property in case anyone is interested in using the date to display somewhere:

```
Public Property Get DateDue() As Variant
  If Not udtProps.CheckedOut Then Err.Raise 438

  DateDue = udtProps.DateDue
End Property
```

The first line of code just makes sure that the property is disabled unless the tape is checked out. After all, if the tape isn't checked out it sure doesn't make sense to see when it is due back in. Otherwise, this routine simply returns the date stored in our object.

OK, now for the more interesting part. When the tape is checked out, we need to make sure to calculate the due date. Most video stores let the customer keep some videos longer than others, but we don't want this to get too confusing. We'll make all the videos in this store be two-day rentals.

We already have a **CheckOut** routine, so all we need to do is add a bit of code to calculate the due date and store it:

```
Friend Sub CheckOut(InvoiceID As Long)
   If Not flgEditing Then Err.Raise 445

   With udtProps
     .CheckedOut = True
     .DateDue = DateAdd("d", 2, Now)
     .InvoiceID = InvoiceID
   End With
   flgDirty = True
End Sub
```

Recording the Late Fee

With this code, we've got everything set up to maintain the due date in each **Tape** object. All that remains is to add any late fees to the customer's list of fees.

The first instinct, at this point, is to create a **LateFee** object as a child of the **Customer** object. This makes a lot of sense, and fits very well into the whole object design concept. The trick is to not only look at this from the object perspective, but also to analyze this from a client/server perspective. This means we need to make sure that the UI processing is in the UI and the data processing is close to the database.

What really happens when we add a late fee during the check in process? It actually boils down to adding a record in a table somewhere to record that fee. To do this with objects, we'd probably have the following steps:

❑ Instantiate the **Invoice** object to find the customer ID
❑ Instantiate the **Customer** object
❑ Add a **LateFee** object to the **LateFees** collection
❑ Call **ApplyEdit** on the **Customer** object to save it and its children

When we consider that a fair amount of network traffic occurs to load the invoice, the customer, and then all the old late fee objects, it sure seems like a lot of work just to add one record to a table. And it is. If there is no compelling reason to create these objects, we can come up with a much more efficient solution.

The closer to the database that we can get the process of adding a record to a table, the faster things will run. Following this train of thought, it would be best if the code that stores the **Tape** object into the database could also just add this late fee record into the appropriate table. This code is already interacting with the database, and so it can directly access data from the invoice and customer - without the overhead of instantiating entire objects.

This means that we'll just add a flag to our UDT so we know enough to apply the late fee when needed.

```
Private Type TapeProps
  TapeID As Long
  VideoID As Long
  Title As String * 30
  CheckedOut As Boolean
  DateAcquired As Variant
  DateDue As Variant
  LateFee As Boolean
  InvoiceID As Long
End Type
```

This flag will start out **False** in any new object, so all we need to do is set it to **True** when appropriate:

```
Public Sub CheckIn()
  If Not flgEditing Then Err.Raise 445

  With udtProps
    .CheckedOut = False
    .InvoiceID = 0
    If DateDiff("d", .DateDue, Now) > 0 Then _
      .LateFee = True
  End With
  flgDirty = True
End Sub
```

The final change we'll make is in the **ApplyEdit** and **ChildApplyEdit** methods. Here are the **ApplyEdit** changes:

```
Public Sub ApplyEdit()
  If flgChild Then If Not flgChildEditing Then Err.Raise 445
  If Not flgChild And flgNew Then Err.Raise 445
  If Not flgEditing Then Err.Raise 445

  If Not flgChild Then
    If flgDeleted Then
      ' code to delete the object's data goes here
      flgNew = True
      flgDeleted = False
    ElseIf flgDirty Or flgNew Then
      If Not IsValid Then Err.Raise 445
      ' save object to database if appropriate
      If udtProps.LateFee Then
        ' add the late fee to the customer
      End If
      ' save object state
      LSet udtSave = udtProps
      flgNew = False
    End If
    flgDirty = False
  End If
```

```
      flgEditing = False
   End Sub
```

As usual, we just have a comment anywhere there might be database code. The actual code to add
the late fee record will vary depending on the physical architecture of the application, so we'll look
at some specific examples in chapters 8 and 10.

The **ChildApplyEdit** changes are just as exciting:

```
Friend Sub ChildApplyEdit(VideoID As Long)
   If Not flgChildEditing Then Err.Raise 445
   If Not IsValid Then Err.Raise 445

   If flgDeleted Then
     ' code to delete the object's data goes here
     flgNew = True
     flgDeleted = False
   ElseIf flgDirty Or flgNew Then
     udtProps.VideoID = VideoID
     ' save object to database if appropriate

     If udtProps.LateFee Then
        ' add the late fee to the customer
     End If

     ' save object state
     LSet udtChild = udtProps
     flgNew = False
   End If
   flgDirty = False
   flgChildEditing = False
End Sub
```

Once we've added the database handling code in these two methods, we have everything all set to
handle the recording of late fees for a customer. That's only half the battle, though, since we still
need to implement a special line item on our invoices to charge the customer for the late fee on their
next videotape rental.

Invoice: Another Parent Object

Let's now implement the **Invoice** object itself. Like the **Video** object, this is a parent object, and so
we have to add a little code to manage our child objects. Still, we went over all the concepts involved
when we implemented the **Video** object, so we can fly through the code here.

Setting up the Invoice Object

As usual, add a **Business** class module to the **VideoObjects** project. Set its Name property to
Invoice and its Instancing property to 5-Multiuse.

The UI will be creating **Invoice** objects using the **Customer** object's **CreateInvoice** method,
but the user may still choose to pull up an invoice after it has been added to the system, so Multiuse
is appropriate.

Updating the Template Code

Now run through the template code, and make the following changes. By now, these should be old hat - with one exception! (I haven't listed the areas of code that don't need changing.)

```
Option Explicit

Event Valid(IsValid As Boolean)

Private Type InvoiceProps
  InvoiceID As Long
  CustomerID As Long
  CustomerName As String * 50
  CustomerPhone As String * 25
End Type

Private udtProps As InvoiceProps
Private udtSave As InvoiceProps

Private objItems As InvoiceItems

Private flgDirty As Boolean
Private flgNew As Boolean
Private flgDeleted As Boolean
Private flgEditing As Boolean
Private WithEvents objValid As BrokenRules

Public Sub BeginEdit()
  If flgEditing Then Err.Raise 445

  ' save object state
  LSet udtSave = udtProps

  flgEditing = True

  objItems.BeginEdit
End Sub

Public Sub CancelEdit()
  If Not flgEditing Then Err.Raise 445

  flgEditing = False
  flgDeleted = False
  ' restore object state
  LSet udtSave = udtProps
  objItems.CancelEdit
End Sub

Public Sub ApplyEdit()
  If Not flgEditing Then Err.Raise 445

  If flgDeleted Then
    ' code to delete the object's data goes here
    flgNew = True
    flgDeleted = False
  ElseIf flgDirty Or flgNew Then
    If Not IsValid Then Err.Raise 445
    ' save object to database if appropriate
```

```
               ' save object state
         LSet udtSave = udtProps

         flgNew = False
      End If
      flgDirty = False
      flgEditing = False

      objItems.ApplyEdit udtProps.InvoiceID

End Sub

Private Sub Class_Initialize()
   Set objValid = New BrokenRules
   flgNew = True

   Set objItems = New InvoiceItems

   ' if we know any rules are broken on startup
   ' then add code here to initialize the list
   ' of broken rules
   '
   ' objValid.RuleBroken "RuleName", True
   objValid.RuleBroken "Customer", True

End Sub


Public Sub Load(InvoiceID As Long)

   If flgEditing Then Err.Raise 445
   If Not flgNew Then Err.Raise 445

   flgNew = False
   ' code to load the object goes here
   objValid.RuleBroken "Customer", False
   objItems.Load udtProps.InvoiceID

End Sub
```

Customer Object Reference

The only new concept here is the use of **objValid**, the **BrokenRules** object, to track whether the **Invoice** has a valid **Customer** object associated with it. In the **Class_Initialize** routine, we assume that we don't have a valid **Customer** object, since when we first create an **Invoice** object it won't have any **Customer** object associated with it.

In the **Load** method, however, we have some code that assumes we *do* have a valid **Customer**. After all, if the **Invoice** object was saved, it must have had a valid **Customer** object - and so when we're restoring it from the database it should still be valid.

Invoice Properties

Our invoice object has a number of properties. The **InvoiceID** property is the same as all the other ID properties we've implemented so far: it relies on the ID value being set when the object is first saved to the database:

```
Public Property Get InvoiceID() As Long
    InvoiceID = udtProps.InvoiceID
End Property
```

We discussed, earlier, how the **Invoice** is a parent object having line items as child objects. In order for the UI to add line items to the invoice, we need to expose the **InvoiceItems** collection for its use:

```
Public Property Get InvoiceItems() As InvoiceItems
    Set InvoiceItems = objItems
End Property
```

As with the **Video** and **Tapes** objects, the **Invoice** object will rely heavily on the **InvoiceItems** object to manage the child objects.

Read-only Properties from Other Objects

The next few properties are more interesting. A couple of times, earlier in the chapter, we discussed how valuable it can be to include read-only properties on an object that provides data belonging to another object. These properties are actually part of the **Customer** object, but they're virtually always used on any invoice display - so we'll make them read-only properties for ease of use and performance reasons. Add these properties to the **Invoice** class:

```
Public Property Get CustomerID() As Long
    CustomerID = udtProps.CustomerID
End Property
```

```
Public Property Get CustomerName() As String
    CustomerName = Trim$(udtProps.CustomerName)
End Property
```

```
Public Property Get CustomerPhone() As String
    CustomerPhone = Trim$(udtProps.CustomerPhone)
End Property
```

We'll go into how these fields are initially loaded in a short while. In Chapters 8 and 10, we'll see how these fields are actually brought in from the database.

Calculated Properties

Any invoice involves the collection of money. In our case, the invoice needs to have a total amount for all the line items, plus any applicable sales tax amount, and then a final total to charge the customer. All three values hinge, almost entirely, on getting a total amount for all the line items: a value we'll refer to as a **subtotal** for the invoice.

This is one of those cases where the **Invoice** object will let the **InvoiceItems** collection object do quite a lot of the work. We'll discuss this collection object in a bit, and we'll take a closer look at the implementation of its **SubTotal** method. Suffice it to say that it calculates the total amount due for all the line items, and returns it for our use here:

```
Public Property Get SubTotal() As Double
   SubTotal = objItems.SubTotal
End Property
```

Once we have a subtotal for the invoice, the rest is easy. Sales tax is simply a percentage calculation based on the subtotal and rounded to the nearest penny:

```
Public Property Get Tax() As Double
   Tax = Val(Format$(objItems.SubTotal * 0.065 + .0005, "0.00"))
End Property
```

> *The rounding technique we're using here is quite common in dealing with financial values, although it looks a bit odd at first glance. In particular, you may be wondering why we're adding `.0005` to the value before rounding it with `Format$()`. To see why it's important, try running the following line of code in the Immediate window:*
>
> > `? Format$(.0045,"0.00")`
>
> *We'd expect to get a result of 0.01, since the 5 should round up the 4 to a 5 and that should, in turn, round up the right-most 0 to a 1. This doesn't happen; instead, the result is 0.00.*
>
> *Now try this line:*
>
> > `? Format$(.0045+.0005,"0.00")`
>
> *Now we get the desired result of 0.01. Just one of those little tricks that comes in useful from time to time.*

With both a subtotal and a tax amount, calculating the total due in an invoice is as simple as adding the two together:

```
Public Property Get Total() As Double
   Total = SubTotal + Tax
End Property
```

Notice how we use the **SubTotal** and **Tax** properties themselves within this property. This is intentional: we want to ensure that any business rules or processing that happens in those properties is also applied to the calculation of the total. So in this case, we're getting the same rounding effect on the tax amount as when the UI code retrieved it via the **Tax** property, without duplicating the code to do the rounding.

Creating an Invoice Object

Our **Invoice** object so far has only one method outside the ones from the business object template code and that's the **Initialize** method. This method is called in the **Customer** object's **CreateInvoice** routine that we created much earlier in the chapter. I'll show that code again here, so it's easy for us to see what's going on:

```
Public Function CreateInvoice() As Invoice
   Dim objInvoice As Invoice

   Set objInvoice = New Invoice
   objInvoice.Initialize Me
   Set CreateInvoice = objInvoice
   Set objInvoice = Nothing
End Function
```

The only way to add a new invoice to the system is through this method on the **Customer** object. This is important, since any invoice must have a customer, and this mechanism determines that we have one to work with when we're setting up the **Invoice** object.

The **Customer** object calls our **Invoice** object's **Initialize** method, passing itself as a parameter. This means that our method can pull any information it needs right off the **Customer** object - very slick:

```
Friend Sub Initialize(Renter As Customer)
   With Renter
     udtProps.CustomerID = .CustomerID
     objValid.RuleBroken "Customer", .IsNew
     udtProps.CustomerName = .Name
     udtProps.CustomerPhone = .Phone
     objItems.LoadFees .CustomerID
   End With
End Sub
```

Of course, the routine is set up as **Friend**, since it will only be called from the **Customer** object. After all, we don't want to let the UI developer call this routine directly, we want to make sure they've identified a valid customer first.

The routine is not complex: it simply copies the **CustomerID**, **Name** and **Phone** properties from the **Customer** object into the **Invoice** object itself.

There is also a check that the **Customer** object really is valid:

```
objValid.RuleBroken "Customer", .IsNew
```

Obviously, we have a **Customer** object; but to be truly valid it can't be a new customer. We need to make sure the customer data is in the database. Fortunately, that's easily determined by checking the **IsNew** property of the object, since **IsNew** will always return **False** if it's been saved to the database.

Also notice the call to **objItems.LoadFees**:

```
objItems.LoadFees .CustomerID
```

We'll look more closely at this method when we implement the **InvoiceItems** collection object. Its purpose is to ensure that we add line items to the invoice for all outstanding late fee records associated with the customer. This routine accepts the **CustomerID** field as a parameter so that it can find those records and create line item objects for them.

Once the **Initialize** method has been called, the **Invoice** object is all set. Of course, the user will undoubtedly add some line items for the tapes that are being rented, but that's handled through the **InvoiceItems** collection object.

InvoiceItem: An Interface Class

Before we get into the collection object itself, let's take a look at the child objects that it will contain. These are a bit more complex than the simple **Tape** object that we implemented earlier in the chapter, since we now have two different things we need to represent.

Our line items will be either a tape that's being rented (**InvoiceTape**) or a late fee (**InvoiceFee**) that needs to be paid. This is shown in the following figure:

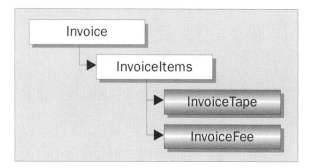

Each object is different, but they do have substantial similarities.

In Chapter 1, we discussed how objects can have multiple interfaces. All objects have their default interface, composed of the **Public** properties and methods we implement. Objects can also have other interfaces, created through the use of the **Implements** keyword. This technique is called **interface inheritance**.

Now we're going to use some of that background to add a common interface, **InvoiceItem**, to both of our new invoice line item objects. The **InvoiceItem** interface will have all the properties and methods that are common to both types of line item, while each line item object's default interface will have properties and methods specific to that type of item.

We'll also discuss some limitations that Visual Basic has imposed on the **Implements** keyword. While it is very powerful, there are some things it doesn't handle as well as we might hope.

Setting up the InvoiceItem Class

Add a generic class module to the **VideoObjects** project. Change its Name property to InvoiceItem and set its Instancing property to 2-PublicNotCreatable.

Interface objects typically need to have their Instancing property set to something other than Private. If we attempt to set the property to 1-Private then we can't use the **InvoiceItem** class name in any Public property or method on any other object. If we do so, we'll get a compile error:

'User-defined types and fixed-length strings not allowed as the type of public member of an object module; private object modules not allowed as the type of a public member of a public object module'

InvoiceItem Properties and Methods

The idea behind an interface class like **InvoiceItem** is to build an interface so that many of the operations we'll need to perform on the child objects are included. For instance, we know that we'll need to run through all the child objects adding up the total amount due for each one, indicating a **Total** property. Without a common interface containing this property, we'd have to use late-binding to run through all the child objects.

In such a case, our client code could look something like this:

```
Dim objItem As Object

For Each objItem In colItems
   dblTotal = dblTotal + objItem.Total
Next
```

While this code looks simple enough, it has declared **objItem** as type **Object** - and so it is using late-binding. Not only do we get a serious performance hit, but we've lost the ability to have Visual Basic perform compile-time checking on our call to the **Total** method.

If all the child objects implement the **InvoiceItem** interface, we can use early-binding to accomplish the same thing much faster - and with full compile-time checking by Visual Basic:

```
Dim objItem As InvoiceItem

For Each objItem In colItems
   dblTotal = dblTotal + objItem.Total
Next
```

Possible Set of Properties and Methods

Since **InvoiceItem** is just an interface class, there won't be any code included. The only thing that's important in an object of this type is the declaration of all the properties and methods. As we discussed in Chapter 1, the purpose of an interface class is merely to define the properties and methods that make up the interface - each object implementing that interface needs to supply the code behind each property and method.

We know that **InvoiceFee** and **InvoiceTape** will be child business objects, so we know they'll both have the set of child methods and properties that entail:

```
BeginEdit            CancelEdit
ApplyEdit            Delete
IsValid              IsNew
IsDirty              IsDeleted
ChildBeginEdit       ChildCancelEdit
ChildApplyEdit       ChildLoad
```

Here's where one of the major limitations of **Implements** comes into play. When an object **Implements** the interface of another object, only the **Public** properties and methods come across. Anything declared as **Friend** or **Private** won't show up. At the same time, we have good reasons for declaring a number of these elements using **Friend**; in particular, we don't want them available to any client code!

Final Set of Properties and Methods

This leaves us with a smaller set of interface elements that we can include in our **InvoiceItem** interface object:

```
Option Explicit
```

```
Public Sub BeginEdit()

End Sub
```

```
Public Sub CancelEdit()

End Sub
```

```
Public Sub ApplyEdit()

End Sub
```

```
Public Sub Delete()

End Sub
```

```
Public Property Get IsValid() As Boolean

End Property
```

```
Public Property Get IsNew() As Boolean

End Property
```

```
Public Property Get IsDirty() As Boolean

End Property
```

```
Public Property Get IsDeleted() As Boolean

End Property
```

Of course, we know that we'll have a couple of less generic properties in these objects as well. We'll now add the **Total** property to this object; we've already discussed this property and its role, and all we need to include here is its declaration:

```
   Public Property Get Total() As Double

   End Property
```

To make it easy to display the list of line items, we should also include some form of description for each item:

```
   Public Property Get ItemDescription() As String

   End Property
```

ItemType Property: Indicating the Type of Object

When we're dealing with a common interface and multiple objects that use that interface, it's often very useful to be able to find out just what type of object we're talking to. Once we know what type of object is actually behind the common interface, we can then write code that talks to that object's native interface - in case we need to do anything that isn't supported by the more generic common interface we're implementing here.

For instance, we may want to treat an **InvoiceTape** object differently than an **InvoiceFee** object at times. If we're using the **InvoiceItem** interface to walk through all the line items on an **Invoice**, we'll need some way to find out which type of object we're really working with at any given time.

To support multiple object types, we'll add a property to return the value:

```
   Public Property Get ItemType() As ItemTypes

   End Property
```

Notice that this property returns a value of type **ItemTypes**. A good way of implementing this as an **Enum**, or as a set of enumerated values. We can simply add the declaration of the list at the top of the **InvoiceItem** class module:

```
Option Explicit
```

```
Public Enum ItemTypes
   ITEM_TAPE = 0
   ITEM_FEE = 1
End Enum
```

Since this **Enum** is **Public**, it will be available for our use throughout our project, so we can use it to determine the type of each object without resorting to cryptic numeric values like 0 and 1. We could write code such as this:

```
If objItem.ItemType = ITEM_FEE Then
  Set objFee = objItem
  ' now we can use the native interface of
  ' objFee
End If
```

Now that we have a common interface to implement within each actual child object, it's time to move on. We'll have two child classes, **InvoiceFee** and **InvoiceTape**. Each will have its own native interface, and each will use **Implements** to include the **InvoiceItem** interface as well.

InvoiceFee: A Read-only Child Object

As a child object, **InvoiceFee** will be very similar to the **Tape** object that we implemented earlier:

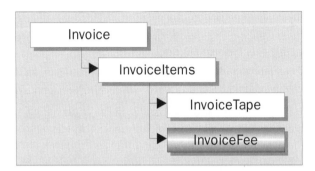

Fortunately, though, the **InvoiceFee** object will never be used as a standalone object like **Tape**. The UI code will never be able to directly create an **InvoiceFee** object; instead, it will need to get at the objects through the **Invoice** object.

This simplifies things, since we need a little less code to keep track of whether or not the object is a child at any given point. At the same time, however, we do still need to provide support for the parent-child relationship - just as we did with the **Tape** object - and so the code will be very similar overall.

Setting up the InvoiceFee Class

Add a new class to the **VideoObjects** project. It's easiest to make it a generic class module to start off. Then just copy the template routines from the **Tape** class into this class, since the differences between these two classes will be fairly minor.

Set the Name property to InvoiceFee, and make the Instancing property 2-PublicNotCreatable.

Rather than going back through all the parent-child relationship code that we covered with the **Tape** object, I'll just highlight the differences in this code as compared to the **Tape** class. Then we'll go through the properties that are specific to this object, and, finally, we'll implement the **InvoiceItem** interface.

Declarations

```
Option Explicit

Event Valid(IsValid As Boolean)
```

```
Private Type FeeProps
   InvoiceID As Long
   FeeID As Long
```

```
   VideoTitle As String * 30
   EnteredDate As Date
   DaysOver As Integer
End Type

Private udtProps As FeeProps
Private udtSave As FeeProps
Private udtChild As FeeProps
```

```
Private flgDirty As Boolean
Private flgNew As Boolean
Private flgDeleted As Boolean
Private flgEditing As Boolean
Private WithEvents objValid As BrokenRules

Private flgChildEditing As Boolean
```

Like any other business object, we've added in a UDT, and the variables based on that type. We'll use these throughout the rest of the code, and we'll review the elements of the UDT as we use each one.

It's also worth noting that the **flgChild** variable is not declared here. Since this object is always a child object, we don't need that variable to keep track of whether or not we are a child.

Updating the Code

These routines ought to be very familiar by now. They are almost the same as the **Tape** object's implementation. The highlighted lines all have a common theme, in that with the **Tape** object they had an extra check to determine if the object was a child or not. In this case, we're can assuming that we're always a child - so those checks have been removed:

```
Public Sub BeginEdit()

   If Not flgChildEditing Then Err.Raise 445

   If flgEditing Then Err.Raise 445

   ' save object state
   LSet udtSave = udtProps
   flgEditing = True
End Sub

Public Sub CancelEdit()

   If Not flgChildEditing Then Err.Raise 445

   If Not flgEditing Then Err.Raise 445

   flgEditing = False
   flgDeleted = False
   ' restore object state
   LSet udtProps = udtSave
End Sub

Public Sub Delete()

   If Not flgChildEditing Then Err.Raise 445

   If Not flgEditing Then Err.Raise 445
```

```
      flgDeleted = True
End Sub
```

The **ApplyEdit** method is simplified even more:

```
Public Sub ApplyEdit()
  If Not flgChildEditing Then Err.Raise 445
  If Not flgEditing Then Err.Raise 445

  flgEditing = False
End Sub
```

In the **Tape** object, this routine had a fair amount of code, but it was all there for when **flgChild** was set to **False**. In this case, **InvoiceFee** is always a child, and so we can remove that entire code block.

There's been no **Load** method so far either. The **Load** method exists in the other objects - so that the client code can create the object and then call **Load** to have the object loaded from the database. This entire sequence of events is invalid if the object is only a child, and so we don't need a **Load** method. We'll still have a **ChildLoad** method, though, which we'll look at in this next bit of code:

```
Friend Sub ChildBeginEdit()
  If flgChildEditing Then Err.Raise 445

  ' save object state
  LSet udtChild = udtProps
  flgChildEditing = True
End Sub

Friend Sub ChildCancelEdit()
  If Not flgChildEditing Then Err.Raise 445

  flgChildEditing = False
  flgDeleted = False
  ' restore object state
  LSet udtProps = udtChild
End Sub
```

Again, these routines ought to be very familiar, as they are directly out of the **Tape** object. The **ChildApplyEdit** routine needs a bit of alteration to fit into our new object. We need to remove these three lines referring to the **LateFee**:

```
      If udtProps.LateFee Then
        ' add the late fee to the customer
      End If
```

We also need to change the parameter that the routine expects from **VideoID** to **InvoiceID** and make sure that value is placed into the UDT variable. Otherwise, the code remains the same:

```
Friend Sub ChildApplyEdit(InvoiceID As Long)
  If Not flgChildEditing Then Err.Raise 445
  If Not IsValid Then Err.Raise 445
```

```
   If flgDeleted Then
      ' code to delete the object's data goes here
      flgNew = True
      flgDeleted = False
   ElseIf flgDirty Or flgNew Then
```

```
      udtProps.InvoiceID = InvoiceID
```

```
      ' save object to database if appropriate
      ' save object state
      LSet udtChild = udtProps
      flgNew = False
   End If
   flgDirty = False
   flgChildEditing = False
End Sub
```

The **ChildLoad** subroutine also needs its parameter changed; in this case, it needs to be **FeeID**:

```
Friend Sub ChildLoad(FeeID As Long)
```

```
   If flgChildEditing Then Err.Raise 445
   If Not flgNew Then Err.Raise 445

   flgNew = False
   ' code to load the object goes here
End Sub
```

The **Tape** object implemented a **SetAsChild** method so that we could tell it to become a child by setting **flgChild** to **True**. **InvoiceFee** is always a child, so we need neither the **flgChild** variable nor the **SetAsChild** method.

The **Class_Initialize** routine needs a minor change. In the **Tape** object, we had some code to indicate that the **DateAcquired** field was invalid. This line of code needs to be removed from the **InvoiceFee** object's code, since it doesn't even have a **DateAcquired** field. I've shown the offending line, here, commented out:

```
   Private Sub Class_Initialize()
      flgNew = True
      Set objValid = New BrokenRules
      ' if we know any rules are broken on startup
      ' then add code here to initialize the list
      ' of broken rules
      '
      ' objValid.RuleBroken "RuleName", True
```

```
      ' objValid.RuleBroken "DateAcquired", True
```

```
   End Sub
```

The remaining business object routines from the template are totally unchanged - so I won't repeat their code here.

InvoiceFee Properties

The **InvoiceFee** object is a read-only representation of a late fee. A customer gets a late fee when they return a tape after its due date. We implemented this in the **Tape** object by adding code to the

CheckIn method that checks the due date. Then, in the code to save the **Tape** object to the database, we noted that we would need some code to add a record in a late fee table associated with the customer.

Since that is the only way a late fee can be added to our system, there will be no mechanism for the UI code to add an **InvoiceFee** object directly. Therefore, each **InvoiceFee** object will be loaded from the database to represent one of those late fee records. Essentially, we're creating objects so that they can be viewed or displayed, but not created or edited.

This property, therefore, replaces **Property Get TapeID** that we've copied across from the **Tape** class:

```
Public Property Get FeeID() As Long
   FeeID = udtProps.FeeID
End Property
```

Like all the other objects, these will have had an ID value assigned when the record was added to the database. This property replaces **Property Get Title** that we've copied across from the **Tape** class:

```
Public Property Get VideoTitle() As String
   VideoTitle = udtProps.VideoTitle
End Property
```

In our UDT, we included a field for the video's title. This is primarily because the system will need to put something on the invoice so that the customer knows what the late fee is for. When we added the late fee record, we knew how many days late the tape was being returned. This property just returns the number of days that were recorded at that time:

```
Public Property Get DaysOver() As Integer
   DaysOver = udtProps.DaysOver
End Property
```

The **InvoiceFee** object represents a fee for some tape that was returned late. In this case, we've put in code to charge $1.50 for each day the tape was late. A full-blown video rental system might have some more complex calculation here, but we'll keep things as simple as possible.

```
Public Property Get Fee() As Double
   Fee = DaysOver * 1.5
End Property
```

Our **Fee** routine calls the **DaysOver** property to get the number of days the tape was overdue. While we could get the same value from **udtProps.DaysOver**, it's always wise to use the object's properties, since we might add some business rules into the property, and then we'd want to make sure that those properties were used in calculating the fee, without duplicating the code.

The first question that a lot of customers will ask is when the late fee occurred. To answer that question, we'll add an **EnteredDate** property:

```
Public Property Get EnteredDate() As Date
   EnteredDate = udtProps.EnteredDate
End Property
```

The date returned, here, is the date that the late fee was recorded in the database. We'll get into the actual database design in Chapter 8, but trust me, this field will be in there.

Finally, we can comment out or delete the code we copied from the **Tape** class that isn't relevant to **InvoiceFee**. The properties are: **Get CheckedOut**, **Let DateAcquired**, **Get Invoice**, **Get DateAcquired** and **Get DateDue**; but we should also comment out or delete the **CheckOut** and **CheckIn** routines in **InvoiceFee**.

Implementing the InvoiceItem Interface

Now that we've got the **InvoiceFee** object implemented, we can add in the code that we need to support the **InvoiceItem** interface. Because we've already implemented the entire object, adding this interface will be quite simple.

Declarations

First, add the **Implements InvoiceItem** line to the top of the **InvoiceFee** class module:

```
Option Explicit

Implements InvoiceItem

Event Valid(IsValid As Boolean)
```

Looking at the Object list in the upper-left of the code window, we find that **InvoiceItem** is one of the options. Choose it as an option, and then look at the Procedure list in the upper-right of the code window. This list now shows all the properties and methods that we added to the **InvoiceItem** class earlier.

The trick in implementing an interface like this is that Visual Basic *requires* that all the properties and methods of that interface are coded within your module. This can be limiting if we don't actually *want* all of them in our new object. Fortunately, we've planned ahead and only included the interface elements that are common to both our child objects in our **InvoiceItem** class.

Implementing the Properties and Methods

Now let's look at the implementation of those interface elements. Many of these properties and methods are duplicated in the object's native interface. What we've done here is to implement the native interface so all those properties and methods contain the code. With those routines already coded, we can just have each routine in the **InvoiceItem** interface call the corresponding routine that we've already written.

For instance, let's look at **InvoiceItem_BeginEdit**:

```
Private Sub InvoiceItem_BeginEdit()
  BeginEdit
End Sub
```

The fact that this routine is declared as **Private** and that the routine name includes **InvoiceItem_** before the normal name is quite usual and normal itself. We discussed how this works in Chapter 1, and it may be worth referring back to that if this seems confusing.

The most interesting aspect of this routine is that it has virtually no code. Instead, we're just deferring the call to the **BeginEdit** method that we've already implemented. There is no sense in duplicating code here to do the same thing, so this makes good sense.

An alternative would be to add a third routine to contain the implementation and have both **BeginEdit** and **InvoiceItem_BeginEdit** call that routine. This is perfectly valid, but adds a lot of extra procedures to the module to accomplish the same goal.

Most of the remaining interface elements are implemented the same way:

```
Private Sub InvoiceItem_ApplyEdit()
  ApplyEdit
End Sub
```

```
Private Sub InvoiceItem_CancelEdit()
  CancelEdit
End Sub
```

```
Private Sub InvoiceItem_Delete()
  Delete
End Sub
```

```
Private Property Get InvoiceItem_IsDeleted() As Boolean
  InvoiceItem_IsDeleted = IsDeleted
End Property
```

```
Private Property Get InvoiceItem_IsDirty() As Boolean
  InvoiceItem_IsDirty = IsDirty
End Property
```

```
Private Property Get InvoiceItem_IsNew() As Boolean
  InvoiceItem_IsNew = IsNew
End Property
```

```
Private Property Get InvoiceItem_IsValid() As Boolean
  InvoiceItem_IsValid = IsValid
End Property
```

We haven't implemented an **ItemDescription** or a **Total** property in our **InvoiceFee** object so far. Instead, we've implemented **Title** and **Fee** properties that do essentially the same function but have more descriptive names. This is still no problem: we'll just call the appropriate property from within the **ItemDescription** and **Total** properties:

```
Private Property Get InvoiceItem_ItemDescription() As String
  InvoiceItem_ItemDescription = VideoTitle
End Property
```

```
Private Property Get InvoiceItem_Total() As Double
  InvoiceItem_Total = Fee
End Property
```

Implementing the ItemType Property

The only remaining property to be implemented is **ItemType**. This property is a bit different, since it has no analogous property within **InvoiceFee** so far. It doesn't make sense for the **InvoiceFee** interface to include an **ItemType** property, however, since if we have a reference to an **InvoiceFee** object using its native interface then we know what kind of object we have.

ItemType is only useful within the **InvoiceItem** interface, because otherwise we have no way of knowing what kind of object is actually behind the interface. Thus the implementation of this property within the **InvoiceFee** object is simple: it just needs to return **ITEM_FEE** to indicate that it is an **InvoiceFee** object:

```
Private Property Get InvoiceItem_ItemType() As ItemTypes
  InvoiceItem_ItemType = ITEM_FEE
End Property
```

With this simple code, we've added an entire second interface to our **InvoiceFee** object. Any code using our object can now get at it through either the native **InvoiceFee** interface or through the **InvoiceItem** interface, whichever is more appropriate.

InvoiceTape: An Aggregate Child Object

The **InvoiceTape** object is very similar to **InvoiceFee** in most respects. Sure, it has some different properties in its native interface but it, too, will implement the **InvoiceItem** interface - and so client code can use it in exactly the same way as it would use **InvoiceFee**.

Setting up the InvoiceTape Class

We can take advantage of the similarity between the **InvoiceFee** object and what we need for the **InvoiceTape** object. Using the **VideoObjects** project, add a generic class module and copy the business object template routines from **InvoiceFee** into this new module. We won't be changing those very much, so that makes a good start.

Set the Name property to InvoiceTape and the Instancing property to 2-PublicNotCreatable. The UI code will need access to the object, but only through the **Invoice** object, so we don't want to make the routine publicly creatable:

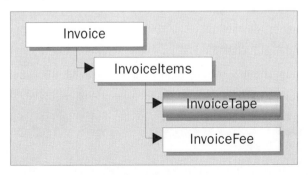

Of course, this object will have its own UDT, but beyond that the general declarations section of the module will be the same as **InvoiceFee**. Here's the UDT for **InvoiceTape**:

```
Private Type InvoiceTapeProps
  InvoiceID As Long
  ItemID As Long
  TapeID As Long
  Title As String * 30
  Price As Double
End Type

Private udtProps As InvoiceTapeProps
Private udtSave As InvoiceTapeProps
Private udtChild As InvoiceTapeProps
```

Then, in the **Class_Initialize()** code, we need to comment out the following line, since this rule isn't relevant to our **InvoiceTape** object:

```
' objValid.RuleBroken "DateAcquired", True
```

The only change to the remainder of the template code is that we need to add a **ChildLoad** method. This is the same as the **ChildLoad** method from the **Tape** object, except we need to pass an appropriate parameter to identify the specific invoice line item:

```
Friend Sub ChildLoad(ItemID As Long)

   If flgChildEditing Then Err.Raise 445
   If Not flgNew Then Err.Raise 445

   flgNew = False
   ' code to load the object goes here
End Sub
```

InvoiceTape Properties

The **InvoiceTape** object's properties are different from **InvoiceFee**, although there are similarities. Still, the fact that they are different highlights the reason it made sense to implement a common interface using **InvoiceItem**.

As usual, this object will have an ID value that's assigned when it is first saved to the database:

```
Public Property Get ItemID() As Long
   ItemID = udtProps.ItemID
End Property
```

To make it easy to display the line item on a screen, we need to make sure that the video tape's title is available. Even though this field originated on the **Video** object, we'll duplicate it here to prevent us from having to instantiate an entire **Video** object just to get it. This is our new version:

```
Public Property Get Title() As String
   Title = udtProps.Title
End Property
```

When a tape is rented, we need to establish a price. In the **Initialize** method, below, we've taken the simple approach of making the default price be $1.99 for all tapes. Still, there are cases where a price needs to be overridden - and so we'll make the **Price** property read-write by implementing a **Property Let**:

```
Public Property Let Price(Value As Double)
  udtProps.Price = Value
  objValid.RuleBroken "Price", (Value < 0 Or Value > 4)
  flgDirty = True
End Property
```

A fair amount of the template code that we included in both **InvoiceFee** and **InvoiceTape** is unused in this program. As we discussed earlier, when we were working with the **InvoiceTape** object, there are certain advantages to leaving this unused code within our objects, such as the facility to enhance our objects at a later date.

It would be quite possible to go through and remove a lot of the code in these objects, since they are very simple.

Applications tend to evolve over time. An object that starts out very simple may become more and more complex, to support new application functionality. Were we to strip each object down to its barest code, eliminating all support for concepts like business rules, editing, and so forth, we'd end up with objects that were difficult to enhance later. While there is some cost associated in having this extra code in each object, it's usually well worth it later when the object needs to be enhanced.

However, while we may want to keep the unused code in **InvoiceTape**, we should comment out or delete the following routines, since they aren't compatible with our **InvoiceTape** properties: **Get FeeID**, **Get VideoTitle**, **Get DaysOver**, **Get Fee** and **GetEnteredDate**.

The **Property Get Price** routine just returns the value stored in **udtProps**, whether that be the $1.99 from the **Initialize** method, or a value entered by the user through the **Property Let** we just implemented:

```
Public Property Get Price() As Double
  Price = udtProps.Price
End Property
```

InvoiceTape Methods

The **InvoiceTape** object represents a tape that is being rented via this invoice. One line item will be added to the invoice for each tape that the customer is renting, so we need to make sure we provide a mechanism for the UI code to easily add new line items.

The **InvoiceItems** collection object will provide an **Add** method, so the UI code can add a line item. The only line items that can be added are those to rent a tape; all the late fee items come from previous tape returns, as we discussed earlier.

Since the line items we'll be adding revolve around a specific tape that's being rented, it makes sense to use a **Tape** object to get any information we'll need for our new line item. To this end, we'll add an **Initialize** method that accepts a **Tape** object as a parameter. The **Tape** object itself will be created in the **InvoiceItems** object's **Add** method, based on the **TapeID** of the tape chosen by the user.

```
Friend Sub Initialize(RentalTape As Tape)
  With RentalTape
    udtProps.TapeID = .TapeID
    udtProps.Title= .Title
    udtProps.Price = 1.99
  End With
End Sub
```

The **Initialize** method itself just copies the properties of interest from the **RentedTape** object into the **udtProps** variable within **InvoiceTape**.

In this case, we've just fixed the price at $1.99 to rent a tape for simplicity. A more comprehensive application might store the price on the **Tape** object, or perhaps base the price on some other more complex criteria.

Implementing the InvoiceItem Interface

As with the **InvoiceFee** object, the code to implement the **InvoiceItem** interface is very straightforward. All the routines, except **ItemType**, just call the appropriate property or method from the **InvoiceTape** object's native interface.

Most of this code is identical to the **InvoiceItem** interface we created for the **InvoiceFee** object:

```
Private Sub InvoiceItem_ApplyEdit()
  ApplyEdit
End Sub

Private Sub InvoiceItem_BeginEdit()
  BeginEdit
End Sub

Private Sub InvoiceItem_CancelEdit()
  CancelEdit
End Sub

Private Sub InvoiceItem_Delete()
  Delete
End Sub

Private Property Get InvoiceItem_IsDeleted() As Boolean
  InvoiceItem_IsDeleted = IsDeleted
End Property

Private Property Get InvoiceItem_IsDirty() As Boolean
  InvoiceItem_IsDirty = IsDirty
End Property

Private Property Get InvoiceItem_IsNew() As Boolean
  InvoiceItem_IsNew = IsNew
End Property
```

```
Private Property Get InvoiceItem_IsValid() As Boolean
   InvoiceItem_IsValid = IsValid
End Property
```

```
Private Property Get InvoiceItem_ItemDescription() As String
   InvoiceItem_ItemDescription = Title
End Property
```

```
Private Property Get InvoiceItem_Total() As Double
   InvoiceItem_Total = Price
End Property
```

The **InvoiceFee** object's **ItemType** property returned **ITEM_FEE**, and the **InvoiceTape** object will have the same code, just returning **ITEM_TAPE** instead:

```
Private Property Get InvoiceItem_ItemType() As ItemTypes
   InvoiceItem_ItemType = ITEM_TAPE
End Property
```

InvoiceItems: A Parent-child Collection Object

Now that we have the child objects ready to go, all that remains is to put together the collection object to manage them. This object is just like the **Tapes** object we implemented earlier, but with one twist: this collection will contain two types of child objects.

There are a number of routines in a parent-child collection object like this that loop through all the child objects. Where possible, we'll use the **InvoiceItem** interface to the child objects for this. Unfortunately, it is the rare case that we can do this, since a lot of the methods we need to call are implemented as **Friend** - so they aren't available to the UI developer; but this also prevented us from making them part of the **InvoiceItem** interface.

Setting up the InvoiceItems Class

Add a new class module to the **VideoObjects** project. Make it a generic class module, then copy all the code from the **Tapes** class into this one. We'll use that code as a base, since it gets us most of the way there.

Set the Name property to InvoiceItems and the Instancing property to 2-PublicNotCreatable. The only time this object should be created is within an **Invoice** object, although it will be used by the UI code through the **Invoice** object's **InvoiceItems** property.

The (General) (Declarations) section should be fine; just change **colTapes** to **colItems** for clarity:

```
Option Explicit
```

```
Private colItems As Collection
```

```
Private flgEditing As Boolean
```

As usual, we'll have a **Class_Initialize** to create the **Collection** object itself:

```
Private Sub Class_Initialize()
    Set colItems = New Collection
End Sub
```

Since this is a collection, we've got the standard **Item**, **Count** and **NewEnum** methods. These are essentially unchanged but for the name of the collection variable:

```
Public Function Item(ByVal Index As Variant) As InvoiceItem
    Set Item = colItems(Index)
End Function

Public Function Count() As Long
    Count = colItems.Count
End Function

Public Function NewEnum() As IUnknown
    Set NewEnum = colItems.[_NewEnum]
End Function
```

Again, remember to use the Tools-Property Attributes menu option to set Item to be the default method and NewEnum with a Procedure ID of −4 and to be hidden.

BeginEdit Method

The **BeginEdit** method needs some work. This is the first case where we loop through all the child objects, so it would be nice to use the **InvoiceItem** interface. Unfortunately, the method we need to call is **ChildBeginEdit**, and it is declared as a **Friend** within each child class. Still, we'll use the **InvoiceItem** interface to get at the **ItemType** property, so it's not a total loss:

```
Public Sub BeginEdit()
    Dim objInvoiceItem As InvoiceItem
    Dim objTape As InvoiceTape
    Dim objFee As InvoiceFee

    If flgEditing Then Err.Raise 445

    For Each objInvoiceItem In colItems
        If objInvoiceItem.ItemType = ITEM_FEE Then
            Set objFee = objInvoiceItem
            objFee.ChildBeginEdit
        Else
            Set objTape = objInvoiceItem
            objTape.ChildBeginEdit
        End If
    Next
    flgEditing = True
End Sub
```

We put each item from the collection into a variable, called **objInvoiceItem**, which is declared as type **InvoiceItem**. This variable uses the **InvoiceItem** interface to whatever child object we're looking at, regardless of whether it is an **InvoiceFee** or **InvoiceItem**. This means that we can use the **ItemType** property to find out with which type of object we are dealing:

```
If objInvoiceItem.ItemType = ITEM_FEE Then
```

From there, we are able to use either **objFee** or **objTape** to get at the native interface of the object. For instance, if we have an **InvoiceFee** object, we just set the **objFee** variable to point to the current item:

```
Set objFee = objInvoiceItem
```

Since **objFee** is declared as type **InvoiceFee**, that's the interface it will use to get at the object. This means that we can now call the native properties and methods from the **InvoiceFee** interface, including those declared as **Friend**:

```
objFee.ChildBeginEdit
```

> The only way to call a property or method declared as **Friend** is to use the default interface. Interface elements declared as **Friend** are not available through other interfaces; nor can they be used through any late-bound variable.
>
> Thus, we can't just declare **objInvoiceItem** as type **Object** and call these methods. If we're going to use the power of the **Friend** keyword then we're going to have to do this extra work.

CancelEdit and ApplyEdit Methods

CancelEdit and **ApplyEdit** run along the same principle, using the **InvoiceItem** interface to find out what type of object we have, and then using a variable of that type to get at the native interface for the object:

```
Public Sub CancelEdit()
  Dim objInvoiceItem As InvoiceItem
  Dim objTape As InvoiceTape
  Dim objFee As InvoiceFee

  Dim lngIndex As Long

  If Not flgEditing Then Err.Raise 445

  flgEditing = False

  For lngIndex = colItems.Count To 1 Step -1
    Set objInvoiceItem = colItems.Item(lngIndex)
    If objInvoiceItem.ItemType = ITEM_FEE Then
      Set objFee = objInvoiceItem
      With objFee
```

```
            If .IsNew Then
                colItems.Remove lngIndex
            .ChildCancelEdit
        End With
    Else
        Set objTape = objInvoiceItem
        With objTape
            .ChildCancelEdit
            If .IsNew Then _
                colItems.Remove lngIndex
        End With
    End If
```

```
    Next lngIndex
End Sub
```

```
Public Sub ApplyEdit(InvoiceID As Long)
    Dim objInvoiceItem As InvoiceItem
    Dim objTape As InvoiceTape
    Dim objFee As InvoiceFee
```

```
Dim lngIndex As Long
```

```
If Not flgEditing Then Err.Raise 445
```

```
    For lngIndex = colItems.Count To 1 Step -1
        Set objInvoiceItem = colItems.Item(lngIndex)
        If objInvoiceItem.ItemType = ITEM_FEE Then
            Set objFee = objInvoiceItem
            With objFee
                If .IsDeleted Then _
                    colItems.Remove lngIndex
                .ChildApplyEdit InvoiceID
            End With
        Else
            Set objTape = objInvoiceItem
            With objTape
                If .IsDeleted Then _
                    colItems.Remove lngIndex
                .ChildApplyEdit InvoiceID
            End With
        End If
```

```
    Next lngIndex
    flgEditing = False
End Sub
```

Delete Method

The **Delete** method is a bit easier. The **InvoiceItem** interface has a **Delete** method and so we don't need to do all that work to find out what type of object we're dealing with. Instead, we'll just declare a variable of type **InvoiceItem**, and use it within the routine.

```
Public Sub Delete()
    Dim objInvoiceItem As InvoiceItem
```

```
    If Not flgEditing Then Err.Raise 445
```

```
      ' code to delete the object's data goes here
      For Each objInvoiceItem In colItems
        With objInvoiceItem

          .BeginEdit
          .Delete
          .ApplyEdit
        End With
      Next
    End Sub
```

Load Method

Our **Load** method is as generic as ever. As with the other objects, the code for this method will be fleshed out in chapters 8 and 10. The only real difference here is that the **InvoiceID** is passed as a parameter, so we can easily find the appropriate records to load into our child objects:

```
    Friend Sub Load(InvoiceID As Long)

      If flgEditing Then Err.Raise 445

      ' here we'll put looping code to load

      ' each of the InvoiceItem objects for the InvoiceID

      ' For Each InvoiceItemID
      '   Set objInvoiceItem = New InvoiceItem
      '   With objInvoiceItem
      '     .SetAsChild
      '     .ChildLoad InvoiceItemID
      '   End With
      '   colItems.Add Item:=objInvoiceItem
      ' Loop
    End Sub
```

Even though the pseudo-code is commented out, it's a good idea to update the comments to reflect the new variable names as shown here. This makes it easier to implement the code when we do add in database access.

Add Method

Remembering back to earlier discussions about adding child objects to the invoice, we decided that it wasn't possible for the UI to add **InvoiceFee** objects. Only **InvoiceTape** objects can be added, one for each tape that the customer is going to rent.

Most video stores have barcode scanners to scan in the video tape's ID number right off the tape case. Following this line of thought, it seems reasonable to expect the UI developer to get this ID value and pass it to our **Add** method when a new line item is to be added to the invoice. So we'll change our **Add** method now.

```
    Public Function Add(TapeID As Long) As InvoiceItem
      Dim objInvoiceTape As InvoiceTape
```

As we've already implemented the **InvoiceTape** object, we know it has an **Initialize** method that expects a **Tape** object as a parameter. Now that we've got the **TapeID** value, it should be easy enough to instantiate the appropriate object:

```
Dim objTape As Tape

Set objTape = New Tape
objTape.Load TapeID
```

Of course, we need to create an **InvoiceTape** child object as well:

```
Set objInvoiceTape = New InvoiceTape
```

Since we already have a **Tape** object, we can just call our new object's **Initialize** event and use **objTape** as a parameter:

```
objInvoiceTape.Initialize objTape
```

The remainder of the routine simply adds the object to the collection of child objects, returns the value to the calling code, and cleans up. Pretty much the same as the **Tapes** object from before:

```
If flgEditing Then objInvoiceTape.ChildBeginEdit

colItems.Add Item:=objInvoiceTape
Set Add = objInvoiceTape
End Function
```

LoadFees Method

We do have a variation on the **Load** method that we need to add to this object. In the **Invoice** object, we have an **Initialize** method that is called by the **Customer** object's **CreateInvoice** routine. This method's purpose is to load the customer's data into a newly created **Invoice** object.

All the late fees for a customer are essentially customer data, and so it's important that, when the customer's data is loaded into the **Invoice** object, the late fees get loaded too. We realized this earlier, and made the **Invoice** object's **Initialize** method call a **LoadFees** method to get those late fee records into the collection:

```
Friend Sub LoadFees(CustomerID As Long)
   If flgEditing Then Err.Raise 445

   ' here we'll put looping code to create
   ' each of the InvoiceFee objects for the CustomerID

   ' For Each InvoiceFeeID
   '    Set objInvoiceFee = New InvoiceFee
   '    With objInvoiceFee
   '       .SetAsChild
   '       .ChildLoad InvoiceFeeID
   '    End With
```

```
'    colItems.Add Item:=objInvoiceFee
' Loop
End Sub
```

As with the other data access routines in this chapter, it's just a few comments. The implementation will vary, and we'll take a look at it later in the book. We do get the **CustomerID** as a parameter, and that should be sufficient to find all unpaid late fees for that customer - so we can load them into **InvoiceFee** objects and add them to the collection.

SubTotal Property

The last thing we need to do with this object is add a **SubTotal** property. The **Invoice** object also has a **SubTotal** property, but it relies on this property to do all the work of adding up the amount due from each line item.

Fortunately, we included a **Total** property on the **InvoiceItem** interface, and so this routine needs merely to loop through all the child objects using the **InvoiceItem** interface to get at that **Total** property.

By adding together all the **Total** properties, we'll arrive at a total due for all the line items on the entire invoice:

```
Friend Property Get SubTotal() As Double
   Dim objItem As InvoiceItem
   Dim dblAmount As Double

   For Each objItem In colItems
     If Not objItem.IsDeleted Then _
        dblAmount = dblAmount + objItem.Total
   Next
   SubTotal = dblAmount
End Property
```

Summary

In this chapter we've looked at how business objects sharing a parent-child relationship can be implemented to give transactional support to the UI, so that no child's state is committed until the parent's state is saved. We've also looked at hybrid child and standalone objects, and at using shared code interfaces to take advantage of the early-binding.

These have been two long chapters, covering many issues specific to the implementation of business objects. Some key types of objects that we have created include:

- Simple business objects
- Objects returning search results for display
- Objects representing a list of text and key values
- Parent business objects
- Child business objects
- Hybrid child and standalone business objects
- Parent-child relationship objects

A lot of the routines in these objects were left with comments to indicate where database access code needs to be added. In the remaining chapters, we will use these objects to illustrate various techniques for database access using the different physical architectures covered in Chapter 4.

Here are the remaining chapters what we'll cover within them:

Chapter 7	Implementing a user-interface with Visual Basic forms
Chapter 8	A single-tier implementation of the data access code
Chapter 9	Implementing a user-interface with Microsoft Excel
Chapter 10	A CSLA implementation with Distributed COM
Chapter 11	Distributing client code with DCOM
Chapter 12	Using Microsoft Transaction Server
Chapter 13	Implementing a user-interface with Active Server Pages

7

Visual Basic Forms as a User-Interface

Overview

In Chapters 5 and 6, we built a fairly simple application to operate a video rental store. Of course, the application was entirely composed of business objects, with no user-interface or data access of any sort. Those were left out intentionally - to illustrate how easy and important it is to design an application's objects first, and deal with the other aspects later.

Throughout the remaining chapters, we'll be looking at how to build a variety of user-interfaces, and how to implement various different data access techniques. Probably the most common style of user-interface will be one built using Visual Basic and regular everyday Visual Basic forms. That's what we're going to cover in this chapter.

While it's certainly possible to create very rich and complex user-interfaces using Visual Basic's forms and an application designed with business objects, we're going to keep the interface in this chapter fairly simple. The logic here is quite straightforward: the most important thing, at this stage, is for us to take a clear look at the basic techniques available when we're designing a UI on top of our business objects. Once we've got the concepts down, we'll be in a position to build new and exciting interfaces for our programs.

As we build the code in this chapter, you'll notice that we're dealing specifically with the details of this, our main example UI, and how our video objects interact with this UI. At the end of this chapter, we'll be able to compile both the business objects and an empty interface shell. In the next chapter, we'll go ahead and implement the object persistence routines that will allow our objects to interact with a database.

VideoUI: A Visual Basic Client Project

The first thing we need to do is put together a Visual Basic project for our forms. All our business objects are contained in the **VideoObjects** project.

As we created it in Chapters 5 and 6, **VideoObjects** is an ActiveX DLL project. While we can add forms to this type of project, the user can't directly run it. We need an **EXE** project of some sort for the user to run.

It's also important to implement the UI outside of the business object DLL, to help maintain the separation of the user-interface from the application itself.

> **We need to keep in mind that the business objects are the application; there may be a number of different user-interfaces that use those objects.**

Our new project has no reason to be an ActiveX server of any sort. All it will contain are code modules that are to be used locally within the UI. That's not to say that it might not contain class modules: it's just that those classes would be for the use of the UI itself, not other applications.

This all boils down to our project being a Standard EXE project. So let's set one up and keep moving.

Open up Visual Basic, choose Standard EXE from the New Project dialog. Then open up the Project Properties window by choosing the Project-Properties menu option to change the Project Name field to **VideoUI**.

The easiest way to implement our user-interface program is to actually add the **VideoObjects** project right into the development environment using a project group. To do this, choose the File-Add Project menu option. Use the Add Project dialog window to select the **VideoObjects** project, and click OK. This will add the **VideoObjects** project to the project window, along with our **VideoUI** project.

The **VideoUI** project should be shown in bold, with the **VideoObjects** shown in a regular font. The bold indicates which project will be run when we press the *F5* key or choose the Run-Start menu option.

Version Compatibility

We're going to add a reference from our **VideoUI** project to the **VideoObjects** project, but before we do this, it's very important that the Version Compatibility setting in the Component tab of the **VideoObjects** Project Properties dialog be set to either Project Compatibility or Binary Compatibility. In this section, we're going to take a good look at why we need to do this:

When we add a reference to an ActiveX Server, Visual Basic records the **global unique ID** (GUID) of the server, and uses it for future references. This GUID value may change each time we recompile the ActiveX server project, causing any client programs to lose their reference to the server.

> *A GUID is a 128-bit structure generated by the Win32 API. The value is created by combining the current date and time with either the ID number from the computer's ethernet card or a randomly-generated value. Microsoft has developed the GUID to provide identification values that are unique in time and space.*

A complex set of rules control how and when the GUID changes, and the Version Compatibility setting is at the heart of these rules. Let's consider this a bit further now.

Interface Changes

We'll talk about the various Version Compatibility settings in a moment, but first let's look at the conditions under which the GUID will change. We can consider an ActiveX server's interface as being composed of all the public interface elements of all the public classes in the server. The interface is basically a contract with all our server's clients. If any part of that interface changes, then the contract could be broken - in which case there is the possibility of a GUID change on the server itself:

Activity	Affect on server GUID
Adding a public class	Depends on Version Compatibility

Table continued on following page

287

Activity	Affect on server GUID
Adding a public property/method to a public class	Depends on Version Compatibility
Changing a public property/method on a public class	New GUID
Removing a public class	New GUID
Removing a public property/method from a public class	New GUID

No Compatibility

When the Version Compatibility setting is No Compatibility, Visual Basic will generate a new GUID value for the ActiveX server each time the project is recompiled. This setting is very difficult to work with when we're testing our server, since each time we recompile the server (ActiveX EXE or DLL) any client projects will lose their reference to the server.

Project Compatibility

With Project Compatibility selected, Visual Basic will generate a GUID the first time the project is compiled, and will attempt to use that same GUID for subsequent compiles, based on the conditions in the table above.

To throw in an extra twist, each public class in the project has a **class ID** (CLSID). A CLSID is a GUID value that represents a class rather than the entire ActiveX server. When we're using the Project Compatibility setting, the CLSIDs for the project's classes are generated each time we compile the server.

Project Compatibility is a very good setting to use during the debugging process. Since the server's GUID remains largely constant, the client programs won't lose their reference to the server. Although the CLSIDs will change each time the server is recompiled, this doesn't cause problems when running the client program within the Visual Basic IDE. Each time the client is run in the IDE, it reconnects its references to specific classes within the server project.

This setting is inappropriate once we've released our ActiveX server to users, or we've moved beyond initial debugging and testing. If the server is recompiled, all the CLSIDs will be regenerated and so we would also need to recompile and redistribute any clients. This can prove to be a serious logistic problem.

Binary Compatibility

Of the three settings, Binary Compatibility is the strictest. With this setting, Visual Basic will make every effort to retain both the server's GUID and all the CLSIDs on each compile. However, changing existing interface elements or removing a class, property, or method, will still result in a new GUID, even with Binary Compatibility selected.

Binary Compatibility is the most appropriate setting for servers that have moved beyond initial debugging and are in production. As long as we don't alter existing properties and methods, or remove any classes, the server's GUID and CLSIDs will remain constant - so any client programs we've distributed will continue to work with the server as it is updated.

Referencing the VideoObjects Project

Now that we've got a handle on GUIDs, CLSIDs, and the various project compatibility settings, we're ready to move on and add a reference from our **VideoUI** project to the **VideoObjects** server.

For a client program to use business objects from an ActiveX server using early-binding, we need to add a reference to the server within the client project. By adding this reference, we're telling the client project to load the server's public interface information from the server's type library.

A type library is a file that contains the definitions for all the public classes (and their public properties and methods) in an ActiveX server. ActiveX EXE and DLL files created by Visual Basic contain this information right inside the EXE or DLL file, but it's still fully accessible to programs that want to communicate with it via COM.

To add a reference to the **VideoObjects** project, select the **VideoUI** project in the Project window and choose the Project-References... menu option:

Find the **VideoObjects** item in the list and check the box to add a reference to it within the project.

Once we've compiled the **VideoObjects** DLL, there will be two **VideoObjects** entries in the list. Make sure the Location shown near the bottom of the window is the **.VBP** file rather than the **.DLL** file.

*If we select the **.dll** file, Visual Basic won't use the project contained in the Visual Basic environment - and so we won't be unable to step through the code when we're debugging.*

VideoMain: MDI form

Most users are very familiar with MDI (multiple document interface) style applications due to the popularity of office suites - almost all of which employ this design. We'll build this interface using an MDI design as well, since it works well to illustrate a number of important concepts about an application built with business objects.

The program will have a main form, **VideoMain**, which is the MDI parent. All the other forms in the application will be either child windows within this form or modal dialog windows to solicit user input. We'll use menus from this main window to give the user access to all the functionality that we'll implement.

To get started, let's add the main form to the project. Choose Project-Add MDI Form. The Add MDI Form dialog should appear. Just click Open to add a regular MDI form to the project:

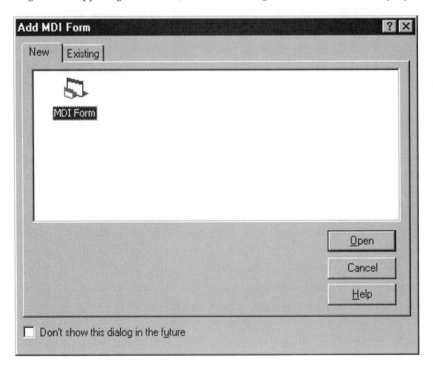

In the form's Properties window, set the **Name** property to **VideoMain**.

Now let's add the menus for the user. We'll put code behind all the menu options through the rest of the chapter, but it's nice to get them set up now so we don't have to worry about it as we go.

Choose the Tools-Menu Editor menu option to bring up the Menu Editor dialog. We won't walk through the details of adding each menu option. As far as the top-level menus go, just set up File (`mnuFile`) and Window (`mnuWindow`). Make the Window menu option a WindowList by checking the option in the dialog.

Under the File menu, set up the following options:

Menu	Sub-menu	Name
Customers		`mnuFileCust`
	Search	`mnuFileCustSearch`
	-	`mnuFileCustLine1`
	New customer	`mnuFileCustNew`
Videos		`mnuFileVideo`
	Search	`mnuFileVideoSearch`
	-	`mnuFileVideoLine1`
	New video	`mnuFileVideoNew`
-		`mnuFileLine1`
New invoice		`mnuFileInvoiceNew`
Check in tape		`mnuFileCheckIn`
-		`mnuFileLine2`
Exit		`mnuFileExit`

Click OK to save the menus.

It would be good to save the project at this point as well. To keep things straight, always save each Visual Basic project in its own directory. This avoids confusion as to which files belong to which projects. When dealing with business object-based applications, it's even more important to keep client applications, such as **VideoUI***, separate from the project containing the business objects - since various other client applications may exist beyond the Visual Basic forms application.*

The only menu item that we can really implement at this point is the code for File-Exit. The rest of the options will require us to design some forms and tap into the business objects. The code behind File-Exit is very simple:

```
Private Sub mnuFileExit_Click()
    Unload Me
End Sub
```

Since **VideoMain** is the parent form, and therefore the first form that we want to get running, we'll set it to be the Startup Object for our UI project. Select the Project-Properties menu option for the UI project, and set the Startup Object to **VideoMain**.

Edit Screens

Our application will need to provide screens so that the user can add and edit the main objects we developed in Chapters 5 and 6. The objects that our users will need to edit are:

- ❏   `Customer`
- ❏   `Video`
- ❏   `Tape`

All of these edit screens will be very similar. However, each one illustrates some differences. `Customer` is a simple business object, while `Video` is a parent of the `Tape` objects. As a result, there are subtle differences involved in developing a form for each type of object.

Creating an Edit Form Template

Just like the business objects themselves, there's a set of code that is essentially common to all the forms that work with our business objects. Rather than starting from scratch with each form we need to create, let's put together that common code - just as we did with the common business object code at the beginning of Chapter 5.

Business Object Support

Compared to the amount of code in the business object, a Visual Basic form will be pretty simple. In fact, that's the whole idea: since the program code itself should be mostly contained within the business objects, the forms should be pretty lightweight.

As a simple template, our form will be pretty bare. We'll build our template using the `Form1` that should already be part of our `VideoUI` project. All it really needs to have are the three buttons, OK, Cancel and Apply. Any data entry and display fields will need to be added based on the properties of each specific business object:

We do need to set some properties to make everything work the way we'd like. Set the Form's **Name** property to `BusForm` to indicate it is for use with a business object.

Name the three buttons `cmdOK`, `cmdCancel`, and `cmdApply`, respectively. Of course, we'll also want to set their captions as shown in the figure. We can leave all their other properties alone: we'll control anything we need to through code.

If you have other application requirements for your forms, you may want to add them to your template as well. For instance, if all your forms have a similar color scheme or graphic image, you can set those properties at this point.

Declarations

Now let's get down to the form's code. We need to declare a business object variable to use within the form. Throughout this code, we'll be using the **Business** class that we'd get by adding a class based on the **Business** template we created in the last chapter.

```
Option Explicit

Private flgLoading As Boolean

Private WithEvents objBusiness As Business
```

The **Business** variable is declared using the **WithEvents** keyword, because we know that our business object will raise at least the **Valid** event that we created. We'll get to the code for that event shortly.

We also declare a **Boolean** variable, **flgLoading**. We'll use this to suppress any activities that we don't want to happen while the object's values are loaded into the form's controls. By setting **flgLoading** to **True** as the form is being loaded, we can put code a check in each routine to avoid any processing that isn't appropriate during the load process. This technique will become very familiar as we go through the template.

Component Method

The form needs a business object to work with. There are two approaches that we can take to this:

1   The form can create the object itself
2   The form can get the object passed to it from some other code

Which approach should we choose?

Having each form create its business object directly seems like a very elegant solution. It means that the code to display the form doesn't need to worry about the object: it can just load and display the form. The problem with this approach is that we have no direct way for our form to edit an existing object that was created from some other source.

Following the second approach, we could write code outside the form to create both the business object and the form. Then we could have that code provide the form with a reference to the business object. Since our form is getting the object passed to it from outside code, it doesn't care if the object is brand new or if it already existed. This provides us with much more flexibility and control.

In this chapter, we'll take this second approach by implementing code behind the MDI form's menu items to create the appropriate business object, load the form, and connect the two together. Our individual forms won't have any code to create objects; instead, they'll rely on our MDI form's code to pass a reference to the object.

This implies that we need to provide a way for the code in the MDI form to pass an object reference to each of our forms. To facilitate this, we'll add a **Component** method to each form:

```
Option Explicit

Private flgLoading As Boolean

Private WithEvents objBusiness As Business

Public Sub Component(BusinessObject As Business)
   Set objBusiness = BusinessObject
End Sub
```

The method is quite simple: all we want to do is receive and store a reference to the business object. Once we've got that reference in **objBusiness**, we'll be able to use the object throughout the rest of the form's code.

Putting the Object's Values on the Form

The first thing we'll probably do with any business object is display the object's property values in controls that are on the form. The best place to do this is in the **Form_Load** routine, since this event fires when the form is loaded but *before* it is actually visible to the user. This means that the values will be in the controls by the time the user sees the form, so there won't be any flickering in the display as the values are copied.

The code we're adding will copy values from the object into the form, and each control's **Change** event will fire as we load it with a value. As we'll see shortly, the **Change** event is the perfect place to put code to copy the control's value into the business object.

The problem, here, is that we're pulling the values directly from the object and into each control. It makes no sense for the control's **Change** event to turn around and copy each value back into the business object. This can become a performance problem. Rather than simply displaying the values in the form, we're also copying the value back into the object - invoking any business rules or other business processing contained within the object.

When we set up the declarations section of our form, we declared a variable named **flgLoading**. If we have our **Form_Load** set **flgLoading** to **True**, then we can add a line at the top of each **Change** routine to exit that routine before the value is copied back into the business object. This way, we won't waste the effort of copying the value out of the business object just to copy it back in:

```
Private Sub Form_Load()
   flgLoading = True
   With objBusiness
      ' load object values into form controls
      'txtText = .Property
      .BeginEdit
   End With
   flgLoading = False
End Sub
```

Notice we make a call to the object's **BeginEdit** method. Since the focus of this form is to allow the user to edit the object's data, we might as well start off assuming that we'll be doing some edits by calling this method right away.

OK, Cancel and Apply Buttons

We need to add code behind the OK, Cancel and Apply buttons to call the appropriate methods on the business object. The OK button needs to apply any changes and then get rid of the form:

```
Private Sub cmdOK_Click()
   objBusiness.ApplyEdit
   Unload Me
End Sub
```

The Cancel button also gets rid of the form, but first it needs to tell the business object to cancel any edits that have been done - by calling the **CancelEdit** method:

```
Private Sub cmdCancel_Click()
   objBusiness.CancelEdit
   Unload Me
End Sub
```

Finally, the Apply button just needs to tell the business object to apply any changes to date. This is as simple as calling the **ApplyEdit** method on the business object. Of course, the **ApplyEdit** method also ends the editing session, and a typical Apply button leaves the user ready to continue editing - so we need to also call the **BeginEdit** method to resume the editing session again:

```
Private Sub cmdApply_Click()
   objBusiness.ApplyEdit
   objBusiness.BeginEdit
End Sub
```

Ideally, the OK and Apply buttons would only be enabled if the object could be saved. We've already implemented an **IsValid** property and a **Valid** event on our business objects, so all we actually need to do is tap into them from our form.

Since there are a couple of places in the form where we'll need to enable or disable these buttons, the easiest thing to do is create a local subprocedure to contain this code. Let's call it **EnableOK**:

```
Private Sub EnableOK(flgValid As Boolean)
   cmdOK.Enabled = flgValid
   cmdApply.Enabled = flgValid
End Sub
```

Now all we need to do is call this routine and send it either a **True** or a **False** to indicate whether the OK and Apply buttons should be enabled or disabled.

In the **Form_Load** event, we created the business object. This is also an excellent place to find out if that business object is valid to start with. Many objects have required fields that will start out at zero length, so they aren't initially valid. The only way to know for sure is to check the object's **IsValid** property:

```
Private Sub Form_Load()
   flgLoading = True
   With objBusiness

      EnableOK .IsValid

      ' load object values into form controls
      'txtText = .Property
      .BeginEdit
   End With
   flgLoading = False
End Sub
```

From this point forward, the business object will raise the **Valid** event any time the object switches from being valid to invalid or vice versa. We therefore need to add some code behind this event to call **EnableOK**. This code is quite simple, since the **Valid** event supplies us with a **Boolean** parameter that indicates whether the object is valid or not - and we just need to pass that along to our local routine:

```
Private Sub objBusiness_Valid(IsValid As Boolean)
   EnableOK IsValid
End Sub
```

Data Entry Fields

Since this is a generic template form, so we don't have any data entry fields. Still, it can't hurt to throw in a quick comment to remind ourselves what the code would look like to handle these fields.

At the very least, we want to use the **Change** event of our control to update the business object with the current data in the entry field. This allows the business object to continually be aware of whether that particular property contains a valid entry - so that the **Valid** event can be raised as needed:

```
'Private Sub Text1_Change()
'   If flgLoading Then Exit Sub
'
'   objBusiness.Text1 = Text1.Text
'End Sub
```

Here, again, is the **flgLoading** variable. Notice how we check the value at the top of the routine, and just exit immediately if it's **True**. This way, the **Form_Load** routine can copy the object's values into the form's controls without invoking the code that copies the form's values back into the business object.

It's also not a bad idea to refresh the form's display, based on the business object's data, in each control's **LostFocus** event. Refreshing the display in the **Change** event is not very practical, since it can wreak havoc with the user's cursor position; but we may still want to keep the display in sync with the object:

```
'Private Sub Text1_LostFocus()
'   Text1.Text = objBusiness.Text1
'End Sub
```

A good example of where this is useful is some field where a business rule dictates that the characters should all be uppercase. The business object would contain code to uppercase the data as it was supplied. Unless the form refreshes the display using the business object's copy of the data, the user may be unaware that their entry was uppercased.

Saving the Form Template

At this point, our form is all set and ready to go. To make it into a template, we need to save the form into the **Template\Forms** directory, under the directory where Visual Basic is installed.

Right-click on **BusForm** in the Project window, and choose the Save BusForm As menu option. Use the Save File As dialog to save the form into the **Template\Forms** directory wherever Visual Basic itself was installed on the system.

Once our new template form has been saved, make sure to remove it from the current project by right-clicking on **BusForm** in the Project window and choosing Remove BusForm.frm.

We can test the template by choosing the Project-Add Form menu option. The **BusForm** template should be an option in the Add Form dialog that appears:

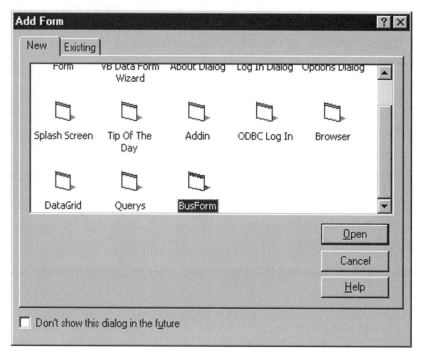

Choose BusForm and click Open to add a new form to our **VideoUI** project - with the buttons and all the code we just added.

CustomerEdit: Simple Editing

Creating the screen to edit the **Customer** object is a good place to begin, since the **Customer** object is pretty basic - being neither a parent nor a child object.

Since this is the first form we've looked at which will communicate with a business object, we'll study it in some detail. For the rest of the forms in the chapter, however, we'll skip over this detail and focus only on the differences.

Since our **BusForm** form template contains the basic code to deal with business objects, we'll use it now to simplify the process of building our **CustomerEdit** form.

Setting up the CustomerEdit Form

In the **VideoProj** project group in Visual Basic, add a form using the BusForm template that we just created.

Set this new form's **Name** property to **CustomerEdit** and the **MDIChild** property to **True**.

Now add the following controls, as shown in the diagram:

Control	Caption	Name
Label	Name	
TextBox		**txtName**
Label	Address	
TextBox		**txtAddr1**
TextBox		**txtAddr2**

Table continued on following page

Control	Caption	Name
TextBox		**txtCity**
TextBox		**txtState**
TextBox		**txtZipCode**
Label	Phone	
TextBox		**txtPhone**

Customizing the Template Code

The template code handles most of the basic operations we'll need to perform on an object, such as loading its data, and the OK, Cancel, and Apply buttons. All we really need to do is change the generic **objBusiness** reference to something more meaningful - such as **objCustomer**, and change the **Business** reference to **Customer**. The easiest way to do this is to use a couple of quick global replace operations using the Edit-Replace menu option.

The following code indicates the lines that are changed by two such global replacements:

```
Option Explicit

Private flgLoading As Boolean

Private WithEvents objCustomer As Customer


Public Sub Component(CustomerObject As Customer)
   Set objCustomer = CustomerObject
End Sub

Private Sub Form_Load()
   flgLoading = True
   With objCustomer

      EnableOK .IsValid
      ' load object values into form controls
      'txtText = .Property
      .BeginEdit
   End With
   flgLoading = False
End Sub

Private Sub cmdOK_Click()
   objCustomer.ApplyEdit

   Unload Me
End Sub

Private Sub cmdCancel_Click()
   objCustomer.CancelEdit

   Unload Me
```

```
      Unload Me
  End Sub

  Private Sub cmdApply_Click()
     objCustomer.ApplyEdit
     objCustomer.BeginEdit
  End Sub

  Private Sub EnableOK(flgValid As Boolean)
    cmdOK.Enabled = flgValid
    cmdApply.Enabled = flgValid
  End Sub

  Private Sub objCustomer_Valid(IsValid As Boolean)
    EnableOK IsValid
  End Sub

  'Private Sub Text1_Change()
  '  If flgLoading Then Exit Sub
  '
  '  objCustomer.Text1 = Text1.Text
  'End Sub

  'Private Sub Text1_LostFocus()
  '  Text1.Text = objCustomer.Text1
  'End Sub
```

The only other thing we need to do is extend the **Form_Load** routine that came with the template. It would be nice if we could set the form's caption based on the business object. If the object is new, then the caption is set to a generic value; otherwise, the customer's name is placed in the caption. We also need some extra code added to copy the object's properties to the appropriate fields on the form:

```
  Private Sub Form_Load()
    flgLoading = True
    With objCustomer
      EnableOK .IsValid

      If .IsNew Then
        Caption = "Customer [(new)]"
      Else
        Caption = "Customer [" & .Name & "]"
      End If

      txtName = .Name
      txtAddr1 = .Address1
      txtAddr2 = .Address2
      txtCity = .City
      txtState = .State
      txtZipCode = .ZipCode
      txtPhone = .Phone

      .BeginEdit
    End With
```

```
      flgLoading = False
   End Sub
```

Adding Code Behind Controls

With the basics of our form all set, we can move on and put code behind each of our controls.

Name TextBox

We're going to put a fair amount of code behind the **TextBox** controls to illustrate how we can create a responsive interface. You'll then be free to choose to implement a simpler or a more complex interface, simply by eliminating code or extending some of these concepts.

In order to provide the user with instant feedback as they press each key, we'll put some code behind the **txtName_Change** event:

```
Private Sub txtName_Change()
   Dim intPos As Integer

   If flgLoading Then Exit Sub
   On Error Resume Next
   objCustomer.Name = txtName
   If Err Then
      Beep
      intPos = txtName.SelStart
      txtName = objCustomer.Name
      txtName.SelStart = intPos - 1
   End If
End Sub
```

In general, this routine copies the value of the control into the business object, allowing the business object to validate the entry with each change. In Chapter 5, we made our business objects either raise an error or raise the **Valid** event when an invalid entry is made. For instance, if the field has a length limit, and the new value exceeds that limit, then our business object raises an error back to the form.

The first activity in this routine is to check the **flgLoading** variable:

```
   If flgLoading Then Exit Sub
```

When the form is loading, and all the object's values are being copied into each control for display, we don't want to be copying the value right back into the object. As we discussed earlier, our solution is to set a flag, **flgLoading**, to be **True** at the start of our **Form_Load**, and then **False** at the end. This way, we can check **flgLoading** to find out if we're currently loading values in during the **Form_Load** - or if we've actually gone past that point. If **flgLoading** is **True** then we know that values are still being loaded into the form.

Given that we're not loading values into the form, the next couple of lines enable error trapping in the routine, and copy the control's current value into the business object:

```
   On Error Resume Next
   objCustomer.Name = txtName
```

By using the **On Error Resume Next** statement, here, we can simply check the **Err** value right after setting the value in the object. If the object raises an error, **Err** will contain some non-zero value and we can handle the error. In this case, we know that the only error that could occur is that the length of the **Name** field is too long for the object:

```
If Err Then
  Beep
  intPos = txtName.SelStart
  txtName = objCustomer.Name
  txtName.SelStart = intPos - 1
End If
```

If the value is too long, we just beep the workstation's speaker and restore the control's value to the value contained in the object. We use the **intPos** variable to keep the cursor's position within the text in the same location that it was before the user pressed the last key.

Although it isn't required in the **txtName** control, it's always wise to use the **LostFocus** event to copy the business object's value into the control:

```
Private Sub txtName_LostFocus()
  txtName = objCustomer.Name
End Sub
```

The reason for this will become more apparent with some of the other controls we'll look at in this section. It's a good idea to always include this code in the **LostFocus** event to be consistent across all controls. If, at a later stage, some processing is added to the **Name** property of the **Customer** object, the form will already have the code in this event to properly present the user with the results of the processing. For example, perhaps we later decide to add code to capitalize the first letter of each word. This code would copy the changed value from the business object to the form as the user leaves the field.

Address, City and Phone TextBoxes

The two **Address** Textbox controls, the **City** Textbox control, and the **Phone** TextBox control, all work exactly like the **Name** TextBox we just looked at. I'll include the code here, but we won't go through it in detail as it is, essentially, the same code all over again:

```
Private Sub txtAddr1_Change()
  Dim intPos As Integer

  If flgLoading Then Exit Sub
  On Error Resume Next
  objCustomer.Address1 = txtAddr1
  If Err Then
    Beep
    intPos = txtAddr1.SelStart
    txtAddr1 = objCustomer.Address1
    txtAddr1.SelStart = intPos - 1
  End If
End Sub

Private Sub txtAddr1_LostFocus()
  txtAddr1 = objCustomer.Address1
End Sub
```

```
      Private Sub txtAddr2_Change()
        Dim intPos As Integer

        If flgLoading Then Exit Sub
        On Error Resume Next
        objCustomer.Address2 = txtAddr2
        If Err Then
          Beep
          intPos = txtAddr2.SelStart
          txtAddr2 = objCustomer.Address2
          txtAddr2.SelStart = intPos - 1
        End If
      End Sub

      Private Sub txtAddr2_LostFocus()
        txtAddr2 = objCustomer.Address2
      End Sub

      Private Sub txtCity_Change()
        Dim intPos As Integer

        If flgLoading Then Exit Sub
        On Error Resume Next
        objCustomer.City = txtCity
        If Err Then
          Beep
          intPos = txtCity.SelStart
          txtCity = objCustomer.City
          txtCity.SelStart = intPos - 1
        End If
      End Sub

      Private Sub txtCity_LostFocus()
        txtCity = objCustomer.City
      End Sub

      Private Sub txtPhone_Change()
        Dim intPos As Integer

        If flgLoading Then Exit Sub
        On Error Resume Next
        objCustomer.Phone = txtPhone
        If Err Then
          Beep
          intPos = txtPhone.SelStart
          txtPhone = objCustomer.Phone
          txtPhone.SelStart = intPos - 1
        End If
      End Sub

      Private Sub txtPhone_LostFocus()
        txtPhone = objCustomer.Phone
      End Sub
```

State and ZipCode TextBox Controls

Not surprisingly, the code for the **State** and **ZipCode** TextBox controls is no different from what we've seen so far:

```
     Private Sub txtState_Change()
       Dim intPos As Integer

       If flgLoading Then Exit Sub
       On Error Resume Next
       objCustomer.State = txtState
       If Err Then
         Beep
         intPos = txtState.SelStart
         txtState = objCustomer.State
         txtState.SelStart = intPos - 1
       End If
     End Sub

     Private Sub txtState_LostFocus()
       txtState = objCustomer.State
     End Sub

     Private Sub txtZipCode_Change()
       Dim intPos As Integer

       If flgLoading Then Exit Sub
       On Error Resume Next
       objCustomer.ZipCode = txtZipCode
       If Err Then
         Beep
         intPos = txtZipCode.SelStart
         txtZipCode = objCustomer.ZipCode
         txtZipCode.SelStart = intPos - 1
       End If
     End Sub

     Private Sub txtZipCode_LostFocus()
       txtZipCode = objCustomer.ZipCode
     End Sub
```

You may remember that, in Chapter 5, we added code in the **Customer** business object to make sure that the **State** value was uppercased. This is a good illustration of why we have the code in the **LostFocus** event. Suppose we enter a value into the form as shown in this diagram:

305

Notice that the value entered by the user is in lowercase. Now, when the user moves to another field, the **LostFocus** event will fire, copying the object's data back into the form's TextBox:

Similarly, the **ZipCode** field is reformatted by the **Customer** object's code, and the result is copied into the control within the **LostFocus** event.

Adding Code to VideoMain

For now, we'll just look at the code for the File-Customers-New Customer menu option.

> *The Search menu option will invoke a different form, which will use our* **Customers** *collection object. We'll deal with that later.*

Here's the code for the File-Customers-New Customer menu option:

```
Private Sub mnuFileCustNew_Click()
  Dim objCustomer As Customer
  Dim frmCustomer As CustomerEdit

  Set objCustomer = New Customer
  Set frmCustomer = New CustomerEdit

  frmCustomer.Component objCustomer
  frmCustomer.Show
End Sub
```

This code is wonderfully simple. We just declare two variables: one for the form, and the other for the **Customer** object. Then we simply create instances of the form and object, using the **New** keyword:

```
Set objCustomer = New Customer
Set frmCustomer = New CustomerEdit
```

All that remains is for us to use the form's **Component** method to provide the form with a reference to the new object, and then to show the form to the user:

```
frmCustomer.Component objCustomer
frmCustomer.Show
```

If we look back at the **Component** method in the form, it just stores the object reference in a form-level variable for later use. The **Show** method causes the **Form_Load** event routine to be run, and the code we put in that **Form_Load** routine copies the object's data into the form's controls before the user gets to see the form itself.

VideoEdit: Editing a Parent Object

The **Video** object is more complex than the **Customer** object in a couple different ways. First, it's a parent object, having **Tape** objects as children. Second, it contains two **TextList** objects that are available through the **Categories** and **Ratings** properties.

Accordingly, the **VideoEdit** form will also need to be a bit more complex. It will need to provide an interface to list, add, edit and remove the **Tape** objects. Additionally, it will have a couple of ComboBox controls so that the user can choose a category and a rating from the list of valid options provided by the **Video** object.

Setting up the VideoEdit Form

The process of adding any edit form is virtually identical to what we've seen for the **Customer** form. We won't go through an explanation of the code in detail, since it's now well within our grasp to set up the basic form and functionality.

Add a form to the **VideoUI** project using the BusForm template. Set the **Name** property to **VideoEdit** and the **MDIChild** property to **True**. Use Edit-Replace to replace **objBusiness** with **objVideo** and to replace **Business** with **Video**.

Now add controls as shown in the following figure.

This form uses the `ListView` *control, which is not available on the ToolBox by default. To add it to your toolbox, right-click on the ToolBox and choose the* Components *option. Then find and include the Microsoft Windows Common Controls option from the list.*

Control	Caption	Name
Label	Title	
TextBox		`txtTitle`
Label	Release date	
TextBox		`txtRelease`
Label	Studio	
TextBox		`txtStudio`
Label	Category	
ComboBox		`cmbCategory`
Label	Rating	
ComboBox		`cmbRating`
Frame	Tapes	
ListView		`lvwTapes`
CommandButton		`cmdAdd`
CommandButton		`cmdEdit`
CommandButton		`cmdRemove`

The ListView Control

We need to set up the ListView control's properties.

If there is one control that causes Visual Basic to crash frequently, it's the ListView control. It is a good idea to always save immediately before and after doing anything with this control, to prevent a lot of frustration over lost work.

Open up the `VideoEdit` form. Right-click on the `lvwTapes` control, and choose the Properties menu option. On the General tab, we need to change the `View` property to 3-lvwReport:

Then use the Column Headers tab to add the columns titles TapeID, Purchased, and Rented.

Updating the Template Code

The only routine that needs to be changed from the template code, at this point, is the **Form_Load** routine. We'll add some code to display the title of the video in the form's caption, and we'll load the video object's properties to the appropriate fields on the form:

```
Private Sub Form_Load()
   flgLoading = True
   With objVideo
      EnableOK .IsValid

      If .IsNew Then
        Caption = "Video [(new)]"
      Else
        Caption = "Video [" & .Title & "]"
      End If
      txtTitle = .Title
      txtRelease = .ReleaseDate
      txtStudio = .Studio

      .BeginEdit
   End With
   flgLoading = False
End Sub
```

TextBox Controls

The **Title** and **Studio** fields will have code that's very similar to the code for the TextBox controls in the **CustomerEdit** form. The logic of this code should therefore be familiar:

```
Private Sub txtTitle_Change()
  Dim intPos As Integer

  If flgLoading Then Exit Sub
  On Error Resume Next
  objVideo.Title = txtTitle
  If Err Then
    Beep
    intPos = txtTitle.SelStart
    txtTitle = objVideo.Title
    txtTitle.SelStart = intPos - 1
  End If
End Sub

Private Sub txtTitle_LostFocus()
  txtTitle = objVideo.Title
End Sub

Private Sub txtStudio_Change()
  Dim intPos As Integer

  If flgLoading Then Exit Sub
  On Error Resume Next
  objVideo.Studio = txtStudio
  If Err Then
    Beep
    intPos = txtStudio.SelStart
    txtStudio = objVideo.Studio
    txtStudio.SelStart = intPos - 1
  End If
End Sub

Private Sub txtStudio_LostFocus()
  txtStudio = objVideo.Studio
End Sub
```

TextBox Control with a Date Value

At first glance, the **txtRelease** control would appear to be just another text box. It is, however, quite different: the underlying property in the **Video** object is a date, and our date properties behave a bit differently than simple text fields.

In particular, the user can enter virtually anything into the field and the business object won't raise an error. Instead, the business object validates the entry each time to see if it is a valid date. As we coded it in Chapter 5, we used the **IsDate()** method to determine if the value could be converted to a date or not.

The business object raises the **Valid** event to tell the form whether all the values in the object are okay. The template code for this form handles the **Valid** event by enabling or disabling the OK and Apply buttons, so the user can't try to accept the form if the **Video** object isn't valid.

This doesn't leave a lot for us to do behind the control itself. We know that the **Video** object won't raise an error on this property, so all we really need to do is copy the current value into the object on each **Change** event:

```
Private Sub txtRelease_Change()
```

```
    If flgLoading Then Exit Sub
    objVideo.ReleaseDate = txtRelease
End Sub
```

Of course, the **Video** object converts the value into a **Variant** with a **Date** data type, so in our **LostFocus** event we need to copy that value out of the object and into the control:

```
Private Sub txtRelease_LostFocus()
   txtRelease = objVideo.ReleaseDate
End Sub
```

*By default, Visual Basic displays values of type **Date** using the system's predefined 'Short Date' setting. Typically, this is good, because it provides a localized display for the date, based on the user's preferences.*

*If our application has different needs for date displays then this would be an appropriate place to use the **Format$()** method to convert the date into the format we require.*

Categories and Ratings ComboBox Controls

As we've discussed, the **Video** business object implements a couple of list-based properties: **Categories** and **Ratings**. These properties both require that the UI provide a valid entry; that is, one contained within the **Categories** or **Ratings** lists respectively.

To make it easy for the UI developer to implement a robust interface, we implemented the **Categories** and **Ratings** properties so that the UI can get access to these lists of valid options. These lists are stored in objects of type **TextList**, which provides a read-only list of the values, and their keys, for use by the UI developer.

Loading the ComboBox Values

The first thing we need to do is load the two ComboBox controls with the values from the TextList objects. Once this is done, things get easy, because the user can only select options from the list - so we don't have to worry about them choosing a value that the business object will reject.

> This does mean that the two ComboBox controls must have their **Style** property set to **2-Dropdown List**.

To minimize the amount of code in the form, it's a good idea to implement a **LoadCombo** method with the code we need to copy the contents of a **TextList** object into a **ComboBox** control:

```
Private Sub LoadCombo(Combo As ComboBox, List As TextList)
   Dim vntItem As Variant

   With Combo
     .Clear
     For Each vntItem In List
       .AddItem vntItem
     Next
     If .ListCount > 0 Then .ListIndex = 0
```

311

```
    End With
  End Sub
```

This routine clears the control's contents, then uses a **For Each** to loop through all the items in the **TextList** object, adding each one to the control with the **AddItem** method. Once the control is loaded, and if it contains any elements, we set the **ListIndex** to **0** so that the user sees the first element in the list right away.

> *This routine is generally useful in many applications. It may be a good idea to put it into a code module so you can be easily reuse it. Better still, you could include it as a method of a custom **ComboBox** control. For more information about creating such controls, see the Wrox Press book* Instant Visual Basic 5 ActiveX Control Creation *(ISBN 1-861000-23-5).*

Now we just need to add some code in the **Form_Load** routine to load the two controls (I'll explain why they're commented out straight after the code):

```
Private Sub Form_Load()
  flgLoading = True
  With objVideo
    EnableOK .IsValid
    If .IsNew Then
      Caption = "Video [(new)]"
    Else
      Caption = "Video [" & .Title & "]"
    End If
    txtTitle = .Title
    txtRelease = .ReleaseDate
    txtStudio = .Studio

    ' LoadCombo cmbCategory, .Categories
    ' LoadCombo cmbRating, .Ratings

    .BeginEdit
  End With
  LoadTapes
  flgLoading = False
End Sub
```

These lines just use the **LoadCombo** routine to copy the values from the **Video** object into the form's controls.

> *We'll comment these lines out, for now, because we haven't implemented the persistence code in Chapter 8. Only when the persistence code is in place will **objVideo.Categories** and **objVideo.Ratings** have been initialized from the database.*

If this is an existing object, the **Category** and **Rating** properties will have specific values. Our **LoadCombo** routine defaults the values to the first item in each list, but that won't be valid if the business object already has a value. As with the other controls on the form, we need to add code to set the ComboBox controls to the current value from the business object. Add these lines to the **Form_Load** event:

```
    ' LoadCombo cmbCategory, .Categories
```

```
'    cmbCategory.Text = .Category
'    LoadCombo cmbRating, .Ratings
'    cmbRating.Text = .Rating
```

Updating the Business Object

Since the list that the user can choose from comes directly from the business object, we don't need to worry about screening the values or having the **Video** object reject the value due to a business rule. This makes the code behind the controls very simple.

With the ComboBox Style property set to 2-Dropdown List, the **Change** event never fires. Instead, the **Click** event fires any time the value in the control is changed; so we'll just put the code behind the **Click** event instead:

```
Private Sub cmbCategory_Click()
  If flgLoading Then Exit Sub
  objVideo.Category = cmbCategory.Text
End Sub

Private Sub cmbRating_Click()
  If flgLoading Then Exit Sub
  objVideo.Rating = cmbRating.Text
End Sub
```

When we authored the **Video** business object, we wrote it to accept the text value from the list rather than the key value. This was intentional, so that the UI developer doesn't have to worry about maintaining both a list of text values and corresponding keys. This way, the UI code can just put the text values into the list and return those values to the business object - very simple.

We also don't need to worry about the **LostFocus** event, since the values are predetermined by the **TextList** object, so the **Video** object won't have altered the values in any way that would need to be refreshed on the screen.

Maintaining Child Objects

Perhaps the most interesting thing about the **Video** object is that it is the parent of zero or more **Tape** objects. We implemented this by adding a **Tapes** object, which is a customized collection object that manages the parent-child relationship between **Video** and **Tape**.

The **Video** object provides a property, **Tapes**, that can be used by the UI developer to gain access to the child objects. Through the **Tapes** property, the **Video** object provides a reference to the **Tapes** object containing its children.

Using the **Tapes** object, the UI code can display, add, or remove **Tape** objects. All of these activities are controlled by the **Tapes** object, so it shouldn't be possible for the UI code to create invalid child objects.

Displaying a List of Tapes

Earlier, we configured a **ListView** control named **lvwTapes**. Now we'll use this control to display the list of **Tape** objects owned by the **Video** object.

Let's create a routine to display the **Tape** objects' values in the ListView. There will be a number of places within the program where we'll want to refresh the list of items in the view, so it makes a lot of sense to put this code in a central routine within the form:

```
Private Sub LoadTapes()
  Dim objTape As Tape
  Dim itmList As ListItem
  Dim lngIndex As Long

  lvwTapes.ListItems.Clear
  For lngIndex = 1 To objVideo.Tapes.Count
    Set itmList = lvwTapes.ListItems.Add _
      (Key:=Format$(lngIndex) & "K")
    Set objTape = objVideo.Tapes(lngIndex)
    With itmList
      If objTape.IsNew Then
        .Text = "(new)"
      Else
        .Text = objTape.TapeID
      End If
      .SubItems(1) = objTape.DateAcquired
      .SubItems(2) = IIf(objTape.CheckedOut, "Yes", "No")
    End With
  Next
End Sub
```

The first thing we do here is clear the contents of the ListView:

```
lvwTapes.ListItems.Clear
```

Since we'll be calling this routine repeatedly within the form's code, we need to make sure that we're starting with a blank slate each time.

Then we loop through each item in the **Tapes** collection using a **For Next** loop:

```
For lngIndex = 1 To objVideo.Tapes.Count
```

We want to store the index value for each **Tape** object in the ListView control's **Key** value so that we can use it later to easily get at the specific element in the list. If we used a **For Each**, then there would be no way to access each element's index value, so we're reduced to using this slower approach.

In order to display each line in a ListView control, we need to create **ListItem** objects for each line. This is done through the **Add** method of the **ListItems** object owned by the **ListView** control:

```
Set itmList = lvwTapes.ListItems.Add _
    (Key:=Format$(lngIndex) & "K")
```

The **Add** method returns a reference to the new **ListItem** object. It also accepts various parameters; in our case, we're setting the object's **Key** value. The key value we're providing is the index of the item from the **Tapes** collection, in a string format, with the letter 'K' appended to the end.

> *Even if we convert a numeric value to a string when setting a* **ListItem** *object's* **Key** *value, it will convert it back to a number, making it difficult to deal with later. To prevent this conversion, we can stick a letter on the end of the numeric value so that the overall value appears to be alphanumeric. Later on, we'll use the* **Val()** *command to easily pull the numeric value back out of the key when needed, since* **Val()** *converts all numbers until it hits the first non-numeric character.*

Now that we have a **ListItem** object ready to be loaded with values for display, we need to get the **Tape** object so that we have the actual values. The easiest way to do this is to use a local variable to store the reference to the **Tape** object:

```
Set objTape = objVideo.Tapes(lngIndex)
```

Now we're ready to load the values for display:

```
With itmList
  If objTape.IsNew Then
    .Text = "(new)"
  Else
    .Text = objTape.TapeID
  End If
  .SubItems(1) = objTape.DateAcquired
  .SubItems(2) = IIf(objTape.CheckedOut, "Yes", "No")
End With
```

If the **Tape** object is new, we put (new) in the Tape ID column; otherwise, we use the object's ID value. Then we load the **DateAcquired** value into the display, and put either Yes or No in the Rented column, based on the **Tape** object's **CheckedOut** property.

That pretty much wraps up the routine. Let's go through the rest of the code and insert the calls to load the display where needed. The most obvious place is in the **Form_Load**, since that's where we copy all the other values from the **Video** object on to the form:

```
Private Sub Form_Load()
  flgLoading = True
  With objVideo
    EnableOK .IsValid
    If .IsNew Then
      Caption = "Video [(new)]"
    Else
      Caption = "Video [" & .Title & "]"
    End If
    txtTitle = .Title
    txtRelease = .ReleaseDate
```

```
      txtStudio = .Studio
      LoadCombo cmbCategory, .Categories
      cmbCategory.Text = .Category
      LoadCombo cmbRating, .Ratings
      cmbRating.Text = .Rating
      .BeginEdit
   End With
```

```
LoadTapes
```

```
   flgLoading = False
End Sub
```

As the user adds new **Tape** objects, they'll be displayed in the list with a Tape ID value of (new). When the user clicks the Apply button, these objects will be saved to the database, and they'll be assigned actual ID values. We need to refresh the display once this is complete, so the user can see the new ID values displayed - rather than (new):

```
Private Sub cmdApply_Click()
   objVideo.ApplyEdit
   objVideo.BeginEdit
```

```
LoadTapes
```

```
End Sub
```

We'll also need to call **LoadTapes** when we add, edit, or remove a tape from the list. Let's go through and look at the code to handle these functions.

Adding a Tape

The user indicates that they want to add a new tape by clicking on the Add button:

```
Private Sub cmdAdd_Click()
  Dim frmTape As TapeEdit

  Set frmTape = New TapeEdit
  frmTape.Component objVideo.Tapes.Add
  frmTape.Show vbModal
  LoadTapes
End Sub
```

The code behind this button creates a **TapeEdit** form (which we'll look at next) for the user to work with. It then creates a new **Tape** object and provides a reference to the new object for the **TapeEdit** form, using the form's **Component** method:

```
frmTape.Component objVideo.Tapes.Add
```

To create a new **Tape** object, we need to use the **Tapes** object's **Add** method. This function creates and initializes a new **Tape** object and returns a reference to that object for our use.

In Chapter 6, we implemented this process in such a way that the object wasn't actually added to the **Tapes** collection until the new **Tape** object's **ApplyEdit** method was called. This way, if the user clicks the Cancel button on the **TapeEdit** form, the blank **Tape** object won't be added to the **Tapes** collection accidentally.

The routine then shows the **TapeEdit** form:

```
frmTape.Show vbModal
```

When the user is done, having clicked either the OK or Cancel button, the **LoadTapes** routine is called to refresh the list and display the newly added **Tape** object.

Editing a Tape

Editing a **Tape** object is just as easy:

```
Private Sub cmdEdit_Click()
   Dim frmTape As TapeEdit

   Set frmTape = New TapeEdit
   frmTape.Component _
      objVideo.Tapes(Val(lvwTapes.SelectedItem.Key))
   frmTape.Show vbModal
   LoadTapes
End Sub
```

In this case, we don't need to create a new **Tape** object; instead, we use the **Key** value we stored in the ListView control to quickly retrieve the appropriate object from the **Tapes** collection:

```
frmTape.Component _
   objVideo.Tapes(Val(lvwTapes.SelectedItem.Key))
```

When we loaded the key value into the **ListItem** object, we concatenated the numeric index value with the letter 'K' to force it to be an alphanumeric value. Fortunately, the **Val()** function returns the numeric value of all the characters in a string until it finds a non-numeric character. This makes it easy to retrieve the numeric index value of the item the user selected - so we can use it to pull out a reference to the underlying **Tape** object within the collection.

Removing a Tape

Removing a tape from the list is even easier:

```
Private Sub cmdRemove_Click()
   objVideo.Tapes.Remove Val(lvwTapes.SelectedItem.Key)
   LoadTapes
End Sub
```

Again, we use the **Val()** function to retrieve the index value of the item the user selected. Using this index value, we just need to call the **Remove** method on the **Tapes** collection object, and it will remove the **Tape** object from the list. We then call **LoadTapes** so that our list is updated on the form.

The removal of an item from the list will be undone if the user then clicks the Cancel button on the **VideoEdit** screen. This is because, in Chapter 6, we built the **Tapes** object so that it didn't actually remove any objects until the **ApplyEdit** method was called. So now, when the user clicks Cancel, we'll cause the **CancelEdit** method to be called, which will restore any deleted **Tape** objects to the collection.

Adding Code to VideoMain

Back in the **VideoMain** form, the File-Videos-New Video menu option needs to contain the following code:

```
Private Sub mnuFileVideoNew_Click()
   Dim objVideo As Video
   Dim frmVideo As VideoEdit

   Set objVideo = New Video
   Set frmVideo = New VideoEdit

   frmVideo.Component objVideo
   frmVideo.Show
End Sub
```

Like the New Customer menu option, this code creates an instance of the **VideoEdit** form and a new instance of a **Video** object. It then uses the **VideoEdit** form's **Component** property to provide the form with a reference to the new object, and shows that form to the user.

TapeEdit: Editing a Child Object

In the **VideoEdit** form's code, we provided support for adding and editing **Tape** objects. This was done with a **TapeEdit** form, so we'd best build that form at this point.

The **TapeEdit** form will be child's play compared to the others we've looked at. Excuse the pun, but this works out well since it's designed to edit a child object.

Setting up the TapeEdit Form

As with the other forms, add a new form to the **VideoUI** project using the **BusForm** template. Set its **Name** property to **TapeEdit**. Since we'll be displaying this form in a modal fashion, set its **BorderStyle** to 3-Fixed Dialog. Add controls to make the form appear as shown here:

Control	Caption	Name
Label	Tape ID	
Label		**lblTapeID**
Label	Purchase date	
TextBox		**txtAcquired**
Label	Rented out	
Label		**lblRented**

Make sure to set the **BorderStyle** property to 1-Fixed single on the **lblTapeID** and **lblRented** controls to get the proper appearance.

As with the other forms, change the template code to work with the relevant business object; in this case, globally change **objBusiness** to **objTape**, and change every instance of the **Business** data type to **Tape**. Then change the **Form_Load** method as follows:

```
Private Sub Form_Load()
    flgLoading = True
    With objTape

        If .IsNew Then
            Caption = "Tape [(new)]"
        Else
            Caption = "Tape [" & .Title & "]"
            txtAcquired.Locked = True
            txtAcquired.BackColor = lblTapeID.BackColor
        End If
        lblTapeID = .TapeID
        txtAcquired = .DateAcquired
        lblRented = IIf(.CheckedOut, "Yes", "No")

        EnableOK .IsValid
        .BeginEdit
    End With
    flgLoading = False
End Sub
```

For the most part, this should look very familiar at this point - with one exception. In Chapter 6, we implemented the **Tape** object's **DateAcquired** property to be editable only when the object is new. This means that when an existing **Tape** object is brought up to be edited, this field can't be altered.

To make this visually apparent to the user, we've added some code to change the behavior of the **txtAcquired** control when the **Tape** object is not new:

```
txtAcquired.Locked = True
txtAcquired.BackColor = lblTapeID.BackColor
```

This code sets the control's **Locked** property to **True**, preventing the user from editing the field in any way. We also set the **BackColor** property to the background color of one of the label controls (typically gray), making it very apparent to the user that the field can't be edited.

This code may appear to replicate some business logic in the form. Why did we go through the work of making the property only editable when the object is new only to turn around and put similar code into the form?

We've considered this question once or twice already in earlier chapters. Ultimately, the answer is that we want to make the UI very friendly. We could just allow the business object to enforce the rule, but that would leave the user with no visual way to know that the field wasn't editable. They wouldn't know there was a problem until they tried to edit the field and got an error message.

Another alternative would be to *only* enforce the business rule in the UI, leaving the business object out of the picture. The problem with this approach is that our Visual Basic UI may not be our only user-interface using the business object. Some other UI developer might not be as thorough in implementing this rule - meaning that we could easily end up with the value being changed when it shouldn't be.

By keeping the business rule in our object, we can prevent the user from editing this field when it is inappropriate, regardless of the particular UI being used. At the same time, it makes a lot of sense for our UI to provide the user with a visual indication that the field isn't editable, thus providing a more friendly and pleasant user experience.

> **Just because a business rule is implemented in the object, that doesn't mean we shouldn't take steps to make the user's interface as rich and friendly as possible.**

TextBox Control

The **txtAcquired** control represents a date property, just like the **txtRelease** control did on the **VideoEdit** form. The code is virtually identical; only the object and control names have changed:

```
Private Sub txtAcquired_Change()
  If flgLoading Then Exit Sub
  objTape.dateacquired = txtAcquired
End Sub

Private Sub txtAcquired_LostFocus()
  txtAcquired = objTape.dateacquired
End Sub
```

List Screens

Now that we've implemented all the functionality to add customers, videos, and tapes, we need to let the user bring up existing data to be viewed or edited. In Chapter 5, we built a couple of list objects to make this as easy as possible: **Customers** and **Videos**.

The objects' **Load** methods accept search criteria as parameters. They then act as collection objects, returning **CustomerDisplay** or **VideoDisplay** objects as elements of the collection as appropriate.

CustomerSearch: Criteria Entry

Before we can display the content of the **Customers** object, we need to load it with values from the database. This is done using the object's **Load** method, which accepts search criteria as parameters: either **Name** or **Phone** or both.

Setting up the CustomerSearch Form

Add a new form to the **VideoUI** project. Don't use the business form template in this case, as the form we're building now will be much simpler than that template would create. Set the **Name** property to **CustomerSearch** and the **BorderStyle** to 3-Fixed Dialog.

Add controls to make the form appear as shown.

Control	Caption	Name
Label	Name	
TextBox		**txtName**
Label	Phone	
TextBox		**txtPhone**
CommandButton	OK	**cmdOK**
CommandButton	Cancel	**cmdCancel**

Putting Code behind the CustomerSearch Form

We want to make forms that just retrieve criteria from the user to work as much like an object as possible. This will allow us to just show the form to the user, let them enter their input, and click either OK or Cancel. Either way, the form won't unload; rather, it will just hide itself and expose some **Public** properties so that the client code can find out what the user did on the form:

```
Option Explicit

Private flgOK As Boolean

Private Sub cmdCancel_Click()
  flgOK = False
  Hide
End Sub

Private Sub cmdOK_Click()
  flgOK = True
  Hide
End Sub
```

In this case, we expose an **OK** property so that the client code can find out if the user clicked OK or Cancel:

```
Public Property Get OK() As Boolean
  OK = flgOK
End Property
```

We'll also expose **Name** and **Phone** properties to return the values that the user entered into the form's controls:

```
Public Property Get ResultName() As String
  ResultName = txtName
End Property

Public Property Get ResultPhone() As String
  ResultPhone = txtPhone
End Property
```

Adding Code to VideoMain

To see how this form is used, let's look at some of the code behind the File-Customers-Search menu option within the **VideoMain** form:

```
Private Sub mnuFileCustSearch_Click()
  Dim frmSearch As CustomerSearch
  Dim objCustomers As Customers

  Set frmSearch = New CustomerSearch
  With frmSearch
    .Show vbModal
    If .OK Then
      Set objCustomers = New Customers
      objCustomers.Load .ResultName, .ResultPhone
      ' display the Customers object in a display form
      Set objCustomers = Nothing
    End If
  End With
  Unload frmSearch
  Set frmSearch = Nothing
End Sub
```

This code creates an instance of our criteria form, **CustomerSearch**, and shows it to the user. Using the values entered by the user, we create a **Customers** object and pass those values to its **Load** method. At this point, our **Customers** object should contain a list of all the customers who match the criteria supplied by the user.

CustomerList: Search Results Display

Now that we have the user's search criteria, and we've used the **Customers** object's **Load** method to retrieve the list of matching data, we can display the information. We'll keep this as simple as possible. In some applications, we may need to build a more sophisticated form, but this will illustrate the basic principals that will be used.

Setting up the CustomerList Form

Add a new form to the **VideoUI** project. Again, don't use the business form template, as this form will be quite simple. Name the form **CustomerList** and set its **BorderStyle** to 3-Fixed Dialog.

Add controls to make the form appear as follows:

Control	Caption	Name
ListView		**lvwItems**
CommandButton	OK	**cmdOK**
CommandButton	Cancel	**cmdCancel**

Use the ListView control's properties window to change the View to 3-lvwReport, and set up two columns: Name and Phone.

Putting Code behind the CustomerList Form

In a very real sense, a form that displays a list of values so that the user can select one is basically just another way of gathering criteria - or user input. Whichever customer the user selects, in this window, that information will just be used as input to the **Load** method of a **Customer** object so that it can be edited.

Based on this view of the form, we'll treat it just like we did the **CustomerSearch** form in terms of implementation. When the user clicks OK or Cancel, the form won't **Unload**, but instead **Hide** itself - and the calling code can find out what the user chose by using Public properties on the form.

Displaying the Data

Add the following code to the **CustomerList** form:

```
Option Explicit

Private objCustomers As Customers
Private lngID As Long

Public Sub Component(objComponent As Customers)
   Dim objItem As CustomerDisplay
   Dim itmList As ListItem
   Dim lngIndex As Long

   Set objCustomers = objComponent
   For lngIndex = 1 To objCustomers.Count
     With objItem
       Set objItem = objCustomers.Item(lngIndex)
       Set itmList = _
         lvwItems.ListItems.Add(Key:= _
         Format$(objItem.CustomerID) & " K")
       With itmList
         .Text = objItem.Name
         .SubItems(1) = objItem.Phone
       End With
     End With
   Next
End Sub
```

This code implements a **Component** method to allow the client code to provide a reference to a **Customers** object. Within this method, we've put the code to copy the items from the **Customers** collection into the ListView control for display to the user.

Each item returned from the **Customers** object is a **CustomerDisplay** object, which provides **Name** and **Phone** properties.

The code to load the **ListView** control is virtually identical to the code we used to load the **Tape** objects into the **VideoEdit** form. However, with the **Tape** objects we simply used the index value of each object from the collection as the **Key** value in our **ListView** control. Here, we're going to store the **CustomerID** value as the **Key** value instead. This way, when the user selects an item from our list, we can easily retrieve the **CustomerID** value from the control and use it to load the appropriate **Customer** object.

The item's **Name** and **Phone** properties are placed in the **ListItem** object to be displayed:

```
Set itmList = _
  lvwItems.ListItems.Add(Key:= _
  Format$(objItem.CustomerID) & " K")
With itmList
  .Text = objItem.Name
  .SubItems(1) = objItem.Phone
End With
```

Code behind the Controls

The OK and Cancel buttons hide the form rather than unloading it. They also set a module-level variable, **lngID**, to hold the ID value of the object chosen by the user. The Cancel button stores a **0** to indicate no selection, while the OK button stores the index value of the item from the **Customers** collection object - by retrieving the value from the key value of the **ListView** control:

```
Private Sub cmdCancel_Click()
  lngID = 0
  Hide
End Sub

Private Sub cmdOK_Click()
  On Error Resume Next
  lngID = Val(lvwItems.SelectedItem.Key)
  Hide
End Sub
```

Public Property - the Selected Customer

This form only needs to provide the ID value for the **Customer** object that the user has selected:

```
Public Property Get CustomerID() As Long
  CustomerID = lngID
End Property
```

Since we stored the **CustomerID** property value as the key for each item in the **ListView** control, we were easily able to retrieve that value when the user clicked the OK button. That code stored the value in the module-level variable **lngID**, so all we need to do within this property is provide that value to the client code.

Adding Code to VideoMain

Now we can look at the entire code behind the File-Customers-Search menu option, back in our **VideoMain** form. We've already looked at the code to bring up the criteria form, so we can move on to add the code to bring up the **CustomerList** form:

```
Private Sub mnuFileCustSearch_Click()
  Dim frmSearch As CustomerSearch
  Dim frmList As CustomerList
  Dim objCustomers As Customers
  Dim objCustomer As Customer
```

```
      Set frmSearch = New CustomerSearch
   With frmSearch
      .Show vbModal
      If .OK Then
         Set frmList = New CustomerList

         Set objCustomers = New Customers
         objCustomers.Load .ResultName, .ResultPhone

         With frmList
            .Component objCustomers
            .Show vbModal
            If .CustomerID > 0 Then
               Set objCustomer = New Customer
               objCustomer.Load .CustomerID
               ' create and set up a CustomerEdit form
               Set objCustomer = Nothing
            End If
         End With
         Unload frmList
         Set frmList = Nothing

         Set objCustomers = Nothing
      End If
   End With
   Unload frmSearch
   Set frmSearch = Nothing
End Sub
```

This new code creates an instance of the **CustomerList** form and uses its **Component** property to provide it with a reference to the **Customers** object we'd already loaded. The code then checks the resulting **CustomerID** property on the form to see if the user selected a valid customer to be edited.

If the user selected a customer from the list, then the **CustomerID** value will be greater than zero. In this case, we create a new **Customer** object and pass its **Load** method the ID value from the **CustomerList** form:

```
         Set objCustomer = New Customer
         objCustomer.Load .CustomerID
```

All that remains now is to add some extra code to bring up the **CustomerEdit** form and give it a reference to the **Customer** object we just loaded:

```
Private Sub mnuFileCustSearch_Click()
   Dim frmSearch As CustomerSearch
   Dim frmList As CustomerList

   Dim frmCustomer As CustomerEdit

   Dim objCustomers As Customers
   Dim objCustomer As Customer

   Set frmSearch = New CustomerSearch
   With frmSearch
      .Show vbModal
      If .OK Then
         Set frmList = New CustomerList
         Set objCustomers = New Customers
```

```
      objCustomers.Load .ResultName, .ResultPhone
      With frmList
        .Component objCustomers
        .Show vbModal
        If .CustomerID > 0 Then
            Set frmCustomer = New CustomerEdit

            Set objCustomer = New Customer
            objCustomer.Load .CustomerID

            frmCustomer.Component objCustomer
            frmCustomer.Show

            Set objCustomer = Nothing
        End If
      End With
      Unload frmList
      Set frmList = Nothing
      Set objCustomers = Nothing
    End If
  End With
  Unload frmSearch
  Set frmSearch = Nothing
End Sub
```

With the completion of this code, the user can now add and edit customers at will.

*We could easily base a Delete menu option on the code for the search menu option. Instead of bringing up the **CustomerEdit** form, we'd just call the **Customer** object's **Delete** method, and away it would go.*

VideoSearch: Criteria Entry

The **VideoSearch** form should work just like the **CustomerSearch** form. We won't go through this form in any detail, as it's very straightforward.

The two TextBoxes are called **txtTitle** and **txtStudio**, respectively. Here's the code to support this form:

```
Option Explicit

Private flgOK As Boolean

Public Property Get OK() As Boolean
  OK = flgOK
End Property
```

```
    Public Property Get ResultTitle() As String
      ResultTitle = txtTitle
    End Property

    Public Property Get ResultStudio() As String
      ResultStudio = txtStudio
    End Property

    Private Sub cmdCancel_Click()
      flgOK = False
      Hide
    End Sub

    Private Sub cmdOK_Click()
      flgOK = True
      Hide
    End Sub
```

VideoList: Search Results Display

Again, the **VideoList** form is virtually identical to the **CustomerList** form. The primary difference is that the **Videos** object returns **VideoDisplay** objects for each item in the list whereas the **Customers** object returned **CustomerDisplay** objects. Beyond that, the form's code performs the same function, displaying the list to the user and providing a Public property so that the client code can retrieve the user's selection.

Setting up the VideoList Form

Create the form to appear as shown here:

The column headers for the **ListView** control should be set to Title and Release date. The code behind this form is shown here:

```
Option Explicit

Private objVideos As Videos
Private lngID As Long

Public Sub Component(objComponent As Videos)
  Dim objItem As VideoDisplay
  Dim itmList As ListItem
  Dim lngIndex As Long

  Set objVideos = objComponent
  For lngIndex = 1 To objVideos.Count
    With objItem
      Set objItem = objVideos.Item(lngIndex)
      Set itmList = _
        lvwItems.ListItems.Add(Key:= _
        Format$(objItem.VideoID) & " K")
      With itmList
        .Text = objItem.Title
        .SubItems(1) = objItem.ReleaseDate
      End With
    End With
  Next
End Sub

Public Property Get VideoID() As Long
  VideoID = lngID
End Property

Private Sub cmdCancel_Click()
  lngID = 0
  Hide
End Sub

Private Sub cmdOK_Click()
  On Error Resume Next
  lngID = Val(lvwItems.SelectedItem.Key)
  Hide
End Sub
```

Main Menu Code for Video Search

We also need to add some code to the **VideoMain** form behind the File-Video-Search menu option. This code will make use of both the **VideoSearch** and **VideoList** forms, as well as the **Videos** object:

```
Private Sub mnuFileVideoSearch_Click()
  Dim frmSearch As VideoSearch
  Dim frmList As VideoList
  Dim frmVideo As VideoEdit
  Dim objVideos As Videos
  Dim objVideo As Video

  Set frmSearch = New VideoSearch
```

```
   With frmSearch
     .Show vbModal
     If .OK Then
        Set frmList = New VideoList
        Set objVideos = New Videos
        objVideos.Load .ResultTitle, .ResultStudio
        With frmList
           .Component objVideos
           .Show vbModal
           If .VideoID > 0 Then
              Set frmVideo = New VideoEdit
              Set objVideo = New Video
              objVideo.Load .VideoID
              frmVideo.Component objVideo
              frmVideo.Show
              Set objVideo = Nothing
           End If
        End With
        Unload frmList
        Set frmList = Nothing
        Set objVideos = Nothing
     End If
   End With
   Unload frmSearch
   Set frmSearch = Nothing
End Sub
```

This code is very similar to that used for the File-Customers-Search menu option. We use the **VideoSearch** form to get the search criteria from the user, and we then provide the criteria to the **Videos** object's **Load** method. Once the **Videos** object has retrieved the data from the database, we create an instance of the **VideoList** form and use its **Component** method to give it a reference to the **Videos** object.

Transaction Support

So far, we've seen how to create forms that work with our business objects to add new objects, edit existing objects, and display lists of data. All the objects we've worked with so far represent simple business entities: a customer, a video title, a tape.

In addition to our simple business entities, we have a set of objects that support the concept of an invoice. Adding an invoice is typically considered a transaction, so the **Invoice** object represents a transaction rather than a simple business entity. We also need to support the concept of checking in a tape when the customer returns it - which also qualifies as a form of transaction.

Let's look at how we can create a UI to support these two transactions.

InvoiceEdit

While adding an **Invoice** object is considered to be a transaction, there is no difference in code from the UI developer's viewpoint. We can treat this like any other form that edits a business object. This means that the **InvoiceEdit** screen will work just like the **CustomerEdit** and **VideoEdit** forms that we implemented earlier in the chapter.

Setting up the InvoiceEdit Form

Since this form will primarily be editing a business object, use the business object form template to add a form to the **VideoUI** project. Set the **Name** property to **InvoiceEdit** and the **MDIChild** property to **True**.

Now add controls to the form as shown here:

Control	Caption	Name
Label	Invoice number	
Label		**lblInvoiceID**
Label	Customer name	
Label		**lblName**

Table continued on following page

Control	Caption	Name
Label	Customer phone	
Label		**lblPhone**
Frame	Invoice items	
ListView		**lvwItems**
CommandButton	Add	**cmdAdd**
CommandButton	Edit	**cmdEdit**
CommandButton	Remove	**cmdRemove**
CommandButton	OK	**cmdOK**
CommandButton	Cancel	**cmdCancel**
CommandButton	Apply	**cmdApply**

Set the **BorderStyle** property of the **lblInvoiceID**, **lblName** and **lblPhone** controls to 1-Fixed single.

We also need to set some of the properties of the ListView control in this form. Right-click on the control and choose Properties from the context menu. Now set the **View** property to 3-lvwReport and, under the Column Headers tab, add the column titles Type and Description.

As with the edit screens we built earlier, we need to change all instances of **objBusiness** to refer to the relevant business object. In this case, globally change **objBusiness** to **objInvoice** and change all the instances of **Business** to **Invoice** in the template code. The **Form_Load** method will also need to be modified to copy the **Invoice** object's property values into the form's controls:

```
Private Sub Form_Load()
   flgLoading = True
   With objInvoice
     EnableOK .IsValid

     If .IsNew Then
       lblInvoiceID = "(new)"
     Else
       lblInvoiceID = .InvoiceID
     End If
     lblName = .CustomerName
     lblPhone = .CustomerPhone

     .BeginEdit
   End With
   flgLoading = False
End Sub
```

Other than the line items on the invoice, there aren't any fields for the user to edit. The **Customer** object's **CreateInvoice** method not only creates the **Invoice** object, but it also provides it with the basic information that's displayed on the screen. The rest of the information is based on the **InvoiceItem** child objects that the user adds later.

Child Object Support

Like the **Video** object, the **Invoice** object is a parent to other objects. The **Invoice** object is a bit more complex, however, since the child objects might be both **InvoiceFee** and **InvoiceTape** objects. Using traditional programming techniques, we'd probably need extra code to deal with this case. Since we're using object-oriented techniques, however, we can avoid any extra work.

When we implemented these objects, we created them both to provide an **InvoiceItem** interface. This means that each of these objects has two interfaces. The **InvoiceFee** object has an **InvoiceFee** interface *and* an **InvoiceItem** interface. Likewise, the **InvoiceTape** object has both an **InvoiceTape** interface and an **InvoiceItem** interface. Since both objects have an **InvoiceItem** interface, we can create code to work with just that interface - and we won't care what particular type of object it really is. This is an application of both multiple interfaces and polymorphism, all in one shot.

Displaying the Child Objects

As with the **VideoEdit** form, we'll add a **LoadItems** routine to copy the child object's properties into the **ListView** control for display:

```
Private Sub LoadItems()
  Dim objItem As InvoiceItem
  Dim itmList As ListItem
  Dim lngIndex As Long

  lvwItems.ListItems.Clear
  For lngIndex = 1 To objInvoice.InvoiceItems.Count
    Set itmList = lvwItems.ListItems.Add _
      (Key:=Format$(lngIndex) & "K")
    Set objItem = objInvoice.InvoiceItems(lngIndex)
    With itmList
      .Text = IIf(objItem.ItemType = ITEM_FEE, _
        "Late fee", "Rental")
      .SubItems(1) = objItem.ItemDescription
      .SubItems(2) = Format$(objItem.Total, "0.00")
    End With
  Next
End Sub
```

Notice that the **objItem** variable is declared as type **InvoiceItem**. Even though the child objects will be of either the **InvoiceFee** or **InvoiceTape** types, we can treat them all as **InvoiceItem** objects because they implemented that interface. The beauty of this is that we could add more types of child business objects and we wouldn't have to change this display routine at all.

We'll need to call the **LoadItems** routine from a number of places within the form, starting with the **Form_Load** routine:

```
Private Sub Form_Load()
  flgLoading = True
  With objInvoice
    EnableOK .IsValid
    If .IsNew Then
      lblInvoiceID = "(new)"
    Else
      lblInvoiceID = .InvoiceID
    End If
    lblName = .CustomerName
    lblPhone = .CustomerPhone
    .BeginEdit
  End With
```

LoadItems

```
  flgLoading = False
End Sub
```

We'll add the call to **LoadItems** elsewhere as we get to each routine.

Adding InvoiceTape Objects

Unlike the display routine, we do need to have different support for each type of child object that we need to add to the **Invoice** object. This is because we'll need to provide an interface for the user to add the information that's customized to the child business object.

We'll keep the code behind the **Add** button as simple as possible. The only type of line item the user can add to the invoice is a tape rental. To add this line item, the only piece of information that is absolutely required is the tape's ID value. This would probably be scanned off the tape with a barcode reader, so we'll just prompt the user for this value using the **InputBox$()** command:

```
Private Sub cmdAdd_Click()
  Dim frmItem As InvoiceTapeEdit
  Dim strID As String

  strID = InputBox$("Scan the tape ID", "Tape ID")
  If Val(strID) = 0 Then Exit Sub
```

If no number is supplied, we'll just exit the subroutine. The typical reason this value would be **0** is if the user clicked the Cancel button in the input box.

Now that we've got a tape's ID value, we can create an instance of a form to edit the line item:

```
Set frmItem = New InvoiceTapeEdit
```

This form's name is **InvoiceTapeEdit**. It's another basic business object edit form, so use the **BusForm** template and add the controls as shown here:

Control	Caption	Name
Label	Title	
Label		lblTitle
Label	Price	
TextBox		txtPrice

Set the **BorderStyle** property of the **lblTitle** control to 1-Fixed single.

As with the edit screens we built earlier, we need to change the code behind it so that all instances of **objBusiness** refer to the relevant business object.

In this case, globally change **objBusiness** to **objInvoiceTape**, and change all the instances of **Business** to **InvoiceTape** in the template code. The **Form_Load** method will also need to be modified to copy the **Invoice** object's property values into the form's controls:

```
Private Sub Form_Load()
   flgLoading = True
   With objInvoiceTape
     EnableOK .IsValid

     lblTitle = .Title
     txtPrice = .Price

     .BeginEdit
   End With
   flgLoading = False
End Sub
```

Now that we've got a form to work with, we can use its **Component** method to provide it with a reference to a new **InvoiceTape** line item:

```
On Error Resume Next
   frmItem.Component objInvoice.InvoiceItems.Add(Val(strID))
```

The new object is created using the **Add** method of the **InvoiceItems** object from the **InvoiceEdit** form's **Invoice** object. We implemented this **Add** method in Chapter 6 so that it accepts a tape ID value as a parameter and builds the line item based on that ID.

The **On Error Resume Next** is important, since the **Add** method we've called might raise an error. In particular, if the ID value entered by the user is invalid, we'll get an error; equally, if the tape has already been rented out on another invoice, we'll get another error. The following code checks to see if there was an error, and responds appropriately for each error:

```
If Err Then
   If Err = vbObjectError + 1100 Then
     MsgBox "Tape is already checked out", vbExclamation
   Else
     MsgBox "Invalid tape id", vbExclamation
   End If
```

```
      Set frmItem = Nothing
      Exit Sub
   End If
```

If we didn't get an error, we show the form to the user so they can edit the line item as needed. In this case, all they can change is the price. As with the other child objects we've worked with, if they click the Cancel button then the object won't be added to the **InvoiceItems** collection:

```
   frmItem.Show vbModal
```

Finally, we just need to refresh the display of the child objects so that the new object will be shown to the user on the screen:

```
      LoadItems
   End Sub
```

Editing Line Items

As with adding items, we need to check the line item's type when editing. The only type of line item the user can edit are the **InvoiceTape** items. With the **ListView** control the user might select an **InvoiceFee** line item to edit, so we need to check for this and handle it appropriately.

The first thing we need to do is get a reference to the object corresponding to the item the user selected on the screen. We'll put the reference to the object in **objItem**, which is of type **InvoiceItem**:

```
   Private Sub cmdEdit_Click()
      Dim frmItem As InvoiceTapeEdit
      Dim objItem As InvoiceItem

      Set objItem = _
        objInvoice.InvoiceItems(Val(lvwItems.SelectedItem.Key))
```

The **InvoiceItem** interface provides an **ItemType** property that we can use to determine the type of the object the user selected. If it's of type **ITEM_TAPE**, we can use the **InvoiceTapeEdit** form to allow the user to edit the object; otherwise, we'll just display a message so the user knows they can't edit late fee line items:

```
      If objItem.ItemType = ITEM_TAPE Then
        Set frmItem = New InvoiceTapeEdit
        frmItem.Component _
          objInvoice.InvoiceItems(Val(lvwItems.SelectedItem.Key))
        frmItem.Show vbModal
        LoadItems
      Else
        MsgBox "Only tape rental items can be edited", _
          vbInformation
      End If
   End Sub
```

Removing Line Items

Both the **InvoiceTape** and **InvoiceFee** objects provide support for being deleted, so the code behind the Remove button won't have to care which type of line item the user selected. This means the code is pretty much identical to the code we used on the **VideoEdit** form:

```
Private Sub cmdRemove_Click()
   objInvoice.InvoiceItems.Remove Val(lvwItems.SelectedItem.Key)
   LoadItems
End Sub
```

Setting up the Menu Option

As with the forms we've put together earlier in the chapter, the **InvoiceEdit** form expects to be provided with an **Invoice** object through its **Component** method. In Chapter 6, we implemented the **Invoice** object as PublicNotCreatable, with the intent that the UI code would be using the **CreateInvoice** method of the **Customer** object to add any **Invoice** objects.

This makes sense, since the typical video rental transaction starts by identifying the customer and then adding the invoice. Our application should follow this model to make it as easy as possible for the user. When the user chooses the File-New invoice menu option, they should be prompted to choose a customer; then the **InvoiceEdit** form should come up.

This whole process is very similar to what happens with the File-Customers-Search menu option. We need to present the criteria screen and then the CustomerList screen. Where we displayed the **CustomerEdit** before, we'll change the code to create a new **Invoice** object and bring up the **InvoiceEdit** screen.

All of the following code is new to our **VideoMain** form, so it all needs to be entered. However, I've only highlighted those lines that are different from the code for our File-Customers-Search menu option; this way, you can see the similarity between them more easily:

```
Private Sub mnuFileInvoiceNew_Click()

   Dim frmSearch As CustomerSearch
   Dim frmList As CustomerList
   Dim objCustomers As Customers
   Dim objCustomer As Customer

   Dim objInvoice As Invoice
   Dim frmInvoice As InvoiceEdit


   Set frmSearch = New CustomerSearch
   With frmSearch
     .Show vbModal
     If .OK Then
       Set frmList = New CustomerList
       Set objCustomers = New Customers
       objCustomers.Load .ResultName, .ResultPhone
       With frmList
         .Component objCustomers
         .Show vbModal
         If .CustomerID > 0 Then
```

```
        Set frmInvoice = New InvoiceEdit

        Set objCustomer = New Customer
        objCustomer.Load .CustomerID
        Set objInvoice = objCustomer.CreateInvoice

        frmInvoice.Component objInvoice
        frmInvoice.Show
```

```
      End If
    End With
    Unload frmList
    Set frmList = Nothing
    Set objCustomers = Nothing
    End If
  End With
  Unload frmSearch
  Set frmSearch = Nothing
End Sub
```

Checking in a Tape

Our menu also provides a File-Check in tape menu option to allow the user to check in a tape that has been rented. When the customer returns a tape, the user should just have to enter the tape's ID value into the system to have it recorded as returned.

To keep this as simple as possible, we'll just use the **InputBox$()** command to prompt the user for the tape's ID value. If the user clicks the Cancel button, we'll get a value of **0**; and if we do get a **0** result, we'll just exit the subroutine:

```
Private Sub mnuFileCheckIn_Click()
  Dim strID As String
  Dim objTape As Tape

  strID = InputBox$("Scan tape ID", "Check in tape")
  If Val(strID) = 0 Then Exit Sub
```

Once we have an ID value, we can create a **Tape** object and use its **Load** method to retrieve the object's data from the database:

```
  Set objTape = New Tape
  On Error Resume Next
  objTape.Load Val(strID)
```

The **Load** method could return an error if the user has provided an ID value that is invalid. By using **On Error Resume Next** before calling the **Load** method, we can then check the **Err** value to see if an error occurred. If we do get an error, we can react by informing the user that the supplied ID value isn't valid:

```
  If Err Then
    MsgBox "Invalid tape ID", vbExclamation
    Exit Sub
  End If
  On Error GoTo 0
```

If we don't get an error then we know we have a **Tape** object that's loaded with information from the database. At this point, we can use the **CheckIn** method to indicate that the tape is no longer rented out to a customer.

We'll also include some code to make sure the tape is in fact checked out by using the **CheckedOut** property. While this is a business rule that is enforced within the business object, we'll add code in the form as well - just to make sure the user has a more pleasant experience with our application. The **Tape** object will raise an error if we call the **CheckIn** method on an object that isn't checked out; but, rather than trapping that error, we'll head it off by using the **CheckedOut** property:

```
    With objTape
      If .CheckedOut Then
        .BeginEdit
        .CheckIn
        .ApplyEdit
      Else
        MsgBox "Tape is not checked out", vbExclamation
      End If
    End With
    Set objTape = Nothing
  End Sub
```

The calls to **BeginEdit** and **ApplyEdit** are necessary because we built the **CheckIn** method, in Chapter 6, to provide some support for being rolled back by the **CancelEdit** method.

Running the UI

We've finished developing our UI for the moment, and we should be able to compile both the business objects and the empty interface shell that we've developed in this chapter.

If you run the **VideoUI** project, you'll see the **VideoMain** MDI form load, and various menu options

Of course, these menu items won't be very active, at the moment, because we haven't implemented any persistence code behind them. Nevertheless, we've really achieved something in this chapter: we now have a full UI, our business objects are interacting with that UI, and we're ready to bring our Video Rental system to life in the next chapter.

Summary

In this chapter, we've covered some basic concepts behind building a user-interface to work with our business objects. This interface was constructed with Visual Basic forms. We looked at a number of different types of interface:

- ❑ Editing simple business objects
- ❑ Editing parent objects
- ❑ Editing child objects
- ❑ Transaction objects

We also saw how we can easily add form templates to our Visual Basic environment. We used one such template to build a number of the forms that edit business objects.

We can use this interface as we go through the remaining chapters and implement data access code for our objects. Once we've finished the next chapter, we'll have a fully working single-tier application. In addition, we'll be able to use the code we've developed here to create another interfaces using Microsoft Excel.

8

Implementing Single-Tier or Two-Tier Data Access

Overview

So far, in our journey through business objects for Visual Basic, we've built an application from business objects and we've created a user-interface to work with those objects. Of course, the application isn't very useful yet, since none of the business objects have any code to retrieve or save their state in a database.

In Chapter 4, we discussed a number of different physical architectures. The simplest architecture we've identified is a single-tier where the client directly accesses the files that contain the database. Using Visual Basic, this type of access is typically done using DAO (Data Access Objects). Fortunately for us, as Visual Basic programmers, DAO is also a practical technology we can use when we're developing two-tier applications, where the client communicates directly with a data server such as Microsoft SQL Server. This is especially true with the advent of ODBCDirect, included with DAO 3.5, which in turn is included with Visual Basic 5.0.

Also, in Chapter 4, we looked at the various techniques we can use to implement object persistence, including:

- ❏ Putting the data access code in each object
- ❏ Using an object manager to provide data access
- ❏ Putting the data access in a data-centric business object

Of these techniques, the first is the simplest: to include the data access code within each business object. This technique is only useful in single-tier or two-tier physical architectures, but it does have the advantage of being the easiest to implement and understand.

As a great introduction to implementing object persistence, in this chapter we'll keep the data access code inside the business objects themselves and use DAO to work with the database. We'll use a Microsoft Access database, so that anyone with Visual Basic can implement this code.

The techniques and principals that we'll use here are easily adaptable to a two-tier setting. The DAO code will need to be slightly modified to work with ODBCDirect, or we might choose to totally change the code to use RDO or ADO. In any case, the code changes will be pretty minimal, and the underlying concepts will remain the same.

Object State

One of the key concepts in making an object persistent is the concept of *state*. We discussed this earlier in the book, but a quick refresher is probably in order, since this concept is so important.

Objects are composed of three basic concepts:

- ❑ **Interface** - The interface is composed of the object's public properties and methods.
- ❑ **Implementation** - The implementation is basically the code that makes the interface work. This is the code behind each property or method that implements the desired behaviors.
- ❑ **State** - The object's state is the core set of data values that make up the object. These are the values that must be saved to and restored from a database, such that the object can be destroyed and recreated based on those values. Note that the object may well have other data values and properties that are derived from these core data values.

Each individual object is unique and has an underlying set of data that makes it so. Often an object can be represented by a single row of data within a table, although there are exceptions. An object's state must always contain a unique identifier that can be used as a primary key value when retrieving the object's data from the database. This unique identifier may not always be made available to client programs through the object's interface, although we did make it available in all the business objects we built in Chapter 5.

An Approach to Persistence

In this chapter, all the objects will contain the code they need to retrieve, add, update, and delete themselves from within the database. We've already implemented **Load**, **Delete** and **ApplyEdit** methods in our objects, with the intent of making it easy to add this database code.

All the data access code will be hidden from the UI code. The business objects will manage all database activity behind the scenes. In our video rental store example, the **VideoUI** interface project won't even have a reference to the DAO library: it will let the **VideoObjects** DLL handle all the details of data access.

In Chapter 9, we'll see how the database code can be moved out of the UI-centric business objects and into data-centric objects. This will allow us to make the data access code run on an application server rather than directly on the client workstation. As we discussed in Chapter 4, this is a much more scalable solution than including the code directly in the objects, since it puts the data access code much closer to the data source.

Keeping scalability in mind, it's a good idea to put all the data access code in private routines within each object rather than directly in the **Load**, **Delete** and **ApplyEdit** methods. This not only makes the code clearer overall, but will make it easier to take the data access code out of the business objects and move them to an application server later.

Retrieving Data

All of our objects need to be able to load their state from the database. We'll create a private **Fetch** routine in each object to contain the code to retrieve the data.

Earlier, we defined an object's state as being its core data. We also noted that each object's state includes a unique identifier that can be used as the primary key when retrieving the object's data from the database. Our **Fetch** routine will accept this key value as a parameter, making it very easy to go to the database and find the correct data to bring back.

The following is an example of a very basic **Fetch** method for an object with an **ID** and a **Name** field. All the **Fetch** methods that we'll implement in our objects will follow this basic pattern.

Don't worry about entering this code, we'll get around to that when we make our video rental store objects persistent later in the chapter.

```
Private Sub Fetch(ObjectID As Long)
    Dim rsObject As Recordset
    Dim strSQL As String

    strSQL = "SELECT NAME FROM TABLE WHERE OBJECTID=" & ObjectID
    Set rsObject = dbData.OpenRecordset(strSQL, dbOpenSnapshot)
    With rsObject
      udtProps.ObjectID = ObjectID
      udtProps.Name = .Fields("Name")

      objValid.RuleBroken "Name", False

      .Close
    End With
    RsObject.Close
    Set rsObject = Nothing
  End Sub
```

The subroutine accepts an **ObjectID** value as a parameter. In this example, the value is of type **Long**, but it could be of any data type able to represent the primary key that we'll use to find the data in the database.

Building a SQL Statement

The next thing we need to do is use this **ID** value to build a SQL statement so we can retrieve the appropriate data from the database.

```
strSQL = "SELECT NAME FROM TABLE WHERE OBJECTID=" & ObjectID
```

This example SQL statement is not complex; it just retrieves the data from the table using a simple **WHERE** clause. If our object's data is scattered across multiple tables, we might have to join the tables together to get at all the fields.

Opening a Recordset

Now that we have a SQL statement, we can use it to create a recordset using the **OpenRecordset** method on a **Database** object. We'll discuss how to open the database in our **VideoObjects** project later in the chapter, but for now we'll just use a **Database** variable named **dbData**:

```
Set rsObject = dbData.OpenRecordset(strSQL, dbOpenSnapshot)
```

It is best to put the SQL statement into a string variable and then use it to create a recordset. This makes debugging easier, since we can set a breakpoint on this line and very easily use the Immediate window to look at the full SQL statement. It is certainly possible to build the SQL statement right in the OpenRecordset statement, but then it would be very difficult to use the Immediate window to see the SQL statement.

Since the only thing we're going to do with the data in this recordset is to store it in the object's local variables, we don't need read-write access to the data. This is why the code creates a snapshot-style recordset by using the **dbOpenSnapshot** flag.

Copy Data Fields to the Object

Using the recordset we just created, we can easily write code to copy the data from the recordset into the object's local variables. All our objects store their state in a variable named **udtProps,** which is based on a user-defined type (UDT); so we've followed that implementation here:

```
With rsObject
  udtProps.ObjectID = .Fields("ObjectID")
  udtProps.Name = .Fields("Name")
```

If we assume that the data loaded from the database is valid then we can also run through any rules that we marked as broken in the object's **Initialize** subroutine and mark them as unbroken. This is pretty typical, since usually the only way the data gets into the database is through our objects; so when the data is read back in, it's fair to assume that it's still as valid as when it was written out:

```
    objValid.RuleBroken "Name", False

    .Close
  End With
End Sub
```

Handling Errors

We have no error-trapping code in this routine. Believe it or not, that is intentional, since if an error is encountered while loading the object's data, we'll want to raise the error up to the UI code. That way, an appropriate message can be displayed to the user. Visual Basic's default behavior for unhandled errors in an object is to raise it up to the calling code, so the easiest thing we can do is just take the default.

The most likely error we'll get in this code is if the **ObjectID** value doesn't return a record in the database. As soon as we try to use the recordset we'll get an error, and that error will be automatically raised by Visual Basic right back up to the code in the UI. This makes it very easy for the UI developer to trap that error and let the user know what happened in whatever way is appropriate for the interface.

Adding/Updating Data

Not every object needs to be able to save itself to the database. Some objects are read-only and typically come from data entered through other objects or from other applications. On the other hand, many objects do need to be able to save themselves in the database. To support this operation we'll add a **Private Save** subroutine to those objects.

We're combining the add and update operations together because the code required for them is so similar. When using the data object models such as DAO or RDO, the difference between adding a record or updating a record is just a couple lines. The vast bulk of the code is identical either way, since both operations need to copy the object's values into the record and call an update method on the data object.

The basic structure of the **Save** routine is pretty straightforward. The following example is based on the same simple object we looked at with the **Fetch** subroutine, where the object's data is composed of an **ID** value and a **Name** field:

```
Private Sub Save()
  Dim rsObject As Recordset
  Dim strSQL As String

  If flgNew Then
    strSQL = "TABLE"
    Set rsObject = dbVideo.OpenRecordset(strSQL, dbOpenTable)
    rsObject.AddNew
  Else
    strSQL = "SELECT * FROM TABLE WHERE OBJECTID=" & ObjectID
    Set rsObject = dbData.OpenRecordset(strSQL, dbOpenDynaset)
    rsObject.Edit
  End If
  With rsObject
    .Fields("Name") = udtProps.Name
    .Update
    If flgNew Then
      .Bookmark = .LastModified
      udtProps.ObjectID = .Fields("ObjectID")
    End If
    .Close
  End With
End Sub
```

The first thing we need to do is determine whether we're adding or updating the object to the database. Fortunately, our object maintains the **flgNew** variable to indicate whether it represents data in the database or whether it contains data that's not in the database yet.

Adding Data

If **flgNew** is **True**, we can directly open the appropriate table in the database and call the **AddNew** method to add a new record to the table:

```
If flgNew Then
   strSQL = "TABLE"
   Set rsObject = dbData.OpenRecordset(strSQL, dbOpenTable)
   rsObject.AddNew
```

We're using the **dbOpenTable** parameter on the **OpenRecordset** method because it's the fastest way to add a record to an Access database. Opening a table directly doesn't require the JET engine to do any queries or retrieve any data, whereas opening a dynaset would involve more work.

> To adapt this to work in a two-tier setting, we'd have to open a **Dynaset**, since it isn't possible to open a table directly on any ODBC data source. Instead, we can use the **Execute** method on the **Database** object and supply a SQL statement to directly insert the data. This does, typically, provide better performance through ODBC than working with a recordset.

Updating Data

If **flgNew** turns out to be **False**, we are updating existing data in the database:

```
Else
   strSQL = "SELECT * FROM TABLE WHERE OBJECTID=" & _
     udtProps.ObjectID
   Set rsObject = dbData.OpenRecordset(strSQL, dbOpenDynaset)
   rsObject.Edit
End If
```

In this case, we'll simply create a dynaset-style recordset by using the **dbOpenDynaset** parameter. The SQL statement needs to select all the data fields we'll be updating and have a **WHERE** clause to make sure we get a record with a matching **ID** value.

Once we've got a dynaset to work with, we can call its **Edit** method to indicate we're going to change the data and we're all set.

Copying the Field Values

Using the recordset we obtained through either opening the table or the Dynaset, we can simply copy the object's internal data values into the recordset:

```
With rsObject
   .Fields("Name") = udtProps.Name
   .Update
```

We don't want to copy the **ObjectID** value, of course, since it's the primary key and thus can't be changed. We do, however, need to copy all the other data elements that comprise the object's state.

After the data values are copied into the recordset, we can call the recordset's **Update** method to actually put the data into the database. If we're updating the database then we're pretty much all done; but if we're adding data, there's a bit more work to do.

Retrieving the New Primary Key

All of the objects we created in Chapter 5 were designed with a numeric ID value. In all these objects, the assumption we made was that the ID value would be assigned by the database when the object was first saved out. This is easily accomplished with most databases, since they almost all provide a mechanism to automatically generate a sequentially ascending number. In Microsoft Access, this type of field is called an Autonumber.

By making each object's ID field an Autonumber within the database, we ensure that the database will provide a unique numeric ID value when a new record is added to the table. The trick is that this ID value is *in the database*, not in our object. Once the object has been saved to the database, it is no longer a 'new' object, so all our code assumes that the object knows its ID value.

Using DAO, this is easy to accomplish. All we need to do is set the recordset's **Bookmark** property to the **LastModified** property to move the current record to the one we just added. Bookmark operations are very fast, so there's only a very small performance hit for this move:

```
If flgNew Then
  .Bookmark = .LastModified
  udtProps.ObjectID = .Fields("ObjectID")
End If
```

Once the current record has been set to the one we just added, we can copy the ID value from the recordset back into the object's internal variable. This way the object's internal state should completely match the data stored in the database, right down to the newly created primary key value.

Deleting Data

Many of our objects will also need to be removed from the database through their **Delete** methods. This means we need to provide a routine along the lines of **Fetch** and **Save** to manage the removal of an object's data from the database. Of course, **Delete** is a reserved word, so we need to choose a different name. Instead, we'll use the name **DeleteObject** within these objects.

Of the operations we've looked at so far, the delete operation is typically the simplest:

```
Private Sub DeleteObject(ObjectID As Long)
   dbData.Execute "DELETE FROM TABLE WHERE OBJECTID=" & ObjectID
End Sub
```

Like the **Fetch** subroutine, this one requires that the object's ID value be passed as a parameter. From there it's easy, since all we need to do is use the **Database** object's **Execute** method to run a SQL **DELETE** statement.

Setting up the VideoObjects Project

Now that we've looked at the basic approach and concepts that we'll use to save each object to the database, let's move on to apply them to our sample application.

One of the biggest benefits in using component-oriented design is that we can isolate many application changes to a specific component, leaving the others unchanged and perhaps even unaware that anything has been changed. While this isn't always possible, we can certainly minimize the impact of changes and even eliminate them in some cases.

To illustrate how this is possible, in this chapter we'll add the code to make our objects persistent by altering just the **VideoObjects** component, leaving the **VideoUI** interface project entirely alone and unaware of the changes.

Therefore, all the changes we'll be making to the code through the rest of this chapter will be within the **VideoObjects** project. The **VideoUI** project that we created in Chapter 6 will continue to work without change - but we'll see our UI becoming more effective as we implement the code that will allow our business objects to begin saving and retrieving data.

Referencing the DAO Library

Most Visual Basic developers are very familiar with DAO, since both DAO and full support for Access databases are provided with Visual Basic right out of the box. This should make it fairly easy for us to implement everything in this chapter.

To use DAO within a Visual Basic project, we need to add a reference to the DAO object library. Open up the **VideoObjects** project and make sure the Microsoft DAO 3.5 Object Library is selected within the Project-References menu option. Now we'll be able to use all the objects and constant values from the DAO library within the **VideoObjects** project.

The Database Connection

In the **Fetch**, **Save** and **DeleteObject** routines that we built earlier in this chapter, that we built earlier, the code assumed that there was a pre-existing database connection. In our example code, this was a variable named **dbData**. We'll want to provide the same persistent data connection within our **VideoObjects** project. Opening a database through DAO can be an expensive operation in terms of performance. Ideally we'd open a connection to the database when the program starts up and leave it open until the program is closed.

Database Variable - dbVideo

For a variable to be available across all modules within a Visual Basic project, it must be declared as a **Public** variable in a BAS module. Normally it's best to avoid such global variables, but there are a few cases where they are required- and this is one of those cases.

Open the **VideoObjects** project, add a standard code module and name it **VOmain**. Then add a declaration for a **dbVideo** variable as type **Database**.

```
Option Explicit

Public dbVideo As Database
```

Opening the Database

Now that we have a database variable, all that remains is to open the database when the program starts up. More accurately, we need to open the database before any objects inside our **VideoObjects** ActiveX DLL are created. After all, if the client program never uses any of our objects we don't need to worry about opening the database.

Fortunately for us, Visual Basic makes this very easy to implement. An ActiveX DLL can have a **Main** subroutine in a code module, and that subroutine can be set as the project's startup routine. Then, when the client program attempts to create the first object from the DLL, Visual Basic will run the **Main** subroutine before the object is created. If we open the database at that time, we can keep it open until the last object from the DLL is terminated.

Within the **VOMain** code module we just created, add a **Public Sub Main** subroutine and have it open the database:

```
Public Sub Main()
    Set dbVideo = OpenDatabase("video.mdb")
End Sub
```

Make sure to choose the Project-VideoObjects Properties menu option and change the Startup Object to **Sub Main**, otherwise this routine won't ever be run.

Setting up the Database

Data access code is pretty useless without a database to work with. We won't go into detail on how to create a Microsoft Access database, although I will lay out the table definitions clearly. For more information on creating an Access database, see the *Beginner's Guide to Access 95* by Wrox Press.

The best approach is to create the database using Microsoft Access itself. This is by far the easiest tool to use when creating Access databases. Alternatively, Visual Basic comes with VisData, the Visual Data Manager. To use this tool, choose the Add-Ins-Visual Data Manager... menu option within Visual Basic.

It's worth noting that we have the luxury of creating the database based on the objects we designed in Chapter 5. This is an ideal situation, since our objects are dictating the design of the database.

In many cases, we'll find that we need to work with a database that already exists. When this happens, we'll need to make the **Fetch**, **Save** and **DeleteObject** methods more complex so they can retrieve and update each object's data in the appropriate fields in the appropriate tables in the database. The reason this might be more complex is that an object's data might be scattered across multiple tables in an existing database, whereas we would otherwise put the data in a single table in an ideal database.

The Customer Table

The **Customer** table will be used to store our **Customer** objects' data. The fields in the table will reflect the elements of the **CustomerProps** UDT we implemented in the **Customer** object:

```
Private Type CustomerProps
  CustomerID As Long
  Name As String * 50
  Phone As String * 25
  Address1 As String * 30
  Address2 As String * 30
  City As String * 20
  State As String * 10
  ZipCode As String * 10
End Type
```

Here are the fields for the **Customer** table:

Field Name	Data Type	Field Size
CustomerID	AutoNumber	Long integer
Name	Text	50
Phone	Text	25
Address1	Text	30
Address2	Text	30
City	Text	20
State	Text	10
ZipCode	Text	10

The **CustomerID** field should be set up as the primary key for the table. Optionally, we might also choose to add indexes for the **Name** and **Phone** numbers, since we know they'll be used as search criteria by the **Customers** object.

The LateFee Table

The only data elements directly subordinate to the **Customer** table are the late fees. While we didn't create a **LateFee** object per se, we did set up the **Tape** object to add records to a list of late fees for the customer and we designed the invoice objects to work with these late fees as well.

Field Name	Data Type	Field Size
FeeID	AutoNumber	Long integer
CustomerID	Number	Long integer

Field Name	Data Type	Field Size
TapeID	Number	Long integer
FeeDate	Date/Time	
PaidDate	Date/Time	
DaysOver	Number	Integer
Paid	Yes/No	
Deleted	Yes/No	

This table's primary key is the **FeeID** field. There should also be an index for the **CustomerID** field since we know this will be the field used by the invoice process to retrieve records. The **Paid** field will also be used, since we'll only be pulling non-paid records into the invoice.

The **CustomerID** field is important, as it is the link between this table and the parent **Customer** table. Had we created a **LateFee** object, it would have been a child of the **Customer** object, and the tables in the database reflect this relationship as well.

The **TapeID** field is important since we'll need to provide the tape's title as a property on the **InvoiceFee** object. The **DaysOver** field is also used by the **InvoiceFee** object so it can calculate the total amount due the customer because of the late fee.

The two date fields, **FeeDate** and **PaidDate**, have been added to illustrate that the database may contain information that is not directly used by an object's logic. The **FeeDate** field will correspond to the **EnteredDate** property of the **InvoiceFee** object, but other than filling in the date, our object has no use for the **PaidDate** field.

Even if the store decides not to charge a customer for a late fee, they probably want to know how many times a customer returned tapes late. Because of this, we've added a **Deleted** flag to the table. This way we'll never actually delete a late fee record, but instead we'll mark it as deleted. Then the customer won't have to pay the fee, but the record remains in the table for later reporting.

The Video Table

Like the **Customer** table, this table will hold objects. In this case, it will hold the **Video** object, whose state is contained in a type named **VideoProps**:

```
Private Type VideoProps
    VideoID As Long
    Title As String * 30
    ReleaseDate As Variant
    Studio As String * 30
    Category As Long
    Rating As Long
End Type
```

The table layout corresponds to the UDT:

Field Name	Data Type	Field Size
VideoID	AutoNumber	Long integer
Title	Text	30
ReleaseDate	Date/Time	
Studio	Text	30
Category	Number	Long integer
Rating	Number	Long integer

As usual, the **VideoID** field is the primary key. Our **Videos** object uses the **Title** and **Studio** fields as criteria so we'll want to create indexes for them.

The Tape Table

Like the **LateFee** table, the **Tape** table is a child of another table. In this case, it's a child of the **Video** table, so it will contain a **VideoID** field to link the two together. The table's fields are based on the **Tape** object's state:

```
Private Type TapeProps
    TapeID As Long
    VideoID As Long
    Title As String * 30
    CheckedOut As Boolean
    DateAcquired As Variant
    DateDue As Variant
    LateFee As Boolean
    InvoiceID As Long
End Type
```

This table has a couple of changes to what we've seen so far. The **Title** field in the UDT will actually come from the **Video** table, as the **Tape** table doesn't contain a **Title** field. As we implemented it in Chapter 5, the **Title** property on the **Tape** object is read-only, specifically because it's a value that really comes from another object's table.

The **LateFee** variable is also a change. While we have included it in the object's state, it won't actually be saved to, or restored, from the database. While this might not make a lot of sense now, it will when we move the persistence code to an application server in Chapter 9.

The rest of the fields map directly to the table:

Field Name	Data Type	Field Size
TapeID	AutoNumber	Long integer
VideoID	Number	Long integer

Field Name	Data Type	Field Size
CheckedOut	Yes/No	
DateAcquired	Date/Time	
DateDue	Date/Time	
InvoiceID	Number	Long integer

The **TapeID** is the primary key for each record.

Our **Tape** objects always have a **Video** object as their parent. Our database needs to reflect this relationship as well. To support this we include the **VideoID** value in this table as well. It is a foreign key to the **Video** table, allowing us to easily determine which **Tape** objects belong to a given **Video** object.

The **InvoiceID** field doesn't need an index, since it shouldn't be used as a lookup into this table; rather, our code will use this value to find the corresponding invoice record.

The Category and Rating Tables

The **Category** and **Rating** tables are used to load the two **TextList** objects within the **Video** object. As such, they are simple tables with just an ID value and a field for the text label.

The **TextList** object is read-only, so these tables will need to be edited through some other mechanism. For instance, we might choose to create business objects to represent a **Category** and a **Rating** and use those objects to support editing of the tables. Alternatively, we can just use Microsoft Access to directly edit the tables, since they are so simple and change so rarely.

It doesn't matter much whether we create a primary key or any indexes for these tables, since we'll always be pulling in their entire contents to populate the **TextList** object.

The Category Table

Field Name	Data Type	Field Size
CategoryID	Number	Long integer
Category	Text	20

The Rating Table

Field Name	Data Type	Field Size
RatingID	Number	Long integer
Rating	Text	5

The Invoice Table

Our **Invoice** object will need a table to store its state. Like most of our other objects, the **Invoice** object stores its state in a UDT variable:

```
Private Type InvoiceProps
   InvoiceID As Long
   CustomerID As Long
   CustomerName As String * 50
   CustomerPhone As String * 25
End Type
```

Like the **LateFee** table, this table will contain some fields that aren't included directly in the object's UDT. Our **Invoice** object has properties for **Subtotal**, **Tax** and **Total** to indicate the monetary amounts due on the invoice. While we don't need to store these values in the table for the **Invoice** object's use, they are very valuable in case the user wants to create reports directly from the database. This is not uncommon, and so many objects will save out information that will never be read back into the object just to make it easier for reporting or other applications:

Field Name	Data Type	Field Size
InvoiceID	AutoNumber	Long integer
CustomerID	Number	Long integer
Subtotal	Number	Double
Tax	Number	Double
Total	Number	Double

The **InvoiceID** field should be set as the primary key. Our objects don't provide any mechanism to look up all invoices for a customer, so we may not need to create an index for the **CustomerID** field. On the other hand, such an index would probably be used by any reporting that the user might want and so, in that light, it may be valuable. So we'll make **CustomerID** an index.

Our object's **Save** subroutine will store the appropriate values in the **Subtotal**, **Tax** and **Total** fields. The **Fetch** subroutine won't need to load them back in, however, since we implemented the **Invoice** object to recalculate those values each time the properties are accessed.

The InvoiceTape Table

Our final table is a child table of the **Invoice** table. Our **Invoice** object actually supports two types of child objects, **InvoiceFee** and **InvoiceTape**. The **InvoiceFee** objects are based on the **LateFee** table we already created, so all that remains is to provide a table to store the **InvoiceTape** objects:

```
Private Type InvoiceTapeProps
   ItemID As Long
   TapeID As Long
   Title As String * 30
   Price As Double
End Type
```

Like the **Tape** object, this object's UDT contains a **Title** field that won't actually be stored in the table. The **Title** property on the object is read-only as the value comes from the **Video** table, even though it is part of this object's state:

Field Name	Data Type	Field Size
InvoiceID	Number	Long integer
ItemID	AutoNumber	Long integer
TapeID	Number	Long integer
Price	Number	Double

The primary key for this table is the **ItemID** field. There should be an index for the **InvoiceID** field since that is the field that we'll use to retrieve the records for a specific invoice.

The **TapeID** field will be used to find the appropriate record in the **Tape** table, so it won't be used as criteria when retrieving records from this table. Thus no index should be required on that field.

Making Simple Objects Persistent

Now that we've established the basic concepts and the database design out of the way, we should be ready to move on to modifying our objects from Chapter 5. To start with, we'll go through the simplest object, **Customer**. Then we'll move on to look at some of the more complex objects, such as the **Tape** and **InvoiceTape** child objects.

The Customer Object

The simplest business object we created in Chapter 5 was the **Customer** object. This object is neither a parent nor a child: it's a standalone object that needs to be added, updated, and removed from the database as appropriate.

We've already looked at the basic **Fetch**, **Save** and **DeleteObject** methods, so we won't rehash the details of how they work. Here's the code for these routines in the **Customer** business object:

```
Private Sub Save()
  Dim rsCustomer As Recordset
  Dim strSQL As String

  If flgNew Then
    strSQL = "CUSTOMER"
    Set rsCustomer = dbVideo.OpenRecordset(strSQL, dbOpenTable)
    rsCustomer.AddNew
  Else
    strSQL = "SELECT * FROM CUSTOMER WHERE CUSTOMERID=" & _
      CustomerID
    Set rsCustomer = dbVideo.OpenRecordset(strSQL, dbOpenDynaset)
    rsCustomer.Edit
  End If
```

```
    With rsCustomer
      .Fields("Name") = udtProps.Name
      .Fields("Address1") = udtProps.Address1
      .Fields("Address2") = udtProps.Address2
      .Fields("City") = udtProps.City
      .Fields("State") = udtProps.State
      .Fields("ZipCode") = udtProps.ZipCode
      .Fields("Phone") = udtProps.Phone
      .Update
      If flgNew Then
        .Bookmark = .LastModified
        udtProps.CustomerID = .Fields("CustomerID")
      End If
      .Close
    End With
End Sub

Private Sub DeleteObject(CustomerID As Long)
    dbVideo.Execute "DELETE FROM CUSTOMER WHERE CUSTOMERID=" & _
      CustomerID
End Sub

Private Sub Fetch(CustomerID As Long)
    Dim rsCustomer As Recordset
    Dim strSQL As String

    strSQL = "SELECT * FROM CUSTOMER WHERE CUSTOMERID=" & _
      CustomerID
    Set rsCustomer = dbVideo.OpenRecordset(strSQL, dbOpenSnapshot)
    With rsCustomer
      udtProps.CustomerID = .Fields("CustomerID")
      udtProps.Name = .Fields("Name")
      udtProps.Address1 = .Fields("Address1")
      udtProps.Address2 = .Fields("Address2")
      udtProps.City = .Fields("City")
      udtProps.State = .Fields("State")
      udtProps.ZipCode = .Fields("ZipCode")
      udtProps.Phone = .Fields("Phone")

      objValid.RuleBroken "Name", False
      objValid.RuleBroken "Phone", False

      .Close
    End With
End Sub
```

The more interesting parts of this are the changes we need to make to the code we put together in Chapter 5 - so that these three new subroutines get called at the appropriate times.

Loading the Customer Data

The **Fetch** subroutine retrieves the object's data from the database and copies it into the object's local variables. This routine requires a parameter be passed; in particular, it requires the **CustomerID** value, so that it can be used to create a SQL **SELECT** statement to find the record in the **Customer** table.

From the UI developer's viewpoint, the **Customer** object gets its data when the object's **Load** method is called. Not coincidentally, the **Load** method also requires that the **CustomerID** value be passed as a parameter.

We'll add a call to the **Fetch** subroutine within the **Customer** object's **Load** method. We need to relay the **CustomerID** parameter supplied by the UI code down into the **Fetch** routine:

```
Public Sub Load(CustomerID As Long)
   If flgEditing Then Err.Raise 445
   If Not flgNew Then Err.Raise 445

   Fetch CustomerID

   flgNew = False
End Sub
```

It is important that **flgNew** be set to **False** *after* the **Fetch** subroutine is complete. This is because the **Fetch** routine could raise an error in the case that the supplied ID value doesn't correspond to a customer record. If this happens, we don't want to erroneously mark the object as having been loaded by setting the **flgNew** variable to **False**.

Again note that we don't have any error handling of our own in this routine. If an error occurs during the call to the Fetch routine, Visual Basic will raise it back to our Load routine. Since our Load routine has no error trapping code, Visual Basic will then raise the error back to the code that called the Load routine. This should be the UI code, where the UI developer should be trapping the error.

By trapping the error in the UI, we can most easily handle it in whatever way is appropriate for the particular UI. For instance, we may want to show the error in a message box, or write it to a log file or entirely ignore it - all of which is up to the specific UI.

Adding/Updating the Customer Data

Just as the UI developer expects that the object's data will be loaded by the **Load** method, they also expect that the object's data will be stored when the **ApplyEdit** method is called. This will get more complicated with child objects, but with a simple object such as **Customer**, such as **Customer** we'll want to call the **Save** routine within the **ApplyEdit** method's code:

```
Public Sub ApplyEdit()
   If Not flgEditing Then Err.Raise 445

   If flgDeleted Then
      ' code to delete the object's data goes here
      flgNew = True
```

```
      flgDeleted = False
   ElseIf flgDirty Or flgNew Then
     If Not IsValid Then Err.Raise 445
     ' save object to database if appropriate
```

Save

```
     ' save object state
     LSet udtSave = udtProps
     flgNew = False
   End If
   flgDirty = False
   flgEditing = False
End Sub
```

Notice that the **Save** method is called before we save the object state by copying **udtProps** into **udtSave**. There is a good reason for this.

Look back at the **Save** routine we just implemented. Near the bottom of the routine, we have code to copy the **CustomerID** back into the object from the database when the object is new:

```
If flgNew Then
  .Bookmark = .LastModified
  udtProps.CustomerID = .Fields("CustomerID")
End If
```

Since this actually made a change to the object's state, we'll want to make sure it gets saved into the **udtSave** variable along with all the other data in **udtProps**.

If we don't do this, and the UI code calls the **CancelEdit** method, we'd lose the **CustomerID** value when **udtSave** was copied back into **udtProps**. This would lead to a bug, since the UI code could then call **ApplyEdit** and our object would not know its own ID value- so it would try to update the wrong customer record in the database.

Deleting the Customer Data

The question of where to call the **DeleteObject** routine is a bit trickier. Our object has a **Delete** method, and it might seem appropriate to just delete the object using that method. We discussed this a little in Chapter 5, however, where we wanted to make sure that the **CancelEdit** method would undo the **Delete** operation.

In order to support the ability to cancel the **Delete** method, we chose to set a flag, **flgDeleted**, within the **Delete** method, and hold off actually deleting any data until the **ApplyEdit** method was called. That way, the **CancelEdit** method can just reset **flgDeleted** back to **False** and it will be as though the **Delete** method were never called:

```
Public Sub ApplyEdit()
  If Not flgEditing Then Err.Raise 445

  If flgDeleted Then
    ' code to delete the object's data goes here
```

DeleteObject udtProps.CustomerID

```
    flgNew = True
    flgDeleted = False
```

```
      ElseIf flgDirty Or flgNew Then
        If Not IsValid Then Err.Raise 445
        ' save object to database if appropriate
        Save
        ' save object state
        LSet udtSave = udtProps
        flgNew = False
      End If
      flgDirty = False
      flgEditing = False
   End Sub
```

As the **DeleteObject** method may result in an error for some reason, it's important not to reset the **flgNew** and **flgDeleted** variables until after the call to **DeleteObject**. By resetting **flgNew** to **True**, we're indicating that the object doesn't correspond to any data in the database. Therefore, we've effectively got a brand new object, though one loaded with some pre-existing data. Since the object is basically new, we'll also want to reset the **flgDeleted** variable to **False** to make it practical to continue using the object.

Making Parent and Child Objects Persistent

Now that we've seen how to make a simple business object persistent, let's move on to something more complex. The **Video** object is a parent to **Tape** objects. This parent-child relationship is managed by the **Tapes** object, as we discussed in Chapter 5.

The **Video** and **Tape** objects are both persistent business objects, while the **Tapes** object is merely a collection of individual **Tape** objects. This means that both the **Video** and **Tape** objects will contain **Fetch**, **Save** and **DeleteObject** routines. The **Tapes** object doesn't have a corresponding table, so it doesn't need these routines. Instead, it needs to make sure to call the appropriate methods on the child **Tape** objects so they each get saved out to the **Tape** table.

The Video Object

The **Video** object is a parent to **Tape** objects. We implemented this relationship by having the **Video** object own a **Tapes** object and having that **Tapes** object manage all the child **Tape** objects.

Since we moved most of the complexity of dealing with the child objects off to the **Tapes** object, the **Video** object doesn't have to worry about these details. We've already altered the **Video** object's **BeginEdit**, **CancelEdit**, **ApplyEdit**, **Delete** and **Load** methods so they make appropriate calls to the same routines within the **Tapes** object. The **Tapes** object then worries about getting the appropriate action taken care of in all the child objects.

Therefore, the **Video** object's **Fetch**, **Save**, and **DeleteObject** routines only need to deal with the **Video** object itself, so they are no different from the basic routines we looked at earlier in the chapter:

```
Private Sub Save()
   Dim rsVideo As Recordset
   Dim strSQL As String
```

```
      If flgNew Then
        strSQL = "Video"
        Set rsVideo = dbVideo.OpenRecordset(strSQL, dbOpenTable)
        rsVideo.AddNew
      Else
        strSQL = "SELECT * FROM Video WHERE VideoID=" & VideoID
        Set rsVideo = dbVideo.OpenRecordset(strSQL, dbOpenDynaset)
        rsVideo.Edit
      End If
      With rsVideo
        .Fields("Title") = udtProps.Title
        .Fields("ReleaseDate") = udtProps.ReleaseDate
        .Fields("Studio") = udtProps.Studio
        .Fields("Rating") = udtProps.Rating
        .Fields("Category") = udtProps.Category
        .Update
        If isNew Then
          .Bookmark = .LastModified
          udtProps.VideoID = .Fields("VideoID")
        End If
        .Close
      End With
    End Sub

    Private Sub DeleteObject(VideoID As Long)
      dbVideo.Execute "DELETE FROM Video WHERE VideoID=" & VideoID
    End Sub

    Private Sub Fetch(VideoID As Long)
      Dim rsVideo As Recordset
      Dim strSQL As String

      strSQL = "SELECT * FROM Video WHERE VideoID=" & VideoID
      Set rsVideo = dbVideo.OpenRecordset(strSQL, dbOpenSnapshot)
      With rsVideo
        udtProps.VideoID = .Fields("VideoID")
        udtProps.Title = .Fields("Title")
        udtProps.ReleaseDate = .Fields("ReleaseDate")
        udtProps.Studio = .Fields("Studio")
        udtProps.Rating = .Fields("Rating")
        udtProps.Category = .Fields("Category")

        objValid.RuleBroken "Title", False

        rsVideo.Close
      End With
    End Sub
```

Loading the Video Data

As with the **Customer** object, we'll call the **Fetch** routine from within the **Load** method.

```
Public Sub Load(VideoID As Long)
  If flgEditing Then Err.Raise 445
  If Not flgNew Then Err.Raise 445


  Fetch VideoID
  objTapes.Load VideoID
```

```
      flgNew = False
   End Sub
```

Notice how we load the **Video** object's data, then the **Tapes** object is told to load all the child objects, and finally we set **flgNew** to **False**. This way, if the **Video** object fails to load, we won't waste effort in trying to load all the child objects; and if any of the load process fails, we won't indicate that the object represents data from the database by changing the value of **flgNew**.

Adding, Updating and Deleting the Video Data

Likewise, the **Save** and **DeleteObject** methods will be called from within the **ApplyEdit** method, as they were within the **Customer** object.

```
Public Sub ApplyEdit()
   If Not flgEditing Then Err.Raise 445

   If flgDeleted Then
      ' code to delete the object's data goes here
      DeleteObject udtProps.VideoID
      flgNew = True
      flgDeleted = False
   ElseIf flgDirty Or flgNew Then
      If Not IsValid Then Err.Raise 445
      ' save object to database if appropriate
      Save
      ' save object state
      LSet udtSave = udtProps
      flgNew = False
   End If
   objTapes.ApplyEdit udtProps.VideoID
   flgDirty = False
   flgEditing = False
End Sub
```

The call to **ApplyEdit** is echoed to the **Tapes** object so it can make sure the appropriate method is called on all the child objects as well.

Now that we have our **Video** persistence code in place, we can some code that we put on hold from within our UI. You may recall, from Chapter 7, how we commented out some lines from the **VideoEdit** form that accessed information that would only become available once object persistence was implemented. The code we can enable is within the **Form_Load** method of the **VideoEdit** form. Change the following lines:

```
Private Sub Form_Load()
   flgLoading = True
   With objVideo
      EnableOK .IsValid
      If .IsNew Then
         Caption = "Video [(new)]"
      Else
         Caption = "Video [" & .Title & "]"
      End If
      txtTitle = .Title
```

```
            txtRelease = .ReleaseDate
            txtStudio = .Studio

            LoadCombo cmbCategory, .Categories
            cmbCategory.Text = .Category
            LoadCombo cmbRating, .Ratings
            cmbRating.Text = .Rating

            .BeginEdit
        End With
        LoadTapes
        flgLoading = False
    End Sub
```

The Tapes Object

The **Tapes** object is not a persistent business object. That is, the **Tapes** object doesn't save itself to any table in the database. Instead, its job is to manage all the child **Tape** objects, making sure they are loaded, saved and deleted as appropriate.

We just saw how the **Video** object echoes the calls to the **Load**, **ApplyEdit** and **Delete** methods down to the **Tapes** object. The **Tapes** object just turns around and calls the appropriate methods on each child object in the collection.

We covered this process in great detail in Chapter 5, so we won't revisit it here. The key thing to keep in mind is which methods get called on the **Tape** objects when each method is called on the **Tapes** collection object.

When the **Load** method is called on the **Tapes** object, it calls the **ChildLoad** method for each child object. The **ApplyEdit** method calls **ChildApplyEdit** on each child, and the **Delete** method calls the **Delete** method on each child.

Loading the Tape Objects

The **Tapes** object's **Load** method bears some further examination. In Chapter 5, we just put comments into this routine, since its actual implementation was dependent on having a database. Now we'll replace those comments with some code.

The **ChildLoad** method of the **Tape** object requires that the **TapeID** value be passed as a parameter. This implies that the **Tapes** object's **Load** method must have a list of **TapeID** values to use when calling each of the child object's **ChildLoad** methods. Add the following code to the **Load** method of the **Tapes** object:

```
    Friend Sub Load(VideoID As Long)

        Dim rsTape As Recordset
        Dim strSQL As String
        Dim objTape As Tape

        If flgEditing Then Err.Raise 445

        strSQL = "SELECT TapeID FROM Tape WHERE VideoID=" & VideoID
        Set rsTape = dbVideo.OpenRecordset(strSQL, dbOpenSnapshot)
        Do While Not rsTape.EOF
```

```
        Set objTape = New Tape
        With objTape
           .SetAsChild
           .ChildLoad rsTape("TapeID")
        End With
        colTapes.Add Item:=objTape
        rsTape.MoveNext
    Loop
    rsTape.Close
End Sub
```

Getting these values isn't difficult. We can simply create a recordset that contains the **TapeID** values for all the tape records that have the right **VideoID**:

```
strSQL = "SELECT TapeID FROM Tape WHERE VideoID=" & VideoID
Set rsTape = dbVideo.OpenRecordset(strSQL, dbOpenSnapshot)
```

Then we can loop through this recordset, creating a new **Tape** object for each record:

```
Do While Not rsTape.EOF
    Set objTape = New Tape
```

We can then tell each **Tape** object that it is a child using the **SetAsChild** method, as we discussed in Chapter 5. Once we've made it a child object, we can call its **ChildLoad** method with the **TapeID** value to load that object with the right data from the **Tape** table:

```
With objTape
  .SetAsChild
  .ChildLoad rsTape("TapeID")
End With
```

All that remains is to add the fully loaded child object to the **Tapes** object's internal collection and move on to the next record:

```
    colTapes.Add Item:=objTape
    rsTape.MoveNext
Loop
```

Removing Tape Objects

We also need to implement the **Tapes** object's **Remove** method. In Chapter 5, we just created this routine with some comments, since its implementation was dependent on access to a database. We're now ready to implement the **Remove** method.

To remove a **Tape** object from the database, we need to call its **Delete** method and then call **ChildApplyEdit** to commit the deletion. All of this is handled by allowing the UI code to directly call each **Tape** object's **Delete** method to flag the object for deletion. If the UI code then calls the **ApplyEdit** method on the **Video** object, all the **Tape** objects flagged for deletion will be removed from both the database and the collection.

So we'll start by declaring the flag variable which will mark the **Tape** object for deletion. Add the following line to our **Tapes** object:

```
Option Explicit

Private colTapes As Collection
Private colDeleted As Collection
```

Now we can add our **Remove** method to the **Tapes** object:

```
Public Sub Remove(Byval Index as Variant)
    Dim objTape As Tape

    If Not flgEditing then Err.raise 445
    Set objTape = colTapes.Item(Index)
    objTape.Delete
    colDeleted.Add Item:=objTape
    colTapes.Remove Index
End Sub
```

First, we create our own reference to the **Tape** object that needs to be removed, through **objTape**, and call its Delete method to flag it for deletion:

```
Set objTape = colTapes.Item(Index)
objTape.Delete
```

Then we simply add the deleted object to the **colDeleted** collection and remove it from the **colTapes** collection:

```
colDeleted.Add Item:=objTape
colTapes.Remove Index
```

The Tape Object

The **Tape** object is probably our most complex object. It is a child object, each one being owned by a **Video** object. But to make things even more difficult, the **Tape** object can be used as a standalone object like the **Customer** object, so it not only has code to support being a child, but also code to support being a standalone entity.

Adding the Persistence Methods to Tape

Either way, the **Fetch**, **Save** and **DeleteObject** routines are required. The process of loading and saving data to the database isn't affected by how the object is being used. In either case, the object's state is being written out to the database or read back in. At the same time, the **Tape** object has some special requirements in these routines.

The Save Method

Add the following code to the **Tape** object:

```
Private Sub Save()
```

```
      Dim rsTape As Recordset
      Dim rsVideo As Recordset
      Dim strSQL As String

      If flgNew Then
        strSQL = "Tape"
        Set rsTape = dbVideo.OpenRecordset(strSQL, dbOpenTable)
        rsTape.AddNew
      Else
        strSQL = "SELECT * FROM Tape WHERE TapeID=" & TapeID
        Set rsTape = dbVideo.OpenRecordset(strSQL, dbOpenDynaset)
        rsTape.Edit
      End If
      With rsTape
        .Fields("VideoID") = udtProps.VideoID
        .Fields("CheckedOut") = udtProps.CheckedOut
        .Fields("DateAcquired") = udtProps.DateAcquired
        .Fields("DateDue") = udtProps.DateDue
        .Fields("InvoiceID") = udtProps.InvoiceID
        .Update
        If flgNew Then
          .Bookmark = .LastModified
          udtProps.TapeID = .Fields("TapeID")
        End If
        .Close
      End With
      strSQL = "SELECT TITLE FROM Video WHERE VideoID=" & _
        udtProps.VideoID
      Set rsVideo = dbVideo.OpenRecordset(strSQL, dbOpenSnapshot)
      udtProps.Title = rsVideo("Title")
      rsVideo.Close
    End Sub
```

When we designed the **Tape** table, we intentionally didn't provide fields in the table to store the **Title** or **LateFee** elements from the **TapeProps** UDT. The **LateFee** variable is a flag to indicate whether to create a late fee record, something we'll talk about shortly.

The **Title** value actually comes from the **Video** table. It is a read-only property of the **Tape** object, so it can't be changed through the **Tape** object. Therefore, we have no reason to write out the **Title** value from the object to the database.

We do need to read the **Title** value in from the database to get it into our object. This is particularly important for a new **Tape** object; otherwise, it might not have the correct **Title** value. To make sure we always have the correct title, we'll read the value in from the **Video** table after we've saved out the **Tape** object's data:

```
strSQL = "SELECT TITLE FROM Video WHERE VideoID=" & _
  udtProps.VideoID
Set rsVideo = dbVideo.OpenRecordset(strSQL, dbOpenSnapshot)
udtProps.Title = rsVideo("Title")
rsVideo.Close
```

This process is not unlike reading in the primary key value generated by the database after we've added a new record, but in this case we're doing the lookup against a different table. The end result is that we retrieve the video's title and put it into the **Tape** object's state, **udtProps**.

The DeleteObject and Fetch Methods

Now add the following code to our **Tape** object:

```
Private Sub DeleteObject(TapeID As Long)
  dbVideo.Execute "DELETE FROM Tape WHERE TapeID=" & TapeID
End Sub

Private Sub Fetch(TapeID As Long)
  Dim rsTape As Recordset
  Dim strSQL As String

  strSQL = "SELECT Tape.*,Video.Title " & _
    "FROM Tape INNER JOIN Video ON " & _
    "Tape.VideoID = Video.VideoID " & _
    "WHERE TapeID=" & TapeID
  Set rsTape = dbVideo.OpenRecordset(strSQL, dbOpenSnapshot)
  With rsTape
    udtProps.TapeID = .Fields("TapeID")
    udtProps.VideoID = .Fields("VideoID")
    udtProps.Title = .Fields("Title")
    udtProps.CheckedOut = .Fields("CheckedOut")
    udtProps.DateAcquired = .Fields("DateAcquired")
    udtProps.DateDue = .Fields("DateDue")
    udtProps.InvoiceID = .Fields("InvoiceID")

    objValid.RuleBroken "DateAcquired", False

    rsTape.Close
  End With
End Sub
```

The **Fetch** routine is a bit different to anything we've seen so far. Again we come back to the read-only **Title** property on the **Tape** object. There is no field on the **Tape** table for **Title**, because this value actually comes from the **Video** table. To load this value into the **Tape** object's state, we need to get it from that table; in this case, we add a **JOIN** to the SQL statement we're using to retrieve the object's data:

```
strSQL = "SELECT Tape.*,Video.Title " & _
  "FROM Tape INNER JOIN Video ON " & _
  Tape.VideoID = Video.VideoID " & _
  "WHERE TapeID=" & TapeID
```

If we were trying to stick with a pure object-oriented design, this would be a problem. From an object-oriented viewpoint, it's far better to create an instance of a **Video** object and get the **Title** value from that object rather than directly reading it from the database. By getting the value from a **Video** object, we'll automatically get the benefit of any business logic that the **Video** object might contain for dealing with the **Title** field.

Unfortunately, there can be a very serious performance hit for loading up an entire object just to get at one field, especially when we compare it to the quick performance of adding a simple **JOIN** to our SQL statement to get the same result. The easiest way to create these SQL statements is to use the query designer in Microsoft Access; otherwise, they'll need to be written by hand.

> The trick is to remember that we're creating a client/server application using objects. If we put object-oriented design ahead of the client/server constraints we'll create an elegant but exceedingly slow application.

Tape as a Standalone Object

When the **Tape** object is being used as a standalone object, the **flgChild** variable is set to **False**. In this case, the object will be used by the UI code just like any other standard business object, and the calls to **Fetch**, **Save** and **DeleteObject** will be made in the **Load** and **ApplyEdit** methods as normal. Of course, they can only be called if **flgChild** is **False**:

```
Public Sub Load(TapeID As Long)
    If flgChild Then Err.Raise 445
    If flgEditing Then Err.Raise 445
    If Not flgNew Then Err.Raise 445
```

```
    Fetch TapeID
```

```
    flgNew = False
End Sub
```

```
Public Sub ApplyEdit()
    If flgChild Then If Not flgChildEditing Then Err.Raise 445
    If Not flgChild And flgNew Then Err.Raise 445
    If Not flgEditing Then Err.Raise 445

    If Not flgChild Then
      If flgDeleted Then
        ' code to delete the object's data goes here
```

```
        DeleteObject udtProps.TapeID
```

```
        flgNew = True
        flgDeleted = False
      ElseIf flgDirty Or flgNew Then
        If Not IsValid Then Err.Raise 445
        ' save object to database if appropriate
```

```
        Save
```

```
        If udtProps.LateFee Then
          ' add the late fee to the customer
        End If
        ' save object state
        LSet udtSave = udtProps
        flgNew = False
      End If
      flgDirty = False
    Else
      If Not objParent Is Nothing Then
        objParent.AddChild Me
        Set objParent = Nothing
      End If
    End If
    flgEditing = False
End Sub
```

Tape as a Child Object

If **flgChild** is **True** then the **Tape** object is acting as a child to a **Video** object. In this case the behavior of the object changes. In particular, the **Load** method disables itself entirely by raising an error:

```
If flgChild Then Err.Raise 445
```

The **ApplyEdit** method isn't disabled, but the majority of its code is contained within an **If...Then** statement that checks **flgChild**:

```
If Not flgChild Then
```

These behavioral changes prevent the UI code from directly causing the **Tape** object to interact with the database when it's acting as a child of a **Video** object.

> **The underlying principle is that child objects should only interact with the database when their parent object tells them to do so.**

As we've just seen, the **Tapes** object calls the **ChildLoad** and **ChildApplyEdit** methods to make each child **Tape** object to interact with the database. The code in each of these routines is very similar to the **Load** and **ApplyEdit** methods in a normal object, but they are only called by the parent collection object.

ChildLoad

The **ChildLoad** method calls the **Fetch** routine to load the object's data:

```
Friend Sub ChildLoad(TapeID As Long)
    If flgChildEditing Then Err.Raise 445
    If Not flgNew Then Err.Raise 445

    ' code to load the object goes here
    Fetch TapeID

    flgNew = False
End Sub
```

This is no different than when **Fetch** is called from the **Load** method; however, this call is invoked by the **Tapes** object rather than the UI code.

ChildApplyEdit

The **ChildApplyEdit** method makes appropriate calls to **DeleteObject** or **Save**:

```
Friend Sub ChildApplyEdit(VideoID As Long)
    If Not flgChildEditing Then Err.Raise 445
    If Not IsValid Then Err.Raise 445
```

```
      If flgDeleted Then
         ' code to delete the object's data goes here
```
```
         DeleteObject udtProps.TapeID
```
```
      flgNew = True
      flgDeleted = False
   ElseIf flgDirty Or flgNew Then
      ' save object to database if appropriate
      udtProps.VideoID = VideoID
```
```
      Save
```
```
      If udtProps.LateFee Then
         ' add the late fee to the customer
      End If
      ' save object state
      LSet udtChild = udtProps
      flgNew = False
   End If
   flgDirty = False
   flgChildEditing = False
End Sub
```

Before we call the **Save** routine, the **VideoID** that was passed as a parameter is copied into **udtProps** so it is part of the object's state. This is important, since this value is the primary key of the parent object and thus is a key part of our object's identity. With this value set, we're able to call the **Save** routine knowing that our object contains all the information needed to save the data into the database.

Creating Late Fee Records

The **Tape** object has another unique feature. When a **Tape** object's **CheckIn** method is called, it indicates that the tape has been returned by the customer and is being checked back in, to be available for rental.

Causing a Late Fee

This routine checks the current date against the date the tape was due back from the customer, and, if the tape is overdue, it sets a flag to indicate that a late fee record needs to be created. The code that we entered to handle this in Chapter 5 is highlighted here:

```
Public Sub CheckIn()
   If Not flgEditing Then Err.Raise 445

   With udtProps
      If Not .CheckedOut Then _
         Err.Raise vbObjectError + 1101, "Tape", _
         "Tape is not checked out"
      .CheckedOut = False
```
```
      If DateDiff("d", .DateDue, Now) > 0 Then _
         .LateFee = True
```
```
   End With
   flgDirty = True
End Sub
```

The code only sets a flag, it doesn't create the late fee record on the spot. This is because the user might click Cancel when the late fee shouldn't be saved. Instead, it sets a flag so we can create the late fee record when the **ApplyEdit** method is called.

Writing the Late Fee Record

Before we get into those details, we should look at the code that actually creates the late fee record. We need to put all this code into the **Tape** class module in a routine called **SaveLateFee**:

```
Private Sub SaveLateFee()
   Dim rsLateFee As Recordset
   Dim rsInvoice As Recordset
   Dim strSQL As String

   strSQL = "SELECT CUSTOMERID FROM INVOICE WHERE INVOICEID=" & _
      udtProps.InvoiceID
   Set rsInvoice = dbVideo.OpenRecordset(strSQL, dbOpenSnapshot)
   strSQL = "LateFee"
   Set rsLateFee = dbVideo.OpenRecordset(strSQL, dbOpenTable)
   rsLateFee.AddNew
   With rsLateFee
      .Fields("CustomerID") = rsInvoice("CustomerID")
      .Fields("TapeID") = udtProps.TapeID
      .Fields("FeeDate") = Now
      .Fields("DaysOver") = DateDiff("d", udtProps.DateDue, Now)
      .Fields("Paid") = False
      .Update
      .Close
   End With
   rsInvoice.Close
   Set rsInvoice = Nothing
   Set rsLateFee = Nothing
End Sub
```

This routine is just regular DAO code. Since the late fee is for a customer, the **LateFee** table has a **CustomerID** field that we need to fill in. Our **Tape** object has no **CustomerID** field, but it does have an **InvoiceID** and we can find out which customer is recorded on that invoice. To do this, we simply retrieve the **CustomerID** field from the **Invoice** table:

```
strSQL = "SELECT CUSTOMERID FROM INVOICE WHERE INVOICEID=" & _
   udtProps.InvoiceID
Set rsInvoice = dbVideo.OpenRecordset(strSQL, dbOpenSnapshot)
```

Then we can move on to create a new record in the **LateFee** table:

```
strSQL = "LateFee"
Set rsLateFee = dbVideo.OpenRecordset(strSQL, dbOpenTable)
rsLateFee.AddNew
```

Given the new record, all that remains is to set the appropriate values into the recordset's fields and call the **Update** method to write them to the database:

```
With rsLateFee
   .Fields("CustomerID") = rsInvoice("CustomerID")
   .Fields("TapeID") = udtProps.TapeID
```

```
.Fields("FeeDate") = Now
.Fields("DaysOver") = DateDiff("d", udtProps.DateDue, Now)
.Fields("Paid") = False
.Update
```

Calling SaveLateFee

The **SaveLateFee** routine we just created will create the late fee record with all the right data. Of course, we need to make sure to call the **SaveLateFee** routine at the appropriate points in the **ApplyEdit** and **ChildApplyEdit** methods.

The only time we need to worry about late fees is when the customer has returned a video tape and it is being checked in. We implemented a **CheckIn** method in the **Tape** object in Chapter 5.

The **Tape** object's **CheckIn** method is available when the **Tape** object is not a child. In fact, this is the intended purpose behind allowing the object to be used in a standalone fashion. We want to make it easy for the user to supply the tape's ID value, load the tape from the database and check it in.

The **Tape** object's **CheckIn** method determines whether a late fee needs to be applied. If it does, the **udtProps.LateFee** variable is set to **True**.

In the **Tape** object's **ApplyEdit** method we can see if the tape has been checked in by using the **udtProps.LateFee** variable. In this case, we know that we need to call the **SaveLateFee** method to create the late fee record:

```
Public Sub ApplyEdit()
  If flgChild Then If Not flgChildEditing Then Err.Raise 445
  If Not flgChild And flgNew Then Err.Raise 445
  If Not flgEditing Then Err.Raise 445

  If Not flgChild Then
    If flgDeleted Then
      ' code to delete the object's data goes here
      DeleteObject udtProps.TapeID
      flgNew = True
      flgDeleted = False
    ElseIf flgDirty Or flgNew Then
      If Not IsValid Then Err.Raise 445
      ' save object to database if appropriate
      Save
      If udtProps.LateFee Then
        ' add the late fee to the customer
```

```
        SaveLateFee
```

```
      End If
      ' save object state
      LSet udtSave = udtProps
      flgNew = False
    End If
    flgDirty = False
  Else
    If Not objParent Is Nothing Then
      objParent.AddChild Me
      Set objParent = Nothing
    End If
```

```
      End If
      flgEditing = False
   End Sub
```

Although we don't envision the user checking in a tape by bringing it up as a child object, it doesn't hurt to add the code to support such an action. Where it is easy to provide flexibility to the UI developer it is usually a good idea to do so. It's hard to envision how our objects will be used somewhere down the line, so the more flexible they are, the easier it will be to get them to meet future requirements.

To this end, we'll also add the call to **SaveLateFee** in the **ChildApplyEdit** method:

```
   Friend Sub ChildApplyEdit(VideoID As Long)
      If Not flgChildEditing Then Err.Raise 445
      If Not IsValid Then Err.Raise 445

      If flgDeleted Then
         ' code to delete the object's data goes here
         DeleteObject udtProps.TapeID
         flgNew = True
         flgDeleted = False
      ElseIf flgDirty Or flgNew Then
         ' save object to database if appropriate
         udtProps.VideoID = VideoID
         Save
         If udtProps.LateFee Then
            ' add the late fee to the customer
```

> **SaveLateFee**

```
         End If
         ' save object state
         LSet udtChild = udtProps
         flgNew = False
      End If
      flgDirty = False
      flgChildEditing = False
   End Sub
```

Now when the **Tape** object is saved, either through **ApplyEdit** or **ChildApplyEdit**, a late fee record will be created if necessary.

Persisting Polymorphic Objects

The **Invoice** object and its child objects, **InvoiceTape** and **InvoiceFee**, are similar to the **Video** and **Tape** objects, but with a twist. Where the **Video** object has only one type of child object, the **Invoice** object has two.

The **Invoice** object's children are managed by the **InvoiceItems** collection object. As with the **Video** object, this means that pretty much all the complexity of handling the child objects has been moved out of the **Invoice** object. The **Invoice** object just calls methods on the **InvoiceItems** object, as appropriate, to get all the child objects loaded, deleted or saved.

The Invoice Object

As with our other objects, the **Invoice** object implements the **Fetch**, **Save** and **DeleteObject** subroutines. Since each child object will handle its own data access, the **Invoice** object's subroutines only need to deal with the **Invoice** object itself:

```
Private Sub Save()
  Dim rsInvoice As Recordset
  Dim strSQL As String

  If flgNew Then
    strSQL = "Invoice"
    Set rsInvoice = dbVideo.OpenRecordset(strSQL, dbOpenTable)
    rsInvoice.AddNew
  Else
    strSQL = "SELECT * FROM Invoice WHERE InvoiceID=" & InvoiceID
    Set rsInvoice = dbVideo.OpenRecordset(strSQL, dbOpenDynaset)
    rsInvoice.Edit
  End If
  With rsInvoice
    .Fields("CustomerID") = udtProps.CustomerID
    .Fields("Subtotal") = Me.SubTotal
    .Fields("Tax") = Me.Tax
    .Fields("Total") = Me.Total
    .Update
    If IsNew Then
      .Bookmark = .LastModified
      udtProps.InvoiceID = .Fields("InvoiceID")
    End If
    .Close
  End With
  strSQL = "SELECT NAME,PHONE FROM Customer " & _
    "WHERE CustomerID=" & udtProps.CustomerID
  Set rsInvoice = dbVideo.OpenRecordset(strSQL, dbOpenSnapshot)
  udtProps.CustomerName = rsInvoice("Name")
  udtProps.CustomerPhone = rsInvoice("Phone")
  rsInvoice.Close
End Sub

Private Sub DeleteObject(InvoiceID As Long)
  dbVideo.Execute "DELETE FROM Invoice WHERE InvoiceID=" & _
    InvoiceID
End Sub

Private Sub Fetch(InvoiceID As Long)
  Dim rsInvoice As Recordset
  Dim strSQL As String

  strSQL = "SELECT Invoice.*,Customer.Name,Customer.Phone " & _
    "FROM Invoice INNER JOIN Customer ON " & _
    "Invoice.CustomerID = Customer.CustomerID " & _
    "WHERE InvoiceID=" & Format$(InvoiceID)
  Set rsInvoice = dbVideo.OpenRecordset(strSQL, dbOpenSnapshot)
  With rsInvoice
    udtProps.InvoiceID = .Fields("InvoiceID")
    udtProps.CustomerID = .Fields("CustomerID")
    udtProps.CustomerName = .Fields("Name")
    udtProps.CustomerPhone = .Fields("Phone")
    rsInvoice.Close
```

```
    End With

    objValid.RuleBroken "Customer", False
End Sub
```

As with the **Video** object, the **Invoice** object will call the **Fetch** routine in its **Load** method. It calls the **Save** and **DeleteObject** routines from within the **ApplyEdit** method:

```
Public Sub Load(InvoiceID As Long)
   If flgEditing Then Err.Raise 445
   If Not flgNew Then Err.Raise 445

   Fetch InvoiceID
   objValid.RuleBroken "Customer", False
   objItems.Load udtProps.InvoiceID
   flgNew = False
End Sub


Public Sub ApplyEdit()
   If Not flgEditing Then Err.Raise 445

   If flgDeleted Then
      ' code to delete the object's data goes here
      DeleteObject udtProps.InvoiceID
      flgNew = True
      flgDeleted = False
   ElseIf flgDirty Or flgNew Then
      If Not IsValid Then Err.Raise 445
      ' save object to database if appropriate
      Save
      ' save object state
      LSet udtSave = udtProps
      flgNew = False
   End If
   flgDirty = False
   flgEditing = False
   objItems.ApplyEdit udtProps.InvoiceID
End Sub
```

Each routine also echoes the method call down to the **InvoiceItems** collection object, just as we did with the **Video** object.

The Invoice Child Objects

The **InvoiceItems** collection can contain two different types of object, **InvoiceTape** and **InvoiceFee**. However, both of these objects implement the **InvoiceItem** interface, so we're able to use them as though they were the same class when we can use them as **InvoiceItem** objects - which is where polymorphism comes into play.

Unfortunately, a shared interface such as **InvoiceItem** can't contain anything other than **Public** properties and methods. This is because the **Implements** keyword only brings the **Public** properties and methods from the base class into the class implementing the interface.

In the child objects, the **ChildLoad**, **Delete** and **ChildApplyEdit** methods aren't **Public**, since we don't want the UI code to have access to them. Therefore, we were unable to include them in the **InvoiceItem** interface.

The InvoiceItems Collection

What this boils down to is that, in Chapter 5, we did some extra work in the **InvoiceItems** collection object to handle each type of child object differently.

We covered this in great detail in Chapter 5, so we won't go over it again here. In the end, the **InvoiceItems** object directly calls each child object's **ChildLoad**, **Delete** and **ChildApplyEdit** method when its **Load**, **LoadFees** and **ApplyEdit** methods are called by the **Invoice** object.

As with the **Tapes** object, the **InvoiceItems** object doesn't implement the **Fetch**, **Save** or **DeleteObject** routines. It doesn't have any data of its own that needs to be saved to the database; instead, it just needs to make sure all the child objects interact with the database as appropriate.

The **Tapes** object's **Load** method contained code to get the ID values for each child and then to create each child object using those ID values. We need to do the same thing with the **InvoiceItems** object, but with a bit more complexity since we have two types of child objects.

Loading the Late Fee Objects

Within the **InvoiceItems** object, we have a **LoadFees** method to load all the late fee objects. In Chapter 5, we simply put comments in this routine, as it can't be implemented without access to a database. We'll replace those comments here with the following code:

```
Friend Sub LoadFees(CustomerID As Long)

    Dim rsItems As Recordset
    Dim objInvoiceFee As InvoiceFee
    Dim strSQL As String


    If flgEditing Then Err.Raise 445


    strSQL = "SELECT FEEID FROM LATEFEE " & _
        "WHERE DELETED=FALSE AND PAID=FALSE AND " & _
        "CUSTOMERID=" & CustomerID
    Set rsItems = dbVideo.OpenRecordset(strSQL, dbOpenSnapshot)
    Do While Not rsItems.EOF
        Set objInvoiceFee = New InvoiceFee
        objInvoiceFee.ChildLoad rsItems("FeeID")
        colItems.Add Item:=objInvoiceFee
        rsItems.MoveNext
    Loop
    rsItems.Close

End Sub
```

This routine gets the **CustomerID** value as a parameter. The **Invoice** object provides this **CustomerID** when it calls the **LoadFees** method, since it knows which customer owns the invoice. The late fee records are all owned by a customer, so this field is used in the **WHERE** clause of the SQL statement to retrieve the correct records:

```
strSQL = "SELECT FEEID FROM LATEFEE " & _
  "WHERE DELETED=FALSE AND PAID=FALSE AND " & _
  "CUSTOMERID=" & CustomerID
```

The **WHERE** clause also contains checks to make sure we don't retrieve records for late fees that have already been paid, or for those that have been deleted. On an invoice we only want to include late fees that need to be paid by the customer.

Using the resulting list of **FeeID** values, we can loop through the recordset, creating and loading an **InvoiceFee** object for each record:

```
Do While Not rsItems.EOF
  Set objInvoiceFee = New InvoiceFee
  With objInvoiceFee
    .ChildLoad rsItems("FeeID")
    If flgEditing Then _
      .ChildBeginEdit
  End With
  colItems.Add Item:=objInvoiceFee
  rsItems.MoveNext
Loop
```

Unlike the **Tape** object, the **InvoiceFee** object has no **SetAsChild** method, since the **InvoiceFee** objects are always child objects.

Loading the Tape Rental Objects

Similarly, we need the **Load** method to load the **InvoiceTape** objects. Again, in Chapter 5 we commented the pseudo-code for this routine; now we'll replace that with actual code.

This method would only be used to bring up an old **Invoice** object, perhaps for display or reporting reasons:

```
Friend Sub Load(InvoiceID As Long)

  Dim rsItems As Recordset
  Dim objInvoiceTape As InvoiceTape
  Dim strSQL As String


  If flgEditing Then Err.Raise 445


  strSQL = "SELECT ITEMID FROM INVOICETAPE " & _
    "WHERE INVOICEID=" & InvoiceID
  Set rsItems = dbVideo.OpenRecordset(strSQL, dbOpenSnapshot)
  Do While Not rsItems.EOF
    Set objInvoiceTape = New InvoiceTape
    objInvoiceTape.ChildLoad rsItems("ItemID")
    colItems.Add Item:=objInvoiceTape
    rsItems.MoveNext
```

```
        Loop
        rsItems.Close
    End Sub
```

Like the other **Load** methods we've looked at, this one creates a recordset containing all the primary key values for the child objects; in this case, **InvoiceTape** objects. Then each child object's **ChildLoad** method is called, and the loaded object is added to the **InvoiceItems** object's collection.

The InvoiceFee Object

The **InvoiceFee** object is rather interesting. This object represents data in a table that is not so much related to an invoice as it is related to a customer. **InvoiceFee** illustrates how powerful this whole object-oriented approach can be, since we are able to create an object model that makes a set of data, a customer's unpaid late fees, appear to be part of an invoice.

To pull this off, we need to take extra care to build the **Fetch**, **Save** and **DeleteObject** so they work with the data correctly. First though, we need to update the object's **FeeProps** UDT.

Adding the Paid Flag

When we created our table earlier in the chapter, we added a field to indicate if the late fee had been paid. While this field is not part of the object's interface, it is part of the implementation. The **InvoiceFee** object needs to update this field as it is saved, to indicate that the late fee has been paid via an **Invoice** object.

The **FeeProps** UDT needs to have a **Paid** variable added to track the current value of the field. We'll also add a PaidDate field to match the one we added to the table earlier. Again, this field will be updated as the InvoiceFee object is saved to indicate when the late fee was paid:

```
    Private Type FeeProps
        InvoiceID As Long
        FeeID As Long
        VideoTitle As String * 30
        EnteredDate As Date
        DaysOver As Integer
        Paid As Boolean
        PaidDate As Date
    End Type
```

We'll use these fields in the **Fetch** and **Save** methods we're about to implement. They aren't used anywhere else in the object, so they provide a good illustration of how our objects sometimes perform entirely data-centric activities. Setting the **Paid** and **PaidDate** fields is a consequence of adding the **InvoiceFee** object to an Invoice object, but the process is not something the UI is directly involved with. Instead, it's entirely handled by our data-centric code in the **Fetch** and **Save** methods.

The Fetch Method

Let's look at the **Fetch** routine first.

```
Private Sub Fetch(FeeID As Long)
   Dim rsLateFee As Recordset
   Dim strSQL As String

   strSQL = "SELECT LateFee.*, Video.Title " & _
      "FROM (LateFee INNER JOIN Tape ON " & _
      "LateFee.TapeID = Tape.TapeID) " & _
      "INNER JOIN Video ON Tape.VideoID = Video.VideoID " & _
      "WHERE LateFee.FeeID=" & Format$(FeeID)
   Set rsLateFee = dbVideo.OpenRecordset(strSQL, dbOpenSnapshot)
   With rsLateFee
      udtProps.FeeID = .Fields("FeeID")
      udtProps.VideoTitle = .Fields("Title")
      udtProps.EnteredDate = .Fields("FeeDate")
      udtProps.DaysOver = .Fields("DaysOver")
      udtProps.Paid = .Fields("Paid")
      If Not IsNull(.Fields("PaidDate")) Then _
         udtProps.PaidDate = .Fields("PaidDate")
      .Close
   End With
End Sub
```

Overall, this routine is not much different from what we've seen in the other objects. The big difference is in the SQL statement, since this object has a **Title** property that needs to come from the **Video** table:

```
strSQL = "SELECT LateFee.*, Video.Title " & _
   "FROM (LateFee INNER JOIN Tape ON " & _
   "LateFee.TapeID = Tape.TapeID) " & _
   "INNER JOIN Video ON Tape.VideoID = Video.VideoID " & _
   "WHERE LateFee.FeeID=1"
```

The only field we have to work with is the **TapeID** field, but that only gets us to the **Tape** table. From there, we need to use the **VideoID** field on the tape record to do a **JOIN** on the **Video** table so we can get the **Title** value.

The DeleteObject Method

The **DeleteObject** routine is even more different than the others we've seen. Instead of removing a record from the table, this routine just changes the **Deleted** field on the record to **True** so the late fee is marked as being deleted but still exists in the table for later reporting:

```
Private Sub DeleteObject(FeeID As Long)
   Dim rsLateFee As Recordset
   Dim strSQL As String

   strSQL = "SELECT DELETED FROM LateFee WHERE FeeID=" & FeeID
   Set rsLateFee = dbVideo.OpenRecordset(strSQL, dbOpenDynaset)
   With rsLateFee
      .Edit
      .Fields("Deleted") = True
```

```
            .Update
            .Close
        End With
    End Sub
```

The Save Method

The **Save** routine for this object doesn't actually save the object's state as much as it sets a couple fields on the related **LateFee** record. The overall structure of the routine is the same as we've seen before:

```
    Private Sub Save()
        Dim rsLateFee As Recordset
        Dim strSQL As String

        If flgNew Then
            strSQL = "LateFee"
            Set rsLateFee = dbVideo.OpenRecordset(strSQL, dbOpenTable)
            rsLateFee.AddNew
        Else
            strSQL = "SELECT * FROM LateFee WHERE FeeID=" & _
                udtProps.FeeID
            Set rsLateFee = dbVideo.OpenRecordset(strSQL, dbOpenDynaset)
            rsLateFee.Edit
        End If
        With rsLateFee
            .Fields("Paid") = udtProps.Paid
            .Fields("PaidDate") = udtProps.PaidDate
            .Update
            If flgNew Then
                .Bookmark = .LastModified
                udtProps.FeeID = .Fields("FeeID")
            End If
            .Close
        End With
    End Sub
```

The difference is more a philosophical one than a physical one. The **InvoiceFee** object doesn't directly represent the **LateFee** table's data; it is more a user of the record. So the **Save** method is less saving the object's state to a table than it is updating the table to reflect the results of a transaction where the late fee was paid by the customer.

Calling the Persistence Methods

The **InvoiceFee** object's **Fetch** routine will be called by a **ChildLoad** method. We've already added code in the **InvoiceItems** object's **LoadFees** method to call a **ChildLoad** method as it creates each **InvoiceFee** object. Now we need to add that code to the **InvoiceFee** object:

```
    Friend Sub ChildLoad(FeeID As Long)
        If flgChildEditing Then Err.Raise 445
        If Not flgNew Then Err.Raise 445

        ' code to load the object goes here
        Fetch FeeID
        flgNew = False
    End Sub
```

The **DeleteObject** and **Save** routines will be called, as usual, from within the **ChildApplyEdit** method:

```
Friend Sub ChildApplyEdit(InvoiceID As Long)
   If Not flgChildEditing Then Err.Raise 445
   If Not IsValid Then Err.Raise 445

   If flgDeleted Then
      ' code to delete the object's data goes here
      DeleteObject udtProps.FeeID

      flgNew = True
      flgDeleted = False
   ElseIf flgDirty Or flgNew Then
      udtProps.InvoiceID = InvoiceID
      ' save object to database if appropriate
      Save

      ' save object state
      LSet udtChild = udtProps
      flgNew = False
   End If
   flgDirty = False
   flgChildEditing = False
End Sub
```

The **ChildApplyEdit** method is called for each child object by the **InvoiceItems** collection object.

The InvoiceTape Object

The **InvoiceTape** object is very much a typical child object. It has an **InvoiceTape** table to hold each object's state data, and its **Fetch**, **Save** and **DeleteObject** routines work primarily with that table. Since this object is always a child object, there is no **SetAsChild** method as with the **Tape** object, so things are somewhat simpler.

The **Fetch**, **Save** and **DeleteObject** routines work primarily with the **InvoiceTape** table, although the **Title** field is brought in from the **Video** table as it was in the **InvoiceFee** object.

The Save Method

Let's start with the **Save** method:

```
Private Sub Save(InvoiceID As Long)
   Dim rsInvoiceTape As Recordset
   Dim rsVideo As Recordset
   Dim strSQL As String

   If flgNew Then
      strSQL = "InvoiceTape"
      Set rsInvoiceTape = dbVideo.OpenRecordset(strSQL, _
         dbOpenTable)
      rsInvoiceTape.AddNew
   Else
      strSQL = "SELECT * FROM InvoiceTape WHERE ItemID=" & _
         Format$(ItemID)
```

```
      Set rsInvoiceTape = dbVideo.OpenRecordset(strSQL, _
        dbOpenDynaset)
      rsInvoiceTape.Edit
    End If
    With rsInvoiceTape
      .Fields("InvoiceID") = InvoiceID
      .Fields("TapeID") = udtProps.TapeID
      .Fields("Price") = udtProps.Price
      .Update
      If IsNew Then
        .Bookmark = .LastModified
        udtProps.ItemID = .Fields("ItemID")
      End If
      .Close
    End With
    strSQL = "SELECT Video.Title " & _
      "FROM Tape INNER JOIN Video ON " & _
      "Tape.VideoID = Video.VideoID " & _
      "WHERE Tape.TapeID=" & udtProps.TapeID
    Set rsInvoiceTape = dbVideo.OpenRecordset(strSQL, _
      dbOpenSnapshot)
    udtProps.Title = rsInvoiceTape("Title")
    rsInvoiceTape.Close
  End Sub
```

This **Save** routine is a bit different from others we've seen, in that it accepts a parameter. This is typical of **Save** routines for child objects, since they need to receive the primary key value of their parent object. In this case, the parent object is the **Invoice** and so the **InvoiceID** is the parameter.

The **InvoiceID** is then stored in the table so we can use it later to retrieve the child record within the **Fetch** routine:

```
      .Fields("InvoiceID") = InvoiceID
```

This code takes care of saving each line item into the InvoiceTape table. Of course, each invoice line item refers to a specific tape that's being rented. We also need to make sure and update that tape's data.

Checking Out a Tape

In Chapter 5, we implemented a **CheckOut** method on our **Tape** object. This method takes care of indicating that the **Tape** object is currently checked out to a **Customer**. With the **Save** method we just implemented, our **InvoiceTape** object takes care of creating an invoice line item, but it also should make sure to call the **Tape** object's **CheckOut** method so the **Tape** object knows it has been rented.

Since this process involves a bit of code, we'll create a small subroutine in the **InvoiceTape** object to take care of checking out the tape:

```
    Private Sub CheckOut(InvoiceID As Long)
      Dim objTape As Tape

      Set objTape = New Tape
      objTape.Load udtProps.TapeID
```

```
    With objTape
      .BeginEdit
      .CheckOut InvoiceID
      .ApplyEdit
    End With
    Set objTape = Nothing
  End Sub
```

This routine creates an instance of the appropriate **Tape** object by using the **TapeID** field from the line item. It then puts the **Tape** object in edit mode with **BeginEdit**, calls the **CheckOut** method, and applies the change with the **ApplyEdit** method.

We just need to call this routine from the **InvoiceTape** object's **Save** method. We'll add this call near the bottom of the **Save** method we just implemented in the **InvoiceTape** object:

```
    rsInvoiceTape.Close
```
```
    CheckOut InvoiceID
```
```
  End Sub
```

With this code, our **InvoiceTape** objects now not only create an invoice line item, but they also make sure the **Tape** object is checked out. This is a good example of object interaction, in that we are able to take advantage of the **CheckOut** behavior of the **Tape** object from within the **InvoiceTape** object.

DeleteObject and Fetch Methods

The **DeleteObject** code for our object is quite straightforward, and so is the **Fetch** routine:

```
Private Sub DeleteObject(ItemID As Long)
  dbVideo.Execute "DELETE FROM InvoiceTape WHERE ItemID=" & _
    Format$(ItemID)
End Sub

Private Sub Fetch(ItemID As Long)
  Dim rsInvoiceTape As Recordset
  Dim strSQL As String

  strSQL = "SELECT InvoiceTape.*, Video.Title " & _
    "FROM (InvoiceTape INNER JOIN Tape ON " & _
    "InvoiceTape.TapeID = Tape.TapeID) " & _
    "INNER JOIN Video ON Tape.VideoID = Video.VideoID " & _
    "WHERE InvoiceTape.ItemID=" & ItemID
  Set rsInvoiceTape = dbVideo.OpenRecordset(strSQL, _
    dbOpenSnapshot)
  With rsInvoiceTape
    udtProps.ItemID = .Fields("ItemID")
    udtProps.TapeID = .Fields("TapeID")
    udtProps.Title = .Fields("Title")
    udtProps.Price = .Fields("Price")
    rsInvoiceTape.Close
  End With
End Sub
```

These routines are called from within the **InvoiceTape** object's **ChildLoad** and **ChildApplyEdit** methods.

Calling the Persistence Methods

We don't have to worry about the **Load** or **ApplyEdit** methods at all with this object, since these are always child objects, and those two methods will never cause the objects to interact with the database:

```
Friend Sub ChildApplyEdit(InvoiceID As Long)
   If Not flgChildEditing Then Err.Raise 445
   If Not IsValid Then Err.Raise 445

   If flgDeleted Then
      ' code to delete the object's data goes here
      DeleteObject udtProps.ItemID
      flgNew = True
      flgDeleted = False
   ElseIf flgDirty Or flgNew Then
      ' save object to database if appropriate
      Save InvoiceID
      ' save object state
      LSet udtChild = udtProps
      flgNew = False
   End If
   flgDirty = False
   flgChildEditing = False
End Sub
```

The **Fetch** routine will be called from a **ChildLoad** method. We've already added code in the **Load** method of the **InvoiceItems** object to call this method, but we still need to add some code to this method in the **InvoiceTape** class:

```
Friend Sub ChildLoad(ItemID As Long)
   If flgChildEditing Then Err.Raise 445
   If Not flgNew Then Err.Raise 445

   ' code to load the object goes here
   Fetch ItemID

   flgNew = False
End Sub
```

This method is essentially the same as any of the other **Load** or **ChildLoad** methods we've implemented so far in this chapter.

385

Making Read-only Objects Persistent

The final set of objects we need to cover are the read-only objects that we built in Chapter 5. The **Customers** and **Videos** objects are designed to return lists of information to the UI so the UI developer can create a screen displaying a list of the items.

This list might be used either for simple display or as selection criteria to load a **Customer** or **Video** object. The UI we designed in Chapter 6 uses these objects to provide a list of items for the user to choose from for editing.

The **TextList** object is more generic, providing a list of text values for use in populating **ComboBox** or **ListBox** controls. The list of values is also used to validate data entry into certain properties on an object. For instance, our **Video** object provides **Categories** and **Ratings** properties for the UI to populate **ComboBox** controls, and also uses the **TextList** objects to make sure the **Category** and **Rating** values entered by the user are valid.

In all of these cases, the data in the objects is provided in a read-only fashion. The UI code can't change or update any of the data. This means that we won't need to provide **Save** or **DeleteObject** routines within these objects. All we'll be doing is loading information into the object from the database, so the only routine that we need to worry about is the **Fetch** routine.

The Customers Object

In Chapter 5, we implemented what was essentially a skeleton of the Customers object. Much of this object relies on the data access code to actually operate, so we'll really flesh it out in this section.

Loading the Customers Object's Data

The **Customers** object provides a **Load** method with two optional parameters, **Name** and **Phone**. The UI developer can call this method to cause the object to load itself with data matching those parameters, with the expectation that they'll be used as matching criteria to return a list of customer information. This is where we'll call our **Fetch** routine, relaying the two parameters along as well. Add this line to the **Customers** object:

```
Public Sub Load(Optional Name As String, _
   Optional Phone As String)
   ' load data from database
   Fetch Name, Phone

End Sub
```

*We're not using the **IsMissing()** function to check to see if both **Name** and **Phone** were supplied. This is because both parameters are typed as **String**, and **IsMissing()** is only valid for optional parameters of type **Variant**. With optional parameters of other data types the function will always return **False**, even if the client code didn't actually supply a value. Just one of those idiosyncrasies of Visual Basic 5.0...*

The **Customers** object's **Fetch** routine takes the parameters and uses them to build a SQL **SELECT** statement to find any matching customer data in the **Customer** table:

```
Private Sub Fetch(Name As String, Phone As String)
   Dim rsCustomer As Recordset
   Dim strSQL As String
   Dim strWHERE As String
   Dim objDisplay As CustomerDisplay

   strSQL = "SELECT CUSTOMERID, NAME, PHONE FROM CUSTOMER"
   If Len(Name) > 0 Then _
      strWHERE = "NAME LIKE '" & Name & "*' "
   If Len(Phone) > 0 Then
      If Len(strWHERE) > 0 Then
         strWHERE = strWHERE & " AND PHONE LIKE '" & Phone & "*'"
      Else
         strWHERE = "PHONE LIKE '" & Phone & "*'"
      End If
   End If
   If Len(strWHERE) > 0 Then _
      strSQL = strSQL & " WHERE " & strWHERE
   Set rsCustomer = dbVideo.OpenRecordset(strSQL, dbOpenSnapshot)
   Do While Not rsCustomer.EOF
      Set objDisplay = New CustomerDisplay
      With objDisplay
         .CustomerID = rsCustomer("CustomerID")
         .Name = rsCustomer("Name")
         .Phone = rsCustomer("Phone")
         colDisplay.Add objDisplay
         Set objDisplay = Nothing
         rsCustomer.MoveNext
      End With
   Loop
   rsCustomer.Close
End Sub
```

We're not doing anything particularly fancy here. If the user supplied a **Name** value, we add it to the **WHERE** clause along with a wildcard character. The same goes for the **Phone** value: if the user supplied a value, we stick a wildcard on the end and add it to the clause. In both cases, we use the **LIKE** keyword to cause the JET engine to do a wildcard match against the fields in the table.

> *If we are writing this code to go against an ODBC data source, we'll need to make sure to use the '%' character instead of the '*' character for the wildcard match.*

The **SELECT** statement only returns the three values that we'll be providing through the **CustomerDisplay** object's properties, **CustomerID**, **Name** and **Phone**. While restricting the number of fields returned in a **SELECT** statement doesn't impact performance much when dealing with an Access database, it is critical in a two-tier setting using an ODBC data source.

Once we've got a SQL statement to work with, we open a recordset; in this case, a **Snapshot** to retrieve the data:

```
Set rsCustomer = dbVideo.OpenRecordset(strSQL, dbOpenSnapshot)
```

At this point, the **Fetch** routine looks a lot like the others we've built in this chapter. The code loops through the recordset, creating a **CustomerDisplay** object for each record in the list:

```
Do While Not rsCustomer.EOF
    Set objDisplay = New CustomerDisplay
```

The **CustomerDisplay** object has no **Load** method and, in fact, we've already retrieved all the data we need to populate the **CustomerDisplay** objects. In Chapter 5, we implemented **Property Let** routines for each **Property Get**, but we made them all with **Friend** scope. That way, they can be given values by the **Customers** object, but the values can't be changed by the UI code, since **Friend** properties aren't available outside the ActiveX server itself:

```
With objDisplay
   .CustomerID = rsCustomer("CustomerID")
   .Name = rsCustomer("Name")
   .Phone = rsCustomer("Phone")
   colDisplay.Add objDisplay
   Set objDisplay = Nothing
   rsCustomer.MoveNext
End With
Loop
rsCustomer.Close
End Sub
```

This code sets the **CustomerDisplay** object's properties from the recordset, adds the object to the **Customers** object's collection, and moves on to the next record.

Updating the Customers Object's Item Method

The **Customers** object, as we implemented it in Chapter 5, has only comments in its **Item** method. This is because we didn't know, at the time, how the **CustomerDisplay** objects would be loaded, since the implementation can vary depending on how we handle persistence.

Now that we've implemented the **Customers** object's **Fetch** routine, we know how it works. Our new **Fetch** routine loads the data from the database and creates a **CustomerDisplay** object for each record from the database. In the end, the **colDisplay** collection contains a list of **CustomerDisplay** objects, all ready for use.

With this implementation, our **Customers** object's Item method is very simple, since all it needs to do is return the appropriate item from **colDisplay**:

```
Public Function Item(ByVal Index As Variant) As CustomerDisplay
    Set Item = colDisplay(Index)
End Function
```

The Videos Object

The **Videos** object has a **Load** method and a **Fetch** routine just like the **Customers** object. We'll include the code here, but we won't go through it in detail since the process is identical to what we just implemented with the **Customers** object.

The Load Method

Again, the **Load** method accepts parameters to be used as criteria to find any matching records. These parameters are relayed to the **Fetch** subroutine for its use.

```
Public Sub Load(Optional Title As String, _
  Optional Studio As String)
  ' load data from database

  Fetch Title, Studio

End Sub
```

The Fetch Method

The **Fetch** routine takes the parameters and builds a SQL **SELECT** statement that is used to open a recordset with all the matching records. A **VideoDisplay** object is created for each row in the recordset, its properties are loaded from the recordset's data, and the object is added to the collection:

```
Private Sub Fetch(Title As String, Studio As String)
  Dim rsVideo As Recordset
  Dim strSQL As String
  Dim strWHERE As String
  Dim objDisplay As VideoDisplay

  strSQL = "SELECT VideoID, TITLE,RELEASEDATE FROM Video"
  If Len(Title) > 0 Then _
    strWHERE = "TITLE LIKE '" & Title & "*' "
  If Len(Studio) > 0 Then
    If Len(strWHERE) > 0 Then
      strWHERE = strWHERE & " AND STUDIO LIKE '" & Studio & "*'"
    Else
      strWHERE = "STUDIO LIKE '" & Studio & "*'"
    End If
  End If
  If Len(strWHERE) > 0 Then _
    strSQL = strSQL & " WHERE " & strWHERE
  Set rsVideo = dbVideo.OpenRecordset(strSQL, dbOpenSnapshot)
  Do While Not rsVideo.EOF
    Set objDisplay = New VideoDisplay
    With objDisplay
      .VideoID = rsVideo("VideoID")
      .Title = rsVideo("Title")
      .ReleaseDate = rsVideo("ReleaseDate")
      colDisplay.Add objDisplay
      Set objDisplay = Nothing
      rsVideo.MoveNext
    End With
  Loop
  rsVideo.Close
End Sub
```

The Item Method

As with the **Customers** object, we need to update the **Item** method of our **Videos** object. In Chapter 5, we just put comments in this routine, but here we'll put in some code:

```
Public Function Item(ByVal Index As Variant) As VideoDisplay
    Set Item = colDisplay(Index)
End Function
```

Our **Fetch** routine creates a **VideoDisplay** object for each record retrieved from the database. It then loads each **VideoDisplay** object into the **colDisplay** collection, so our **Item** method merely needs to return the appropriate **VideoDisplay** object from the collection on request.

The TextList Object

The **TextList** object is a bit different, though still quite similar to what we've seen. Like all the other objects, it has a **Load** method that calls the **Fetch** routine.

```
Friend Sub Load(ListName As String)
    Fetch ListName
End Sub
```

It may seem odd that we bother to have a separate **Fetch** routine if the **Load** method is only a single line of code to call that routine. Why not include the code from the **Fetch** routine right into the **Load** method? If we had no intention of moving the data access code to an application server later, it might make sense to put the code into the **Load** method. However, we'll be moving this code to another object in Chapter 9, so we're doing this to make it easier later.

In writing this routine, we've made some specific assumptions that are very important. We're assuming that the **ListName** parameter will be the same as the name of the table containing the data. We're also assuming that the table's layout has a first column with a unique ID value and a second column where the text value is displayed.

Since we designed both the **Category** and **Rating** tables this way, we can make these assumptions. If we have a more complex data design we may have to make this routine more complicated to compensate.

Like most of our other **Fetch** subroutines, this one opens a recordset to retrieve a list of values from the table. In this case, we're opening the whole table as a Snapshot by using the **ListName** parameter in the **OpenRecordset** statement:

```
Private Sub Fetch(ListName As String)
  Dim strSQL As String
  Dim rsList As Recordset

  Set rsList = dbVideo.OpenRecordset(ListName, dbOpenSnapshot)
  Do While Not rsList.EOF
    colList.Add Format$(rsList(1)), Format$(rsList(0))
    colKeys.Add Format$(rsList(0)), Format$(rsList(1))
    rsList.MoveNext
  Loop
  rsList.Close
End Sub
```

Then we loop through all the elements in the recordset, loading both the **colList** and **colKeys** collections. The **colList** collection is loaded with the text values being the Item and the ID value from the table being the collection's Key:

```
Do While Not rsList.EOF
   colList.Add Format$(rsList(1)), Format$(rsList(0))
```

The **colKeys** collection is loaded with the ID value from the table as the collection's Item and the text value from the table as the Key. This is exactly the reverse of the **colList** collection:

```
      colKeys.Add Format$(rsList(0)), Format$(rsList(1))
      rsList.MoveNext
   Loop
   rsList.Close
End Sub
```

After all the values have been loaded into both collections, we close the recordset and the object is ready for use.

Now we've implemented the persistence code for our **TextList** object, we can update some code that we began to develop in Chapter 5 that was dependent upon this persistence. In the **Video** object's **Class_Initialize** method, we noted that we needed to set our **udtProps.Category** and **udtProps.Rating** variables with data from the database. We've had to wait until now to update this code, because we read the data from the **TextList** objects within the **VideoEdit** form. So add the following lines to the **Class_Initialize** method of the **Video** object:

```
      Set objCategories = New TextList
      objCategories.Load "Category"
      udtProps.Category = objCategories.Key(objCategories(1))

      Set objRatings = New TextList
      objRatings.Load "Rating"
      udtProps.Rating = objRatings.Key(objRatings(1))
```

These lines store the first item from the Category and Rating tables within our **udtProps.Category** and **udtProps.Rating** variables by reading the data we've just read in from the Load method of our **TextList** variables.

Summary

Given the material we've covered in this chapter (as well as Chapters 5 and 6), we now have a fully functional application - which is no small achievement. The business objects provide the application's logic, and we have a user-interface developed with Visual Basic forms.

In this chapter, we added the final piece of the puzzle, giving the objects the ability to save and restore themselves from the database.

We looked at techniques to persist a number of different types of object:

❑ Simple objects
❑ Parent objects
❑ Child objects
❑ Parent-child relationship objects
❑ Read-only objects

The techniques that we've used in this chapter are fairly limiting in terms of scalability, since the data access code is right inside each object and thus would be running on each client workstation. On the other hand, the approach is very simple to implement, so it can be a good solution for a single-tier or 2-tier setting.

There are some flaws in this approach when it comes to database transactions. It is technically possible to save a **Video** record, then have one of the **Tape** objects saves fail, leaving us with questionable data in the tables. This can be overcome by adding *BeginTrans* and *CommitTrans* statements in strategic locations within our objects. We didn't address this issue within the chapter, so we could keep the focus on the process of saving and restoring the objects' data.

In Chapters 9 and 10, we'll revisit object persistence, moving the **Fetch**, **Save** and **DeleteObject** routines for each object off to an application server. We will further address performance, scalability, and transactional support in those chapters.

9

Using Microsoft Office as an Interface

Overview

One of the major benefits of designing our application as a component that contains business objects is that we can easily change the user-interface. We can even go so far as to have multiple user-interfaces to the same application code.

In Chapters 5 and 6, we built an application using business objects, and in Chapter 8 we added code so that those objects can save and restore themselves from a database. In Chapter 7, we implemented a user-interface to the application using Visual Basic forms and controls.

To illustrate just how powerful component-oriented application design can be, in this chapter we'll build a user-interface to some of our objects from within Microsoft Office 97. We'll be using Microsoft Excel as our environment, but most of the concepts we'll cover in this chapter can be easily translated to Microsoft Word, PowerPoint and Project.

We won't be replacing the entire user-interface that we built in Chapter 7; instead, we'll focus on some of the specific approaches that we can take when we're using Excel as an interface to our application's business object components.

Compiling the VideoObjects Project

In Chapter 7, we used Visual Basic 5.0's ability to load multiple projects into a single environment using a project group. If we want to develop user-interfaces using tools other than Visual Basic 5.0, however, we'll need to compile our project into an actual binary component so that the other tool can access it. With the **VideoObjects** project, we compile it into an ActiveX DLL.

To compile the project, open up Visual Basic and load the **VideoObjects** project into the environment. Then choose the File-Make VideoObjects.dll... menu option:

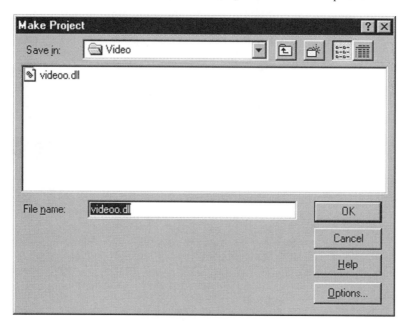

In this example, we'll name the DLL **videoo.dll** rather than **VideoObjects.dll**. You can name it either way as you choose.

> *I always try to make my compiled components follow the old DOS 8.3 file naming convention. Sure it is outdated and limiting, but it's amazing how many places you'll go where they have old Novell servers or workstations running DOS or Windows 3.x. Even though the components aren't useful on those machines, they get in the way and you end up renaming the files to fit in an 8.3 name.*

Once you've compiled the DLL, make sure to save the **VideoObjects** project. It will have recorded the location of the file we just created and will use that file to maintain project compatibility - as we discussed in Chapter 7.

Using a User Form as an Interface

Microsoft Office 97 comes with VBA (Visual Basic for Applications) built right into all its applications.

> **Creating an interface using VBA is very similar to creating an interface with Visual Basic itself.**

This shouldn't be surprising, since VBA is a subset of Visual Basic. The underlying language used by all VB programmers is the language provided by VBA.

In this section, we'll see how to create an interface to our business objects using Excel. The other applications in the Microsoft Office suite have the ability to create the same interface just as easily, so we could easily apply the same concepts to Word or PowerPoint and develop a similar interface, if that was required.

Creating the Interface

We'll walk through the process of adding a form within Excel, so we can add a customer using our **Customer** business object. As we'll see, the process is remarkably similar to adding such a form to our **VideoUI** project from Chapter 7.

Once we've built the form, we'll see how we can make that form available to the user from within Excel. There are many ways to do this but, to keep things fairly simple, we'll just add a button to a spreadsheet that brings up the form - so the user can add a customer to the database.

Opening the VBA Editor

To use VBA within Excel, we need to open up the Visual Basic Editor. First things first, though; you'll need to open up Excel before we can go any further.

Within Excel, choose the Tools-Macro-Visual Basic Editor menu option or press *Alt-F11*. Either way, after a short pause you should see the editor appear on your screen:

Not surprisingly, it looks very similar to the familiar Visual Basic 5.0 interface that we work in all the time. It has a Project window, a Properties window, and even an Immediate window for use with debugging.

We'll use this environment to develop an interface to our **Customer** business object.

Adding a Reference to VideoObjects

As with the **VideoUI** project we developed in Chapter 7, we'll need to add a reference to the **VideoObjects** server. Earlier in this chapter, we compiled the **VideoObjects** project into a DLL - so we should be all ready to add a reference to our **VideoObjects** from within this new environment.

Choose the Tools-References... menu option to bring up the References dialog:

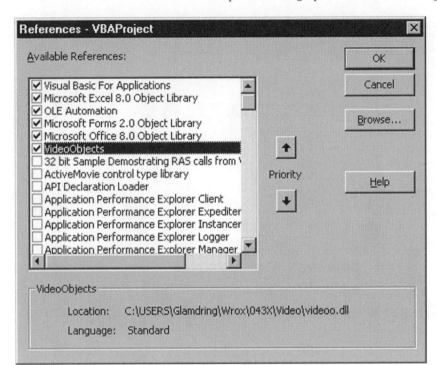

Find the **VideoObjects** entry in the list and check the box to its left. Then click OK to add a reference to the server.

Adding a UserForm

Now that we have a reference to our server, we can move on to building the interface itself. The VBA Editor environment is not as advanced or friendly as the Visual Basic 5.0 IDE, but it does provide the basic functionality that we'll need to build the interface.

Chapter 9

Choose the Insert-UserForm menu option to add a form to the project:

A new form, **UserForm1**, is added to the Project window and is displayed in the edit area. A Toolbox, similar to the Visual Basic Toolbox, will appear - so we have a palette from which we can add controls to the form.

Using the Properties window, change the Name of the form to **CustomerEdit** and the Caption property to **Add a customer**.

Adding Our Controls

Within the new form, we need to add controls so that the user can enter the customer information. To continue my emphasis on the similarity between forms within Office and forms within Visual Basic itself, let's make this form look as close as possible to the **CustomerEdit** form we created in Chapter 7:

Add the controls as shown, using the following naming scheme.

Control	Caption	Name
Label	Name	
TextBox		**txtName**
Label	Address	
TextBox		**txtAddr1**
TextBox		**txtAddr2**
TextBox		**txtCity**
TextBox		**txtState**
TextBox		**txtZipCode**
Label	Phone	
TextBox		**txtPhone**
CommandButton	OK	**cmdOK**
CommandButton	Cancel	**cmdCancel**
CommandButton	Apply	**cmdApply**

Click on the OK button and change its **Default** property to **True**. Then click on the Cancel button and change its **Cancel** property to **True**. This will make the buttons respond appropriately to the *Enter* and *Escape* keys if they are pressed by the user.

Code Behind the Form

If you glance back at the **CustomerEdit** form in Chapter 7, you will notice that this form looks virtually identical. Even more importantly, all the controls are laid out the same and have the same names. This is far from coincidental, and we'll make use of these similarities right now.

Copying the Code from Chapter 7

Bring up Visual Basic itself and open up the **VideoUI** project. In the Project window, click on the **CustomerEdit** form and open up its code window.

Select all the text behind the **CustomerEdit** form and choose Edit-Copy. To quickly select all the text, you can use the Edit-Select All menu option. Note that you'll need Full Module View on to see all the code in the class at once.

Now switch back to the Visual Basic Editor and double-click on the **CustomerEdit** form there to bring up its code editing window. Paste the contents of the clipboard, the code from Chapter 7, into this new form's code window.

I won't repeat the code here; you can look back to Chapter 7 to see what it looks like, how it works, and why we did things the way we did.

Adapting the Code for Excel

The events behind the **UserForm** are not identical to those behind a regular Form. This is also true of the controls. These controls are different from their Visual Basic counterparts; there are also some different events, some with different names.

The biggest difference that affects us is that there is no **Load** event for the form. Without this event, there's no easy way to know when to load the object's property values into the form's controls. The best compromise, in this case, is to load the controls when the form's **Component** property is set:

```
Public Sub Component(objComponent As Customer)
   Set objCustomer = objComponent
   flgLoading = True
   With objCustomer
     EnableOK .IsValid
     If .IsNew Then
       Caption = "Customer [(new)]"
     Else
       Caption = "Customer [" & .Name & "]"
     End If
     txtName = .Name
     txtAddr1 = .Address1
     txtAddr2 = .Address2
     txtCity = .City
     txtState = .State
     txtZipCode = .ZipCode
     txtPhone = .Phone
     .BeginEdit
   End With
   flgLoading = False
End Sub
```

This is the code that was in the **Form_Load** routine. Of course, that routine is no longer needed - since there's no **Load** event to fire it.

All the events used by our controls still exist, except for **LostFocus** on the **TextBox** controls. This event does still exist; but in VBA it's called **AfterUpdate** instead. If we perform an Edit-Replace and change all the occurrences of _LostFocus to _AfterUpdate this problem will be fixed as well. For instance, the **txtName_LostFocus** routine should become:

```
Private Sub txtName_AfterUpdate()
```

With those small changes, we have brought an entire form's worth of code from Visual Basic 5.0 into a Form in Microsoft Office. Pretty incredible.

Testing the Interface

At this point, we've got a form in Excel that lets us add and edit **Customer** objects. Now we need to test it, and also come up with a way for users to bring up the form.

Testing the Interface in the Editor

It's quite easy to test a form from within the VBA Editor, although it may not be very obvious where to start, since our form requires that the **Component** property be set to a new **Customer** object before the form is shown to the user - and that requires a bit of code.

Fortunately, this environment makes this reasonably easy. All we need to do is create a small test subroutine to create the **Customer** object, set the **Component** property and show the form.

Adding Code to a Code Module

To add this routine, we need to open a code window in which to type. This is easy: choosing the Insert-Module menu option. The result should be an empty code window named Book1.xls – Module1 (code).

Now we can add our test routine by typing the following code.

```
Option Explicit

Public Sub Test()
  Dim objCustomer As Customer
  Dim frmCustomer As CustomerEdit

  Set objCustomer = New Customer
  Set frmCustomer = New CustomerEdit

  frmCustomer.Component objCustomer
  frmCustomer.Show
End Sub
```

The code in the Test subroutine should look pretty familiar, since it's the same as the code in the File-Customers-New Customer menu option from Chapter 7:

```
Private Sub mnuFileCustNew_Click()
   Dim objCustomer As Customer
   Dim frmCustomer As CustomerEdit

   Set objCustomer = New Customer
   Set frmCustomer = New CustomerEdit

   frmCustomer.Component objCustomer
   frmCustomer.Show
End Sub
```

Running the Test Routine

If you look at the toolbar in the VBA Editor window you'll see the standard Run, Pause and Stop buttons for debugging, just like in the Visual Basic 5.0 IDE. My first assumption upon seeing them was that they'd work just like the ones in Visual Basic.

Actually, they work similarly, but with an important difference. When you click the Run button, or press *F5*, the editor will run the code for the routine where the cursor is located.

This means that we can simply click anywhere in the code for the Test routine, as long as the cursor is located somewhere in that code, and press *F5*. The VBA Editor will run the Test routine, creating a **Customer** object and a **CustomerEdit** form. The form's **Component** property will be set, and the form will be displayed.

We should now be able to use the form to add a customer - just like the interface we created in Chapter 7. Notice how the **State** field is automatically made uppercase, and the **ZipCode** field gets automatically formatted, just like in the Visual Basic forms interface.

> The rules within the business object are enforced within this interface just as thoroughly as with the Visual Basic forms interface. This is because we are using the same underlying business logic contained within the **VideoObjects** component.

Once you've added a customer or two using this interface, switch back to the **VideoUI** program we created in Chapter 7. You should be able to bring up these new customers to view and edit them there. There's no difference between customers added in Excel or within Visual Basic, since both interfaces utilize the same underlying business objects.

Perhaps even more importantly, neither interface has any idea about how the data is actually stored in the database. Both of them rely entirely on the objects to manage those details, making it possible to entirely rewrite or change the database access with no impact on the UI at all.

Adding a Button to a Spreadsheet

OK, so now we know we've got a working form within Excel. All that remains is to make the form available to the user. As I've indicated, we'll do this by simply adding a button to a spreadsheet, or as Excel calls them, a worksheet.

Adding a Button to a Worksheet

There are a couple different ways to add controls to a worksheet. We can add a button as a control, or as an element of an Excel Form. In this case, we'll add the button as an element of an Excel Form, since that will make it easy to tie right into the work we've done so far.

To add the button, choose the View-Toolbars-Forms menu option in Excel. This will bring up the Forms palette:

Now we can use this palette to add a button to the worksheet - just as we would add a button to a Visual Basic form. Click on the button icon in the palette, then click and drag within the worksheet to create and size the control.

As soon as you release the mouse after drawing the button on the worksheet, Excel will bring up the Assign Macro dialog so we can associate a macro with the button:

Fortunately, for us, macros in Microsoft Office 97 are simply Visual Basic subroutines that are located in code modules. They do have to be declared as **Public** subroutines, however, just like we did with the **Test** subroutine earlier.

In fact, we can see that **Test** is listed as a valid macro within the workbook. Just click the **Test** option from the list and then click OK. This will associate the button with the **Test** subroutine that we built earlier.

Setting the Button's Caption

The button's caption probably reads Button 1, so we'll want to change that. If we move the mouse over the text in the control the cursor should change to the standard I-beam for text editing. Just click to get an edit cursor within the control and we can then change the caption text to read Add customer:

Now you can click the close box in the upper-right corner of the Form palette. This will switch Excel back to a normal user mode from the form editing mode we've been in so far.

Trying the Button

Now, when we move the mouse over the Add customer button, the cursor should change to a pointing finger. If you click the button, it will run the associated macro; in this case, that macro is our **Test** routine.

Of course, the **Test** routine creates a **Customer** object and a **CustomerEdit** form, sets the **CustomerEdit** form's **Component** property, and shows the form. This means that any time the button is clicked our form will appear, allowing the user to add a **Customer** object.

Excel always shows forms modally, so we don't need to worry about the user opening dozens of copies at the same time. If the user clicks anywhere else within Excel when the **CustomerEdit** form is displayed, they'll just get a beep: the rest of the application is locked out.

Using a Document to View Objects

In the first section of this chapter, we looked at how easily Visual Basic forms can be translated into forms within Microsoft Office. Now we'll move on to see how information can be pulled from objects for display within other applications.

This second approach is much more closely allied to whichever Office application we happen to be working on. Our previous example used a type of form that was consistent across all the Office applications; that form could therefore be moved from Excel to Word with relative ease.

In this second example, however, we'll be creating a report using Excel's abilities to display information. To move this report from Excel to Word, for example, would require substantial changes to the interface code we're about to write. In many ways, though, this second approach is more powerful, since it allows us to tap into the strengths of each Office application.

The objects we designed in Chapters 5 and 6 were focused on providing editing and transaction capabilities for our system. We didn't put a lot of thought into making it easy to display information about our objects. Even so, it should be possible to develop a spreadsheet that lists all the video tapes in our inventory and shows their current status. We'll then have a basic report that shows which tapes are available and when the others are due back from the customers.

If this type of display is a requirement for any of our applications, we can choose to design specific read-only objects to provide the necessary information. This is especially true if we're dealing with a three-tier architecture, since we'd then want to optimize the data retrieval process so that all the data we wanted to display was pulled back in one shot.

The way our objects are implemented currently, each object will retrieve its own data. This means the data will come back in small chunks, one object at a time - very slow in a distributed setting.

Building the Report

Since we've already got Excel up and running, and our workbook has a reference to the **VideoObjects** component, we'll continue to use the same workbook that we used in our earlier example.

Like the previous example, we'll rely on our business objects to do most of the work, but in this case we'll just use a regular Excel workbook for the interface. We won't be developing any forms or using any controls except the button to launch our report.

Also as with the previous example, we'll be writing an Excel macro using VBA to generate the report. The code will therefore look very familiar to any VB programmer.

The first thing we need to do is get back to the VBA Editor within Excel. If you still have it running, then just switch to it; otherwise, choose the Tools-Macro-Visual Basic Editor menu option to bring it up.

Earlier in the chapter, we added a code module, **Module1**. This module should contain our **Test** macro that brings up the **CustomerEdit** form. We'll just add the report code to this code module, since it's already set up and ready to go.

Bring up the **Module1** code window by double-clicking the Module1 entry in the Project window. Now let's add a macro subroutine named **VideoList**.

```
Public Sub VideoList()

End Sub
```

Printing Column Titles

To make our report readable, we need to add column headers or titles. This is also an excellent opportunity to look at some simple code that puts text into a worksheet:

```
Public Sub VideoList()
    Columns("A:D").Select
    Selection.ClearContents

    Range("A1").Select
```

```
      ActiveCell.FormulaR1C1 = "Video title"
      ActiveCell.Font.Bold = True
      Range("C1").Select
      ActiveCell.FormulaR1C1 = "Acquired"
      ActiveCell.Font.Bold = True
      Range("D1").Select
      ActiveCell.FormulaR1C1 = "Status"
      ActiveCell.Font.Bold = True
      Range("A1").Select
```

```
End Sub
```

Clearing the Columns

The first couple of lines are there to make sure the columns where we're going to put in the report don't already have text in them. The first line selects all of columns from A through to D:

```
Columns("A:D").Select
```

The other line clears the contents of those columns, leaving them empty and ready for our report:

```
Selection.ClearContents
```

Adding the Titles

The rest of the code is quite repetitive. For each column title, we move the current selection to the cell that should contain the text:

```
Range("A1").Select
```

Once the correct cell is selected, the text is inserted. What we're really inserting is an Excel formula, but simple text is just displayed without any processing by Excel:

```
ActiveCell.FormulaR1C1 = "Video title"
```

To set the column titles apart from the other text, the current cell's contents are set to a bold font:

```
ActiveCell.Font.Bold = True
```

The last line in the routine, so far, just sets the current cell back to the far upper left, A1. This gives us a nice consistent starting point for the code we'll add next.

By this point, you can probably see that programming inside Excel is really no different from programming in Visual Basic with any other object. Excel and all its parts are just a group of objects that are available for your use as a programmer. Of course, to program effectively inside Excel, we need to learn what all the objects are and what they can do. That's pretty much equivalent to learning a whole new language!

The easiest way to figure out how to use Excel's object is to use the macro recorder to record a macro while you manually walk through the steps you need to do. Then you can go back and read the VBA code contained in the macro to figure out how it works.

Adding a Button

Now that we've got a start on our macro, let's add a button to the worksheet so we can try it out. Again, we'll add a button by using the Forms palette and just make it run our **VideoList** macro routine.

Switch to Excel and bring up the Forms palette by choosing the View-Toolbars-Forms menu option. Choose the Button option and click and drag to put a button on the Sheet1 worksheet.

When you release the mouse button, the Assign Macro dialog should appear:

Choose the **VideoList** macro and click OK. Now the button is connected to the macro, so all that remains is to set the button's caption. Change the button's caption to read List video titles.

Now, if we click the button we can watch as Excel clears out columns A through D and puts our column headers across the top. As we continue to build our report, we'll be able to click the button to see the results of the changes as we make them.

Listing the Video Titles

The first thing we need to do is get a list of all the video titles in the inventory. Fortunately, we created a **Videos** object that can do just that; all we need to do is call its **Load** method with no parameters and it will return a list of all the video titles in the system:

```
Public Sub VideoList()

    Dim objVideos As Videos
    Dim objDisplay As VideoDisplay


    Columns("A:D").Select
    Selection.ClearContents
```

```
      Range("A1").Select
      ActiveCell.FormulaR1C1 = "Video title"
      ActiveCell.Font.Bold = True
      Range("C1").Select
      ActiveCell.FormulaR1C1 = "Acquired"
      ActiveCell.Font.Bold = True
      Range("D1").Select
      ActiveCell.FormulaR1C1 = "Status"
      ActiveCell.Font.Bold = True
      Range("A1").Select
```

```
      Set objVideos = New Videos
      objVideos.Load
      For Each objDisplay In objVideos
        With objDisplay
          ActiveCell.Offset(1,0).Range("A1").Select
          ActiveCell.FormulaR1C1 = .Title
        End With
      Next
```

```
    End Sub
```

The **Videos** object is a **Collection** object whose items are objects of type **VideoDisplay**. The first thing we need to do is create the **Videos** object and get it loaded with data from the database:

```
      Set objVideos = New Videos
      objVideos.Load
```

Then we can loop through the collection and print the **Title** property for each **VideoDisplay** object it contains. To do this, we use a **For Each...Next** syntax to loop through the collection and retrieve each **VideoDisplay** object:

```
      For Each objDisplay In objVideos
        With objDisplay
          ActiveCell.Offset(1,0).Range("A1").Select
          ActiveCell.FormulaR1C1 = .Title
        End With
      Next
```

The line that sets the current cell is a bit different from anything that we've seen so far. Instead of using an absolute reference, such as **A2**, this code uses a relative reference. It indicates an offset from the current cell, specifying how far down, then across, to move the current cell:

```
      ActiveCell.Offset(1, 0).Range("A1").Select
```

If you click the List video titles button at this point, you should get a list of video titles from your database. Here's what the display looks like with my sample data:

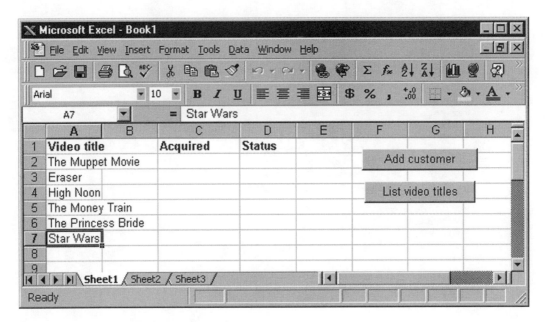

Listing the Tapes and their Status

Now that we have a list of video titles we just need to add code to list all the tapes for each title and show their status. Fortunately, one of the properties of the **VideoDisplay** object is the **VideoID**.

We can use this property as a parameter to the **Load** method of a **Video** object. Once we have a **Video** object, we can use its **Tapes** property to list all the child **Tape** objects for that **Video**, including their status based on the **CheckedIn** property of the **Tape** object:

```
Public Sub VideoList()
    Dim objVideos As Videos
    Dim objDisplay As VideoDisplay

    Dim objVideo As Video
    Dim objTape As Tape

    Columns("A:D").Select
    Selection.ClearContents

    Range("A1").Select
    ActiveCell.FormulaR1C1 = "Video title"
    ActiveCell.Font.Bold = True
    Range("C1").Select
    ActiveCell.FormulaR1C1 = "Acquired"
    ActiveCell.Font.Bold = True
    Range("D1").Select
    ActiveCell.FormulaR1C1 = "Status"
    ActiveCell.Font.Bold = True
    Range("A1").Select

    Set objVideos = New Videos
    objVideos.Load
    For Each objDisplay In objVideos
```

```
        Set objVideo = New Video
        objVideo.Load objDisplay.VideoID
        With objVideo
            ActiveCell.Offset(1,0).Range("A1").Select
            ActiveCell.FormulaR1C1 = .Title

            ActiveCell.Offset(1,2).Range("A1").Select
            For Each objTape In .Tapes
              With objTape
                ActiveCell.FormulaR1C1 = .DateAcquired
                ActiveCell.Offset(0, 1).Range("A1").Select
                If .CheckedOut Then
                  ActiveCell.FormulaR1C1 = "Due back " & _
                    Format$(.DateDue, "Short date")
                Else
                  ActiveCell.FormulaR1C1 ="Available"
                End If
              End With
              ActiveCell.Offset(1, -1).Range("A1").Select
            Next
        End With

        ActiveCell.Offset(0, -2).Range("A1").Select
      Next
    End Sub
```

Now, for each **VideoDisplay** object, we can turn right around and create an actual **Video** object:

```
        Set objVideo = New Video
        objVideo.Load objDisplay.VideoID
        With objVideo
```

The **Title** property that we display can come from the **Video** object itself rather than from the **VideoDisplay** object at this point, though the line of code to display the value doesn't change.

Because we need to indent the list of tape information to column C, we have a line of code to move the current cell to the right by 2:

```
        ActiveCell.Offset(1,2).Range("A1").Select
```

Then, we can just loop through all the **Tape** objects contained in the **Video** object's **Tapes** collection:

```
        For Each objTape In .Tapes
          With objTape
```

The first thing we display for each tape is the date it was acquired. We've already moved the current cell to the right spot, so we can just display the value and move the cell to the right by one in preparation for displaying the tape's status:

```
          ActiveCell.FormulaR1C1 =.DateAcquired
          ActiveCell.Offset(0,1).Range("A1").Select
```

To make the display more useful, we've also added some code to print the due date for any tape that is currently rented, or the word 'Available' for those that aren't rented out:

```
If .CheckedOut Then
  ActiveCell.FormulaR1C1 = "Due back " & _
    Format$(.DateDue, "Short date")
Else
  ActiveCell.FormulaR1C1 ="Available"
End If
```

Of course, we need to move the current cell down one and to the left, so things are positioned properly for the next tape's acquired date:

```
End With
ActiveCell.Offset(1, -1).Range("A1").Select
```

Once all the **Tape** objects have been displayed, we need to exit the loop and move the current cell to the left by 2. That should return it to column A, where it needs to be in order to display the next **Video** object's **Title** property:

```
    Next
  End With
  ActiveCell.Offset(0, -2).Range("A1").Select
Next
End Sub
```

The VideoList Report

Now, if we click the List video titles button, we'll get the full report, including the column headers, the video titles, and the status of each tape:

Summary

In this chapter, we implemented a second interface to our business objects, one that easily coexists with the Visual Basic forms interface that we created in Chapter 7. The new interface was created using Microsoft Excel, but could have been implemented with Word, PowerPoint, Access or Project, with as much ease.

The key concept when thinking about Microsoft Office 97 is that all the applications in the suite use VBA (Visual Basic for Applications) as their macro language. VBA is, literally, the same language used by Visual Basic 5.0, and so it's easy to translate a Visual Basic UI into forms within Office.

As we saw in our second example, we can also implement an interface using the unique capabilities of each particular Office application. We still use VBA to write the interface code, but the abilities, strengths, and weaknesses of each application are different and will impact the nature of the interface in each case.

This chapter has illustrated not only how easily we can create user-interfaces using Microsoft Office, but also how powerful the concept of component-oriented design really is. By developing our applications as a collection of business objects in one or more components, we make it very easy to add new, specialized user-interfaces without any danger of breaking existing interfaces.

Client software, such as a Visual Basic form, Excel, or any other application, need not know the details of data access or business logic. They only need to deal with each object's properties and methods. Using these, they can be used to easily and safely create whatever user interfaces are required.

Using Data-Centric Business Objects

Overview

Now we're ready to have some serious fun. We have a fully functional program with persistent business objects and two user interfaces, but it is designed as a single-, or at most two-, tier application.

In this chapter we'll move the persistence code from the business objects into a separate ActiveX EXE. We can then put this program on a central application server machine to be used by client workstations, with, possibly, the database server on yet another machine - thus achieving a physical three-tier implementation.

We'll look at the issues involved in actually running our new ActiveX EXE on another machine in Chapter 11. In this chapter we'll keep the focus on splitting the UI-centric and data-centric behaviors of each object to create our new out-of-process server.

In Chapter 4 we covered a number of different techniques that we can use to make objects persistent. Then, in Chapter 8, we took the simplest of those techniques and enhanced our objects to save and restore themselves from the database directly.

The last technique we looked at in Chapter 4 involved adding **SetState** and **GetState** methods to our persistent objects to load and retrieve each object's core data, or state. The ability to move an object's state around as a single entity, in this case a string variable, is very important since it means we can send an entire object across a network in a single call.

Each COM call has a substantial performance penalty associated with it, and, when these calls are handled through DCOM, the penalty is even worse. When designing an application where an object's data must be sent to another program through DCOM, it is very important to minimize the number of properties and methods called on each object.

Splitting Out Behaviors

If we look at a simple business object, say the **Customer** object from Chapter 5, it is composed of an interface, internal data and behaviors, as the following diagram shows:

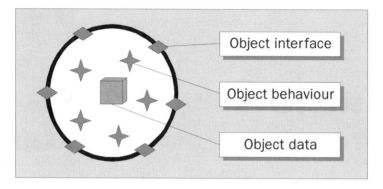

Let's now look more closely at the behaviors of our business objects, and in particular, at those we implemented in Chapter 8.

Separate UI from Persistence

We can really divide the behaviors of those objects into two distinct parts. There are behaviors that service the UI, and those that exist to manage the object's persistence.

The behaviors that manage the object's persistence are contained primarily in the **Fetch**, **Save** and **DeleteObject** subroutines within the object. Virtually all the other code exists to allow the object to support a rich UI for the user.

What we really want to do is take our single object and break it into two objects, both with the same internal data, but each with specific interface elements and behaviors:

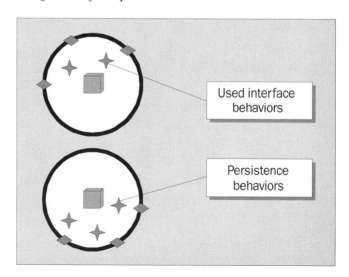

We discussed this concept back in Chapter 2, referring to one half of the object as a UI-centric business object and the other half of the object as a data-centric business object.

The UI-centric business object provides the UI support, containing the properties and methods of our current object along with many of the behaviors.

The data-centric business object implements the behaviors needed to support persistence.

By splitting each business object in two, we can keep the bulk of our business processing close to where it is needed. The UI-centric business object can reside near the UI itself, providing good performance and allowing us to create a rich, interactive user interface. The data-centric business object can reside closer to the data source, again providing for good performance and allowing us to implement powerful data access algorithms with minimal network overhead.

Splitting the Object's Behavior

Given this approach, we need some way to easily split each business object into two parts. Separating the behaviors themselves is not terribly difficult. All we need to do is create a new object to contain the data-centric processing and move the data-oriented routines from our original business object into the new object.

For instance, if we consider the **Customer** object from Chapter 8, it contains both UI-centric and data-centric routines. We can create a new object, **CustomerPersist**, and move the **Save**, **Fetch** and **DeleteObject** routines to this new object. We'll look at exactly how to do this as we go through this chapter.

By doing this, we make it so our **Customer** object only contains UI-centric behaviors; that is, all the data-centric routines have been removed. At the same time, our new **CustomerPersist** object gets all the data-centric behaviors, but none of the UI-centric routines.

This effectively gives us two objects that work together to provide the functionality that we had in the original **Customer** object from Chapter 8. Of course each object will need access to the same set of data in order to work.

Moving the Object's State

The question then, is how do we easily move the object's internal data, or state, between the UI-centric and data-centric business objects? Given that we'll be sending this data over a network, our primary constraint is performance and so it is important to move the data very efficiently.

This is where the **GetState** and **SetState** methods come into play. As we saw in Chapter 4, by using the **LSet** statement to implement these methods we can create very efficient routines to convert data from the detailed user defined types that contain the object's data into a simple string variable.

If we add **GetState** and **LetState** methods to *both* of these objects, we can move their data back and forth with ease:

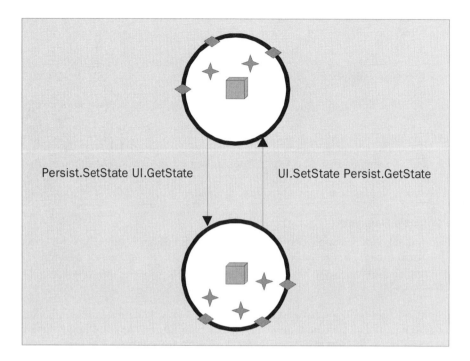

For instance, to copy the objects state from the UI down to the persistence object we can just write:

```
PersistenceObject.SetState UIObject.GetState
```

The reverse is as simple. To copy the state from the persistence object back to the UI object we can write:

```
UIObject.SetState PersistenceObject.GetState
```

Remember that the UI-centric and data-centric objects here are really two halves of the same object. By implementing **SetState** and **GetState** on both the UI-centric and data-centric objects we make it very easy to move the object's data back and forth between the two halves.

Client Calling Server

By using the **GetState** and **SetState** methods to copy the data as shown, it doesn't appear to matter whether the method calls are in the UI object, the persistence object or some other part of the program. For instance, if we want to move the object's state data from the data-centric object to the UI-centric object we'd use the following code:

```
UIObject.SetState PersistenceObject.GetState
```

We might write this line of code in the UI-centric object, the data-centric object or some code outside of either object. In a sense it doesn't matter, since the line of code would be the same in all three cases.

In reality however, it does matter where we put the code to move the object's state data back and forth. We are creating a client/server system here, and we need to establish the roles each object will play. As we discussed in Chapter 4, our Component-based Scalable Logical architecture puts the UI-centric objects on the client workstation and the data-centric objects on an application server machine:

With this architecture it seems clear that our UI-centric business objects are clients of the data-centric business objects. This means that the UI-centric objects are the active objects; they initiate all activity, asking the data-centric objects for services when needed.

Following this model, we'll put the code to move the state data between the two objects into the UI-centric objects. This way they can send the data to the data-centric object before calling any methods that need the data and retrieve the state data from the data-centric objects after each method is called.

Setting up a Server Project

We will need a place to put the new objects we'll be creating to hold the persistence behaviors. Since this program will be running on an application server machine, let's call the program **VideoServer**.

> **In Chapter 11 we'll make the data-centric objects on our application server machine available to other machines on the network via DCOM. To make this easy, we'll put them in an ActiveX EXE.**

We'll be dealing with scalability and multi-user issues when we discuss Microsoft Transaction Server in Chapter 12. For now we'll just focus on creating a server program that can be used by a single client workstation. This way we'll be able to keep the examples simpler and better demonstrate the concepts we need to cover regarding distributing objects. At the end of this chapter we'll have a distributed three-tier application, but there will still be quite a lot of work left to do before it is ready for use in a 'real' setting.

To get started, we need to bring up Visual Basic and create a new ActiveX EXE project. Name the project **VideoServer**.

Using DAO in VideoServer

Since all the code to handle persistence will be in this new project, it's only sensible that we'll need to take appropriate steps to give the project access to our database.

We'll leave the database in Microsoft Access for this chapter. To do a real n-tier implementation we'd need to modify the code to work with SQL Server, Oracle or another database. In Chapter 12 we'll change the code to work against SQL Server using ODBCDirect to get the full impact of using MTS in an n-tier setting.

To use DAO within this project we need to bring up the project's references dialog and check the DAO 3.5 entry from the list.

Opening the Database

Now we need to add some code to open the database when the server is started up. This code will be the same as we used in Chapter 8 within the **VideoObjects** project, since we'll be opening the same database. As with the **VideoObjects** project, this code needs to be placed in a code module within the project. Name this module **VOmain** and add the following code:

```
Option Explicit

Public dbVideo As Database

Public Sub Main()
  Set dbVideo = OpenDatabase("video.mdb")
End Sub
```

We need to make sure that **Sub Main** is the **VideoServer** project's startup option as well. To do this, bring up the project's properties window and change the Startup Object property to **Sub Main**.

Making Simple Objects Persistent

Customer Object

With an understanding of the basic theory of breaking our object into two parts, let's apply it to the **Customer** object to see how it works.

What we'll do here is add the **GetState** and **SetState** methods to both the UI-centric **Customer** object and the data-centric **CustomerPersist** object. Then we'll move the **Fetch**, **Save** and **DeleteObject** subroutines out of the **Customer** object itself and put them into the new **CustomerPersist** object. Once that's done, we can change the **Customer** object to call the methods on our new object.

Adding GetState and SetState to Customer

We've already looked at some basic **GetState** and **SetState** methods back in Chapter 4. These will follow right along the same lines, but with some slight differences.

Moving the UDT

Open up the **VideoObjects** project in Visual Basic and bring up the **Customer** class module. At the top we have a UDT to hold the object's state. We'll need this UDT both here and in the **CustomerPersist** object we'll be creating shortly.

While we could duplicate the code by declaring it as a **Private** type in each class, it is much easier to move the UDT to a central BAS module that can be shared between the **VideoObjects** and **VideoPersist** projects. By storing the UDT in one file, we have a greater level of confidence that both projects will be using the same definition.

Add a new code module to the project and name it **VideoTypes**. Then move the UDT from the **Customer** class module into the new module and change it to a **Public** type.

```
Option Explicit

Public Type CustomerProps
    CustomerID As Long
    Name As String * 50
    Phone As String * 25
    Address1 As String * 30
    Address2 As String * 30
    City As String * 20
    State As String * 10
    ZipCode As String * 10
End Type
```

Once we've saved this new code module to disk we can bring up the **VideoServer** project and use the Project-Add File menu option to add this very same file to that project as well. This way both our **VideoObjects** and **VideoServer** projects will have the same file, so we know they'll have the same UDTs.

Adding IsNew, IsDeleted and IsDirty

As it stands, the UDT contains all the object's basic data. However, our object also keeps track of whether it is new, changed or deleted. It is important information that should be available to the code that translates our object to and from a database.

For instance, in the **Fetch** routine in **Customer** we use the **flgNew** variable to know whether to add or update the record. Since we're moving the **Fetch** routine to another object, we need to make sure we make the value of **flgNew** available to that object.

This can be easily accomplished by adding three variables to the UDT to hold these values.

```
Option Explicit

Public Type CustomerProps
    CustomerID As Long
    Name As String * 50
    Phone As String * 25
    Address1 As String * 30
    Address2 As String * 30
    City As String * 20
```

```
         State As String * 10
         ZipCode As String * 10
      IsNew As Boolean
      IsDeleted As Boolean
      IsDirty As Boolean
   End Type
```

We'll add code to maintain these variables when we implement the **GetState** and **SetState** methods in a later section.

Creating the CustomerData Type

In our new **GetState** and **SetState** methods we'll be using the **LSet** command to copy data from our **CustomerProps** UDT variable into another variable based on a UDT that just contains a string buffer. This new UDT will be called **CustomerData**, and its string variable needs to have the same length as the **CustomerProps** UDT. We covered this in detail in Chapter 4, so we won't repeat the discussion here.

Declare **CustomerData** as follows

```
   Public Type CustomerData
      Buffer As String * 193
   End Type
```

The GetState Method

As we implemented it in Chapter 5, our **Customer** object stores all of its state data in a variable named **udtProps**. This variable is based on the UDT, **CustomerProps**.

The **GetState** method is a **String** function that translates the data in **udtProps** into a single buffer and returns it as a result. In its simplest form, our **GetState** method is basically a call to the **LSet** command, as in Chapter 4. Add this code to the **Customer** object:

```
   Private Function GetState() As String
      Dim udtData As CustomerData

      LSet udtData = udtProps
      GetState = udtData.Buffer
   End Function
```

However, we've added the **IsNew**, **IsDeleted** and **IsDirty** variables to the **CustomerProps** UDT and we need to load their values based on the values of **flgNew**, **flgDeleted** and **flgDirty**. So we need to make the following changes to the code in **Customer**:

```
   Private Function GetState() As String
      Dim udtData As CustomerData

      With udtProps
         .IsDeleted = flgDeleted
         .IsNew = flgNew
         .IsDirty = flgDirty
      End With
```

```
      LSet udtData = udtProps
      GetState = udtData.Buffer
   End Function
```

Note that here in the **Customer** object, **GetState** is a **Private** method. The UI developer doesn't need to have any access directly to an object's internal data, in fact providing such access eliminates the benefits of encapsulation.

The **GetState** and **SetState** methods will only be used to copy the object's data to and from the persistence object. All the calls to the persistence object will be handled within the **Customer** object's code and so the only place from which we're able to call these methods is from within the **Customer** object itself.

The SetState Method

Like the **GetState** method, **SetState** makes use of the **LSet** command to copy data from one UDT variable to another. In this case we'll be copying a string buffer into our detailed **udtProps** variable. Add this **SetState** method to the **Customer** object:

```
   Private Sub SetState(Buffer As String)
      Dim udtData As CustomerData

      udtData.Buffer = Buffer
      LSet udtProps = udtData
   End Sub
```

Unlike the **GetState** method, this method doesn't need to deal with the **IsNew**, **IsDeleted** and **IsDirty** variables. Those values are needed by the persistence object, but they are really copies of the **Customer** object's **flgNew**, **flgDeleted** and **flgDirty** variables. These variables are owned and maintained by the **Customer** object and so we don't want them to change because of the persistence object. Effectively, we are providing them as read-only values to the persistence object for its use.

Creating the CustomerPersist Object

Now that we've got the **Customer** object itself all ready to go, we can move on to create the new data-centric business object, **CustomerPersist**.

As we discussed earlier in the chapter, **CustomerPersist** will also have **GetState** and **SetState** methods. Since it will need to store the state data as it retrieves and stores it in the database, it will have its own **udtProps** variable, also based on the **CustomerProps** UDT.

We'll also move the **Fetch**, **Save** and **DeleteObject** methods from the **Customer** class into this new class.

Adding the CustomerPersist Class

To create the class module, open the **VideoServer** project, choose the Project-Add Class Module menu option to add a generic class module to the project. Set its Name property to CustomerPersist and make sure its Instancing is set to 5-Multiuse.

Declaring udtProps in CustomerPersist

Like the **Customer** object, the **CustomerPersist** object will need access to the values from the **CustomerProps** UDT. To be consistent, we'll just declare a **udtProps** variable within this class like that within **Customer**:

```
Option Explicit

Private udtProps As CustomerProps
```

The **CustomerProps** UDT is declared in our **VideoTypes** code module that we've included in both this project and the **VideoObjects** project.

Adding GetState to CustomerPersist

To get data out of **udtProps**, so it can be loaded into the **Customer** object itself, we'll provide a **GetState** method within **CustomerPersist**. This needs to be a **Public** method, since the **Customer** object will be calling the method.

```
Public Function GetState() As String
   Dim udtData As CustomerData

   LSet udtData = udtProps
   GetState = udtData.Buffer
End Function
```

This is just a basic **LSet** of the values in **udtProps** into the string buffer defined by the **CustomerData** UDT.

Adding SetState to CustomerPersist

Likewise, we need a **SetState** method so the **Customer** object can send its state buffer to the **CustomerPersist** object. This buffer needs to be copied into the **udtProps** variable so that the detailed values are available for use within the **Fetch**, **Save** and **DeleteObject** methods.

```
Public Sub SetState(ByVal Buffer As String)
   Dim udtData As CustomerData

   udtData.Buffer = Buffer
   LSet udtProps = udtData
End Sub
```

The parameter, **Buffer**, is declared using the **ByVal** keyword. This is an important performance consideration when implementing out-of-process ActiveX servers and even more important when using DCOM. In a call to a normal Visual Basic subroutine, parameters are passed by reference, meaning that changes to the parameter value in the subroutine affect the original variable that was passed as a parameter.

When a parameter is passed to an object's method through COM or DCOM a simple reference can't be sent, so COM copies the variable's data to the ActiveX server and provides it as a parameter. Microsoft wanted to make COM transparent to the programmer however, so even though the value was not passed by reference they wanted to simulate the effect. To do this, the parameter is copied *back* from the ActiveX server to the client once the method call is complete. This means in the default case, where parameters are passed by reference, they are copied both *to* and *from* the ActiveX server on each method call.

> Using the `ByVal` keyword in the parameter's declaration indicates to COM that the parameter value doesn't need to be copied back from the ActiveX server to the client program. When we are dealing with large string buffers this is a very important consideration and so we should pretty much always use `ByVal` when declaring parameters on `Public` methods of ActiveX EXE projects.

By storing the object's data in a local UDT variable, **udtProps**, and using **GetState** and **SetState** methods to move the data in and out we have created an object with a duplicate of the **Customer** object's data.

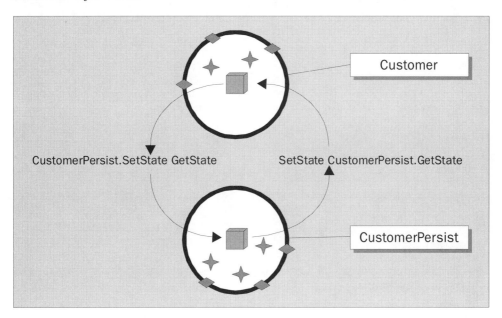

This is very powerful, because now we can add methods and properties to this new object and they can act on the exact same data as in the **Customer** object itself.

We are now ready to move the **Fetch**, **Save** and **DeleteObject** subroutines from the **Customer** object over to the new **CustomerPersist** class.

*The easiest way to work with the examples in this chapter is to open Visual Basic twice, with
our **VideoProj** project group from Chapters 7 and 8 in one instance and the new
VideoServer project in the other. Unfortunately it is not very practical to have more than
one EXE type project within a single project group, since only one of them can be set as the
startup project. Any other EXE projects would be ignored by Visual Basic were we to run the
project in the IDE.*

In the **Customer** class our three persistence methods were **Private**, but we need to make them
available for use by the **Customer** object now that they are in the **CustomerPersist** class. To
make this possible, we'll change all three to **Public** methods in the class as we move the code.

Moving Save to CustomerPersist

The **Save** routine needs a bit of work, though not much. It makes reference to **flgNew**, the variable
that indicates if the object is new or not. We need to change the references to this variable so they
refer instead to **udtProps.IsNew**. The **GetState** method in the **Customer** class makes sure this
value is correct before it is sent over to the **CustomerPersist** object.

We'll also need to change the way the **SELECT** statement is generated. When we built this code back
in Chapter 8, we used the **CustomerID** property from the object in the statement:

```
strSQL = "SELECT * FROM CUSTOMER WHERE CUSTOMERID=" & _
   CustomerID
```

That property isn't available over in the **CustomerPersist** object and so we need to change the
code to use the **CustomerID** value from **udtProps**, as shown below:

```
Public Sub Save()

   Dim rsCustomer As Recordset
   Dim strSQL As String


   If udtProps.IsNew Then

      strSQL = "CUSTOMER"
      Set rsCustomer = dbVideo.OpenRecordset(strSQL, dbOpenTable)
      rsCustomer.AddNew
   Else
      strSQL = "SELECT * FROM CUSTOMER WHERE CUSTOMERID=" & _
         udtProps.CustomerID

      Set rsCustomer = dbVideo.OpenRecordset(strSQL, dbOpenDynaset)
      rsCustomer.Edit
   End If
   With rsCustomer
     .Fields("Name") = udtProps.Name
     .Fields("Address1") = udtProps.Address1
     .Fields("Address2") = udtProps.Address2
     .Fields("City") = udtProps.City
     .Fields("State") = udtProps.State
     .Fields("ZipCode") = udtProps.ZipCode
     .Fields("Phone") = udtProps.Phone
     .Update
      If udtProps.IsNew then
```

```
      .Bookmark = .LastModified
      udtProps.CustomerID = .Fields("CustomerID")
    End If
    .Close
  End With
End Sub
```

The same is true for the **IsNew** flag, since that value is now in **udtProps.IsNew** rather than being stored in a **Private** variable.

Moving the DeleteObject Method

The **DeleteObject** method was simple to begin with, and so the only change we need is making it **Public** rather than **Private**:

```
Public Sub DeleteObject(ByVal CustomerID As Long)
  dbVideo.Execute "DELETE FROM CUSTOMER WHERE CUSTOMERID=" & _
    CustomerID
End Sub
```

Moving the Fetch Method

The **Fetch** routine will require some small changes. Like the **Save** method, this routine contains some code that assumes it is running inside the **Customer** object itself. In particular, we have included calls to the **objValid** object to check whether or not our object's rules are broken.

The **objValid** object is private to the **Customer** object itself and is not available in the **CustomerPersist** object. We need to remove those lines from the **Fetch** routine and move them back into the **Customer** object. Here's the code for the **CustomerPersist** object's **Fetch** method:

```
Public Sub Fetch(ByVal CustomerID As Long)
  Dim rsCustomer As Recordset
  Dim strSQL As String

  strSQL = "SELECT * FROM CUSTOMER WHERE CUSTOMERID=" & _
    CustomerID
  Set rsCustomer = dbVideo.OpenRecordset(strSQL, dbOpenSnapshot)
  With rsCustomer
    udtProps.CustomerID = .Fields("CustomerID")
    udtProps.Name = .Fields("Name")
    udtProps.Address1 = .Fields("Address1")
    udtProps.Address2 = .Fields("Address2")
    udtProps.City = .Fields("City")
    udtProps.State = .Fields("State")
    udtProps.ZipCode = .Fields("ZipCode")
    udtProps.Phone = .Fields("Phone")

    .Close
  End With
End Sub
```

We originally called the **Fetch** subroutine in the **Customer** object's **Load** method. This is where we now need to move the calls to **objValid**. Here's the code for the **Customer** object's **Load** method back in the **VideoObjects** project:

```
Public Sub Load(CustomerID As Long)
   If flgEditing Then Err.Raise 445
   If Not flgNew Then Err.Raise 445

   Fetch CustomerID

   objValid.RuleBroken "Name", False
   objValid.RuleBroken "Phone", False

   flgNew = False
End Sub
```

Calling CustomerPersist from Customer

At this point we have a **CustomerPersist** object that can be used to retrieve, save and delete a **Customer** object's data within the database. Using the **GetState** and **SetState** methods we can efficiently copy the object's data from **CustomerPersist** to **Customer** and back again.

All that remains is to go through the **Customer** object itself and change any calls to the **Fetch**, **Save** and **DeleteObject** subroutines so the methods of **CustomerPersist** are used instead. Fortunately, we only need to change two methods in **Customer** - **ApplyEdit** and **Load**.

Calling DeleteObject from ApplyEdit

All adding, updating and deleting of an object's data is handled through the **ApplyEdit** method. It is in this method that we called the **DeleteObject** and **Save** subroutines. All we need to do is change this code to create a **CustomerPersist** object and call the appropriate method on that object instead.

In the **Customer** object's **ApplyEdit** method we need to change the call to **DeleteObject**.

```
Public Sub ApplyEdit()
   Dim objPersist As CustomerPersist

   If Not flgEditing Then Err.Raise 445

   Set objPersist = New CustomerPersist
   If flgDeleted Then
      ' code to delete the object's data goes here
      objPersist.DeleteObject udtProps.CustomerID
      flgNew = True
      flgDeleted = False
   ElseIf flgDirty Or flgNew Then
      If Not IsValid Then Err.Raise 445
      ' save object to database if appropriate
      Save
      ' save object state
```

```
        LSet udtSave = udtProps
        flgNew = False
     End If

     Set objPersist = Nothing

     flgDirty = False
     flgEditing = False
  End Sub
```

This change is pretty easy. We declare **objPersist** and create an instance of a **CustomerPersist** object. Then, instead of calling a private **DeleteObject** subroutine, we just make a simple change to call the **objPersist.DeleteObject** method.

Calling Save from ApplyEdit

Of course, **DeleteObject** is pretty simple. It doesn't require any values from **udtProps**, only the ID value passed as a parameter. The call to the **Save** method, though, is a different story. Make the following changes to the **ApplyEdit** method in the **Customer** object:

```
     ElseIf flgDirty Or flgNew Then
        If Not IsValid Then Err.Raise 445
        ' save object to database if appropriate

        With objPersist
          .SetState GetState
          .Save
          If flgNew Then SetState .GetState
        End With

        ' save object state
        LSet udtSave = udtProps
        flgNew = False
     End If
```

It's pretty obvious that we need to change the call to the **Save** subroutine to call **objPersist.Save** instead. Before we can call the method though, it is critical that our **Customer** object's state be copied down to **objPersist** by using the **SetState** method:

```
     With objPersist
       .SetState GetState
```

What is even less obvious is that there are times when we need to retrieve the persistence object's state *after* the **Save** method has been called.

Our object's **CustomerID** field doesn't actually contain a meaningful value until after the object has been saved to the database. We are relying on the database to assign the ID value during the add process, and then the code in the **Save** method retrieves the newly assigned value:

```
     If udtProps.IsNew Then
       .Bookmark = .LastModified
       udtProps.CustomerID = .Fields("CustomerID")
     End If
```

Of course the **udtProps** where this value just got stored is inside the **CustomerPersist** object, not the **Customer** object. Thus, if the object is new when the **Save** method is called it is very important to pull the state back from **CustomerPersist**:

```
If flgNew Then SetState .GetState
```

With this small code change, we've altered the **Customer** object so it sends its state data to the **CustomerPersist** object and calls its **Save** method. The **Save** method is the same code we implemented in Chapter 8, and so we know it will save the object's data the way we desire. We then retrieve the resulting state data if needed to update the **Customer** object with the current values.

Calling Fetch from Load

The changes to the **Customer** object's **Load** method are very comparable. We just need to create an instance of the **CustomerPersist** class, call its **Fetch** method and retrieve the state data using the **GetState** method:

```
Public Sub Load(CustomerID As Long)
    Dim objPersist As CustomerPersist

    If flgEditing Then Err.Raise 445
    If Not flgNew Then Err.Raise 445

    Set objPersist = New CustomerPersist
    With objPersist
      .Fetch CustomerID
      SetState .GetState
    End With
    Set objPersist = Nothing

    objValid.RuleBroken "Name", False
    objValid.RuleBroken "Phone", False

    flgNew = False
End Sub
```

As with the **Save** method, the **Fetch** method is the same code we implemented in Chapter 8, so we are loading the object's data the same way we were before, just in a different object. By copying the object's data from the persistence object back to the **Customer** object we've accomplished the same functionality, but now we can put the data access code on a different computer.

Making List Objects Persistent

The **Customer** object provided a good example of making a simple, singular object persistent by using a separate persistence object. The techniques we used are pretty straightforward in that case, but what if we have an entire list or collection of data that we need to persist?

We have a number of examples, including the **TextList** object, the **Customers** and **Videos** objects. The **Tapes** and **InvoiceItems** objects probably also fit this category, but since they are child objects, they have their own twist as well.

What we'll focus on now are the read-only list objects. Later on, we'll discuss child objects and use the same techniques. However, child objects bring a lot of additional complexity, and so we'll tackle the easy objects first.

The challenge with objects that are lists of other objects, or that are collections of data, is that we can't afford to pull back each individual object or element across the network. Each DCOM call has a lot of overhead, and if we make a call for each element in the list we could be in trouble. Imagine if the list contains dozens, hundreds or even thousands of elements.

> *Let's look at some statistics in support of this assertion. Don Box quotes inproc object method calls as being 28,000 faster than a remote object on the same LAN (Source: MSJ vol. 12 no. 5). And in Richard Grimes' Professional DCOM, he tests multiple method calls (e.g. ten calls to send ten strings) against to a single big method call (that is send all ten strings with one call). The total time for the multiple calls was five to ten times longer than the single big method call.*

Instead we need to find a way to bring across all the elements in a single DCOM call. The problem is that with list objects, each object's state is not fixed. With the `Customer` object we know exactly how big the object's state will be and so we can easily convert it to a buffer. With a list of elements we don't know how many elements there might be and so it becomes much harder.

Buffer Object

To help deal with this problem, we can use a utility object that efficiently collects all the elements from a list into a single `String` buffer. If we put the `String` buffer back into this object it can efficiently unpack the buffer, providing easy access to each element in the list. We'll call this the `Buffer` object.

Designing the Object

The `Buffer` object makes some assumptions. The most notable assumption is that each element will have a state or some data that is in a `String` variable. We'll also assume that each element's data is the same length as all the other elements. This works well when dealing with most database information, since the data is basically fixed length in any case.

The object also assumes that the developer has some rough idea of the number of elements that will be added to the buffer. The exact number isn't required, just a rough idea.

Focus on Performance

It is very important to realize why we are building this object in the first place – performance. Most programs retrieve lists of data to be displayed to the user. We populate `ComboBox` and `ListBox` controls in almost every program. Having lots of lists can dramatically slow down a conventional Visual Basic form's load-time; and pulling the data across DCOM and into an object is even worse. The challenge behind designing this object is to come up with a solution that is fast but still effective.

Because of this constraint, there's no error trapping in the object. The focus is entirely on performance and so we're assuming that the client code will use it as intended.

If you use this class in your applications you can feel free to add error trapping, but be aware of the ramifications on performance!

String Handling in Visual Basic

One question to consider is whether we need to go through the work of building a class to handle the buffer. After all, it would be a simple matter to just declare a dynamic string variable and append each element's data into that variable. If they are fixed length elements, it is easy enough to pull them back out on the other end.

Actually this is basically what the **Buffer** object will do, but there is a serious trick involved to get good performance.

> **Visual Basic's string handling is incredibly slow, and string concatenation ranks right at the top of the list when it comes to performance problems.**

To get any measure of performance at all, we need to avoid string concatenations while building the buffer. Fortunately, Visual Basic provides an excellent mechanism we can use to add elements to a buffer with no concatenation.

Most people are familiar with the **Mid$()** function. They use it to return a portion of a string variable like this:

```
strNew = Mid$(strOld, 4, 3)
```

What many people don't know is that **Mid$()** can also be used to put text *into* a string in a specific location:

```
Mid$(strOld, 4, 3) = "ABC"
```

This technique does require that the target string variable is already long enough to hold the data. In this example, **strOld** would need to be at least seven characters long before this statement or the text wouldn't be put into the variable. The easiest way to get a pre-sized string is to use the **Space$()** command.

```
strOld = Space$(7)
```

This is why we want a class. The class needs to pre-size a buffer, then use **Mid$()** to insert each element into the string. Along the way it needs to keep track of the current position in the buffer and possibly resize the buffer if we try to add more elements than will fit in the current buffer.

Creating the Buffer Class

We'll want to use the **Buffer** class in both the **VideoObjects** and **VideoPersist** projects. If we use it in **VideoPersist** to pack together a list of elements, we can then create a **Buffer** object in **VideoObjects** to unpack those elements from the buffer.

A good approach is to use the same technique we are using with the **VideoTypes** BAS module. Create a single **Buffer.cls** file and include it in both projects. This way we only have one source file to maintain, and both projects are kept in sync.

In the **VideoPersist** project add a new class module. Set its Name property to Buffer and its Instancing property to 1-Private. While we'll be sending the **String** buffer created by this object across the network, the **Buffer** object itself will only be used within this project.

Initializing the Buffer Object

As we mentioned earlier, the **Buffer** object needs to make some assumptions about the data it is being given. The first assumption is that all the element data will be the same length. That is, each element's data will have a fixed length that is the same as all the other elements. The **Buffer** object also requires that the user provide an estimated count of the number of elements that will be added to the list.

Declaring Variables

To store these values we'll use - what else? - a UDT:

```
Option Explicit

Private Type BufferProps
   Length As Integer
   EstCount As Long
   MaxCount As Long
   Count As Long
End Type

Private Type BufferData
   Buffer As String * 8
End Type
```

The UDT also includes the current maximum number of elements that will fit in the buffer and a count of the number of elements currently in the buffer.

We've included an overlay, **BufferData**, for use with the **LSet** command later. This will be used in the object's **GetState** method.

We'll also declare a constant to be one longer than the length of **BufferData**:

```
Private Const BUFFER_START = 9
```

We can use this constant to mark the start of the data in our buffer. This way, the first eight characters of our string are reserved to hold the UDT we just defined, and the rest of the buffer can be used to hold the elements of the list.

Of course, we need to declare a variable to act as the buffer:

```
Private strBuffer As String
```

And we need a variable to hold the object's data, based on the UDT:

```
Private udtProps As BufferProps
```

Finally, we need a variable to store the current location in the buffer.

```
Private lngPos As Long
```

As we add each element to the buffer we need to increment this value to point to the next empty slot where we'll add the next element.

The Initialize Method

Once the client code has created an instance of the **Buffer** object to add elements, the first thing they need to do is tell the object the length of each element and the estimated number of elements that will be added. To support this, we'll implement an **Initialize** method that takes these values as parameters:

```
Public Sub Initialize(Length As Integer, EstimatedCount As Long)
   With udtProps
      .Length = Length
      .EstCount = EstimatedCount
      .MaxCount = EstimatedCount
      .Count = 0
      strBuffer = Space$(BUFFER_START + .MaxCount * .Length)
      lngPos = BUFFER_START
   End With
End Sub
```

The routine stores the length and estimated count parameters in **udtProps**. It also sets **MaxCount** to the estimated count and sets **Count** to zero since we know there is nothing in the buffer.

The next line uses the **Space$()** command to pre-size the buffer. The buffer needs to be big enough to hold the estimated number of elements based on the supplied size. We also need to add room at the beginning of the buffer to fit the data in **udtProps**.

```
strBuffer = Space$(BUFFER_START + .MaxCount * .Length)
```

Finally we need to set **lngPos** so it points at the first character in the buffer where we can add data. The **BUFFER_START** constant is used to make sure we leave enough room at the beginning of the string to fit the **BufferProps** UDT.

Adding Elements

Though this class is not based on a native Visual Basic collection object, it is very much like a collection in many ways. Because of this, we'll emulate the interface from the **Collection** object.

The Add Method

To add an element to the buffer the client code can use the **Add** method. This method accepts a **String** parameter that contains the element's data. Note that there is no checking of the assumption that the data supplied is of a fixed length that matches the length from the **Initialize** method call.

If the supplied data is too short it will be inserted, with spaces filling in the remaining space. If the data is too long it will be automatically truncated by the call to **Mid$()**.

```
Public Sub Add(Data As String)
   With udtProps
      Mid$(strBuffer, lngPos, .Length) = Data
      lngPos = lngPos + .Length
      .Count = .Count + 1
   End With
End Sub
```

The **Mid$()** command is used to insert the data into the appropriate location in **strBuffer**. Then **lngPos** is incremented by the length indicated in the **Initialize** method call, so we are all set to add the next element. And of course the **Count** value is incremented by one to indicate that we've added an element.

Extending the Buffer

As shown, the **Add** method will work great - assuming that the estimated count provided in the **Initialize** method was correct. It will even work if the estimate is too big, since the buffer will have extra room. Where it won't work is if the estimate is too small and the buffer runs out of room. Subsequent attempts to add data to the buffer will fail, resulting in lost data. The answer is to extend the buffer as needed:

```
Public Sub Add(Data As String)
   With udtProps

      If .Count = .MaxCount Then
         strBuffer = strBuffer & _
            Space$(udtProps.EstCount / 2 * udtProps.Length)
         .MaxCount = .MaxCount + udtProps.EstCount / 2
      End If

      Mid$(strBuffer, lngPos, .Length) = Data
      lngPos = lngPos + .Length
      .Count = .Count + 1
   End With
End Sub
```

As shown, we've set it up so the buffer is extended by half the original length, assuming that the estimated count isn't off by more than 50%. Even if it is off by more than that amount, the buffer would just extend again.

After all the talk about avoiding concatenation, we've used it here. This isn't a problem, though, since, if we are provided with a reasonable estimated count, the buffer probably won't need to be extended. Even if it does, it probably won't extend many times, certainly far less than if we concatenated each element into the buffer individually.

GetState and SetState Methods

Now that we've got the object set up to build the buffer, we need to provide a mechanism to copy that buffer across the network. As with our other objects, this one will have **GetState** and **SetState** methods. In this case, however, the same class will exist in both projects and so we'll be effectively cloning the object entirely from one machine onto another machine using this technique.

> *Of course, this assumes we've remembered to include the* **Buffer** *class module into both the* **VideoObjects** *and* **VideoServer** *projects.*

GetState Method

The **GetState** method basically returns the value in **strBuffer**. However, we want to send the data in **udtProps** as well, and so the first thing we need to do is use **LSet** to copy that value into a string buffer. Then we can use **Mid$()** to put that buffer in the first few characters of **strBuffer**. Remember that we saved room at the start of the buffer for just this data.

```
Public Function GetState() As String
   Dim udtData As BufferData

   LSet udtData = udtProps
   Mid$(strBuffer, 1, Len(udtData.Buffer)) = udtData.Buffer
   GetState = Left$(strBuffer, lngPos)
End Function
```

We're using the **Left$()** function to only return the portion of **strBuffer** that actually contains data. This way, if the estimated count of elements was way too big, or if we extended the buffer and didn't use all the space, we don't return blank space. Remember that the result of the **GetState** method will probably be sent across the network via DCOM and so we don't want to send any more data than is absolutely necessary.

SetState Method

The **SetState** method can just do the reverse. It gets a buffer as a parameter, pulls the first few characters out and uses **LSet** to put them into **udtProps**.

```
Public Sub SetState(Buffer As String)
   Dim udtData As BufferData

   udtData.Buffer = Mid$(Buffer, 1, Len(udtData.Buffer))
   LSet udtProps = udtData
   strBuffer = Buffer
End Sub
```

Using these two routines, we can copy a buffer containing an entire list of elements from one machine to another as a single **String** variable:

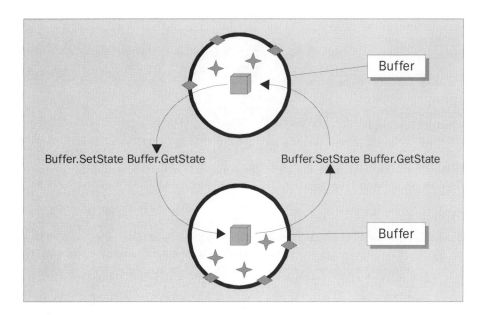

Retrieving Elements

Once we've copied the **String** buffer across the network we can use the **SetState** method to put it back into a **Buffer** object. This effectively creates a clone of the original **Buffer** object, with all the data and internal values set and ready to go.

Now we need to implement some mechanism for the client code to pull the elements of the list back out of the buffer. Again we'll emulate the Visual Basic **Collection** object's interface by implementing similar properties.

Item Property

To retrieve a single element from the buffer we'll implement an **Item** property. This property will accept a numeric index to indicate which element to retrieve:

```
Public Property Get Item(Index As Long) As String
  Item = Mid$(strBuffer, BUFFER_START + (Index - 1) * _
    udtProps.Length, udtProps.Length)
End Property
```

Since all we need to do is return the original string value that we were given through the **Add** method, we can just use **Mid$()** to pull out that section of **strBuffer** and return it.

Informational Properties

The **Buffer** object provides some basic informational properties. These are read-only, but are important to the code that is using the object to retrieve data.

It is important to know how many elements exist in the buffer. The **Count** property provides that value.

```
Public Function Count() As Long
   Count = udtProps.Count
End Function
```

As a convenience, we'll provide the **Length** value.

```
Public Function Length() As Long
   Length = udtProps.Length
End Function
```

There are cases where the client code may not know the length of each element and this property can provide that information easily.

Updating Elements

The final bit of functionality that we'll add to the object is the ability to update an individual element in the buffer. The reason this is important will become clear when we get to discuss child objects later in the chapter. For now, let's just look at how the update capability is implemented.

We already have a **Property Get Item** routine to retrieve an element's data from the buffer. To keep some level of symmetry, let's create a **Property Let Item** routine to handle the update process.

```
Public Property Let Item(Index As Long, Buffer As String)
   Mid$(strBuffer, BUFFER_START + (Index - 1) * _
      udtProps.Length, udtProps.Length) = Buffer
End Property
```

This is basically just the reverse of the **Property Get**, using **Mid$()** to put data into **strBuffer** in the right spot rather than pulling it out.

TextList Object

The **Buffer** object isn't too complex, but it provides a very nice mechanism by which we can copy an entire list of elements from one object to another. Let's try it out as we update the **TextList** object to retrieve its data through a persistence object.

In concept we'll be doing the same thing here that we did with the **Customer** object earlier. We'll create a **TextListPersist** object in the **VideoPersist** project, then move the **TextList** object's **Fetch** routine to the new object.

Of course we'll have to do a bit of extra work, since the **Fetch** method will now need to load its results into a **Buffer** object and then the **TextList** object will need to receive that **Buffer** object's state data and unpack it.

Creating TextListPersist

Open up the **VideoPersist** project in Visual Basic and add a new class module to the project. Change its Name property to TextListPersist and make sure its Instancing property is 5-Multiuse.

Most of our simple business objects use a UDT to hold their state data. However, list objects typically hold an entire list of information and so they are a bit more complex.

Rather than a UDT, we'll store the object's state in a **Buffer** object. Let's declare that in the class module.

```
Option Explicit

Private objBuffer As Buffer
```

Adding a UDT for the TextList Data

Because of the way we implemented it, the **Buffer** object expects that each individual element's data will be the same length. The easiest way to handle this is to put each element in a UDT, use **LSet** to copy that data into a string and then add that string to the **Buffer** object.

Bring up the **VideoTypes** BAS module. We'll need this UDT in both the **VideoPersist** and **VideoObjects** projects, since we'll use it to unpack the data in the **Buffer** object when we get to the **TextList** object's **SetState** method. Enter both the detailed UDT and the matching string buffer UDT.

```
Public Type TextListProps
   Key As String * 30
   Item As String * 255
End Type

Public Type TextListData
   Buffer As String * 285
End Type
```

We've put some arbitrary, but reasonably large, lengths on both the **Key** and the **Item** fields. As we move this code to other applications we may be able to reevaluate the sizes to make them fit the specific data better.

Moving the Fetch Routine to TextListPersist

Because the **TextList** object is read-only, the only data access routine it contains is **Fetch**. It has no **Save** or **DeleteObject** since they aren't needed in a read-only setting. This makes our job easier, since we only need to worry about moving that one routine.

Move the **Fetch** subroutine code from the **TextList** object over to the new **TextListPersist** object. The code needs some changes as shown here:

```
Public Sub Fetch(ByVal ListName As String)

   Dim rsList As Recordset

   Dim udtProps As TextListProps
   Dim udtData As TextListData

   Set objBuffer = New Buffer
   objBuffer.Initialize Len(udtData), 50

   Set rsList = dbVideo.OpenRecordset(ListName, dbOpenSnapshot)
   Do While Not rsList.EOF
```

```
    With udtProps
        .Item = rsList(1)
        .Key = rsList(0)
    End With
    LSet udtData = udtProps
    objBuffer.Add udtData.Buffer
            rsList.MoveNext
    Loop
    rsList.Close
End Sub
```

Let's review the changes to the code to see what we've done. First, the **Fetch** routine was a **Private** subroutine, but now it will need to be available to the **TextList** object via DCOM and so it needs to be a **Public** method.

```
Public Sub Fetch(ByVal ListName As String)
```

In the original **Fetch** subroutine, we took the results of the recordset and stored them directly in a **Collection** object for later use. Now we need to put each element in the **TextListProps** UDT and then store that in our **Buffer** object. This means we need variables for both **TextListProps** and **TextListData**.

```
Dim rsList As Recordset
Dim udtProps As TextListProps
Dim udtData As TextListData
```

We've already declared **objBuffer** as type **Buffer**, but we do need to create an actual instance of the object.

```
Set objBuffer = New Buffer
objBuffer.Initialize Len(udtData), 50
```

We've also called the **Initialize** method on the **Buffer** object, providing it with the length of the UDT that we'll be using for each element and an estimated count of the number of items. Fifty items is probably way too high, but it is better to make this value a bit too big than too small.

Now we're ready to build the recordset and start looping through each item that is returned from the database. We'll take each item and copy the key and item values into the **udtProps** variable, then use **LSet** to copy that into a single string variable.

```
Set rsList = dbVideo.OpenRecordset(ListName, dbOpenSnapshot)
Do While Not rsList.EOF
    With udtProps
        .Item = rsList(1)
        .Key = rsList(0)
    End With
    LSet udtData = udtProps
```

Once the element's data is in a single string, we can just use **objBuffer**'s **Add** method to add the data to the **Buffer** object. Then we can loop to the next row in the recordset and do the same thing.

```
      objBuffer.Add udtData.Buffer
      rsList.MoveNext
    Loop
    rsList.Close
  End Sub
```

In the end, our **Buffer** object contains the data from the entire recordset.

Adding GetState to TextListPersist

After the **Fetch** method is called, the **Buffer** object, **objBuffer**, will contain the entire list of data from the database. We need to implement a **GetState** method so the **TextList** object can easily retrieve this list of data. Fortunately, the **Buffer** object has already consolidated all the data into a single string that we can get from its **GetState** method, so our new object doesn't need to do any work to speak of.

```
Public Function GetState() As String
  GetState = objBuffer.GetState
End Function
```

Updating TextList

As with the **Customer** object earlier in the chapter, we need to make some changes to **TextList** so it calls the **Fetch** method on the **TextListPersist** object instead of calling a local **Fetch** subroutine. We also need to do a bit more work in this case, since we need to copy the resulting data into our internal **Collection** object.

Load Method in TextList

The original **Load** method simply called the **Fetch** subroutine and left it at that. Our new **Load** routine will have a bit more code, since it needs to create an instance of **TextListPersist**, call its **Fetch** method and then use its **GetState** method to retrieve the resulting data.

```
Friend Sub Load(ListName As String)

  Dim objPersist As TextListPersist

  Set objPersist = New TextListPersist
  With objPersist
    .Fetch ListName
    SetState .GetState
  End With
  Set objPersist = Nothing

End Sub
```

SetState Subroutine

The real work comes in the **SetState** routine however, since it is this routine that needs to unpack the resulting data. The string that we are passed as a parameter is actually the state string from the **Buffer** object in **TextListPersist**.

```
Private Sub SetState(ByVal Buffer As String)
  Dim objBuffer As Buffer
  Dim lngIndex As Long
```

```
      Dim udtProps As TextListProps
      Dim udtData As TextListData

      Set objBuffer = New Buffer
      objBuffer.SetState Buffer
      With objBuffer
        For lngIndex = 1 To objBuffer.Count
          udtData.Buffer = objBuffer.Item(lngIndex)
          LSet udtProps = udtData
          With udtProps
            colList.Add Format$(.Item), Format$(.Key)
            colKeys.Add Format$(.Key), Format$(.Item)
          End With
        Next
      End With
  End Sub
```

The way we designed the **Buffer** object was to be able to accept such a state string and effectively become a clone of the original **Buffer** object, so to start with we've declared a **Buffer** variable.

```
Private Sub SetState(ByVal Buffer As String)
   Dim objBuffer As Buffer
```

Since we're looping through each element, we need an index variable as well. For each element we pull out of the **Buffer** object we need to unpack it by using the **TextListProps** and **TextListData** UDTs that we added to the **VideoTypes** BAS module earlier.

To create a 'clone' of the original **Buffer** object, we just need to create an instance of a **Buffer** object, then use its **SetState** method to pass it the string buffer that we were given as a parameter:

```
Set objBuffer = New Buffer
objBuffer.SetState Buffer
```

The **Buffer** object itself has code in the **SetState** method to pull out the object's data, including the length and number of elements in the list.

Now we can just loop through all the elements in the **Buffer** object. Each element will be put into the **udtProps** variable using **LSet** and then those values can be used to populate our two **Collection** objects. The **TextList** object stores everything twice, once for a normal lookup of an item by its key and then again so we can look up a key based on the item's value.

```
  With objBuffer
    For lngIndex = 1 To objBuffer.Count
      udtData.Buffer = objBuffer.Item(lngIndex)
      LSet udtProps = udtData
      With udtProps
        colList.Add Format$(.Item), Format$(.Key)
        colKeys.Add Format$(.Key), Format$(.Item)
      End With
    Next
  End With
End Sub
```

That clinches it. The **TextListPersist** object loads the information from the database into a **Buffer** object. The **TextList** object takes the **Buffer** object's state and uses it to create a clone of the original **Buffer** object. From there, it just loops through the elements in the **Buffer** object, loading them into its internal data store just like the original **Fetch** subroutine of Chapter 8.

Display Lists

Our application has two other read-only list objects - **Customers** and **Videos**. Like **TextList**, these objects have a **Fetch** subroutine that retrieves data from the database and copies it into a collection. There is a difference, however, in that the collection actually contains simple child objects instead of the simple key-value pairs of the **TextList** object.

The changes to both objects will be virtually identical, so we'll only walk through the **Customers** object's code. The **Videos** object can be modified by following the same steps.

CustomersPersist Object

As usual, we need to create a new object in the **VideoPersist** project to hold the data access code. We'll call this one **CustomersPersist**, make sure its Instancing property is set to 5-Multiuse so the **Customers** object can create it when needed.

Create a UDT for each Element

As with the **TextList** object, we'll need to create a couple of UDTs to store each element's data and to support the **LSet** copy of the data into a buffer. Of course, each element will be copied into a **Buffer** object, but we'll get to that in a bit.

```
Public Type CustDisplayProps
   CustomerID As Long
   Name As String * 50
   Phone As String * 25
End Type

Public Type CustDisplayData
   Buffer As String * 77
End Type
```

This declaration goes into the **VideoTypes** BAS module so it is available to both the **VideoPersist** and **VideoObjects** projects. The **VideoPersist** project will use it to load the **Buffer** object, while **VideoObjects** will use it to pull the data back out of the **Buffer** object and use it as needed.

The **CustomersPersist** object, like the **TextListPersist** object, will store its state data in a **Buffer** object, so we'll need to declare that in that **CustomersPersist** class module.

```
Option Explicit

Private objBuffer As Buffer
```

The Fetch Routine

Next we need to move the **Fetch** subroutine from the **Customers** object into the **CustomersPersist** object and convert it into a **Public** method for use by the **Customers** object.

Like the **TextList**'s **Fetch** method, the **Customers** object's routine directly loads its internal data from the recordset. We'll need to modify this code to load the recordset data into our **Buffer** object instead, then make the **Customers** object's **SetState** method put the data into the object's internal variables.

```
Public Sub Fetch(ByVal Name As String, ByVal Phone As String)
    Dim rsCustomer As Recordset
    Dim strSQL As String
    Dim strWHERE As String

    Dim udtData As CustDisplayData
    Dim udtProps As CustDisplayProps

    strSQL = "SELECT CUSTOMERID, NAME, PHONE FROM CUSTOMER"
    If Len(Name) > 0 Then _
        strWHERE = "NAME LIKE '" & Name & "*' "
    If Len(Phone) > 0 Then
        If Len(strWHERE) > 0 Then
            strWHERE = strWHERE & " AND PHONE LIKE '" & Phone & "*'"
        Else
            strWHERE = "PHONE LIKE '" & Phone & "*'"
        End If
    End If
    If Len(strWHERE) > 0 Then _
        strSQL = strSQL & " WHERE " & strWHERE
    Set rsCustomer = dbVideo.OpenRecordset(strSQL, dbOpenSnapshot)

    Set objBuffer = New Buffer
    objBuffer.Initialize Len(udtData.Buffer), 100

    Do While Not rsCustomer.EOF

        With udtProps
            .CustomerID = rsCustomer("CustomerID")
            .Name = rsCustomer("Name")
            .Phone = rsCustomer("Phone")
        End With
            LSet udtData = udtProps
            objBuffer.Add udtData.Buffer

        rsCustomer.MoveNext
    Loop
    rsCustomer.Close
End Sub
```

The original code created a **CustomerDisplay** object for each row in the recordset, then copied the data into that object and added it to a private collection object. The changes we've made here just copy each row's data into **udtProps**, **LSet** that into **udtData** and then add the data to **objBuffer**, the **Buffer** object.

Add GetState

With the recordset's data copied into the **Buffer** object, we are all ready to create a **GetState** method so that the **Customers** object can retrieve the data. The **Buffer** object already provides us with a **GetState** method, so we can simply delegate the call down to that object to get the data.

```
Public Function GetState() As String
  GetState = objBuffer.GetState
End Function
```

Customers Object

The **Customers** object itself needs to be changed a bit as well. Of course, its **Load** method was used to call a local **Fetch** subroutine and so we'll need to modify that routine. Also we need to add a **SetState** method. This method will accept the result from **CustomersPersist** and will unpack it into a collection of **CustomerDisplay** objects, just like the original **Fetch** routine did with the recordset results.

Load Method

The **Load** method needs to create an instance of **CustomersPersist**, then call its **Fetch** method. Once that is done, we can use the **GetState** method on **CustomersPersist** to retrieve the resulting data and put it into the **SetState** method of the **Customers** object itself.

```
Public Sub Load(Optional Name As String, Optional Phone As String)
    Dim objPersist As CustomersPersist

    Set objPersist = New CustomersPersist
    With objPersist
      .Fetch Name, Phone
      SetState .GetState
    End With
    Set objPersist = Nothing
End Sub
```

The changes to this routine are just like the changes we made to the **Load** method of the **TextList** object.

SetState Routine

As with the **TextList** object, the bulk of the work occurs in the **SetState** method. It is here that we unpack the **Buffer** object, using **LSet** to copy each element's data into **udtProps** and from there into a **CustomerDisplay** object.

```
Private Sub SetState(ByVal Buffer As String)
    Dim objBuffer As Buffer
    Dim objDisplay As CustomerDisplay
    Dim lngIndex As Long
    Dim udtData As CustDisplayData
    Dim udtProps As CustDisplayProps

    Set objBuffer = New Buffer
    With objBuffer
      .SetState Buffer
```

```
        For lngIndex = 1 To .Count
          Set objDisplay = New CustomerDisplay
          udtData.Buffer = .Item(lngIndex)
          LSet udtProps = udtData
          With objDisplay
            .CustomerID = udtProps.CustomerID
            .Name = Trim$(udtProps.Name)
            .Phone = Trim$(udtProps.Phone)
            colDisplay.Add objDisplay
            Set objDisplay = Nothing
          End With
        Next
      End With
      Set objBuffer = Nothing
    End Sub
```

We should be able to make similar changes to the **Videos** object, creating a matching
VideosPersist object. Since all these objects are read-only, they are pretty easy to deal with. We
don't need to worry about updating data or deleting records, just pulling back the information in the
most efficient manner possible.

Making Child Objects Persistent

At this point we've basically adopted the following sequence of events:

❑   Pull out the data access code
❑   Put it into another object in another project
❑   Modify the original object to call methods on the new persistence object

It's basically the same regardless of whether the object is read-write, read-only or even when it is just
a list of data.

Now let's get into the complicated stuff - child objects. This is where things get very interesting and
more than a little tricky.

On one level we can view child objects as being very much like the **CustomerDisplay** objects we
just loaded in the previous section. The persistence object can just load them into a **Buffer** object
and send them across the network. But then who unpacks the buffer? The parent object? Or,
perhaps, our custom collection object?

Who packs up the child objects to send them back to the persistence object when the user clicks OK
or Apply? Worse still, suppose the child object's data is updated during the update process, how do
we get the resulting changes back into the objects?

Our implementation in Chapter 8 was painfully simplistic. When each object saves itself to the
database it is very easy for the object to update any changed data or do any other database work
required. That's good, but for performance reasons we can't allow each child object to save itself to
the database individually. Suppose there are hundreds of child objects? - that would translate into an
awful lot of calls across DCOM, bogging down performance and leading to some very unhappy
users.

Instead, we need to load all the objects into a **Buffer** object and move them back and forth as a unit. At first glance this doesn't seem too complex. However, it can get tricky when it comes to handling real-world objects.

For example, after we've added a child Tape object we need to retrieve that object's state to get the **TapeID** value assigned by the database. If we've packaged *all* our child objects into a single buffer we don't necessarily want to retrieve the data for Tape objects that already existed, only for those that are newly added.

In our application we have a couple of parent-child relationships. The **Video** and **Tape** objects have that relationship, as do the **Invoice** and **InvoiceItem** objects. The concepts and techniques that we'll employ here work in both cases, so we'll just go through the **Video** and **Tape** objects. The implementation of the **Invoice** object and its children can be extrapolated from there.

Making the Video Object Persistent

The **Video** object is the parent of our **Tape** objects. However, we can basically think of it as a simple business object like **Customer**. The hard work comes in when we make the collection of **Tape** objects persistent, but we'll get through the easy part first.

Global UDTs

Since we'll be moving the **Video** object's data back and forth between the **VideoObjects** and **VideoPersist** projects, we need to provide a global UDT to hold that data. This means taking the **VideoProps** UDT from the **Video** class module and putting it into the **VideoTypes** BAS module.

Moving the VideoProps UDT

Don't forget to add variables to store the values of **flgNew**, **flgDeleted** and **flgDirty**. We'll use these when we build the **VideoPersist** object and in the **GetState** method of the **Video** object.

```
Public Type VideoProps
    VideoID As Long
    Title As String * 30
    ReleaseDate As Date
    Studio As String * 30
    Category As Long
    Rating As Long

    IsNew As Boolean
    IsDeleted As Boolean
    IsDirty As Boolean
End Type
```

Adding a VideoData UDT

We also need to create a **VideoData** UDT so we can use **LSet** to copy the detailed data from **VideoProps** into a single **String** buffer.

```
Public Type VideoData
    Buffer As String * 80
End Type
```

The VideoPersist Object

As with the **Customer** object, we'll need to split out the persistence code into a new object. In the **VideoPersist** project create a new class module named **VideoPersist** and set its Instancing to 5-Multiuse.

The process to support making the **Video** object persistent is the same as we used for the **Customer** object earlier on in the chapter. All we'll do is move the **Fetch**, **Save** and **DeleteObject** methods from **Video** to **VideoPersist** and make them **Public** in scope. Of course, we'll add **GetState** and **SetState** methods as well.

```
Option Explicit

Private udtProps As VideoProps

Public Sub Save()
  Dim rsVideo As Recordset
  Dim strSQL As String

  If udtProps.IsNew Then
    strSQL = "Video"
    Set rsVideo = dbVideo.OpenRecordset(strSQL, dbOpenTable)
    rsVideo.AddNew
  Else
    strSQL = "SELECT * FROM Video WHERE VideoID=" & _
      udtProps.VideoID
    Set rsVideo = dbVideo.OpenRecordset(strSQL, dbOpenDynaset)
    rsVideo.Edit
  End If
  With rsVideo
    .Fields("Title") = udtProps.Title
    .Fields("ReleaseDate") = udtProps.ReleaseDate
    .Fields("Studio") = udtProps.Studio
    .Fields("Rating") = udtProps.Rating
    .Fields("Category") = udtProps.Category
    .Update
    If udtProps.IsNew Then
      .Bookmark = .LastModified
      udtProps.VideoID = .Fields("VideoID")
    End If
    .Close
  End With
End Sub

Public Sub DeleteObject(ByVal VideoID As Long)
  dbVideo.Execute "DELETE FROM Video WHERE VideoID=" & VideoID
End Sub

Public Sub Fetch(ByVal VideoID As Long)
  Dim rsVideo As Recordset
  Dim strSQL As String
  Dim rsTape As Recordset

  strSQL = "SELECT * FROM Video WHERE VideoID=" & VideoID
  Set rsVideo = dbVideo.OpenRecordset(strSQL, dbOpenSnapshot)
  With rsVideo
    udtProps.VideoID = .Fields("VideoID")
    udtProps.Title = .Fields("Title")
```

```
      udtProps.ReleaseDate = .Fields("ReleaseDate")
      udtProps.Studio = .Fields("Studio")
      udtProps.Rating = .Fields("Rating")
      udtProps.Category = .Fields("Category")

      rsVideo.Close
    End With
  End Sub

  Public Sub SetState(ByVal Buffer As String)
    Dim udtData As VideoData

    udtData.Buffer = Buffer
    LSet udtProps = udtData
  End Sub

  Public Function GetState() As String
    Dim udtData As VideoData

    LSet udtData = udtProps
    GetState = udtData.Buffer
  End Function
```

The Video Object

The **Video** object itself needs to be updated as well. In particular, we need to change the **ApplyEdit** and **Load** methods to use the **VideoPersist** object's methods instead of private subroutines. We also need to add **GetState** and **SetState** methods as we did with the **Customer** object.

Updating ApplyEdit in Video

The changes to the **ApplyEdit** method are basically the same ones we made to the **Customer** object's **ApplyEdit** method.

```
Public Sub ApplyEdit()
    Dim objPersist As VideoPersist

    If Not flgEditing Then Err.Raise 445

    Set objPersist = New VideoPersist
    If flgDeleted Then
      ' code to delete the object's data goes here
      objPersist.DeleteObject udtProps.VideoID

      flgNew = True
      flgDeleted = False
    Else 'If flgDirty Or flgNew Then
      If Not IsValid Then Err.Raise 445
      ' save object to database if appropriate

      With objPersist
        .SetState GetState
        .Save
        If flgNew Then SetState .GetState
      End With
```

```
    ' save object state
    LSet udtSave = udtProps
    flgNew = False
  End If
  objTapes.ApplyEdit

  Set objPersist = Nothing

  flgDirty = False
  flgEditing = False
End Sub
```

Updating Load in Video

Likewise, the **Load** method just needs simple enhancement.

```
Public Sub Load(VideoID As Long)

  Dim objPersist As VideoPersist

  If flgEditing Then Err.Raise 445
  If Not flgNew Then Err.Raise 445

  ' code to load the object goes here

  Set objPersist = New VideoPersist
  With objPersist
    .Fetch VideoID
    SetState .GetState
  End With
  Set objPersist = Nothing

  objValid.RuleBroken "Title", False

  flgNew = False
End Sub
```

The call to the **RuleBroken** method of **objValid** shown here was originally in the **Fetch** subroutine. When that routine was moved out of the **Video** object the reference to **objValid** became useless and so this line had to move to the **Load** routine.

```
  objValid.RuleBroken "Title", False
```

Adding GetState to Video

The **GetState** method copies the values of **flgNew**, **flgDeleted** and **flgDirty** into **udtProps**, then uses **LSet** to copy the object's state into a single **String** buffer.

```
Private Function GetState() As String
  Dim udtData As VideoData

  With udtProps
    .IsDeleted = flgDeleted
    .IsNew = flgNew
    .IsDirty = flgDirty
  End With
  LSet udtData = udtProps
```

```
      GetState = udtData.Buffer
   End Function
```

Adding SetState to Video

As with **Customer**, the **SetState** method is even simpler. All it does is copy the buffer into **udtProps** using the **LSet** command.

```
Private Sub SetState(Buffer As String)
   Dim udtData As VideoData

   udtData.Buffer = Buffer
   LSet udtProps = udtData
End Sub
```

Marshaling the Tape Objects

So now we're down to brass tacks. The parent object is all set and ready to go, we just need to figure out how to manage the child objects. The key word in that sentence is *manage*. In Chapter 6 we built an object specifically to manage the child objects, the **Tapes** object. What we're about to do here is just an extension to the management job that the **Tapes** object already handles.

Our **Tape** objects provide both child behaviors and regular business object behaviors. For the most part a **Tape** object is a child of the **Video** object. However, we also allow the UI to bring up a **Tape** object by itself for the purpose of calling the **CheckIn** method. This way we can create a UI that prompts the user for a tape's ID number to directly check in the tape.

Right now we'll focus exclusively on the child object behaviors so it is clear exactly how to handle child objects. Later on we'll go back through and add in the code to allow the **Tape** object to retrieve and update its data directly so the UI can use the **CheckIn** method.

As we discussed earlier, the driving force behind this whole endeavor is performance. We need to come up with some mechanism by which all the **Tape** objects can be sent through DCOM in a single method call. If each **Tape** object makes its own calls via DCOM our application's performance will be terrible.

Instead of each child object making the calls, we'll put this code into the **Tapes** object. It can collect all the child object's state data together into a **Buffer** object and send that across the network to a **TapesPersist** object. The **TapesPersist** object can then break the **Buffer** object apart and get each object updated in the database.

What we are doing here is an example of *marshalling* the data. We are choosing to marshal all the data from the child objects together into a single unit that we can send over the network. The work of marshalling will be handled by the **Tapes** object, though each individual **Tape** object will have to provide and update its own state data.

Updating the Tape Object

Adding GetState to Tape

The first thing we need to do is provide a way to get each individual **Tape** object's state data into and out of the object. As with our other objects, we'll do this by implementing **GetState** and **SetState** methods in the object.

We need to move the **TapeProps** UDT into the **VideoTypes** BAS module and create a **TapeData** UDT so we can convert the detailed properties into a single **String** buffer.

```
Public Type TapeProps
    TapeID As Long
    VideoID As Long
    Title As String * 30
    CheckedOut As Boolean
    DateAcquired As Date
    DateDue As Date
    LateFee As Boolean
    InvoiceID As Long

    IsNew As Boolean
    IsDeleted As Boolean
    IsDirty As Boolean
End Type


Public Type TapeData
    Buffer As String * 60
End Type
```

The **GetState** method is the same as the methods we've implemented in the **Customer** and **Video** objects. The only significant difference is that the method is declared as **Friend** rather than **Private**. This is because the **Tapes** object will be getting and setting each **Tape** object's state and so will need access to the method.

```
Friend Function GetState() As String
    Dim udtData As TapeData

    With udtProps
      .IsNew = flgNew
      .IsDeleted = flgDeleted
      .IsDirty = flgDirty
    End With
    LSet udtData = udtProps
    GetState = udtData.Buffer
    flgNew = False
End Function
```

Adding SetState to Tape

The **SetState** is also declared as **Friend**, but is otherwise quite familiar.

```
Friend Sub SetState(Buffer As String)
    Dim udtData As TapeData
```

```
   udtData.Buffer = Buffer
   LSet udtProps = udtData
   flgNew = False
   objValid.RuleBroken "DateAcquired", False
End Sub
```

Since the **SetState** will only be called when data is being provided from the database to the object, we've included code to mark any data-oriented rules as unbroken.

```
   objValid.RuleBroken "DateAcquired", False
```

This code was in the **Fetch** subroutine, but as with our previous objects, the **Fetch** subroutine will be moved to the persistence object and so this code needs to be moved. In the **Customer** and **Video** objects we moved it to the **Load** method, but since **Tape** is a child object, the **Load** method isn't going to be used.

The **SetState** method is therefore the ideal location to indicate the rule is unbroken, since we know the data supplied is valid because it has just come from the database.

> *The assumption that the data coming from the database is only valid if we are certain that there are no other applications working with the data. If there is any form of data access other than through our business objects we might need to add extra data validation in either our UI-centric object's **SetState** method or in the data-centric object's **Fetch** method.*

Updating the Tapes Collection Object

Adding GetState to Tapes

The **Tapes** object itself will need **GetState** and **SetState** methods as well. These will be a bit different, since the 'state' of the **Tapes** object is really the collected states of all the **Tape** objects.

Let's look at the **GetState** method first.

```
Private Function GetState() As String
   Dim objBuffer As Buffer
   Dim objTape As Tape

   Set objBuffer = New Buffer
   Set objTape = New Tape
   objBuffer.Initialize Len(objTape.GetState), 20
   For Each objTape In colTapes
     objBuffer.Add objTape.GetState
   Next
   For Each objTape In colDeleted
     objBuffer.Add objTape.GetState
   Next
   GetState = objBuffer.GetState
   Set objBuffer = Nothing
End Function
```

To start off we need to create a **Buffer** object, **objBuffer**. The hard part in this case is to initialize the new object. We need to know the length of the elements we'll be adding to the **Buffer**. There are many ways to get this length. Here we've simply created a new **Tape** object and taken the length of its **GetState** method's result.

Next we just need to loop through the **Tape** objects and add each one's state to the **Buffer** object.

```
For Each objTape In colTapes
    objBuffer.Add objTape.GetState
Next
```

What might not be entirely obvious is that we also need to add the states of each **Tape** object that has been moved to the **objDeleted** collection. These particular **Tape** objects have their **flgDeleted** flags set to **True**, but to get actually deleted from the database we need to send them across to the persistence object as well.

```
For Each objTape In colDeleted
    objBuffer.Add objTape.GetState
Next
```

After having added all the individual **Tape** object's states to the **Buffer** object, we can simply return the **Buffer** object's state as the result of this **GetState** method.

```
    GetState = objBuffer.GetState
    Set objBuffer = Nothing
End Function
```

Adding SetState to Tapes

The **SetState** method is also a bit unusual when compared to the others we've seen. A while ago we discussed how bidirectional updates of the child objects were tricky. Here we come face to face with the issue.

When we go to save a group of **Tape** objects we send them all to the persistence object as a group. The problem is that each item's data may change while it is interacting with the database. For instance, a new **Tape** object gets an ID value as it is being saved. How does that new ID value get back into the **Tape** object itself?

All the child object states come back from the persistence object in a single **Buffer** object. In fact, that **Buffer** object is what we use in this **SetState** routine. The challenge is to figure out which child object needs to be updated from each element in the **Buffer**.

In this case we'll take the easy way out. Rather than trying to identify and update individual **Tape** objects, we'll just drop the reference to all the child objects, effectively destroying them all. Then the **SetState** code can just recreate the collection of child objects based on the current content of the **Buffer** object.

```
Private Sub SetState(ByVal Buffer As String)
    Dim lngIndex As Long
    Dim objTape As Tape
    Dim objBuffer As Buffer
```

```
    Set colTapes = Nothing
      Set colTapes = New Collection
      Set colDeleted = Nothing
      Set colDeleted = New Collection
```

These last four lines create new **Collection** objects for **colTapes** and **colDeleted**. This means that we no longer have a reference to the old objects and so they will terminate. Since those **Collection** objects are the only things with references to the child **Tape** objects, all of those objects will terminate as well.

Using these new and empty **Collection** objects, we can loop through the elements in the **Buffer** object, creating a new **Tape** object for each item.

```
    Set objBuffer = New Buffer
    objBuffer.SetState Buffer

    For lngIndex = 1 To objBuffer.Count
      Set objTape = New Tape
      With objTape
        .SetAsChild
        .SetState objBuffer.Item(lngIndex)
      End With
      colTapes.Add Item:=objTape
    Next
  End Sub
```

In the end we've fully rebuilt the collection of child **Tape** objects based on the **Buffer** object's data. This means that the **Tape** objects are all populated with current and correct data from the database, including any new or updated data that might have come into play during the process of adding or updating the objects into the database.

Creating the Data-Centric Tape Objects

What we've done so far should enable us to take all the data from all the **Tape** objects and marshal it into a single **String** buffer that we can send over the network. The process also works in reverse, in that we can accept a **String** buffer and rebuild all the child **Tape** objects based on the data provided.

As with our other business objects, we also need to create data-centric business objects in the **VideoPersist** project to restore, save and delete the child objects' data. Since we've got all the child object data into a single **String** buffer, we'll design our data-centric objects to work with the same **String** buffer, making it easy to transfer our objects' data back and forth between the UI-centric and data-centric objects.

We need a data-centric object for the **Tapes** object to work with, one that can accept and provide a buffer containing all the child objects' data. We also need an object that knows how to save and restore the **Tape** objects themselves. While it would certainly be possible to combine these functions into a single object, it is much more maintainable and readable to keep them separate.

The TapesPersist Object

The **Tapes** object needs a corresponding object in the **VideoPersist** project that can accept the **String** buffer, unpack it and save each element's data. This object also needs to have a **Fetch** method to retrieve all the child objects' data, pack it into a buffer and provide it to the **Tapes** object upon request.

In many ways this object will be very much like the **TextListPersist** and **CustomersPersist** objects that retrieved lists of data earlier in the chapter. The big difference is that this object will also need to be able to write data back out to the database. Also, the actual database code will not be contained in this object, but rather will be contained in a **TapePersist** object that we'll get to later.

Setting up TapesPersist

Add a new class module to the **VideoPersist** project and name it **TapesPersist**. Make sure its Instancing is set to 5-Multiuse, since the **Tapes** object will be creating and working with this object.

Like the persistence objects we created earlier to handle lists of data, this object's state is basically a **Buffer** object, so we'll need to declare and create this object before we can use it.

```
Option Explicit

Private objBuffer As Buffer

Private Sub Class_Initialize()
  Set objBuffer = New Buffer
End Sub
```

Adding SetState and GetState Methods to TapesPersist

It will also need **GetState** and **SetState** methods. All these methods need to do is copy the **Buffer** object's state into or out of **objBuffer** as appropriate, so we'll let the **Buffer** object itself do most of the work here.

```
Public Sub SetState(ByVal Buffer As String)
  Set objBuffer = New Buffer
  objBuffer.SetState Buffer
End Sub

Public Function GetState() As String
  GetState = objBuffer.GetState
End Function
```

Adding a Fetch Method to TapesPersist

Our existing **Tapes** object's **Load** method contains code to retrieve the list of **TapeID** values from the database for all the records that have the appropriate **VideoID**. This routine will provide the basis for the **TapesPersist** object's **Fetch** method.

Like the original routine, this new routine will create a recordset containing all the valid **TapeID** values from the database. It will then loop through all those ID values, invoking a **Fetch** method to load each **Tape** object's data.

```
Public Sub Fetch(ByVal VideoID As Long)
    Dim strSQL As String
    Dim rsTape As Recordset
    Dim objPersist As TapePersist

    strSQL = "SELECT TapeID FROM Tape WHERE VideoID=" & VideoID
    Set rsTape = dbVideo.OpenRecordset(strSQL, dbOpenSnapshot)
    Set objPersist = New TapePersist
    Set objBuffer = Nothing
    Set objBuffer = New Buffer
    With objPersist
        objBuffer.Initialize Len(.GetState), 20
        Do While Not rsTape.EOF
            .Fetch rsTape("TapeID")
            objBuffer.Add .GetState
            rsTape.MoveNext
        Loop
    End With
    Set objPersist = Nothing
    rsTape.Close
End Sub
```

The big difference is that instead of creating a **Tape** object and calling its **Fetch** method, we are now creating a **TapePersist** object and using its **Fetch** method. Once we've called the **Fetch** method we can use the **GetState** method to retrieve that item's state data and add it to **objBuffer**.

Adding a Save Method to TapesPersist

The **Save** method is a bit more interesting, especially when compared to our earlier methods of this type.

We need to rebuild the **Buffer** object so it contains any changes to each **Tape** object's data. Along the way we want to remove the deleted objects from the buffer since there's no reason to keep them once the data has been removed from the database.

Rather than trying to update the existing **Buffer** object, **objBuffer**, we'll create a new empty **Buffer** object. Elements that are deleted aren't copied into the new buffer, while those that have been added or updated are copied into the buffer once the database activity is complete.

When we're done, the new **Buffer** object contains only data from valid **Tape** objects. The deleted elements are not present, and all the data for the individual elements will include any changes made during the add, or update, process. Now when the **Tapes** object retrieves the **Buffer** object it will actually get the revised and correct data for the **Tape** objects.

The following code creates a **TapePersist** object, which we'll use to save each **Tape** object's data as we loop through the list from the **Buffer** object. It also creates and initializes this new **Buffer** object into which we'll be copying all the updated elements.

```
Public Sub Save(ByVal VideoID As Long)
    Dim objPersist As TapePersist
    Dim objUpdatedTapes As Buffer
    Dim lngIndex As Long
```

```
      Set objUpdatedTapes = New Buffer
    With objBuffer
       objUpdatedTapes.Initialize .Length, .Count
    End With
    Set objPersist = New TapePersist
    For lngIndex = 1 To objBuffer.Count
      With objPersist
         .SetState objBuffer.Item(lngIndex)
         .SaveChild VideoID
         If Not .IsDeleted Then _
            objUpdatedTapes.Add .GetState
      End With
    Next
    Set objPersist = Nothing
    Set objBuffer = objUpdatedTapes
  End Sub
```

Now we're ready to work with the **Tape** object data itself. But remember back to where we loaded the elements in the **Buffer** object. We included those that need to be added and updated to the database as well as those that are to be deleted. In our previous **Save** methods we only had to worry about elements being saved, but now we've got to handle those being deleted as well.

The problem is that we have no easy access to the detailed values for each element. To get at the detailed fields we'd have to use **LSet** to copy the buffer into the **TapeProps** UDT. This is an expensive operation just to get at the **IsDeleted** flag, and so we've taken another approach.

Instead of making this routine more complex, we've left it up to the **TapePersist** object to handle the messy details. Rather than calling either **Save** or **DeleteObject** methods on **TapePersist**, we're calling a new method named **SaveChild**. This routine will need to make the determination as to whether the object should be saved or deleted.

```
         .SaveChild VideoID
```

Once each element has been updated into the database we need to copy its state data into our new **Buffer** object, **objUpdatedTapes**. Deleted objects should not be copied into this object - after all, the goal is to have **objUpdatedTapes** contain updated state data for objects that continue to be valid.

To handle this, we'll add an **IsDeleted** property to the **TapePersist** object. Then we can use this property to determine whether the element should be added into the new **Buffer** object.

```
         If Not .IsDeleted Then _
            objUpdatedTapes.Add .GetState
```

The final step is to make sure the **TapesPersist** object's state is updated to contain the new **Buffer** object. By doing this, our client **Tapes** object can use the **GetState** method to retrieve the updated elements.

```
         Set objBuffer = objUpdatedTapes
```

The TapePersist Object

Of course the code we just implemented needs a **TapePersist** object in order to work. This object will contain the code that actually loads and updates the **Tape** object's data into the database, along with our new **SaveChild** method and **IsDeleted** property.

Setting up TapePersist

Add a new class module to the **VideoPersist** project and name it **TapePersist**. Set its Instancing property to 1-Private. This object is created and used by the **TapesPersist** object, so we don't need to expose it to the outside world.

*Admittedly we'll need to expose it later, to make the **Tape** object itself able to use the methods implemented here. For right now I want to keep focused on the process of saving child objects.*

Like the single object persistence objects we've built so far, this one's state is composed of a UDT containing the **Tape** object's data. We've already moved the **TapeProps** and **TapeData** UDTs to the **VideoTypes** BAS module, so we're all set to use them in **TapePersist**.

```
Option Explicit

Private udtProps As TapeProps
```

Adding SetState and GetState to TapePersist

We also need to implement **GetState** and **SetState** methods to retrieve and set the object's data into the UDT variable.

```
Friend Sub SetState(Buffer As String)
  Dim udtData As TapeData

  udtData.Buffer = Buffer
  LSet udtProps = udtData
End Sub

Friend Function GetState() As String
  Dim udtData As TapeData

  LSet udtData = udtProps
  GetState = udtData.Buffer
End Function
```

Moving Fetch to TapePersist

Next, move the **Fetch**, **Save** and **DeleteObject** methods from **Tape** into this object. We'll handle these a bit differently than before. The **Fetch** method will need to be **Friend**, since it is directly called from the **TapesPersist** object.

```
Friend Sub Fetch(TapeID As Long)
  Dim rsTape As Recordset
  Dim strSQL As String
```

```
      strSQL = "SELECT Tape.*,Video.Title " & _
        "FROM Tape INNER JOIN Video ON Tape.VideoID = " & _
        "Video.VideoID " & _
        "WHERE TapeID=" & TapeID
    Set rsTape = dbVideo.OpenRecordset(strSQL, dbOpenSnapshot)
    With rsTape
      udtProps.TapeID = .Fields("TapeID")
      udtProps.VideoID = .Fields("VideoID")
      udtProps.Title = .Fields("Title")
      udtProps.CheckedOut = .Fields("CheckedOut")
      udtProps.DateAcquired = _
        IIf(IsNull(.Fields("DateAcquired")), 0, _
        Fields("DateAcquired"))
      udtProps.DateDue = IIf(IsNull(.Fields("DateDue")), 0, _
        .Fields("DateDue"))
      udtProps.InvoiceID = .Fields("InvoiceID")

      rsTape.Close
    End With
End Sub
```

Other than changing its scope to **Friend**, the **Fetch** method is unchanged from the **Tape** object.

> Throughout the code for this object, no parameters use the **ByVal** keyword, although the methods may be **Public**. This is because the object itself is **Private**, so even the **Public** methods can't be called by code outside the immediate Visual Basic project. Using **ByVal** here would be a detriment to performance rather than providing the benefits we see when passing parameters across process boundaries or network connections.

Moving Save to TapePersist

The **Save** method can remain **Private** in scope. We'll be calling it from the **SaveChild** method rather than directly from the **TapesPersist** object, so it doesn't need to be available outside this class.

```
    Private Sub Save()
      Dim rsTape As Recordset
      Dim rsVideo As Recordset
      Dim strSQL As String

      If udtProps.IsNew Then
        strSQL = "Tape"
        Set rsTape = dbVideo.OpenRecordset(strSQL, dbOpenTable)
        rsTape.AddNew
      Else
        strSQL = "SELECT * FROM Tape WHERE TapeID=" & udtProps.TapeID
        Set rsTape = dbVideo.OpenRecordset(strSQL, dbOpenDynaset)
        rsTape.Edit
      End If
      With rsTape

        .Fields("VideoID") = udtProps.VideoID
```

```
              .Fields("CheckedOut") = udtProps.CheckedOut
              .Fields("DateAcquired") = udtProps.DateAcquired
              .Fields("DateDue") = udtProps.DateDue
              .Fields("InvoiceID") = udtProps.InvoiceID
              .Update

          If udtProps.IsNew Then

              .Bookmark = .LastModified
              udtProps.TapeID = .Fields("TapeID")
          End If
          .Close
      End With
      strSQL = "SELECT TITLE FROM Video WHERE VideoID=" & _
          udtProps.VideoID
      Set rsVideo = dbVideo.OpenRecordset(strSQL, dbOpenSnapshot)
      udtProps.Title = rsVideo("Title")
      rsVideo.Close


      If udtProps.LateFee Then
        ' add the late fee to the customer
        SaveLateFee
      End If

  End Sub
```

The first couple of changes in this routine are the same old thing we've done with the others, replacing **flgNew** with **udtProps.IsNew**. This last change is quite different however.

In the original **Tape** object, we had code in the **ApplyEdit** method to call the **SaveLateFee** subroutine if a late fee was indicated by the **udtProps.LateFee** variable.

```
          If udtProps.LateFee Then
            ' add the late fee to the customer
            SaveLateFee
          End If
```

Moving SaveLateFee to TapePersist

The **SaveLateFee** routine actually goes out to the database and adds a record to the **LateFee** table. Since we're moving all the code that works with the database out of the **VideoObjects** project, the **SaveLateFee** subroutine needs to be moved as well, and so does the code that calls it.

The **SaveLateFee** routine can be moved from the **Tape** object to the **TapePersist** object directly and without change. We may change where we've called it from, but it still needs to do the exact same thing it was doing before.

```
      Private Sub SaveLateFee()
        Dim rsLateFee As Recordset
        Dim rsInvoice As Recordset
        Dim strSQL As String

        strSQL = "SELECT CUSTOMERID FROM INVOICE WHERE INVOICEID=" & _
          udtProps.InvoiceID
        Set rsInvoice = dbVideo.OpenRecordset(strSQL, dbOpenSnapshot)
        strSQL = "LateFee"

        Set rsLateFee = dbVideo.OpenRecordset(strSQL, dbOpenTable)
```

```
      rsLateFee.AddNew
      With rsLateFee
        .Fields("CustomerID") = rsInvoice("CustomerID")
        .Fields("TapeID") = udtProps.TapeID
        .Fields("FeeDate") = Now
        .Fields("DaysOver") = DateDiff("d", udtProps.DateDue, Now)
        .Fields("Paid") = False
        .Update
        .Close
      End With
    End Sub
```

Moving DeleteObject to TapePersist

Like the **SaveLateFee** routine, the **DeleteObject** routine can be moved from **Tape** to **TapePersist** unchanged.

```
    Friend Sub DeleteObject(TapeID As Long)
      dbVideo.Execute "DELETE FROM Tape WHERE TapeID=" & TapeID
    End Sub
```

Adding an IsDeleted Property to TapePersist

The final step in the process is to create the **SaveChild** method and the **IsDeleted** property. Let's look at the **IsDeleted** property first, since it is so simple.

```
    Friend Property Get IsDeleted() As Boolean
      IsDeleted = udtProps.IsDeleted
    End Property
```

The **TapePersist** object's state is stored in the **udtProps** variable, just like the **Tape** object itself. Thus, its **IsDeleted** property can simply return the value of the **IsDeleted** variable within **udtProps** and we're all set.

Adding SaveChild to TapePersist

The **SaveChild** method isn't all that complex either. Back in the **Save** method of the **TapesPersist** object we called this method instead of the **Save** or **DeleteObject** methods because the **TapesPersist** object had no easy way of knowing whether this particular **Tape** object needed to be saved or deleted.

Now that we're inside the **TapePersist** object and the object's state is contained in the **udtProps** variable this is trivial. We can directly examine the **IsDeleted** value and make a determination as to whether we need to delete the object or call the **Save** subroutine.

```
    Friend Sub SaveChild(VideoID As Long)
      With udtProps
        If .IsDeleted Then
          DeleteObject .TapeID
        ElseIf .IsDirty Or .IsNew Then
          .VideoID = VideoID
          Save
        End If
      End With
    End Sub
```

Updating the Tapes and Tape Objects

At this point the objects in **VideoPersist** are ready to roll. The **TapesPersist** object will accept all the data for the **Tape** objects and will use the **TapePersist** object to retrieve or update them as appropriate.

We've already incorporated **GetState** and **SetState** methods into both the **Tapes** and **Tape** objects, but there are some other changes we need to make before we're all done.

The Tapes Object

In the **Tapes** object we just need to make a couple of changes. In particular, we need to add code so the **TapesPersist** object's methods are called when needed.

Updating ApplyEdit in Tapes

In the **ApplyEdit** method we used to just loop through all the child **Tape** objects and tell each one to do its own **ApplyEdit** operation. Now we need to add some code to collect all the child object's state data by using the **GetState** method we wrote earlier. Then we need to send this data down to the **TapesPersist** object and let it get everything updated.

```
Public Sub ApplyEdit(VideoID As Long)

    Dim objPersist As TapesPersist

    If Not flgEditing Then Err.Raise 445

    Set objPersist = New TapesPersist
    With objPersist
      .SetState GetState
      .Save VideoID
      SetState .GetState
    End With
    Set objPersist = Nothing

    flgEditing = False
End Sub
```

This is a far cry from the code we had in here before. In fact this is a whole lot simpler. The reason is largely that we are rebuilding all the child **Tape** objects when the data is retrieved from the **TapesPersist** object.

```
    SetState .GetState
```

Our **SetState** method drops all references to the child objects, thus terminating them. It then loops through the results from the **TapesPersist** object and builds new **Tape** objects with the updated data. This implicitly produces updated child objects as well as removing any deleted objects from memory.

Updating Load in Tapes

Likewise, the **Load** method becomes much simpler. Where it used to access the database to retrieve a list of ID values for the child objects, it now simply calls the **TapesPersist** object's **Fetch** method and lets that object deal with all the details.

```
Friend Sub Load(VideoID As Long)
    Dim objPersist As TapesPersist

    If flgEditing Then Err.Raise 445

    Set objPersist = New TapesPersist
    With objPersist
      .Fetch VideoID
      SetState .GetState
    End With
    Set objPersist = Nothing
End Sub
```

The Tape Object

The changes to the **Tape** object are very easy to implement. In reviewing what we've done to the **ApplyEdit** and **Load** methods of the **Tapes** object, we can see that they no longer call **ChildApplyEdit** or **ChildLoad** on each **Tape** object. Instead they rely on the **SetState** method to get data into or out of each child object.

This means we can simply remove the **ChildApplyEdit** and **ChildLoad** methods from the **Tape** object. If they aren't called there's no reason to retain them.

Making the Tape Object Make Itself Persistent

If we try to recompile the project at this point we'll get some errors in the **Tape** class module. It still has some references to the **Fetch**, **Save** and **DeleteObject** subroutines that we've moved to the **TapePersist** object.

That's because we've focused entirely on the concept of making child objects persistent. Our **Tape** object is more than just a child object however. It is a kind of hybrid, able to fetch and update its data directly as well as through the child mechanism that we've just implemented.

Now that we've got all the parent-child persistence out of the way, let's go back through the **Tape** and **TapePersist** objects and make the final changes.

Make TapePersist Public

First off, because the **Tape** object is a hybrid, it will need direct access to the **TapePersist** object. Simple child objects wouldn't have this access, but in this case it is required.

Updating the Scope of TapePersist

Bring up the **VideoPersist** project and select the **TapePersist** class module in the Project window. Change the Instancing property of the class to 5-Multiuse. This will allow the **Tape** object to directly create instances of the class as needed.

Updating the Scope of the TapePersist Methods

Now we need to run through the existing methods on the **TapePersist** object and make sure their scope is still in line with what we need. We need to make sure that the methods we'll be calling from the **Tape** object are **Public** and that all the others are either **Private** or **Friend**.

Method	Old scope	New scope
SaveChild	Friend	Friend
Save	Private	Public
DeleteObject	Private	Public
Fetch	Friend	Public
SaveLateFee	Private	Private
SetState	Friend	Public
GetState	Friend	Public

Updating ApplyEdit in Tape

Now that we know the **Tape** object has access to the methods it will need from **TapePersist** we can simply alter the code that called the **Fetch**, **Save** and **DeleteObject** subroutines. Instead of calling local subroutines we'll change the code to create a **TapePersist** and use the methods on that object instead.

The **ApplyEdit** method of the **Tape** object needs to be modified in the following manner:

```
Public Sub ApplyEdit()
    Dim objPersist As TapePersist

    If flgChild Then If Not flgChildEditing Then Err.Raise 445
    If Not flgChild And flgNew Then Err.Raise 445
    If Not flgEditing Then Err.Raise 445

    If Not flgChild Then
        If flgDeleted Then
            ' code to delete the object's data goes here
            Set objPersist = New TapePersist
            objPersist.DeleteObject udtProps.TapeID
            Set objPersist = Nothing

            flgNew = True
            flgDeleted = False
        ElseIf flgDirty Or flgNew Then
```

```
          If Not IsValid Then Err.Raise 445
          ' save object to database if appropriate

          Set objPersist = New TapePersist
          With objPersist
            .SetState GetState
            .Save
            If flgNew Then SetState .GetState
          End With
          Set objPersist = Nothing

          ' save object state
          LSet udtSave = udtProps
          flgNew = False
        End If
        flgDirty = False
      Else
        If Not objParent Is Nothing Then
          objParent.AddChild Me
          Set objParent = Nothing
        End If
      End If
      flgEditing = False
    End Sub
```

Updating Load in Tape

Likewise, the **Load** method needs to be changed.

```
      Public Sub Load(TapeID As Long)

        Dim objPersist As TapePersist

        If flgChild Then Err.Raise 445
        If flgEditing Then Err.Raise 445
        If Not flgNew Then Err.Raise 445

        If Not flgChild Then
          ' code to load the object goes here

          Set objPersist = New TapePersist
          With objPersist
            .Fetch TapeID
            SetState .GetState
          End With
          Set objPersist = Nothing

        End If
        flgNew = False
      End Sub
```

Removing Data Access from VideoObjects

With these changes, the **TapePersist** and **Tape** objects can now work together to directly retrieve and update data from the database. At this point we should have the same functionality as we had in Chapter 8, but all the data access is handled by the **VideoPersist** ActiveX server rather than by the **VideoObjects** DLL itself.

If we apply similar changes to the **Invoice** object and its child objects then none of the objects in the **VideoObjects** project will contain any data access code at all.

With that achieved, we can remove the **VOMain** code module from the **VideoObjects** project. This module contained the code to declare **dbVideo** and to open the database. We no longer need any access to the database in this project.

We can also remove the reference to the DAO library from the project. Choose the Project-References... menu option and uncheck the DAO item in the References list.

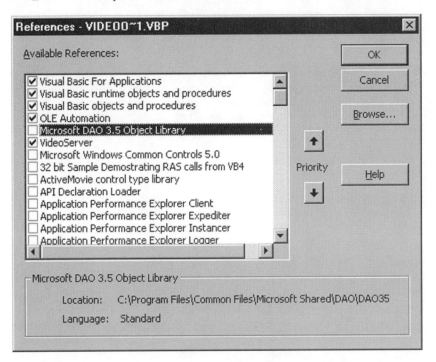

If we don't remove this reference the project will continue to require the DAO libraries to be present and loaded when the program is running. This consumes unneeded resources on the client workstation and would generally be sloppy programming in any case.

Summary

Here, at the end of the chapter, we should be able to run the **VideoUI** client, or the Excel client we created in Chapter 9 for that matter. The clients will work with the business objects in **VideoO.dll** as always, without change.

Of course the business objects themselves will now be communicating through COM to the **VideoPersist** server application. At this point that application will be running on our client workstation along with our UI application, but we've effectively separated our UI-centric objects from our data-centric objects nonetheless.

In Chapter 11 we'll take the **VideoPersist** server and run it on a separate application server machine, using DCOM to allow communication between the client workstation and the application server. Then in Chapter 12 we'll convert it to run inside Microsoft Transaction Server. This will provide our application with much greater scalability, as well as providing transaction support for our database activity.

Finally, in Chapter 13 we'll look at implementing a Web interface to our business objects by using Active Server Pages.

Distributing Objects using DCOM

Overview

In Chapter 10 we took the video rental business objects we created in Chapter 8 and split the data persistence routines into separate data-centric business objects. We put the data-centric objects into an ActiveX EXE server named **VideoServer**. By having each of our business objects split into two parts, a UI-centric object and a data-centric object, we have changed our video rental application to follow the CSLA architecture we established in Chapter 2.

As we left it in Chapter 10, however, our data-centric objects remain on the client workstation, so we are still running in, at most, a two-tier physical environment as shown in the following figure:

Client workstation	Presentation tier
	UI-centric objects
Application server	Data-centric objects
Database server	Data services tier

In this chapter we'll move closer to a three-tier physical architecture, by seeing how we can run our **VideoServer** program on an application server. This will move the data-centric business objects off the client workstation and onto a separate machine. If we were to have the database running on a third machine we'd have a full three-tier physical implementation.

We won't worry about setting up an actual database server until Chapter 12, since in this chapter we'll focus on running the **VideoServer** program on the application server machine. This means is that we'll need to have a machine separate from our client workstations that is accessible through a network. This machine will act as our application server.

Application Server Issues

Of course, effectively running our objects on an application server is no small feat. An application server needs to support many concurrent client workstations within the limitations of the CPU, memory and database connections. Usually this involves creation of a pool manager, database-connection management and, maybe even record-locking management.

Distributing an application's processing across multiple machines is complex. There are many issues involved, including performance and support for many concurrent users. The topic is complicated enough for me to devote two chapters to covering the basics alone.

In Chapter 10, we made changes to the code so that the **VideoServer** project handles all the data access. Our UI-centric business objects remain in the **VideoObjects** in-process server, but they rely on the data-centric objects in **VideoServer** to communicate with the database. We can now look at running the **VideoServer** program on an application server machine. The **VideoObjects** and **VideoServer** ActiveX servers will communicate with each other using DCOM.

Since our **VideoServer** program uses a database connection we have to worry about multiple users using the same connection, or each user establishing. Also, we still haven't addressed any database transaction issues. Even in our implementation from Chapter 10, when a **Video** object is saved and one of its **Tape** objects fails to save then nothing should be saved. Our current code would leave some data saved and some not.

Many of these issues are typically addressed by developing a pool manager to coordinate and control the use of the server's objects. On the Visual Basic CD there is a sample pool manager project, PoolMngr, that we can use to start developing our own pool manager. The PoolMngr project is very complex, and if we look at it, we can swiftly see why we'd want to think twice before implementing our own pool manager.

Fortunately, Microsoft has released the Microsoft Transaction Server (MTS) product to take care of many of these details, as these issues should really form part of the operating system. In Chapter 12 we'll deal with pool management and other application server issues by putting our data-centric objects into an ActiveX DLL that can be used within MTS.

Rather than pursuing a homemade pool manager in this chapter, we're just going to look at how to use DCOM to distribute the **VideoServer** program to another machine. In Chapter 12 we'll use MTS (Microsoft Transaction Server) to address many of the application server issues we just mentioned.

Building the VideoServer Project

In Chapter 10 we developed the **VideoServer** project on the same machine as the **VideoObjects** and **VideoUI** projects. This is an easy approach, as we can test everything on one machine without having to worry about remote registration and other DCOM concerns.

Now, however, we need to go through the process of moving the **VideoServer** program to another machine. The first thing we need to do is make some changes to the **VideoServer** project itself.

Bring up the **VideoServer** project in Visual Basic. The changes we need to make are all within the Project Properties dialog, so choose the Project-VideoServer Properties... menu option.

Unattended Execution

On the General tab, check the Unattended Execution option. This option is important for any server program.

This option prevents Visual Basic from displaying any message boxes from the program and it makes sure you haven't included any forms or controls in your project. This is important because message boxes or other display elements will cause the program to expect user input. Of course the program is running on a server, not on the user's workstation and so there'd be no one there to provide the input, and typically this would hang the server program.

Multi-threading

Visual Basic allows us to create programs that run in multiple threads of execution. This means that we can have a single program running in a single process, but that program may have multiple threads running at the same time.

Visual Basic uses apartment-model threading, which means that each thread lives in its own 'apartment'. To our code, an apartment seems like a separate process from any other apartment – there's no shared memory, no global variables between threads, and so on. In reality all the threads are running inside the same process, but to each thread that's not how it appears.

> *Multi-threading is mostly important if we intend to run our* **VideoServer** *program on a computer with more than one CPU. On a computer with only one CPU, only one thread can run at a time, whereas with multiple CPUs it is possible for each CPU to be running a different thread - all at the same time.*

Fixed Thread Pool

By default, Visual Basic selects this option, so our program runs in a thread pool composed of a single thread. What this means is that the program will then run as it normally would, since all programs get a single thread of operation whether they are unattended or not.

We can raise the number of threads in the pool if we'd like. By doing this we are allowing Visual Basic to create more than one thread within the program's process. If we increase the thread pool count, the program's objects will be created in different threads as time goes on. There is no way to predict which of the objects will be created in which thread, Visual Basic assigns them to threads using a round-robin algorithm.

The key thing is that each thread acts like a process. This means each thread gets its own global **dbVideo** variable and **Sub Main** runs once when the thread starts up.

In our case this is less than ideal. Since many objects may run inside a single thread, but each thread has its own **dbVideo** we'll have many objects sharing a single database connection. This can lead to conflicts between clients, since different objects may be owned by different clients. Especially if we add **BeginTrans** and **CommitTrans** statements to our data access code we'll find that our objects start committing transactions from other clients, and all sorts of messiness will follow.

Thread per Object

The other option we are given is to have one thread for each object running in the server process. More accurately, there will be one thread for each *externally created* object. The **TapesPersist** object will get its own thread, but when it creates a **TapePersist** object, that object will run inside the same thread since it wasn't created by an external entity.

The threads we're talking about here work the same as with a thread pool. Each thread gets its own global **dbVideo** variable and runs **Sub Main** when it starts up.

The big difference here is that, when a client creates an object, that object runs in its own memory space, with its own database connection. Obviously this isn't ideal for large numbers of clients, since we could end up with a very large number of database connections.

However, we'll use this approach here since it is the simple way to support a number of clients without the complexity of creating a pool manager. Since each thread gets its own database connection, we don't need to worry about two clients trying to use our server at the same time and ending up using the same database connection. With this approach, each client will create its own object, and that object will automatically get its own thread - and thus its own memory and database connection.

Click the Thread per object option as shown in the figure:

Creating Remote Server Files

If we're going to run this program on a remote server we need some way of making each client aware of what the server can do and where to find it on the network. This is handled by a couple of key files that Visual Basic will create for us.

Choose the Component tab in the Project Properties dialog and click on the Remote Server Files option.

With this selected, Visual Basic will create the appropriate files next time we compile this project.

TLB File

Our clients will need to know what the ActiveX server can do. What this really means, is that the client program needs to know the interface definition of the server, basically a list of its classes and their properties and methods.

This is less a Visual Basic issue than a COM issue, because all COM servers should make this information available regardless of what language was used to develop them. They don't have to do this, but it makes the server much easier to work with when it comes to writing client programs. To make the information available, most COM servers provide a **type library** file, usually with a TLB extension.

This type library contains the definitions for all the classes and their interfaces. Using the information in this file, a developer can find out the names and data types of all the parameters, return values and anything else that is important when developing a client program.

With the Remote Server Files option checked in a project's properties, Visual Basic will create a TLB file for us that contains all this information for our program. This file is created each time the project is compiled.

VBR File

The other file that is created with the R̲emote Server Files option is a VBR file. This file is specific to Visual Basic, and provides the mechanism by which the client workstation can register the ActiveX server in its registry.

When the program is running on a server machine it needs to be registered on the server. The thing is, it also needs to be registered on each client workstation along with some extra information about network connections to the server and so forth.

We'll talk about setting up a client shortly, and this VBR file will be a key piece of that discussion.

Binary Compatibility

The last item we need to change is also on the Component tab of the Project Properties dialog. In Chapter 7 we discussed how the Version Compatibility options work and what they do in general terms.

So far we've been using either P̲roject Compatibility or B̲inary Compatibility during development of our programs. This is the Visual Basic default and typically works great – during development.

When we start putting components on different machines things get more complex. While it is certainly possible to stick with Project Compatibility and still use DCOM to access your ActiveX server, it is much easier to get everything working by using Binary Compatibility.

As we discussed in Chapter 7, Binary Compatibility effectively freezes the GUID values for the program itself, along with all its classes. Project Compatibility freezes the program's GUID, but not the class GUIDs, or CLSIDs. As we register the **VideoServer** program on the server and then on multiple clients, everything will be much simpler if none of the GUID values for the program are changing.

We'll need to have compiled the program at least once before we can switch to Binary Compatibility. After we've compiled it, we need to make a copy of the EXE file. Once we've done that we can return to the Project Properties window and click the B̲inary Compatibility option.

Then set the filename of the compatible server to the copy of the original EXE. In this example we've simply used the copy and paste options in Explorer to create a copy. It is important to use a copy of the server for compatibility rather than the server itself because our actual server EXE is recreated each time we compile the program. It is possible for Visual Basic to get confused and lose the server's GUID values if we make our server's EXE also be the compatible server.

> Make sure to save the project after making all these changes. We'll also want to make sure to recompile the project at least once after we've changed the **Unattended Execution** and **Remote Server File** options so they take effect.

Check the Database Location

Keep in mind that we're going to be installing the server program on an application server somewhere on our network. For our DAO code to continue to work we need to double check the code in **Sub Main** to make sure the database location is correct on the application server machine.

The dangerous part about putting code in an ActiveX server's **Sub Main** is that if it fails we won't get any meaningful error messages from Visual Basic. All we'll get is a generic OLE Automation error telling us that our object couldn't be created.

In this case, if the database fails to open an error will be raised, but all we'll see is a generic and unenlightening error message on the client. This type of problem can lead to hours of searching for solutions only to find that the problem was as simple as an error in **Sub Main**.

A good solution to this is to trap any errors in **Sub Main** and write them to a log file.

```
Public Sub Main()
```

```
      On Error GoTo ErrHandler

    Set dbVideo = OpenDatabase("e:\projects\ch7\video.mdb")

    Exit Sub

  ErrHandler:
    App.LogEvent Err.Description & " (" & Err.Number & ")", _
      vbLogEventTypeWarning

  End Sub
```

In the code shown here, we are using Visual Basic's **App** object's **LogEvent** method to write the message to the Windows NT application event log. If we have this program running under Windows 95 the message will be written to a log file in the Windows system directory.

Installing VideoServer on the Server

Now that we've got the **VideoServer** ActiveX server project ready to roll we can proceed to installing it on the server machine.

If you are using something other than NT on your application server the overall process to get everything set up will be similar. However, only NT will provide you with the full range of network protocols for your clients to connect through, and NT is substantially more stable and scalable than other versions of Windows. These are important considerations when setting up an application server.

It's possible we've been developing the software right on the application server machine. Typically this isn't a good practice, but it certainly simplifies things. We'll be going through the process of moving the program to the server machine and getting it registered. If we've developed the program on the server machine then it is already there and it is already registered, and we can skip past the next section.

Installing VideoServer

Before we can make the server program available to client workstations we need to install it on the application server computer. Assuming we didn't develop the program on that computer and that we don't have Visual Basic itself installed on the server computer, we'll need to install a number of files onto that machine.

Things can be simpler if we've got Visual Basic itself, or possibly other Visual Basic applications, already installed on the server machine. In this case all the supporting files for Visual Basic and probably for DAO will already be installed and all we need to do is install and register the **VideoServer** server.

In fact, it can be very confusing to do our development on either the server machine or a client machine. When we compile the applications Visual Basic writes entries into the registry. When we install programs through a Setup program it writes entries into the registry. These entries are almost guaranteed to get messed up and leave us unable to do anything productive at all.

481

Ideally we'd develop your components on one or more development machines and then use a Setup program to get them placed onto your server and client workstations.

Using the Setup Wizard

If we don't know that all the required files exist on the application server computer we'll need to use the Setup Wizard or some equivalent tool to install all the Visual Basic and DAO support files along with our program file on the machine.

We're not going to go through the process of using the Setup Wizard in detail. There's really only one panel in the wizard that is important for our needs.

Install as a Shared Component

Launch the wizard and go through all the panels until we reach the Shared ActiveX Application panel.

It's not that we need to change anything from the default, but this is a key panel for setting up our server.

The Install as a shared component option is appropriate for a shared server like **VideoServer**. Our program is not a full-blown application; in fact it is totally useless without a client program to use it.

Remote Automation

The second question is trickier because the wording is so complex. Basically the question is whether the server will be accessed using Remote Automation as in Visual Basic 4.0. The only time you'd answer Yes would be if you plan to get at this program via Remote Automation, otherwise answer No.

> *Remote Automation is useful in two areas. The most typical use is for 16-bit client workstations, which have no support for DCOM. The other use is for Windows 95 workstations that don't have a TCP/IP connection to our application server. DCOM for Windows 95 only supports the TCP/IP network protocol, so if we're not using that protocol on our network we'll need to use Remote Automation.*

In this chapter we'll assume we're using DCOM, not Remote Automation, and so No is appropriate.

Completing the Install

Once we've completed the process of running the Setup Wizard, just take the resulting installation files and install the program on the application server. This will put all the required files in the correct directories and get them registered as needed.

That's not the last step, because the component still needs to be set up to work with DCOM. We'll get to that shortly.

> It's wise not to install a new version of an ActiveX component on a machine where one is already installed. First uninstall the component by using its uninstall program. Worse, though, is deleting a registered server. When Explorer tells you that the server is registered and you say Yes to moving it to the Recycle Bin, it will helpfully change the `LocalServer32` path to point to the Recycle Bin. Now when you empty the bin, the registry will be wrong.

Manual Registration

For subsequent installations or upgrades to an ActiveX component we can handle the register and unregister process manually. If all the required support files are in place and properly registered we can just unregister the old program, copy in the new version and register it.

Unregister the Previous Version

To unregister a previous installation of **VideoServer,** go to the Windows Start menu and choose the Run option. Then run the **VideoServer** program itself using the **/UNREGSERVER** switch on the command line.

Copy and Register the New Version

Once we're sure that the program is no longer registered, we can copy the upgraded version into place and register it using a similar technique.

Choose the Run option from the Windows Start menu and run the program using the **/REGSERVER** switch on the command line. This will register the program in the Windows registry.

DCOM Configuration

Once the appropriate version of the **VideoServer** ActiveX server is installed and registered on the application server machine all we need to do is get it set up for DCOM. This isn't a difficult thing to do; in fact it is pretty much all set to go by default. The only thing we typically need to do is set the security permissions on the **VideoServer** server so clients can create and use its objects.

DCOM provides a program, **Dcomcnfg.exe**, that we can use to set the permissions on our server program. By default there is no icon or shortcut to this program. To run it, choose the Run option from the Windows Start menu and enter **dcomcnfg**.

Enabling DCOM

The program provides three tabs. The first thing we need to do is make sure that DCOM is actually enabled on this computer. It is by default, but it is well worth checking to make sure someone hasn't disabled it, as we may think that our program doesn't compile, when, in reality, DCOM just isn't enabled.

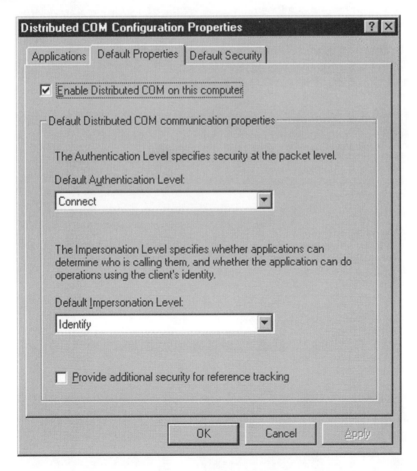

Choose the Default Properties tab and check to make sure the Enable Distributed COM on this computer option is checked.

> The other options on this panel are important, but should be set to workable values by default. For more details about these options you can refer to *Professional DCOM Programming* (ISBN 1-816000-60X) from Wrox Press.

Setting VideoServer Permissions

Once we're sure that DCOM is enabled on this computer we can move on to setting the permissions on the **VideoServer** ActiveX server. The default security settings don't allow remote users to start up or use objects within a server. This is typically a good thing, since we probably don't want people starting up any old server and using its objects.

Selecting the VideoServer Application

We need to switch back to the Applications tab and select the **VideoServer** server from the list displayed there.

Don't be confused by the fact that it also displays a class name, in this case **CustomerPersist**. Even though the program displays one of the server's classes in the list, we are really operating on the server itself rather than any specific class inside the server.

Once we've chosen the server, click on the <u>P</u>roperties... button to bring up the properties for **VideoServer**.

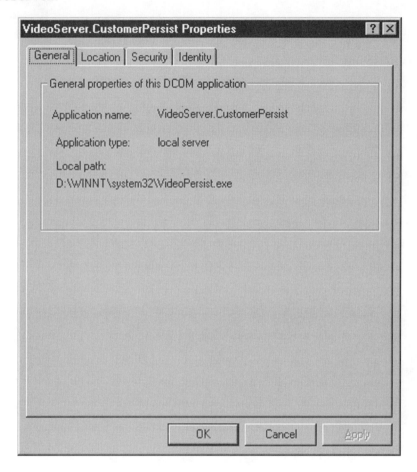

The General tab displays information about the ActiveX server, including its name, whether it is running 'local' or 'remote' and the path to the component itself. The path can be quite useful during debugging, as we can use this to make sure that DCOM is running the program we think it is running.

For instance, things can get very complex if we don't uninstall the program before reinstalling or recompiling it. We can end up with duplicate entries for the server in the registry and it can be difficult to know which one is which without referring back to the path.

Setting VideoServer Permissions

For our purposes at the moment, however, we are interested in the Security tab. The default security won't allow client workstations to use the **VideoServer** server, so we need to switch the options on this server to use custom permissions. This is true for both accessing and launching the server application as shown in the figure.

For both the access and launch permissions we need to click on the Edit... button and customize the permissions. The changes are the same for both permissions, so we'll just walk through the steps, then they need to be repeated for both cases.

Click the Edit... button to
bring up the Registry Value
Permissions dialog.

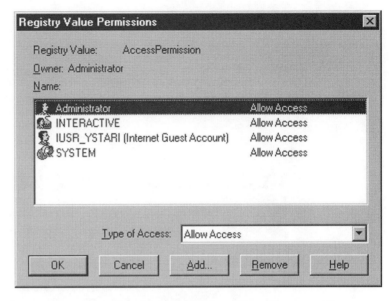

By default, the only users that have any access are ones local to this machine. We can set the
permissions as required by the specific environment, but the easiest approach is to add the Everyone
group to this list. Keep in mind that this opens up the server machine for anyone to start our object –
something that might not be desirable for anything beyond testing.

To do this, click the Add...
button to bring up the Add
Users and Groups dialog.

Then double-click the Everyone entry on the list and click OK. The result should be that the Everyone group is added to the list of people who can either access or launch the **VideoServer** server application.

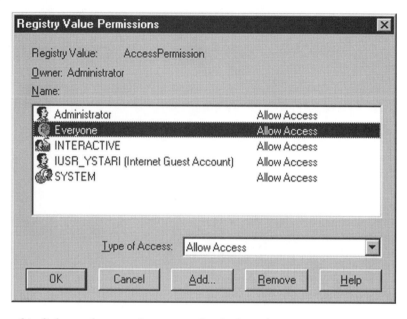

Click OK on this dialog and repeat the process for the launch permissions.

Set the Identity Account

There is one last thing we need to change. On the main screen, switch to the Identity tab. By default the user account is set to The launching user. This option means that our server application will be run under the user account of the user logged into the client workstation.

If that user has no account on our NT server, they won't be able to run our server application – thus they won't be able to get at our objects.

This setting can also cause performance issues, since DCOM will start up a separate process for each user account that accesses our server. This happens regardless of the threading model or instancing settings that we have set up in our project or its objects.

The best thing to do is to choose to run the server under a specific user account, supplying the user and password information on this tab:

This way, DCOM will run our server program under this user account, regardless of who each client might be. Also, all client users will have their objects running within the same process – subject to the threading and object instancing settings we chose when developing our out-of-process server.

Building the VideoObjects Project

Throughout the last chapter, we've been developing the **VideoObjects** project with a reference to either the **VideoServer** project itself, or the **VideoServer** EXE file. At this point we need to change this reference to use the **VideoServer** project's TLB, or type library, file.

Using the TLB File from VideoServer

The TLB file is the final authority on the **VideoServer** server's public interface and GUID values for identification. This is the file that will be defining the **VideoServer** server on each client workstation where your program will be running. Thus it is very important that our client project, **VideoObjects**, also use the TLB file to get its information.

Before going any further, we'll need access to the most recent TLB file for **VideoServer**. If it is not already on our development machine, we'll want to copy it to the Windows 95 **\System** directory or the Windows NT **\System32** directory as appropriate. This is the location that the TLB file will end up being installed by the setup program we'll be creating shortly and so we might as well put it there as well.

Changing the VideoObjects Server's Reference

To make this change, bring up the **VideoObjects** project in Visual Basic and open its Project References dialog. Deselect the **VideoServer** entry from the list. By looking at the Location field at the bottom of the panel we can tell whether it is using the VBP or EXE file to gets its information.

> *Before switching the reference, we need to make sure that* **VideoServer** *is not registered on our development machine. If we're developing* **VideoObjects** *on a different machine than* **VideoServer** *we probably don't have a problem, but if we've been developing on the same machine then* **VideoServer** *will be registered. Before trying to add a reference to our TLB file we need to dereference* **VideoServer** *using by running* **VideoServer.exe** *with the* **/unregserver** *command-line switch.*

Next, click the Browse button and select the **VideoServer.TLB** file. An entry will be added to the list of available references so we can check it and we're all set.

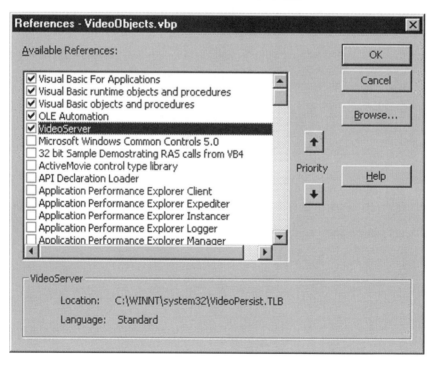

The Location field near the bottom of the dialog shows that the reference is now using a TLB file to get its information.

Setting up the Client

Though **VideoServer** is installed and configured on the application server machine, we still need to make it available to every client machine that needs to use it. This means that we need to register **VideoServer** on each client in a special way so that the client workstation knows to find the server's objects via DCOM.

There are two ways we can do this, either by using a setup tool such as the Visual Basic Setup Wizard or manually using a program supplied with Visual Basic called **Clireg32.exe**.

Using the Setup Wizard

In previous versions of Visual Basic, the Setup Wizard has been pretty inflexible and undependable. While the wizard is much improved in Visual Basic 5.0, it is still not perfect. One problem is that one of the areas where it falls down on the job is in dealing with ActiveX DLL projects that reference a remote ActiveX server, just as our **VideoObjects** DLL references the **VideoServer** server. Another is that the entries in the **Setup.1st** file for remote files don't have the necessary remote computer entries.

This doesn't prevent our use of the wizard, it just means that we need to work around the problem when we build our installation set.

Creating a Dependency File for VideoObjects

We'll be creating a setup program to install the client program, **VideoUI**. However, **VideoUI** requires the **VideoObjects** DLL, **Videoo.dll**, in order to run and so this file will be included automatically by the wizard in the **VideoUI** setup program.

Visual Basic 5.0's Setup Wizard uses a DEP file, or dependency file, to make sure it has any required support files for each ActiveX component that is included for setup. This means that the wizard will expect a DEP file to exist for the **VideoObjects** ActiveX component so it can make sure it gets any support files required by the DLL.

Here's where the wizard's bug enters the picture. The **VideoObjects** component requires the **VideoServer** server, and there's a step in the Setup Wizard to identify **VideoServer** as being required. The problem is that identifying **VideoServer** here does us no good, because the dependency won't flow through to the **VideoUI** installation like it is supposed to.

> Not only do we need to identify **VideoServer** as being important for **VideoObjects**, but we'll need to identify it *again* when we create the setup program for **VideoUI**!

Copy the VideoServer TLB File

Before going any further we need to make sure that the development machine has access to the required files from **VideoServer**. Both the current TLB and VBR files should be copied to the Windows 95 **\System** directory or the Windows NT **\System32** directory. These files will be used by the setup wizard to define the **VideoServer** server for the dependency file.

Generate Dependency File

Creating a dependency file is basically the same as creating a regular setup program. Run the Setup Wizard and choose the **VideoObjects** project file.

Then select the Generate Dependency File Only option as shown in the figure. When we click the Next button, Visual Basic will bring up a warning message about the **VideoServer.tlb** file.

In our case the file does indeed refer to a remote automation component (that is, working on a separate machine), so we can click Yes. When we do this, Visual Basic brings up yet another dialog to remind us to manually add this component to the list of required files later.

This might seem confusing – after all we are using DCOM, not Remote Automation, and yet we are telling the Setup Wizard that we're using a remote automation component. This is simply a terminology holdover from older versions of Visual Basic, so while it's confusing it is basically harmless.

Adding a Reference to VideoServer

When we click OK the wizard will think for a bit and bring up the ActiveX Server Components panel.

Click the Add Remote... button on this panel to add the **VideoServer.VBR** file. We should be presented with a standard dialog to select the file, so navigate to the appropriate directory and select the **VideoServer.VBR** file.

The wizard will bring up a dialog to get the Remote Connection Details for the **VideoServer** server.

The Remote Transport option will default to DCOM, which works just great for us. When using DCOM we don't need to provide much information, just the name or network address of the application server machine. The Network Protocol and Authentication Level fields are used only for Remote Automation.

Enter in the name of our application server computer and click OK.

Completing the Setup Wizard

The rest of the wizard is just like creating a setup program, except that instead what is created is a DEP file for the **VideoObjects** ActiveX component. The file will be named **Videoo.DEP**, using the same name as the DLL file.

The final step is to check that the DEP file is in the same directory as the registered copy of **Videoo.dll** file. If we have multiple copies of **Videoo.dll** on the machine only one will be registered and so that is the directory where the file needs to exist.

> *The Windows registry is an interesting thing. While everything in the registry is ultimately identified by a GUID value, there are also human-readable text names for most items, including ActiveX servers. The trick is this: when a program tries to access an ActiveX server, it does so by name, not by GUID. The first step is to translate the name into a GUID and go from there.*
>
> *The registry can only have one entry for any given human-readable name, so for all practical purposes a given ActiveX server can only be in the registry once.*

Setup for VideoUI

Now we're ready to create an actual setup program for the **VideoUI** client program. We'll make use of the dependency file that we just created for **VideoObjects** in this process, and we'll also end up manually adding a reference to the **VideoServer.VBR** file since the Setup Wizard won't correctly retrieve the information from the **Videoo.DEP** file.

Start the Setup Wizard and select the **VideoUI** project file. The wizard should automatically find the **Videoo.dll** requirement and display it in the ActiveX Server Components panel.

497

Adding a Reference to VideoServer

Here we need to add the **VideoServer.VBR** file, as we did with the **VideoObjects** project. One would think that the Setup Wizard would realize that we already set up the **VideoServer** server through the **VideoObjects** project's DEP file, but it doesn't catch everything and we need to do it by hand.

Click on Add Remote... and select the **VideoServer.VBR** file. We'll be presented with the Remote Connection Details dialog where we need to enter the network name of the application server machine.

Just proceed through the rest of the wizard from there. When we get to the File Summary panel we should see that the **Videoo.dll** along with the two **VideoServer** files, VBR and TLB, are included in the list.

Fixing the Setup.lst file

As with previous versions of the Visual Basic Setup Wizard, this one has more than one problem we need to work around. When setting up a client install for a DCOM server, the wizard forgets to include the remote server connection information for our VBR file. Without this information, the setup will fail to install our software on the client workstations.

The setup process relies on the **Setup.lst** file for all the information about what to install, where to install it and how it should be installed. We'll need to edit this file using Notepad or some other text file editor before trying to install any clients.

Bring up the **Setup.lst** file and look for the **[Files]** section of the file. We're looking for the line that deals with our **VideoPersist.VBR** file. It will appear something like this (though each file entry is all on one line):

```
File2=1,,videoo.dl_,videoo.dll,$(WinSysPath),$(DLLSelfRegister),$(Shared),10/28/1997
16:21:42,152576,1.0.0.0,"","",""
File3=1,,VideoPersist.VB_,VideoPersist.VBR,$(WinSysPath),$(Remote),$(Shared),10/25/19
97 0:26:16,8395,,"","",""
```

This last line is just fine; we won't need to change it. However, there should be *another* line immediately following this one to indicate the DCOM connection information. Let's add this line to the file. Again, remember that the original text is really all on one line, it just doesn't fit here due to space constraints:

```
File3=1,,VideoPersist.VB_,VideoPersist.VBR,$(WinSysPath),$(Remote),$(Shared),10/25/19
97 0:26:16,8395,,"","",""
Remote3="YSTARI",,1,DCOM
```

Of course the server name, **YSTARI**, will need to be changed to reflect the name of the application server in our particular environment.

Once this change has been made, save out the **Setup.1st** file and we should be all ready to install our clients.

Completing the Client Install

Once the wizard and our manual modifications to **Setup.1st** are complete we should have a setup program that we can run on our clients. This setup program will install the **VideoUI** client program and the **VideoObjects** DLL. It will also add the required entries in the system's registry so the **VideoServer** server will be available through DCOM.

It's also worth noting that the **VideoServer.TLB** and **VideoServer.VBR** files will be installed into the Windows 95 **\System** or Windows NT **\System32** directory on each client workstation.

Using CLIREG32

If we change and recompile the **VideoServer** project, Visual Basic will create new VBR and TLB files. There may be cases where we change a server like this, but where we don't need to change and redistribute the **Videoo.dll** file. For instance, perhaps we've added functionality to **VideoServer** for some other client DLL and **Videoo.dll** wasn't affected.

In a case like this we may choose to manually update the client machine's registries with the new **VideoServer** server information rather than using the Setup Wizard to create a setup program to handle it.

Unregister VideoServer

If we've already got the remote **VideoServer** server registered on this client it is important to unregister it before proceeding. Just like any other registry activity, if we register an already-registered program and the uuids (CLSID, TypeLibID, IID and AppID) are different from the previous version, we are asking for double entries in the registry and all sorts of confusion.

In the **\Clisvr** directory under your Visual Basic installation there is a program named **Clireg32.exe**. This program will register and unregister a remote server by using its VBR and TLB files.

It is easiest to run this program from the DOS prompt, though we can use the Run option from the Windows Start menu as well.

The command to unregister the server is:

```
CLIREG32.EXE C:\WINNT\SYSTEM32\VIDEOPERSIST.VBR -u
```

Copy VideoServer's TLB and VBR Files to \System32

After we've unregistered the remote server, we can proceed to update the VBR and TLB files in the Windows system directory. To do this, just copy the updated **VideoServer.TLB** and **VideoServer.VBR** files into the client workstation's Windows system directory. This will be **\System** for Windows 95 or **\System32** for Windows NT.

Most likely we'll be replacing existing files with the new ones, though we can certainly use this technique to register a remote server for the first time as well. If this is a first time installation we won't have to unregister the server of course.

Register VideoServer.VBR

Once the TLB and VBR files are in place we are ready to register the remote server on the client.

The command to register a remote server is:

```
CLIREG32.EXE C:\WINNT\SYSTEM32\VIDEOPERSIST.VBR
```

The program will display a copyright dialog, then move on to the dialog shown in the figure.

In our case we'll want to switch the Remote Transport to Distributed COM and enter the Network Address of our application server machine.

The end result here is the same as if we'd run our earlier setup program on this client workstation. The **VideoServer** ActiveX server is registered as a remote client, with DCOM knowing how to find and invoke the server when needed.

Summary

Here, at the end of the chapter, we should be able to run the **VideoUI** client, or the Excel client we created in Chapter 9 for that matter. The clients will work with the business objects in **Videoo.dll** as always, without change.

Of course the UI-centric business objects themselves will now be communicating through DCOM to the **VideoServer** server application that is running on our application server machine.

Due the highly-efficient marshalling we implemented in Chapter 10 to transfer data to and from the application server, we should find that performance is barely degraded when compared to running the **VideoServer** server on the same machine as the client. Obviously this will vary greatly depending on the network configuration and load.

In Chapter 12 we'll take the **VideoServer** server and convert it to run inside Microsoft Transaction Server. This will provide our application with much greater scalability, as well as providing transaction support for our database activity.

Then in Chapter 13 we'll look at implementing a web interface to our business objects by using Active Server Pages.

12

Running Server Components in MTS

Overview

In Chapters 10 and 11, we converted our video rental store application from a one or two-tier implementation into a three-tier implementation, using DCOM between the client and application server, and arranging for the application server to access the database.

Technically, our implementation, though a three-tier logical architecture, was physically two-tier, since the application server used a JET database. It is easy to change the code to talk to a SQL database, such as Oracle or Microsoft SQL Server, something we're going to do in this chapter, when we can count it as a physical three-tier implementation.

Our focus was clearly on the important issues surrounding how the client objects communicate with the application server. Without a solid foundation for this communication, our application would have suffered from serious performance problems as a result of networking and DCOM overhead.

To sustain that focus, we intentionally ignored some important issues:

- ❑ Scalability of an application for a large number of clients
- ❑ Multi-user support
- ❑ Database transactions - where a series of operations on the database is only committed to disk if all its calls succeed.

Now that we've gone through the basic principles of communication between client and server machines, we're ready to properly consider these issues.

In this chapter, we'll use Microsoft Transaction Server (MTS) on our application server machine to address these issues. This will require some modification to the **VideoServer** project, but there'll be no impact on our client-side business objects or UI code, which illustrates one of the main benefits of our distributed architecture.

> **Throughout this chapter, we'll be using Microsoft Transaction Server version 1.1. At the very least, we'll want to make sure that we've applied the version 1.0 service pack if we're running MTS 1.0, because the original release was missing some key features we'll be relying on in this chapter.**

We'll start off by taking a good look at the issues of scalability, multi-user support and database transactions. We'll then move on to consider the some of the philosophy and practical implications of MTS objects, before we get down to the really interesting task of getting our **VideoServer** server running on MTS.

Supporting Multiple Clients

Until fairly recently, we'd have had to provide scalable multi-user support by implementing a pool or queue manager of some sort. This manager would create and maintain our server-side objects, making them available to clients on request, but with a level of control on the server - for example, for user access and resource allocation.

This manager would also need to provide some form of database-connection pooling. Opening a database connection can be a time consuming process. If a new connection needs to be opened each time a client tries to use an object, our performance will suffer greatly. To avoid this, some entity on the server (usually the pool manager) keeps a pool of open database connections for general use by server-side objects.

Keeping Objects Alive

From a performance standpoint, it's very important that the **VideoServer** objects don't disappear every time a client is done with them. There's a fair amount of overhead in starting a new process under Windows. If the **VideoServer** server is not running when a client makes a request, Windows needs to run this server to start a new process. As soon as no clients are talking to the server the process would shut down, putting us back at having to start a new process for the next client.

On the other side of the coin, the application server machine has only so much memory, and the CPU can handle only so many threads before performance degrades. If we keep all our server programs and their objects loaded all the time, such that there are enough for all our clients, the server machine will probably run out of memory, or CPU, or both. These performance problems will get worse as we scale up the application across the enterprise, or the Internet.

Microsoft recognized that this was a universal problem for designers of distributed systems. The result is MTS, which provides us with a solution to the problem of managing the demands of multiple clients for our objects. Microsoft has recognized the importance of these services and so they intend to incorporate MTS directly into the NT operating system.

MTS has been described as a *transactional ORB*. We'll talk about the transactional part later, but the ORB description directly applies to what we're talking about here. ORB stands for **object request broker**, which is basically a piece of software that manages objects on a server machine and provides a standard way to access them from clients. MTS may or may not qualify as an ORB, but it certainly provides us with a way to manage our server-side objects - without having to write our own object-management software.

We can put our **VideoServer** ActiveX server into MTS, and it will help us manage the demands of multiple users by creating instances of our objects when they are requested from clients.

To the client, it appears that the object was just created by DCOM, just as we saw in Chapters 10 and 11; but behind the scenes, it's MTS that does all the work. The benefit, here, is that MTS doesn't let the objects disappear from memory when the clients release them.

> Actually, MTS 1.1 and earlier versions *do* release objects when each client is done with them. While MTS retains a reference to the ActiveX DLL itself for a time, the object-pooling feature of MTS isn't implemented in version 1.1.

The next time a client requests an instance of the object, MTS provides a reference to the *existing* object. This can produce a huge performance benefit, since the object is already loaded and running, and we avoid the overhead of starting a process and getting the object initialized.

Keeping the DLL Loaded

The basic functionality of keeping our ActiveX server loaded in memory for a few minutes is totally transparent, that is we don't perform any special coding for our program to take advantage of this feature!

Of course, the server DLLs aren't kept around forever. If MTS did that, the server machine would run out of memory. Instead, MTS can be set to keep inactive DLLs around for a certain number of minutes; then they are released.

The default setting is three minutes of inactivity before an ActiveX server DLL is unloaded from memory.

Keeping Objects Loaded

If we want *specific objects* within our server to remain loaded in memory, we must add some code to the objects themselves. Since our server itself remains loaded anyway, the only time we need to keep a specific object loaded is when that object has a significant amount of processing that takes place when it's initialized.

*The objects in our **VideoServer** server don't have **Class_Initialize** routines, so we obviously don't have to worry about lengthy processing as our objects are created. In fact, many of our objects won't require MTS to keep them loaded in memory. The big performance gain is typically in keeping the DLL itself loaded rather than any specific object.*

For one of our objects to indicate that it can be pooled by MTS, it needs to meet a couple of criteria. First, we need to implement the **ObjectControl** interface so that MTS can call into our object. We also need to make sure that our object resets itself when it's deactivated by MTS, that is each time a client is done working with our object. Let's look at that now.

To implement the **ObjectControl** interface, we'll use the **Implements** keyword at the top of our class module. This requires that we add a reference to the MTS type library DLL, **Mtxas.dll**. The **ObjectControl** interface consists of the following methods:

Method	Description
Activate	This method is called by MTS when our object is provided to a client. If the object was just created, this method occurs after the **Class_Initialize** and **CanBePooled** method calls. If the object was recycled this method occurs after the **Deactivate** method.
Deactivate	This method is called by MTS when a client is done with our object. After MTS calls **Deactivate**, our object may be recycled (in which case **Activate** will be called) or destroyed (in which case **Class_Terminate** will be called).
CanBePooled	This method is called by MTS once - as our object is instantiated. First, the **Class_Initialize** occurs, followed by a call to **CanBePooled** and then a call to the **Activate** method.

Once we've implemented **ObjectControl**, our object will need to support the three methods in its interface, **Activate**, **Deactivate** and **CanBePooled**. If **CanBePooled** returns the value of **True**, MTS will pool this object. We'll go through this, in more detail, later in the chapter.

> Remember that this functionality is not supported by MTS 1.1 or earlier. MTS does call the CanBePooled method of our object, but ignores the value. We are covering this method here because it is valuable to implement the routine in preparation for the day that MTS does support object recycling.

If we've indicated that our object can be pooled by returning a **True** value from the **CanBePooled** method then our object has a bit more work to do. In particular, a pooled object is rarely terminated, but rather it is kept around and used by one client after another.

Of course, each client will expect the object to act as though it had just been created, so the object will need to ensure that any internal state data, usually stored in module-level variables, is reset whenever a client is done with the object.

This is where the **Activate** and **Deactivate** methods of the **ObjectControl** interface come into play. When an object is provided to a client, MTS calls that object's **Activate** method - so the object can do any initialization that is required. Likewise, when an object is returned to the pool of available objects, MTS calls its **Deactivate** method so that the object can reset its state or do any other cleanup work that might be needed.

Activate and **Deactivate** also play a role in supporting transactions, so we'll see more of them later in the chapter.

Limiting the Number of Objects

Many pool managers provide a way to limit the number of objects created on the application server. MTS, on the other hand, provides no mechanism to limit the number of objects that can exist at any given time.

If two clients request the same object at the same time, MTS will create two instances of the object so that each client can have one. A new object is created every time a client requests an instance and there isn't one already available. This means that if a couple of hundred clients request the same object, MTS might try to create a couple of hundred instances of the object!

> *This may seem like an unlikely scenario, but consider an object that verifies a user's identity. This object could be used as users log into an application, and at the beginning of the workday there may be hundreds of users trying to log in within a very small span of time.*

The long term answer for MTS appears to be in future versions of Windows NT, where MTS can spread the objects across several NT machines in a cluster. This would be transparent to the client applications, but would allow a form of load balancing across several machines - hopefully allowing MTS to create enough objects to handle the peak load.

Database Connections

The other major performance concern deals with database connections. Opening a connection to a database can take quite a bit of time - often enough time to be a performance problem for our end users.

MTS provides a solution to this problem as well, in the form of database connection pooling. This means that when an object opens a connection to the database, and then closes it when it's done, MTS steps in and actually keeps the connection open. The next time an object needs a connection to the database, MTS transparently provides one of the pre-opened connections when the object makes its call to ODBC to get a connection.

> *ODBC 3.5 also provides database connection pooling outside MTS. This means we can gain the benefits of database connection pooling without using MTS if we so desire.*

Note that we're talking ODBC. That is because MTS only pools ODBC connections, so this feature doesn't help a program that's using an ISAM database such as JET. Also, only ODBC 3.0 or higher provides the features used by MTS to handled connection pooling. If you don't have at least an ODBC 3.0 driver for your database, this feature will not be available.

Assuming that our program is using an ODBC connection to the database, we don't need to do any special coding to take advantage of the database connection pooling. MTS provides this feature to our objects in an entirely transparent fashion. The only thing we might actually want to do is change our program to keep any database connections open for as short a time as possible. After all, MTS will keep the connection open for us, so the next time we want one it will be right there for us.

Database Transactions

Our application in Chapter 10 provided no support for database transactions. For instance, when we saved a **Video** object and all its **Tape** objects, it was possible for one of the **Tape** objects to fail to save. If this were to happen, we could end up with some objects saved and others not, and our database would contain inaccurate and incomplete data.

Ideally, we'd start a database transaction before saving the **Video** object, then commit it once all the **Tape** objects were saved. If any problems occurred during the save process, we could then roll back the entire transaction, resulting in nothing being saved. While we could certainly handle this by adding a bit of code to our **VideoServer** server to support transactions, we intentionally left this out of the picture until now so we could see how MTS handles the problem.

Earlier, we noted that MTS is sometimes described as a *transactional ORB*. We've already discussed the ORB part of the description, so let's look at its transactional support.

Just as MTS slips in to provide database connection pooling, it also slides in between our program and ODBC to provide database transactions on our behalf. Behind the scenes, things are a bit more complex. MTS actually uses Microsoft's Distributed Transaction Coordinator (DTC) to handle the transactions; but for our purposes, it's enough to know that we can tell MTS which objects require or support transactions and modify each object to indicate whether it completed successfully. MTS will handle the details from there.

If any of our data access doesn't go through ODBC, then we can't rely on MTS to provide transaction support for that data access. For instance, if one of our objects writes to a simple text file, then MTS does nothing to help us roll back our changes or even know that we need to roll them back ourselves.

To implement this feature, we're required to make some changes to our application: both in the **VideoServer** and the **VideoObjects** projects. MTS needs to know which objects perform actions as a result of other objects, so they can all be coordinated as a transaction. We'll get into the specific details later in this chapter.

MTS Objects

MTS was designed with a certain philosophy of how an application server should be constructed. To make objects fit seamlessly into the MTS environment, it's easiest to adopt and follow that philosophy in our object design.

There are two key points to designing an MTS-ready object. First, the objects should be stateless, meaning that they don't retain any information inside the object between method calls. Second, the client code should minimize the amount of time that it retains a reference to any object in MTS. The same is true for any references that server objects hold on any other objects in MTS.

Stateless Objects

All the objects we've worked with so far, in this book, have had a concept of state. All our business objects retain some form of state throughout their life, usually making the state data available to client programs through properties. Even our server objects in **VideoServer** have a concept of state, receiving and providing this data through the **SetState** and **GetState** methods. The state data is then used in the implementation of the object's methods.

The basic philosophy of MTS indicates that objects should not retain state. Instead, objects should provide methods that accept parameters with all the data they'll need to function. Then, when the method is complete, the object should retain no information: instead relying on the calling code to provide any required data as parameters for subsequent method calls.

While the concept of stateless objects is very important, it can reduce our objects to nothing more than a collection of self-contained procedures. This means that the objects running inside of MTS don't meet the normal definition of an object, being composed of an interface, behaviors and, of course, state.

We've intentionally designed the objects so far in this book to have state, including those in the **VideoServer** server. There is a tradeoff here. Objects with state are much more powerful and flexible, and are able to provide more functionality on the application server. On the other hand, stateless objects fit better into a transactional scheme, where the goal is to get in, call a function, and get out as fast as possible.

> Basically, it boils down to stateful objects having more capabilities, with stateless objects providing better performance.

As we go through this chapter, we'll look at how to implement our objects in MTS, while leaving them with a concept of state. We'll really implement a compromise solution though, because although our objects retain state, they are designed to only maintain that state during the short time that the client business object is interacting with the server.

Short Reference Retention

Our other main design concern is that references to any objects running inside MTS should be retained for as little time as possible. After all, the objects running inside the MTS environment are most likely in demand by many clients.

If a reference is held to a server object by one client, or by another object in MTS, it is unavailable for use by any other objects. Because of this, any other requests for an instance of that class will result in a new object being created, thus incurring an overhead to create and initialize the new object.

As we'll see when we discuss transaction processing, an object running in MTS can become available for use by other clients even if the original client doesn't release its reference to the object. However, in the simple case where we are trying to put an object into MTS with as few modifications as possible, it is important that the clients retain their references for as short a period of time as possible.

The faster an object reference is released, the faster the object will become available for recycling.

Recycling is the term used by MTS to describe making the object available for another client. It only occurs when an object has indicated it can be pooled using the **CanBePooled** method from the **ObjectControl** interface. Once a client is done with an object, or the object indicates it is done with its work, it will be recycled back into the pool of available objects.

In many ways, this concept of short reference retention goes hand in hand with stateless objects. At its core, the MTS philosophy is that a client should get a reference to an object, make a method call and release the reference, with the object retaining no information between method calls.

Our server objects in the **VideoServer** project are designed with reference retention in mind. Our business objects get a reference to an object, set its state, make a method call, retrieve its state and release the reference. However we can basically follow the same scheme that MTS desires – quickly in and out of any server-side object, making it available for use by other clients as soon as possible.

ActiveX DLL Servers

Objects that are to run in MTS must be contained in an ActiveX DLL. By default, MTS will create instances of the objects from within the DLL such that they run in a process controlled by MTS itself, though it can create instances of objects that are running in another process, such as IIS. By residing in a DLL, our objects allow MTS to handle issues such as creation, termination and threading.

Our **VideoServer** server is an ActiveX EXE. Since DCOM can only create instances of objects from an EXE server, that was our only choice. MTS 'tricks' DCOM - making DCOM believe that it can create instances of objects from a DLL. Of course, DCOM ends up talking to MTS, and it is MTS that creates the objects from the DLL.

If we're going to move our server-side objects into MTS, we'll need to convert the **VideoServer** project to an ActiveX DLL. Fortunately, this is a very simple change, and we'll get into the details later in the chapter.

Context

One of the more advanced, but very important concepts for objects running in the MTS environment is that of **context**. When MTS provides a reference to an object, it also creates another object behind the scenes. This other object exists to maintain the context in which our object will run.

Every object that's running in the MTS environment has one of these **ObjectContext** objects associated with it. This object allows MTS to provide both database transaction support and security features to our objects.

Transactions

Context includes information about any current transaction that is taking place. We already discussed transactional support and what it can do for us. This context object is a key part of how MTS implements transactions.

The context object waits for each object that is part of the transaction to indicate whether it succeeded or failed. If it succeeded, our object will call the **SetComplete** method on the context object; if it failed, it will call the **SetAbort** method. Either way, the context object ends up knowing whether or not all the objects involved in the transaction succeeded. If they did not, MTS uses DTC to roll back any database changes performed by any of the objects.

Later in the chapter, we'll see how we can use the context object to provide transactional support for our **Video** object and its children. We'll make some changes to the objects in both the **VideoServer** and **VideoObjects** servers so they take advantage of the MTS context object to run within a transaction.

Security

Another function of the context object is that of security. MTS implements security on two levels. With MTS, we can restrict which users can access specific interfaces or specific objects. We can also add code to our objects to restrict their behavior - based on the role of the client that's working with the object.

MTS security is handled through a concept of **roles**. A role can have a list of Windows NT users or user groups assigned to it. Then we can set MTS to allow only certain roles to have access to our objects or object interfaces. Within our object's code, we can also check the current client's role by calling the **IsCallerInRole** method of the MTS context object.

> *We won't get into MTS security in this chapter. It can be a very complex and involved topic, and it's best addressed by a book specifically about implementing components in MTS.*

Object Creation and References

Another area where MTS imposes some constraints is when we're creating objects or passing references to objects as parameters or return values of methods. When an object is created within the MTS environment, MTS needs to know about that object so it can create a context object for it - and so it can manage it appropriately.

In this section, we're only going to discuss objects created by other objects that are running in the MTS environment. What we're concerned with here are objects created by other MTS objects, and references to MTS objects, that might be passed back to the client.

Object Lifetimes in MTS

Objects within the MTS environment have different lifetimes than other objects. In particular, MTS may keep objects around long after a client has released its reference by placing it into the pool of available objects.

Also, an object may become available for use by another client even though the first client still retains a reference to it. If the object has called the **SetComplete** or **SetAbort** methods of the **ObjectContext** object, then MTS will instantly deactivate that object and make it available for use by other clients. If the first client tries to use its reference to the object, it may actually get a different or new instance of that object instead of the one it was using before.

Creating MTS Objects with Visual Basic

To make all these capabilities possible, it's important that MTS be aware of what objects are created and which clients hold references to them. Visual Basic provides two ways to create objects: the **New** keyword and the **CreateObject** method. MTS works with each of these differently, and also provides a third method for creating an object: **CreateInstance**. Let's take a look at these three methods now.

The New Keyword

The **New** keyword acts just like **CreateObject** when creating an object from another ActiveX server, but it actually bypasses some COM processing when it creates an instance of a class that's within the same ActiveX server.

The **New** keyword *must* be used to create objects from classes with Instancing properties of 1-Private or 2-PublicNotCreateable. If we try to use **CreateObject** to create instances of these classes, it's treated as though an external client were trying to create the object - and since they can't be created by external clients, we'll get an error.

For classes that can be publicly created, the exact opposite is true. Because the **New** keyword sometimes bypasses COM, we should *never* use it to create objects with Instancing properties of 3 or higher.

If we create an object with the **New** keyword, that object will be created without MTS support. It will run inside the same thread and context as our current object, but MTS doesn't know it's there, and in fact it doesn't care. The object will function as regular code, like that found in a BAS module within the component.

Any attempt to pass a reference to an object created with the **New** keyword will fail, regardless of the **Instancing** property set on the class. And as soon as we try to provide a reference to this object - to a client or other MTS object - MTS will notice that we're attempting to provide a reference to something it doesn't know about, and it will prevent the reference from working.

The CreateObject Method

Another way we can create objects using Visual Basic is the **CreateObject** method. **CreateObject** *always* uses COM to create instances of a class, regardless of whether that class is in the current ActiveX server or in a different server. **CreateObject** is always acceptable within the MTS environment, although it doesn't offer all the capabilities that we might want.

When an object is created using **CreateObject**, it's as if that object were created by a client, even though it may actually have been created by another object inside MTS. This is perfectly acceptable from the viewpoint of our objects and also MTS.

The caveat with using **CreateObject** is that the object reference returned should not be passed back to a client. The creating object can use the reference all it wants, without any problem; but that reference should not be provided to any other objects or clients as a parameter or the result of a function.

The CreateInstance Method

CreateObject references not only shouldn't be passed back to clients, but objects created this way don't provide MTS security or transaction support. In these cases, we want to create each new object such that it will inherit the current object's context information about security and transactions.

This is where the **ObjectContext** object's **CreateInstance** method comes into play. **CreateInstance** is called just like **CreateObject**, but behind the scenes it does some extra work.

When a new object is created with **CreateInstance**, MTS copies the creating object's context information to the new object's **ObjectContext** object. This means that the new object's context has the same security and transaction environment as the creating object.

As we'll see when we implement the **VideoPersist** and **TapePersist** objects with transactional support, the use of **CreateInstance** is an integral part of the process.

References to objects created using **CreateInstance** can be safely passed back to clients or to other MTS objects. Since MTS itself was part of the creation process for these objects, everything is all set for MTS to manage any client references created through **CreateInstance**.

Error Handling

The final design concern for MTS objects that we need to cover is error handling. This is because MTS handles errors within objects very differently from DCOM. In particular, MTS has no facility for raising errors from an object back across the network to the client program.

In our **VideoServer** project, we didn't take any steps to handle errors that might be encountered while accessing the database. This was intentional, since any errors that might occur would automatically be raised back through DCOM to the client. Then the client would be able to trap and deal with the error as desired.

With MTS, things are different. If our object gets an error, it will be raised up to MTS. Rather than returning the error that was raised, MTS will return a generic error message back to the client. The error description will indicate that the method failed, with no explanation as to why or what might have happened.

This means that we need to come up with some mechanism by which we can know what error occurred on the server-side objects. Whether we choose to return that information to the client or write it to a log on the server is up to us; but either way, we need to come up with some mechanism to handle errors.

In this chapter, we're going to opt for a fairly straightforward solution. Rather than developing a scheme for returning the details of an error back to the client, we'll alter our objects to write the error description to Windows NT's application event log. This is quite easy under Visual Basic 5.0, since the built-in **App** object now has a **LogEvent** method that will write entries into the event log.

We'll let MTS raise the generic error back to the client so the client knows that something went wrong. In the event than an error does occur in our server code, as developers, we can just look in the NT event log to get the details. Windows NT provides the Event Viewer application just for this purpose, so this is a very nice facility to tap into for server-side applications.

Getting VideoServer Ready for MTS

Now that we've got the basics of MTS down, let's move on to get our **VideoServer** ActiveX server running in the MTS environment.

To keep things simple, it is best to make a copy of the **VideoServer** server code into a new directory. We'll be making a number of changes to this program, not the least of which is changing it from an ActiveX EXE to an ActiveX DLL. While we could certainly just change the current program over, this approach will give us an opportunity to illustrate how little impact MTS will have on the client code - so we'll make both the **VideoServer** EXE and the new DLL available at the same time.

VideoServer Properties

Bring up the copy of **VideoServer** project in Visual Basic. We'll actually make a couple of changes to the project at this point, both in the Project Properties dialog.

Changing to an ActiveX DLL

Choose the Project-VideoServer Properties... menu option to bring up the Properties dialog. On this screen, we'll change the Project Type field to ActiveX DLL, as shown here:

Changing the Project Name

Now change the Project Name field to VideoServerMTS. This way, the new DLL version of our server will have a different name than the original EXE server, and they can both be registered on our clients at the same time without conflicting.

> Instead of modifying the existing **VideoServer** server, we're basically creating a brand new server, **VideoServerMTS**, that provides the same functionality.

Unattended Execution and Threading Model

In Chapter 11 we selected the Unattended Execution option in the **VideoServer** server. This option makes sure that our server has no forms or controls and redirects any calls to the **MsgBox** method so they're written to a log file.

We still want this behavior within MTS, since the **VideoServerMTS** server will be running on a server machine, not the user's machine. So we'll leave this option turned on in this new ActiveX server project.

The Threading Model for **VideoServer** was set to Apartment Threaded. With this setting, our ActiveX EXE server was able to create a new thread each time a client requested an instance of our server's objects. Essentially, this provided our **VideoServer** server with a way to support multiple concurrent clients, although not nearly as well as MTS would.

> At this time, MTS doesn't support the Apartment Threading model. In the documentation, this issue is mentioned and Microsoft recommends implementing servers using the Apartment Threading model anyway - since it doesn't hurt. At some future point, with any luck, MTS will support this threading model, and then our server will be all ready to take advantage of it.
>
> With support for apartment threading, MTS will be able to efficiently run a large number of our server's objects in various threads. At this time, without apartment threading, MTS must either run all our objects in a single thread or create multiple processes, one for each object. The ability to run many objects in a single process, but with multiple threads, will be a significant performance benefit.

At this point, we've got the project switched over to a DLL with a new server name, so click the OK button and save the project.

Compatible Server

Since we're creating a new server, we need to switch our project's compatible server from the old EXE to our DLL.

First, bring up the project's properties dialog and make sure the Version Compatibility setting is changed to No Compatibility. We discussed compatibility settings in some detail back in Chapter 7.

Our **VideoServer** DLL currently has a GUID that identifies the server to any clients. Since we are trying to create a new server, **VideoServerMTS**, we need to make sure it gets assigned a different GUID, otherwise our client programs will get our two servers, each with the same GUID, confused.

By setting the Version Compatibility to No Compatibility and recompiling the program we'll cause Visual Basic to assign a new GUID to our **VideoServerMTS** DLL.

> **This is important, because we need to compile our DLL, just the one time, without compatibility - so it creates new GUID values for the MTS-based server, the classes and the interfaces.**

The next step in this process is to compile our project to create **VideoServerMTS.DLL**. Just choose the File-Make VideoServerMTS.dll menu option and go from there.

As we did in Chapter 11 with the **VideoServer** DLL, use the Windows Explorer to make a copy of this new DLL, so we can use the copy for our compatible server. Once that's complete, bring up the project's properties dialog again, and change the Version Compatibility setting back to Binary Compatibility. Select the copy of our new DLL to be the compatible server.

Make sure to save the project once we've made this change. This will ensure that subsequent compiles of the project will retain the GUID values for the ActiveX server, its classes and their public interfaces.

> **As we discussed in Chapter 11 with the VideoServer ActiveX EXE server, it's very important to use Binary Compatibility to keep these GUID values constant. Any time the values change, we'll need to reregister the ActiveX server on all our client workstations - or our application will cease functioning.**

Object Creation and References

Visual Basic provides us with two ways to create objects:

- The **New** keyword
- The **CreateObject** method

Normally we can choose to use either of these techniques to create our objects. Once we have a reference to an object we can use it as we wish, including passing the reference as a parameter to other objects or routines within our application.

When using MTS, there are some constraints placed on how we can create objects and work with our object references. We discussed the basics of these constraints earlier, so now let's see how they impact our project.

We're fortunate in that the **VideoServerMTS** project contains no objects that return references to other objects, or that pass such references as parameters. This simplifies our task somewhat, since we don't need to worry about making sure those references are appropriate for use by clients.

Using CreateObject Instead of New

What we do need to change are all the cases where the **New** keyword is used to create objects that are to be used by other objects within MTS. Objects created using the **New** keyword are not properly controlled by MTS, so the recommendation is quite definitely not to use it. Instead, we should use the **CreateObject** method to create these objects.

Using CreateObject

For instance, the **TapesPersist** object's **Fetch** method contains code that creates a **TapePersist** object:

```
Set objPersist = New TapePersist
```

The **TapePersist** class has an Instancing property of 5-Multiuse, so we can't continue to use the **New** keyword to create the object. Therefore, we'll change this line of code to use the **CreateObject** method:

```
Set objPersist = CreateObject("VideoServerMTS.TapePersist")
```

> *While this is technically true, and this change is recommended, it is possible to continue to use the **New** keyword. If we leave the **TapesPersist** routine alone, allowing the **TapePersist** object to be created with the **New** keyword, the program will continue to run just fine. However, if we watch the activity on the server, using the MTS Explorer we'll cover later, we find that it appears as though no **TapePersist** object was ever created. This is because objects created with the **New** keyword aren't noticed by MTS.*

Calling Friend Properties and Methods

There's an important caveat to making this change to **CreateObject**. Any interface elements declared using **Friend** scope will no longer be available for use in any objects created using **CreateObject**.

> ***Friend** scope implies that properties and methods are only available to other code running in the same ActiveX component as the object.*

Normally, **CreateObject** would create an object such that **Friend** elements continue to work just fine. In the MTS environment, however, when we use **CreateObject** the new object will be created in such a manner that any attempt to call a **Friend** property or method will result in an error.

This comes into play in the **VideoServerMTS** project as well. For instance, in the **TapesPersist.Save** method, we create an instance of **TapePersist**. This was done with the **New** keyword, but now it should be done with **CreateObject**:

```
Set objPersist = CreateObject("VideoServerMTS.TapePersist")
```

However, this routine also makes a call to a method on the **TapePersist** object that has **Friend** scope:

```
For lngIndex = 1 To objBuffer.Count
  With objPersist
    .SetState objBuffer.Item(lngIndex)
    .SaveChild VideoID
    If Not .IsDeleted Then _
      objUpdatedTapes.Add .GetState
  End With
Next
```

This method is declared as **Friend** because we didn't want to expose it for use by the **Tape** object itself: that is, it's only appropriate for calling from the **TapesPersist** object. Unfortunately, the only solution to our dilemma is to change its scope to **Public** within the **TapePersist** class. We'll just have to live with the fact that the method has a broader scope that we'd prefer:

```
Public Sub SaveChild(VideoID As Long)
```

Our object contains a number of properties and methods declared with **Friend** scope. When we create an object with **CreateObject** we are using late binding, and that means we can't call anything that's not **Public** in scope. This means that we don't need to change *all* our properties and methods from **Friend** to **Public**, only those that are called using late binding. And this includes any method call where an object is created using **CreateObject**.

Using the New Keyword

As we noted earlier, we do need to continue using the **New** keyword to create **Private** objects. The **TapesPersist** object's **Fetch** method also creates a new **Buffer** object using the **New** keyword:

```
Set objBuffer = New Buffer
```

We should leave this code alone. If we try to create the **Buffer** object using **CreateObject**, or the **ObjectContext** object's **CreateInstance** method, we'll get an error. Either of these approaches will attempt to create the object as if from an external client, and the **Buffer** class has an Instancing property of 1-Private, so external clients can't create or reference it.

With the **New** keyword, the **Buffer** object will be running in the same environment and with the same context object as the **TapesPersist** object itself. From the viewpoint of MTS, our **Buffer** object is just some code that's being used by **TapesPersist**, and not an actual object at all.

ODBC Data Sources

At this point, our new project is technically able to run in the MTS environment. However, as it stands it wouldn't take advantage of the database-connection pooling provided by MTS, because we're still using a JET database and MTS only provides connection pooling for ODBC 3.0 data sources.

Three-tier Architecture

Obviously, this is a very desirable feature, and one that we want to make use of in our program. Besides, if we switch from a JET database to Microsoft SQL Server, we'll have a more scalable implementation with potential for client workstations, an application server running MTS and a database server running SQL Server.

RDO and ODBCDirect

Visual Basic 5.0 provides us with two built-in data access methods for using ODBC data sources. The older of the two is Remote Data Objects (RDO). With Visual Basic 5.0, Microsoft added ODBCDirect, which is basically RDO with a thin interface on top to make it look like regular Data Access Objects (DAO).

ODBCDirect does virtually no work; it just provides us with a way to use RDO by calling methods and properties that match DAO. As a result, there's almost no performance difference between RDO and ODBCDirect. Both technologies provide very fast access to ODBC data sources from within our programs.

Now comes the question: which to use? A full answer would best left to a book on data access rather than a book on distributed business objects. For our purposes, we can look at RDO as being a tiny bit faster and providing more direct access to ODBC features. And we can look at ODBCDirect as being the easiest way to convert an existing application with a JET database to use an ODBC data source.

In this case we'll convert our program to use ODBCDirect; either solution will provide very good performance, but ODBCDirect will require the least amount of code changes to our objects. In fact, the only changes we need to make are to the open database and open recordset calls.

Switching from JET to SQL Server

Before we get into the details of our Visual Basic code changes, we need to do bit of groundwork.

For this chapter, we'll move our JET database into a Microsoft SQL Server 6.5 database by using the Access 97 Upsizing Wizard. This wizard is freely available from Microsoft - it will quickly move our entire database, including tables, indexes, relationships and data, from an Access 97 database into a SQL Server database.

> There is a caveat with the move from Access to SQL Server. One of our tables, `Tape`, is a reserved word within SQL Server, so the wizard automatically renames the table to `Tape_`. While this is not a big problem, it does mean that our program's SQL statements that reference the `Tape` table will need to be slightly altered to reference `Tape_` instead.

We'll also need a SQL Server user ID for use within our application. Let's create a user id, **VideoApp**, which has access to our new tables in SQL Server. This user's password is 'password' for simplicity. Obviously, we'd probably want a less obvious password in a real application, but this will work for our test project.

There are a couple of other changes you need to make to the SQL queries used in VideoServer. Firstly, all references to Boolean False values need to be changed to 0s. This occurs in **InvoicePersist.LoadFees**. Secondly, the SQL wildcard character searches in the **Fetch** method calls of **CustomersPersist** and **VideosPersist**, need to change from **LIKE '**`search_string*`**'** to **LIKE '**`search_string%`**'**.

Database Connections

The **VideoServer** project currently has a **Sub Main** that opens the database; the database is then left open for as long as the server program is running. This is a good approach for our EXE server, but with MTS providing database-connection pooling, it's actually counterproductive. Since MTS keeps the database connections alive even when we aren't using them, it's best to release our reference to any connection as soon as possible after we're done using it.

As a result, we'll actually change the **Sub Main** and also create an **OpenDB** function that returns a connection to the database. Instead of holding a global connection to the database, we'll declare **dbVideo** within each class module, so the connections are localized to each class.

Then we can call **OpenDB** at the top of each method, and **dbVideo.Close** at the bottom of that method. This way, we'll only be retaining a reference to a database connection for a very short time, making that connection available for use by other objects as much as possible.

Changes to VOmain

VOmain is the BAS module that contains our **Sub Main** routine and the declaration of **dbVideo** as a global **Database** variable. Since we'll now be declaring **dbVideo** in each class module, we can remove that declaration here. We'll also change **Sub Main** to no longer open the database:

```
Option Explicit

Public Sub Main()
  DBEngine.DefaultType = dbUseODBC
End Sub
```

Instead of opening the database, **Sub Main** now simply changes the DAO **DBEngine** object's **DefaultType** property to indicate that we want our default workspace to use ODBCDirect. With this change, any commands that rely on the default workspace, such as **OpenDatabase**, will use ODBCDirect instead of JET to get at the database.

The OpenDB Function

Since we'll be opening a connection to the database at the top of every method, it makes a lot of sense to create a single **OpenDB** routine to contain the appropriate code. We'll always open the database the same way, so this is definitely common code.

Basically, this routine just needs to call **OpenDatabase** and return the result to the caller of the function:

```
Public Function OpenDB() As Database
    Set OpenDB = OpenDatabase("VIDEO", dbDriverNoPrompt, False, _
        "ODBC;DATABASE=Video;UID=VideoApp;PWD=password;DSN=VIDEO")
End Function
```

This **OpenDatabase** command is quite different than the one we used to access the JET database. The parameters we've set are described in the following table:

Parameter	Meaning
Name	**VIDEO** is the DSN for our ODBC data source.
Options	The **dbDriverNoPrompt** tells ODBC not to prompt the user for login information when our **Connect** string is incomplete or invalid. Instead, a trappable error would be returned to our program.
Read-only	We'll set this to **False**, since we do want to be able to write to the database.
Connect	This is a standard ODBC connect string which supplies the DSN, user id and password for the database connection.

Of course, MTS doesn't provide any descriptive error information back to a client in the case of failure. This is a good place to start adding in some error handling, since it is often difficult to get everything set up to open an ODBC connection on the first try. Rather than trying to come up with a fancy mechanism to return error information to the client machine, we're going to take the easy way out and simply write an entry into the Windows NT application event log using the **App.LogEvent** method provided by Visual Basic:

```
Public Function OpenDB() As Database

    On Error GoTo errhandler

    Set OpenDB = OpenDatabase("VIDEO", dbDriverNoPrompt, False, _
        "ODBC;DATABASE=Video;UID=VideoApp;PWD=password;DSN=VIDEO")

    Exit Function

errhandler:
    App.LogEvent "VideoServerMTS OpenDB - " & _
        Err.Description & "(" & Err.Number & ")", vbLogEventTypeError
    Err.Raise vbObjectError

End Function
```

The error handler simply uses the **LogEvent** method to record a message into the event log. The **vbLogEventTypeError** constant indicates that the event indicates an error.

We then call **Err.Raise** to raise an error back to the calling code. Remember that MTS will intercept this error and actually return a generic error message, so it doesn't matter much what error we raise here. In this case, we've simply raised the base error value for errors in objects, **vbObjectError**.

In an actual application it may be worth returning a more descriptive error message. While the description will be ignored with current versions of MTS, we can yet hope that some future version of MTS will support more robust error handling.

Declaring dbVideo in each Class

Now we need to go through and declare **dbVideo** within each class module where any data access is done. This is as simple as adding a declaration at the top of the module. For instance, the **CustomersPersist** module will have the following change:

```
Option Explicit

Private dbVideo As Database

Private objBuffer As Buffer
```

Updating the DeleteObject Methods

We need to go through all our objects and make some changes to their methods. At the very least, our code was written with the assumption that the database was opened as the server program started up and was available for use at any time. With our new scheme, each method needs to call the **OpenDB** routine at the top, and then close **dbVideo** at the bottom with **dbVideo.Close**.

The simplest of the methods to change are the **DeleteObject** methods. They all need to be changed in the same manner. For example, here are the changes to the **CustomerPersist** object's **DeleteObject** method:

```
Public Sub DeleteObject(ByVal CustomerID As Long)
    Set dbVideo = OpenDB
    dbVideo.Execute "DELETE FROM CUSTOMER WHERE CUSTOMERID=" & _
        CustomerID
    dbVideo.Close
End Sub
```

Nothing extraordinary here. By using ODBCDirect with a **Database** object, we've made the change from a JET database to an ODBC data source almost transparent.

Updating the Fetch Methods

We need to add calls to **OpenDB** to all our object's **Fetch** methods as well. However, we're going to implement another change in the **Fetch** method's code. When working with an ODBC connection, we have access to some new types of recordset beyond the typical **Dynaset** and **Snapshot**. One of these new types is the **forward only cursor**, which is the fastest type of cursor for data that's going to be read from the database by scanning the recordset from top to bottom.

All our **Fetch** methods are read-only, and all of them start at the top of the recordset and read in all their data by using the **MoveNext** method to scan sequentially through the results. This is exactly the scenario where a forward only cursor makes sense, so we'll change our **OpenRecordset** calls to open this new type of recordset rather than opening the **Snapshot** recordsets that they were opening.

As with the **DeleteObject** methods, all the **Fetch** methods will be changed in the same way. For instance, the **VideosPersist** object's **Fetch** method will be changed as follows:

```
Public Sub Fetch(Title As String, Studio As String)
   Dim rsVideo As Recordset
   Dim strSQL As String
   Dim strWHERE As String
   Dim udtProps As VideoDisplayProps
   Dim udtData As VideoDisplayData
```

```
Set dbVideo = OpenDB
```

```
strSQL = "SELECT VideoID, TITLE,RELEASEDATE FROM Video"
If Len(Title) > 0 Then _
   strWHERE = "TITLE LIKE '" & Title & "*' "
If Len(Studio) > 0 Then
   If Len(strWHERE) > 0 Then
      strWHERE = strWHERE & " AND STUDIO LIKE '" & Studio & "*'"
   Else
      strWHERE = "STUDIO LIKE '" & Studio & "*'"
   End If
End If
If Len(strWHERE) > 0 Then _
   strSQL = strSQL & " WHERE " & strWHERE
```

```
Set rsVideo = dbVideo.OpenRecordset(strSQL, dbOpenForwardOnly)
```

```
Set objBuffer = New Buffer
objBuffer.Initialize Len(udtData.Buffer), 100
Do While Not rsVideo.EOF
   With udtProps
      .VideoID = rsVideo("VideoID")
      .Title = rsVideo("Title")
      .ReleaseDate = rsVideo("ReleaseDate")
      LSet udtData = udtProps
      objBuffer.Add udtData.Buffer
      rsVideo.MoveNext
   End With
Loop
rsVideo.Close
```

```
dbVideo.Close
```

```
End Sub
```

Again, by using ODBCDirect and a **Database** object, we've made the transition from JET to ODBC almost entirely transparent. At the same time, we're taking advantage of the incredible performance gains to be had by using RDO to gain access to the ODBC data source. The use of the forward only cursor can buy us significant performance gains, especially on large data sets.

Updating the Save Methods

Our **Save** methods will require a bit more work. The first thing that all our **Save** methods do is determine whether the object is being added or updated in the database.

When an object is added, we open a table-type recordset, since that's the fastest way to add a record to a JET database. For instance, the **InvoicePersist** object's **Save** method contains the following code:

```
If udtProps.IsNew Then
  strSQL = "Invoice"
  Set rsInvoice = dbVideo.OpenRecordset(strSQL, dbOpenTable)
  rsInvoice.AddNew
Else
  strSQL = "SELECT * FROM Invoice WHERE InvoiceID=" & _
    udtProps.InvoiceID
  Set rsInvoice = dbVideo.OpenRecordset(strSQL, dbOpenDynaset)
  rsInvoice.Edit
End If
```

When using an ODBC data source, it isn't possible to open a table-type recordset. Therefore, we'll need to alter the code that opens the table-type recordset so that it opens a recordset that's legal with an ODBC data source. The **InvoicePersist** code would change to the following:

```
strSQL = "SELECT * FROM Invoice WHERE InvoiceID=" & _
  udtProps.InvoiceID
Set rsInvoice = dbVideo.OpenRecordset(strSQL, dbOpenDynaset)
If udtProps.IsNew Then
  rsInvoice.AddNew
Else
  rsInvoice.Edit
End If
```

This code still isn't quite complete. Earlier, we noted that ODBCDirect is a thin layer on top of RDO. When RDO opens a connection to a database, it always defaults to a read-only database cursor, and the same is true of ODBCDirect. This means that any time we want to open a recordset for editing, we need to specify that we want to be able to write to the result. Make the following changes:

```
Set rsInvoice = dbVideo.OpenRecordset(strSQL, dbOpenDynaset, _
  0, dbPessimistic)
```

The **dbPessimistic** constant indicates that we want to lock the database for writes using a pessimistic scheme. The default is **dbReadOnly**. Other options include:

Option	Description
dbOptimistic	Lock the database for writes using optimistic locking. Much like **LockEdits=False** for a JET database.
dbOptimisticValue	Use optimistic locking, checking the data values for changes before saving our changes.
dbOptimisticBatch	Create a local batch cursor that can be changed locally and then updated as a batch back into the database.

Beyond this change, we need to call **OpenDB** at the top and **dbVideo.Close** at the bottom of each method. We'll need to apply these same changes to the **Save** methods in all our objects in the **VideoServerMTS** project:

```
CustomerPersist          TapePersist
CustomersPersist         TextListPersist
VideoPersist             InvoicePersist
VideosPersist            InvoiceTapePersist
TapesPersist             InvoiceFeePersist
```

One further change to **TapesPersist** is necessary. In the **Save** method, we loop through each **Tape** object and save it using the **TapePersist** object. The problem is that we only perform a **objPersist.GetState** call if the **Tape** isn't to be deleted. The successful code should call **GetState** so **SetComplete** can be set:

```
Public Sub Save(ByVal VideoID As Long)
   Dim objPersist As TapePersist
   Dim objUpdatedTapes As Buffer
   Dim lngIndex As Long

   On Error GoTo errhandler
   Set objUpdatedTapes = New Buffer
   With objBuffer
      objUpdatedTapes.Initialize .Length, .Count
   End With
   Set objPersist = objContext.CreateInstance( _
      "VideoServerMTS.TapePersist")
   For lngIndex = 1 To objBuffer.Count
      With objPersist
         .SetState objBuffer.Item(lngIndex)
         .SaveChild VideoID

         If Not .IsDeleted Then
            objUpdatedTapes.Add .GetState
         Else
            .GetState
         End If

      End With
   Next

   ...

End Sub
```

With these changes, the **VideoServerMTS** server is now completely converted to use ODBCDirect. We'll now automatically get the benefit of MTS database connection pooling.

Handling Errors

When we were discussing the design concerns for objects that will run in the MTS environment, we mentioned that errors are handled differently by MTS than standard DCOM. We'll need to alter our code to compensate for these differences, or our **VideoServerMTS** server will be virtually impossible to debug.

When an unhandled error occurs in a component within the MTS environment, MTS will intercept the error and raise a generic error message back across DCOM to the client. This means that although our client knows something went wrong, it has no way of finding out any details.

There are various ways to handle this when we're designing an object to run in MTS. We can design all our methods with a mechanism to return a success code and possible error message. Alternatively, we could implement a utility object where error information could be stored and then retrieved by the client. The simplest solution is to log the error information on the server machine itself, then let MTS return the generic error back to the client.

We've already tipped our hand with the error handler we added to the **OpenDB** function in the last section. In this section, we'll be implementing pretty much the same style of error handling throughout the **VideoServerMTS** project.

We'll need to make essentially the same changes to each method of our objects. The changes are not complex: adding an **On Error Goto** statement at the top of the routine to invoke error trapping, and then implementing an error handler at the bottom of the routine to log the error into the Windows NT event log.

> *As a bit of useful and somewhat related information, Visual Basic 5.0 imposes a substantial performance hit if we use a **Resume** statement in our error handling code. More accurately, the Visual Basic 5.0 native code compiler imposes the hit, since running programs in interpreted mode with **Resume** still work great.*
>
> *The native code compiler normally provides no way for a program to arbitrarily jump to any point in code. Of course, the **Resume** statement (especially **Resume Next**) could cause program execution to resume at just about any point in the code. To support this, the native code compiler adds code before and after each line of code so it can resume at that location if needed.*
>
> *So, in general, it's good to avoid the use of the **Resume** keyword in any component that we compile using the native code compiler. If we need the **Resume** keyword, we're probably better off compiling our component to P-code and letting the Visual Basic interpreter take care of it - since we won't have to take the performance hit of all this extra code added by the native code compiler.*

The code we'll add to our objects' methods will be the same. As an example, let's look at the **DeleteObject** method of the **CustomerPersist** object:

```
Public Sub DeleteObject(ByVal CustomerID As Long)
  On Error GoTo errhandler

  Set dbVideo = OpenDB
  dbVideo.Execute "DELETE FROM CUSTOMER WHERE CUSTOMERID=" & _
    CustomerID
  dbVideo.Close

  Exit Sub

errhandler:
  dbVideo.Close
  App.LogEvent "Customer Delete - " & Err.Description & " (" & _
    Err.Number & ")", vbLogEventTypeError
  Err.Raise vbObjectError

End Sub
```

The key part of this new code is the call to the **LogEvent** method of the **App** object. When running under Windows NT, the **LogEvent** method writes an entry into the NT application event log. We can then use the Windows NT Event Viewer application to view the entries that were written into the log.

Once we've written the log entry, we can just raise an error to MTS. It doesn't really matter what error we raise to MTS, since it will just raise a generic error back to the client, regardless of what error we raise. In this case, we're simply raising the base **vbObjectError** value:

```
    Err.Raise vbObjectError
```

Note that we didn't bother to include a description of the error. As with the error number, the description is ignored by MTS. It will provide its own description for the error that it raises back to the client.

> *It's important to add this code to all the **Public** methods of all our server's objects – other than those objects with Instancing set to 1-Private. A generic error will still be returned to the calling code, but at least we'll have a record of the actual error stored in the application event log so we can debug the problem.*

Running VideoServerMTS in MTS

Once we've implemented the changes from the previous section, we're all ready to put our server into the MTS environment.

Later in this chapter, we'll see how we can use **ObjectContext** to implement transactional support for saving the **Video** object and its child objects; but for now, we can just put the **VideoServerMTS** server into MTS and immediately gain the benefits of object and database connection pooling.

Installing the Server in MTS

Moving an ActiveX server into the MTS environment is literally as simple as drag-and-drop. It is an amazingly simple process. Let's go through the steps.

Copy the DLL to the Server machine

First off, we need to make the **VideoServerMTS.dll** file available to the application server machine that is running MTS. We can do this by copying the DLL to the application server machine's hard drive. There is no need to manually register the DLL on the application server, we'll let MTS register it for us, as we'll see shortly.

> *In fact, the easiest way to work with MTS is to have Visual Basic 5.0 installed on the MTS server machine. MTS provides a Visual Basic add-in that automatically updates the appropriate registry entries when the DLL is recompiled. If we're doing our development on a separate machine, we'll need to manually refresh the component on the server each time we recompile the DLL, and recopy it to the MTS server machine.*

Using the Transaction Server Explorer

Once the DLL is available to the MTS server machine, bring up the Transaction Server Explorer using the Windows Start menu.

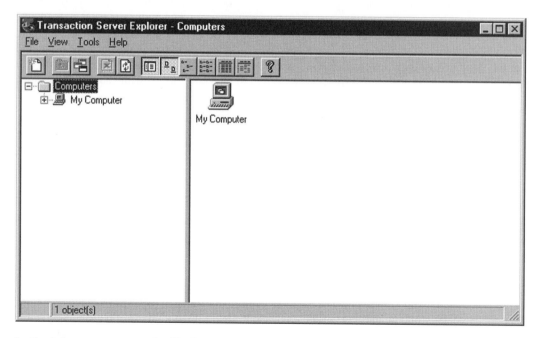

In the left pane, open up the My Computer entry and select the Packages Installed entry from the list. MTS comes with a couple of pre-built packages, as shown in the figure.

In MTS, a **package** is a way of containing related components. Microsoft has indicated that MTS 2.0 will allow packages to contain selected objects from within an ActiveX DLL, but, at this time, packages must contain all the objects from any DLL included in the package.

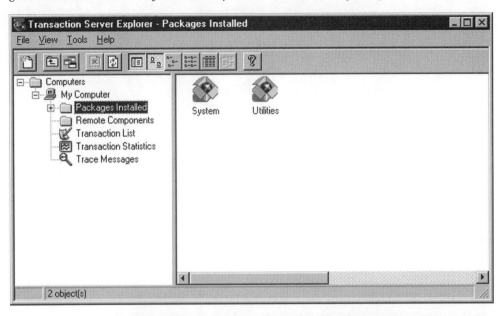

Adding a New Package

We need to add a new package for our server, so choose the File-New menu option. MTS will bring up a wizard to guide us through the process of adding the package. On the first panel, we need to indicate whether we're importing an existing package or creating a new one. Since our **VideoServerMTS** server has never been placed in MTS before, we need to create a new package to hold it:

Next, we need to supply a name for the package. In this case, let's enter the name as
`VideoServerMTS`, just like the name of our DLL. There's no requirement that the names match,
but here it makes sense:

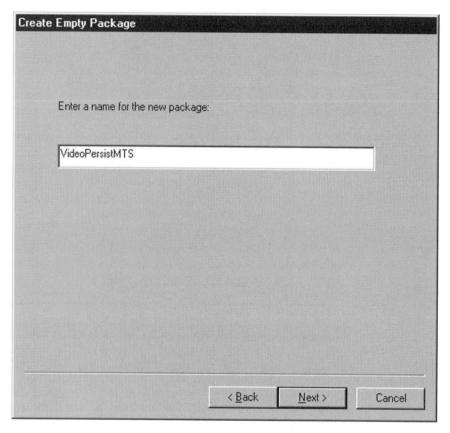

On the next panel, we need to provide MTS with information about the NT user under which the
component will be running. We can then supply a specific user and password, or allow MTS to
install the component to run under the currently log-on. In our case, we're logged into the server as
Administrator, so we're going to select the first option:

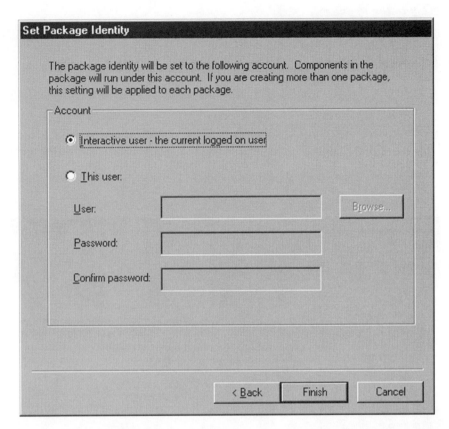

When we click Finish, MTS will add a new package to the list of packages shown in the explorer window:

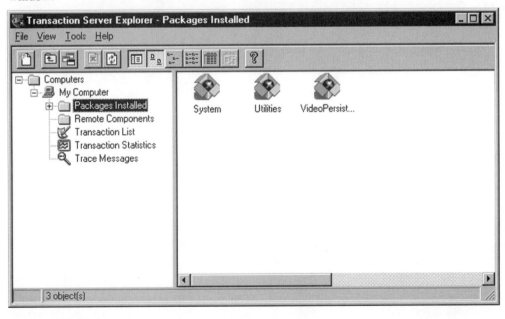

Copying the DLL into the Package

Now comes the drag-and-drop part of the process. In the left pane, expand the Packages Installed item and then expand the VideoServerMTS item. We'll see entries for both the Components and Roles that belong to this package.

The Roles entry is where we'd set up security for this package. In this case we'll just accept the default security settings.

What we are concerned about is the Components item, since this is where we need to install our objects. Select the Components item in the left pane, then simply drag the **VideoServerMTS.dll** file from the Windows NT Explorer into the right pane of the Transaction Server Explorer. The result will be a listing of all the classes contained in our DLL, shown as components of this package in MTS:

With these few steps, we've installed our server program into MTS. Now all we need to do is get the server registered on our client machine and switch our **VideoObjects** project to reference our MTS server rather than the **VideoServer** EXE server from Chapter 10.

Creating the Client Setup

In Chapter 11, we created a client setup program using Visual Basic's Setup Wizard. That wasn't too difficult, but with MTS the process is even simpler.

MTS provides a very easy way to take a package that's installed on one server and move it to another MTS server. Along with the information needed to copy the package to anther server, MTS also creates a client install program all at the same time.

If we select the VideoServerMTS package in the left pane of the Transaction Server Explorer, we can then select the File-Export Package menu option. This will bring up a dialog to prompt us where the package information is to be exported:

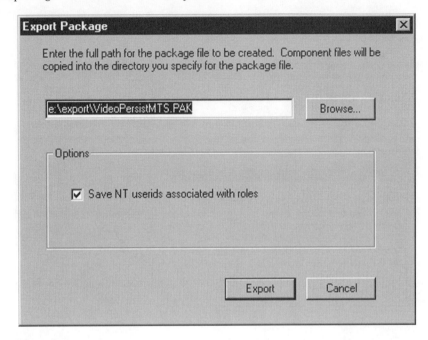

When we click the Export button, MTS will create the PAK file in the directory we've indicated. The PAK file can be used to import our package into another installation of MTS. In addition, MTS will also create a `clients` subdirectory beneath the directory where the PAK file is placed, for the client install program.

The client install program will have the same name as the PAK file, but it will be an executable program. Everything needed to install and register the required software on the client will be included in this self-installing EXE file. All we need to do is get the program to the client workstation and run it.

> *With Visual Basic components, the client installation will not only register the server on the client, but it will also copy the* ***VideoServerMTS.dll*** *file itself on to the client's hard drive.*

Once the installation program has been run on the client, our **VideoServerMTS** server will appear as a valid option for use by ActiveX client programs. DCOM will transparently route any calls to the server across the network to our MTS server machine. From there, they'll be routed to the appropriate object in our server.

Making VideoObjects Use the New Server

With **VideoServerMTS** registered on our client workstations, all that remains is to change our **VideoObjects** project so that it references **VideoServerMTS** rather than **VideoServer**.

Since both servers provide the same classes, with the same properties and methods, we don't need to make any code changes to the **VideoObjects** project at all. Of course, the **VideoUI** project doesn't even know about the **VideoServer** project in the first place, so it won't need any changes either.

Bring up the **VideoObjects** project in Visual Basic. Then open up the project's references dialog:

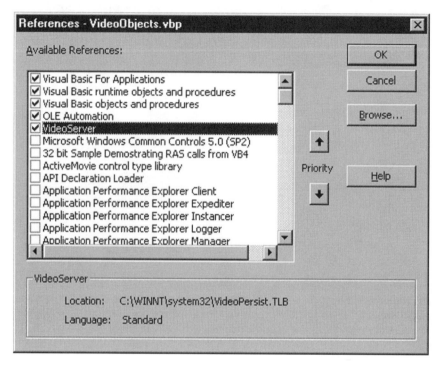

Deselect the **VideoServer** option. We no longer need to use our ActiveX EXE server via DCOM, since we'll now be using our new MTS-based server.

Page down through the list to find the **VideoServerMTS** option, and select it. This will cause our **VideoObjects** project to reference the new server running in MTS:

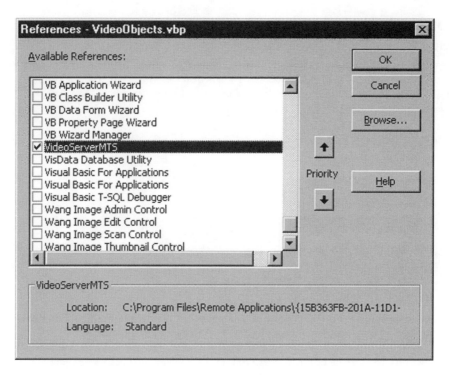

Now save and recompile this project. At this point, we should be able to run the **VideoUI** client program, and everything should work.

> *There will be a noticeable pause the first time we choose a menu option that retrieves or saves data, since MTS will need to start up our server. After that, however, we should find that the application is quite responsive.*
>
> *By default, if we let the server sit idle for three minutes, MTS will release our server. The next user trying to retrieve or save data from the database will incur the same pause while MTS reloads our server into memory again.*

MTS Transactions

What we've achieved so far, in this chapter, works well for non-transactional objects such as **CustomerPersist**. Each method in **CustomerPersist** only performs a single database operation: retrieving, updating or deleting a single record in the database. There's no need to worry about database transactions when we're working with a single record.

But this is not the case with the **Video** object and its child **Tape** objects. When we save a **Video** object through the **VideoPersist** object, it not only updates a single record; but the overall transaction also includes the corresponding updates to all of its child **Tape** objects. Each **Tape** object is saved through a **TapePersist** object, which updates another record.

ObjectContext Objects

MTS provides a mechanism by which we can implement a transaction to protect any updates to the **Video** object and its child objects. The best way to view transactions in MTS is to consider that one of the objects is the 'parent' object that owns the transaction. All other objects are subordinate to that object. The parent object is the one that is created by the base client; in this case, our **VideoObjects** code.

A Hierarchical View of Transactions

We already have a hierarchy with our objects on the **VideoObjects** side:

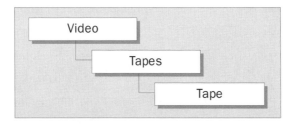

If we follow the same scheme on the MTS side, our parent object would be the **VideoPersist** object, and it would be responsible for creating the **TapesPersist** object.

As it stands now, our **TapePersist** object is created by the **TapesPersist** object. This is fine, since it's created by a child of the **VideoPersist** object, and it would be part of any transaction initiated by the **VideoPersist** object.

Getting an ObjectContext Reference

Earlier in the chapter, we discussed how MTS transparently creates a context object for each one of our objects it creates. This means that it automatically creates a context object for our **VideoPersist** object, and another for each **TapePersist** object we might create.

We can easily get access to this context object from within our objects. Open the **VideoServerMTS** project in Visual Basic, and bring up its References dialog. MTS provides a DLL we can reference from within our project to provide us with access to the **ObjectContext** object and its interface. Scroll through the list of servers to find and select the Microsoft Transaction Server 1.0 Type Library entry.

With this reference, we can add code in any one of our methods to get a reference to the **ObjectContext** associated with our persistence object:

```
Dim objContext As ObjectContext
```

Along with the **ObjectContext** class, the reference to **Mtxas.dll** provides us with a method, **GetObjectContext**. This method will return a reference to the current object's context object:

```
Set objContext = GetObjectContext
```

In the next section, we'll see how we can get a reference to the context object each time our object is activated. Using this technique, we can have access to the **objContext** variable at all times within our object's code.

Linking Context Objects

As we discussed earlier in this chapter, context objects provide us with access to both the security and transaction features of MTS. Our transaction effectively spans the **VideoPersist**, **TapesPersist** and **TapePersist** objects. In order for MTS to provide transactional support, the context objects behind each of our persistence objects need to be aware of each other.

This is where things get interesting, since the only way the context objects can know about each other is if the client only creates the first persistence object. Each time the client program creates an object in MTS, we get a new – totally separate – context for our object.

If, on the other hand, an object running within MTS creates another object, we can link the new object's context to the original object. This is shown in the following figure:

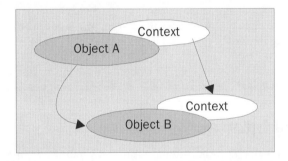

In this figure, object **A** creates object **B**. Since both objects are running within MTS, a link is established between object **A**'s context and the context of object **B**. This link between context objects is what allows MTS to make sure all our objects properly work together to complete the transaction.

> To support transactions, all subsequent server-side objects involved in the transaction must be created by one server-side object.

Creating Objects from the Client

As it stands in our application right now, the client code in **VideoObjects** directly creates and uses the **VideoPersist** and **TapesPersist** objects. Both objects are created using the **New** keyword within the **VideoObjects** project, and then the code uses various methods of both objects.

The problem with this is that we'll get two context objects, one for **VideoPersist** and another for **TapesPersist**, that know nothing about each other. From the MTS perspective, it's as though two different clients were using objects within the server, so there's no way for it to link these two context objects or support any form of transaction.

We'll cover a solution to this problem later in the chapter, but for now let's focus on getting the **TapesPersist** and **TapePersist** objects working together.

In the final analysis, the base client (in this case our **VideoObjects** code) can only *create* a single MTS object. From that point forward, all other MTS objects must be created by other MTS objects using the **CreateInstance** method.

References to these objects may be returned to the base client and used. Since they were created by other objects with **CreateInstance**, they already have a properly-configured context object, so it doesn't matter what code calls their methods.

Using CreateInstance

As we discussed, all the objects in a transaction must be created by other objects on the MTS server. We can't use the **New** keyword or the **CreateObject** command to create these objects, as those techniques won't link the context object of the new object back to that of the creating object. Instead, we need to use the **CreateInstance** method on our context object to create each subsequent object.

For instance, in the **TapesPersist** object, both the **Fetch** and **Save** methods create **TapePersist** objects using the **New** keyword. These routines need to be changed to use **CreateInstance**, as shown here:

```
Set objPersist = objContext.CreateInstance("VideoServerMTS.TapePersist")
```

The ObjectControl interface

Earlier in the chapter, we saw that objects wishing to support pooling (when MTS itself provides it) would need to implement the **ObjectControl** interface. Through this interface, our object will implement three methods: **Activate**, **Deactivate** and **CanBePooled**. Pooling uses the **CanBePooled** method, but we can also make very good use of the **Activate** and **Deactivate** methods to support transactions.

> We'll need to make these changes to all three objects. We'll go through the steps with the **VideoPersist** object, and you can follow suit on the other two.

As we discussed earlier, the first thing to do is make sure that **Mtxas.dll** has been added to the **VideoServerMTS** project's references.

We need to use the **Implements** keyword at the top of the class to indicate that we want to implement a new interface:

```
Option Explicit

Implements ObjectControl

Private objContext As ObjectContext
```

```
Private dbVideo As Database
Private udtProps As VideoProps
```

We've also added the declaration of a variable to store a reference to our context object. We'll set this value shortly.

Once the **Implements ObjectControl** statement has been added, Visual Basic will expect us to add implementations for all elements of that interface. In this case, we need to add three methods. We'll look at these methods now.

ObjectControl_CanBePooled

The **CanBePooled** method simply returns a **Boolean** value to indicate whether our object is set up for pooling. In our case, let's return **False** just to be on the safe side:

```
Private Function ObjectControl_CanBePooled() As Boolean
   ObjectControl_CanBePooled = False
End Function
```

> *To be safely pooled, our object would need to ensure that it reset its internal state upon deactivation, but we don't currently support that.*

ObjectControl_Activate

The **Activate** method is more important to our transaction. This method is called by MTS each time our object is about to be used by a new client. Since we've indicated our object is not to be pooled, this will only get called when our object is created. If we were using pooling, it would be called right before a new client began using our object.

In any case, we'll want to use this method to initialize anything our object will need each time it is used:

```
Private Sub ObjectControl_Activate()
   Set objContext = GetObjectContext
End Sub
```

The **Activate** method call is the first time that we can access our object's context object - as we can't gain access to the context object within the **Class_Initialize** event.

We'll need the context object in a few places within our code, and so this is an ideal spot to get a reference to the context object and keep it until we are deactivated.

The code here simply gets a reference to our context object using the **GetObjectContext** method, supplied by referencing the MTS type library. We've stored the reference in **objContext**, the variable we declared at the top of the class module.

ObjectControl_Deactivate

MTS will call our **Deactivate** method when the object is done with its work. If we were creating an object to support pooling, this would be the routine where we'd reset all module-level variables to the state they were in when the object was first created.

In our case, we'll use this opportunity to release the reference to our context object:

```
Private Sub ObjectControl_Deactivate()
   Set objContext = Nothing
End Sub
```

The object may or may not ever be reactivated, and so it isn't appropriate to retain a reference to the context object beyond the call to **Deactivate**. In fact, **Deactivate** is the last point at which our reference to the context object continues to be valid. If our object is now terminated, the context object reference won't be valid in the **Class_Terminate** event, regardless of whether we drop the reference here.

Indicating Transaction Status

Time out for a bit of theory. We've already discussed some of the philosophy followed by MTS and how ideal objects should function. An ideal MTS object is totally stateless, with each method being totally atomic - meaning nothing is retained between calls to the object. This means that it won't matter if a client calls a method on one object and another method on a different object of the same class.

Our objects are definitely not stateless, nor are our methods atomic. MTS considers our objects to be stateful, and we need to indicate to MTS that this is the case. MTS makes certain assumptions about stateless objects; most importantly, there is no guarantee that MTS will continue to provide the same object to a client across multiple method calls.

Suppose MTS has two **VideoPersist** objects, and our client calls **Fetch** on one, but then MTS swaps the two objects - and so the client ends up calling **GetState** on the other. With stateless objects, this is perfectly acceptable, and in fact there's no guarantee that MTS won't do that to us.

Calling DisableCommit

MTS assumes that all objects are stateless unless told otherwise. That's where the **DisableCommit** method on the **ObjectContext** object comes into play.

While the details are more complex, what **DisableCommit** effectively does is tell MTS that an object is stateful and that it is in an indeterminate state until either **SetComplete** or **SetAbort** are called. We'll talk about those two in a moment.

We know our objects are always stateful, so we can just call **DisableCommit** right away in the **Activate** method:

```
Private Sub ObjectControl_Activate()
   Set objContext = GetObjectContext
```

```
objContext.DisableCommit
```
```
End Sub
```

By making this call, we're ensuring that a client will have a reference to the same **VideoPersist** object until either the client releases the reference or the object calls either **SetComplete** or **SetAbort**. During this time, MTS won't attempt to automatically commit any database activity or make any assumptions that the object is operating successfully.

Calling SetComplete and SetAbort

SetComplete and **SetAbort** are methods on the **ObjectContext** object. These methods are called by our object to indicate that we've done all our work. **SetComplete** indicates that everything went successfully within this object, while **SetAbort** indicates that something went wrong and that the transaction must be rolled back.

A call to **SetComplete** doesn't guarantee that the transaction will be committed. If any object in the transaction calls **SetAbort**, the entire transaction will be rolled back, including any work done by objects that called **SetComplete**. Only if all the objects call **SetComplete** then MTS will commit the transaction, including all the work done by all objects.

> It's very important to understand that as soon as **SetComplete** or **SetAbort** are called, the object is deactivated. Even though a client might *think* it retains a reference to the object, that object is gone. Subsequent method calls by the client may be routed to a new or a different instance of the object.

Since our objects are stateful, we must make sure we don't call **SetComplete** or **SetAbort** until we're sure that the client has gotten what it needs from the object. As soon as **SetComplete** is called, the client will be working with a new instance of the object; so if it didn't get everything it needed first, we'll be in trouble.

SetComplete

For instance, if the client calls the **Fetch** method on **VideoPersist**, we must not call **SetComplete** at the bottom of the **Fetch** routine. Were we to do that, the client would get an entirely different object when it called **GetState** to retrieve the data that was retrieved.

In fact, if we look at the **VideoPersist** object and how it's used, we always call **GetState** as the last operation on the object. If we've got to call **GetState**, that means we didn't get an error earlier in the process and so everything was successful. This meets the conditions for calling **SetComplete**, so let's just add the call to **SetComplete** into the **VideoPersist** object's **GetState** method:

```
Public Function GetState() As String
  Dim udtData As VideoData

  LSet udtData = udtProps
```

```
      GetState = udtData.Buffer
      objContext.SetComplete
End Function
```

The only case where we interact with a persistence object and don't end by calling **GetState** is when we're deleting the object. If we call the **DeleteObject** method we are all done - we don't subsequently call **GetState**. This means that we need to call **SetComplete** within the **DeleteObject** method as well:

```
Public Sub DeleteObject(ByVal VideoID As Long)
   On Error GoTo errhandler
   Set dbVideo = OpenDB
   dbVideo.Execute "DELETE FROM Video WHERE VideoID=" & VideoID
   dbVideo.Close

   objContext.SetComplete

   Exit Sub

errhandler:
   dbVideo.Close
   App.LogEvent "Video DeleteObject - " & _
     Err.Description & "(" & Err.Number & ")", vbLogEventTypeError
   Err.Raise vbObjectError
End Sub
```

SetAbort

SetAbort is a bit more pervasive. If our object fails, at any point, then we need to call **SetAbort** to indicate to MTS that something went wrong. Fortunately, we've already added error handlers to all our **Public** methods, so we can simply add a call to **SetAbort** to each error handler.

For instance, the error handler in the **VideoPersist** object's **DeleteObject** method should be changed as indicated here:

```
Public Sub DeleteObject(ByVal VideoID As Long)
   On Error GoTo errhandler
   Set dbVideo = OpenDB
   dbVideo.Execute "DELETE FROM Video WHERE VideoID=" & VideoID
   dbVideo.Close
   objContext.SetComplete
   Exit Sub

errhandler:
   dbVideo.Close
   objContext.SetAbort

   App.LogEvent "Video DeleteObject - " & _
     Err.Description & "(" & Err.Number & ")", vbLogEventTypeError
   Err.Raise vbObjectError
End Sub
```

If we call **SetAbort** every time our object fails, then not only will we raise an error back to the client to indicate there was a problem, but we'll have indicated to MTS that there was a problem. Based on this call, MTS will automatically roll back any transaction that might be in progress.

Referencing TapesPersist

With those changes, our **VideoPersist**, **TapesPersist** and **TapePersist** objects should be all ready to run within a transaction. We do have a significant outstanding issue, however, with how our client code gets references to the **VideoPersist** and **TapesPersist** objects.

Since our client can only create a single MTS object and still support transactions, we need to come up with some way for the **VideoObjects** code to get at both a **VideoPersist** and a **TapesPersist** object, but only create one of them.

> *The type of transaction we're demonstrating here is called an* automatic transaction, *and it is the preferred type in MTS.*
>
> *We can also implement manual transactions by having the client use another component provided with MTS that allows the client code to control the transaction. Essentially, what happens is that the client calls a method on this object to start a transaction, then uses it to create other MTS objects on the client's behalf. Once the client is done with all its work, it calls another method on the object to commit the transaction.*
>
> *The problem with this approach is that all the responsibility lies in the client code. If we wanted to author another client, we'd have to support transactions there too. The preferred approach is to have the MTS objects take care of transactions themselves so the client code doesn't worry about it at all.*

Add TapesPersist Method to VideoPersist

Keeping in mind the hierarchical view of transactions we discussed earlier, it is the **VideoPersist** object's job to provide a way for our client code to get a reference to a **TapesPersist** object.

To support this, we can simply add a **TapesPersist** method to the class. To create an object that exists within an existing transaction, we need to use the context object's **CreateInstance** method to create the new object:

```
Public Function TapesPersist() As VideoServerMTS.TapesPersist
    Set TapesPersist = _
        objContext.CreateInstance("VideoServerMTS.TapesPersist")
End Function
```

The call to the **CreateInstance** method is the same as to **CreateObject**, but it allows MTS to take care of details behind the scenes. In this case, we're relying on MTS to copy the **VideoPersist** object's transaction information to the context object of the new **TapesPersist** object so it, and the objects it creates, can participate in the transaction.

Because we've changed the public interface of our ActiveX server, we'll need to reregister the server on our clients. Once we've recompiled the **VideoServerMTS** project, and refreshed MTS with the new DLL, we'll need to export the package from MTS. This will produce the EXE that must be run on the client to register the current version of the server.

> Make sure to uninstall the **VideoServerMTS** program from any client before installing the new version. If we don't uninstall first, we're inviting disaster, as the Windows registry may end up with multiple conflicting entries for our server.

Changes to the VideoObjects Project

With the new and updated **VideoServerMTS** server running in MTS and registered on our clients, we need to move on and update the **VideoObjects** project to support the transaction processing. Right now, our client code directly creates both **VideoPersist** and **TapesPersist** objects from within MTS as shown in the following figure:

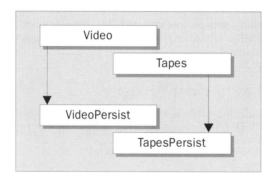

We need to change this behavior so that the **TapesPersist** object is created using the **VideoPersist** object's new **TapesPersist** method as shown here:

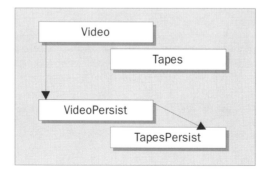

We also need to make some other changes to make sure that our **VideoPersist** object's **SetComplete** method isn't called before all the **Tape** objects are saved. In our existing code we call **SetComplete** in each object's **GetState** method.

Right now, the **VideoPersist** object's **GetState** is called before we've allowed the **Tapes** object to save its child objects. Since that takes place after **VideoPersist** has called **SetComplete**, the child objects are not saved as part of the overall transaction. We need to rearrange our client code to make sure all the child objects are updated before we allow our transaction's parent object, **VideoPersist**, to call **SetComplete**.

Update the Video Object

In the **Video** class, we need to change the **Fetch** and **ApplyEdit** methods. Both of these methods create and use a **VideoPersist** object, and then they call the **Tapes** object so it can retrieve or update all the child **Tape** objects.

Instead of having the **Tapes** object directly create an instance of **TapesPersist**, we'll modify the **Video** object to create the **TapesPersist** object and pass it to the **Tapes** object.

In the **Video** object's **ApplyEdit** method, we'll change the call to the **Tapes** object's **ApplyEdit** method so we pass a new **TapesPersist** object as a second parameter. This **TapesPersist** object is created using our new method on the **VideoPersist** object:

```
    With objPersist
       .SetState GetState

       .Save
    End With

       ' save object state
       LSet udtSave = udtProps
       flgNew = False
    End If

    objTapes.ApplyEdit udtProps.VideoID, objPersist.TapesPersist
    If Not flgDeleted Then _
       SetState objPersist.GetState

    Set objPersist = Nothing
    flgDirty = False
    flgEditing = False
 End Sub
```

Also note how we've moved the call to the **VideoPersist** object's **GetState** down in the routine so that it's after we've made the call to the **Tapes** object's **ApplyEdit**. The **GetState** method is where **VideoPersist** calls **SetComplete**, so that's effectively the end of any transaction. Thus it is critical that we've made any other calls related to the transaction, such as **objTape.ApplyEdit**, before calling **GetState**.

We also need to change the **Load** method. The changes here are basically the same as in **ApplyEdit**:

```
Public Sub Load(VideoID As Long)
   Dim objPersist As VideoPersist

   If flgEditing Then Err.Raise 445
   If Not flgNew Then Err.Raise 445

   ' code to load the object goes here
```

```
    Set objPersist = New VideoPersist
    With objPersist
      .Fetch VideoID
      objTapes.Load VideoID, .TapesPersist
      SetState .GetState
    End With
    Set objPersist = Nothing

    objValid.RuleBroken "Title", False

    flgNew = False
End Sub
```

Again, we're passing a reference to a new **TapesPersist** object as a second parameter. We've also moved the call to the **VideoPersist** object's **GetState** method so it happens after the call to the **Tapes** object's **Load** method.

Even though the **Load** methods do not update the database they will be part of a transaction. As we'll see shortly, MTS considers objects to be part, or not part, of transactions, regardless of the specific methods we are calling on each object. This means that even processes that retrieve read-only data from the database will be part of a transaction if one is set up for the objects.

Update the Tapes Object

In the **Tapes** class module, we need to change the **ApplyEdit** and **Load** methods to accept a second parameter, and use that object rather than creating one directly.

The **ApplyEdit** method originally declared a local **objPersist** and created a **TapesPersist** object with the **New** keyword. Now it will get the object passed as a parameter:

```
Public Sub ApplyEdit(VideoID As Long, _
  objPersist As TapesPersist)

    If Not flgEditing Then Err.Raise 445

    With objPersist
      .SetState GetState
      .Save VideoID
      SetState .GetState
    End With

    flgEditing = False
End Sub
```

We've changed this routine quite a bit, by adding the parameter, but also by removing the code to declare, create and dereference our **TapesPersist** object.

The same is true for the **Load** method. Where it used to declare and create a new object, it will now get that object passed as a parameter from the **Video** object:

```
Friend Sub Load(VideoID As Long, objPersist As TapesPersist)

    If flgEditing Then Err.Raise 445

    With objPersist
```

```
        .Fetch VideoID
        SetState .GetState
    End With
End Sub
```

We've also removed the line that created the instance of **TapesPersist**, since we're getting the reference as a parameter.

Establishing a Transaction

We have changed the **VideoServerMTS** project and its classes so they follow the rules for transaction processing and object reference passing. We've changed the **VideoObjects** code to behave as required by only directly creating a single MTS object, and by calling the **GetState** method of **VideoPersist** after all other work is done.

All that work got our program ready to support transactions. Now all that remains is to flip the final switch so MTS knows to use our objects in a transactional context. MTS makes this very easy to do: we just need to set some properties on our objects using the Transaction Server Explorer.

Bring up the explorer and navigate to the **VideoServerMTS** package's Component display:

VideoPersist Object

Now right-click on the **VideoPersist** object in the right pane. Choose the Properties option from the menu to bring up the object's property sheet:

Select the Transaction tab to view the transaction properties for this object. This panel provides four options to choose from. By default, the last option, Does not support transactions, should be selected:

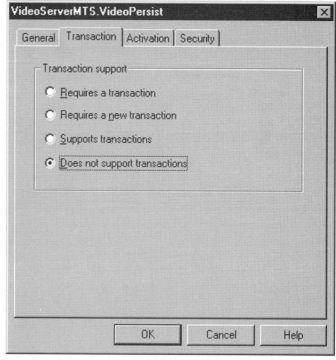

Each option has special significance, as described in the following table:

Option	Description
Requires a transaction	This means that the object must run within a transaction. If one is already started, it will join it; but if the object is created outside the context of an existing transaction then a new transaction will be started.
Requires a new transaction	With this option, any time an instance of this object is created, it will start a new transaction. This will happen regardless of whether it was created by an object within an existing transaction or not.
Supports transactions	This option indicates that the object is programmed to support transactions but does not require one. If this object is created by another object within a transaction then it will participate in that transaction. If it is created outside of any transaction then it will run with no problem, just without any transactional support.
Does not support transactions	This is the default option and indicates that the object does not contain the code needed to support transactions. If our object doesn't call **SetComplete** and **SetAbort** then it falls into this category.

We have designed the **VideoPersist** object to be the parent object of a transaction. This means that it should not only require a transaction, but that it should require a new transaction any time it is used:

TapesPersist Object

Bring up the **TapesPersist** object's property sheet, and switch to the Transaction tab. Again, the default will be Does not support transactions. Of course, we've modified this object, so it's ready to fully participate in transactions. Beyond that, this object is responsible for saving a collection of child objects, and we never want that type of database activity to be unprotected.

At the same time, we also know that this object needs to participate in an existing transaction to be created by the **VideoPersist** object. This means we need to set this object's selection to Requires a transaction.

TapePersist Object

The final object that participates in our transaction is the **TapePersist** object. We've modified this object to support transactions, and so we're all ready to save **Tape** objects when they are loaded as children of a **Video** object.

However, we also load **Tape** objects directly so we can call the **CheckIn** method. In this case the **Tape** object won't be loaded as a child, so the **Tape** object will be directly interacting with the **TapePersist** object. When **TapePersist** is called directly from the **Tape** object, it is very much like the **CustomerPersist** object, where there is no real need for a transaction at all.

For the **TapePersist** object, we'll set its Transaction support option to Supports Transactions so that it can participate in the **VideoPersist** object's transaction and yet work with the **Tape** object in a non-transactional setting:

Distributed Transaction Coordinator

The last area we're going to cover is the DTC (Distributed Transaction Coordinator). This is a service that was originally released as part of Microsoft SQL Server 6.0, but is now considered part of MTS.

DTC is used to handle transactions over multiple or distributed databases. It is also what really provides support for transactions within MTS. Of course, as object programmers, we never see DTC - since MTS takes care of those details behind the scenes. Still, it's important to know it's there and being used.

The one time that we might need to worry about DTC is when it isn't started on our MTS server machine, and that's what we'll cover in this section. If the DTC isn't running, we will be unable to create instances of any MTS objects marked as requiring a transaction. In our case, this includes both the **VideoPersist** and **TapesPersist** objects.

> *DTC may be set to automatically start when NT boots up on the server, and if so then we won't need to worry about this issue at all.*

Manually Starting the DTC

To start the DTC, we can use a couple different tools.

SQL Service Manager

If we have SQL Server installed on our server machine, we can use the SQL Service Manager to start the service. We can run this application from the Windows Start menu:

This figure shows the DTC service as being stopped by highlighting the red light in the stoplight.

To start the service, simply double-click on the green light or the words Start/Continue. The status bar at the bottom will indicate first that the service is starting, and then that it is running.

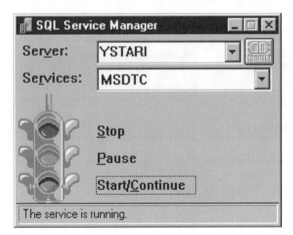

Transaction Server Explorer

If we don't have SQL Server installed on our machine, we can use the Transaction Server Explorer to start and stop the DTC service. We can use the Tools-MS DTC-Start menu option to start the service.

The same menu provides options to pause or stop the service if necessary.

Starting DTC as NT Boots

If we're planning to support transactions on a regular basis, we'll probably want to make sure that the DTC service starts automatically each time Windows NT is booted. This is done using the Services applet from our computer's Control Panel.

If we run the Services applet, we should be able to find the DTC entry in the list of services:

As shown in this figure, MSDTC is currently set up for manual startup. To change this setting, highlight the MSDTC item in the list and click the Startup button to the right. We can then select the Automatic option in the window so the DTC service will be started whenever Windows NT is booted.

Summary

At this point in the book, we've realized our goal of creating a full three-tier physical client/server system. Better still, we've used distributed object technology to accomplish the goal, with our business objects doing some work on the client and some on the application server within MTS.

In this chapter, we moved our persistence server, **VideoServer**, into Microsoft Transaction Server. This provides us with some significant benefits today, including:

❑   Database connection pooling
❑   Transaction support with two-phase commit
❑   Limited object pool management

As MTS matures, we can look forward to better object pooling. We'll also see fault tolerance and load balancing as MTS becomes integrated with Windows NT clustering. Microsoft has indicated that they consider MTS to be a vital piece of their COM strategy.

While it is not there today, Microsoft Transaction Server will very likely enable Visual Basic and other COM-compliant languages to tackle large, mission critical systems.

An Active Server Pages Interface

Overview

From the very beginning of the book, we've been exploring how we can develop our applications so that the user interface is separate from the application itself. In Chapter 7, we implemented a traditional Visual Basic interface to our application. Then, in Chapter 9, we implemented an interface using Excel - without changing the application itself.

Extending that concept, we also separated the application's business logic into two parts - the data-centric and the UI-centric processing. We've done this in two ways, using DCOM directly in Chapters 10 and 11, and most recently using Microsoft Transaction Server in Chapter 12.

Back in Chapter 2, I proposed an architecture where an application is composed of four basic parts:

- ❏ UI
- ❏ UI-centric business objects
- ❏ Data-centric object services
- ❏ Data provider

Hopefully, by now, the benefits of partitioning our application in this manner are clear. With very little effort we've built two different user interfaces and switched from one type of database to another. In a traditional Visual Basic application either change would have most likely meant a significant rewrite of the code. With the techniques we've employed in this book, neither change was particularly difficult.

An HTML User Interface

In this final chapter of the book I want to further illustrate just how easy it is to add radically different user interfaces. I think that most people would agree that a traditional Visual Basic user interface, or even one from Microsoft Office, is very different to what a user would experience using a web browser.

Where the Visual Basic or Office interface is likely to be highly interactive, a browser interface is typically batch-oriented. The user enters a screen's worth of information, clicks a button and the entire screen is processed as a unit. Plus, the user is also provided with useful hyperlinks and friendly navigational capabilities that are often unavailable in a traditional UI.

> *HTML has recently developed into Dynamic HTML (DHTML), available in IE4 and Netscape Communicator 4. The flexibility of traditional UI coding is now available within the browser window, in addition to the excellent text and image handling capabilities found in ordinary HTML. The use of DHTML UIs in 'hybrid' applications is now a real possibility. For more information, I suggest you look at the Microsoft web site and at* Professional IE4 Programming *(ISBN 1-861000-70-7) from Wrox Press.*

To implement this interface we'll use Active Server Pages (ASP). ASP provides us with a *server-side* scripting environment where we can interact with objects on our Web server machine, using them to get information to dynamically build web pages in HTML for our clients.

Designing for the Internet

Following our video rental store scenario, we'll provide an interface that may be available via the Internet. This means that our end users may be using any number of different browsers running under a wide variety of operating systems.

In today's world there is no truly universal client-side scripting tool. Neither JavaScript nor VBScript are guaranteed to run properly across all operating systems and all browsers. This means we can't use any client-side scripting if we want to make sure our user interface will be available to as many of our fictitious store's customers as possible.

VBScript is also known as the Visual Basic Scripting Edition, and is a scripting language with the syntax of Visual Basic.

The same is true for controls or components. ActiveX controls are very powerful, but they also have a limited audience. In the grand scheme of things, few browsers or operating systems support ActiveX controls, and so again we need to avoid using them.

> **Of course, if we're working on an intranet, we can enforce a standard browser type, and, with the right choice of browser, expand the range of technologies available to us. However, to utilize the widest possible client-side applicability, we're going to stick with standard HTML.**

Architecture of the UI

As I'll illustrate later, we can use ASP to construct a user interface where the client workstation sends or receives standard HTML. The user sees displays constructed with HTML and provides information back to the web server using HTML forms or other valid HTML information-passing techniques.

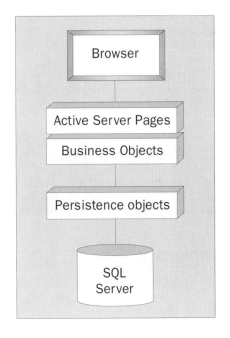

Our ASP scripts are responsible for using the user's input to interact with our business objects in order to generate the HTML to be sent back to the browser. Used this way, our ASP code will be interacting with the business objects in much the same way as the code behind our forms in a traditional Visual Basic application.

In our traditional Visual Basic UI we added code to allow the controls on the form to interact with the business objects. The ASP scripts are no different. They allow the HTML forms to interact with the business objects and provide HTML back to the browser in response to any activity.

The business objects themselves will remain effectively unchanged. We've already implemented the objects to communicate through DCOM with the persistence objects running within an MTS environment. This communication is unaffected by the UI, so it doesn't matter whether the business objects are being used by a Visual Basic interface, Excel or an Active Server Pages script. In each case, the business objects interact with the objects in MTS in exactly the same way.

Active Server Pages

Web developers have been using various techniques to create software on the web server since the very early days of the technology. One of the earliest techniques involved having the web server recognize certain file extensions as being scripts. The server would run this script, providing any arguments from the URL to the script and sending any output from the script back to the user's browser. This was made into a standard called the Common Gateway Interface, or CGI.

While effective, CGI required the use of tools that supported C style input and output and so the development tool set was quite limited. For the most part, only programs that worked on a command line could operate with CGI.

Various workarounds to the limitations of communicating through CGI then started to appear. Microsoft backed ISAPI, which is very similar in concept to CGI, but runs the called programs within the server process for extra performance. It also introduced the notion of an ISAPI filter, a DLL which intercepts each browser request and can decide what content to return.

While ISAPI broadened the number of development tools that could be used for server-side development in Windows, it also suffered from some of the same limitations as CGI; i.e. it was difficult to develop to. Neither technique provides any real environment for scripts.

ASP is one of a number of development environments that attempts to address these shortcomings. ASP uses ISAPI to communicate with the web server itself, but it goes far beyond ISAPI in what it provides to the scripts that run inside its environment.

> *One point to note is that ASP 2.0 (in Beta at the time of writing) supports transactions on MTS 2.0 within the scripting page. This is interesting, but not very relevant here, as the* **VideoObjects** *DLL has transactional support built right into its objects. If we depended on the ASP script to maintain an overall transactional view of the components executing on the page, and roll back or commit based on the success of all the components, we would have reduced the flexibility of our business objects for use in a variety of UIs.*

A Simple ASP Script

Before we get too far into the ASP environment, let's take a quick look at what a script looks like and how it might work. The traditional thing to do is to create a simple 'Hello world' program, and I'd hate to break with tradition.

> *ASP scripts are simple text. You can create them using Visual Interdev, Microsoft FrontPage or any number of other web-authoring tools. Throughout this chapter however, I'll use Notepad to keep things simple and to illustrate that ASP programming doesn't necessarily require complex tools.*

Set up the Script Directory

In order for your web server to realize that files with an ASP extension are programs and not simple HTML we need to set the web directory to have Execute permissions. This is done differently depending on whether you are using Microsoft Internet Information Server (IIS) or Personal Web Server. Since any serious business application should be running under Windows NT, I'll stick to IIS for this demonstration.

Creating a Directory for the Files

Before we get started with IIS itself, we need to make sure we have a physical directory on the disk in which to store our files. I won't go through the details of using the Windows Explorer, suffice it to say we need to create a folder to hold our scripts.

On your web server machine you should (by default) have an **Inetpub\wwwroot** directory where IIS prefers to have all the web files located. On my server this is **d:\Inetpub\wwwroot** and so it is under this directory that I will create a **helloworld** directory, **d:\Inetpub\wwwroot\helloworld**.

> *If this directory is on an NTFS drive you may need to change its permissions so the relevant files are accessible to IUSER_servername (in this example, IUSER_ystari) for Read and Execute. I'll leave those details up to you.*

Microsoft Internet Service Manager

The tool we need to use to manage our web site is the Internet Service Manager. This program will display all the Internet services that are running on our NT machine, or other NT machines that we are allowed to manage. You can run this program from the Windows Start menu. It should be under the Programs-Microsoft Internet Server menu.

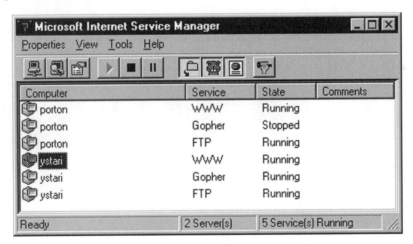

From the main screen, select the service where we'll be running our new script. It needs to be a WWW service, of course, since ASP works only with web servers. Once you've selected the appropriate service, choose the Properties-Service properties menu option to bring up the property sheet for that service.

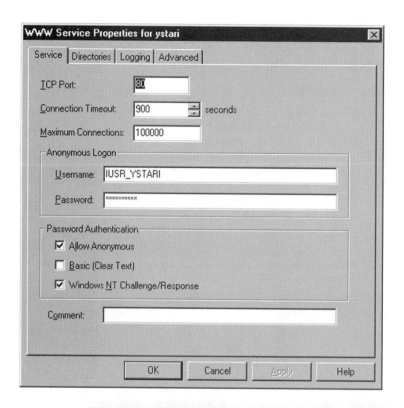

This first tab shows the general configuration for the service you selected. The information we need is found on the Directories tab.

Adding a Directory to IIS

We'll want to add a new directory for our sample program. Click the Add button on the screen to bring up a new Directory Properties sheet.

We need to enter a physical directory name, in my case **d:\Inetpub\wwwroot\helloworld**. This is the directory we created earlier in this section, so its location may be different on your server.

We also need to enter an alias for our new virtual directory. I won't get into a discussion of the difference between home and virtual directories, suffice it to say that, for our purposes in this example and in our video store UI, we'll want to use a virtual directory.

Virtual directories provide an easy way for a user to find our files regardless of where they are physically stored on the server. Users always use the virtual directory name to find the files and IIS does the hard work of finding out where the files are really stored.

> With a virtual directory name of helloworld and my server's name of ystari, the URL to our files will be
> http://ystari/helloworld/filename.

It is also very important that you check the Execute option on the screen. It is this switch that informs IIS that programs within this directory are to be executed rather than downloaded to the user's machine.

When you click OK the new directory will be created and should be visible in the list of directories.

Create the Script

ASP scripts are stored in files with an ASP extension, for example **hello.asp**. They are a mix of HTML and the scripting language of your choice. The default scripting language for ASP is VBScript, which will work great for us.

Simple HTML

The first thing I want to do is demonstrate how HTML can be used in an ASP script. Consider the following:

```
<HTML>
<BODY>
Hello world<P>
```

```
</BODY>
</HTML>
```

This bit of code is HTML to print Hello world in the browser's display. You might find this code in a file with a **.htm** or **.html** extension. You might also find it in a file with a **.asp** extension, since ASP scripts can contain regular HTML.

Bring up Notepad and enter the code from above. Save the file in your **helloworld** directory as **hello.asp**. Now bring up your browser and enter a URL to get at the new file. For example, with my server's name of **ystari**, the URL is:

```
http://ystari/helloworld/hello.asp
```

The browser should come up with the words Hello world on an otherwise blank page.

Adding Code

Other than illustrating how we can have HTML in our scripts, that was not terribly interesting. Now let's extend our script to include some code.

We need to indicate to ASP what sections of our file contain code and what sections contain HTML. This is done by enclosing the code within a set of brackets **<%** and **%>**. These brackets might enclose a single statement or an entire block of code spanning many lines. Either way works just fine as far as ASP is concerned.

Change the text in Notepad as shown.

```
<HTML>
<BODY>
<% For Index = 1 to 5 %>
Hello world<P>
<% Next %>
</BODY>
</HTML>
```

Now save the file and refresh your browser. You should see that we get Hello world displayed five times instead of just once.

ASP interpreted our **For...Next** loop as you'd expect of any such loop in Visual Basic. What might not have been obvious until running the script is that all the HTML within the **For...Next** loop is repeated as though it were part of the code.

Mixing Code and HTML

As a final example, let's incorporate some script code on the same line as our HTML. Change the script as shown here:

```
<HTML>
<BODY>
<% For Index = 1 to 5 %>
Hello world <% =Index %><P>
<% Next %>
</BODY>
</HTML>
```

If you now save and run this script you should see something like the result shown in this figure here:

What we've done is mixed some HTML and some script code together on the same line.

```
Hello world <% =Index %><P>
```

As before, the code is enclosed within the **<%** and **%>** brackets. In this case we are just printing the value of **Index** into the output that goes back to the browser. The syntax **=variable** is a shorthand for printing any value into the output stream being sent to the browser.

Just to show that ASP has done what should; if you view the source of the displayed page, you'll get the following, HTML-only code:

```
<HTML>
<BODY>

Hello world<P>

Hello world<P>

Hello world<P>

Hello world<P>

Hello world<P>

</BODY>
</HTML>
```

The ASP Environment

Scripts running in the ASP environment may be authored using either JavaScript or VBScript. ASP provides developers in either language with a powerful, standard environment with which to create software.

ASP provides support for security, as well as the concept of a *session*, which spans multiple interactions with a single user and the friendly parsing of user input or other arguments on the URL. In fact, ASP supplies five main objects to every script, and these objects provide the scripts with properties and methods to support these advanced concepts:

- ❑ **Application**
- ❑ **Request**
- ❑ **Response**
- ❑ **Server**
- ❑ **Session**

I am not going to go through the details of all these objects. ASP development is a topic for whole books, like Professional Active Server Pages *(ISBN 1-861000-72-3) from Wrox Press. Sample code for the book is available at* **http://rapid.wrox.co.uk**. *I recommend you explore that and the ASP documentation from Microsoft for more detailed information. Within this chapter we'll see how we can latch a simple ASP script into our business object code.*

I will cover selected methods of the **Request**, **Response** and **Server** objects, since we'll be using them to develop our new UI. **Request** and **Response** are the most basic of the objects, providing each ASP script with the ability to receive information from the user and to provide dynamic information back for display in the browser. The **Server** object allows our script to gain access to services provided by the web server itself.

The Request Object

One of the biggest limitations of CGI and ISAPI is that they provide no standard or easy way for the script to get at the information supplied by the user or provided as arguments on the URL. ASP's **Request** object is the answer to this problem.

Script code can use the **Request** object's methods to easily get at any data provided by the user, be it from an HTML form or the URL itself. In our UI we'll use both of these techniques to provide input to the script, so let's look at how this is done.

Request.QueryString

One way to send information to an ASP script is to send it as a parameter on the URL. The syntax for this type of URL is like this:

```
http://server/directory/page.asp?key=value
```

For instance, if we wanted to send a parameter to our **hello.asp** script we might use a URL like:

```
http://ystari/helloworld/hello.asp?count=5
```

Were we to do this, we could alter our ASP script to take advantage of the parameter value to vary the number of times we go through our **For...Next** loop.

```
<HTML>
<BODY>
<% For Index = 1 to Request.QueryString("count") %>
Hello world <% =Index %><P>
<% Next %>
</BODY>
</HTML>
```

As you can see, **QueryString** requires that you indicate the name of the parameter for which you are looking. Alternatively you can use a numeric value to indicate the parameter by position. For instance, to get the third parameter you could use **Request.QueryString(3)**.

You might have also noted that I didn't make any allowances for the data type of the value returned. This is because all values of any variable in ASP are **Variant**. ASP has no concept of data types, so everything is always a **Variant**. As you'll see later in the chapter, we'll need to take some steps to overcome this when we are talking to our objects.

Request.Form

HTML forms are very old, at least in terms of Internet chronology. These forms allow us to create input forms so that the user can enter values into text boxes, select from lists, radio buttons or check boxes and work with combo boxes.

The **Request** object makes it very easy for us to retrieve the values entered by the user into each of the controls in our HTML forms. The **Form** collection of the **Request** object is very similar to **QueryString**, requiring us to indicate which field's data we want to get and returning the corresponding value.

For instance, suppose we have an HTML form with a text box named **txtName**. In our ASP script we can use the value entered by the user as shown:

```
<HTML>
<BODY>
<% For Index = 1 to Request.QueryString("count") %>
<% =Request.Form("txtName") %><P>
<% Next %>
</BODY>
</HTML>
```

Again I am using the **=value** shortcut to include the value returned by **Request.Form** directly into the HTML that is sent back to the browser. The example itself simply prints the contents of the textbox **count** number of times on the returned page.

The Response Object

The **Response** object is the opposite of the **Request** object. Instead of collecting information from the user, the **Response** object is what we use to send information back to the browser.

We've already used the **Response** object by using the **=value** shortcut to send the value of a variable back to the browser as HTML. This is really a shortcut for the **Write** method of the **Response** object.

To see how this can work, let's rewrite our **hello.asp** file so it contains no HTML, only code. Needless to say, this is deliberate overkill - we're just proving a point:

```
<%
Response.Write "<HTML>"
Response.Write "<BODY>"
For Index = 1 to 5
  Response.Write "Hello world" & Index & "<P>"
Next
Response.Write "</BODY>"
Response.Write "</HTML>"
%>
```

Rather than mixing HTML and code, this new script is all code. Of course, we want the resulting output to be HTML, and so I am using **Response.Write** to send all the same HTML code to the output stream.

If you run this script you should get the same result as we had earlier. From the browser's perspective this is no different from our very first page.

The Server Object

Our intent is to use ASP scripting code to create a user interface for our business objects. This implies that our scripts will have access to the business objects so our ASP code can interact with the objects' properties and methods.

One of the **Server** object's methods is **CreateObject**, and it pretty much does what you'd expect. Just like the **CreateObject** method within Visual Basic, you merely send it the ActiveX server name and class name and it returns a reference to the object.

```
Set objVideo = Server.CreateObject("VideoObjects.Video")
```

There are some differences. By default, ASP will only allow you to create objects from an in-process server, not from any out-of-process or remote servers. Fortunately for us, our business objects are contained within a DLL and so we don't need to worry.

However, the fact that our business objects turn right around and create objects on a remote machine is not problematic for ASP. Basically ASP prevents us from *directly* creating out of process server objects, but we can do pretty much whatever we want within the objects in our DLLs.

Updating our ActiveX Servers

Now that we've got the basics of using ASP, let's look at how this new user interface will change our existing ActiveX servers, **VideoObjects** and **VideoServerMTS**.

As far as code changes go, we need to change absolutely *nothing*. Since we've designed our business objects to support a robust and interactive UI, we already have everything we need to support this new UI. Remember that a web-based UI is going to be batch oriented, and for our business objects that means simpler.

We don't have to worry about Cancel or Apply buttons. The only time data will be sent back to the server is if the user clicks an OK button, and so we only need to worry about the case where the user wants to save data or run a search. Our objects already provide access to the properties that can either be displayed in the browser, or set based on data entered by the user.

ASP and Threading Models

Where we do need to make a change is in the threading model of the **VideoObjects** DLL.

ASP is designed to support large numbers of concurrent users from the Internet. Because of this it is highly multi-threaded, allowing powerful server machines to make use of multiple CPUs to service more than one client at the same time. This technique is very important for performance and scalability.

Any DLLs used by ASP scripts should also support multi-threading. If they don't, ASP can only run the DLL in a single thread, regardless of the number of users trying to get at the DLL. The result is that each user's thread needs to send its data over to the DLL's thread each time a property or method is called. The effect of these cross-thread calls is the same as a cross-process call between two ActiveX EXE servers. Performance goes downhill real fast, leaving us with a slow application and some unhappy users.

ActiveX DLLs created with Visual Basic can support a multi-threaded host such as ASP. All we need to do is change a setting in the project's properties and recompile it.

Bring up the **VideoObjects** project in Visual Basic. Choose the Project-VideoObjects Properties... menu option.

Switch the Threading Model to Apartment Threaded as shown. I've also selected the Unattended Execution option since we don't want the DLL code to bring up any unsolicited message boxes or anything that might cause problems on an unattended server.

The Threading Model of **VideoObjects** was set to Single Threaded, which works great when we are using the DLL from a Visual Basic or Excel interface. In that case each client gets the DLL mapped into the client process's memory space. Basically each client gets its own copy of the DLL and so the DLL doesn't need to support more than one thread at a time.

With ASP, however, the DLL will be used within the ASP process itself, but by many threads all at the same time. By changing to Apartment Threaded we have indicated that our DLL should provide support for multiple threads. Not that the DLL itself creates or contains any threads, but when more than one ASP thread uses the DLL, the DLL's code will safely operate for all the threads all at the same time.

Setting the DLL to support Apartment Threading won't cause any problems for our normal clients. Each Visual Basic client or each Microsoft Office client only contains a single thread. The fact that the DLL can support more than one thread is immaterial in this case since we only have one thread, but it doesn't hurt anything to implement this feature.

Don't forget to save these changes and recompile the DLL for this change to take effect.

With this one simple change we've upgraded our entire application to be ready for use by ASP. Now we need to make sure our DLL is available for use by ASP.

Installing the VideoObjects DLL

For our ASP scripts to use the business objects in our DLL we need to make the DLL available to ASP. This means installing the DLL on our web server machine. It also means we need to run the client install program to register the **VideoPersistMTS** objects on the web server machine.

If your web server machine doesn't have Visual Basic, or any Visual Basic programs installed you'll need to use the Setup Wizard (as we did in Chapter 11) to create an installation set for the **VideoObjects** DLL. This will install not only the DLL, but all the required Visual Basic support files with which it needs to operate.

On the other hand, if your web server has all the required Visual Basic support files, you can just copy the DLL to the server's hard drive and register it by hand. In the **\regutils** directory on the Visual Basic 5.0 CD there is a program called **regsvr32.exe**. This program can be used to register an ActiveX DLL without needing a full-blown setup program.

```
regsvr32 videoo.dll
```

We also need to make sure to run the client install program for our MTS components on the web server machine. ASP itself won't be interacting with the objects in MTS, but our **VideoObjects** DLL will need access to them. By running the client install program we'll register our MTS-based objects on the web server machine and our business objects will be able to use them just as they do on any other client workstation.

Displaying Details of a Video

At this point we have our web server machine all set up as a client workstation, with **VideoObjects** and **VideoPersistMTS** both registered. Were we to install our **VideoUI** client program on the web server it should be able to run just like it does on any other client workstation. We are now ready to move on to create our web-based user interface.

The first thing we'll do is create a simple script to display the details about a video title. This seems like a pretty reasonable service that a video store might want to provide to its customers via the Internet. After all, it would be nice to get the details on a video and find out if any tapes are currently available for rental before driving all the way to the rental store.

Creating the Script

To develop this script you can use any tool you'd like. I'm just using Notepad since it will be nothing more than a small text file. You can place this script in any IIS directory you choose, just make sure that directory's Execute option is checked. In my example I am using a directory named **wroxvideo** that I created using the same process we followed earlier in the chapter for the **helloworld** directory.

Creating the Video Object

The first thing we need to do in our script is create a reference to one of our **Video** business objects. To do this we'll use the ASP Server object's **CreateObject** method as we discussed earlier.

```
<%
Set myVideo = Server.CreateObject("VideoObjects.Video")
```

As you can see, we are assigning the reference to the variable **myVideo**. I haven't declared **myVideo** for two reasons. First, VBScript has no concept like **Option Explicit** and secondly it only supports **Variant** data types so it wouldn't matter anyway.

> Note that, if **VideoObjects** references the **VideoServerMTS** DLL from Chapter 12, any errors in the response will not be reset, by default, for three minutes. You may instead want to make sure that **VideoObjects** references the DCOM code we created in Chapter 10.

Loading the Video Object

Now that we have a reference to a **Video** object we can call its **Load** method to tell it to retrieve values from the database. As you may recall, the **Load** method accepts the **VideoID** value as its single parameter. In this case we'll use the ASP **Request** object's **QueryString** method to get the ID value from the URL.

```
myVideo.Load CLng(Request.QueryString("id"))
%>
```

By using the **QueryString** method we have set up our script so we can pass a **Video** object's ID value on the URL. For example:

```
http://ystari/wroxvideo/getvideo.asp?id=3
```

The **QueryString** method is used to retrieve the value of the id parameter from the URL. Here's where we need to watch what we're doing, though, because the value returned by **QueryString** is a **Variant** just like everything else in VBScript, but our **Load** method expects a **Long**.

Were we using early binding in the Visual Basic environment the **Variant** value would automatically be converted to a **Long** and we'd have to do no work. VBScript provides no support for early binding, so our objects will always be late bound. This means that VBScript has no way of knowing that the parameter is supposed to be a **Long**, and thus it doesn't perform type conversion.

To solve this problem we need to manually convert the variable to the correct type. In this case we need to use the **CLng()** function to convert the **Variant** to a **Long**.

Setting the Document Title

At this point we've got a fully loaded **Video** object. Now we can move on to create HTML, along with some code, to display pertinent information about the video title to the user.

The first thing we'll do is indicate the title of our web page. This is done in the **<HEAD>** section of the document by using the **<TITLE>** tag.

```
<HTML>
<HEAD>
<TITLE><% Response.Write myVideo.Title %></TITLE>
</HEAD>
```

What I've done here is mix a bit of HTML with a bit of code. Rather than providing a static title for the document we are using the **Video** object's **Title** property as the title using the Write method of the **Response** object. The VBScript code, as usual, is wrapped within the **<%** and **%>** tags.

The Document Body

With the object loaded, and the document's title set, we are ready to create the body of the document. This is started with the **<BODY>** tag, and I've also inserted a couple of blank paragraphs to leave a bit of space at the top, one in HTML and the second through code.

```
<BODY>
<P>
<%
Response.Write "<P>"
```

The rest of the body of our document will be created from code. Obviously in any real application you'd want a much more complex document, with various graphics, fonts, colors and all the other exciting bells and whistles that come with web documents. In this example I'm avoiding all those things so we can focus directly on the code that generates the dynamic text for the display.

Displaying the Studio and Title

Our first line of output will display the studio where the video was produced along with the video's title.

```
Response.Write myVideo.Studio & " Presents "
Response.Write Chr(34) & myVideo.Title & Chr(34) & "<P>"
```

There are a couple interesting things here. These two lines of code actually create only one line in the display. HTML only breaks lines when we tell it to by using a tag, and the first line here has no tag to break the line.

Both lines use the **&** character for string concatenation, just like Visual Basic itself. I have set this up so the video's title is placed within double quotes. To do this I am using the **Chr()** function, passing the value **34** which is the ASCII value for the double quote character.

Displaying the Rating

In this next bit of code, we'll display the video's rating, along with descriptive text indicating the meaning of the rating. Ideally we might have our business object provide this information, but since it wasn't required for our other interfaces it was not included in the object. Instead we'll use a **Select...Case** statement to display the appropriate text.

We'll now copy the **Rating** property from our **Video** object into a variable. I've prefixed the variable with **str** to indicate it contains a string value. Even though VBScript variables are all **Variant**s, it doesn't hurt to indicate the data type we believe the variable holds to increase our program's readability.

```
strRating = Trim(myVideo.Rating)
Response.Write "This movie is rated '" & strRating & "', "
Select Case strRating
Case "G"
  Response.Write "suitable for general audiences"
Case "PG"
  Response.Write "parental guidance suggested"
Case "PG-13"
  Response.Write "not suitable for children under age 13"
Case "R"
  Response.Write "children under 17 not admitted without parent"
Case "NR"
  Response.Write "not rated - for mature audiences"
End Select
Response.Write "<P>"
```

Again, all this code generates a single line in the display. Only the last line written to the output stream, **<P>**, causes the browser to break to a new paragraph.

Counting the Number of Tapes

By this point you've probably had enough of simply displaying text. The only other piece of critical information our video store's customers will probably want is whether there are any tapes available for rental. Fortunately for us, by loading the **Video** object we have also loaded all its child **Tape** objects.

We can use the **Video** object's **Tapes** collection to scan through all the **Tape** objects and find out which ones have been rented and which are available. This is as simple as using a **For...Each** loop and incrementing a counter, **intAvail**, each time a **Tape** is found that isn't checked out.

```
For Each Tape In myVideo.Tapes
  If Not Tape.CheckedOut Then intAvail = intAvail + 1
Next
```

With the number of available tapes in hand we can use an **If...ElseIf** structure to provide a user-friendly display of the number of tapes.

```
Response.Write "We have "
If intAvail = 0 Then
   Response.Write "no tapes "
ElseIf intAvail = 1 Then
   Response.Write "1 tape "
Else
   Response.Write intAvail & " tapes "
End If
Response.Write "available for rental<P>"
```

Wrapping up the Document

With that, we've created the body of our document. All we need to do now is set our object variable to **Nothing** to release the object and provide the HTML to indicate the document is done.

```
Set myVideo = Nothing
%>
</BODY>
</HTML>
```

Save this file as **getvideo.asp** into the directory where you are storing our new UI. As I mentioned, I am using a directory named **wroxvideo**. Make sure the directory's Execute attribute is checked on, using the Internet Services Manager application.

Running the Script

Running our program is easy. All we need to do is bring up our browser, pretty much any browser will do, and enter the URL to our script file. We do need to pass the ID parameter on the URL line after the **?** symbol. For example:

```
http://ystari/wroxvideo/getvideo.asp?id=3
```

This will cause IIS to invoke ASP. ASP in turn will run our script, executing the code we've included and producing a web page that displays the details about the video with a **VideoID** of 3.

Notice how the title bar of the browser indicates our video's title, while the body of the text in the browser is assembled as we'd expect from the code we just implemented.

While this is a very useful display of information, it is pretty limited in its use. To get any information the user needs to supply the video's ID number. Obviously we can't expect our video store's customers to know the ID value for every video title, so we need to come up with a solution to this problem.

Getting a List of Video Titles

In the UI we created using Visual Basic we included a screen where the user could enter part or all of a video's title or studio and get a list of matching values from the database. This result set was returned through the **Videos** object as a collection of **VideoDisplay** objects.

We can provide the same functionality through our web interface. First we can show the user a form, allowing them to enter part or all of the video's title and studio. Based on the values entered we can load a **Videos** object and display the results for the user.

Better still, we can set up each video title to be a hyperlink back to our **getvideo.asp** script so the user can click on a video title to get details about that specific video. I realize that from a user's perspective I'm presenting these two scripts in reverse order, but I wanted to get the easy one out of the way first and then tackle this one.

A Recursive HTML Form

Using ASP, we can create scripts that present the user with a form, and then send the user's input values back to the *same* script. This can be a very elegant way to package all the code for an HTML form into the same file, making it easy to develop and maintain.

The HTML Form

The first thing we need to look at is the HTML form code itself. I'm not going to get into the details of the HTML in **VideoSearch.html** - suffice it to say that the following HTML code will display a form with two text-input boxes, an Enter button and a Cancel button.

```
<HTML>
<HEAD>
<TITLE>Get Video Criteria</TITLE>
</HEAD>
<BODY>
<FORM ACTION="getvideos.asp" METHOD="POST">
  Title:<BR>
  <INPUT TYPE=TEXT NAME="txtTitle"><P>
  Studio:<BR>
  <INPUT TYPE=TEXT NAME="txtStudio"><P>
  <INPUT TYPE=SUBMIT VALUE="Enter">
  <INPUT TYPE=RESET VALUE="Cancel">
  </FORM>
</BODY>
</HTML>
```

If the user clicks the Cancel button the form is simply reset by the browser; nothing is sent back to the web server. When the user clicks Enter however, the form is posted back to the web server. The results are sent to the URL indicated by the **ACTION** attribute of the **<FORM>** tag.

```
<FORM ACTION="getvideos.asp" METHOD="POST">
```

We'll be naming our script **getvideos.asp**, so this line of code indicates that the contents of the controls on the form are to be sent back to our script file.

Handling the Recursion

Obviously when the user clicks the Enter button they won't be expecting to see the form simply redisplayed. Yet this is what would happen if we don't take some extra steps in our code to see if the script is being run as a result of the Enter button being clicked.

We could add VBScript code to see if the user entered a value in either the Title or Studio fields and use that to branch off to different code. However it is possible the user might not enter a value in either field, and yet we still want to react to the fact that the Enter button was clicked.

The answer lies in the ability of an HTML form to have a hidden 'control', for example:

```
<INPUT TYPE=HIDDEN NAME="hdnAction" VALUE="0">
```

These controls can have a value assigned to them, but they aren't visible to the user. When the Enter button is clicked, the values of all controls on the form are sent back to our script. On the other hand, when a script is run directly, for instance by the user moving to that URL, no control information is provided to the script at all.

If we add code at the top of our script to check for the presence of the hidden control then we can easily know whether our script was invoked through a URL directly, or by the user clicking the Enter button on our form.

```
<%
If Request.Form("hdnAction") = Empty Then
%>
  <HTML>
  <HEAD>
  <TITLE>Get Video Criteria</TITLE>
  </HEAD>
  <BODY>
  <FORM ACTION="getvideos.asp" METHOD="POST">
    <INPUT TYPE=HIDDEN NAME="hdnAction" VALUE="0">

    Title:<BR>
    <INPUT TYPE=TEXT NAME="txtTitle"><P>
    Studio:<BR>
    <INPUT TYPE=TEXT NAME="txtStudio"><P>
    <INPUT TYPE=SUBMIT VALUE="Enter">
    <INPUT TYPE=RESET VALUE="Cancel">
    </FORM>
  </BODY>
  </HTML>
```

```
<%
Else
    ... Code or HTML goes here ...
End If
%>
```

At the top we have an **If...Then** statement that checks to see if the hidden control, **hdnAction**, exists. If we got here by the user clicking on the Enter button the control won't be empty since it will contain the value **0**. In this case VBScript will branch down to the **Else** statement and execute any code found there.

Basically we've created two entire documents within a single file. If the script is run directly from a URL the document will consist of everything from the **If...Then** down to the **Else** statement. On the other hand, if the script is run via the *Enter* key being pressed then the document will consist of everything between the **Else** and **End If** statements.

What we have is the definition of our HTML form at the top and all the code to process the results at the bottom. This structure makes for contained and maintainable HTML forms.

Displaying the List of Videos

Now that we've got the basics of our recursive HTML form put together we need to add the code to process the data entered by the user. To make the results readable we'll present them to the user in an HTML table, displaying both the video's title and its release date.

Creating the Videos Object

As with the **Video** object earlier, we need to use the ASP **Server** object's **CreateObject** method to create an instance of our **Videos** object.

```
<%
Else
    Set myVideos = Server.CreateObject("VideoObjects.Videos")
```

Loading the Object

Once we have a reference to our new object we can call its **Load** method, using the title and studio values entered by the user as criteria. For readability I have included code here to copy the user-supplied values into the variables - **strTitle** and **strStudio**. To get the values from the form's controls we are using the ASP **Request** object's **Form** collection as discussed earlier in the chapter.

```
    strTitle = Request.Form("txtTitle")
    strStudio = Request.Form("txtStudio")
    myVideos.Load CStr(strTitle), CStr(strStudio)
    %>
```

The **Load** method expects that its parameters will be of the **String** data type. Just like the **Load** method of the **Video** object, we need to manually convert our variables to the appropriate type to avoid a type mismatch error from VBScript. In this case we'll use the **CStr()** function to convert the **Variant** variables to the **String** data type.

Setting up the Document

With our object loaded and ready to go, we can start creating the HTML document itself. The first thing we need to do is set the document's title. We'll also indicate that we're starting the document's body and add a line of text indicating what type of information is being displayed.

```
<HTML>
<HEAD>
<TITLE>Video List</TITLE>
</HEAD>
<BODY>
Here is a list of video titles from our wide selection:<P>
```

Building the Table

Onto the table itself. The first thing to do is to use the **<TABLE>** tag to indicate we are building a table. Then we'll add column headers to indicate the contents of each column in the table.

```
<TABLE BORDER=1>
<TR>
<TD>Title</TD>
<TD>Release date</TD>
</TR>
```

Once the table is set up we can use a **For...Each** loop to go through each element in the **Videos** object and display its data. The elements of the **Videos** object are individual **VideoDisplay** objects, each with **VideoID**, **Title** and **ReleaseDate** properties.

```
<%
For Each Video In myVideos
  Response.Write "<TR>"
```

The **<TR>** tag indicates we are starting a new row in the table. We'll want a new row for each element in our **Videos** object.

Adding a Hyperlinked Field

The next few lines are interesting because they are a mix of HTML and VBScript, all jumbled together. In the end they combine to display the video's title in the first column of our new row, with the title itself being a hyperlink back to our **getvideo.asp** script.

```
%>
<TD><A href="getvideo.asp?id=<% =Video.VideoID %>">
  <%= Video.Title %></A></TD>
<%
```

The second line shown here creates the URL reference to the **getvideo.asp** file. It also appends the id parameter, passing the **VideoID** value from the current **VideoDisplay** object. Earlier in the chapter we created the **getvideo.asp** script to look for the ID parameter and use its value as the key when loading the details about the specific video. So by passing the **VideoID** property as that parameter here, we provide the user with a friendly way to get at the **getvideo.asp** script's functionality.

The next line puts the **Title** property of our **VideoDisplay** object into the output stream so it is displayed for the user. Since this value is enclosed within the **<A>** and **</A>** tags it is considered to be a hyperlink and so it will be displayed appropriately in the browser.

Displaying the ReleaseDate Property

The other column of information we'll display to the user is the video's release date from the object's **ReleaseDate** property. The HTML to include this column in the table is quite straightforward.

Once the date is added to the table we need to use the **</TR>** tag to indicate that this row of the table is complete:

```
        Response.Write "<TD>" & Video.ReleaseDate & "</TD>"
        Response.Write "</TR>"
    Next
```

Now that we've added this particular **VideoDisplay** object's data to the table, we can just continue looping through the rest of the elements in the **Videos** object, displaying each one in turn.

Wrapping up the Document

With the table complete, all that remains is to close out both our object and the HTML. As usual, we need to set our object variable to **Nothing** to release our reference to the object. Then we can add the HTML to close out the table, the body of the document and the document itself.

```
        Set myVideos = Nothing
    %>
    </TABLE>
    </BODY>
    </HTML>
<%
End If
%>
```

We mustn't forget to add the **End If** statement as well. Remember that from VBScript's perspective all this code we just wrote exists within the **Else** clause of an **If...Then...Else** statement. If we forget to include the **End If** statement we'll get a compile error when the user tries to access our script file from their browser.

Now save this file in your script directory as **getvideos.asp**. In my case I'm saving it into the **wroxvideo** directory along with the **getvideo.asp** file. It is important that these two files be located in the same directory, since we've implemented hyperlinks from the **getvideos.asp** script back to the **getvideo.asp** script we created earlier.

Running the Script

We can run this script pretty much the same way we ran **getvideo.asp**. Simply enter the URL to **getvideos.asp** as your browser's address. In my case the URL will be

```
http://ystari/wroxvideo/getvideos.asp
```

The browser should come up and display our HTML form, allowing us to enter values for the title and studio, along with options to click the Enter or Cancel button.

If you now enter values into the Title and Studio fields and click the Cancel button you'll see that the browser resets the fields to be blank. There is no network traffic here; the Cancel button is entirely handled by the browser itself.

If, on the other hand, you click the Enter button, with or without criteria, the browser will send the results of the form back to the **getvideos.asp** script. Since the form also includes our hidden control, **hdnAction**, our VBScript code will branch down to the **Else** clause where we can process the values in the Title and Studio fields.

The result will be the display of a table of video titles along with their release dates.

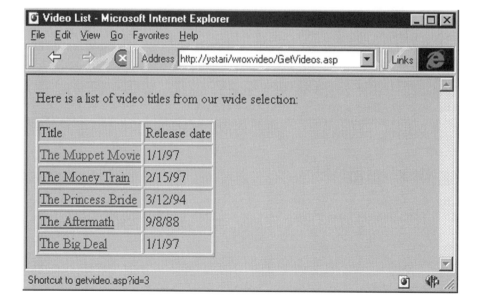

As you can see, all the video titles are hyperlinks. In the figure above, the status bar shows the URL that will be invoked if we click on the first item in the table. This should look familiar, as it is the same URL I entered manually when we were testing the `getvideo.asp` script earlier in the chapter.

If we now click on the first item in the table the browser will send that URL to the web server. This will run our `getvideo.asp` script and should produce the same result we got in our earlier tests.

Summary

In this chapter we've taken a full n-tier client server application and added an entirely new and different user interface with almost no effort. By extending the examples I've shown in this chapter you could easily create a browser-based UI that provides all the capabilities of the Visual Basic interface we created in Chapter 7.

Even better than the ease with which we were able to add this new interface is the fact that the existing interfaces still function. Since our application's behavior is entirely contained within the business objects themselves we can easily and safely add various user interfaces as the needs of the business change.

Regardless of whether our business object's data persistence code is in the objects themselves, in a DCOM server or running in MTS, we always gain these benefits of the separation of the interface from the business objects. And as we've seen through Chapters 8, 10 and 12, it is very easy to move the data persistence processing out of the objects and onto other machines without affecting the business logic or the UI to any significant degree.

Whether you are developing an application for a single PC or for an enterprise-wide distributed network the logical model I've presented in this book will help you. Smaller applications benefit because they are more easily maintained and extended. Larger applications gain those benefits plus scalability and the ability to exploit the resources of both your client workstations as well as server machines. By keeping the UI processing close to the user and the data processing close to the database these applications minimize network load and maximize performance.

Appendix A

Building Objects and Components with Visual Basic

This Appendix is about how to create objects using Visual Basic. We can create them directly, by entering all the code ourselves, or we can use a wizard supplied with Visual Basic. In the first section of this Appendix, we'll take a look at both of these techniques as we implement a basic object.

Once we have a solid handle on creating objects, we'll take a look at the various types of binary component we can create with Visual Basic. Since components are based on objects, we'll make use of our ability to create objects as we build our different components.

Building Objects in Visual Basic

Class modules are the centerpiece of Visual Basic's ability to create objects and components. At first sight, a class module seems like just another code module - it's so similar to a form or code module. Looking more closely, though, there are some substantial differences.

Class modules can contain variables and code, including sub routines, functions and properties. Our programs can't directly use any of these variables or code, however, since a class module just provides a template to be used when creating an **object**.

As an example, let's assume we have a class module that contains code to draw a circle. Say this class module is named **CircleShape** and that it has a **Radius** property and a **Draw** method.

It seems pretty straightforward to use the class something like this:

```
CircleShape.Radius = 200
CircleShape.Draw
```

Unfortunately this won't work because we can't interact with a class module directly. Instead, we first need to create a new object based on the **CircleShape** class:

```
Dim objCircle as CircleShape

Set objCircle = New CircleShape
```

Alternatively, we can combine the statements:

```
Dim objCircle As New CircleShape
```

Then we can use the **MyCircle** *object* to get at the code in the class module:

```
objCircle.Radius = 200
objCircle.Draw
```

Let's look at how to create a class using Visual Basic and its class modules.

Class Modules from Scratch

Creating a class module is as easy as creating a form or code module. While we can create a class module by hand, Visual Basic also provides a wizard to help us out. We'll look at the wizard later; for now let's see how easy it is to just jump in and directly code a class module.

Since we've already discussed a **CircleShape** class, let's look at how we might implement such a class in Visual Basic. Then we'll also create a form with some client code so we can create an object and use the code within our new class.

First off, open Visual Basic and choose to create a Standard EXE project from the New Project dialog. Then choose the Project-Add Class Module menu option. From the Add Class Module dialog, choose the Class Module option and click Open.

In the code window that appears, enter the following:

```
Option Explicit

Private sngX As Single
Private sngY As Single
Private sngRadius As Single
Private frmForm As Form

Public Property Let CurrentX(Value As Single)
   sngX = Value
End Property

Public Property Get CurrentX() As Single
```

```
      CurrentX = sngX
   End Property

   Public Property Let CurrentY(Value As Single)
      sngY = Value
   End Property

   Public Property Get CurrentY() As Single
      CurrentY = sngY
   End Property

   Public Property Let Radius(Value As Single)
      sngRadius = Value
   End Property

   Public Property Get Radius() As Single
      Radius = sngRadius
   End Property

   Public Property Set Form(Value As Form)
      Set frmForm = Value
   End Property

   Public Sub Draw()
      frmForm.Circle (sngX, sngY), sngRadius
   End Sub
```

This code includes everything a **CircleShape** object will need to know in order to function properly. Each **CircleShape** object we create will get its own copy of the **Private** instance variables:

```
Private sngX As Single
Private sngY As Single
Private sngRadius As Single
Private frmForm As Form
```

These variables are not accessible to any code outside of the class module itself.

We control how these values are accessed by implementing **Property Let**, **Property Get** and **Property Set** routines within our code. For instance, the **sngX** instance variable gets its value when the client code provides a value to our object's **CurrentX** property.

```
Public Property Let CurrentX(Value As Single)
   sngX = Value
End Property
```

The complimentary **Property Get** routine allows a client program to retrieve the value of our **sngX** variable.

```
Public Property Get CurrentX() As Single
   CurrentX = sngX
End Property
```

Our class also implements a **Draw** method with the following code:

```
Public Sub Draw()
  frmForm.Circle (sngX, sngY), sngRadius
End Sub
```

Change the name of the class to **CircleShape** in the class module's properties window.

Let's try our new **CircleShape** class by drawing a circle on a form. Open the code window for **Form1** and enter the following:

```
Option Explicit

Private Sub Form_Click()
  Dim objCircle As New CircleShape

  With objCircle
    Set .Form = Me
    .CurrentX = 500
    .CurrentY = 500
    .Radius = 200
    .Draw
  End With
End Sub
```

Note that **Circle** is a reserved word in Visual Basic, so when you type **Dim objCircle** you will need to enter the line like this:

```
Dim objCircle As New CircleShape
```

Notice how easy it is to work with the **objCircle** object. In fact, working with our new object is no different than working with any of Visual Basic's built in objects, such as the **Printer** object, or even a control such as a **TextBox**. In all of these cases, we are simply setting properties and calling methods just as we have done with our **objCircle** object.

Now we can run the project and click on the form. The circle should appear in the upper-left corner.

Though this **CircleShape** class is obviously not a business object like a **Customer** or **Product** might be, it does illustrate just how easy it is to create a class within Visual Basic. Creating a **Customer** class is no more difficult than our **CircleShape** class, it just might have more properties and methods and a bit more code in those routines.

We'll be using the `CircleShape` class module in the next section, so we'll want to save the project at this point. Save the project under the name `CircleDemo` in a directory on the hard drive.

Using the Class Builder

As we've just seen, creating a class from scratch is not terribly difficult. The Enterprise edition of Visual Basic 5.0 also comes with a Class Builder wizard to help create and maintain classes. This wizard provides a structured Windows-style interface that you can use to enter the properties and methods for your classes.

Let's walk through the process of creating our `CircleShape` class using the wizard. We're recreating the same class as above, just using a different approach. Open Visual Basic and choose to create a Standard EXE project from the New Project dialog.

Choose the Project-Add Class Module menu option. From the Add Class Module dialog choose the Visual Basic Class Builder option:

The Class Builder window will now appear as shown in the figure:

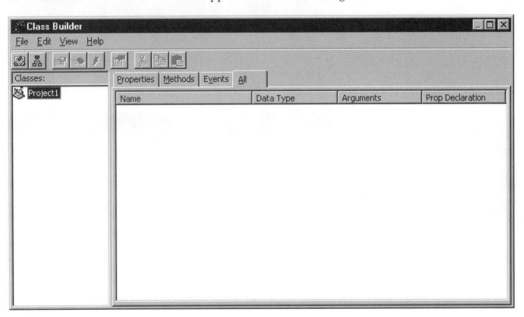

The display on the left shows our project and lists the classes within that project. Of course, the display is pretty empty, since we haven't added any classes. On the right, we have a choice of displays, allowing us to view the properties, methods, and events for the class selected on the left.

Now click the Add New Class button or choose File-New-Class....

We can use this dialog to set the basic properties of our class. Since this is our first class in this project, it is automatically a top-level class. The options in this dialog will change as we create child classes. Change the name of the class to **CircleShape**.

If we click on the Attributes tab, we can enter a description for your class and set up a help context id:

This class description will appear in the Visual Basic object browser, and so it can be very useful - although, for now, we'll leave both these fields blank. Just click OK to return to the Class Builder screen:

Now that we're back at this screen we can see that there are a number of changes to the options. Our new class is shown on the left, and the buttons to add a new property, method, and event are now enabled.

Click the Add New Property to current Class button on the left or choose File-New-Property... to bring up the Property Builder dialog:

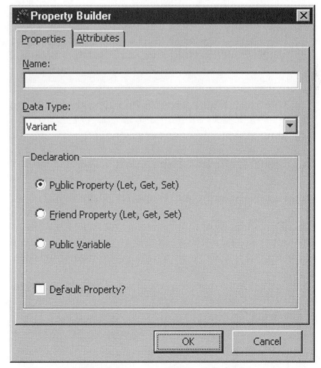

This screen provides all the options we need to set up a property for a class.

Let's name this property **CurrentX** and change the Data Type to **Single**. The possible data types are:

Byte	**Boolean**	**Integer**
Long	**Single**	**Double**
Currency	**Date**	**String**
Variant	**Object**	**Collection**
CircleShape		

All these are the normal Visual Basic data types, except for **CircleShape**. As we add classes to our project through the Class Builder the class names will become available in the list. This means that we can easily create properties that accept or return objects based on our classes.

Notice the options in the Declaration frame. These options control the scope of our property, meaning they control who can see the property. The concept is the same as declaring a variable using the **Private** or **Public** keywords. By default, our property is part of our class's public interface and it will be declared with the **Public** keyword.

We could choose to declare it using the **Friend** keyword, in which case the property would only be available to code within our project. This really only comes into play if we are creating an ActiveX server, since **Friend** properties aren't available to our server's clients.

The third option is a carryover from Visual Basic 4.0, and is another way to create public properties. In the code, this will appear as a **Public** variable. Behind the scenes, though, Visual Basic 5.0 will actually create **Property Let** and **Property Get** procedures for us.

> *The way Visual Basic 5.0 handles* **Public** *variables in class modules is a substantial improvement over Visual Basic 4.0, in terms of documenting classes, since the hidden* **Property Let** *and* **Property Get** *procedures show up in Visual Basic's object browser. On the other hand, in Visual Basic 4.0,* **Public** *variables offered a speed benefit over regular properties, and that benefit has been lost with Visual Basic 5.0's implementation.*

We can also check the Default Property checkbox on one of our properties. This indicates to Visual Basic that the property is to be the default for our class. Most native Visual Basic objects have default properties or methods. For instance, the **TextBox** control's default property is **Text** - so a programmer can just say **MyTextBox = "Hello world"** rather than **MyTextBox.Text = "Hello world"**. Checking this box provides the same feature to our class.

The Attributes tab of this screen is identical to the class attributes, allowing us to enter a description for display in the Visual Basic object browser, and a help context id. We'll leave these blank for now, so just click the OK button.

Using the same technique, add the following properties:

Property	Data Type
CurrentY	Single
Radius	Single
Form	Object

We've encountered a couple of limitations of the Class Builder at this point. First, in the **CircleShape** class that we built from scratch, the **Form** property was write-only (with just a **Property Set**); but the Class Builder doesn't provide this option. Second, we were able to type the **Form** property **As Form** before; but with the Class Builder we have to use the more general and less efficient **Object** data type. We'll fix these problems once we're done with the wizard.

Now all that's left is to add our **Draw** method - so click on the New Method button or choose File-New-Method... to add a new method.

Set the name of the method to **Draw**.

Our **Draw** method has no arguments but, as you can see, this dialog allows you to add, remove and order the arguments for each method. We can also put in a Return Data Type. In our case, we'll leave this blank - so as to create a subroutine rather than a function.

The Declare as Friend and Default Method options work similarly to the same options on the Property Builder dialog that we discussed earlier.

Again, the attributes tab is the same as we've seen, and we'll leave it blank for this example.

Click OK and we'll return to the Class Builder:

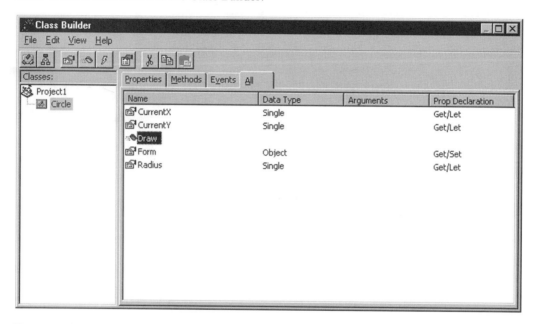

Now just close the Class Builder. The wizard will ask whether we want to update our project, so choose Yes and we'll be on our way. The Class Builder will work a bit at this point and then we should be back in the regular Visual Basic environment, with the code window for our new class displayed.

As we noticed earlier, the Class Builder has some limitations, so we need to clean up some of the code it generated. To start with, it didn't let us make the **Form** property write-only, so we need to remove the following code:

```
Public Property Get Form() As Object
'used when retrieving value of a property, on the right side of an assignment.
'Syntax: Debug.Print X.Form
    Set Form = mvarForm
End Property
```

The other thing the tool didn't let us do was declare the **Form** property as type **Form**; we had to make it type **Object**. Let's fix that now by finding the following routine:

```
Public Property Set Form(ByVal vData As Object)
'used when assigning an Object to the property, on the left side of a Set statement.
'Syntax: Set x.Form = Form1
```

```
        Set mvarForm = vData
    End Property
```

Change the first line so the routine appears like this:

```
Public Property Set Form(ByVal vData As Form)
```
```
    'used when assigning an Object to the property, on the left side of a Set statement.
    'Syntax: Set x.Form = Form1
        Set mvarForm = vData
    End Property
```

And in the declarations section, at the top of the code module, make the following change from
Object to **Form**:

```
Private mvarForm As Form 'local copy
```

Finally, we need to add the code for the **Draw** method:

```
Public Sub Draw()
```
```
    mvarForm.Circle (mvarCurrentX, mvarCurrentY), mvarRadius
```
```
End Sub
```

At this point we can test our new **CircleShape** class using the same test code as in our earlier
example. Open the code window for **Form1** and enter the following:

```
Option Explicit

Private Sub Form_Click()
  Dim objCircle As New CircleShape

  With objCircle
    Set .Form = Me
    .CurrentX = 500
    .CurrentY = 500
    .Radius = 200
    .Draw
  End With
End Sub
```

Now just run this program to see the
results:

Not surprisingly, this circle looks just like the one from the **CircleShape** class we implemented manually. The wizard merely provides us with another tool for developing a basic class module. In many cases it can be quicker and easier to simply enter the code by hand, though the wizard does provide easy access to advanced features such as property and method descriptions.

ActiveX Components

Now that we've gone through the basics of creating classes and objects in Visual Basic, let's look at how objects can be packaged inside components. There are three basic types of ActiveX components:

- ❑ Out-of-process (EXE)
- ❑ In-process (DLL)
- ❑ Control (OCX)

The first two of these are created in an almost identical fashion; but the third type, where we put objects into a control, is rather different.

We'll look at each of these component types in turn and see how they are created. Since our components are based on classes we'll need a class to use in building our components. Since we've already got it implemented, we'll use the **CircleShape** class from the previous section.

There are many issues surrounding when to use each type of component and how they should be designed. We go into those issues throughout the book. Right now, though, let's focus on how each type of component is created.

ActiveX EXEs

To create an out-of-process ActiveX server with Visual Basic, you need to create an ActiveX EXE project. The result will be an executable program, just like any other, except that the program will allow other programs to use some or all of its objects.

To get started, open up Visual Basic and select the ActiveX EXE from the New Project dialog. Visual Basic will create a new project with a single class module called **Class1**. This is one of the differences between this project type and a Standard EXE project, where the default starting point is a form.

We won't be using the **Class1** code module, so right-click on the module in the Project window and remove it from the project.

Adding Our Class

We'll start with the code from our original **CircleShape** class. We saved this file in the **CircleDemo** project, so we should be able to choose the Project-Add File menu option to bring that the **CircleShape** class module into our new project.

We need to make some minor changes to our code for it to work in an out-of-process server. In particular, objects of type **Form** are always private in Visual Basic 5.0. This means that we can't accept a parameter of type **Form** from another program since the compiler will reject it. Since we are creating an ActiveX server for use by other programs we'll need to avoid this problem.

Our **CircleShape** class has a **Form** property that accepts a **Form** type value. We'll have to change this to accept an **Object** value instead to dodge this restriction.

```
Public Property Set Form(Value As Object)
    Set frmForm = Value
End Property
```

And, of course, we'll need to change the declarations section at the top of the module:

```
Private frmForm As Object
```

The Instancing Property

When we are creating an ActiveX server we get to choose how each of our class modules can be used by client programs. This is controlled using the Instancing property for each class module. What we are setting with this property is essentially the scope of our class.

The available instancing properties are:

Instancing Property	Description
1-Private	Used to indicate that the class can only be used within this ActiveX server, and is not available to any other programs or components.
2-PublicNotCreatable	Used to indicate that the class can be used by other programs or components, but that those programs can not create instances of the class. This means that they have to rely on other objects within the server to create this object and return a reference.
3-SingleUse	Used to indicate that the class can be used by other programs or components. Each time they create an object from this class, the object will be created inside a new process; therefore, there is a single use of this class per process.
4-GlobalSingleUse	This is the same as SingleUse except that the client does not create an explicit object from this class, but rather one is created automatically. All the methods and properties of this class are directly available to the programmer as though they were part of the Visual Basic language itself.

Table continued on following page

Instancing Property	Description
5-MultiUse	Used to indicate that the class can be used by other programs and components. All objects created from this class will exist inside the same process, the exact opposite behavior from SingleUse.
6-GlobalMultiUse	Like GlobalSingleUse, this is a way to make the properties and methods of the class appear to be part of the Visual Basic language in the client program. Like MultiUse, though, each client won't load a new process to hold this object: all the clients will get their own object within the same server process.

For our **CircleShape** class, we'll want the Instancing property set to 5-Multiuse so it can be created and used by client programs.

At this point, we could add as many other classes as we desired to the project, and they'd all end up inside the same out-of-process server when we were done. Notice that we can use the Instancing property, for each class, to indicate whether it will be available to other programs or just available within our server itself.

Setting the Project Properties

We're done with the code, so we just need to make a couple of adjustments to the project's properties. Choose Project-Project1 Properties... to bring up this dialog:

We won't go through this entire dialog in detail. There are just a few fields that are important for an ActiveX server, and they are all on this tab:

- ❑ Project Type
- ❑ Project Name
- ❑ Unattended Execution

Project Type

The Project Type is already set for us, since we picked this type of project when we created it. Still, it is worth noting, since we can change our project's type later on if we need to.

> *There are some serious caveats to making such a change, though, so be careful! In particular, switching between ActiveX EXEs and ActiveX DLLs can be tricky. You need to make sure you unregister the existing server before you make the switch. If it was an EXE, run the program using the /UNREGSERVER switch, or if it was a DLL, you'll need to use the Regsvr32.exe utility from the Visual Basic CD with the /U switch.*

Project Name

The Project Name should also be changed. We gave our class the name **CircleShape**, and that will be the name our client code will use to create objects based on the class. However, our ActiveX server itself needs a name. The Project Name field is how we set that up. In this case, let's change the value to read **CircleServer**, since our server is just there to make circles.

When a client program or component uses our server, they'll add it to their project's list of references by using our Project Name. Alternatively, they might use the **CreateObject** function to create an object from our server. For instance:

```
Set objCircle = CreateObject("CircleServer.CircleShape")
```

This line of code creates an instance of our class. To do this it references both the name of our ActiveX server and of our class module.

Unattended Execution

The Unattended Execution option is used to indicate to Visual Basic that this program is intended for use where there is no interactive user. This option is primarily intended for our use in creating ActiveX servers just like the one we are creating now, so we'll want to check this box.

By selecting this option we are telling Visual Basic to help us out by preventing the program from making any attempt to directly interact with a user. We'll be prohibited from having any forms in our project, preventing us from 'accidentally' creating a display that requires user input.

Also, Visual Basic will automatically redirect any **MsgBox** function or method calls such that they are written into the system's event log. Under Windows NT this will be the Application Event log and under Windows 95 this will be a log file in the Windows root directory.

Threading Model

The Threading Model frame let's us tap into Visual Basic 5.0's ability to create multithreaded servers. We discuss multithreading and how it can be useful at various stages in the book where we designing business object servers. For now we'll leave these options alone.

Compiling the Server

To compile our new ActiveX server choose File-Make CircleServer.exe. This doesn't appear any different than compiling any other Visual Basic program, but there are a lot of differences behind the scenes.

Since this is an ActiveX component, Visual Basic automatically adds entries to the Windows registry for our server and each class it contains. These entries are used by any client programs so they can find the server and its classes.

Testing Our Server

Let's quickly run through a client program to test our server. We'll essentially be using the same client program from our earlier examples with the **CircleShape** class, but this new program will use the **CircleShape** class from our new ActiveX server.

Start a new copy of Visual Basic and create a Standard EXE project.

The first thing we need to do is make our program aware of our server. This is done by referencing our ActiveX server within the client program. To do this choose Project-References to bring up the following dialog:

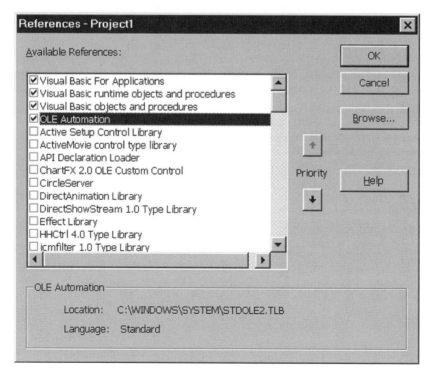

Now scroll down through the list to find the CircleServer entry, click its checkbox on, and click OK.

This will create a reference from our client program to the ActiveX server, making the classes in our server directly available to our client program. To the code in our client it will appear as though all the class modules from the **CircleServer** program were included directly into the client project – except of course that they'll really be running in our out-of-process server.

Now open the code window for **Form1** and enter the following familiar code:

```
Option Explicit

Private Sub Form_Click()
  Dim objCircle As New CircleShape

  With objCircle
    Set .Form = Me
    .CurrentX = 500
    .CurrentY = 500
    .Radius = 200
    .Draw
  End With
End Sub
```

Now we can just run the program and click on the form to see a circle appear as in our previous examples.

Mostly likely we'll see that the circle appears somewhat more slowly than before. This is because Windows has to start up a new process for our ActiveX server before our client program can get the **CircleShape** object to work with.

ActiveX DLLs

In-process servers are created in exactly the same way as out-of-process servers, with just a couple of minor exceptions. These servers are ActiveX DLLs that run within the context of the client's process. This means they technically share the client's memory, though Visual Basic prevents our server's code from directly interacting with the client's code – all the interaction occurs through our objects, as with an out-of-process server.

> If you created the **CircleServer** in the previous example, and you are now going to adapt it to be a DLL, don't forget to unregister **CircleServer.exe** before getting started. To do this, simply use the Run command from the Start menu, and type: *PATH*/circleserver /unregister.

Setting up the Server

To create an in-process server, we need to choose the ActiveX DLL option from the New Project dialog. Just as when we created a new ActiveX EXE project, we're presented with a brand new class module all ready to go. At this point, we can add classes just like we did for our out-of-process server.

We'll use the same `CircleShape` class as before, so choose the Project-Add File menu option and add the `CircleShape` class module from the `ClassDemo` project.

The Instancing Property

An important difference in the class module properties is within the Instancing selections. Classes in a DLL are more restricted in their options than those in an EXE. The available options are:

- 1-Private
- 2-PublicNotCreatable
- 5-MultiUse
- 6-GlobalMultiUse

In particular, the SingleUse and GlobalSingleUse options are missing. This is because in-process servers are literally loaded into the client's process, or memory space. It is not possible to start up a new in-process server to house each object that is created, which is exactly the definition of the single use instancing options.

Project Properties

As with an ActiveX EXE, we'll need to set some properties in the Project Properties dialog for our ActiveX DLL:

Project Type

The Project Type is, of course, ActiveX DLL. In fact, we could have chosen to change the Project Type of our original server from ActiveX EXE to ActiveX DLL rather than creating a new project. Either way, we need to unregister the original server before trying to compile our new version.

Project Name

As with our out-of-process server, we need to set the Project Name value in the Project Properties dialog. This name is used by our client developer to reference our ActiveX server and so we don't want it to read something like **Project1**.

Unattended Execution

We'll want to check the Unattended Execution option in this project as well. This serves exactly the same purpose as our earlier out-of-process server.

Threading Model

The Threading Model frame's options are a bit more restricted here than they were with our ActiveX EXE. This is because a DLL always runs in the context of the client program's process and so it makes use of the threads in that process rather than having its own. Because of this it makes no sense to indicate whether threads will be created for each object or as a pool – all that is handled by the process itself.

Compiling the Server

To compile our new ActiveX server choose File-Make CircleServer.dll. As with our out-of-process server, our DLL is an ActiveX component and so Visual Basic will automatically add entries to the Windows registry for the server and each class it contains.

Testing the Server

If we build **CircleServer** as a DLL, we can use the exact same client program that we used to test the **CircleServer** EXE. It will work without a single change to its code.

Re-referencing the Server

The one thing we will need to do before we can run the client program is re-reference the server using the Project-References menu choice. We need to do this because the server's global unique identifier (GUID) has changed.

Anytime we recompile an ActiveX server project without having a compatible server set up the server's GUID will be regenerated. This is certainly true when you change from an out-of-process to an in-process server. Even though on the screen we are referencing our servers by name, Visual Basic actually references them using the server's GUID behind the scenes.

We discuss GUID values, compatible servers, and other related issues in Chapter 9. In any case, it is a good idea to read through the Visual Basic manuals to get a good feel for how this works before launching into any sizeable project using ActiveX servers. These can be significant development hurdles to overcome without having a good grasp of how GUIDs work.

Running the Test

Other than the server reference everything will operate just like it did in the previous example. You may notice that the program runs faster - it is much easier for Windows to load a DLL than to start up a new process for an EXE.

ActiveX Controls

Out-of-process and in-process ActiveX servers are by far the most common way to package business objects into components. However, Visual Basic 5.0 provides us with the ability to create ActiveX controls, and it is perfectly possible to put business objects in a control.

In general it is a better practice to put our business objects in either in-process or out-of-process servers than in controls. Controls are a specialised form of component, geared towards acting as widgets for use in creating user interfaces. At the same time, there are more mechanisms for distribution of ActiveX controls to our client workstations than exist for either in-process or out-of-process servers and so there are times when placing business objects in a control can be an attractive option.

ActiveX controls also have the restriction that they must be contained within a form. This means that the client program needs to include a form to contain the control. Our in-process and out-of-process servers, on the other hand, can be used by any client regardless of whether they contain a form.

ActiveX controls are quite similar to an in-process server. They are loaded into the client's process, sharing the same memory. There are, however, some significant differences in the interface that you can provide to the client developer when you're implementing an ActiveX control as compared an ActiveX DLL.

Setting up the Server

Using the now familiar **CircleShape** class, I'll walk through the process of creating an ActiveX control to house business objects. The control itself will be invisible at runtime, since we aren't trying to build a screen widget. In this case we're just trying to create an alternative form of component to house our objects.

Open a new project in Visual Basic and choose the ActiveX Control option. Visual Basic will come up with an ActiveX control 'form' for you to work with, which can be used to define the control's runtime user interface.

Setting up the Control

For the most part, we'll simply ignore this interface element, since we're trying to create an invisible control. However, there is at least one interface-related duty we should perform to make our control work.

In particular, we need to change the control's **InvisibleAtRuntime** property to **True** using the property window. This means our control will be visible at design time, so a client programmer can work with it; but it won't be visible to the end user at run time. This is the same way that the **Timer** control works, for example.

We may also want to resize the control to be substantially smaller, or even set its **Picture**
*property to give it a pleasing appearance for the programmer using it at design time. To keep
the focus on the business object aspect, we'll avoid those possibilities in this example. For more
information on ActiveX control development, you can refer to* Instant Visual Basic 5
ActiveX Control Creation *(ISBN 1-861000-235) from Wrox Press.*

While we're working with the control itself, let's give it a descriptive name. Change the control's
name property to **CircleControl**.

Adding the CircleShape Class

Now choose Project-Add File menu option and bring in the **CircleShape** class module from the
CircleDemo project.

As with an ActiveX EXE or DLL, we can add as many classes as we want to this project. An ActiveX
control can contain an entire group of business objects simply by adding those classes to the project.

The Instancing Property

The Instancing options are even more limited than with an ActiveX DLL. The only options available
are 1-Private and 2-PublicNotCreatable. This is because the control itself provides the only public
interface to this type of component. Client programs can't just reach into a control and work with the
classes it contains. This means that we'll have to put methods on the control to provide access to the
business objects inside.

The Instancing property of our **CircleShape** class is automatically set for public use, with the
value 2-PublicNotCreatable.

Adding a Method to get an Object

Now we need to add a method to our control's interface so our client program can ask for a
CircleShape object. To do this, add the following code to the control's code window:

```
Option Explicit

Public Function GetCircle() As CircleShape
    Set GetCircle = New CircleShape
End Function
```

Testing the Control

All that remains is to test what we've done - so we'll add a project directly into the current Visual
Basic session. To do this close down all the edit windows for the control. Don't close Visual Basic
itself, just all the code and form design windows inside the Visual Basic session.

Then choose File-Add Project to get the new project dialog and choose the Standard EXE option.
You should end up looking at a brand new form in a new project, but still within the same Visual
Basic environment where we built the control.

Now simply grab our new control off the toolbox and put it on the form. Since
we didn't change the control's icon, it should appear on the toolbox like this:

Once we've added the control,
our form won't look much
different:

The blank area in the center is our control. Obviously, if we'd been creating a commercial control
then we'd want to put a picture in our control for a production setting. For our current purposes,
however, we're all set.

All that remains is to add some code to the form's code window:

```
Option Explicit

Private Sub Form_Click()
   Dim objCircle As CircleShape

   Set objCircle = CircleControl1.GetCircle
   With objCircle
      Set .Form = Me
      .CurrentX = 500
      .CurrentY = 500
      .Radius = 200
      .Draw
   End With
End Sub
```

This code is very similar to our previous examples, but we need to look at a couple key points.

First off, notice that we are still able to declare our variable as type **CircleShape**. The **CircleShape** class in the control is public - it is just not directly creatable. Since it is public, we can use it as a data type within any form that contains the control.

```
Dim objCircle As CircleShape
```

We did have to eliminate the **New** keyword of course, since we couldn't directly create a **CircleShape** object out of the control. Instead, we've added a new line of code to create the **CircleShape** object by calling the control's **GetCircle** method:

```
Set objCircle = CircleControl1.GetCircle
```

So, with two small changes, we've converted our client program from working with an ActiveX DLL to working with an ActiveX control.

Now just run the program, and click on the form to see the circle show up.

Summary

In this appendix we covered the mechanics of creating objects using Visual Basic. We then took those concepts and used them to create binary components.

We looked at all three types of components we can create in Visual Basic:

- ❑ ActiveX EXEs
- ❑ ActiveX DLLs
- ❑ ActiveX controls

Appendix B
Unified Modeling Language

The Unified Modeling Language (UML) encompasses a number of different notations for different purposes, including the following diagrams:

- Static class
- Sequence
- Use case
- State transition
- Activity
- Component
- Deployment

This appendix will briefly cover static class diagrams as they are represented in the Unified Modeling Language (UML), since they are the only type of UML diagram used in this book are static class diagrams.

Throughout this book, all UML diagrams have been created using Microsoft Visual Modeler. This tool is available from Microsoft to all Visual Basic Enterprise owners. It can be downloaded for free from their web site at
http://www.microsoft.com/vstudio/owner.

Static Class Diagram

Static class diagrams are very similar, in many ways, to standard entity relationship (ER) diagrams used in more traditional analysis techniques. They show the static, or constant, relationships between objects.

Classes

The core of a class diagram is – not surprisingly – the class and its related notation. Let's look at how a class is displayed in UML, then we'll move on to look at how class relationships are displayed.

Class Display

A class, in UML, is shown as a box with the class name near the top center. For example:

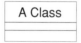

This diagram shows a class named **A Class**. The two lines below the class name separate the spaces where properties and methods will be displayed.

Property Display

Most classes have some attributes, or properties. In UML, we display the properties for a class immediately below the class name, after the first line:

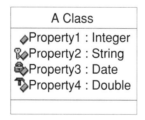

In the diagram we've listed four properties, **Property1**, **Property2**, **Property3** and **Property4**. Each property's data type is shown to the right, after a colon.

The icons to the left of each property indicate scope. In the diagram, each property has been assigned a different scope to illustrate all the possible options. The following table describes each one:

Property	Scope	Description
Property1	Public	Public scope, the same as Visual Basic's **Public** keyword.
Property2	Protected	Visual Basic has no direct analog to this scope. It can be useful in portraying properties with **Friend** scope.
Property3	Private	Private scope, the same as Visual Basic's **Private** keyword.
Property4	Implementation	Visual Basic has no analog to this scope.

Method Display

The methods for a class are displayed below the properties, after the second line in the class box:

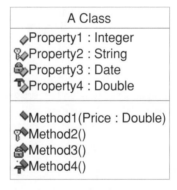

In the diagram we have four methods. The first method, **Method1**, is shown to accept a parameter, **Price**. The other methods do not accept parameters.

As with the properties, the icons to the far left indicate the scope of each method.

Class Relationships

The primary intent of a static class diagram is to show the relationships between classes. We'll go through the common relationships and show the notations used for each.

General Relationship

General relationships cover a lot of ground, including:

- ❑ One object using another
- ❑ One object knowing about another
- ❑ One object creating another

In UML, a general relationship between classes is expressed using the following notation:

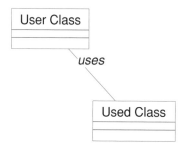

This diagram shows two classes, where the **User Class** is in a relationship where it uses the **Used Class**. Another word could be substituted for **uses** in the diagram to indicate a different type of relationship, for example; **displays**, **owns** or **contains**.

Aggregation

UML provides a special notation to denote aggregation. This is the case where one object is composed of one or more other objects. The notation looks like:

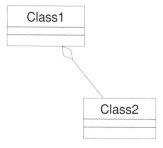

In this case **Class1** is composed of **Class2**. Another way to say this is that **Class2** is aggregated into **Class1**.

Generalization (Inheritance)

Generalization is an analysis technique by which we identify a general class that can be used to create other, more specialized, classes. In UML we can show this relationship as:

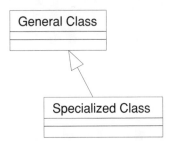

In this diagram the **Specialized Class** is created by inheriting from the **General Class**.

Multiplicity

One key piece of information required by UML for all relationship types is **multiplicity**. Multiplicity indicates how many objects of each class are involved in the relationship.

For instance, take a look at the following diagram:

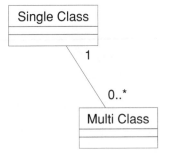

In this diagram, one instance of the **Single Class** has a relationship with zero or more instances of the **Multi Class** class. UML allows us to specify any level of multiplicity, though the common ones include:

Multiplicity	Meaning
0	Zero
1	One
0..*	Zero or more
1..*	One or more

Table continued on following page

Multiplicity	Meaning
n	A particular number
x..y	A range

Technically, UML requires us to indicate multiplicity for each object in a relationship. This is true for all the different types of relationship that we include in a diagram.

Summary

This has been a highly cursory look at UML, intended simply to explain the class diagrams developed in this book to illustrate the VideoStore application. If you want to learn more, I suggest you look at the forthcoming title from Wrox Press, *Instant UML* (ISBN 1-861000-87-1).

Bibliography

Object-Oriented Modeling And Design, by Rumbaugh, Blaha, Premerlani, Eddy, Lorensen.
Published by Prentice Hall, © 1991

The Object-Oriented Enterprise, by Rob Mattinson with Michael J. Sipolt.
Published by McGraw Hill, © 1994

The Tao of Objects, by Gary Entsminger.
Published by M&T Books, © 1995

Professional Active Server Pages, by Various.
Published by Wrox Press, © 1997

Object-Oriented Analysis and Design Using Rational Rose, a custom course by Magdy Hanna,
Dave West and Don Howard. Produced by Software Dimensions, © 1997

Object-Oriented Technology: A Manager's Guide, by David A. Taylor.
Published by Addison-Wesley Publishing Company, Inc., © 1990

Index

Symbols

VideoObjects, compiling, 396
Microsoft Transaction Server (MTS), 474, 506
  VideoServer, 506
    database connections, 509
    database transactions, 510
    MTS objects, 510
    MTS transactions, 537
    object request broker, 506
    ObjectControl, 507
    objects numbers, limiting, 509
    preparing VideoServer, 516
    VideoServerMTS, 516
  VideoServerMTS, 516
    running in MTS, 529
Mid$(), VB string handling
  Buffer object design, 434, 437, 439
mnu..., VideoMain menus, 291
modularity, business objects, 18
module level variables, 9
  scope, 9
MTS. *see* **Microsoft Transaction Server (MTS)**
multiple document interface (MDI), 290
multiple interfaces, objects, 13
  Container, 15
  Implements keyword, 14
  objects, 260
  scope, 15
multi-threading, VideoServer, 476
  options, 476

N

Name property, Customer object, 194
New keyword, MTS objects, 514, 520
NewEnum method, Customers object, 204
NewEnum method, Tapes object, 243
NewEnum method, TextList object, 208
n-tier architecture, 62
  data services, 67

data-centric business objects, 66
  application server, 67
  data sources, 66
UI-centric business objects, 64
user interface, 62

O

object ID, object persistence
  see also **Autonumber, object persistence**
object manager, object persistence, 160
  out-of-process server, object manager as, 161
object persistence, design, 155
  data-centric business objects, 160, 170
  form/BAS module, 156
  object manager, 160
  self-saving objects, 156
object persistence. *see* **persistence, data access**
object request broker (ORB)
  MTS, VideoServer, 506
ObjectControl, VideoServer, 507
  methods, listing, 508
ObjectControl_Activate method, 541
ObjectControl_CanBePooled method, 541
ObjectControl_Deactivate method, 542
ObjectID, object persistence, 345
object-level validation, object and UI example, 140
  BrokenRules class, 141
  canceled edits, 147
  IsValid property, 140
    implementing, 144
  methods, protecting, 152
    disabling methods, 153
  properties, protecting, 152
    read-only properties, 152
    write-once properties, 153
    write-only properties, 155

object-oriented design, 18
  see also **components, component-oriented design** *and* **objects**
  abstraction, 30
  applications, 29
  defining objects, 73
  encapsulation, 30
  identifying objects, 73
  inheritance, 34, 105
    containment, 36, 108
    delegation, 36, 108, 109
    interface inheritance, 34
  Internet, 558
    ActiveX, 559
    client-side scripting, 558
  object persistence, 155
    data-centric business objects, 160, 170
    form/BAS module, 156
    object manager, 160
    self-saving objects, 156
  object relationships, implementation, 94
    aggregate relationship, 100
    generalization relationship, 105
    ownership relationship, 95
    user relationship, 100
  polymorphism, 32
    early binding, 33
    interface inheritance, 32, 33, 260
    late binding, 32
    persistence, 374
  reusability, 18
  use case analysis, 74
    functional decomposition, 74
    functional use case, 77
    requirements use case, 75
    use case formats, alternative, 94
objects
  see also **components** *and* **object-oriented design**
  classes, 8
    class modules, 9
    instances, 8
  definition, 8
  encapsulation, 9
    scope, 9

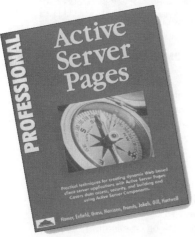

Professional Active Server Pages

Authors: Various   ISBN: 1861000723
Price: $44.95 C$62.95 £41.99

Active Server Pages is simply the easiest way to build dynamic sites. This book assumes you are familiar with simple HTML Web pages, and have at least some knowledge of Visual Basic or VBA. It starts with a full review of the background and workings of this new technology to get you up to speed, then quickly moves on to discuss the ways it can be used in the real world. We take ASP further than other books, showing you just what is possible. There's a discussion of client/server design topics, a full reference section, and plenty of real-world examples. This is one book you just can't afford to be without.

Professional IE4 Programming

Authors: Various
ISBN: 1861000707
Price: $49.95 C$69.95 £46.99

There's no doubt that many people will be using the new version of Microsoft's Internet Explorer browser. As well as supporting Dynamic HTML, the latest and most exciting version of HTML, it also offers lots of other new features. This book looks at what you can do with IE4, and - more importantly for the developer and HTML author - how you can program for it. We cover Dynamic HTML in depth, and explore ways of using the whole Active Desktop environment. This includes Active Desktop Components, dynamic linking to server-side databases, subscriptions and channel technology. Providing you are reasonably familiar with HTML up to version 3.2, and have tinkered with scripting languages before, you'll find everything you need to know here.

Professional SQL Server 6.5 Admin

Authors: Various   ISBN: 1874416494
Price: $44.95   C$62.95   £41.49

This book is not a tutorial in the complete product, but is for those who need to become either professionally competent in preparation for Microsoft exams or those DBAs needing real-world advice to do their job better. It assumes knowledge of databases and wastes no time on getting novices up to speed on the basics of data structure and using a database server in a Client-Server arena.

The book covers everything from installation and configuration right through to the actual managing of the server. There are whole chapters devoted to essential administrative issues such as transaction management and locking, replication, security, monitoring of the system and database backup and recovery. We've used proven techniques to bring robust code and script that will increase your ability to troubleshoot your database structure and improve its performance. Finally, we have looked very carefully at the new features in 6.5, such as the Web Assistant and Distributed Transaction Controller (DTC) and provided you with key practical examples. Where possible, throughout the book we have described a DBA solution in Transact SQL, Visual Basic and the Enterprise Manager.

Professional DCOM Programming

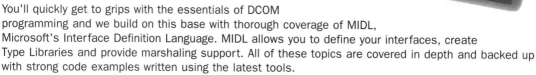

Author: Richard Grimes
ISBN: 186100060X
Price: $49.95   C$69.95   £46.99

The book starts by examining why we need to be able to implement and distribute code objects, and looks at the various systems of distribution that currently exist. It then narrows the focus down to sharing data and functionality on Windows. This leads into an examination of COM, and from there, logically, to DCOM. We show how DCOM builds on the foundations of COM and RPC.

You'll quickly get to grips with the essentials of DCOM programming and we build on this base with thorough coverage of MIDL, Microsoft's Interface Definition Language. MIDL allows you to define your interfaces, create Type Libraries and provide marshaling support. All of these topics are covered in depth and backed up with strong code examples written using the latest tools.

The latter half of the book looks at the design and implementation of distributed applications. Each chapter covers a topic of prime importance to DCOM programmers. Security is fully explained, starting with the NT security model and exploring how it relates to DCOM. You'll then see how to write your DCOM servers as NT services, before being drawn into the murky world of multithreaded applications. The book shows how to use threads in Win32 and in DCOM servers, covers the different threading models and also looks at the issues of passing interface pointers between threads. Finally, you'll see how Microsoft Transaction Server can ease the life of a DCOM developer as well as the new issues introduced by this product

Register Professional Visual Basic 5.0 Business Objects and sign up for a free subscription to The Developer's Journal.

A bi-monthly magazine for software developers, The Wrox Press Developer's Journal features in-depth articles, news and help for everyone in the software development industry. Each issue includes extracts from our latest titles and is crammed full of practical insights into coding techniques, tricks, and research.

Fill in and return the card below to receive a free subscription to the Wrox Press Developer's Journal.

Professional Visual Basic 5.0 Business Objects Registration Card

Name _____

Address _____

_____

_____

City _____ State/Region _____

Country _____ Postcode/Zip _____

E-mail _____

Occupation _____

How did you hear about this book? _____

☐ Book review (name) _____

☐ Advertisement (name) _____

☐ Recommendation _____

☐ Catalog _____

☐ Other _____

Where did you buy this book? _____

☐ Bookstore (name) _____ City _____

☐ Computer Store (name) _____

☐ Mail Order _____

☐ Other _____

What influenced you in the purchase of this book?

☐ Cover Design

☐ Contents

☐ Other (please specify) _____

How did you rate the overall contents of this book?

☐ Excellent ☐ Good

☐ Average ☐ Poor

What did you find most useful about this book? _____

What did you find least useful about this book? _____

Please add any additional comments. _____

What other subjects will you buy a computer book on soon? _____

What is the best computer book you have used this year? _____

Note: This information will only be used to keep you update about new Wrox Press titles and will not be used for any othe purpose or passed to any other third party.

Check here if you DO NOT want a subscription to The Developer's Journal or further support for this book ☐

WROX

WROX PRESS INC.

Wrox writes books for you. Any suggestions, or
ideas about how you want information given in
your ideal book will be studied by our team.
Your comments are always valued at Wrox.

Free phone in USA 800-USE-WROX
Fax (312) 397 8990

UK Tel. (0121) 706 6826 Fax (0121) 706 2967

———— *Computer Book Publishers* ————

NB. If you post the bounce back card below in the UK, please send it to:
Wrox Press Ltd. 30 Lincoln Road, Birmingham, B27 6PA

Supporting you on the web
http://www.wrox.com/

Fast download the source code to your book and collect updates on any errata

Preview forthcoming titles and test out some sample chapters

Get the full, detailed lowdown on any of our books - and read the reviews!

Sign-up for our free newspaper: "Developers' Journal" for Wrox activity, sample chapters and hot info on the industry

Drop into our mirror site at
http://www.wrox.co.uk